Symbol	Meaning*
CT	Transitory real consumption expenditures (10)
CU	Currency (6)
cu	Desired ratio of holdings of currency to demand deposits (6)
Δ	Delta: Change in a variable (3)
δ	Delta: Replacement investment (9)
D	Deposits (6)
d	Marginal propensity to invest (4)
$(\ )_d$	Desired value (3)
DD	Demand (checkable) deposits (6)
DEF	Government budget deficit (11)
DEP	Depreciation (9)
$\dot{(\ )}$	Percentage rate of change in a variable (8)
E	Desired real expenditures; real aggregate demand (3)
$(\ )_E$	Equilibrium value (3)
e	Response of demand for money (transactions demand) to a \$1 change in real income (7)
$(\ )^e$	Expected value (3)
EX	Expectations (4)
EXC	Exchange rate (16)
f	A functional relationship (3) or the production function (12)
FIN	Deposits available for financing (9)
$(\ )^*$	Full employment value of a variable (2)
G	Real government purchases of goods and services (4)
	real consumption expen- ... pur- ...4)
GNP	Gross national product; money value of goods and services produced (1)
h	Response of demand for money to a \$1 change in interest rates (7)
HS	Housing starts (9)
I	Desired and actual real investment expenditures (3)
$\bar{I}$	Autonomous real investment expenditures (3)
i	Nominal interest rates (2,8)
IC	Inflation curve; dynamic aggregate supply curve (expectations-augmented Phillips curve) (13)
ICL	Long-run inflation curve (13)
IM	Imports (16)
INV	Inventories (9)
INV_d	Desired level of inventories (9)
ir	Internal rate of return (9)
IS	Investment-saving curve; points of equilibrium in goods market (5)
K	The stock of capital (9)
K_d	Desired stock of capital (9)
k	Multiplier (3)
k_1	Multiplier excluding effects of induced higher interest rates (8)
k_2	Multiplier including effects of induced higher interest rates (8) or exports and imports (17)
kBB	Balanced-budget multiplier (4)

(Glossary continues inside the back cover)

*Number in parenthesis indicates the chapter in which the symbol is introduced.

Macroeconomics

To accompany the text: Study Guide for *Macroeconomics*
by Burton Abrams, University of Delaware

Macroeconomics

THEORIES AND POLICIES

Sherman J. Maisel

University of California, Berkeley

W • W • Norton & Company

NEW YORK   LONDON

Copyright © 1982 by W. W. Norton & Company, Inc.
All rights reserved.
Published simultaneously in Canada by George J. McLeod Limited, Toronto.
Printed in the United States of America.

Cover photo: Norman McGrath (Hardy, Holzman and Pfeiffer, R.A.)

Library of Congress Cataloging in Publication Data
Maisel, Sherman J.
  Macroeconomics.
  Includes index.
  1. Macroeconomics. I. Title.
HB172.5.M34 1982   339   81-4504
ISBN 0–393–01490–8   AACR2

W. W. Norton & Company, Inc. 500 Fifth Avenue, New York, N. Y. 10110
W. W. Norton & Company, Ltd. 37 Great Russell Street, London WC1B 3NU

1 2 3 4 5 6 7 8 9 0

Contents

Preface

Macroeconomic events constantly make news. Prices, interest rates, output, and employment rise and fall. The economy endures bouts of inflation and recession and, in recent years, a combination of the two known as stagflation. Without a solid grounding in macroeconomic theory, one has little hope of tracing these events back to their causes or evaluating the programs designed to put the economy on an even keel.

What's more, the tools of macroeconomic analysis, properly applied, can be immensely valuable to decision makers—from the corporate executive who recognizes that capital spending programs, wages, and prices are subject to the vicissitudes of the national economy to the government official confronted with vast arrays of data and econometric models to the ordinary individual looking for financial investment opportunities or a home mortgage. Uses of aggregate economic analyses such as these are the focal point of this text.

I started writing with the aim of making current developments in macroeconomic theory available for classroom use while placing the theories in a practical context, and I did not swerve from those aims over three drafts and substantial class testing of the manuscript. For this, as any text, reflects the author's experience—in my own case, teaching economics and finance in a university, developing public policies as a governor of the Federal Reserve, and assisting corporations to formulate forecasting and other programs heavily dependent on macroeconomics. From experience, I have become convinced that understanding can be enhanced by pointing up lively controversies over theory, by treating specific policy actions or case studies, and by examining the alternatives that confront key macro policy decision makers. I have taken just such approaches in this text. In the course of writing it the rapid evolution of the theories of dynamic inflation, of rational expectations, of supply-side economics, and of government spending expanded the concepts necessary for inclusion. The end result is a volume that differs from most other intermediate macroeconomic texts in four principal respects:

• Discussions of price and wage formation, productivity, supply-side economics, and the dynamic inflationary process can no longer simply be grafted onto a discussion of demand. Because these topics form a growing share of modern macroeconomics, they have been thoroughly developed and integrated over several chapters.

• Greater consideration has been given to the topic of money—a key policy issue. When money and monetary policy are treated too briefly, it can appear that economic results follow directly from policy changes by the Federal Reserve. To make absolutely clear the significance of money's role in any policy action, one needs to know what money is and how it changes. As explained by the theory of portfolio selection, alterations in the stock of money influence wealth, the ability to obtain credit, and desires to spend. Precisely how money works through markets to affect output and inflation is traced in detail, showing both why money is so important and why it remains a controversial topic.

• The study of the causes of and possible cures for inflation highlights the roles of expectations, of time, and of the failure of markets to adjust rapidly. Because the development of inflation, what it costs, and possible solutions for it have been unclear, economists have tended to underestimate its significance. Factors such as poor information, rapid shifts in expectations, the time lags before the economy adjusts to new situations, and the impact of divergent relative prices were neglected in analysis.

• President Reagan's "Program for Economic Recovery" has brought to the fore many of the theoretical issues explored in this text. Throughout the volume, I have incorporated discussions of the theoretical underpinnings of the program as well as some of its controversial components. Included are explanations of the theories of the chief exponents of the economic logic of that program—the new classicists, whose views derive both from supply-side economics and rational expectations.

All macroeconomists must be impressed—and at times overwhelmed—by the pace at which the field has been changing. How rapidly new concepts should be introduced into an intermediate text is a matter of judgment. I have tried to include all those which seem necessary to an understanding of the economic developments of the 1980s, at the same time stressing the idea that the field is dynamic and that new theories and understanding will continue to develop under the pressure of time, of shifting concerns, and improved knowledge.

The aim of this text is to teach macroeconomics by relating the development of models and theories to their uses. The careful introduction of new ideas and definitions and the illustration of models by numerical and graphical examples are elements which have proved extremely helpful in my courses. This text is especially planned to provide the tools students need:

• New terms and concepts are defined when they are introduced: they often are illustrated further in applications.

• The basic models of the field are developed through a coordinated set of equations, diagrams, tables, and numerical examples. These numerical and graphical examples, which accompany most equations, have proved particularly useful as learning aids.

• Each model builds upon and utilizes preceding expositions.
• The symbols used throughout follow a single, simple pattern. A glossary and brief description of each symbol can be found inside the front and back covers of the book.
• Questions and problems at the end of every chapter can be used by students to test their comprehension of the major points.
• The chapter summaries help to clarify important ideas.

One problem which faces most instructors is how to adjust a textbook to their own particular teaching needs. Because I assume that few instructors want to be locked into someone else's ideas as to the best allocation of time and order of exposition, I have tried to make this book as flexible as possible. To a large extent, those chapters which supplement the main models have been made as nearly self-contained as possible so that they can be shifted easily from one order to another. For example, many instructors will prefer to develop consumption theory (Chapter 10) along with the consumption function (Chapter 3); others will prefer to complete the model of aggregate demand and supply (Chapters 12 and 13) before introducing the more detailed exposition of the theories of instability in spending (Chapters 9, 10, and 11). In the same way, many may prefer to delay study of the supply of money (Chapter 6) until policy issues are taken up. The book has been planned so that such changes can be made with a minimum of interference to the presentation of the models and their basic logic.

While it should not be difficult to cover all 19 chapters in a full semester course, many instructors on a quarter system will not want to assign the entire book. Some will prefer to omit a few chapters or to assign some chapters only as supplementary reading. If time is limited, the basic theories of macroeconomics can be covered in 12 chapters—namely, Chapters 1–5, 7, 8, 12–15, and 19. The volume is so planned that dropping the other chapters will not interfere with the development of the full domestic models of aggregate demand, aggregate supply, the inflationary process, and policy decisions.

THE ANCILLARIES

Professor Burton Abrams of the University of Delaware has prepared a *Study Guide* to accompany this text. It provides an overview of the basic concepts presented in each chapter as well as more detailed explanations of them, frequently in terms different that those in the text. Important models and their derivations are also reviewed. Multiple-choice, completion, and true-false questions are designed to allow students to verify their understanding of basic concepts and terms. Problem sets and discussion questions encourage students to apply the concepts they have learned.

An *Instructor's Manual* which provides teaching suggestions, answers to the end-of-chapter questions, and a test bank has been prepared by Professor Abrams and myself. It is available to instructors on request to the publisher.

ACKNOWLEDGMENTS

Like all authors, I owe a great debt to those who have contributed to this work. My students at the University of California, who were subjected to duplicated copies of preliminary versions of this text, have been especially helpful as I worked out different forms of exposition. Most of the chapters have been read and commented on by many of my colleagues at Berkeley, including especially Roland Artle, Gillian Garcia, Frances Van Loo, and James Wilcox. Others who have read some or all of the book and whose comments have been extremely valuable, whether or not accepted, include: Burton Abrams, University of Delaware; Alan Deardorf, University of Michigan; James Duesenberry, Harvard; John Karaken, University of Minnesota; Robert Jacobson, Federal Reserve Bank of San Francisco; Bruce Mann, University of Puget Sound; John Pettingal, University of Virginia; Uri Possen, Cornell; James Rhodes, Kansas State; Gordon Sellon, Federal Reserve Bank of Kansas City; Robert Shiller, Pennsylvania, and Theodore Taylor, Texas Tech.

My research assistants, Dmitry Bosky and Anthony O'Brien, have been very helpful. Of particular value have been the sound advice and editorial aid of Mary Shuford and Donald Lamm of W. W. Norton. Having had considerable experience with other publishers, I appreciate how outstanding they are. Above all, the book literally would not have been possible without the constant assistance and encouragement of my wife, Lucy C. Maisel.

Part 1

Introduction and Measurement

1

Introduction

In early 1981, an air of economic crisis pervaded Washington. Policy makers worried about the record pace at which prices had been rising. Unemployment was high also, with the number out of work growing. Financial markets were in turmoil. The government deficit was nearing a record. The prime lending rate of banks—the interest they charge their best customers—had reached 21.5 percent. Long-term interest rates had nearly doubled since 1978, driving the prices of outstanding bonds to record lows. Production was at an all-time high, but its growth during the decade just past had been slower than in previous periods. While rapidly rising production, a slower rate of inflation, and record profits for many firms indicated that immediate prospects were good, such improvements were deemed to be temporary and lacking long-term significance. Some major businesses reported falling profits and fears of bankruptcy. The popular view seemed to be that drastic economic action was required.

The overwhelming concern of the new Reagan administration in its first six months in office was to shift the fundamental course of the United States economy. The Reagan economic policy emphasized the importance of business rather than government actions in determining spending and prices. The government's budget was cut; taxes were reduced, and growth in money slowed. The administration was willing to risk a period of slow growth in order to halt inflation. While the harsh medicine would be distasteful, it was necessary to achieve a healthier economy. As is true in most economic analysis and decision making, contrary views were expressed. Only with hindsight is it possible to evaluate the decisions that were taken and what the best set of policies would have been.

Explaining why the nation was faced with an unsatisfactory choice of economic actions and how similar conditions might be avoided in the future is one of the tasks of macroeconomics. **Macroeconomics** is the study of how our overall economy performs. It deals with causes of inflation, recession, and depression, and ways to combat them. It provides a theoretical and analytical framework to explain what determines output, unemployment, and the general price level; why they are at present levels; how they are likely to move in the future; and what can be done about them. Macroeconomics deals with the broad picture. It can be contrasted with **microeconomics,** which is concerned with the economic behavior of individual economic units such as consumers, firms, and owners of resources. Microeconomics analyzes the setting of prices for particular goods in specific industries and markets. Macroeconomics groups these individual spending units into a limited number of sectors and considers markets in the aggregate. What goods will the economy as a whole demand, and at what prices will they be sold?

Businesses and individuals, as well as the government, must make decisions based on macroeconomic analysis in an effort to achieve their economic goals. Decisions by executives as to whether to build a new plant or introduce a new product are based on estimates of future sales and income. Individual job decisions are related to potential growth. In 1981 the interest rates that banks charged large corporations on loans were at record levels. Related movements in the prices of bonds and common stocks sharply reduced the value of investment portfolios. Families thus were forced to reconsider whether they ought to buy stocks, bonds, houses, or other investments. In 1970 a retired family with an income of $10,000 a year was relatively well off; a decade later that amount would buy only half as much. Such families were rapidly becoming impoverished. Watching what was happening to others, potential retirees had to rethink the dangers of inflation and try to find ways to offset its risks in planning their futures.

People faced with inflation or recession, with soaring prices or loss of jobs, must choose from a wide range of possible alternative actions. An understanding of macroeconomics helps us to cope with economic problems and to predict their consequences. This chapter begins by examining some central issues affecting the economy, businesses, and individuals. Controversies over these questions have received increasing public exposure. People want to know what causes recessions, why prices rise, and what can be done about them. Vehement debates take place over money and interest rates, over government spending, taxes, balancing the budget, and the public debt. Macroeconomics offers a framework, or **model,** to abstract and simplify the enormous number of economic facts with which everyone must deal so that key relationships can be discerned. The framework and theories aid in modeling possible interactions between parts of the economy. Issues can be defined, goals established, costs and benefits of alternatives examined, and actions determined. While general agreement exists as to the form of the framework, disagreements over what should be done are common in specific situations. In this chapter, we will introduce some of these techniques as well as the divergences in views concerning them and their use.

Macroeconomic Issues

In order to identify some of the key macroeconomic issues, let us look at the economic record of the United States for the 51-year period 1929–80. The year 1929 marked the height of a major economic boom, followed shortly by a great crash. The prolonged depression which ensued (called the Great Depression) was a traumatic experience for millions. By 1933 more than a quarter of the labor force could not find jobs. The Depression brought about a complete reshaping of theories as to how the economy works. In addition to a major depression, the period since 1929 has witnessed wars, economic growth, and prosperity. The economy also experienced periods in which output fell and unemployment rose well above normal. It ended with a severe inflation.

GROWTH IN OUTPUT

The 51-year record of the economy shows normal growth interrupted by a number of downturns, each creating unemployment, industrial losses, and a waste of assets and wealth. Figure 1.1 shows the growth in the gross national product (GNP). The **nominal gross national product** is the total money value of goods and services produced by our economy in a year. During this 51-year period, nominal GNP grew by more than 2,400 percent. However, this growth was not as outstanding as that number suggests. The nominal GNP is measured in current or actual dollars. It is not a pure measure of the growth of physical output because it fails to eliminate growth due to price increases. During this period, the price level, measured by changes in the GNP price index, rose by nearly 450 percent. The **real gross national product** is a measure of physical output in **constant dollars**—that is, current-dollar values corrected for changes in prices.[1] During this 51-year period, the real GNP increased about $3\frac{1}{2}$ times or, more precisely, by 360 percent. The population grew as well; nevertheless in 1980, as compared to 1929, almost $2\frac{1}{2}$ times the amount of real goods and services were available for every man, woman, and child in the United States.

Real growth, which determines how fast the standard of living can rise, depends on two separate factors: (1) the number of hours people work and (2) **labor productivity,** the amount of output produced by an hour of work. Productivity rises with technological improvements, more and better capital goods, and more highly skilled labor. The movements in labor productivity for the 1929–80 period are detailed in Figure 1.2. Over the entire period, productivity grew at a rate of 2.2 percent per year. But sharp differences occurred within the period. From 1947 to 1968, the compound growth rate was 3.2 percent. In contrast, in the period 1968–80, the growth rate was less than one-third, or

---

1. The term *output* is used as an equivalent to real GNP. Data in this volume are based on the 1980 revision of the National Income and Product Accounts. See *Survey of Current Business* (December 1980).

under 1.0 percent per year. Herein we find one of the critical macroeconomic issues for the 1980s: What caused the drop in productivity gains? And how can they be recovered? How can growth in productivity be improved?

FIGURE 1.1   **Nominal and Real Gross National Product and the GNP Price Index, 1929–80**

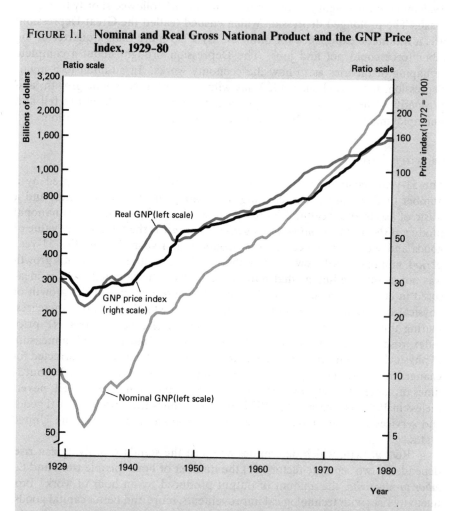

Nominal GNP (measured in current dollars) rose quite steadily except for setbacks during the Great Depression and recessions. However, a considerable amount of the growth was due to higher prices. Real GNP is the nominal (or current-dollar) GNP corrected for price changes. The GNP price index measures the average change in prices. Note that this figure uses a ratio scale. Equal vertical distances show equal percentage changes rather than actual movements. The plotted points are logarithms of values, not actual numbers.
SOURCE: U.S. Department of Commerce.

FIGURE 1.2   **Growth in Productivity 1929–80**
(output per hour, nonfarm business-sector)

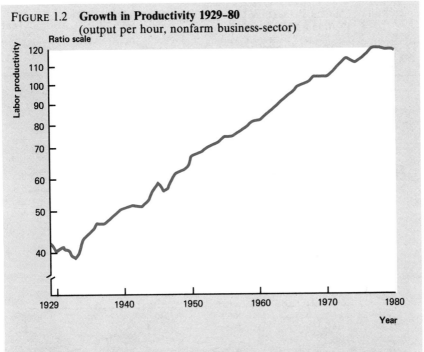

Labor productivity

Ratio scale

1929   1940   1950   1960   1970   1980

Year

Productivity has grown during most periods; it increased at quite a rapid rate following the Great Depression. However, it falls during recessions because those at work are less fully occupied. The much slower rate of growth since 1968 has made increasing productivity a key concern of the 1980s.
SOURCE: U.S. Department of Labor.

INSTABILITY AND LOSSES IN OUTPUT AND EMPLOYMENT

Even when growth occurs, its rate is uneven, as Figure 1.3 demonstrates vividly. The real GNP curve measures the year-to-year changes in output. For macroeconomic analysis, the periods when growth declines carry the most significance; they mark losses in output and increases in unemployment. Such periods of recession or depression began in 1929, 1937, 1945, 1948, 1953, 1957, 1960, 1969, 1973, and 1980. In this 51-year period, ten recessions or depressions affected the economy.

Closely related to movements in output are changes in **unemployment,** the number of workers who are unsuccessfully looking for jobs. When output fails to expand or declines, firms stop hiring workers and then begin to lay off those already at work. Changes in output thus are followed by movements in unemployment. Figure 1.4 pictures the oscillations in the percent of the total labor force that is unemployed. Unemployment is one of the most critical macroeco-

FIGURE 1.3   **Annual Percentage Changes in the Growth Rate of Real Gross National Product, 1929–80**

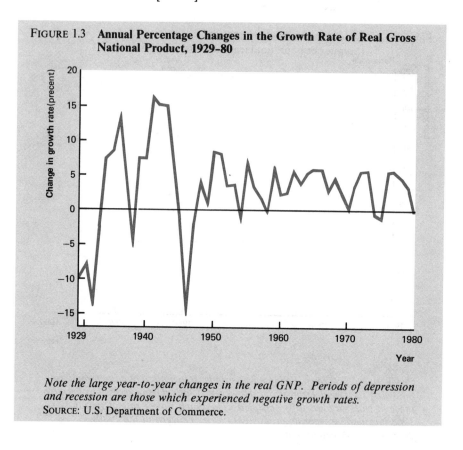

Note the large year-to-year changes in the real GNP. Periods of depression and recession are those which experienced negative growth rates.
SOURCE: U.S. Department of Commerce.

nomic issues. People without jobs suffer individual losses of income, esteem, and well-being. National output is reduced. In the nadir of the Great Depression, unemployment for the year 1933 was more than 25 percent of the labor force. But that figure fell below 1½ percent during World War II. During the 1970s, annual unemployment rates ranged from 4.9 to 8.5 percent.

FULL EMPLOYMENT AND POTENTIAL OUTPUT

One goal of the economy is to reduce unemployment as far as possible; that is, to reach full employment. But in a complex society, it is not possible for everyone seeking a job to find one immediately. Furthermore, unless some slack exists in the work force, prices will rise rapidly. Thus the concepts of full employment and minimum unemployment are the same. *Full employment* and *the natural rate of unemployment* are defined as the level of minimum sustainable unemployment below which the rate of price increases tends to accelerate. *Potential output* is the amount the economy can produce at that point.[2]

2. While in most analysis and, therefore, in this volume, the point of full employment is considered as equivalent to that of the natural rate of unemployment, some economists feel

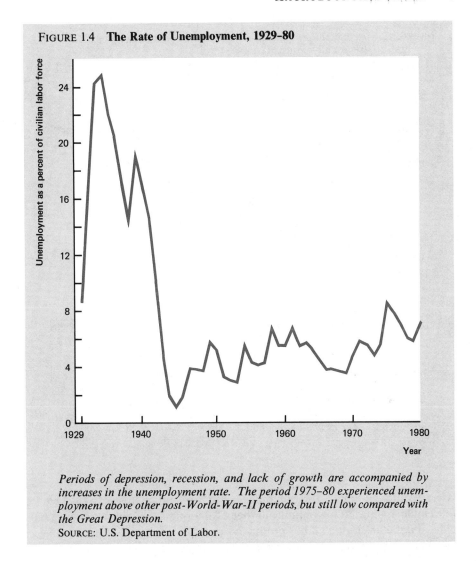

FIGURE 1.4   **The Rate of Unemployment, 1929-80**

Periods of depression, recession, and lack of growth are accompanied by increases in the unemployment rate. The period 1975–80 experienced unemployment above other post-World-War-II periods, but still low compared with the Great Depression.
SOURCE: U.S. Department of Labor.

What level of unemployment will cause inflation to accelerate is a matter of judgment. Translating this level into an equivalent point of maximum potential output also requires an exercise of opinion. Figure 1.5 presents two separate estimates of potential output made by the Council of Economic Ad-

---

strongly that the two should have separate definitions. They believe that in the 1970s factors other than an excess of demand caused prices to accelerate when unemployment was still well above the full-employment level. In their view, a failure to recognize such differences can cause policy errors. See E. F. Denison, "Changes in the Concept and Measurement of Potential Output in the United States of America," General Series Reprint 367, (Brookings Institution, Washington, D. C., 1981) and G. L. Perry, "Inflation in Theory and Practice" *Brookings Papers on Economic Activity* 1(1980):209.

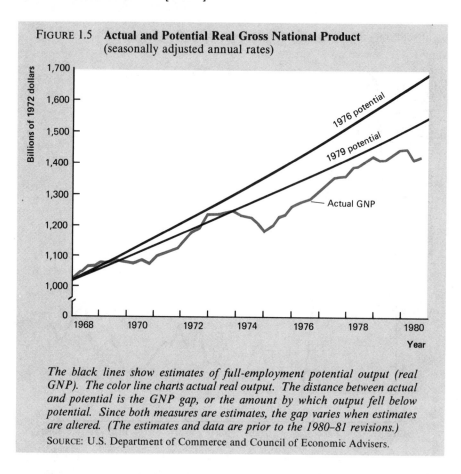

FIGURE 1.5   **Actual and Potential Real Gross National Product**
(seasonally adjusted annual rates)

The black lines show estimates of full-employment potential output (real GNP). The color line charts actual real output. The distance between actual and potential is the GNP gap, or the amount by which output fell below potential. Since both measures are estimates, the gap varies when estimates are altered. (The estimates and data are prior to the 1980–81 revisions.)
SOURCE: U.S. Department of Commerce and Council of Economic Advisers.

visers at different times. The differences arise from judgments as to the level of full employment, the maximum number of man-hours of employment available, and the level which labor productivity would reach at that point—that is, how many hours would be worked and how much output would be produced for each hour.

The divergences between the 1976 and later estimates of potential output cause large differences in the estimated losses from failure to achieve full employment. In 1979, for example, the estimated gap between potential and actual output was reduced by $133 billion, or over $1,700 for every household. The changing estimates highlight a shift in the views of economists and policy makers concerning the most important macroeconomic problems. Prior to the 1970s, most debates centered around ways to influence total (aggregate) demand in the economy. Emphasis was placed on the failure of demand to generate full employment. If the economy produced below potential, action could be taken to raise demand. Increased output and lower unemployment would follow. As the decade progressed, more and more attention was paid to supply and the costs of producing the output needed to meet each level of demand. Revised estimates of potential suggested that the only way to get added output without increasing inflation was by improving total (aggregate) supply. What was needed was not additional demand, but greater productivity, reduction in the natural rate of unemployment, and fewer material and capital bottlenecks in production.

INSTABILITY AND LOSSES IN SECTORS OF THE ECONOMY

While instability of demand causes losses in output and unemployment throughout the economy, the impacts tend to be amplified in specific sectors of the economy. Such amplification can aggravate both declines in real GNP for the entire economy and the costs to particular firms, households, and individuals. Furthermore, variations in costs and benefits derived from actions to curtail demand increase the difficulty of arriving at a consensus on macroeconomic issues. Home construction supplies the most obvious example of how changes in macroeconomic activity affect a major sector. Figure 1.6 charts the year-to-

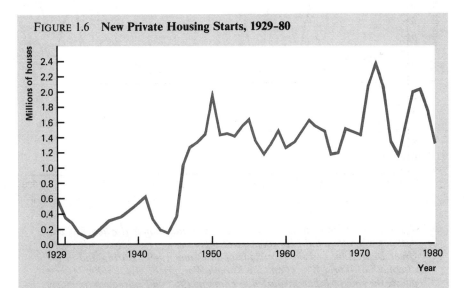

FIGURE 1.6   **New Private Housing Starts, 1929-80**

Some sectors of the economy suffer much wider swings in output and employment than the average. The fluctuations in housing starts shown in this figure are larger than but not untypical of the instability in other sections of the economy producing durable goods and dependent on financing. The ups and downs in output and unemployment cause large losses for business and labor in such industries.

SOURCE: U.S. Department of Commerce.

year movements in housing starts from 1929 to 1980. During this period, homebuilding went through ten cycles. In the Great Depression, output of new units dropped over 80 percent. From one high to the next low, the average fall during this period was over 50 percent.

INFLATION

The problem judged in the 1980s by both experts and nonexperts alike to be the most serious of all is the problem of inflation. **Inflation** is defined as a period of persistent rising general prices. Figure 1.7 shows annual percentage changes in the consumer price index.[3] The increases during the 1940s represent a not

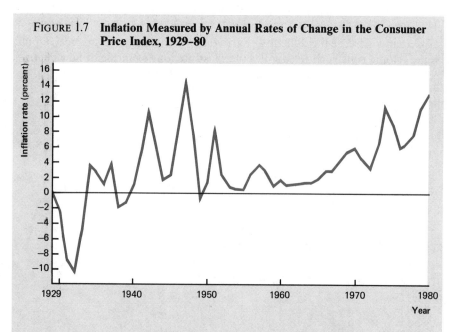

FIGURE 1.7   **Inflation Measured by Annual Rates of Change in the Consumer Price Index, 1929–80**

The rate of inflation increases when demand and output rise too fast and declines when they fall. However, price increases were negative only in the Great Depression and the recessions of 1937 and 1949. During and in the aftermath of World War II and the Korean War, prices rose rapidly. After a pause, the rate of inflation started to climb in 1966 and stayed continuously high by past standards, even though declines in the rate occurred in 1971–72 and in 1976.

SOURCE: U.S. Department of Labor.

3. This index, discussed in Chapter 2, measures changes in a broad range of goods and services.

unusual reaction of prices to wars and shortages. The behavior of prices in the 1970s, however, was a new phenomenon for the United States. Prices rose relentlessly and much more rapidly than in the past.

Inflation is a critical issue because it undermines the usefulness of money as a standard for the economy. No one can be sure what a dollar will buy tomorrow. People find it difficult to plan. When prices change, income is redistributed haphazardly; wages get out of line; creditors are repaid in money worth less than that which they lent; the value of pensions shrinks; interest rates fluctuate widely. Output and productivity fall as business decisions are warped and uncertainty increases. Psychological costs are high both because of uncertainties and because who gains and who loses depends more on hustling or luck than on one's value to society.

If inflation averages 10 percent a year, the amount a dollar can buy falls in half in just over seven years. An indication of how fast inflation actually erodes the purchasing power of money and how widespread it is can be found in Table 1.1. The table compares ten-year rates of inflation and shows what happened to the purchasing power of each country's currency between 1929 and 1979. The near-universality of inflation is obvious. Few countries have escaped. Equally shocking to most of us when we first observe it is the extremely sharp drop in the purchasing power of many currencies. The dollar in 1979 bought only 24 percent as much as the 1929 dollar. Such changes are typical only of the least inflationary countries. In 1979 the French franc, the Italian lira, the Argentin-

TABLE 1.1 **Inflation around the World**

	Change in consumer prices (percent)					Purchasing power of currency (1929 = 100)	
	1929–39	*1939–49*	*1949–59*	*1959–69*	*1969–79*	*1949*	*1979*
United States	−19	72	22	26	98	72	24
France	22	1,540	79	46	134	5	*
Italy	−30	4,598	30	44	216	3	*
Netherlands	−20	112	44	47	97	59	14
Sweden	1	52	53	44	127	65	13
Switzerland	−14	60	12	36	62	73	29
Argentina	50	104	1,088	673	144,704	25	*
Brazil	51	308	300	3,786	1,273	16	*

* Less than 0.01 percent.
SOURCE: International Monetary Fund.

Since World War II inflation has been a nearly universal phenomenon. However, price increases have varied widely among countries and by decades. Corollary to inflation is a drop in the purchasing power of a currency.

ian peso, and the Brazilian cruzeiro were worth less than 0.01 percent of their value in 1929. Statements of how purchasing power has fallen overdramatize the issue somewhat because few people would have held only currency or money assets over the whole period. They would have been transferring back and forth from money to other assets. Consequently, some of their earnings from assets as well as their wages would also have been inflated.

Table 1.1 brings out a number of other interesting facts as well. The period from 1929 to 1939, including the Great Depression, was the only one in which prices fell. While all countries experienced inflation, movements across countries in each decade varied widely. World War II had a tremendous impact. It was felt most in the countries at war, but Sweden and Switzerland, both neutrals, also experienced sharp price increases.

THE FAILURE TO END INFLATION

Table 1.1 raises serious questions about both the ability and the desire of countries to fight inflation. As we shall see, there is nearly complete agreement that inflation cannot continue unless governments provide enough money to permit purchases and sales to take place at the higher price levels. The nearly universal rise in prices in the face of knowledge that it could be halted is at the heart of a great deal of macroeconomic debate. If inflation can be halted by government action, what accounts for the almost worldwide increase in prices shown in the table? Among possible reasons why governments have failed to act may be (1) the problems are too hard to solve, (2) governments are incapable of effective action, or (3) the voters recognize the potential costs to themselves and therefore prefer that politicians and the economic leaders talk about inflation but not do too much about it.

When the tools of macroeconomics are applied to the problem, analysts offer widely different policy suggestions. Governments and central banks hesitate to take drastic actions. When asked, most voters list stopping inflation as one of the most critical problems of the country. But in stating this opinion, they have no clear picture of how an anti-inflation battle must be waged. Specific policy measures, such as raising taxes, cutting government expenditures, or raising interest rates, are thus often opposed by a majority (or at least by a very vocal minority) of those same voters. They fear that they will pay more than their fair share of the costs. Because enough people fear that they will be the ones to pay for the gains of others, consensus is often hard to achieve.

If inflation continues, it is important to know how the future will be affected. Not only will relative prices shift, but interest rates will go up and demand will fluctuate more. Adjusting properly to lower sales, higher interest rates, and less credit may mean the difference between profits and losses, capital gains, or fewer assets. Businesses and individuals who successfully incorporate policies based on the recognition of what can happen if anti-inflationary policies are adopted, as well as what may happen if inflation persists, will do well in either case. When such considerations are neglected or adjustments required by either inflation or recession are too difficult and costly, the results may be disastrous.

STAGFLATION AND DISCOMFORT

In most periods of economic history, problems have been caused either by too little demand leading to unemployment and lack of output, or by excess demand leading to inflation. In the 1970s, however, the United States was subjected to *stagflation*—large doses of simultaneous unemployment (stagnation) and inflation. Reflecting the fact that the ratio of bad news to good in the economic sphere grew as the decade progressed, most economic commentators in the late 1970s shifted from optimism to pessimism.

A simple summary of this deterioration in the mood and sense of well-being of the American people is shown in Figure 1.8. This chart portrays a

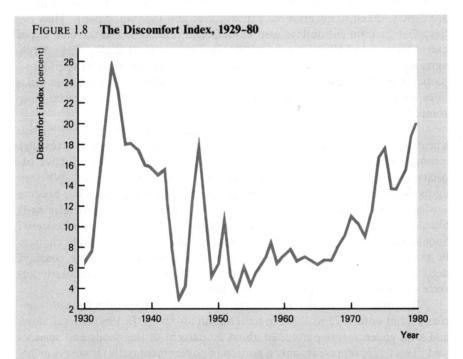

FIGURE 1.8   **The Discomfort Index, 1929–80**

The economy suffered from large-scale unemployment during the Great Depression and later from inflation caused by World War II. The stagflation years 1973–80 witnessed high levels of discomfort, with a postwar record reading of 20.0 in 1980. President Reagan made the high level of this discomfort index a major political issue in his successful election campaign in 1980.

discomfort index, which is derived by adding together the rate of unemployment and the rate of inflation. The inflation rate is measured by the movement of the consumer price index from the same quarter in the previous year. The discomfort index appears to be an accurate reflection of consumers' dissatisfaction with the performance of the economy.

Several facts stand out in the figure. The level of discomfort moved upward to a new plateau in the 1970s. For the decade, the level was twice as high as in the 1960s. Previous highs had been around 10 in 1958 and 1969. But in 1975 the discomfort index averaged over 18, and in 1980 it was 20. Just as striking as the sharp rise in the level of discomfort was the fact that even the best readings for the last half of the 1970s were above the worst experiences of the years between World War II and 1970. Such poor readings had previously been experienced only during the Great Depression following 1929.

GOVERNMENT SPENDING AND TAXES

In the minds of many, the fight against inflation and the economy's discomfort are closely linked to government expenditures and the public debt. They believe that government outlays lead to inefficiency, deficits, and the creation of excess money, and thus have been the principal cause of high prices. While agreeing that when demand is too high, increases in government spending—particularly if they cause the creation of too much money—can result in inflations, most economists hold that the causes and cures of inflation are far more complex.

However, even before inflation became critical, government spending was a heated issue in macroeconomics. Shifts in government outlays and taxes alter income, spending, and output. They influence the economy's productive capacity, efficiency, and growth. They affect the distribution of income. Whether limits should be placed on the amount governments tax and spend has become a widely debated issue. If limits are set, how should they be determined? Should spending and taxes be varied in response to inflations or recessions? Should such shifts be permanent or temporary, and how often should changes be made? In establishing policy, the president and Congress face constant decisions as to whether some taxes and expenditures have a particularly adverse or favorable effect on growth and stability.

Not only has the dollar amount of government spending steadily increased, but until 1975 its share in total output also rose. In 1980 federal, state, and local governments purchased about 20 percent of the goods and services sold. This figure represents only a portion of government outlays; governments also make *transfer payments* for social security, welfare, pensions, interest, and similar outlays. Transfer payments shift money among groups but do not use productive services and, therefore, are not included in the GNP. In 1980, when the federal government purchased about 7.6 percent of all goods and services, transfer payments amounted to more than twice that percentage. In attempting to cut the initial 1982 budget of $739 billion, a key problem facing the Reagan administration was that more than 66 percent of the total budget went for transfers, not purchases of goods and services.

INTERNATIONAL ECONOMIC RELATIONS

Countries buy and sell goods and lend and borrow money abroad. Foreign commerce can have a major impact on the health of the economy and on many businesses and jobs. An obvious example can be found in the long lines at gas stations following the Arab oil embargo. Another is the competitive impact of Japanese cars on domestic auto production. The importance of international economic relations to the United States has been growing steadily.

Major macroeconomic issues arise with respect to the rates at which currencies exchange and to the balance of payments. *Exchange rates,* or the price of one currency in units of another, influence the terms on which goods can be traded, as well as a country's well-being, its prices and inflation rate, and, to some extent, its power in world politics. The *balance of payments* is an accounting record of a country's foreign transactions. A deficit balance of payments means a loss in international reserves. Changes in the balance of payments can lead to movements in exchange rates and can cause both internal and external distortions. Prices, jobs, and income distribution are all affected. Governments come under pressure to alter both domestic and international economic policies. International issues are discussed in detail in Part 6. Until that point is reached, most analysis is in terms of domestic macroeconomic relationships only. The interactions with foreign economies through trade, lending, and investing are set aside and not analyzed until these later chapters.

Macroeconomic Goals and Policies

Macroeconomics explains the causes behind the movements in growth of output and wealth and behind the instability of output, employment, and prices. It also asks what can be done to improve economic results. *Goals* are general views—in some cases, formal statements—of where we would like the economy, or a business, or even a family, to be in some future period. *Policies* are actions taken to help reach goals.

GOALS

It once seemed fairly easy to sum up the goals of the economy, and probably the goals of most businesses and families as well, in the simple statement "more is better." Increased purchasing power would lead to greater satisfaction. However, as the United States and other industrialized countries have become richer, we have learned that richer is not necessarily synonymous with happier or better. Studies show that the ratio of increased human welfare to increased output is far from one to one. In fact, after some level of affluence has been reached, the importance of noneconomic factors in individual satisfaction seems to increase. What one does, how one feels, relationships to others, peace and contentment become more important once one has enough income to attain some adequate level of physical well-being. In the same way, problems of crowding, crime, pollution, and loss of natural beauty reduce satisfaction as economic production expands.

At the end of World War II, the United States adopted the Employment Act of 1946, which contained a relatively simple statement of goals:

> The Congress hereby declares that it is the continuing policy and responsi-
> bility of the Federal Government to use all practicable means consistent
> with its needs and obligations ... to promote maximum employment,
> production and purchasing power.

While the economy's record of stability under the 1946 Act appeared improved, unsatisfactory economic performance in the 1970s led to a debate and to the amendment of the act by a new one, the Full Employment and Balanced Growth Act of 1978 (the Humphrey-Hawkins Act). In this act, the simple six-word goal of the original act was replaced by the following:

> ... to promote full employment and production, increased real income,
> balanced growth, a balanced Federal budget, adequate productivity
> growth, proper attention to national priorities, achievement of an im-
> proved trade balance through increased exports and improvement in the
> international competitiveness of agriculture, business, and industry, and
> reasonable price stability.

Furthermore, this much more complex statement is followed by several hundred words of additional qualifications.

With the 1978 act, the government accepted the task of replacing the generalities which sufficed in the past with more specific targets. The administration and Congress are to review annually basic policies in an effort to determine to what degree they have fostered or hindered the achievement of the goals of the economy. The specific targets for the economy under the 1978 act make the adoption of economic policy far more difficult. Instead of generalities, the new system seeks to gain both political and economic agreement as to the state of the economy, where we would like it to go, and the best way to get there.

Ironically, however, by the time this act was passed, the Carter administration was spending so much time fighting inflation that most of the other goals were neglected. With the election of President Reagan, it became clear that price sta ility would continue to be the primary goal, not merely one among equals.

POLICIES

In a dynamic economy, the government cannot avoid assuming some policy stance. Making no change is as much a policy as taking positive action. Existing government programs and tax laws may bring about surpluses or deficits; they may intensify inflation or aggravate unemployment.

There is no automatic device to regulate the rate at which money is created; a determination must be made as to how much money the economy needs. *Monetary policies* are government actions to influence the stock of money and of bank assets and liabilities. Too much money leads to inflation; too little to financial crisis and depression. Action must be taken to insure that the growth of money follows whatever path has been chosen as best. Recognition of these facts led to the establishment of the Federal Reserve System in 1913 and a grant to it by Congress of authority (subject to congressional review) to control the rate at which money is created.

Another form of government action is *fiscal policy.* It includes the spending and taxing decisions that determine the total level of government programs (whether the budget is in deficit or surplus) and the measures taken to raise the funds the government spends. The Office of Management and Budget, the Treasury, and the Council of Economic Advisers (CEA) are responsible to the president for recommendations as to the most desirable budget. They are also responsible for maintaining current forecasts of where the economy is headed. On the basis of these forecasts, they recommend to the president possible policy changes. Suppose, for example, that a tax cut is under consideration. Before taxes are lowered, analysis must predict the probable effects of such a move. A tax cut may increase the number of jobs, but it can also cause prices to rise. Forecasting which result is most probable, or how much of each, calls for a prediction of what the economic situation will be when the cut becomes effective and an analysis of how the cut will affect spending and output. Any administration's economic policy agencies must coordinate with the Federal Reserve and with the Congress. For this reason, at certain times a change in the amount of money may be a more effective policy than a change in taxes because it can be implemented far more quickly and with less political controversy.

While much of macroanalysis deals with government policies, decisions of businesses and individuals are also important. All interact and influence each other. Exxon's view of where the economy is heading may cause it to postpone building a new refinery. Sears Roebuck may cut its inventories by 10 percent. Such decisions are made by key executives on the basis of their analysis of the economy and what is in store for it. In turn, they thereby help determine where the economy is headed. In the same way, individuals may decide to buy real estate or bonds or hold onto money as a result of their judgments—whether carefully formulated or not—of what will happen to interest rates, prices, and income.

Individual investors, business executives, and voters are constantly faced with decisions that require macroeconomic analysis. Whether formal or so informal that it is not even recognized as a decision, the processes are similar. The current situation is examined for possible alternative actions. Decisions are based on a view as to where the economy is headed and what results would be desirable. To lower taxes, to invest in a refinery or inventory, to look for a job, to buy stocks, to open a business—all of these actions could be called policies. Whether to adopt one or another depends on judgmental forecasts of the economy and on what differences the decisions will make to future well-being.

Macroeconomic Methods

To aid in achieving goals and selecting policies, macroeconomics furnishes a framework and models. Because the amount of data which surround us is too massive and chaotic to be readily understood, economic analysts need a framework. Information must be summarized, simplified, and expressed in a form that brings out essential interrelationships and allows them to be tested and measured. The end results of analysis are *models,* which are simplified explanations or theories of how the economy works. The models are used to forecast the future of the economy and to test conflicting policy views.. If next year's forecast predicts continuing inflation or a recession, should any action be planned? If policies should be altered, what changes would be best? Models try to explain what might happen under alternative policies. For example, would a tax cut next year raise or lower inflation?

If you argue·about a limit on taxes with your neighbor and claim a relationship between government spending and inflation, you are using a simplified model of how the economy may operate. Such descriptive models suffer from several defects. They are often imprecise and difficult to apply. Frequently their assumptions are not stated. They do not progress logically from point to point. Their formulations are so general that time is wasted in semantic confusion. Macroeconomists, increasingly, supplement or supplant descriptive reasoning with mathematical analysis and ˙quantitative statistical techniques. Such models can be tested by seeing how well they can explain past events and if they can make accurate predictions of the future.

A good framework or model improves understanding, forecasts, and decisions. The key quest in building macroeconomic models is to find simplified but accurate representations of the processes through which the aggregate economy operates. This is accomplished by grouping participants into sectors, the components of which react in the same way to economic events. For example, to explain why consumers spend as they do, we don't examine a particular family; we group all families and households together. We don't study the contract between General Motors and the United Auto Workers, but rather, we try to predict average wages and labor income. *The Wall Street*

Journal lists daily several hundred interest rates on individual bonds or Treasury bills. In contrast, most macroeconomic models deal with a single interest rate. However, if a model is large and complex, the differing rates on long-term bonds or on short-term Treasury bills and other specific types of interest may be forecast separately.

The analytical framework of this volume groups economic decisions into three key components: those which influence (1) aggregate demand, (2) aggregate supply, and (3) the inflationary process. The chapters which follow detail the elements which determine their values and present differing views as to the importance of each component. Knowledge of how the economy operates is necessary to explain what is happening, to understand predictions of the future economy, and to analyze conflicting views as to which policies, if any, can be most helpful in achieving national and individual goals.

AGGREGATE DEMAND

Figure 1.9 illustrates graphically an aggregate demand curve. Each point on the *aggregate demand curve* (AD_1) stands for the quantity of output of goods and services that the economy desires to purchase in a given period of time at a particular price level. In the figure, the quantity of output (Q) is measured on

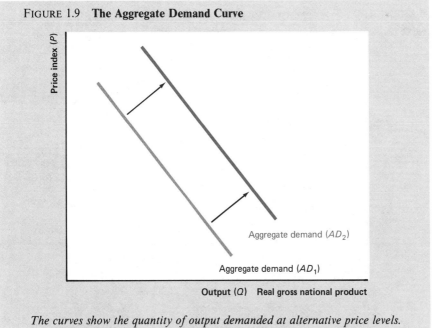

FIGURE 1.9   **The Aggregate Demand Curve**

The curves show the quantity of output demanded at alternative price levels. As price levels rise, the aggregate demand for the real GNP falls.

the horizontal axis. The associated price level (*P*), for each amount of purchases is measured on the vertical axis.

The **position** and **shape** of the *AD* curve depend on the tastes and preferences of consumers, investors, and the foreign sector, as expressed in their desires to spend and to hold money and by the policies of the government with respect to its taxes, expenditures, and creation of money.

The AD_2 curve in Figure 1.9 illustrates a greater willingness of the economy to purchase goods and services at each price level than is true on AD_1. The move from position AD_1 to AD_2 is called a **shift** in aggregate demand. In this case, only the position and not the shape of the demand curve alters. Such shifts are caused by events such as an increase in the amount of money, an increase in government spending or taxes, or a change in the private sector's desires to buy goods or hold money.

AGGREGATE SUPPLY

Figure 1.10 illustrates graphically an **aggregate supply curve** (AS_1), or the schedule of prices at which specific quantities of real goods and services would be supplied. The axes and scales of measurements for *AD* and *AS* are equivalent. The shape of aggregate supply illustrates the way in which costs change as

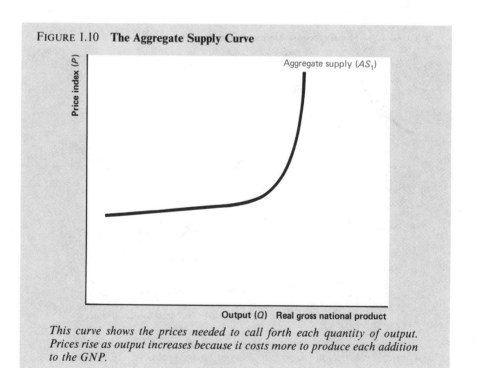

FIGURE 1.10   **The Aggregate Supply Curve**

Price index (*P*)

Aggregate supply (AS_1)

Output (*Q*)   Real gross national product

This curve shows the prices needed to call forth each quantity of output. Prices rise as output increases because it costs more to produce each addition to the GNP.

production moves in response to changes in demand.[4]

The forces influencing aggregate supply include the supply of the factors of production—labor, capital, and materials—and the technology or knowledge and techniques by which they are combined. The *AS* curve shifts as a result of a change in these factors—for example, more women entering the labor force or the rise in international oil prices—as well as a change in technology and the organization of production. One major question is whether the willingness to work more or harder and to invest in capital has declined, causing a critical difference between the economy in the 1980s and that of the 1930s or 1950s.

THE INFLATIONARY PROCESS

Figure 1.11 shows a Phillips curve, one of the schedules developed to help describe the inflationary process. With the growth of inflation, the belief that

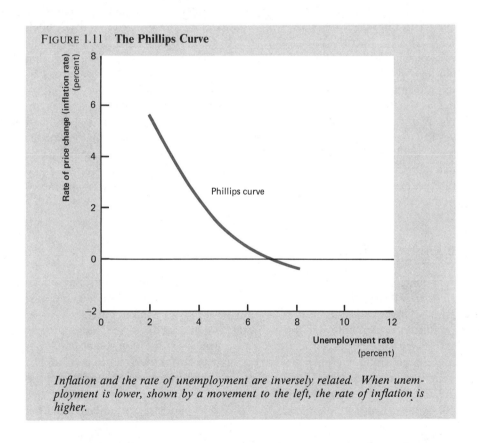

FIGURE 1.11   **The Phillips Curve**

Inflation and the rate of unemployment are inversely related. When unemployment is lower, shown by a movement to the left, the rate of inflation is higher.

4. The curve as drawn is sometimes described as that which prevails in the intermediate run (one quarter to three or four years). Shorter-run *AS* curves are often drawn as horizontal. As the intermediate period extends into the long run, the shape of the curve becomes more vertical.

the economy will produce the same quantity of goods only at ever-higher prices has become a matter of anxiety. As a result, increased attention has been given to possible inflationary processes or forces that lead to continuing upward shifts in aggregate supply and demand.

Phillips curves picture relationships between rates of price change (inflation) and a measure of over- or underutilization of the economy's productive capacity. Each point on a Phillips curve relates unemployment or capacity utilization to a rate of inflation. In Figure 1.11, the rate of price change (the change in prices over the price level, $\frac{\Delta P}{P}$ in percent) is measured on the vertical scale and the level of normal or abnormal utilization of supply on the horizontal.[5] In this Phillips curve, the state of utilization is measured by the unemployment rate. It can also be measured by ratios of output to capacity or similar forces. On each curve other factors, such as expectations and pressures to adjust wages and prices to past or expected movements, are assumed constant.

The Phillips curve shown in Figure 1.11 is only one of many models developed to describe and analyze the dynamic forces which determine the relationships between the rates of inflation and output. The general idea that output and unemployment are related to the rate at which prices change as part of an overall inflationary process must be differentiated from specific Phillips curves which have been derived statistically from past movements. For example, many observers believe that such relationships shift over time (becoming vertical in the long run). Part 5 analyzes numerous issues related to inflation, its costs, and how movements in demand and supply can lead to or combat persistent price increases. Models which include dynamic forces leading to steady rates of price change (inflation) are a necessary part of a complete macroeconomic framework.

Macroeconomic Theories

Aggregate demand depends on decisions to consume and invest. Such decisions are affected by factors like expectations, the amount of money, and government taxes and expenditures. Aggregate supply depends on desires to work, productivity, available resources, capital, and similar factors. Changes in demand and supply influence prices and output. In addition, persistent price movements—inflation—may develop as a result of expectations or from the organization of our wage and price-setting institutions. The schedules of aggregate demand, aggregate supply, and the inflationary process can be fleshed out by the use of theory and history. Past events and data are analyzed in order

---

5. The sign delta (Δ) means "change in." The inside of the front cover lists this and other technical abbreviations to aid in finding their meanings and definitions.

to develop both theories and working models of how the economy operates. These theories and models help identify feasible alternatives and goals.

THE CLASSICAL ECONOMISTS

In the 1930s, much of the Western world experienced a major depression. Unemployment and poverty were rampant. To help analyze these problems, John Maynard Keynes published *The General Theory of Employment, Interest, and Money* in 1936. Keynes was trying to fill a gap in the then-dominant method of economic analysis, which he labeled "classical" and which was based on the writings of David Ricardo, John Stuart Mill, F. Y. Edgeworth, and Alfred Marshall. These men, the most prominent English economists of the nineteenth and early twentieth centuries, gave scant attention to the problems of unemployment and depression, considering such phenomena to be merely temporary lapses from the more basic condition of full use of resources. The classical economists were primarily interested in how the economy could best utilize its scarce resources and in how money influences prices. They were less concerned with what determined the level of total income and output because deviations from full utilization of resources were deemed to be temporary aberrations. As a result, they did not bother to model specifically the factors which determine income.

KEYNES AND THE NEO-KEYNESIANS

Perhaps the most revolutionary element in Keynes's writings was his emphasis on the problem of underemployment and the outline of a framework useful in modeling it. He advanced the concept that the economy might stall at an *equilibrium*—a point without any pressure for change—of less than full employment of labor and productive capacity. Keynes stressed the need to include in theoretical analysis such factors as imperfections in markets, delayed reactions, lack of information, and shifting expectations. He also emphasized the importance of government decisions and institutions. Each of these neglected factors can result in instability and underemployment or inflation.

Keynes's great influence on modern thought is due as much to his emphasis on new questions as to the actual ideas and theories of his simple model. His book led to a fundamental reconstruction of macroeconomics. It had a lasting impact on how the world views the problems of inflation and depression. It introduced in an elemental form a model of *income determination*—that is, a model of the forces that determine the amount of output and income in each period. While income determination has remained at the core of economic analysis, today's views differ considerably from the simple model formulated by Keynes. His ideas have been clarified and modified by neo-Keynesians as a result of numerous factors. Among them are the reactions of neo-Keynesians to acknowledged errors in Keynesian analysis and forecasts, the development of better data and computer techniques and, very importantly, the influence of economists who argued that the Keynesian analysis neglected many important variables. The current models of income determination place far greater emphasis on money, prices, and the factors influencing supply than did the Keynesian models of the 1940s and 1950s. The initial analysis based on Keynes's work emphasized primarily the factors determining aggregate demand. In the Great Depression and World War II, these were by far the most critical variables. With time, the significance of supply and the process of inflation were recognized, and the theories were modified to upgrade the importance of such factors.

MONETARISTS

During the 1960s and 1970s, under the leadership of Milton Friedman of the University of Chicago, many economists vigorously attacked the neo-Keynesians for what they felt was an incorrect view of how income is determined. These economists are called monetarists. While no single body of doctrine exists on which all monetarists agree, several key tenets predominate. Most important is the view that income analysis must give a preeminent role to the quantity of money. Changes in the amount of money play a crucial part in determining the spending decisions of all sectors. In addition, monetarists place a heavy emphasis on the underlying stability of the economy and the basic efficiency of financial markets. Most monetarists believe that, if left to itself and not disturbed by government and Federal Reserve action, the economy would not require special aid or policies.

In contrast, early Keynesian models downplayed money and price changes and emphasized an inherent instability in the system. Money and interest rates were part of the Keynesian framework, but they affected primarily the level of investment. The impact of money on wealth, on expectations, and on consumption was neglected. The effect of price changes on the willingness to spend, save, and invest was inadequately represented as well. Although they developed a theory of the inflationary process based on the existence of excess demand, Friedman and other monetarists also neglected the theory of supply and the way in which changes in demand were split between price movements and output. Since their theories primarily incorporated efficient markets with rapid adjustments, most monetarists assumed, at least until recently, that the bulk of adjustments to demand would occur in prices and not in output.

NEW CLASSICISTS

The inauguration of President Reagan brought to the fore a view of economics which had been developing over the past decade in opposition to the neo-Keynesian and monetarist economists of the mainstream. In the Reagan policy proposals, a good deal of emphasis was placed on supply-side economics and rational expectations. These ideas developed from the analysis of economists whose models are similar in many ways to the classical models with purely competitive markets. In their models, prices and wages react flexibly to changing conditions of supply and demand, while firms and workers formulate their views of the future in a rational manner. Because their approaches have much in common with the classical tradition, these economists have been called the **new classicists.** The term has been applied both to those who emphasize rational expectations and to those who stress the supply side. The classical assumptions lead to a downplaying of most questions concerning the factors influencing aggregate demand, while emphasizing the significance of aggregate supply. The result is a model of the economy that usually operates at full employment. While some instability does occur because of errors made in judging future price movements and necessary output, much of reported unemployment is assumed to be voluntary, reflecting a logical delay of workers in accepting positions while they search for better jobs.

In the opinion of both neo-Keynesians and traditional monetarists, shifts in spending cause fluctuations in output and prices. While the mainstream economists disagree over the factors causing demand to shift and, therefore, over specific policies, they are in accord that inflations and recessions can be reduced if proper policies are followed. In contrast, the new classical view holds that policy changes are likely to be ineffectual in minimizing short-run fluctuations because such movements occur either as a result of mistakes in policies or because of an irreducible level of instability.

As a corollary, improvements must come primarily through increasing the economy's ability to produce goods and services. Since it is assumed that the economy, left to itself, will operate at the best attainable level of demand, what is needed on the demand side is to remove impediments to the economy's natural forces. Possibilities for increasing output do exist, however, through more work and a faster growth in productivity. Greater output can be achieved by reducing government regulations and increasing incentives, particularly through lower taxes. In addition, since fluctuations are caused by inadequate information, new techniques of disseminating knowledge and facts might enhance stability in the future.

AN ECLECTIC APPROACH

This book presents a framework and theories of income determination developed from ideas both of Keynes and of his critics. It places far more emphasis on money, wealth, and prices than the oversimplified traditional Keynesian models. It also emphasizes more strongly factors such as expectations, productivity, and the financial world. Although Keynes did include these in his analysis, they were omitted from the early, simple Keynesian models. Such a framework has been called "the post-Keynesian consensus."[6]

6. G. Haberler, "Critical Notes on Rational Expectations," *Journal of Money, Credit, and Banking* 12 (Nov. 1980):833–34.

Factors which affect the aggregate supply curve are also described in more detail than in either the simple Keynesian or monetarist models. More attention is given to the way in which changes in demand and supply interact with the market's institutions to help determine the level of output, price changes, and inflation. The model presented in this volume also puts more emphasis on business fluctuations or cycles, which was a popular area of work before Keynes. It was greatly neglected in the 1950s and 1960s. By the 1980s economists were once again concerned with the factors causing the economy to move up and down.

Monetarists remain split to some extent over the question of whether such a framework can be utilized successfully. Friedman has used the Keynesian framework well to contrast opposing views as to how the economy works. Other monetarists hold that the framework does not give full scope to their position; that it tends to bias the analysis of income determination because certain interactions are hidden. We feel, with Friedman, that most macroeconomic analysis and debate can be encompassed in the current version of the framework of determination of income, prices, and output. This would include the analysis of the new classicists, but their use of a more limited set of assumptions will often lead to different results. Their emphasis tends to reduce the importance of analysis of periods during which prices and wages are adjusting to new situations. In the long run, the different schools agree that the future state of the economy depends on what growth is achieved in aggregate supply. They disagree on the significance of changes in demand in influencing such growth.

Why Economists Disagree

During the 1960s and 1970s, macroeconomics experienced many ups and downs in public acceptance. At times opinion held that we were on the verge of solving our basic economic problems; at other times a widespread feeling prevailed that the field was badly disorganized and could make only minor contributions to improving economic well-being.

The persistence of inflation disheartened many. Wasn't this proof that macroeconomics was in disarray? If we could explain and predict inflation properly, couldn't it be cured? We have seen why this need not be true. Further explanations will appear as we examine the subject in more detail.

Forecasts during this period contained larger errors than we would have liked. For example, over the 17 years between 1963 and 1980, the principal forecasters made on average (their mean absolute error) an error of about 0.9 percent in their forecasts of the next year's current-dollar GNP. Of course an error that small would be excellent for those setting odds on football or basketball games, but it did not meet the needs for the economy. An error of 0.9 percent can mark the difference between low growth and a recession. It can lead to serious policy errors. This is particularly true because the errors in forecasting output and prices were larger than .9 percent, but they partially offset each other.

The situation most disturbing to many, however, was the frequent lack of agreement among economists as to proper policies. Hard-working, well-informed, and honest individuals kept coming up with widely divergent recommendations as to how best to meet our economic goals. Why do economic policy recommendations vary so much? On the whole, it it is not because of forecasts for next year. In fact, economists of widely differing views do not disagree greatly in their actual forecasts. Yet despite short-term forecasts which do not diverge greatly, policy recommendations are often far apart. As an example, compare the columns written in *Newsweek* by Paul Samuelson, one of our country's foremost neo-Keynesians, and Milton Friedman, a foremost monetarist. While they sometimes agree in their predictions as to where the economy is headed, only rarely do they concur on the proper policy to be followed. Understanding why such eminent economists disagree on policy, despite using similar facts, framework, and methods of analysis, helps us to realize what macroeconomics can and cannot do. The factors which cause their analyses to differ are those which must be watched for, both in making our own analyses and in understanding those of others, whether they be government economists, the president of Dupont, the chairman of the Senate Banking Committee, an investment adviser, or your next-door neighbor.

THE CAUSES OF DISAGREEMENTS

A major source of divergent views is the disagreement among analysts about which goals are most important. Some weigh the dangers of inflation far above those of unemployment. Others take the opposite view; unemployment should have top priority. Part of this divergence originates in the differing significance economists attach to present events as compared to the future. Some emphasize the need to achieve goals in the near short run, while others feel that the state of the economy in five or ten years is the important thing. They are willing to live with bad conditions or high unemployment in the next year or two on the assumption that it is the only way to bring about good long-run results.

Secondly, close watchers of the economy place varying degrees of trust in models and forecasts. An economist who believes in the accuracy of forecasts is more likely to support active policies to influence the economic future.

Closely related to the first two factors are opinions about how well-administered policy actions are likely to be. An economist who believes that whatever policy is adopted will probably be fouled up won't urge much action. This is especially true if the economist believes that there will be serious political delays in adopting a policy. A tax cut postponed for a year may be worse than none at all. An employment program that merely moves people from one public payroll to another won't lower unemployment.

There is widespread disagreement over whether the historical instability of the economy, as seen in the period 1929–80, is an inherent phenomenon caused by our institutions and the shifting expectations of private businesses and individuals or whether it results from errors in governmental policies. Those who believe that the economy is basically stable advocate policy action less frequently, feeling that the economy, left to itself, will perform well. Those who believe the economy is basically unstable will see a more urgent need for policy changes.

Closely related to questions of instability are differences in the model used to explain the economy. Some economists believe that accurate descriptions are possible with simple models. In contrast, others believe that simplified models cannot explain where the economy is and where it is going because they neglect the effects of time, of poor information, of transactions costs, and of market constraints. At one extreme, prices are held to move primarily in reaction to changes in expectations of future prices. These expectations, in turn, depend on anticipated spending changes which stem from current monetary policy. At the other extreme, price and wage changes are believed to result from inertia in the price-wage structure. Wage-earners try to catch up with previous losses in income stemming from prior price increases. Markets for goods and wages are sticky. The economy's adjustment process is slow. Upward momentum of prices may build up and be hard to stop. Prices and wages respond not only to supply and demand, but also to how corporate executives and trade-union leaders react to specific events. Many prices are administered so as to satisfy long-run objectives.

Views also differ as to how expectations or anticipations of future events are arrived at and how rapidly they influence actions. Some believe that markets process and act on information rapidly and efficiently (expectations are **rational**) and conclude that activist government policies can exert only minimal effects. Others point to the poor record of market price forecasts, waves of optimism and pessimism, and lack of knowledge as indications of why government policies can improve the operations of the economy.

In appraisals of more complex models of the economy, estimates vary considerably as to the shape and magnitude of critical relationships. For example, specific studies yield different outcomes as to how income reacts to changes in money or how investment reacts to interest rates. Analysts will arrive at opposing conclusions about the economy depending on which study they accept.

As we examine any suggested policy moves, however, it is well to recognize the fact that differences in policy recommendations seem to depend far more on individual opinions as to what ought to be than on the framework or model employed. When analysts with differing goals, objectives, philosophies, and beliefs about how the economy operates use identical facts, techniques, and procedures, they will end up with contrasting recommendations. Because such differences are substantial and tend to be permanent, students of the economy must understand how they affect opinions and suggestions. Informed decision makers should know how much of the differences in the alternative policies offered can be ascribed to facts and how much to divergent assumptions, views of the economic process, and value judgments. Realizing why people differ in their advice enables us to make better choices. We can evaluate their opinions in formulating our own.

Macroeconomics does not find simple answers to problems. A general model brings out possible relationships. Estimates of the form and magnitude of these relationships become feasible. Students learn what questions to ask and how to analyze potential links among variables. There are few constants in our complex, shifting economy. Today's truth may be tomorrow's error. Those who make good decisions and find correct answers are not constrained by a single approach or theory. They employ a good analytical framework and use it to develop judgment which is then applied to specific situations.

Summary

1. Macroeconomics describes the operations of the economy as a whole. It considers the actions of major sectors—all households, businesses, government, foreign—rather than those of individuals or specific markets, such as those for wheat or steel.

2. One set of key economic issues concerns how to increase growth in the supply of goods and services. Greater inputs of capital, materials, and labor raise the ability of the economy to produce. Improved productivity means that more goods are turned out for each hour worked.

3. Output, employment, and prices have been unstable. Individual jobs, the value of a household's assets, and business profits and losses have fluctuated widely, especially in major sectors of the economy such as financial markets and construction. Macroeconomics attempts to explain what causes instability and how it can be reduced.

4. The 1980s started with a high rate of inflation accompanied by unemployment well above its natural rate at the point of full employment, and with a high amount of output lost because of the failure to produce at full potential. The result was a national sense of discomfort leading to a demand for political action and change.

5. Economic policies are actions taken to help reach goals, which are future economic conditions deemed desirable by the body politic, individuals, and businesses. Economic decision making utilizes models (simplified explanations) of how the economy works to forecast the probable state of the econ-

omy under alternative policies, to permit selection of those which seem most likely to help achieve goals.

6. In order to understand how the economy works and to build explanatory models of the determination of income, output, and prices, economic decisions can be grouped into those influencing aggregate demand, aggregate supply, and the process of inflation. Such models abstract from reality to yield simple theories capable of interpreting the actions of the economy and of predicting its future direction.

7. The general macroeconomic framework contained in this volume can be used to explain a wide variety of views as to how the economy operates. Analysts differ considerably as to which factors they emphasize and in their assumptions about how these factors work. As a result, they frequently end up with divergent policy prescriptions.

8. The study of macroeconomics enables us to see what lies behind the variety of forecasts and policy proposals. With an understanding of how and why particular views are arrived at, we can adjust the analysis and improve our own individual decisions.

Questions for Discussion and Review

1. Can you think of examples of how particular individuals and families have been affected by stagflation?

2. What current sacrifices do you feel are worthwhile in terms of output and jobs to end an inflation? If a failure to cut back at one time means that output will be 10 percent lower five years later, how would that change your estimate?

3. Since models contain only a small amount of information and in a greatly simplified form, we should not expect them to provide accurate explanations or predictions of the economy. Do you agree?

4. Courses in microeconomics present the theory of how producers, consumers, and resource owners make their decisions and interact with each other. At first glance, knowledge of this theory might seem sufficient to understand the workings of the economy. Why, then, are there entire courses and books devoted to macroeconomics?

5. Over the last 20 years macroeconomic theory has been constantly changing, with many propositions once accepted by a majority of economists being discarded or greatly changed. At the same time microeconomic theory has been relatively unchanged. Why do you suppose this is?

6. What are some of the main issues over which macroeconomists disagree? Are these disagreements resolvable in principle?

References

Useful background and source material may be found in:

Council of Economic Advisers. *Economic Report of the President.* Washington, D.C.: Government Printing Office, issued annually.

Business Week, published biweekly.

The Wall Street Journal, published every workday.

Some considerations basic to the material to be covered are discussed in:

Friedman, Milton. "The Methodology of Positive Economics." In *Essays in Positive Economics.* Chicago: University of Chicago Press, 1953.

Johnson, H. G. "The Keynesian Revolution and the Monetarist Counter-Revolution." *American Economic Review* 61 (1971):91–106.

Leijonhufvud, A. "Schools, 'Revolutions,' and Research Programmes in Economic Theory." In *Method and Appraisal in Economics,* edited by S. J. Latsis. Cambridge, England: Cambridge University Press, 1976.

Lucas, R. E. Jr. "Methods and Problems in Business Cycle Theory." *Journal of Money, Credit and Banking* 12 (1980): 695–715.

Morgenstern, O. *On the Accuracy of Economic Observations,* 2nd edition. Princeton: Princeton University Press, 1963.

Solow, R. M. "Alternative Approaches to Macroeconomic Theory: A Partial View." *Canadian Journal of Economics* 12 (1979): 339–54.

2

Measures of the Aggregate Economy

The year 1929, the start of the Great Depression, was the watershed year for the economy and for macroanalysis. It swept away all that had gone before and forever changed economics and the structure of the American and world economies. The lack of demand, leading to large-scale unemployment and untold distress, stimulated the development of methods of analyzing and measuring the economy—a direct result of the need to understand what was happening. The extended depression of the 1930s persisted so long because of ignorance about its extent and causes and what to do about it. As the Great Depression wore on and analysis improved, better techniques of explanation and measurement developed. Because of this new knowledge, when the economy reached a new peak in 1980 and then turned down, only a small minority of observers feared that another major crash would occur. Most felt that enough had been learned so that, if the nation desired, another Great Depression could be prevented; or a recession could be planned and directed by government actions in an attempt to fight inflation.

Before we can analyze and forecast the economy's future, we must be able to measure what is happening. This chapter introduces and explains five important aggregate measures of economic activity:

The gross national product in current dollars (nominal GNP).
The gross national product in constant dollars (real output).
The aggregate price indexes (consumer price index or GNP deflator).
Potential output (full employment or natural rate of unemployment).
Unemployment.

A SET OF FORECASTS

We can get an idea of how these measures are used and their importance by looking at the steady flow of evaluations of past economic performance and of forecasts that signal the approach of the end of the year as reliably as Christmas decorations. They appear in the press, on television, and in statements made by presidents of major corporations and banks. All of the principal measures—namely, nominal GNP, output, prices, and unemployment—are at the core of business and government decision making. More importantly, forecasts are fed into the planning process at all levels of business and government. Next year's budget, sales goals, and production programs are drafted to accord with expectations of where the economy is going.

Most forecasts are prepared from computer models derived from theoretical and statistical analysis of past economic developments. Some forecasts are still prepared from judgmental rather than statistical models. In either case, the forecasters bring their analyses up to date with the latest information on the economy. They make projections of variables such as monetary or fiscal policy, whose values cannot be determined within the model. They adjust, or fine-tune, the model using their interpretation of the significance of recent events.

On the basis of projections from these updated and adjusted models, the forecasters issue predictions for a large number of economic variables covering periods of from one quarter to one to five years into the future. These predictions become the basis for decisions at the executive level of what to do or not to do.

Table 2.1 illustrates how well or poorly a typical set of forecasts performed for the years 1978, 1979, and 1980. The values of the four main ag-

TABLE 2.1   **Examples of Annual Forecasts**

	1978		1979		1980	
	Forecast	*Actual*	*Forecast*	*Actual*	*Forecast*	*Actual*
GNP (billions of dollars)	2,106	2,106	2,303	2,368	2,524	2,574
GNP (billions of 1972 dollars)	1,402	1,384	1,414	1,431	1,408	1,421
Change in GNP price deflator (percent)	6.2	7.4	7.1	8.8	8.4	9.5
Unemployment (percent)	6.1	6.0	6.6	5.8	7.4	7.2

SOURCE: UCLA National Business Forecast

The numbers in the forecast columns are estimates made in November of the previous year. The actual column reports figures as they appear in November of the forecast year. Such forecasts are used in decisions made by businesses and governments.

gregates for these years as forecasted are compared to their actual values. As was typical for the 1970s, projections of the GNP in current dollars, or total expenditures, were quite accurate. But the forecasts of prices (the GNP price deflator) and unemployment contained greater errors. These particular forecasts were prepared by the UCLA Business Forecast Service and were issued in November-December of the year preceding the projection. The forecasts are typical. Other forecasting services show better results in some areas and worse in others. What exactly do the measures in this and similar forecasts cover? Why is knowledge of their content so vital to macroeconomic analysis?

The National Income and Product Accounts

The National Income and Product Accounts were developed in the 1930s to help quantify what was happening in the economy. They have become the center of most of macroeconomics. They provide estimates of how much is being spent, and by whom. The development of these measures has been a major factor in improving analysis of the economy.

From these accounts we obtain estimates of the gross national product (GNP), national income, overall price changes, and real output. The **gross national product** is a measure of the total money value of all final goods and services produced by our economy in a given period of time. The GNP measures not only total production and demand, but also the components which make up both. The accounts aid in explaining why demand and supply shift. When the Ford Motor Company decides on its production for the next quarter, a major influence on its decision will be the expected level of the GNP for that quarter. Ford uses the predicted level of the GNP in its decisions because auto sales, as well as the sales of most other commodities, are highly sensitive to changes in the GNP.

THE CIRCULAR FLOW OF EXPENDITURES AND INCOME

To picture how the GNP is measured, let us start with a simple circular flow model of the economy (Figure 2.1). This model excludes government expenditures and saving by households and businesses. Households purchase goods as varied as bread and washing machines, plus services such as tax advice, health care, or haircuts from the businesses which produce them. Household expenditures are shown at the top of the figure. Money for the purchases flows from left to right, while the goods flow from the businesses to households. One measure of the GNP is simply to count the money value of all expenditures on final products as they occur. This can be done by metering all of the expenditure flows between households and businesses.

It is important in this measurement to count only the value of *final,* not all, goods and services produced. **Final goods and services** are those purchased (and not resold) by their final user in the period. Thus sugar sold to a household is a

FIGURE 2.1   **The Circular Flow: Income as Product and Earnings**

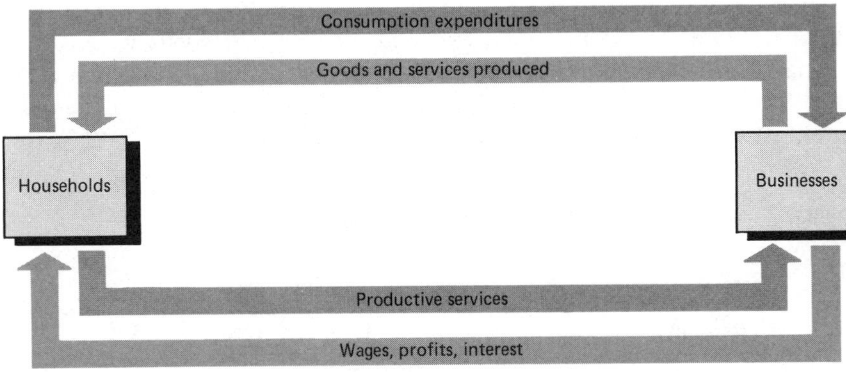

Consumption expenditures

Goods and services produced

Households

Businesses

Productive services

Wages, profits, interest

The GNP is measured by counting the dollars people spend or the goods and services they receive, shown in the upper loop. Counting the amounts received by households for their services—wages, profits, interest, and so on—gives another measure of the total. The flow through the two loops must be equal.

final good, but sugar sold to a candy maker is an ***intermediate good.*** It would be double-counting to add together the value of the candy and the value of the sugar used in its production.

Another way of measuring the GNP is to count the wages, profits, and other income which businesses are paying to households for the resources—labor, capital, land—needed in production. These flows are called ***gross national income.*** These factor earnings are the costs of producing the final product. The value of income paid for the resources will exactly equal the value of the goods produced.

The definitions of double-entry bookkeeping in a firm make costs and the value of product equal. When a business records an amount paid out as income, it simultaneously records the same amount as a cost. The same is true for bookkeeping on a national scale. The value of production is merely the total amount paid out in wages, rent, and interest plus profits. Profits, whether plus or minus, measure the difference between amounts paid for the other factors of production and the amounts received from sales. They serve as a balancing item to make the GNP, whether measured by expenditures or income, identical.

People who follow economic affairs sometimes worry that because of inflation or other reasons, sufficient income will not be earned to buy all goods produced. Figure 2.1 shows why, in a formal sense, this is a needless concern. The amount of income earned exactly equals the cost and value of the goods and services produced. There is always enough income to buy production, no matter what happens to prices or inflation.

This double-accounting format for the economy becomes clearer when we leave the simplified circular flow model and examine Table 2.2, which is a summary of the National Income and Product Accounts for 1980. The right side of the table shows that total expenditures for final goods were $2,627 billion. This is obtained by counting the flow depicted at the top of Figure 2.1. The left side shows the costs or amounts paid out for this production—the bottom part of the diagram. By definition, the two are equal.

TABLE 2.2   **National Income and Product Accounts (1980)**
(in billions of dollars)

Gross National Income		*Gross National Product*		
Wages, Salaries, and		*Households*		
Supplements (W)	1,726			
Rental income of persons (RE)	32	Personal consumption		
Net interest (IN)	180	expenditures (C)		1,670
Corporate profits, adjusted (PR)	182	Durables	210	
		Nondurables	674	
National income (NI)	2,120	Services	786	
Capital consumption allowances		*Business*		
(DEP)	288			
Indirect business taxes and		Gross private investment (I)		395
transfers (TI)	217	Residential construction	104	
Statistical discrepancy and misc		Business fixed investment	295	
($DISC$)	2	Increase in inventories	−4	
		Governments		
		Government purchases of goods		
		and services (G)		535
		Federal	199	
		State and local	336	
		Foreign		
		Net exports of goods and		
		services (X-IM)		27
		Exports (X)	341	
Charges against gross national		Imports (IM)	314	
product	2,627	Gross national product		2,627

SOURCE: U.S. Department of Commerce.

The left side reports earnings by the factors of production (national income) plus costs for depreciation and indirect taxes as well as a small statistical discrepancy. The right side measures goods produced and the sectors which purchased them.

EXPENDITURES BY SECTORS OF THE ECONOMY

The right side of Table 2.2 classifies expenditures by sectors of the economy— households (consumption), business (investment), governments, and foreign (net exports). This is most important for analytical purposes. The division of spending into groups has become a basic tool for explaining changes in the level of the GNP. By grouping decision makers, one can analyze more readily their decisions to spend. Each group is made as homogeneous as possible, in the hope that similar factors will influence all the transactions of that sector, whether in buying goods or supplying resources.

Although we shall consider only the four principal sectors shown in Table 2.2, a few subgroups, such as consumer durables, nondurables, and services, are shown in the further breakdown of the table. These subgroups reflect distinct types of spending decisions. Because in most circumstances replacement of durables such as automobiles and furniture can be delayed if prospects or income become uncertain, expenditures on durables fluctuate more widely and follow somewhat different patterns than spending on bread, clothing, gasoline, and other nondurables. These, in turn, differ from expenditures for medical care, theater tickets, rent, or other consumer services. Excluded from the count because they are not expenditures for goods produced during the period are purchases of used cars, existing houses, and other existing assets. Major forecasting services with massive computers may analyze separately over 20 spending decision groups. The number of subgroupings at the command of an analyst is limited only by time and by available data. The key problem for the analyst is to classify the groups in such a way that their level of spending can be reliably explained and projected.

Consumption.   The first and largest class of expenditure in Table 2.2 is **personal consumption expenditures** (*C*).[1] These represent the bulk of the amount spent on final products by households and nonprofit institutions. Both of these groups are almost always included within the shorthand rubric *consumers.*

Investment.   Although the largest amount of spending in our economy is done by businesses, only a small portion of business expenditures ends up classified as spending for final products, or **gross private investment** (*I*). Most business purchases of goods or services are for intermediate goods, which become part of final sales to consumers or governments. The GNP account includes all gross private investment; depreciation is not subtracted. However, because capital is used up in production, some analysts feel that a better measure of final product is the **net national product** (NNP), which subtracts out estimates of **capital**

---

1. A note on nomenclature: For ease of exposition, a standard nomenclature and a single set of numerical examples are used throughout this book. Each variable or functional relationship is represented by one or a set of letters. The letters make up words and do not imply multiplication. Usually the letters are traditional or are closely related to the sound of the variables. Capital letters are used to represent variables and lowercase letters to represent coefficients of the relationships. Thus, YD is disposable income and kT is the tax multiplier. Bars over letters represent autonomous expenditures, and asterisks mean values at full employment. Thus, C represents consumption and the desire to consume, $\bar{C}$ is autonomous consumption, and C^* is consumption at full employment. Lowercase c is the coefficient of disposable income in the consumption function. With each equation a specific numerical example is usually provided, in which imaginary values are assigned to the coefficients and variables so that solutions can be found. Thus, $\bar{C}$ is usually $300 billion and c is .75.

consumption allowances, or *depreciation* (*DEP*). Since these sums are used up in production they are not available for consumption. But most macroanalysis deals with factors affecting total current expenditures; hence, GNP is the more closely watched and more often cited figure.

The largest subgroup of investment is purchases by businesses of structures and producers' durable equipment. The other two components of investment each have unusual features. Investment in residential construction, includes all spending by households for new homes or for major improvements. Households are considered businesses for this purpose. Investments in inventories may be planned or unplanned. All goods produced in the period and not sold or not used to replace goods withdrawn from the start-of-period inventories are classified as investment expenditures, whether intentional or not. This category shows the widest period-to-period fluctuations of any in the accounts.

It is important to recognize the difference between the meaning of the term *investment* as used in the GNP accounts, which is restricted to purchases of currently produced capital goods, and the more common usage of *investment*, which includes purchases of securities such as stocks and bonds, or existing assets such as older homes. While money spent to buy common stocks may influence the amount of expenditures for new capital goods, the causal path is winding and complex. The same is true for possible relationships between purchases of existing houses and investment in new construction.

Government. Anyone aware of the heated debates over public budgets and expenditures may be surprised at the relatively low magnitude of *government purchases of goods and services* (*G*) shown in Table 2.2. In 1980, total federal government expenditures as shown in the budget and in other parts of the national accounts were over three times as large as the figure shown for federal purchases of goods and services in the table. Furthermore, for all governments, total expenditures were 60 percent higher than *G* in the table. The difference consists of *transfer payments,* which are payments by governments but not expenditures for final products. The federal budget includes sizable transfer payments to individuals, grants-in-aid 'to states and local governments, and interest payments. None of these is included in the table since they are not expenditures for current production. Purchases of goods and services require the use of labor, capital, and land. Such expenditures result in additional output, often in the private sector. On the other hand, transfer payments do not increase output; they reallocate income among groups in the economy. While they have a significant impact on income available to spend, they do not form part of the GNP.

Net exports. The importance of the foreign sector is also distorted by the small magnitude of *net exports of goods and services* (*X-IM*) shown in the table. When the actual levels of exports (*X*) and imports (*IM*) are examined separately, their importance to the economy becomes far more obvious. In most typical presentations of the GNP, exports and imports are netted together, primarily for ease of calculation and exposition. The total of expenditures on final product in the United States can be estimated in either of two ways. In one, the expenditures for domestic goods and services can be added to the amount of export goods produced ($2,286 + $341 = $2,627). This is the total amount of the gross national output produced in the United States. We include Boeing's production of 747s whether they are sold here or abroad. In the second method, the $2,600 billion spent within the country on both domestic and foreign products can be added to the net difference between exports and imports ($2,600 + $341 − $314 = $2,627). We add in Boeing's sales of 747s abroad, but subtract purchases by U.S. airlines of European-made airbuses. Users must beware of underestimating the impact of foreign trade when they see the small net export figure in the GNP accounts. Failing to include Boeing planes sold for export excludes an important segment of the Seattle economy.

GNP. The total expenditures of the four sectors equal the GNP and the amount of effective aggregate demand in a period. The GNP can also be measured as the total value of goods and services produced in a period. By definition, total expenditures must exactly equal the value of the final product, since a good is sold to a consumer, to an investor, to the government, as an export, or is kept in inventory and recorded as a planned or unplanned inventory investment. Counting changes in inventories as part of expenditures insures that expenditures equal the value of final product.

NATIONAL INCOME

The left-hand column of Table 2.2 shows receipts, or **gross national income.** It is the equivalent of the flow at the bottom of Figure 2.1 and, as shown there, must equal expenditures and output of the GNP. The first four items are simple. They include wages and income of individual proprietors (W), rents (RE), interest (IN), and adjusted profits (PR). These are the payments to the factors of production, and their total equals what the Commerce Department defines as "national income."

Reported business profits are after depreciation (DEP) and after adjustments for some failures of corporations to adjust their books for inflation. However, sums to cover capital consumption (depreciation) are included in the prices of goods sold. Therefore, they appear as an additional charge against the GNP. Some other income is also received by governments through **indirect business taxes** (TI), as, for example, taxes on business property. Finally, a few minor adjustments are made. Most important of these is one for statistical discrepancies ($DISC$). These discrepancies occur because the two sides of the National Income and Product Accounts are estimated from different statistical sources. The National Accounts draw data from millions of individual units. Since the two sides are not forced into equality by auditors, as is done in a unified accounting system, minor errors in estimation arise and are shown as a statistical discrepancy.

DISPOSABLE INCOME

The fact that the two sides of the National Income and Product Accounts are equal by definition tends to obscure rather than clarify variables which cause changes in income and output. Most important among the variables affecting consumption is the level of income available for spending which is called *disposable income.* As Table 2.3 shows, the amount which households have available to spend or not as they see fit is significantly less than the national income.

TABLE 2.3   **National and Disposable Income (1980)**
(in billions of dollars)

National income	2,120
Less corporate profits tax (*TPR*)	−80
Less undistributed profits (*PRU*)	−47
Less contributions for social security (*BSS*)	−204
Plus government and business transfers and interest paid by government (*TR*)	+371
Personal income	2,160
Less personal taxes (*TP*)	−338
Disposable personal income (*YD*)	1,822

SOURCE: U.S. Department of Commerce

Disposable income is the amount available to households for spending. National income measures factor earnings, but households do not receive or keep it all. Some is retained by businesses; some goes to governments. Household funds are increased, however, by transfer and government interest payments.

Incomes received by households differ from total national income because households do not receive certain types of income. Businesses pay taxes on their profits to the government (*TPR*). In addition, undistributed profits (*PRU*) are amounts which businesses do not pay out to their stockholders. Businesses also make contributions to social security (*BSS*). These amounts paid to the government for social security benefit individuals but are not available for spending.

Not all adjustments are subtractions from available funds. Amounts which can be spent are increased when households receive transfer payments from government and businesses, interest paid by the government, and other minor sums. As noted previously, transfer (*TR*) payments are income paid by governments or businesses to those who render no current service in return, as in the case of government pensions to veterans and retired civil servants. While such payments may be desirable in promoting the public welfare, because they are not payments for goods or services being produced currently, they are excluded from the GNP. To make these transfer payments, tax money is collected from some and transferred to others. Taxes reduce the ability to spend of those from whom they are collected, while recipients of the transfer payments will have more to spend.

Personal income is the amount left after these adjustments have been made to national income. However, not all personal income is available for individuals to spend. Households must first pay taxes to the government out of this income. Thus, only after personal taxes (*TP*) are subtracted from personal income do we arrive at available disposable income (*YD*), one of the most critical variables in macroeconomics.

THE CIRCULAR FLOW REVISITED

Macroeconomics depends heavily upon analyses of the components of the GNP. Fundamental to income analysis is the necessary equality of the two sides of the GNP accounts. The first two columns of Figure 2.2 illustrate again the necessary relationships between expenditures on gross output and gross

FIGURE 2.2   **The Circular Flow Revisited**

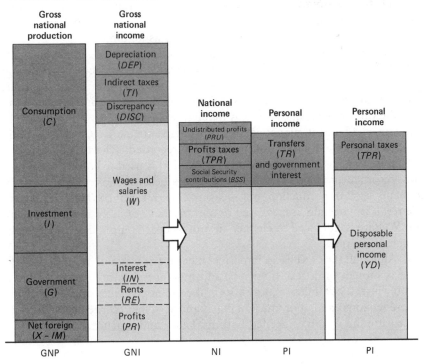

Gross expenditures are identical to gross national production and gross national income earned. Subtracting depreciation, indirect taxes, and the statistical discrepancy from the GNI leaves national income. Subtracting undistributed profits, profit taxes, and social security contributions from national income and adding transfers and government interest payments yields personal income. After personal taxes are paid, the remainder is disposable personal income.

income. The second column also details the reductions needed to transform gross receipts to (net) national income. The remainder of Figure 2.2 relates national and disposable income. The amount of personal disposable income greatly influences spending and, therefore, production. Households do not receive all national income because businesses pay taxes to governments and do not distribute some profits. On the other hand, personal income is augmented by receipts of transfer payments, including interest paid by governments. The sums available for households to spend are reduced by personal tax payments. The remainder is disposable income—the amount consumers can spend or save.

NET WELFARE

While increasing and stabilizing the GNP are frequently cited as national goals, economists recognize that there are important values which are not included in the GNP. The GNP excludes such important services as those performed by housewives or by do-it-yourself repairs and construction because they are not market transactions and it would be hard to assign a monetary value to them. Earnings from off-book work or work not reported in order to evade taxes is also not included and seems to be expanding. The same is true of other illegal activities such as the distribution of drugs such as heroin.

As the country's wealth grows, more people substitute leisure time satisfactions for work and the ability to purchase goods and services. Their welfare is enhanced thereby; yet the GNP goes down. Some costs of production, such as urbanization, are offsets not shown by the GNP. Increasing crime detracts from the value of central city life. A plane trip with every seat full is worth less than one on a half-full plane; yet no adjustments are made. Costs of pollution of air and water are great, but they are not recorded. The number of safety devices in plants is increasing. But when capital is used to correct these problems, recorded productivity falls. This occurs because more goods and labor are being used in production, but measured output in the GNP does not rise. The result is a decline in measured output per hour of labor input (productivity). Welfare is enhanced by cleaner air, but recorded output does not rise, even though prices may.

Although the GNP is an imperfect measure of welfare, it can nonetheless serve as a rough yardstick. It must be adjusted for population increases and for possible biases, but unless major shifts in the excluded values occur, the general picture remains valid. For much of macroanalysis, the recorded changes suffice to measure the variables needed both in theory and practice.

Price Indexes

The gross national product of the United States—the value of total spending—rose by more than a trillion dollars between 1975 and 1980. This change in value reflected two separate forces at work: (1) greater production of physical goods and services and (2) their sales at higher prices. For analysis, we must be able to separate the change in expenditures measured in current dollars into its component parts—movements in physical (real) output and movements in prices.

Price movements are measured by *price indexes,* which are comparisons of the average prices of a set of goods and services in two or more years. A widely used price index is the *consumer price index* (CPI) which monthly compares prices of a weighted market basket of goods commonly purchased by families. Movements in the CPI are used to adjust wages, social security and pension plans, and many other contracts. The incomes of a growing number of people are cost-of-living adjusted (COLA) and thus are directly affected by how the CPI measures price changes. The CPI is also frequently used to measure changes in the purchasing power of the dollar.

When prices rise, a dollar buys less. Purchasing power, or the value of money, falls. Economists measure changes in the value of money with a price index. The value of a dollar, or its purchasing power in terms of a selected base year, is found by dividing the dollar by a price index. This is demonstrated by the following example:

	1949	1959	1967	1969	1980
Consumer price index (1967 = 100)	71.4	87.3	100	109.8	246.5
Dollar divided by index ($\frac{100}{\text{CPI}}$)	$\frac{100.0}{71.4}$	$\frac{100.0}{87.3}$	$\frac{100}{100}$	$\frac{100.0}{109.8}$	$\frac{100.0}{246.5}$
Purchasing power of a dollar in terms of 1967 base ($\frac{100}{\text{CPI}} \times 100$)	140	115	100	91	41

Using 1967 as the base year, the consumer price index rose from 71.4 percent in 1949 to 246.5 percent in 1980. The purchasing power of the dollar fell in terms of 1967 dollars from $1.40 in 1949 to 41¢ in 1980. A 1980 dollar was worth 29¢ in terms of the 1949 dollar. (Changing base years does not affect relationships, as will be explained shortly.)

THE CONSUMER PRICE INDEX

A table showing price changes for a group of particular commodities or services would mean very little. To make it useful, it must be summarized in some way. Prices do not change in an identical, or even similar, manner. If they did, indexes would not be needed, since any price could represent all the others. Instead, some prices rise while others fall. Some move rapidly while others barely change. In 1977, apartment rents were 17 percent higher than in 1974. Farm crop prices, on the other hand, were down 14 percent, while used-car prices were 49 percent higher. (Differences for a single year in changes in major components of consumer prices are shown in Figure 2.3.) Given changes like these, to comprehend what is happening in prices, some summary or representative measure is needed to express the different movements.

Indexes are obtained by a "weighted" averaging of prices or price changes in each period. Usually weights are assigned to commodities in accordance with some estimate of the economic importance of the commodity in the field for which a measure is desired. The consumer price index uses weights based on surveys of money spent and goods and services purchased by American urban households. Movements of the averages, or indexes, can be more readily understood and analyzed than can changes in individual prices.

CONSTRUCTING AN INDEX

A simplified example of how price indexes are constructed is found in Table 2.4. For this hypothetical index, consumers are assumed to buy only three items: beef, dresses, and doctors' services. A consumer expenditure survey in 1980 found that, on average, a family bought 50 pounds of beef, 5 dresses, and made 1 visit to the doctor. The table shows the prices of each item and expenditures both for each item and in total. Expenditures are equal to the quantity (Q_1) times the price (P_1) per item. When added together, consumer expenditures in 1980 were found to be $340.

In 1983, only a survey of prices is conducted. A hypothetical budget is

TABLE 2.4   **A Hypothetical Consumer Price Index**

	1980			1983		
Item	Quantity (Q_1)	Price (P_1)	Expenditures $(Q_1 P_1)$	1980 Quantity (Q_1)	1983 Prices (P_2)	Expenditures at 1983 prices for 1980 quantities $(Q_1 P_2)$
Beef	50 pounds	$ 2.20	$110.00	50 pounds	$ 2.64	$132.00
Dresses	5 each	40.00	200.00	5 each	44.00	220.00
Doctor Visits	1 each	30.00	30.00	1 each	45.00	45.00
Total			$340.00			$397.00

$$\text{Price index} = \frac{\text{1983 expenditures at 1983 prices for 1980 quantities}}{\text{1980 expenditures}} = \frac{\Sigma Q_1 P_2}{\Sigma Q_1 P_1}$$

$$= \frac{397}{340} = 1.17 \times 100 = 117.$$

Each good or service contained in a typical market basket is priced at intervals. These prices times the initial quantities equal the expenditures needed to purchase the market basket in each period. Dividing the calculated expenditures needed in a period by those of the base period and multiplying by 100 yields a price index. Other market baskets (weights) will yield different estimates of changes in the price level.

found by multiplying the quantity (Q_1) of each item from the 1980 calculations by the new prices (P_2). Added together, these values estimate how much it would cost in 1983 to buy the same market basket of goods as was purchased in 1980. This is done even though it is recognized that the actual quantities purchased in 1983 are almost certain to be different.

In the second part of the table, the price index is calculated. The amount that would have to be spent for the 1980 basket at 1983 prices ($\Sigma Q_1 P_2$) is divided by the 1980 expenditures ($\Sigma Q_1 P_1$). The index is 1.17 or, when multiplied by 100 (as is usually done to permit reading in percentages), the reading is 117. Prices are said to have risen by 17 percent. This represents an average of the single price increases ranging from 10 percent for dresses up to 50 percent for doctors' services. The index is a weighted average of price changes, with the weights determined by the initial expenditure survey.[2]

WEIGHTS IN THE CPI

In the CPI, as in our hypothetical example, goods and services are weighted by the importance of each type of expenditure in a typical consumer's market basket. The weights and the commodities included are selected after a sample survey of households. Weights assigned are based on a category's percentage of total expenditures in the survey. The weights remain constant until a new survey is made, after ten years or so, and the weights are adjusted. In 1977, the CPI was moved to weights found in a 1972–73 survey.

Errors or biases creep in because the system of weighting becomes unrepresentative over time. Weights and measures should change as new products are introduced, as the quality of goods changes, and as spending habits alter— partly as a result of differences in relative price increases. With much higher gas prices, people are more inclined to drive slowly and to use forms of transportation other than the automobile. With such a substitution, the weight assigned to gasoline prices based on the use of cars before the Organization of Petroleum Exporting Countries (OPEC) began the rapid run-up in the price of crude oil will be too large for later periods.

The introduction of new goods causes a related but different form of bias. Consider the advent of color TV sets, of video recorders, or of calculators. Consumers quickly increased purchases of these new items; yet the market basket on which the index was based did not include these goods for a considerable period after they were introduced. Improper weights are not the only problem. Damage is even greater because, as is typical of new products, prices of such commodities tend to drop rapidly as their use spreads. Price indexes will vary depending on when new products are introduced.

How urban Americans spend their money and the vast differences in price

---

2. Thus the consumer price index takes the following form (Σ is the sign of summation):

Period 1	Period 2	Period 3
$\dfrac{\Sigma Q_1 P_1}{\Sigma Q_1 P_1}$	$\dfrac{\Sigma Q_1 P_2}{\Sigma Q_1 P_1}$	$\dfrac{\Sigma Q_1 P_3}{\Sigma Q_1 P_1}$

changes among components are illustrated by Figure 2.3. The segmented circle shows the relative importance of various components for December 1979. The energy segment includes 5.6 percent for gasoline and 4.6 percent for fuel. When household furnishings and fuels are added to shelter, we find that more than 43 percent of all expenditures go for housing. Transportation, including gasoline, is the next largest component, ranging from 18 to 20 percent for particular groups. Food at home, which used to be the most important, is only 12.2 percent; but when meals away from home and alcoholic beverages are added, this total becomes 18.7 percent.

The bars in the figure show the great variety of price movements. In 1979 apparel rose at a rate of only 5.5 percent compared to 37.4 percent for energy costs. These differences in prices make weights extremely significant in determining movements of average prices.

The Gross National Product in Constant Dollars

The GNP as measured in the National Income and Product Accounts is not in physical (or real) terms. Expenditures for such items as haircuts, gasoline, aircraft carriers, and all other products are valued at current market prices. These individual expenditures are then added together to get the GNP total. The CPI and other price indexes are employed to convert values of goods and services measured in current dollars in the GNP to values in constant (base-year) dollars. The ratio of the current- to constant-dollar values of the total GNP is called the *GNP implicit price deflator.* The process of correcting the nominal GNP for price changes yields two of the most important macroeconomic gauges: (1) the *deflated or constant-dollar GNP* measures movements in real output and (2) the GNP price deflator provides the broadest measure of changes in the economy's price level.

THE PROCESS OF DEFLATION TO REAL QUANTITIES

Between two years, a change in hair style might increase the number of haircuts. Higher prices could result in lower gas sales. Aircraft carrier production would rise or fall on the basis of national defense needs. The difference in spending between years may reflect either a higher price for some items, a difference in the level of physical output, or both. To get a measure of real output, these differences among goods must be taken into account. The process of obtaining a measure of real output and of average price changes consists of five steps:

1. Recording expenditures in current dollars for each good and service.
2. Measuring price changes for each item; that is, constructing a price index for each, with the identical base period (1972 in the following example).
3. Deflating each item by dividing its expenditures in a period by its price relative to the base. This results in an estimate of the item's value of output

FIGURE 2.3   **Importance of Categories in the Consumer Price Index, 1979**

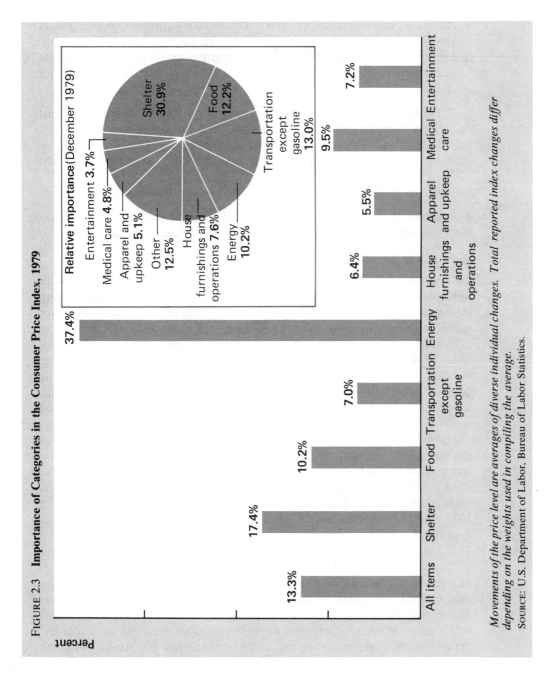

Relative importance (December 1979)

Shelter 30.9%

Food 12.2%

Transportation except gasoline 13.0%

Energy 10.2%

House furnishings and operations 7.6%

Other 12.5%

Apparel and upkeep 5.1%

Medical care 4.8%

Entertainment 3.7%

All items 13.3%

Shelter 17.4%

Food 10.2%

Transportation except gasoline 7.0%

Energy 37.4%

House furnishings and operations 6.4%

Apparel and upkeep 5.5%

Medical care 9.5%

Entertainment 7.2%

Percent

Movements of the price level are averages of diverse individual changes. Total reported index changes differ depending on the weights used in compiling the average.
SOURCE: U.S. Department of Labor, Bureau of Labor Statistics.

expressed in constant (base-year) prices. Such constant-dollar estimates are spoken of as measures of real output.

4. Adding all real outputs in a period to obtain total output in constant dollars valued relative to the base period. This is the measure of total real output.

5. Dividing the nominal GNP in a period by the constant-dollar GNP for the same period. This ratio multiplied by 100 is an index of implicit price changes.

For example, to correct, or deflate, the amount spent for haircuts, it must be divided through by the price index of haircuts. If $50 million were spent on haircuts in 1985 and the price index for haircuts on a 1972 base was 250, an estimate of the production of haircuts in constant 1972 dollars would be $20 million ($\frac{50}{2.5} = 20$). A similar correction would be made for each type of expenditure in the GNP. The addition of all of the constant-dollar expenditures yields an estimate of each year's total GNP production in constant dollars.

While a constant-dollar GNP should be obtained in this way, the variety and number of items contained in the GNP is simply too large to make this method workable. To collect price data for all items would be an overwhelming task. Instead, the Department of Commerce uses available indexes, obtaining price indexes for each principal component from various sources. Each major spending stream is then translated into an estimate of production in constant dollars by dividing current-dollar output by the relevant individual price index. For example, to estimate the output of consumer goods and services in constant dollars, a limited number of components of the CPI is utilized, while constant-dollar residential construction is arrived at by dividing current-dollar expenditures by an index of residential construction costs. All of the deflated components are then added together to obtain the total real GNP.

This process can be followed in Table 2.5. The first two columns contain the actual-, or current-dollar, expenditures for consumer durables, residential construction, federal purchases, and all other items in both 1972 and 1977. The third column contains a price index for each of these expenditures obtained from another source. For example, the price index of consumer durables in 1977 was 129.2 percent of its 1972 base. In the fourth column, each individual expenditure component is deflated by its own price index. Thus, when the $178.8 billion of consumer durable spending in 1977 is divided by the index of 129.2, the result in the fifth column is an estimate of 1977 expenditures of $138.4 billion in 1972 dollars. These estimates are added together to obtain the total level of real output in current dollars. The table points up that great differences can occur in the analysis when real expenditures replace current-dollar ones. While all categories show large increases in current dollar expenditures, in real terms housing output (residential investment) and the quantity of federal government purchases of goods and services both declined over this period.

TABLE 2.5   **Deflation of Nominal GNP to GNP in Constant Dollars**

	Nominal expenditures		1977 price index for commodity (P_2) (1972 = 100)	Process of deflation $\left(\dfrac{Q_2P_2}{Price\ index\ (P_2)}\right)$	1977 real expenditures (Q_2) (in billions of 1972 dollars)
	1972 GNP Q_1P_1 (in billions of current dollars)	1977 GNP Q_2P_2			
Durable personal consumption	111.1	178.8	129.2	$\dfrac{178.8}{129.2}$ =	138.4
Residential investment	63.8	95.8	158.0	$\dfrac{95.8}{158.0}$ =	60.6
Federal purchases of goods and services	101.7	143.9	142.9	$\dfrac{143.9}{142.9}$ =	100.7
All other goods and services	909.3	1,499.5	139.9	$\dfrac{1,499.5}{139.9}$ =	1,072.0
Total GNP	1,185.9	1,918.0	139.8		1,371.7

GNP implicit price deflator for 1977:

$$P_2 = \frac{GNP_2}{.Q_2} = \frac{1918.0}{1371.7} \times 100 = 139.8$$

> *GNP accounts report the current value of goods and services produced. Current dollar figures for each component are divided by an applicable price index (such as parts of the CPI). A value divided by a price index expresses that part of the GNP in dollars of a constant purchasing power. The constant dollar estimates for each sector are added to obtain the GNP in constant dollars. Nominal GNP for a period divided by the constant dollar GNP (Q_2) for the period yields the GNP implicit price index.*

THE GNP IMPLICIT PRICE DEFLATOR

In each year the implicit deflator (*P*), or GNP price index, is the ratio of nominal GNP in current dollars to real GNP (*Q*) measured in constant dollars. Thus, at the bottom of Table 2.5, the GNP deflator is calculated for 1977. In the second column, the value of the GNP in current dollars is summed. Similarly, all of the deflated (constant-dollar) expenditures in the fifth column are totaled. Dividing column 2 by column 5 (× 100) yields the implicit price index for 1977 of 139.8. This says that prices in 1977 were 39.8 percent above 1972.

The figure for the price index is circled in the body of the table to show that it is not the sum of the figures above it. The index is called implicit because the GNP deflator has no predetermined weights as does the CPI. The weight of a good or service in each year depends on the value of the expenditures for that item in that year. As a result, the weight for an item will vary from year to year. In a poor auto year, since the share of autos in total expenditures will be reduced, the effect of any change in auto prices will be reduced also. If a cattle shortage leads to soaring beef prices, the effect on the GNP price index will be less than that on the CPI. In the latter, the higher prices will be multiplied by a fixed weight of cattle, even though fewer are being purchased. In the implicit index, this reduction in sales automatically causes beef to have a lower weight.

SHIFTING THE BASE YEAR

In some studies of output you will find tables showing that the real GNP grew from $323.6 billion (in 1958 dollars) in 1949 to $476.7 billion (in 1958 dollars) in 1959. Other tables show that the growth from 1949 to 1959 was from $489.8 billion to $721.7 (in 1972 dollars). Although the amount of output appears to differ, in fact it does not. The Department of Commerce shifted the base year in which the constant dollar output was calculated. Such shifts in the base occur periodically.

While deflating by means of price indexes changes measurements from nominal to real terms, the choice of a specific base year in which to denominate the final price-corrected measure and the readings for the price deflator index is quite arbitrary. The choice of a base year affects the units in which quantities are expressed, but not the measured changes. Thus the GNP deflator in 1972 can be expressed as either 151.4 on a 1958 base or 100 on a 1972 base, while 1958 prices were 100 on the earlier base and 66.04 on the 1972 base. At first glance, the movements seem dissimilar, but you can check to see that prices increased 51.4 percent no matter how expressed. Similarly, output rose by 47.3 percent from 1949 to 1959 on either base.

The hypothetical figures below show how the base can be shifted from one period to another without affecting comparisons. (One can use 1980 or 1983 for a base even if weights are based on 1972–73 or any other year.) In this example, divide each of the figures on a 1980 base by 125, the number required to make 1983 equal to 100. When this is done, as in the second row, the index has a new 1983 base.

	1980	1983	1985
Base is: (1980 = 100)	100	125	150
Base is: (1983 = 100)	80	100	120

The measured percentage changes are the same on either base.

Use of Indexes to Correct for Inflation

In periods with shifting prices, analysis is seriously affected when *nominal* (current-dollar) values are deflated to *real* (constant-dollar) values—that is,

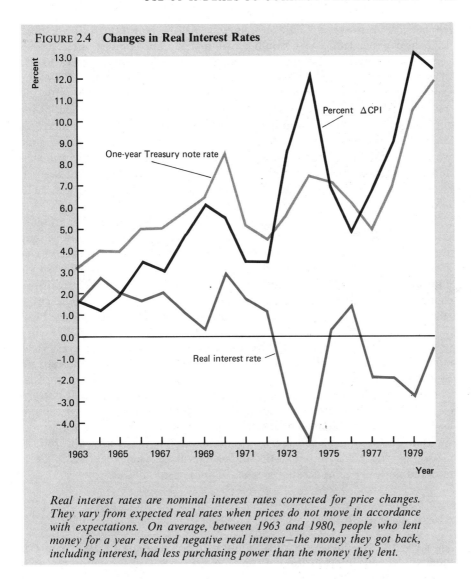

FIGURE 2.4   **Changes in Real Interest Rates**

Real interest rates are nominal interest rates corrected for price changes. They vary from expected real rates when prices do not move in accordance with expectations. On average, between 1963 and 1980, people who lent money for a year received negative real interest—the money they got back, including interest, had less purchasing power than the money they lent.

when prices are expressed in dollars with the same purchasing power over time. Failure to look behind price changes to see how they affect decisions can lead to serious errors. Price indexes are also used frequently in wage or other bargains in attempts to make payments in different years represent equivalent purchasing power. When indexes are used for such purposes, the manner of their construction can cause major variations in amounts paid and received.

REAL AND NOMINAL INTEREST RATES

Interest rates are a good example of the need to adjust nominal to real values. Although lending contracts are made in nominal dollars, experience shows that lenders and borrowers adjust decisions to reflect the real returns they expect. Take the case of a lender who would be willing to accept 4 percent interest for a year's loan of real dollars. What should she do if she expects prices to rise during the period of the loan? She lends $100 and wants to be paid $104 of the same purchasing power. If during the year prices rose 4 percent, the $104 she got back at the end of the year would buy only the same amount of goods as the $100 originally lent. She would receive no real interest; the price increases would have wiped out any interest earnings. To earn a real 4 percent, she would have had to ask roughly 8 percent in nominal interest. Both the principal and interest received back would have to be deflated in order to find the real interest rate. What she lent and what she got back would have to be compared in dollars of a constant purchasing power.

Experience shows that while lenders do attempt to obtain higher nominal interest rates in order to offset anticipated changes in purchasing power, they are not always successful because of uncertainties about future price movements. How interest rates and price changes compared from 1963 to 1980 is illustrated in Figure 2.4. The curve labeled "Percent ΔCPI" shows percentage changes in the CPI from the previous to the current December. The curve labeled "One-year Treasury note rate" shows the interest that would have been received from an investment the previous December in one-year U.S. Treasury notes. The bottom line, labeled "Real interest rate," shows this interest yield minus the change in prices. It approximately measures the real interest rate earned in each year. Real interest rates are much lower than people assume who only consider nominal rates. Nominal interest rates averaged 5½ percent over real rates. The difference consists of lost purchasing power. Although lenders may try to obtain compensation for price changes, they do not always succeed. In addition to a considerable variation around the average real return, in several years yields from investing in these securities were negative. Interest rates did not fully compensate for losses in purchasing power.

COST-OF-LIVING ADJUSTMENTS

The consumer price index contains a number of potential biases. Its estimate of inflation depends on its method of construction. Every time inflation becomes meaningful, the CPI comes under attack as being an unsuitable gauge of real income. Since at least one-quarter of income recipients in the United States have direct cost-of-living adjustments (COLA) and many more use the CPI as a gauge in wage bargaining and price setting, distortions of the index cause immediate tension among large segments of the population.

Two such distortions became obvious in 1979 and 1980. Some idea of their significance can be seen in Table 2.6, which shows that in 1979, the categories "homeownership" and "energy" accounted for nearly 60 percent of the increase in prices that year, even though in 1972–1973 they were only about 32 percent of consumer expenditures. While they rose at rates of 19.8 percent

TABLE 2.6   **Effect of Weights on Measures of Average Movements in the Consumer Price Index, December 1978–December 1979**

Item	Weight (December 1978)	Percent Change in Item	Percent Item is of Total Change in CPI
Homownership	23.56	19.8	35.1
Energy	8.50	37.4	23.9
All others	67.94	8.0	41.0
Total	100.00	13.3	100.0

SOURCE: U.S. Bureau of Labor Statistics.

How a price change affects the overall index depends on its importance (weight) and magnitude. Because of their importance and large size, changes in the price of owning a home accounted for more than a third of reported inflation in 1979. Because they rose so much, energy prices (even though their importance was only 8.5 percent) made up nearly a quarter of the total.

and 37.4 percent respectively, all other expenditures rose by 8 percent. If energy and homeownership had risen only as fast as the remainder, estimates of inflation and the consequent increases granted to hold real income constant would have been 8 instead of 13.3 percent, or 40 percent smaller. While 40 percent overstates the amount of bias, most observers agree that the CPI did distort people's views of inflation. Even though later offsetting movements were probable, the economy was worse off than if a more accurate gauge had been available. The biases in the cost-of-living adjustments arose from two different causes.

The substitution bias.   The energy component carried too large a weight because rapid increases in costs after the 1972–73 survey caused people to use less energy. They made substitutions—for instance, walking instead of driving, or wearing sweaters instead of turning up the thermostat. Multiplying the initial base-year weights, instead of reduced weights reflecting actual uses, by the new prices distorted the total estimate of how much money people required to maintain a standard of living. This is called a **base-year** or **substitution bias.**

The investment aspects of ownership.   A second major distortion arises from treating housing as a normal consumer good and giving no weight to its investment aspects. Home ownership is a large factor in the CPI because the majority of families own homes, and mortgage payments form a high percentage of most family budgets. But many people believe that the CPI gives too large a weight to the prices at which new houses sell and that it fails to consider that real mortgage costs are reduced by the rising value of houses.

1. In the CPI, the change in the prices paid by *new* owners is multiplied by weights derived from budget data for *all* homeowners. Yet, relatively few households—less than 6 percent of the total—buy a house in any year. A rise

in the selling price of houses does not change the budget expenditures of owners who do not make a change. In fact, rising house prices increase their wealth and make them better off. Yet the CPI is incorrectly used as an indicator of a need for more income to maintain their standard of living.

2. Much of the increased price of interest to new borrowers reflects a general rise in the price level. Higher interest payments are matched by similar price increases in the value of houses. That is why people are willing to make large mortgage payments. They expect to recover their increased expenses when they sell their house at a higher price. The real expense of occupying a house is reduced by the amount owners gain through their ownership. The CPI includes the increase in nominal interest rates, but makes no adjustment for the reduction in the cost of living which results from the increases in the value of the property for which the interest rates are being paid.

The inclusion of homeownership and energy costs in the CPI led to perverse initial results in attempts to fight inflation. When interest rates and energy prices were raised in order to reduce consumption and damp down demand, the CPI immediately shot up. The rise in the CPI led to higher wage demands and higher future prices, partially offsetting the anti-inflationary forces. On the other hand, opposite effects were experienced in 1981, when the CPI reported a sharper reduction in inflation than actually occurred. Reported inflation plunged because the excess estimates of 1980 were followed by downward-biased estimates in 1981.

Full Employment-Potential Output

The National Income and Product Accounts yield measures of both actual output and the price level. For many purposes we need, in addition, a measure of potential (full-employment) output. The Employment Act of 1978 set as a national goal the promotion of "full employment and production." To achieve this goal and to gauge how well or poorly the economy is performing we must be able to measure actual compared to potential output.

Full employment, potential output, and the natural rate of unemployment are at an identical point on the aggregate supply curve. When output increases beyond the point of potential, prices begin to accelerate. To find full employment, one must examine the shape of aggregate supply and the ability of the economy to increase production. At full employment, expansion may be limited either by a shortage of labor or by bottlenecks and shortages of capital and materials.

THE RELATIONSHIP OF FULL EMPLOYMENT TO AGGREGATE SUPPLY

The line Q_1^* in Figure 2.5 marks a point of full employment under the assumption that the curve AS_1 represents the supply situation in the economy. (Recall that an asterisk is used throughout this volume to indicate the point of full employment.) To the right of this point, additional output can be produced

FIGURE 2.5   **Aggregate Supply and Full Employment**

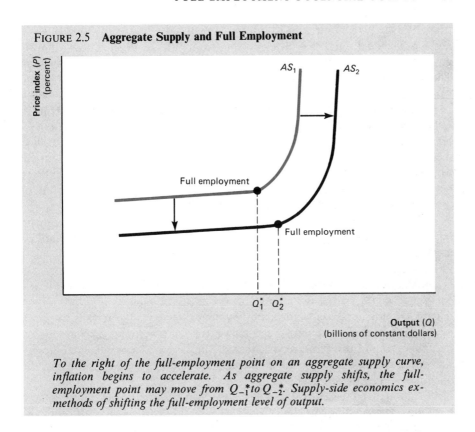

To the right of the full-employment point on an aggregate supply curve, inflation begins to accelerate. As aggregate supply shifts, the full-employment point may move from Q_{-1}^* to Q_{-2}^*. Supply-side economics ex- methods of shifting the full-employment level of output.

only with accelerating costs. To produce more, less efficient labor has to be used; overtime pay must be raised; the capital stock and other resources are stretched; sellers of commodities in limited supply must be paid higher prices. Higher prices are needed to match these increased costs.

The point of full employment (Q^*) varies with the available factors of production—labor, capital, and resources. Aggregate supply, and therefore the point of full employment, can be shifted. Policies to increase supply can alter both the location and the shape of the curve. AS_2 represents such a shift, with the point Q_2^* the new measure of full employment and potential output. (Part 5 discusses in detail factors influencing the position and shape of aggregate supply. If productivity increases and bottlenecks are straightened out, the point of full employment can be moved to the right. The result will be increased production with a reduced danger of inflation.)

EMPLOYMENT AND UNEMPLOYMENT

Key measures underlying estimates of potential output and full employment are the Labor Department's estimates of the labor force and its division into those at work and the unemployed. The *labor force,* defined as the total number of employed and unemployed workers, grew at an annual rate of 2.4 percent from 1973 to 1978, compared to rates of growth of 1.7 percent from 1959–68 and a projected annual rate of 1.1 percent from 1985 to 1990. These differing growth rates affected growth in total output and the level of full employment. They are due to changes in the age structure of the population and in desires to work.

Employment and unemployment data are estimated by the Bureau of Labor Statistics from a monthly sample conducted by the Census Bureau of all households in the United States. This survey attempts to measure the employment status of all persons 16 years old or over. By asking whether people are at work or are looking for work, the survey divides the population into (1) those not in the labor force, (2) those who are employed, and (3) the unemployed, or those who do not have jobs but are seeking work.

The **unemployment rate** is the percentage of the civilian labor force who report they do not have a job but are looking for one. The level of unemployment changes when people get or lose jobs or when they enter or leave the labor force. None of these concepts is unambiguous. A student or housewife may decide she would like a job. When she starts to look for work, even if only for a part-time job, the size of the labor force is increased. If she finds work immediately, employment rises and unemployment does not. If she fails to find a job, she is reported as unemployed. However, if she becomes discouraged by her failure to find work and reports that she has stopped looking, even though she would still like a job if she could find one, both the labor force and the unemployment rate are decreased.

Although increases in unemployment usually mean that fewer people have jobs, this need not be the case. When the labor force expands, both the number of workers with jobs and the rate of unemployment can grow at the same time. The labor force has increased for two main reasons:

1. Growth in population, particularly in the working age groups. About 70 percent of the increase in the labor force between 1974 and 1978 was due to a larger population of working-age people.
2. A change in the **labor participation rate,** the percentage of those of working age who report that they are in the labor force and are either employed or seeking work. This accounts for about 30 percent of the increased labor force. A major change in our economy has been an increase in the labor-participation rate for adult women. After hovering close to 37 percent in the mid-1950s, the rate then grew, accelerating greatly during the 1970s. In 1978, the labor force participation rate of adult women passed the 50 percent level. This more than offset the decline in the labor force participation rate of adult men, which fell from 88 percent to under 80 percent. (Men stayed in school longer and retired earlier.)

FULL EMPLOYMENT

Estimates differ among analysts and over time as to the minimum level of unemployment possible before the job market exerts additional upward pressure on wages and prices. This minimum level depends on time needed to search for jobs, on the skills or lack of skills and the location of those seeking work, and on the pressure (economic or social) society puts on the unemployed to accept less desirable jobs.

The number out of work at the point of full employment increased as the percentage of recent entrants into the labor force grew. This growth of less skilled workers, which forms the basis of the CEA's assumption of higher unemployment at full employment, is expected to reverse during the 1980s. Improving job markets and skills can lower the unemployment level at which prices start to rise. More controversial are suggested changes in unemployment compensation, minimum wages, social security, and other social programs which many believe have raised unemployment rates at full employment well above the CEA's assumptions.

In addition to an estimate of the number of workers at full employment, potential output is based on the number of hours each will work. The average number of hours worked on a job has dropped steadily. The typical work week is shorter. There is less overtime. The greater participation in the labor force of teen-agers, married women, and elderly men who are more likely to want to work part-time has helped to lower the average hours worked per job.

FULL EMPLOYMENT AND CAPITAL

The previous discussion focused on the job market as the primary factor determining the full-employment level. At full employment, the number out of work is at the minimum level necessary to prevent an acceleration in prices. Usually this is also the point where all who want jobs can obtain them. But it is possible that the point of full employment, instead of being determined in the job market, could be set by the amount of available capital equipment. If a shortage of capital equipment developed, some people would be seeking work but, because their employment would lead to an inefficient use of capital and higher costs, they could not be hired without an acceleration of prices. The economics of production causes full employment of capital to be substantially below the theoretical barrier where technology would limit the use of equipment, just as full employment of labor is less than 100 percent of the labor force.

As an example of the difference between an economic and a technological barrier, consider a plant working $1\frac{1}{2}$ shifts. Even if no technical reason hindered moving to a two-shift basis of production, such a change might be economically unfeasible if hiring the extra work force for the additional partial shift was very expensive. But with sufficiently high demand, the plant can work a full second shift. Output can be pushed above the optimum economic point, engendering higher costs and inflationary price increases.

The full-employment level for capital as a whole is sometimes estimated at 86 percent of reported capacity. When use rises above this percentage, price accelerations develop equivalent to those that occur when labor is overemployed.[3] What causes this price acceleration when output is still well below

3. *1978 Economic Report of the President* (Washington, D.C.: U.S. Government Printing Office, 1978), p. 160.

rated capacity and still further below the maximum technological effort? Apparently, although average use of capacity may still be low, some industries will be producing above their individual optimums. Their prices begin to rise before other industries reach their optimum. As a result, the point of full potential is below 100 percent of capital capacity.

Most estimates show that, through 1980, a shortage of labor always preceded that of capital. Thus capital as a limit on potential output was not applicable. However, in periods such as 1968 and 1973, when both capital and labor were close to full employment, their interaction led to more rapid price increases. This experience, together with the related drop in productivity, has led to a major push for more capital. One of the claims has been that the shortage of capital has been serious enough to set the point of full employment and potential output below where it would be if its location depended on the job market alone.

Uncertainty about Potential Output

The amount of potential output varies with the point of full employment, with the number of hours the labor force desires to work, and with productivity. Uncertainty about each of these three factors leads to differing estimates of potential output. Figure 1.5 presented two CEA estimates of potential output. Chapter 15 presents a wide variety of competing estimates. In each of these cases, estimates differ as to how much labor can be hired before prices start to accelerate and as to how much will be produced per labor-hour.

Hours worked.   The amount of labor that will be offered at or near existing real wages depends on the maximum number who want work and the number of hours each worker offers at these wages. Maximum employment depends also on minimum unemployment. At full employment some people will still be out of a job and looking for work, either because it takes time to change and find jobs (frictional unemployment) or because they cannot match their skills to available job openings (structural unemployment).

Productivity.   The slow growth of potential output in the 1970s was due to a sharp drop in the growth rate of labor productivity rather than in the available hours of work. Productivity rose at the rate of 2.6 percent per year from 1950 through 1968, but between 1973 and 1980 it grew at only .5 percent a year. The factors causing these changes in productivity are discussed in more detail in Chapter 15.

THE DIFFERING ESTIMATES

The concept of potential output was introduced in the January 1962 *Report of the Council of Economic Advisers.* It assumed the minimum level of unemployment to be 4 percent, although it was hoped this could be lowered by training and improvements in the labor market. Mid-1955, when prices de-

FIGURE 2.6   **The Gap between Actual and Potential Output**

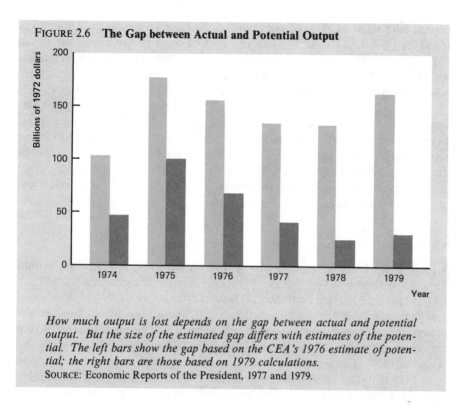

How much output is lost depends on the gap between actual and potential output. But the size of the estimated gap differs with estimates of the potential. The left bars show the gap based on the CEA's 1976 estimate of potential; the right bars are those based on 1979 calculations.
SOURCE: Economic Reports of the President, 1977 and 1979.

clined as unemployment approached this level, was chosen as a reasonable estimate of the level of attainable GNP. The rate of growth in potential was assumed to be 3.5 percent from 1952 through 1962, 3.75 percent through 1968, 4 percent through 1975, and 3.75 percent thereafter.

Until 1973 the estimates seemed adequate. In that year, however, inflation accelerated even though output was well below estimated potential. For this and other reasons, the CEA reexamined their prior judgments. As a result, in 1977 they revised downward their estimates of potential output. They reduced projected growth rates after 1968 to 3.5 percent. While the labor force was growing faster than expected, they raised the rate of unemployment at full potential to 4.9 percent and lowered the estimated growth rate of productivity.

The failure of inflation to decelerate with excess unemployment in 1977 and 1978 led to another reexamination. The 1979 CEA Report lowered the estimated growth in potential output to 3 percent from 1973 to 1983. The rate of unemployment at full potential was raised to 5.1 percent from 1975 to 1978. (Chapter 15 shows that other analysts consider this to be low.) The growth rate in productivity for 1973–78 was pegged at 1 percent—well under previous levels.[4] The result of these changes was to reduce drastically the estimated gap between actual and potential output. Figure 2.6 illustrates this reduction. The

4. P. K. Clark, "A New Estimate of Potential GNP," in *Hearings*, Joint Economic Committee (U.S. Congress, 1978).

revised data show an average gap of only $33 billion (constant 1972 dollars) in the years 1977–79. The 1980–81 GNP revisions reduced this estimated gap to $29.4 billion. Many have argued that better estimates of potential output would show that the economy in this period was actually producing above potential and the resulting pressures were accelerating the inflation rate.

The decline in estimates of potential output is one of the many reasons why so much more attention is being paid to methods of increasing supply. Every 1 percent growth in output means over $25 billion of added goods and services available to the economy. The fall in productivity caused a loss in estimated potential output of over $150 billion a year by 1980. Obviously, great advantages would accrue to most families if the trends could be reversed and potential output increased.

PROJECTED POTENTIAL OUTPUT IN 1990

A projection of where the economy will be in ten years is a vital input into corporate planning. In many cases plants presently in the design stage will not yet have reached the height of their usefulness after ten years, and in other cases they may not even be broken in. Because of these lags, to fill these needs, projections of potential output for anywhere from 5 to 20 years into the future are common. Table 2.7 shows such a projection made in 1978 covering the period to 1990. The table shows that output grew at a 4.3 percent annual rate from 1959 to 1968 and at a 2.7 percent rate from 1968 to 1977. For 1977–85, projected growth is 3.9 percent per year, and it is at a 3.2 percent rate for the

TABLE 2.7   **Actual and Projected Average Annual Rate of Change in Real GNP, Labor and Productivity: 1959–90**

(percent)

	Actual		Projections	
	1959–68	1968–77	1977–85	1985–90
GNP (1972 dollars)	4.3	2.7	3.9	3.2
Labor force (including military)	1.7	2.1	1.8	1.1
Unemployment rate	−0.2	0.4	−0.3	−0.1
Civilian jobs	1.9	1.8	2.2	1.2
Hours paid per job	−0.4	−0.4	−0.3	−0.3
Total hours paid	1.7	1.4	2.2	1.1
Productivity	2.8	1.5	1.9	2.4

SOURCE: V. A. Personich, "Industry Output and Employment: BLS Projections to 1990," *Monthly Labor Review* (April 1979), p. 4. (May contain rounding errors, because periods are combined.)

Growth in potential output (measured by GNP in 1972 dollars) depends on the rate of increase in total hours of work and productivity—the bottom two lines. Hours of paid work will increase with the number of jobs (labor force minus unemployment) and will decrease if hours per job continue to fall.

final five years. Some of the slowdown in the growth rate of potential output will be recovered according to this projection.

What are the underlying factors at work? The large increases in unemployment and the decline in the growth rate of productivity which occurred between 1968 and 1977 are the starting point for the projection. Note that the rate of growth in output (GNP in 1972 dollars) in this period was only about 60 percent of that in the previous decade. The slow growth in output contrasted with a rapid labor force growth of 2.1 percent per year. Because the armed forces declined by 1.4 million persons, the growth in the civilian labor force was still larger. But unemployment nearly doubled; it averaged 3.6 percent in 1968 and 7.0 percent in 1977. The run-up in unemployment resulted in the number of hours worked (total hours paid) growing at a rate of only 1.4 percent, compared to the previous 1.7 percent. A slower rise in productivity, combined with the slower growth in jobs, gave the 40 percent smaller rate of growth in output.

The projections from 1977 to 1990 assume that unemployment will decline to 4.7 percent in 1985 and to 4.5 percent in 1990. At the same time, improvements in productivity will speed up, although even in the last five years of the decade, its growth will be less than in the 1959–68 period.

Based on a rapid expansion in the labor force (1.8 percent per year) and a considerable drop in unemployment, the number of jobs and total hours paid are projected to grow at an average 2.2 percent per year between 1977 and 1985—the highest for any period covered. On the other hand, while the rate of growth in productivity is predicted to improve, it stays below earlier rates. The increased hours worked, with a moderate rate of improvement in productivity, yield the forecast rate of expansion in output of 3.9 percent for 1977–85 and 3.2 percent for 1985–90. Look especially at the last five years, 1985–90. Those born in the post-World-War-II baby boom will already have entered the labor force. The change in minimum unemployment is slight. As a result, growth in the labor force and in new jobs drops. Hours worked expand only half as fast as in the previous period. Even though improvements in productivity are predicted to speed up, total potential output expands at a slower rate.

Table 2.7 and its analysis demonstrate again the key differences in the major macroeconomic measures which will appear throughout the remainder of this volume. We measure output and growth in terms of constant-dollar or real GNP. Output depends on hours worked and on productivity. However, nominal GNP, or expenditures in current dollars, also expands because of price increases as well as the growth in real goods and services. To measure the effect of the price movements on expenditures and to obtain estimates of the real GNP, it is necessary to use price indexes.

Summary

1. The gross national product (GNP) measures the total money value of all final goods and services produced by the economy in a period of time. The GNP also equals the total expenditures of the economy on final goods and

services. Expenditures can be classified by major sectors so that the GNP equals the sum of spending by households, businesses, governments, and foreign. GNP = $C + I + G + (X\text{-}IM)$.

2. The GNP also equals gross national income. This includes all claims by the factors of production plus indirect business taxes, depreciation, and an account to balance statistical discrepancies. Disposable income is the amount families have available to spend or not. It equals factor income increased by receipts from transfer payments and reduced by taxes paid and undistributed profits.

3. The consumer price index is a weighted index of price changes using a fixed, or market-basket, weighting system. It can become biased if the weights become unrepresentative of current expenditures. The GNP price deflator uses implicit rather than fixed weights.

4. Price indexes can be used to deflate nominal measures such as the GNP, money payments, and interest rates in order to obtain estimates of quantities expressed in constant dollars of the same purchasing power. These values are spoken of as real values.

5. A variety of price indexes are used to deflate current-dollar expenditures in the GNP to obtain a measure of the GNP in each period in terms of dollars of a constant purchasing power. This real or constant-dollar GNP is used as a measure of output in the economy. The ratio of nominal GNP in current dollars to real GNP in constant dollars is the implicit GNP price deflator, a key measure of movements in the price level.

6. Potential output is the amount that can be produced without an acceleration of costs and prices. It is determined by the area in which full utilization of the supply of labor or capital occurs. It changes with the amount of labor and capital in the economy and with their productivity.

7. The amount of employment and unemployment is measured by surveys of the population. Respondents say whether they have a job, are looking for one, or are not in the labor force. The point of full employment is a concept similar to that of potential output. All those who want work can find it with the exception of a minimum level of fractional and structural unemployment, but costs are not driven up by an excess of demand. In the 1970s, jobs and employment expanded quite rapidly. On the other hand, estimates of unemployment at the full-employment level were raised because of shifts in the structure of the labor force.

Questions for Discussion and Review

1. Since the purchase of a shoe-making machine, like the purchase of leather, serves no purpose other than aiding in the manufacture of shoes, why do we include one in our measure of GNP and not the other?

2. Which of the following transactions would be included in a proper measure of GNP:
    (a) Payment of rent by a supermarket
    (b) Purchase of flour by a baker
    (c) Purchase of a used car
    (d) Your sale of class notes to a fellow student
    (e) Purchase of an oven by a baker
    (f) Payment to a barber for a haircut
    (g) Payment to an arsonist for destroying a building

3. Discuss GNP as a measure of welfare.

4.

	1950	1967		1980
	P (dollars)	Q (units)	P (dollars)	P (dollars)
Food	20	5	30	40
Housing	30	2	32	60
Clothing	10	6	11	15

From the above chart, calculate:
    (a) The CPI for each year (assume 1967 as the base year)
    (b) The value of the dollar in each year in terms of the base year

5. What problems can arise in using the CPI? What can be done to correct this?

6. How is potential output defined? In general, is it possible to estimate a single value for potential output?

7. Is it possible for the number of unemployed persons to increase without the unemployment rate rising?

References

Barro, R. J., and S. Fischer. "Recent Developments in Monetary Theory." *Journal of Monetary Theory* 2(1976):133–67.

Christ, C. F. "Judging the Performance of Econometric Models of the U.S. Economy." *International Economic Review* 16:54–74.

Clark, P. K. "A New Estimate of Potential GNP." In *Hearings,* Joint Economic Committee. U.S. Congress, 1978.

Gordon, R. J. "Recent Developments in the Theory of Inflation and Unemployment." *Journal of Monetary Economics* 2(1976):185–219.

Kendrick, J. W. *Economic Accounts and Their Uses.* New York: McGraw-Hill, 1972.

Nordhaus, W., and J. Tobin. "Is Growth Obsolete?" In National Bureau of Economic Research, *50th Anniversary Colloquium V.* New York: Columbia University Press, 1972.

Okun, A. M. "Inflation: Its Mechanics and Welfare Costs." *Brookings Papers on Economic Activity* 2(1975):351–90.

U.S. Department of Commerce, *The National Income and Product Accounts of the United States, Survey of Current Business* (December 1980) and supplements.

Part 2

Equilibrium in the Goods Market

3

Income and Expenditures: A Simplified Model

The ability to predict and account for the amount the economy will spend next year is basic to intelligent decision making. Will the desire to spend exceed the level of potential output and aggravate inflationary pressures? Or will aggregate demand fall short of the economy's ability to produce, leading to deflationary pressures and unemployment? Rather small changes in the desire to spend are significant in determining whether the economy experiences prosperity or recession and more or less inflation.

Changes in aggregate demand, income, and prices begin with shifts in the spending desires of one of the four key sectors—households, businesses, governments, and foreign. For example, people may increase their desires to buy new houses if house prices are expected to be higher in the future. Changes in such variables then bring about a new equilibrium of all desires to spend and of income in the goods market. In analyzing movements in expenditures, it is useful to divide them into (1) changes in spending desires engendered by *autonomous* forces—that is, those independent of income—and (2) those changes which are induced by a shift in the level of income. In fact, the largest share of increases or decreases in spending comes from the second category. The equilibrium level of spending is the result of a group of interdependent decisions to spend and produce. A change in one sector's spending alters the income and spending of every other sector. To explain why aggregate demand shifts and where it will end up, we need to understand these interrelationships. An introduction to the analysis of aggregate demand can start with a simplified model of the factors which determine equilibrium in the ***market for real goods.*** The chapters of Part 2 describe the forces which bring about equilibrium in the real goods market and cause real spending desires to move up and down.

This chapter introduces in an elementary form a model to describe the mutual determination of income and spending. This initial version of the model of income determination is greatly simplified, utilizing only two sectors—households and businesses—to explain what determines the equilibrium of income and how it shifts. The main concepts include:

> Equilibrium and disequilibrium.
> The desire to spend.
> The consumption function and its components.
> The circular flow: identities and unplanned spending.
> The equilibrium level of expenditures.
> Leakages and injections (saving equals investment).
> The multiplier (the multiplication of spending shifts).
> Lags and dynamic analysis.

Equilibrium and Disequilibrium

EQUILIBRIUM

The heart of economic analysis is the concept of equilibrium. Aggregate demand and aggregate supply shift as a result of external shocks or policy actions.

FIGURE 3.1   **Equilibrium of Aggregate Demand and Supply**

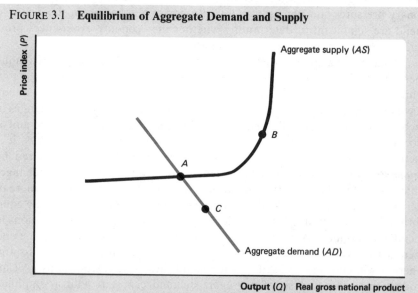

Point A marks an equilibrium intersection. It indicates the amount the economy demands and supplies of real output measured on the horizontal axis at the price level measured on the vertical axis. If prices were lower, as at C, demand exceeding supply at that price would cause prices to rise. Excess supply, as at B, would force prices back to A.

The ensuing changes in output and prices depend upon the point at which equilibrium is regained and on the path the economy takes to get there. **Equilibrium** is basically a state of balance. In an equilibrium situation, there is no tendency for change. The willingness of the economy to spend and to produce, as expressed in the underlying schedules, is satisfied. At the equilibrium level A in Figure 3.1, suppliers are willing to produce the amounts demanded by spenders. If prices were higher (as at point B), suppliers would want to produce more, but demanders would not take all the additional output. If prices were lower (point C), the demand for goods and services would exceed the amount producers want to supply. Only at the intersection is the market in equilibrium.

Figure 3.2 provides an illustration of the effects of shifts in demand curves from AD_1, to AD_2, then AD_3. Such shifts could be the result of a change in any factor, such as an increased desire to consume, higher government spending, or more money. Two new equilibrium points, D and E, are shown at the intersections of the new demand curves with the original supply curve. When aggregate demand shifts, the shape of the aggregate supply curve will determine how much of the additional spending will go into price increases and how much into greater output. In the figure, the impact of moving from equilibrium A will be quite different depending on whether the new point reached is D or E. At point D, almost all of the increased spending results in greater output, with only slight price movement. Between A and D the supply curve is nearly horizontal. At

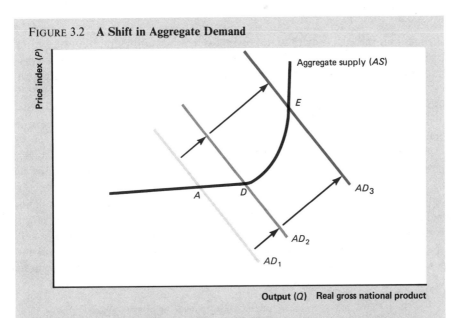

FIGURE 3.2   **A Shift in Aggregate Demand**

A shift in aggregate demand, as from AD₁ *to* AD₂, *results in a new equilibrium, point* D, *with more output at a slightly higher price level. Because of the slope of the supply curve, if demand shifts to* AD₃, *the new equilibrium* E *would require much higher prices.*

point E, most of the increase in spending is reflected in a rise in prices, with a smaller percentage going to added output. Between D and E the supply curve becomes nearly vertical.

A shift in demand can bring about either desirable or undesirable effects. As the figure shows, to find which will occur, one must look at the new equilibrium. If resources are fully utilized, added demand will result primarily in higher prices. If resources are unemployed, jobs and output rather than prices will be raised by the added demand.

Macroeconomic theory analyzes the forces which determine the position of equilibrium and cause it to move. The shapes of the demand and supply curves determine where they meet and, therefore, the level of output and prices. Either of the two curves can shift as a result of **shocks,** which are unexpected changes in one or some of the variables which determine the shape or position of either curve. In macroeconomic models, **variables** are those components whose values change fairly rapidly. **Exogenous variables** are those whose values are determined outside the structure of the model. An auto strike, which reduces income and output, is an example. Their values are inserted into the model in order to explain what happens. **Endogenous variables** are those whose values are determined and explained by the relationships within the system. The level of consumption depends on income; therefore it is an endogenous variable.

DISEQUILIBRIUM

The fact that the economy may not be in a state of equilibrium, but away from it for short or long periods, is important in the analysis of many problems, particularly that of inflation. **Disequilibrium** is a situation in which prices or wages do not move sufficiently to keep demand and supply in equilibrium. It is also called a **failure of the market to clear.** Quantities of output and unemployment vary a great deal because prices change too little or too late to permit employment of available resources.

Many reasons are advanced for the existence of disequilibrium. It takes time to adjust to change. There may be a lack of information or frictions in markets. Decision makers must "search" for the new equilibrium—a process that can be lengthy and expensive. Markets may have ratchets in them. (This analogy is derived from ratchet gears, in which a device prevents reversal of motion.) Prices may move up when demand increases but are unable to fall when demand declines.[1] Even when unemployment in the construction industry has been as high as 20 or 25 percent, new union contracts have required

---

1. R. J. Barro and S. Fischer, "Recent Developments in Monetary Theory," *Journal of Monetary Economics* 2(1976): 133–67; R. J. Gordon, "Recent Developments in the Theory of Inflation and Unemployment," *Journal of Monetary Economics* 2(1976): 185–219; A. M. Okun, "Inflation: Its Mechanics and Welfare Costs," *Brookings Papers on Economic Activity* 2(1975): 351–90.

higher, not lower, wages. For whatever reason, the length of time from one equilibrium to the next and the path which the economy follows in its adjustment must enter into all predictions and judgments as to the results of actions.

STATICS AND DYNAMICS

The movements in the demand curves and in the equilibrium levels illustrated in Figure 3.2 are examples of analysis by use of *comparative static models.* In such models, a change in an exogenous variable, such as added government spending or new investment resulting from a technological innovation, alters aggregate demand and causes the economy to shift from one equilibrium (as at *A*) to a new one (as at *E*). A comparison of the equilibrium positions of the economy before and after the change enables one to explain the total effect of such exogenous movements on the economy. Comparative statics analyzes the direction and magnitude of a change when all of the related movements it has caused have worked their way through the economy. If the economy gets stuck in a disequilibrium situation, the explanations of the model will be wrong. Furthermore, comparative static models do not describe the path of the economy between the two equilibrium positions, nor do they tell how long it will take to reach a new point.

　　To explain what happens between the time a change occurs and that when the new equilibrium position is reached, *dynamic analysis* must be employed. In dynamic analysis, time and the process of change are recognized specifically. Thus, dynamic analysis gives some insight into the path the economy takes in moving from one equilibrium to another. In a dynamic model, each variable carries a time designation. Dynamic models will also err in their predictions if markets fail to clear. Appendix 3.2 illustrates how time is designated and specifically introduced into dynamic models.

SOME PROBLEMS WITH EQUILIBRIUM

While the concept of movements to a new equilibrium is basic to macroanalysis, it is not always easy to apply it. Macroeconomic theories and statistical analysis leave open many questions of fact. The economy and the demand and supply schedules are too dynamic to be pinned down exactly. Estimates both of the shape and of potential shifts must be recognized as falling within a band of uncertainty.

　　A related problem is that analysts are never certain whether the economy is in disequilibrium or in a state of temporary or stable equilibrium. In economics, equilibriums are usually in flux. We know within the limits of our statistics what the GNP is in any given year or quarter, but we do not know whether or not the economy is in fact in equilibrium at any given moment. Statistically, the GNP must balance; production and spending must be equal. But this balance is simply one of definition; there is no certainty that equilibrium actually exists.

A further difficulty is that the premises upon which decisions were based may not be realized. Producers may get stuck with unwanted inventories; savers may desire to spend more but are not able to find goods that please them. Significant delays or lags may occur between movements in the forces leading toward an equilibrium and the reaching of the new point. Although such tendencies may be operating to drive the economy up and down, the statistical equality may hide the pressures.

In a dynamic economy so many factors cause the schedules to shift that it may be that we are always in the process of pursuing a stable situation without ever reaching it. The statistical measures of the economy are like the stop-action shots shown in sports events on television. Everything in the picture is seen in a fixed position, not necessarily in equilibrium. However, careful scrutiny can give some idea of the forces or pressures that have been at work, and they may help as well to predict the future.

It is also important to recognize that equilibrium situations are not necessarily satisfactory ones. When a new equilibrium is predicted, it must be examined to see whether it approaches the economy's goals. Many macroeconomic issues deal with policies which might be adopted in an effort to replace unsatisfactory equilibriums with more desirable ones.

The Desire To Spend

Each sector has a specific desire to purchase a given amount of real goods and services at each level of real income. For example, the amount of consumer goods households want to buy differs at each income level. We designate both the sum of goods they desire to purchase and those they do buy by the letter C. The sum total of all desires to spend is called *real aggregate demand* (E) and it expresses the amount of real goods and services the economy wants and plans to purchase at each level of real income (Y). It also equals the actual expenditures the economy realizes in a period. Any independent (autonomous) shift in a sector's desire to spend causes a movement in real aggregate demand and income. Where income and expenditures end up depends on both the size of the shifts (or shocks) and on the amount of income-induced spending. This in turn is determined by the shape of existing relationships between income and spending desires, both for each sector and for the aggregate.

In general, explanations of expenditures begin by analyzing how a sector determines its spending and saving. The theories of the consumption and investment functions describe these decisions. These functions also spell out how exogenous shifts in spending are multiplied. To obtain a fuller explanation, however, the simple theory must be augmented by analysis of those variables most likely to cause the simplified income-spending schedules to shift.

SIMPLIFYING ASSUMPTIONS

The model of the determination of spending desires presented in this chapter makes five simplifying assumptions which are relaxed in later chapters.

1. Only two sectors—households and businesses—are considered. Since no government and no foreign sectors exist, total spending equals consumption plus investment. Neither government expenditures nor net exports are present.
2. The aggregate supply curve is completely elastic.[2] As a result, any change in spending leads to an equal increase in real output and, simultaneously, in real earned income.
3. All analysis is in real terms. The effect of price movements is not considered until Chapter 8.
4. Businesses do not save and there are no taxes or transfer payments. This means that total earned income equals disposable income.
5. The level of investment is autonomous. It is independent of both the level of output and of interest rates.

INCOME-INDUCED OR PASSIVE EXPENDITURES

While expenditures on some goods—primarily durables—shift radically in dynamic situations, other expenditures are made in a more orderly fashion. A major segment of demand appears to react in an almost passive manner to the disposable income received by the decision-making sectors. Spending primarily dependent on income receipts moves more regularly and predictably than other expenditures. When consumption expenditures are compared to spending on investment goods, the former are found to move far less erratically. Much of this difference arises from the far greater importance of income-induced (passive) factors in consumption spending.

The more stable relationship of consumption and income is a basic aid in predicting and explaining the economy's movements. Even when forecasters make poor predictions, their ability to do well in estimating consumption minimizes their errors. For example, Table 3.1 shows the average error made by five of the most widely followed national forecasters in predicting the real GNP and its components for the year ending in the first quarter of 1975. This period produced the worst forecasts in 25 years. But note that the errors in predicting expenditures for the different sectors were very uneven. Consumer spending on nondurables and services was 56 percent of total spending, but it accounted for less than 10 percent of the total error. The errors in prediction of government purchases of goods and services were equally small. The three investment

2. In graphical terms, the economy is assumed to be in the sector from A to B on an aggregate supply curve.

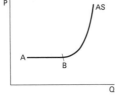

These assumptions are implicit in most elementary statements of the determination of income and output.

TABLE 3.1   **Errors in Forecasts 1974: Q1 to 1975: Q1**
(in billions of constant 1972 dollars, four-quarter change)

	Forecast	Actual	Error	Percent of total error	1975: Q1 Percent of total expenditures
Total real GNP	18.0	−50.5	68.5	100	100
Consumer nondurables and services	8.4	1.7	6.7	10	56
Consumer durables	2.7	−10.0	12.7	19	9
Business investment	4.1	−12.5	16.6	24	10
Residential investment	5.6	− 9.1	14.7	21	3
Inventory investment	−2.4	−22.3	19.9	29	−2
Net exports	−4.9	0.1	−5.0	−7	2
Government purchases	4.6	1.7	2.9	4	22

Consumer nondurables and services made up 56 percent of expenditures (fifth column), but accounted for only 10 percent of the forecast errors (fourth column).

categories, which accounted for 11 percent of spending, made up three-fourths of the total error. Forecasts of purchases of consumer durables, which are actually a form of investment, were in an intermediate category.

Such differences are typical of most macroeconomic analysis. The forecasts of consumer and government expenditures are far better than those for the investment or foreign sectors. The differences in the ability to predict reflect the importance or lack of importance of income in determining the sector's spending. When income is the critical variable, estimates tend to be good. When other variables are more important, success is more elusive.

The Consumption Function

The relationship between consumption and income is a convenient base for examining the determinants of aggregate demand. Household consumption expenditures are by far the largest component of the GNP. (Consumption was 65 percent of the GNP in 1980; see Table 2.2.) Furthermore, knowledge of how spending and income interact in the consumption sector can be applied to other spending decisions, such as the relationship between income and investment, income and taxes, income and imports.

A THEORETICAL CONSUMPTION FUNCTION

A *consumption function* expresses the relationship between the amount people desire to spend on consumption goods or services and disposable income. In

FIGURE 3.3   **The Consumption Function**

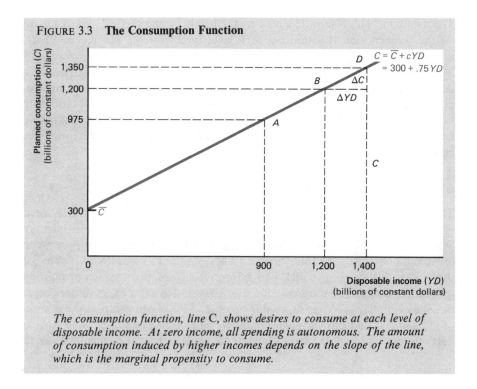

The consumption function, line C, shows desires to consume at each level of disposable income. At zero income, all spending is autonomous. The amount of consumption induced by higher incomes depends on the slope of the line, which is the marginal propensity to consume.

general functional form, this is stated as

$$C = f(YD), \qquad\qquad 3.1$$

where consumption (C) is a function (f) of disposable income (YD). In macroeconomics, functional notation is used to indicate that a relationship exists between two or more variables. Such general statements give no indication of the exact form or size of the relationships, which may in fact be quite complex. In this volume, most functional relationships are stated in a simple linear form so that they can be readily interpreted and manipulated.[3] The examples should be recognized as indicative but not exact. At the points were actual functions used in applied models are examined, they will be found to be more complex.

The general and numerical functional examples can easily be connected to the diagrams and tables expressing the same relationships. Line C in Figure 3.3 represents a theoretical consumption function. Each point on this curve shows the value of output that consumers desire to buy at a certain level of disposable income. At point D, for example, the desired level of consumption is

3. In a linear equation, the coefficients are assumed to be constants. The lines expressing the relationship between two variables are straight. Their slope remains the same—it is constant—throughout.

$1,350 billion. This is found by reading the height on the vertical axis of a point on the consumption function above a level of disposable income of $1,400 billion found on the horizontal axis.

This figure represents a theoretical consumption function because, like a demand or supply curve, it assumes that all other forces influencing the propensity to consume remain constant. It expresses only the simple relationship between consumption and disposable income. The curve in the figure is in real terms (constant dollars) and is derived from aggregate data representing the entire household sector.[4]

MARGINAL PROPENSITY TO CONSUME

The first two columns of Table 3.2 show the same information as that presented graphically in Figure 3.3. Both represent the economy's consumption function. While these numbers are simplified, they resemble the relationship between consumption and disposable income. The remaining columns in Table 3.2 show other information which can be derived from the basic consumption schedule or curve. The third column shows how much extra expenditure occurs out of each dollar of extra disposable income. This relationship at the margin of income is called the **marginal propensity to consume** (*mpc*), defined as that part of every additional dollar of income that will be spent on consumption, or

$$mpc = \frac{\Delta C}{\Delta YD}. \qquad \text{3.2}$$

The slope of the consumption line tells how much consumption changes for each increment of income. It is illustrated by the move from point B to point D in Figure 3.3. Because a straight line has a constant slope, on this diagram the marginal propensity to consume is the same at all income levels. The curve and the table both show consumption changing by $75 billion for each movement of $100 billion in income. Thus the slope of the consumption function equals

$$\frac{\Delta C}{\Delta YD} = \frac{75}{100} = .75.$$

The final two columns show the saving schedule, or the amount of planned saving and the marginal propensity to save at each income level.

AVERAGE PROPENSITY TO CONSUME

In addition to the marginal propensity to consume, the **average propensity to consume** (*APC*), or the proportion of income consumed by households in any

4. Appendix 3.1 at the end of this chapter describes how empirical consumption functions are derived from actual data by the use of regression analysis.

TABLE 3.2   **Consumption and Saving Schedules**
(in billions of constant 1972 dollars)

Disposable income (YD)	Planned consumption expenditures (C)	Marginal propensity to consume $(\frac{\Delta C}{\Delta YD})$	Average propensity to consume $(\frac{C}{YD})$	Planned Saving (S)	Marginal propensity to save $(\frac{\Delta S}{\Delta YD})$
800	900	$\frac{75}{100}$	1.125	−100	$\frac{25}{100}$
900	975	$\frac{75}{100}$	1.083	−75	$\frac{25}{100}$
1,000	1,050	$\frac{75}{100}$	1.050	−50	$\frac{25}{100}$
1,100	1,125	$\frac{75}{100}$	1.022	−25	$\frac{25}{100}$
1,200	1,200	$\frac{75}{100}$	1.000	0	$\frac{25}{100}$
1,300	1,275	$\frac{75}{100}$	.981	25	$\frac{25}{100}$
1,400	1,350	$\frac{75}{100}$	.964	50	$\frac{25}{100}$

Households' plans to consume (second column) or to save (fifth column) depend on their income (first column). The marginal propensities to consume (third column) and to save (sixth column) show how much they want to consume or save out of each addition to income.

period, can also be important in analysis. The average propensity to consume is the level of consumption divided by the level of income, or

$$APC = \frac{C}{YD}. \qquad\qquad 3.3$$

This is shown in the fourth column of Table 3.2. At an income level of $1,400 billion, the APC is

$$\frac{C}{YD} = \frac{1,350}{1,400} = .964.$$

The table demonstrates that because of the positive autonomous consumption, the average propensity to consume falls as income rises, even with a constant marginal propensity to consume. This information can also be derived from the diagram of the consumption function. In Figure 3.3 the APC is simply the height of consumption at a given point divided by the income at that point (the vertical distance from the axis divided by the horizontal distance). For example, at point B the APC is $\dfrac{1,200}{1,200} = 1$ and at point A it is $\dfrac{975}{900} = 1.083$. At all points to the left of point B in Figure 3.3 the average propensity to consume will be greater than 1; to the right, less than 1.

The relationship between the average and marginal propensities will depend on whether or not the constant (autonomous) factor is positive or negative and on the size and shape of the income coefficient. In the case of Figure 3.3 and Table 3.2, the APC will decline asymptotically toward the mpc.

AUTONOMOUS AND INDUCED EXPENDITURES

The information in Figure 3.3 can be used to specify an equation expressing the consumption relationship. Study of the diagram shows that consumption will not be zero even when income is zero, since people must consume to live. In this case, at zero income consumption equals $300 billion. Such expenditures which are independent of the level of income (or of interest rates) are called *autonomous* (and, as noted, are designated by a bar over the related value).

The amount of consumption at any level of income equals autonomous expenditures plus an amount which varies with income in accordance with the *mpc*. The term *induced* is applied to expenditures whose amount depends upon income. The total relationship then is

$$C = \overline{C} + cYD \qquad\qquad C = 300 + .75(YD). \qquad\qquad \textbf{3.4}$$

What consumption will be at any income level can be found from the curve, the table, or the equation. The coefficient of the level of income in the equation, or c, is another representation of the marginal propensity to consume. It determines how much the desire to consume will change with disposable income. That total consumption equals the autonomous and induced amounts can be checked by substituting the values at any point of the table into equation 3.4. Thus with all data in billions of dollars at an income level of 1,200:

$$C = 300 + \frac{75}{100}(1,200) = 1,200.$$

The consumption schedule of the table, the consumption function in the diagram, and the algebraic equation all contain identical information. The amount of desired consumption depends on the level of income.

THE AMOUNT OF CONSUMPTION

It is possible now to visualize what happens when explanations and predictions of consumption are made. At any time, consumption expenditures depend on the position and shape of the consumption function and on the income which households receive. Each point on the curve reflects the amount of autonomous expenditures ($\overline{C}$) and the amount of income induced consumption (cYD). Because households desire to consume more at higher income levels, the amount of consumption may increase merely as the result of a growth in income. Thus Table 3.2 shows that the desire to consume will be $1,200 billion when income is $1,200 billion and will be $1,350 billion when YD is $1,400 billion. If income rises, expenditures move up the curve to the higher level.

Planned consumption can also shift as a result of alterations in autonomous consumption desires or of the *mpc*. Even with income constant, consumers might decide to spend $50 billion less at all income levels, so $\overline{C}$ would fall to $250 billion. Substituting this changed value in equation 3.4 shows planned consumption of $1,150 billion if YD remains at $1,200 billion. Similarly, in an effort to beat inflation, households might decide to spend 80 percent of income instead of the assumed 75 percent. The higher c would raise spending at all income levels.

The Circular Flow

Spending sectors will not have their desires fulfilled unless expenditures and income received from this spending are equal. The consumption function

FIGURE 3.4   **The Circular Flow of Income and Goods**

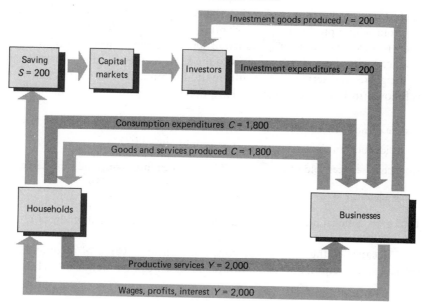

Households can make purchases or save. The GNP equals total expenditures, C + I (in color in the upper loop). While saving must equal investment expenditures, if desired saving does not equal desired investment, the flow through the loops and the GNP will alter.

shows how households split income between spending and not spending. But it does not tell the whole story. To illustrate the interdependence of income and demand and their link to spending desires and to saving and investment, Figure 3.4 depicts again a simplified circular flow model of the economy. In this model, the simple circular flow for households found in Figure 2.1 has been expanded to include a saving and investment sector. The other simplifying assumptions remain. Households now have a choice. They can divide the income they earn (Y) into expenditures for consumption goods (C) and saving (S). **Saving** is income they fail to spend for whatever reason. By definition, there are only two possible uses for income earned. The income of households is identically equal to consumption plus saving:

$$Y \equiv C + S. \hspace{4cm} 3.5$$

The figure also adds another decision-making process. Investors can decide to purchase investment goods (I). They can obtain funds for their investments in the capital markets. For example, they can sell bonds or stock or issue mortgages or notes to get funds. The second line in the figure shows them using the amounts not spent by households for investment expenditures. The top line shows the reverse flow of investment goods produced.

NECESSARY IDENTITIES IN THE CIRCULAR FLOW

Each stream in the circular flow is balanced by another. Thus, income earned (Y) from selling productive services must exactly equal the productive services sold. In turn, the value of productive services equals the value of the goods produced with them. This sum is also the same as the amount of money spent on the goods and services. The information summarized in the circular flow is as follows (in billions of constant 1972 dollars):

Income earned (Y)	2,000	Goods and services	
is identical to		produced (Q)	2,000
		are identical to	
Productive services sold (Y)	2,000	Expenditures on goods and services	
		Consumption (C)	1,800
is identical to		Investment (I)	200
		are identical to	
Total gross national income (Y)	2,000	Total gross national product (Y)	2,000

Because of the balancing items, the measured value of income earned, services sold, output, and expenditures must always be identical.[5] Thus

5. The symbol Y is used to represent the GNP. Because they are identical, it is also commonly substituted for income earned and services sold. In Chapters 3–7, which assume all relationships are in real, not nominal, terms, it can also be substituted for output (Q)

$$Y \equiv Q \equiv C + I$$

and

$$I \equiv Y - C. \hspace{4cm} \textbf{3.6}$$

This also must exactly equal the identity of income earned and spent or saved:

$$Y \equiv C + S$$

or

$$S \equiv Y - C. \hspace{4cm} \textbf{3.7}$$

This identity can be subtracted from the equal identity of income produced and expenditures in order to obtain another identity, namely, saving equals investment:

$$I \equiv Y - C \hspace{4cm} \textbf{3.6}$$

minus

$$S \equiv Y - C \hspace{4cm} \textbf{3.7}$$

equals

$$I \equiv S \hspace{4cm} \textbf{3.8}$$

The construction of the income accounts and the method of measuring the circular flow insure that realized saving and investment must always be equal.

SPENDING MAY NOT BE IN EQUILIBRIUM

The levels of spending and income are in constant flux. The circular flow does not remain constant, but expands or contracts. Analyses of the pressures acting either to retain spending at its current level or to move it to a new equilibrium are used to predict whether demand and income will rise or fall, and by how much. Equilibrium exists when the total demand for goods and services equals the amount produced.

Central to understanding how the circular flow shifts is the recognition of the difference between an identity and an equilibrium. In both cases, spending equals income and investment equals saving. But in the income accounts, these equalities result from the statistical and accounting conventions used. Because income and output are equal does not mean an equilibrium prevails. Pressures may be building up leading to change.

All goods produced and not purchased by consumers are, by definition, investment expenditures. All income received and not spent by consumers is defined as saving. While the accounts for the period must balance, the identities give no clue as to whether or not the situation is in equilibrium and will continue to be. The data alone do not inform us whether those making spending decisions are satisfied or whether they will act to change the level of income. To answer questions about equilibrium or disequilibrium and the trend of future spending, we must examine the desires or spending schedules of the household and business sectors.

How are the definitional identities of expenditures and income and of saving and investment related to an equilibrium of demand? No fixed channel guarantees that the amount the economy wants to spend will be identical to what is produced in any period or that the amount some want to save will be equal to what others want to invest. But relationships do exist between the amount the economy wants to consume or save and its income and the amount it plans to invest and its income. If at a given income level, spending and producing desires or saving and investment plans are not equal, income will expand or contract, bringing about an equality of the desires. It is the pressures to move to a new equilibrium because of unfulfilled or changed spending plans that must be recognized and used to predict next period's expenditures and income. Such changes in the circular flow occur even though an examination of the accounts at any time shows that spending and income and saving and investment appear equal. Because of definitions, their totals are the same, but they are not necessarily in equilibrium.

Let us differentiate between the concepts of actual expenditures (Q_a) or output, actual saving (S_a), and actual investment (I_a), all of which are the amounts in a period recorded in the National Income and Product Accounts, and planned expenditures (Y_p), planned saving (S_p), and planned investment (I_p) which result from the interaction of specific saving and investment functions and the level of income. In place of the term *actual* one can also speak of **realized** values, which include both a **planned** and an **unplanned** component. To the degree that realized expenditures differ from desired or planned, the economy will not be at equilibrium. The unplanned and undesired spending or saving exerts pressures on the circular flow to change.

The accounting identities require that actual output or income and expenditures be equal and realized saving and investment must also be equal:

$$Q_a \equiv Y_a \qquad\qquad 3.9$$
and
$$S_a \equiv I_a. \qquad\qquad 3.10$$

However, actual production need not equal planned expenditures, and planned saving need not equal planned investment. It is possible that

$$Q_a \neq Y_p$$
and
$$S_p \neq I_p.$$

If such inequalities exist, they will cause the level of output and income to move.

Assume, for example, that businesses produce $2,000 billion of goods and services in a period, in the belief that consumers desire to purchase $1,800 billion and investors want to buy $200 billion. In fact, however, consumers spend only $1,750 billion and actually save (S_a) $250 billion. Businesses would find that instead of their planned $200 billion investment, they would have realized investments of $250 billion. Actual investment would equal actual output less actual consumption expenditures:

$$I_a = Q_a - C_a \qquad I_a = 2,000 - 1,750 = 250, \qquad \textbf{3.11}$$

and actual saving would equal actual investment:

$$S_a = I_a \qquad 250 = 250, \qquad \textbf{3.12}$$

but neither planned expenditures nor planned investment would equal the realized amounts. Adding the plans to consume and invest need not give the actual output:

$$Q_a \neq C_p + I_p \qquad 2,000 \neq 1,750 + 200.$$

Because production exceeded desired spending, undesired investment in inventories takes place:

$$I_a = 250$$

and

$$I_p = 200,$$

so

$$I_a - I_p = 50.$$

The actual investment includes an undesired component of $50 billion. Their excess inventories will cause producers to cut production, hoping to sell their unplanned investment in inventories. This action will push the economy toward a new equilibrium—one where planned and actual spending are equal and the total demand for goods equals the amount produced. How far it will move can be found by analyzing where the new equilibrium will occur.

The Equilibrium Level of Expenditures

At the equilibrium level of spending (Y_E—the subscript E indicates an equilibrium value), no tendency to change exists because the economy desires to spend all it receives as income and to purchase aggregate output. There is no pressure to expand or contract production. Planned investment and saving are equal, as are planned and actual saving and planned and actual investment.

At equilibrium:

Planned spending equals income produced	$E = Q$
Planned investment equals planned saving	$I_p = S_p$
Planned investment equals actual investment	$I_p = I_a$
Planned saving equals actual saving	$S_p = S_a$

Such an equilibrium is pictured at the $2,000 billion level in Table 3.3. The equilibrium level of the GNP will shift if spending sectors change their desires. Why and how does this occur?

TABLE 3.3   **Determination of the Level of Expenditures**
(in billions of constant 1972 dollars)

Levels of output and earned income $(Q = Y)$		Planned consumption schedule (C)	+	Planned investment schedule (I)	=	Planned spending level (E)
1,200		1,200		200		1,400
1,400		1,350		200		1,550
1,600		1,500		200		1,700
1,800		1,650		200		1,850
2,000	=	1,800	+	200	=	2,000
2,200		1,950		200		2,150
2,400		2,100		200		2,300

Only at $2,000 billion are planned expenditures and output equal. If output is lower, excess demand causes production to expand. If output is higher, unwanted inventory accumulation leads to a cutback in production.

In this table, the first column shows levels of output (Q) and earned income (Y). (Because taxes are assumed absent, earned income (Y) is the same as disposable income $[YD]$.) The second column shows the amount households want to consume at each income level. The relationship is based on the comsumption function of equation 3.4 and Table 3.2. The third column shows the desire to invest at each income level. In this case, planned investment is autonomous $(\bar{I} = 200)$ and is the same at all incomes. The last column gives the real aggregate demand for goods and services (E) at each income level. It is the sum of the desires to spend of the individual sectors $(C + I)$, or

$$E = C + I. \qquad\qquad 3.13$$

Before seeing how new equilibriums come about, we can study Table 3.3 to find the equilibrium where planned spending exactly equals income produced—where producers will supply exactly the output demanded. This equilibrium point is $2,000 billion. The tendency toward stability can be tested. What if businesses produced $2,400 billion of goods and services? This would appear as output and disposable income in the first column. But would this amount of production be purchased? The remaining columns show that it would not. At an income of $2,400 billion, the economy would plan to spend (E) only $2,300 billion. Producers would receive less than they paid out; losses would occur and, in the next period, less would be produced. Income paid out would fall until it reached $2,000 billion, when again there would be no tendency to change. The same thing would occur if we start at the $1,600 billion level. Here desired spending exceeds the amount produced. There is a tendency for income to expand until it reaches the satisfactory or equilibrium level.

FINDING EQUILIBRIUM BY DIAGRAMS

The way in which equilibrium is determined may also be described through the use of diagrams (Figure 3.5). First, look at panel A. Here the consumption function of Figure 3.3 and Table 3.2 is presented again in the line labeled C, or E_1. In the simplified model, all income received is available for spending; it is both income earned and disposable income. Reflecting this fact, the horizontal axis is labeled Y rather than YD. It is also labeled Q because, in accordance with the circular flow, income earned and output are identical.

At each income level, the planned level of investment is added to the desired level of consumption in order to obtain the real aggregate demand line marked $C + I$, or E_2. This shows how much all sectors of the economy plan to spend at each level of income. Thus, at an income level of $1,400 billion, the desire to consume is $1,350 billion, to which is added the desire to invest of $200 billion, to yield the point H on the aggregate demand ($C + I$) line of $1,550 billion.

The same information is contained in panel B; but here, the real aggregate demand line ($C + I$) is derived in a different way which yields other useful information. First, note where the line starts. It originates at a level determined by all autonomous spending desires (in this case $\overline{C} + \overline{I}$ or $500 billion). This is the amount of spending which, in theory, would occur even if income were zero. It is autonomous spending ($\overline{A}_2$). Aggregate demand equals the autonomous amount at the intercept plus an additional amount determined by the level of income and the amount of spending induced by that income. This additional spending depends on the slope of the spending function, or c in this simple model. At each level of earned income, how much will be demanded depends on the intercept, the slope of the line, and the available income. Of course, the planned spending lines (E_2) in both panels, whether labeled $\overline{C} + cY + \overline{I}$ or $\overline{A}_2 + cY$ are identical.

To find how much the economy will spend at equilibrium, the figure can be used to relate planned spending with output and income earned. The horizontal scale is labeled both income and output to emphasize that the two are always the same. Figure 3.5 also introduces a 45° line ($E = Q$) on which vertical and horizontal distances are equal. Consequently, at any point on this line one can read off the amount of output, of income earned, and a level of demand. For example, point D is on the 45° line; therefore, $OG = GD$. Since OG measures $1,400 billion on the horizontal output scale, the amount of output at D is $1,400 billion. The distance between H and D (1,550 − 1,400) shows the amount by which real aggregate demand (E_2) exceeds output when income (also OG) is $1,400 billion. Now note where the planned expenditure curve (E_2) crosses the 45° line at point F. Planned spending equals output. The demand for and output of goods and services are exactly equal, as is the income earned from that output.

With the aggregate demand (E_2) and the 45° lines it is possible to check and see which points on Figure 3.5 are not in equilibrium and how the economy will move from them. At the designated points on Figure 3.5A, the following information can be read off:

	Expenditures (in billions of constant dollars)		
	D	F	J
Output (Q)	1,400	2,000	2,400
Consumption (C)	1,350	1,800	2,100
Planned I	200	200	200
Unplanned I	−150	0	100

Each point on the 45° line equals the actual level of output. The height of the line C shows consumption and that of the $C + I$ line shows planned expenditures for a level of income and output measured either on the horizontal scale or the 45° line. The distance between output and planned expenditures shows unplanned expenditures. At point J, output exceeds aggregate demand by $100 billion. This is not a stable situation. Unwanted inventories accumulate as businesses cannot sell all they produce. To bring the economy into equilibrium (Y_E in the figure), output will contract. In the same way, no level to the left of F (such as H) will be satisfactory. Inventory investment is less than planned. Expansionary forces will increase output to the level of planned expenditures. Only at point F, where aggregate demand and output are $2,000 billion, do planned expenditures equal output and income earned. Neither producers' nor purchasers' plans are frustrated. This is the equilibrium point.

EQUILIBRIUM BY A NUMERICAL EXAMPLE

In addition to the numerical example of the table and figure, equilibrium can be found by substituting the equations for the consumption and investment schedules in the expenditure identity. The identity is

$$Y \equiv C + I, \qquad\qquad\qquad 3.14$$

FIGURE 3.5   **Determination of Equilibrium Expenditures and Income**

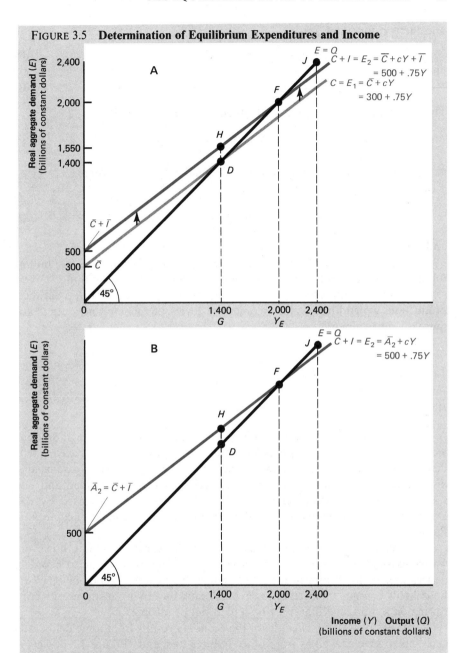

The planned spending (E)—or real aggregate demand—line is the sum of planned consumption and investment at each income level. It equals autonomous spending ($\bar{A}$) plus induced spending (cY). At equilibrium, F, planned spending, output, and income are equal.

and the two functions are

$$C = \overline{C} + cY \qquad C = 300 + .75Y \qquad\qquad \textbf{3.15}$$

and

$$I = \overline{I} \qquad I = 200. \qquad\qquad \textbf{3.16}$$

The substitution gives aggregate demand (since $E = C + I$).

$$E = \overline{C} + cY + \overline{I} \qquad E = 300 + .75Y + 200. \qquad\qquad \textbf{3.17}$$

At equilibrium, planned expenditures will equal output and income ($E = Q = Y_E$), so Y_E can be substituted for E and Y:

$$Y_E = \overline{C} + cY_E + \overline{I} \qquad Y_E = 300 + .75Y_E + 200 \qquad\qquad \textbf{3.18}$$

and since $.25Y_E = 500$, $Y_E = 2{,}000$.

Thus the numerical example also yields an equilibrium of $2,000 billion for income and expenditures. All three techniques say the same thing. Given schedules of the desires to spend along with the necessary relationship between production, expenditures, and income, the levels of income and output are mutually determined.

Leakages and Injections

THE SAVING FUNCTION

A complete kit for analyzing spending changes includes several additional tools. Closest to the consumption function in concept is the *saving function* (S), defined as the relationship between the amount people desire to save and disposable income. Saving can also be defined as income received and not spent. In fact, this latter definition ($YD - C$) is the method used by the Department of Commerce to calculate saving in the National Income and Product Accounts.

Thinking of demand merely as a decision to consume or not, however, wastes useful information. Some decisions not to spend are due to people's desires to save for future needs. Rather than buy current goods or services, households commit themselves to savings plans by buying insurance or borrowing on a mortgage that must be repaid out of income.

The desire-to-save schedule for the economy results from some deliberate decisions to save as well as from other failures to spend. Figure 3.6 depicts a saving function. The line S is a graph of the function

$$S = \overline{S} + sY \qquad S = -300 + .25\,Y. \qquad\qquad \textbf{3.19}$$

Like the consumption function, $\overline{S}$ is autonomous saving and s is the **marginal propensity to save,** or the slope of the saving function. At any time, the marginal

FIGURE 3.6   **A Saving Function Used to Find Equilibrium Expenditures and Income**

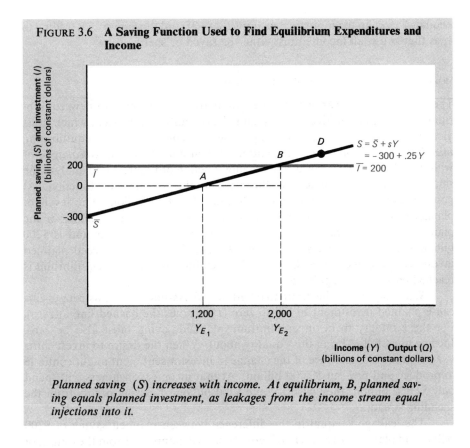

Planned saving (S) increases with income. At equilibrium, B, planned saving equals planned investment, as leakages from the income stream equal
injections into it.

propensities to save and to consume are complements, summing to one. When
an extra dollar of income is received, it must be either consumed or saved.

The equation for the saving function can be derived from the consumption function. Saving equals income not consumed:

$$S \equiv Y - C. \qquad\qquad\qquad \textbf{3.20}$$

The consumption function,

$$C = \overline{C} + cY \qquad\quad C = 300 + .75Y \qquad\qquad \textbf{3.4}$$

is substituted in equation 3.20:

$$S = Y - \overline{C} - cY \qquad\quad S = Y - 300 - .75Y.$$
$$S = -\overline{C} + (1 - c)Y \qquad\quad S = -300 + (1 - .75)Y. \qquad \textbf{3.21}$$

From the equality of equations 3.19 and 3.21, note that $\overline{S}$ equals $-\overline{C}$ and

s equals $1 - c$. In the numerical example, $s = .25$ and the $mpc = .75$; adding to 1, as they must, all income must either be saved or spent.

MOVEMENTS TO A NEW SPENDING EQUILIBRIUM

The saving function can also be used to analyze movements to new equilibriums. It is an alternative to the planned expenditure approach, which must yield identical results. This technique uses the concept that, in equilibrium, *injections* or additions into the spending stream must be equal to *leakages,* or withdrawals from it. Let us use the saving function of Figure 3.6 to analyze the shifts in aggregate demand just illustrated by the consumption function. At point *B,* the figure displays an equilibrium of $2,000 billion. The levels of planned saving and investment are equal, as shown by the meeting of the planned-saving and planned-investment lines ($\bar{I}$ is autonomous and is $200 billion at all income levels). At point *D,* desired saving will exceed planned investment. Income will leak out of the spending stream until equilibrium is reached once again at point *B.*

What happens if the desire to invest drops? Assume that disastrous events cause planned investment to fall to zero ($\bar{I}$ becomes the dashed line at zero). For the economy to be in equilibrium, planned saving must also be zero. Income must fall to bring this equality about. When the desire to invest shifts to zero, producers unaware of the change in investor sentiment might continue to produce and pay out $2,000 billion. At that income, consumers will spend only $1,800 billion; they wish to save $200 billion. Leakage occurs from the spending stream.

The leakage is equal to the difference between planned saving of $200 billion and planned investment of zero. What will happen? From the output of $2,000 billion, only $1,800 billion will be sold; the remaining $200 billion will end up as undesired and unplanned inventories. Actual saving still equals actual investment. But this situation is not stable. Businesses do not reach their goals; they are overinvesting in the form of unplanned inventory accumulation. To get back to a more desirable situation, producers will cut back on output. They will continue to cut back, and leakages from the spending stream will take place until, finally, the desires to invest and to save are once again equal. Leakages from the spending stream persist and do not stop until the new equilibrium income of $1,200 billion, or point *A* on the diagram, is reached.

The Multiplier

The expansions and contractions in income which result from exogenous changes in spending are examples of one of the most important principles in the theory of aggregate demand. When any sector increases its spending, the total growth in income and output will be a multiple of the initial increase. A similar multiplication occurs if the sector reduces its demand. If U.S. Steel builds a billion-dollar complex, the added national income will amount to a good deal more than its investment expenditures. This multiplication of exogenous shifts in spending is a factor which is significant in explaining instability in the aggregate economy.

Any autonomous change in spending *induces* additional amounts. The *multiplier* (k) is the number by which any change in autonomous spending is magnified to provide the total change in income. Suppose that investment in energy and energy-related industries increases by $200 billion a year as a result of new regulatory and tax policies and subsidies. How much will total demand for goods and services grow? Recalling all the limiting assumptions of the simplified model, note that this is equivalent to the cases just discussed. Analysis of the kind they contain, when buttressed by actual rather than assumed coefficients, can yield the answers sought.

For example, Table 3.3 and Figures 3.5 and 3.6 illustrate an autonomous increase in investment spending ($\Delta \bar{I}$) of $200 billion compared to the case in which consumption only was considered. The change in the equilibrium level of income (ΔY_E) which results is $800 billion. In other words, the $200 billion change in autonomous spending is magnified to a $800 billion increase in income, or by a factor of 4. This is the particular multiplier (k) which results from the spending schedules in those examples.

The diagram showing the determination of total spending (Figure 3.7) makes clear the reason for this multiplication. When an autonomous shift in spending takes place, consumers move to higher levels of expenditures along a preexisting schedule—the consumption function. They spend more because they have a desire to do so which can be realized when they receive more income. Income expands to a point where the desire to save exactly equals the greater desire to invest. The total growth in output (ΔQ) and income (ΔY) equals the increased expenditures on investment (ΔI) plus those for consumption (ΔC):

$$\Delta Q = \Delta Y = \Delta \bar{I} + \Delta C \qquad \Delta Y = 200 + 600 = 800. \qquad \textbf{3.22}$$

To find the multiplier, the change in equilibrium income (ΔY) can be divided by the movement in autonomous spending ($\Delta \bar{I}$) which caused it:

$$k = \frac{\Delta Y}{\Delta \bar{I}} = \frac{\Delta \bar{I} + \Delta C}{\Delta \bar{I}} = \frac{200 + 600}{200} = 4. \qquad \textbf{3.23}$$

Look at the consumption function—the lower line marked *C*—in Figure 3.7. This is the same function diagrammed in Figures 3.2 and 3.5. From the diagram or from Table 3.3 we can see that at an income of $1,200 billion, consumers desire to spend $1,200 billion; at $1,600 billion the desire to consume is $1,500 billion; when income is $2,000 billion, consumers want to spend $1,800 billion.

The lower line shows that if the only autonomous spending is consump-

FIGURE 3.7   **The Multiplier**

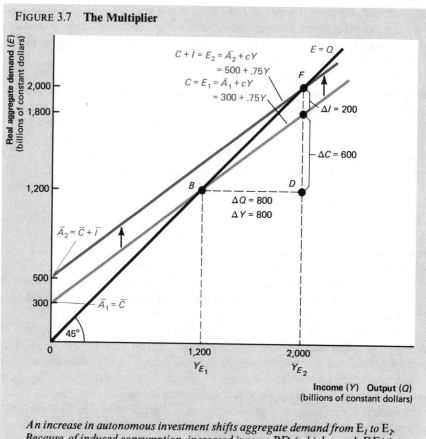

An increase in autonomous investment shifts aggregate demand from E_1 to E_2. Because of induced consumption, increased income BD (which equals DF) is a multiple of the added autonomous spending. The components of DF are the additional I and C, and they show how much of the new income comes from each source. The multiplier is the total over the autonomous increase or, in this example, $k = \dfrac{\Delta Y}{\Delta \bar{I}} = \dfrac{800}{200} = 4.$

tion, equilibrium income will be $1,200 billion. The consumption function has the intercept $\bar{A}_1 = \bar{C} = \$300$ billion. It has a slope equal to $c = .75$. Notice what happens when $200 billion of desired autonomous investment is added to the desire to consume at each income level. The intercept $\bar{A}_2$ now equals $\bar{C} + \bar{I}$, or $500 billion, and the slope is unchanged. The line of aggregate demand has shifted to E_2. Equilibrium is no longer $1,200 billion because, at that level, desires to spend exceed output. Producers will expand output. A new equilibrium, Y_{E_2} is reached at $2,000 billion. To reach that point, output and income have expanded (ΔQ) by $800 billion. At this new level of output and income, consumers are able to fulfill their desire to spend of $1,800 billion. The change in income of $800 billion resulting from the $200 billion added desire to invest has induced an increase in consumption of $600 billion.

Lags and Dynamic Analysis

In modern macroanalysis, a crucial factor is the recognition that time can play a substantial role in determining the path to a new equilibrium. Many theories of inflation and of cyclical instability are based on the concept of delays in adjustment. Delays can cause prices to continue to rise even after the initial impulse has dissipated or dynamic relationships may cause the economy to turn up or down without any new shock from outside forces.

LAGS

The analysis of dynamic relationships recognizes that the effects of altered decisions cannot be felt immediately. When an autonomous shift in spending occurs, it will take some time before all of the induced effects appear. Families and households must adjust to new situations. The period of adjustment is called a *lag* in the timing of spending or any other action.

In a snapshot of the economy, as in a quarterly GNP report, many spending decisions will not have had a chance to affect the spending for that period. The economy may be moving toward a new equilibrium but that will not be reflected in the statistical facts. For example, in a typical empirical model, it is estimated that families spend from 25 to 30 percent of any increase in income in the first quarter they receive it; from 50 to 60 percent in the first year; and the remainder is spread out up to three years. In estimating the impact of factors affecting consumption, care must be taken to estimate this time period over which effects will be felt. Lags must be included.

The concept of lags can be demonstrated through the process by which income contracts or expands until planned saving equals planned investment. The previous analysis compared equilibrium levels of income before and after new spending desires. However, neither the discussion nor the diagrams gave any indication of how long it would take to reach the new level nor of the path by which it would be reached. In the example, did the induced rise in consumption take place simultaneously with the postulated increase in the desire to invest? Evidently not. When demand increased, the output of investment goods had to be expanded, causing incomes to grow through higher wages, interest, and profits. It took time before the recipients of the new incomes could increase their purchases. In other words, lags exist between changes in demand and production, between production and receipt of income, and between income and changed expenditures. The length of these lags determines how long it takes before a new equilibrium is reached.[6]

No simple or single lag exists. Production takes time. Each factor receives and spends its income uniquely. Higher wages may be paid out in a week or two, whereas profits might not be distributed for a year or more. For

---

6. See W. L. Smith and R. L. Teigan, *Readings in Money, National Income, and Stabilization Policy,* revised ed. (Homewood, Ill.: Irwin, 1970), p. 25.

analytic purposes, however, it is easier to think in terms of decisions being made in some average period.

This concept of distinct periods can be used to trace the induced increase in expenditures. In the initial period, an increase in demand raises output, and payments for the new investment goods augment income, but no new consumption takes place. By the end of the first period, people have received all the new income from the investment purchases. They must decide whether or not to spend it. By how much will they increase their spending in the second period? That depends on their consumption function and marginal propensity to consume. If, as in the specific example, they habitually spend three-quarters of any new income, for each $100 of additional income they receive in the first period, they will spend $75 and save $25 in the second period. As this money is spent, it leads to additional output and income for the factors producing consumption goods in the second period. When the third period starts, households again have to decide how much of their new income to spend. Again, they will decide in accordance with their marginal propensity to consume.

DERIVING THE MULTIPLIER BY PERIOD ANALYSIS

The way in which the amount of new income and the multiplier in any period depend on lags can be readily observed in Table 3.4. To underscore the fact

TABLE 3.4   **The Dynamics of Spending Injection: The Multiplier**
(billions of constant dollars at annual rates)

Period	Decisions to invest and consume					Decisions to save and consume				
	Investment ΔI_1	+	Consumption ΔC_1	=	Income produced ΔQ_1	=	Income received ΔY_1	=	Planned consumption ΔC_2	+	Planned saving ΔS_2
1	200	+	0	=	200		200	=	150	+	50
2	200	+	150	=	350		350	=	263	+	87
3	200	+	263	=	463		463	=	347	+	116
4	200	+	347	=	547		547	=	410	+	137
5	200	+	410	=	610		610	=	458	+	152
.	.		.		.		.		.		.
.	.		.		.		.		.		.
.	.		.		.		.		.		.
Final period	200	+	600	=	800		800	=	600	+	200

An autonomous increase in spending (first column) raises output (third column) and income (fourth column). Households divide the added income into next period's consumption or planned saving in accordance with their mpc. Output rises to match added demand and continues to expand until added investment equals the planned additions to saving. The multiplier is the additional output (third column) at equilibrium over the added autonomous spending.

that it is the additional or marginal spending that is involved, Table 3.4 has been constructed by subtracting the initial level of spending from the total in each period, so that the table records only the changes in spending which result from an autonomous increase. It is assumed that the level of desired investment permanently shifts up by $200 billion in each period.

In Table 3.4, investment expenditure, output, and income are each increased in the first period by $200 billion. At the end of the first period, households decide what to do with their extra income.[7] They increase their consumption in accordance with their marginal propensity to consume times the amount of additional income received in the period, which is (ΔI_1). Thus, in the second period their additional consumption is $C_2 = c\Delta I_1$. For the second period, the total increase in income consists of added investment plus the added consumption, or

$$\Delta Q_2 = \Delta I_2 + c\Delta I_1 \qquad 350 = 200 + .75(200). \qquad \textbf{3.24}$$

Again, this extra income is divided into planned saving and added consumption, which increases output and income in the next period:

$$\Delta Q_3 = \Delta I_3 + c(\Delta I_2 + c\Delta I_1) \qquad 463 = 200 + .75[200 + .75(200)], \qquad \textbf{3.25}$$

or, removing the parenthesis,

$$\Delta Q_3 = \Delta I_3 + c\Delta I_2 + c^2\Delta I_1 \qquad 463 = 200 + .75(200) + .75^2(200). \qquad \textbf{3.26}$$

The table illustrates income growing until it finally reaches a level of maximum expansion. In any period, how much income exceeds that of the period before the rate of investment rose depends on (1) the size of the autonomous rise in spending $(\Delta \bar{I})$ and (2) the amount of induced consumption $(\ldots c\Delta I_2 + c^2\, \Delta I_1)$, which is determined by the *mpc* and the number of periods since the autonomous shift occurred. Thus, in period n, consumption spending is influenced by the additional income of each prior period. However, the influence of a period decreases with time at a geometric rate. In general, if investment increases autonomously by a fixed amount in each period, the additional income in period n equals

$$\Delta Q_n = \Delta \bar{I}_1 + c\Delta \bar{I}_2 + c^2\Delta \bar{I}_3 + c^3\Delta \bar{I}_4 \ldots,$$

or, since all changes in investment are equal, $\Delta \bar{I}$ can be factored out,

7. The period in which action occurs is designated by a subscript. Thus Q_1 is output of the first period. Y_1 is income earned in the first period. It is available in the second period for second period's consumption, C_2, or second period saving, S_2. Investment in the third period would be I_3. A more complete explanation of lags can be found in Appendix 3.2 at the end of this chapter.

$$\Delta Q_n = \Delta \bar{I}(1 + c + c^2 + c^3 + \ldots).$$ 3.27

The added income equals the change in investment times a series which forms a geometric progression. Because the marginal propensity to consume is less than one, we know from elementary algebra that this series has a value of $\frac{1}{1 - c}$. Replacing the series in equation 3.27 by this value and using Y in place of Q gives the expression

$$\Delta Y = \Delta \bar{I} \frac{1}{1 - c}$$ 3.28

Dividing the equation by the autonomous change in spending gives the multiplier

$$\frac{\Delta Y}{\Delta \bar{I}} = \frac{1}{1 - c} = k$$ 3.29

or the multiplier is seen to be $\frac{1}{1 - c}$ or $\frac{1}{1 - mpc}$.

With knowledge of the multiplier, the actual amount demand and income will have increased in the final period when the full series has worked itself out is found to be

$$\Delta Y = \Delta \bar{I} \frac{1}{1 - c} \qquad\qquad \Delta Y = 200(\frac{1}{1 - .75}) = 800.$$

While, in theory, it will take an infinite number of periods for this entire expansion to take place, most of the effects will be felt in a limited time.[8]

---

8. Experiment with consumption functions having other slopes. The steeper the slope, the greater will be the magnification resulting from any increase in investment or any autonomous expenditure $(\bar{A})$. The increase in consumption ΔC will be $c\Delta Y$ or $\Delta \bar{A} \frac{c}{1 - c}$. Thus, if $\Delta \bar{A}$ is $200 billion and $c = .8$, consumption will increase by $800 billion. The multiplier,

$$k = \frac{\Delta \bar{A} + \Delta C}{\Delta \bar{A}} = \frac{200 + 800}{200} = 5.$$ 3.30

On the other hand, if $c = .5$, consumption will increase by only $200 billion. The multiplier,

$$k = \frac{\Delta \bar{A} + \Delta C}{\Delta \bar{A}} = \frac{200 + 200}{200} \text{ is } 2.$$

CONTRASTING A PERMANENT INCREASE AND A SINGLE INJECTION
OF AUTONOMOUS SPENDING

The multiplier process is presented graphically in Figure 3.8. In the first period, only the change in investment occurs. In the second period, the increased income of the prior period leads to an expansion of consumption which is shown by the box $c\Delta I_1$. The total added income of the second period consists of the induced consumption plus a new injection of investment (ΔI_2). In the third period income consists of a third injection (ΔI_3) plus more induced consumption. Some of the added consumption is the stream flowing from the initial investment ($c^2\Delta I_1$); some comes from the second period's investment ($c\Delta I_2$). The effect of the initial investment and its decreasing impact on consumption in later periods is shown by the bottom set of boxes, each of which contains ΔI_1. The effects of the second period's injection are traced by the second box in each period, those containing ΔI_2. The total increase in income for a period, which is shown by the total height of a column, depends on the new investment in that period plus its consumption. The total increase in a period's consumption can be considered as the result of either the consumption function times the additional income of the previous period or, equivalently, it is the amount of consumption induced by all prior injections of investment less the leakages through past saving.

Does the injection of a constant amount of added investment in each period mean that income keeps increasing? Figure 3.8 shows that this does not happen. The income level stabilizes at a new height which is determined by the amount of added investment and the multiplier resulting from the actual marginal propensities to consume and save. The multiplication comes to an end because there is a leak in the spending stream in each period. Some of the income received is saved rather than being spent. In fact, the multiplied effect stabilizes when the leakage through saving exactly equals the added injection from investment. When the multiplier finally reaches its limit, the amount of planned saving finally equals the amount of investment.[9]

9. To reflect the leakage-injection concept, the multiplier is frequently expressed as the reciprocal of the marginal propensity to save. Again, this statement can be derived directly from the equality of added saving and investment in equilibrium:

$$\Delta S = s\Delta Y = \Delta \overline{I} \qquad\qquad .25\,\Delta Y = \Delta \overline{I}. \qquad\qquad \textbf{3.31}$$

To find the multiplier, divide equation 3.31 by $s\Delta\overline{I}$:

$$\frac{s\Delta Y}{s\Delta\overline{I}} = \frac{\Delta\overline{I}}{s\Delta\overline{I}} \qquad\qquad \frac{\Delta Y}{\Delta\overline{I}} = \frac{1}{s}$$

and

$$k = \frac{\Delta Y}{\Delta\overline{I}} = \frac{1}{s} \qquad\qquad k = \frac{\Delta Y}{\Delta\overline{I}} = \frac{1}{.25} = 4 \qquad\qquad \textbf{3.32}$$

or

$$k = \frac{1}{s} = \frac{1}{1-c} \qquad\qquad k = \frac{1}{.25} = \frac{1}{1-.75} = 4. \qquad\qquad \textbf{3.32 and 3.29}$$

FIGURE 3.8   **The Dynamics of Spending Injections**

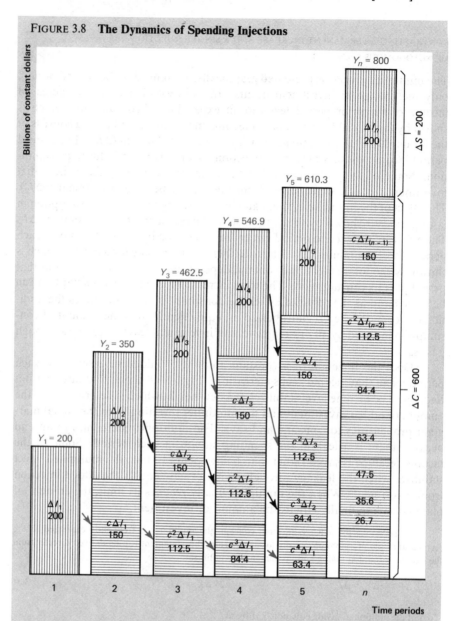

A new investment, $\Delta \overline{I}$, raises income. In the next period, consumption rises in accordance with the mpc. Output rises still more as a result of a second increase in investment. Income continues to rise as consumption expands, reflecting a higher output from both $\Delta \overline{I}$ and C. Finally, in period n, total leakages (planned saving) equal the injection of that period, so no further expansion occurs.

What would happen if instead of investment shifting up by $200 billion in each period, it rose by this amount and then dropped back immediately to its previous level? Figure 3.8 and Table 3.5 bring out the difference between a permanent increase in the level of autonomous spending and a single or one-shot increase. Table 3.5 illustrates the latter situation. In the first period, investment and income produced both rise by $200 billion. In the second period investment falls back to zero, but because the extra $200 billion earned is available to be spent or saved, people, in accordance with the consumption function, consume an additional $150 billion and save $50 billion. The increase in income compared to period zero is now $150 billion. This again results in more consumption and more saving. By the end of the series, all of the added initial injection will have leaked out. All spending streams are back at their starting point, zero. If we now cumulate all the added spending, as in the bottom row, we find

$$\Delta Y = \Delta \bar{I} + \Delta C \qquad 800 = 200 + 600. \qquad \textbf{3.22}$$

The level of spending stays above its previous base until the leakages or amount of saving is $200 billion—equal to the entire added autonomous injection. This movement is illustrated by the bottom set of boxes in Figure 3.8. The first box shows the initial I. The declining ones thereafter show the injection's impact on consumption, which falls to zero by the final period. Adding the initial invest-ment to the induced consumption in each period gives the cumulative increase in income of $800 billion.

TABLE 3.5 **The Dynamics of a One-Shot Increase in Investment**
(billions of constant dollars)

Period	Investment	Consumption	Saving	Income
		(increase compared to base period)		
0	0	0	0	0
1	200	0	0	200
2	0	150	50	150
3	0	112.5	37.5	112.5
4	0	84.4	28.1	84.4
.	.	.	.	.
.	.	.	.	.
Final	0	0	0	0
cumulativeΣ	200	600	200	800

In contrast to a continuous injection of autonomous spending, after a oneshot increase, spending gradually returns to its initial level. This happens when higher incomes no longer induce added consumption because the original autonomous injection has completely leaked out of the circular flow. The amount of leakage in each period depends on the size of the saving function(s) which is .25 in the table.

Summary

1. One of the most significant concepts in analyzing aggregate demand or the desires to spend of the economy is that if spending units receive additional income, they will raise their spending in accordance with preexisting patterns of behavior that can be observed and predicted.

2. One of the most important of such aggregate relationships is the con-sumption function, which expresses the desire to spend out of income for the household sector, holding all other spending influences constant. From the consumption function, one can determine the desired extra spending resulting from each dollar of added income, called the marginal propensity to consume, as well as the average relationship at any level between consumption and income, called the average propensity to consume. The saving function and the marginal propensity to save are the complements of consumption, since any dollar of income is either consumed or saved.

3. The circular flow illustrates the necessary connections between ex-penditures, output, and income. By definition, identities exist relating compo-nents of the GNP. Real output is the same as total expenditures and total income. Since investment goods are defined as those goods produced and not sold to consumers (in the model which excludes the government) and since saving is defined as income received by consumers from the production of all goods less the amount they spend for consumption, actual investment and saving must be equal.

4. However, the desire to produce and to spend or to invest and save need not be equal. Desired spending changes in any sector lead to a new equilibrium point for the economy. During the process through which the economy reaches a new equilibrium, periods of temporary disequilibrium will occur. The plans or desires to spend may not equal production. For example, there may be unplanned disinvestment in inventories. If consumption expenditures exceed the amounts businesses expected and produced, they might meet the demand through a reduction of inventories. As they increase production to meet the new demand and to replace inventories, incomes will rise; so will spending. Equilibrium will be reached when desired and actual spending are again equal; no unplanned investment exists. The path to and the level of the new equilib-rium can be found by comparing the equilibrium levels of spending before and after a shift or by tracing the path to the new level through period analysis. Thinking in terms of periods makes clearer the concepts of lags and speed of adjustment.

5. The process to a new equilibrium can also be analyzed in terms of injections into the income stream and leakages from it. When a new dollar of spending is injected into the income stream, it will continue to circulate, in-creasing jobs, income, and further spending. There is a limit on its impact, however, because people will not spend some of their added income; they will

save it instead. Equilibrium is reached when planned saving, including that from the added income, again equals planned investment.

6. If an initial shift in spending occurs, it will be multiplied. The added spending becomes income of the factors of production, and they in turn fulfill their pre-existing desires to spend, evidenced by their spending schedules. The size of the multiplier depends on the marginal propensity to consume. It is equal to $\dfrac{1}{1-c}$. In other words, the multiplier depends on the amount of extra income consumers desire to spend. Since the marginal propensity to save is the complement of the *mpc*, the multiplier is also equal to $\dfrac{1}{s}$.

Questions for Discussion and Review

1. Suppose a budget survey has been conducted yielding the following results:

Income level in 1980	Consumption Expenditures in 1980 (billions of dollars)
5,000	5,100
10,000	8,850
20,000	16,350
50,000	38,850
75,000	57,600
100,000	76,350

   (a) Graph the consumption function.
   (b) Calculate for each income group:
      (1) *mpc*
      (2) *APC*
      (3) saving
      (4) *mps*
   (c) If the pattern indicated in the survey continued, what would be the value of *APC* for the million-dollar-a-year income group?

2. How would the economy be affected if businessmen were always able to forsee accurately future demand for their products?

3. Give both an algebraic and an economic explanation of why the multiplier is one or greater.

4. If the whole of income were always spent, what would the value of the multiplier be?

5. Consider an economy described by the following relations (quantities in billions of constant dollars):
$$C = 300 + .80Y$$
$$I = \bar{I} = 300$$
   (a) What is the equilibrium level of income?

(b) What is the value of the investment multiplier?

(c) Suppose that in period 1, $\bar{I}$ increases to 400, and that in period 2 and in all periods thereafter it returns to 300. How much additional output will eventually be induced? What will be the equilibrium level of income toward which income and output are heading?

6. If the desire of individuals to save increases, what happens to the equilibrium level of income?

References

Havrilesky, T. M., and J. T. Boorman. *Current Issues in Monetary Theory and Policy,* 2nd edition. Arlington Heights, Ill.: AMH Publishing Co., 1980.

Mansfield, E. *Economics,* 3rd edition. New York: Norton, 1980. Chapters 10 and 11.

Schultze, C. L. *National Income Analysis,* 3rd edition. Englewood Cliffs, N.J.: Prentice-Hall, 1971).

Smith, W. L., and R. L. Teigan. *Readings in Money, National Income, and Stabilization Policy,* revised edition. Homewood, Ill.: Irwin, 1970.

APPENDIX 3.1   Regression Analysis

Macroeconomics describes the relationships among aggregate economic variables. In this volume, these relationships are described in several ways: (1) verbally, (2) by use of diagrams, (3) by use of simple algebraic equations, (4) by numerical examples, and (5) at times by actual cases of models fit by practitioners in the field through the use of regression analysis. Regression equations are used primarily to replace qualitative with quantitative information. In most macroeconomic discussions, the models and general equations that are used tend to be based on casual empiricism and are *a priori.* It is important to know whether these hypotheses can be confirmed by the actual data. Do the equations in fact provide an adequate representation of what has been happening?

Examine the dots in Figure 3.9.[10] Each dot represents an amount of consumption in a year measured on the vertical or *y*-axis and the amount of income in the same year measured on the horizontal or *x*-axis. The location of the dots bears out the theory that a relationship exists between these two variables. When one is low the other is likely to be low and vice versa. In this case, consumption is called the **dependent variable** because it is assumed that its value depends on income, the **independent variable.**

REGRESSION

In order to find the relationship between a dependent and independent variable, a line can be drawn or an equation calculated for the line which best

10. This figure is the same as Figure 10.1. More detailed analysis of this relationship appears accompanying that figure.

FIGURE 3.9   **A Regression of the Consumption Function, 1946–80**

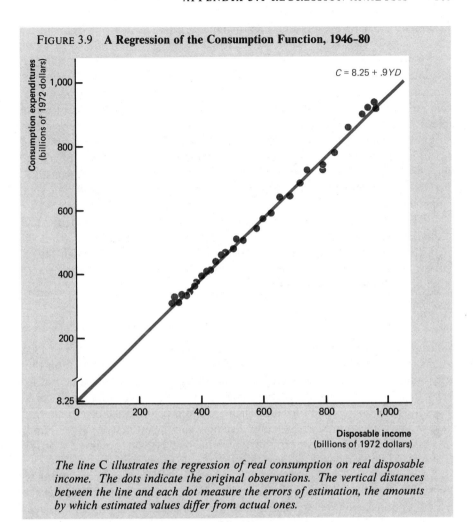

The line C illustrates the regression of real consumption on real disposable income. The dots indicate the original observations. The vertical distances between the line and each dot measure the errors of estimation, the amounts by which estimated values differ from actual ones.

describes (fits) the relationship. Such a line, labeled C in Figure 3.9, is called a *regression.* The equation of this line in terms of its intercept and slope is called the *regression equation.* Either estimates the average value for the dependent variable corresponding to each value of the independent variable.

The process of finding the line or equation which best fits a series of related values is called *regression analysis.* There can be more than one independent variable affecting the dependent variable included in the equation, and the form of the relationship can be extremely complex. In equation 3.33, an actual regression equation is calculated for data covering the years 1947–80. This equation is

$$C = 8.25 + .897\,YD \qquad R^2 = .999. \qquad\qquad \textbf{3.33}$$

The values in this equation and in similar ones used as illustrations come from the simple linear regression equation, usually written:

$$y = b_0 + b_1 x + u. \tag{3.34}$$

(Note that the y in this equation is not used to represent income. It represents a random dependent variable, while the x represents any independent variables.) The equation states that in a period the value of y, the dependent variable, is equal to a constant (b_0) plus the value of the regression coefficient (b_1) times the value in that period of x, the independent variable, plus u, a random variable or error term with an expected value of zero. The constant (b_0) equals the intercept of the regression line, and the regression coefficient (b_1) equals the slope of the line.

The regression equation or line can be used to estimate an expected value of the dependent variable for any value of the independent variable. Thus in 1970 disposable personal income (YD) was \$751.6 billions in constant 1972 dollars. Substituting this amount in equation 3.33 tells us that the expected value of consumption outlays would be

$$682.4 = 8.25 + .897(751.6).$$

In fact, the reported consumption was \$672.1 billion. This agrees with expectations. The value of a single observation of the dependent variable from the regression equation is not expected to equal exactly the reported value but to equal it only on average of all the observations. A scatter of points exists around the regression line. Because of the random disturbance or error term, there will be some unpredictable difference between the estimated value, y, and the actual observation. However, the high value of R^2 (to be explained shortly) in this equation leads us to believe that the u's, or errors, will be small.

Estimating the actual values of the constant and regression coefficients is done by fitting a **least-squares equation** to the observations of y at different levels of x.[11] As noted, Figure 3.9 is a graph of the individual observations for each pair of y's and x's. The y values are consumption and the x values are disposable income. What a least-squares regression equation does is to insure that the sum of the squares of the distances from the regression line to the observations are a minimum.

11. The least-squares line of regression is found by solving two equations called the normal equations, which are

$$\Sigma y = n b_0 + b_1 \Sigma x. \tag{3.35}$$

$$\Sigma x y = b_0 \Sigma x + b_1 \Sigma x^2. \tag{3.36}$$

The inputs in equation 3.35 are the sums of each observation of the dependent (Σy) and independent variables (Σx) and the number of observations (n) together with the regression coefficients being solved for (b_0 and b_1). Equation 3.36 uses the sum of the cross-products ($\Sigma x y$) for each observation of the variables, the sum of the independent variable (Σx), and the sum of the squares of the independent variables (Σx^2).

In 1979, when *YD* was 1,011.5, the observed consumption expenditures were 930.8. The distance between the actual observation and the regression line at an income of 1,011.5 was

$$930.8 - 8.25 - .897(1,011.5) = 15.2.$$

It is the square of this distance $(15.2)^2$ from the regression line to each observation that is minimized in fitting the least-squares regression.

EXPLAINED VARIATION

On the same line and coming right after the statistical statement of the consumption function is another measure, namely R^2, or the **coeffecient of determination.** It is a measure of how well the regression equation "explained" the relationship. The higher the R^2, the closer the association between the dependent and independent variables.

The **variance** of a set of values is defined as the arithmetic average of the squares of the difference between the individual values and their mean $(\bar{y})$. It is

$$\frac{\Sigma(y_i - \bar{y})^2}{n}.$$

The coefficient of determination is the proportion of the total variation in y explained by the regression equation when $\hat{y}$ is the value estimated from the regression (the "hat", , is used to designate the estimated value); that is, the value on the regression line for a specific value of x. Then $\Sigma(\hat{y}_i - \bar{y})^2$ is the total amount of variation explained by the regression:

$$R^2 = \frac{\Sigma(\hat{y}_i - \bar{y})^2}{\Sigma(y_i - \bar{y})^2} = \frac{\text{explained variation}}{\text{total variation}} = 1 - \frac{\text{unexplained variation}}{\text{total variation}} \qquad \textbf{3.37}$$

If all the variation were explained, the R^2 would be 1. If none were explained, it would be zero.

The above explanation of linear regression is in terms of only a single independent variable. In fact, however, models often assume that the level of the dependent variable results from influences of more than one independent variable. In this case, instead of a simple single regression equation, the econometricians or statisticians use **multiple regression.** Multiple regression is basically the same form of analysis just explained, but instead of a single regression coefficient and independent variable, there may be several, as in the following form:

$$y = b_0 + b_1 x_1 + b_2 x_2 + b_3 x_3 \ldots b_n x_n + u. \qquad \textbf{3.38}$$

In this, the estimate of the dependent variable will depend on each of the regression coefficients and the values taken by all of the independent variables at a given time. The R^2 in the case of multiple regression has the same meaning as when there is only a single independent variable. It tells how much of the total variation is explained by the complete multiple regression equation.

APPENDIX 3.2   A Note on Lags

Economic dynamics dates each variable according to the period in which it occurred. By convention, the current period is given the subscript 0 (or the subscript is left off). Prior periods are shown with minus subscripts increasing with distance from the current period, while future periods are numbered and indicated by plus signs. Thus, to show total consumption in a two-year period which includes the current quarter, three future quarters, and four past quarters, a summation of the data would appear as

$$\sum_{+3}^{-4} C_i = C_{+3} + C_{+2} + C_{+1} + C_0 + C_{-1} + C_{-2} + C_{-3} + C_{-4}. \qquad \textbf{3.39}$$

The Greek letter Σ (sigma) is used to signify the summation of a series. The period over which it is summed is indicated with the subscript as the starting point and the superscript as the ending point. The subscripts and superscripts appear directly below and above the Σ.

EMPIRICAL ESTIMATES OF LAGS

A common problem in economic dynamics is to explain how spending in a period will be influenced by changes in income occurring in prior periods. For example, this quarter's consumption will depend on both the levels of disposable income received in this quarter and also, because of lags, it will be influenced by the amount of disposable income received in previous quarters. The three most common methods of estimating such lags are (1) inclusion of prior observations of the values of the independent variable directly in the regression equation, (2) the use of geometric or Koyck lags, and (3) the use of Almon techniques or lags.

LAGGED INDEPENDENT VARIABLES

The use of previous values of the independent variable is simple. For example, a model may say that this quarter's consumption depends on income in this quarter and last quarter. In this case, the regression equation would be

$$C_0 = b_0 + b_1 YD_0 + b_2 YD_{-1}. \qquad \textbf{3.40}$$

When the equation is fit, each quarter's C would be regressed on the current value of YD and the value of YD in the previous quarter. The resulting equation would resemble

$$C = 22.2 + .62\,YD_0 + .29\,YD_{-1}. \tag{3.41}$$

The process of calculating the equation of best fit simultaneously determines the lag relationship between current and previous income.

GEOMETRIC OR KOYCK LAGS

Another common assumption is that the effect of past periods will diminish at a geometric rate. To calculate a model with a lag of this form, one need not use all past observations of the independent variable. All that is required is one independent variable, while the second independent variable is found from the previous period's observation for the dependent variable. This special transformation to a geometric lag was innovated by L. M. Koyck and bears his name. Thus, to relate consumption to all past income, one can use an equation of the form:

$$C_0 = b_0 + b_1 YD_0 + b_2 C_{-1}. \tag{3.42}$$

Current consumption depends on current income and is related to some portion of the previous period's consumption. In turn, the previous period's consumption depends on income in that period and on C in the second period back. In effect, the function says that consumption depends upon the income of all prior periods, with the effect of income decreasing geometrically.

The speed with which the influence of income is felt depends on the coefficient b_2[12]. This coefficient is one minus the speed of adjustment from the previous level to the new one which results from an increase or decrease in income. Kuh and Schmalensee present a typical consumption function of this form (using per capita real consumption and per capita real disposable income). It is

$$C = .60\Delta Y + .21\,Y_{-1} + .77\,C_{-1} \qquad R^2 = .998. \tag{3.43}$$

According to this equation, consumption will go up by 60 percent of the current quarter's increase in disposable income. The short-run marginal propensity to consume is .6. The increase in this quarter's income also affects next quarter's consumption. It does this in two ways. This quarter's income is higher and, according to the second term in the equation, that raises next quarter's consumption. The third term shows that the higher consumption in this quarter will also raise next quarter's consumption. This regression is a form of the Koyck geometric lag, in which the impact of income decays over time. The actual long-run *mpc* when equilibrium is finally reached is 0.924.

---

12. Those interested in the exact form in which the various lag equations relate to each other can consult E. Kuh and R. L. Schmalensee, *An Introduction to Applied Macroeconomics* (Amsterdam: North Holland, 1973).

ALMON LAGS

Another common approach to estimating lags is through the use of a technique developed by Shirley Almon.[13] Under this technique, the estimator inserts a few restrictions in the computer (such as on the intercept), the form of the lags, and the number of terms for the independent variable. The weights for each period are then calculated by a complex computer program which allows coefficients on the variable to take a wide variety of values. The person doing the regression analysis usually examines the results of early estimates and then introduces additional restrictions into new estimates. The results may show lags of from one to twenty or more periods. As an example, equation 10.6 reflects the results of a use of this technique. In that example, consumption in a period is influenced by the amount of wealth over 12 periods and stock values over 7 periods.

The use of Almon lags tends to increase the R^2 for a model. Some believe it also may give a more realistic picture of the relationship between two factors. Others object to its use because they feel the results depend too much on the subjective judgment of the person performing the estimation process.

13. S. Almon, "The Distributed Lag between Capital Appropriations and Expenditures" *Econometrica* 33 (1965): 178–96.

4

Expanding the Simple Model

The simple model of the preceding chapter concentrated on one critical factor influencing aggregate demand—the importance of spending movements induced by changes in income. But this model does not say much about other issues that are also central to macroeconomics, such as the role of the government, dynamic instability, and the effect of expectations on spending. Swings in government spending or taxes often speed up movements in demand. They may accelerate inflation or shorten or deepen recessions through their initial impact and their multiplied influence on the circular flow of spending.

Of all sectors, investment expenditures experience the widest fluctuations. One reason is that shifts in aggregate demand change the desired amount of investment. The multiplier is larger than it would be if only consumption had an induced component. The fact that government revenues also expand and contract with the GNP creates difficulties in balancing the budget. Furthermore, unless tax rates are altered, the income-induced changes in revenues can cause large swings in real aggregate demand.

Expectations of future conditions may also cause massive shifts in spending and inflationary pressures. People speed up or slow down purchases in accordance with their beliefs as to where the economy is headed. The effects of changes in expectations may be good or bad. Their importance, for example, was dramatized in 1980, when interest rates reached record levels. During that period, the avowed aim of the Federal Reserve (supported by the rest of the government) was to administer such a severe shock to the economy that expectations of inflation and, therefore, aggregate demand would be drastically revised. To this end, tight monetary policy was accompanied by the widest consensus since 1932 that the federal budget ought to be balanced.

To explain how these and other actions influence aggregate demand, the simple model must be expanded to make room for other variables. Additional factors will be introduced one by one to show how they affect demand and then supply. Their impacts will bring about different equilibriums than in the simple models. This chapter introduces the topics of the government's influence on demand and the economy's influence on government budgets, as well as the impact of shifting expectations on spending. It broadens the concept of consumption movements induced by income changes to add those induced in governments and businesses. The result is a supermultiplier that reflects all income-induced effects. The major issues examined in this chapter include:

> The central role of aggregate demand.
> The government's direct influences on aggregate demand.
> Equilibrium and the multiplier of government expenditures.
> Equilibrium and the multiplier of government taxes and transfers.
> Government expenditures in wartime: The multiplier in action.
> Changes in the marginal propensity to spend and the multiplier.
> Taxes and transfers as a function of income.
> Expectations.
> Expectations and spending.

The Central Role of Aggregate Demand

Until recently, most research effort in macroeconomics was devoted to explaining aggregate demand. Time spent analyzing aggregate supply and the inflation process was minimal. Numerous and varying reasons have been advanced to explain the relative emphasis on only one blade of the demand-supply scissors. Knowledge of how to explain and influence supply or the process of inflation is limited. With expanded research, such information may improve, but at the present time, what achievements can be expected from supply management remain uncertain.

In contrast, after much study, economists agree on the general shape of the demand curve and the forces that influence it. While arguments take place over the relative significance of particular variables and which should be changed at a specific time, such conflicts do not undermine the basic accord. Major depressions and hyperinflations are the pathological manifestations of aberrant aggregate demand. They reflect extreme imbalances. History shows that the level of demand can be influenced by policy actions. Thus major depressions are not a necessity Inflations can be halted.

THE GREAT DEPRESSION

The Great Depression lasted ten years, from 1929 to 1939. In 1933, the GNP stood at only about half of its 1929 peak. Real output did not regain its previous height until 1939. In the entire decade of the 1930s, the unemployment rate averaged nearly 20 percent. Men walked or rode the rails from city to city looking for any type of work. The popular song, "Brother, Can You Spare a Dime?" was descriptive of actual conditions. Many families existed on minimal foods that lacked necessary nutrition, and there were many instances of actual starvation.

The carnage in the business and financial world was also unprecedented. Between 1930 and 1933, over 8,000 banks went under. Millions of families saw their savings wiped out. Business bankruptcies reached record levels. In 1933 the average price of common stocks dropped to about 10 percent of its 1929 peak. Many people who had bought stocks on margin never got out of debt. In 1933 over 250,000 mortgages were foreclosed. The only thing that enabled many families to keep their homes was that lending institutions couldn't handle all the property with which they were saddled; they were better off having families occupy the buildings without paying than they were having them vacant and rapidly deteriorating.

Those who had food and jobs were frightened. Most people saw poverty striking their friends and neighbors; few seemed immune. The best policy seemed to be to hunker down and hope that things would improve. Steps taken to raise aggregate demand were hesitant and subject to long debate. The dominant philosophy prior to the New Deal was opposed to direct government action in the economic sphere. Only after it was seen how war expenditures lifted demand and raised output and income did observers become convinced that the problem of the Depression was a lack of demand and that demand shortages could be licked.

HYPERINFLATIONS

At the opposite extreme from major depressions are hyperinflations. In Germany after World War I and in Hungary and China after World War II, excess demand pulled prices up to incredible levels. In Germany in 1923, prices were over 30 billion times as high as they had been in 1919. In Hungary, the value of the pengö fell by more than 1.0×10^{30}—a figure that would require the width of this page to write out.

In hyperinflations the whole social system falls apart. Production grinds to a halt. Literally baskets of money are needed to buy small amounts of goods. Households rush to spend their income before its value drops further. Stores and factories are better off hoarding materials than producing goods with them. Again, however, experience shows that when excess demand is halted, economies can return to normal.

Fortunately, both major depressions and hyperinflations remain rare events; but they show how the economy can be dominated by demand movements. Even though demand in normal times is a less overwhelming force, changes in the amount that spending sectors demand remain critical in determining income and output for the economy.

The Government's Direct Influences on Aggregate Demand

Depressions and inflations start when demand falls too low or rises too high compared to available supply. To what degree should governments shift their spending and taxing plans to combat inflations and recessions? When the excess or shortage of demand is not extreme, popular and professional arguments abound over this issue. All agree that changes in government expenditures and taxes can directly shift aggregate demand. Debates center mainly around what indirect effects arise from shifts in the budget and what other types of policies, if any, could better be applied in particular circumstances.

In the analysis of government expenditures, spending on goods and services must be differentiated from transfer payments. When the government increases its purchases of goods and services, the initial impact falls on the level of production. A missile manufactured by Lockheed increases the GNP, as does the pay of the airman who fires it. In addition, Lockheed workers and the military personnel receive income which they can spend. However, when the retired airman receives a pension check, it is counted as a transfer payment. The GNP does not increase when he receives this government check. Disposable income does rise, however, since he has more income to spend, and thus desires to spend go up. Because they do not result in an increase in output, transfer payments (TR) are not included in government expenditures on goods and services (G). Instead, because their economic impact resembles that of taxes, with a reversed sign, in analysis they are subtracted from taxes (TA). When the term *taxes* (T) is used, even though transfers are not mentioned specifically, it is defined throughout this volume as the net amount of taxes less transfers. Thus

$$T = TA - TR. \qquad \qquad \textbf{4.1}$$

In our analysis, we first add autonomous government purchases, taxes, and transfers to the simplified model of the determination of income and real aggregate demand. Later we reverse the process and ask how government budgets are affected by income changes and how this influences demand. Because the simple, naive models explaining government spending or taxing introduced in this chapter are incomplete, caution must be exercised in attempting to draw policy conclusions until after the introduction of such variables as interest rates, credit, and aggregate supply.

EXPANDING THE CIRCULAR FLOW

The manner in which governments affect income can be demonstrated by including a government sector in the circular flow diagram of the previous chapter (Figure 4.1). In this diagram, only income and expenditure flows

FIGURE 4.1   **The Circular Flow of Expenditures and Income Including a Government Sector**

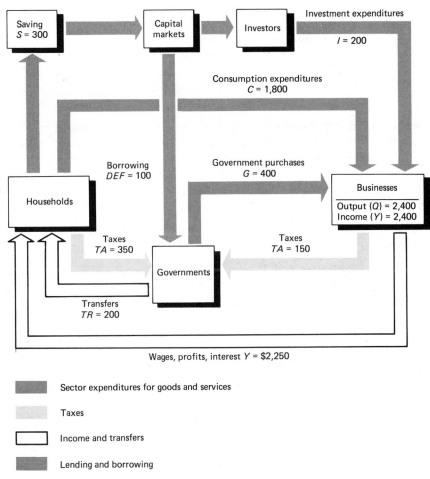

Sector expenditures for goods and services

Taxes

Income and transfers

Lending and borrowing

Governments purchase goods and services. Taxes pay for purchases and for transfer payments. Government deficits offset private saving; surpluses increase saving in the economy. Spending and taxing decisions alter the circular flow and induce changes in the demand of the other sectors.

appear; the additional and equal flows of productive services are not diagrammed. (The numbers are illustrative only; actual government data are given in Chapter 2.)

The government receives income from taxes levied against households ($350 billion) and businesses ($150 billion). It purchases $400 billion of goods and services from business.[1] It also pays $200 billion in transfer payments. These transactions result in a government deficit calculated as follows:

Purchases of goods and services		$400
Taxes	$500	
Minus transfer payments of $200		
Net taxes and transfers		$300
Deficit		$100

The deficit is funded by borrowing in the capital market. Disposable income of consumers totals $2,100 billion ($2,250 from business less $150 in net taxes and transfers to the government). Households divide their income into $1,800 billion of consumption expenditures and $300 billion of saving. Businesses are in balance also; expenditures and business receipts are $2,400 billion. They pay out $2,250 to households and $150 billion to the government.

THE IDENTITIES INCLUDING THE GOVERNMENT

The expanded circular flow illustrates some new necessary identities in the GNP accounts. The expenditures of the three sectors by definition must be identical to the amount of output and income earned from that output:

$$C + I + G \equiv Q \equiv Y \qquad 1{,}800 + 200 + 400 = 2{,}400. \qquad \textbf{4.2}$$

The income earned from this production divides into three components: consumption, saving, and net taxes and transfers.[2]

$$Y \equiv C + S + T \qquad 2{,}400 \equiv 1{,}800 + 300 + 300. \qquad \textbf{4.3}$$

The other identities also become slightly more complex. Consumption expenditures can be subtracted from each side of 4.2 and 4.3 to give:

$$Y - C \equiv I + G \qquad \text{and} \qquad Y - C \equiv S + T$$

or, since sums equal to the same amount are equal to each other,

$$I + G \equiv S + T \qquad 200 + 400 \equiv 300 + 300. \qquad \textbf{4.4}$$

---

1. Showing all purchases of goods and services from business is not quite accurate. The government sector actually produces goods and services (education, military forces) itself. It purchases labor from households for this purpose.
2. Business saving occurs as well as personal saving. If business saving were shown separately, part of the income attributed to households would appear to flow directly to the capital market.

In the expanded model, injections include investment and government expenditures. These amounts added to the income stream must exactly equal the amount not spent by consumers, which are the leakages in the form of saving and taxes.

Another point to note is that **government surpluses or deficits** in the GNP are the difference between revenues (T) and expenditures (G), or $T - G$. When G is subtracted from both sides of equation 4.4, it becomes apparent that private investment in the accounts must exactly equal private saving plus a government surplus or less a deficit:

$$I \equiv S + (T-G) \qquad 200 \equiv 300 + (300-400). \qquad \textbf{4.5}$$

Again, equilibrium exists when aggregate demand exactly equals production and income earned or when planned injections equal planned leakages as well as actual injections and leakages. The government surplus or deficit affects the capital market: it either adds to or offsets part of personal and business saving. In a more complete model which includes interest rates, this capital-market effect can be extremely significant.

Equilibrium and the Multiplier of Government Expenditures

When the government buys more goods and services, equilibrium spending shifts in the same way that it does when autonomous changes occur in investment or consumption. The same multiplier applies. In fact, most multiplier analysis has been concerned with how movements in government expenditures and taxes induce changes in the private sector.

The concept of the multiplier leaped into prominence during the debates over public spending during the Great Depression. It was used to justify government expenditures by showing that the entire gap between the existing level of income and a more desirable level did not have to be filled by the government. The increase in income put into the spending stream by the government would be multiplied. No sooner had the concept been developed in the Depression context than it was recognized that the multiplication of exogenous spending could also cause inflation. In wartime, governments buy huge amounts of weapons and supplies. The recipients of this income step up their consumption. Total demand exceeds the ability of the economy to produce. Unless the multiplier is reduced by greater saving, whether private or government, excess demand drives up prices.

A CHANGE IN GOVERNMENT SPENDING

What happens when autonomous government purchases ($\overline{G}$) are added to those of households and investors? The curve of total planned expenditures (E) now

FIGURE 4.2 **Determination of Equilibrium Expenditures and Income with Autonomous Investment and Government Spending**

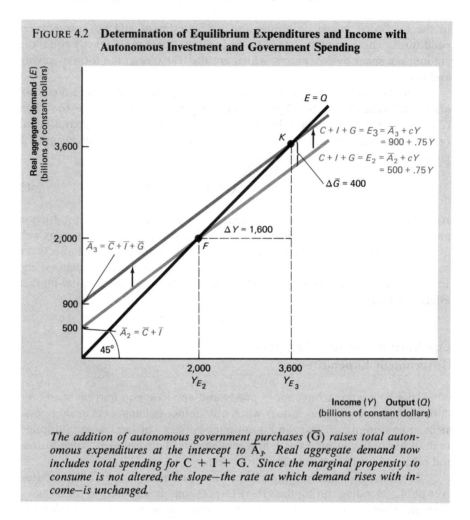

The addition of autonomous government purchases ($\overline{G}$) raises total autonomous expenditures at the intercept to $\overline{A}_3$. Real aggregate demand now includes total spending for $C + I + G$. Since the marginal propensity to consume is not altered, the slope—the rate at which demand rises with income—is unchanged.

includes the desires of three sectors ($C + I + G$) rather than only two ($C + I$). Total autonomous spending ($\overline{A}_3$) consists of the autonomous factors from each ($\overline{C} + \overline{I} + \overline{G}$) assuming initially an absence of taxes. The result of adding $\overline{G}$ is pictured in Figure 4.2. The intercept of the real aggregate demand curve shifts up from $\overline{A}_2$ to $\overline{A}_3$. Since no change has occurred in the marginal propensity to spend (c) the slope remains the same. Equilibrium on the new curve E_3 ($\overline{A}_3 + cY$) is at point K.

How much equilibrium shifted can be found from the general equation and the numerical example. Chapter 3 showed that the amount income increases depends on the size of the autonomous shift and on the amount of induced spending. Dividing the total of the two (the change in income) by the autonomous change yields the multiplier. In this case, adding $400 billion of autonomous government spending raises $\overline{A}$ from 500 to 900. Equilibrium income increases by the autonomous plus the induced increase. Initially, equilibrium was

$$Y_{E_2} = \overline{A}_2 + cY_{E_2} \qquad\qquad Y_{E_2} = 500 + .75\,Y_{E_2} = 2{,}000. \qquad\qquad 4.6$$

After the autonomous increase, it becomes

$$Y_{E_3} = \overline{A}_3 + cY_{E_3} \qquad\qquad Y_{E_3} = 900 + .75\,Y_{E_3} = 3{,}600. \qquad\qquad 4.7$$

Total income has increased by $1,600 billion, the horizontal distance between points F and K in Figure 4.2.

The increase in autonomous spending ($\Delta\overline{G}$) has raised total spending by $1,600 billion or, in accordance with the definition of the multiplier,

$$k = \frac{\Delta Y}{\Delta\overline{G}} = \frac{1600}{400} = 4. \qquad\qquad 4.8$$

This result, of course, can also be obtained by using the multiplier relationship developed in Chapter 3, which shows that the size of the multiplier depends on the amount of induced spending, which is determined by the marginal propensity to spend (c):

$$k = \frac{1}{1 - c} = \frac{1}{1 - .75} = 4. \qquad\qquad 4.9$$

The figure, the equilibrium equation, and the multiplier give identical results.

Equilibrium and the Multiplier of Government Taxes and Transfers

What if, instead of increasing purchases of goods and services, governments alter transfer payments or taxes ($\overline{T}$)? The answers will differ because such expenditures do not directly increase output. When the government buys an airplane from Boeing, the amount of production ($\overline{G}$) rises. When it makes a social security payment, the recipient has a higher income but the transaction is not part of production. In the same way, when a tax reduction raises income, its effect on the GNP depends on what the taxpayer does with the added income. If everyone saves, no change in spending occurs; the injection through lowered taxes all leaks out through added saving.

Calculating the change in equilibrium or the multiplier of an autonomous change in taxes or transfers is slightly more complicated than for a change in spending. Two alternative techniques are used:
1. Measure the change in autonomous spending ($\Delta\overline{A}$) which occurs as a result of autonomous change in taxes ($\Delta\overline{T}$). Insert this change in spending into the

equilibrium equation to find the amount of induced spending. [Equivalently, multiply the autonomous change by the spending multiplier $(k\Delta\overline{A})$.]

2. Use a different multiplier, called the **tax multiplier** (kT), defined as the number by which an autonomous change in taxes or transfers is magnified to give the total change in income:

$$kT = \frac{\Delta Y}{\Delta \overline{T}}. \qquad\qquad 4.10$$

AN AUTONOMOUS CHANGE IN TAXES OR TRANSFERS

How does a change in taxes and transfers differ from a change in government purchases? When taxes are raised, how much will spending drop? When autonomous taxes go up, they reduce the disposable income $(Y - \overline{T})$ from which consumers make their spending decisions. Instead of being able to spend the amount earned, Y, the most they can spend is $(Y - \overline{T})$. If the desire to spend is not altered, consumption becomes

$$C = \overline{C} + c(Y - \overline{T}). \qquad\qquad 4.11$$

Consumption is not lowered by the full amount of the tax. Some of the tax $(s\overline{T})$ is funded by a reduction in saving:

$$\Delta\overline{T} = c\Delta\overline{T} + s\Delta\overline{T}. \qquad\qquad 4.12$$

The amount autonomous spending falls depends on the amount by which taxes are increased and on how much consumers would have spent from that income, or by $-c\Delta\overline{T}$. The tax change lowers $\overline{A}$, the intercept of the $C + I + G$ line, by $c\overline{T}$. For example, Figure 4.3 shows that the intercept is reduced from $\overline{A}_3$ to $\overline{A}_4$ $(\overline{C} + \overline{I} + \overline{G} - c\overline{T})$ compared to Figure 4.2. Equilibrium falls from K to L.

Again, the general equation and the numerical example show the size of the decrease from the income at K of \$3,600 billion. The level of autonomous spending, A_3, is reduced by \$150 billion $[c\Delta\overline{T} = .75(200)]$ when taxes increase by \$200 billion. The new equilibrium Y_{E_4} in Figure 4.3 consists of the autonomous and induced spending:

$$Y_{E_4} = \overline{A}_4 + cY_{E_4} \qquad Y_{E_4} = 750 + .75\,Y_{E_4} = 3,000, \qquad 4.13$$

or, by using the spending multiplier (k),

$$\Delta Y = \frac{1}{1 - c}(-c\Delta\overline{T}) \qquad\qquad 4.14$$

$$\Delta Y = \frac{1}{1 - .75}\,[-.75\,(200)] = 4(-150) = -600.$$

FIGURE 4.3   **Determination of Equilibrium Expenditures and Income with Autonomous Taxes**

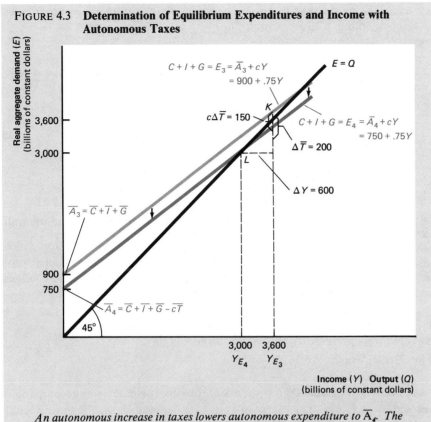

An autonomous increase in taxes lowers autonomous expenditure to $\overline{A}_4$. The drop ($c\Delta\overline{T}$) is less than the increase in taxes. When taxes rise, people lower expenditures in accordance with their desire to spend (c). Accordingly, taxes are funded partly through lower spending and partly through reduced saving ($\Delta\overline{T} = c\Delta\overline{T} + s\Delta\overline{T}$ and $c + s = 1$).

THE TAX MULTIPLIER

Instead of first estimating the fall in autonomous spending and applying the spending multiplier to it, the same results can be obtained by multiplying the tax multiplier (k_T) directly to the change in taxes and transfers. The tax multiplier can be calculated by the same procedure used previously to find the spending multiplier. The change in spending due to an autonomous change in taxes equals its direct impact and the amount of change in induced spending:

$$\Delta Y = -c\Delta\overline{T} + c\Delta Y \qquad \Delta Y = -.75(200) + .75\Delta Y = -600. \qquad \textbf{4.15}$$

The tax multiplier is found by moving the term with an income change to the left and dividing through by the autonomous change in taxes, in accordance with the definition of the tax multiplier:

$$(1 - c)\frac{\Delta Y}{\Delta \overline{T}} = - c(\frac{\Delta \overline{T}}{\Delta \overline{T}}) \qquad (1 - .75)\frac{\Delta Y}{\Delta \overline{T}} = -.75(\frac{200}{200})$$

and

$$kT = \frac{\Delta Y}{\Delta \overline{T}} = \frac{- c}{1 - c} \qquad kT = \frac{\Delta Y}{\Delta \overline{T}} = \frac{- .75}{1 - .75} = -3. \qquad \textbf{4.16}$$

The change in income is -3 times the increase in taxes, the result shown in Figure 4.3 and by equation 4.14.

The tax multiplier $(\frac{- c}{1 - c})$ has the opposite sign from the spending multiplier. An increase in taxes is a leakage from the income stream. How much smaller kT is than the spending multiplier, k, depends on the marginal propensity to spend, which determines how much autonomous spending changes and which appears in the numerator of kT.[3]

Government Expenditures in Wartime: The Multiplier in Action

Every major war in which the United States has participated was accompanied by a serious inflation. The excess of aggregate demand shows the multiplier at work. These episodes reflect heightened demand by the military and a multiplication of that demand because of increased civilian incomes. The fact that higher government expenditures had a multiplied impact on total demand was recognized as a danger when World War II started. The new theory of income determination showed that while military expenditures had to rise, their inflationary impact could be reduced if the expenditure multiplier could be partially offset by a tax multiplier with its opposite sign and impact.

For this reason, at the beginning of World War II, Keynes and other economists urged strongly that action be taken to increase both taxes and private saving. While some effort was made along these lines, on the whole the demand engendered by those receiving income from the new government spending was neutralized primarily through rationing and controls over materials, production, and prices. People were forced to save more than they wanted to simply because they could not obtain goods with their added income. When the war ended, the lid was removed and normal consumption relationships again took over. Spending grew rapidly, causing prices to shoot up.

3. The difference between the two multipliers means that if both government purchases and taxes rise by the same amount, income will increase although the deficit does not change. This phenomenon is called the **balanced-budget multiplier** and is explained in Appendix 4.1.

PAYING FOR THE VIETNAM WAR

This economic history was much on the minds of those responsible for deciding how to pay for a new war when American troops began to be sent overseas to Vietnam in large numbers and expenditures began to mount rapidly at the end of 1965. No one knew how much the war would cost, but it would clearly be expensive. The economy was producing at nearly full potential. Unemployment stood at 4.2 percent. A growing labor force and increased productivity would make some room for expansion. But would it suffice to cover both the added war spending and the increased consumption which would arise from the added income? Most economists thought not. Even a balanced-budget multiplier could give problems. They strongly urged that disposable income be curtailed through higher taxes and expenditure cuts in nonmilitary spheres.

Because tax increases are always difficult to implement and because the war was unpopular, the political decision was to take no direct fiscal action and to muddle through. Demand could be held in check mainly by tight money and high interest rates. In September 1966, to halt excessive investment and take some of the pressure off monetary policy, the Johnson Administration asked and received permission to suspend the investment tax credit. Government revenues rose with income but not as fast as expenditures.

Table 4.1 shows what happened to the economy during the two years following the decision not to raise taxes or cut other government expenditures. In real terms, national defense expenditures rose $15.6 billion (1958 dollars), or 35 percent. Other federal government expenditures fell, but state and local

TABLE 4.1   **Gross National Product in 1958 Prices**
(in billions of 1958 dollars)

Expenditure	1965: Q4	1967: Q4	Change
Consumption	409.9	433.2	+23.3
Investment and net exports	107.2	105.8	−1.4
Total government	117.3	140.4	23.1
National defense	44.5	60.1	15.6
Other federal	14.8	14.3	−0.5
State and local	58.0	66.0	8.0
Total gross national product	634.4	679.4	45.0
Implicit price deflator (1965: Q4 = 100)	100.0	106.4	+6.4%

Government expenditures rose rapidly during the first two years of the Vietnam War, as shown in the final column. In response to higher incomes, consumption expenditures also rose. The multiplier is the total change in GNP divided by the autonomous increase in A ($\Delta G + \Delta I$) or for this period it was approximately 2.1 $\left(\dfrac{45.0}{23.1 - 1.4} \right)$.

spending went up primarily because the postwar baby boom was raising the demand for education, particularly at the more expensive advanced levels. On the other hand, a near financial panic, brought about by higher interest rates and the temporary repeal of the investment tax credit, caused real investment to fall somewhat. Net exports also dropped. The net total of government actions plus those of investors resulted in an autonomous increase in nonconsumption spending of $21.7 billion.

The total increase in GNP was $45 billion. This, divided by the change in autonomous expenditures of $21.7 billion, yields a simple multiplier of 2.1 for this period. A multiplier of this size is about what was predicted by the large-scale econometric models in existence and used in analysis during the debates of 1965. Later we shall see that such a simple multiplier cannot be used for detailed analysis because it neglects, among other factors, the effect of taxes and price changes. Still, it does provide a simplified explanation of what went wrong in this period.

Aggregate demand grew at a rate 15 to 20 percent faster than potential output. The increase in spending on the war might have been handled through normal growth. But when it was multiplied, the total increase in demand was simply too great. Aggregate spending exceeded the point of full employment or potential output through the middle of 1969. Inflation accelerated. The rate of price increases due to this excess demand was nearly three times its prewar rate.

During the World-War-II and Vietnam periods, analysts correctly predicted the inflationary results of autonomous increases in expenditures not covered by additional taxes. However, the political battles to raise taxes were lost. Both liberal and conservative legislators fought against tax increases. While it is possible that they were not convinced of the inflationary dangers they were creating, most observers felt that Congress judged it a safer political solution to risk inflation and its consequences. It would be hard to trace inflation back to any specific votes. In contrast, a vote to raise taxes could be pointed to immediately as the source of the decline in the real incomes of some citizens.

Changes in the Marginal Propensity to Spend and the Multiplier

Our discussion of induced spending and the multiplier has thus far been limited to the marginal propensity to consume. However, induced consumption makes up only part of the expenditures which vary with income. Investment too has an induced component. In addition, we will note when we examine the foreign sector that the levels of imports and the balance of trade are highly responsive to changes in the GNP. Income effects on government revenues also play a critical role in the determination of real aggregate demand. When all of these factors are included, the marginal propensity to spend and save from the GNP differs considerably from the simple consumption function. Still, the basic idea prevails that autonomous shifts in expenditures are multiplied by a factor that depends on how much the economy chooses to spend or save from an additional dollar of income.

As significant for analysis as supermultipliers is the fact that the marginal propensity to spend can shift. For example, shifting expectations or a response to new sociological or psychological developments can raise or lower the amount spent from each addition to income. What happens when the marginal propensity to spend changes? A shift in the propensity to spend alters the slope of the real aggregate demand curve. This contrasts with the shift in autonomous spending which moves the intercept but not the slope or multiplier. An increase in the propensity to spend rotates the curve upward and increases the multiplier. How this works can be illustrated by considering the part of investment which varies with income. The general principles observed in analysis of induced consumption continue to prevail.

THE INVESTMENT-INCOME FUNCTION

Let us introduce some investment spending which is induced by the level of income. The marginal propensity to invest out of income can be designated d. To avoid extraneous factors, we return to the simple model with only consumption and investment and with income equal to disposable income. The investment function then consists of an autonomous part ($\bar{I}$) and an income-induced component of dY, or

$$I = \bar{I} + dY \qquad I = 200 + .05(Y). \qquad \textbf{4.17}$$

Combining this investment function with the consumption function increases the level of both autonomous and income-induced plans to spend:

$$E = \bar{C} + cY + \bar{I} + dY \qquad E = 300 + .75Y + 200 + .05Y \quad \textbf{4.18}$$

or

$$E = \bar{A} + (c + d)Y \qquad E = 500 + (.75 + .05)Y.$$

We designate marginal propensities to spend from income as m. In this case, m equals .80, the sum of the propensities to consume and invest ($c + d$).

Figure 4.4 illustrates what happens when induced investment effects are added to a demand curve (such as E_2 in Figure 4.2). Both lines E_2 and E_5 start at the same point because autonomous expenditures ($\bar{A}_2$) are the same. However, the slope of the new line is steeper. With a larger marginal propensity to spend (m), induced expenditures are higher at each positive income level. Furthermore, because the line has rotated upward, the distance between the real aggregate demand curves widens. The amount of additional planned spending grows larger at each higher income level. The actual equilibrium moves from F to M.

FIGURE 4.4   **Determination of Equilibrium Expenditures and Income When The Marginal Propensity to Spend Rises**

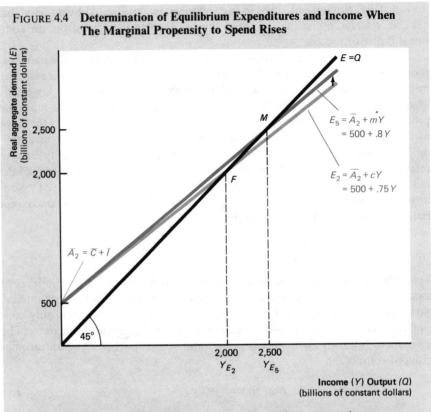

The inclusion of income-induced investment expenditures in real aggregate demand shifts the marginal propensity to spend and the slope of total planned expenditures (E). Equilibrium increases, as does the multiplier.

THE SHIFT IN THE MULTIPLIER

With a larger marginal propensity to spend, the amount of multiplication increases and equilibrium is higher for any amount of autonomous spending. Total planned expenditures (E) include both the autonomous and income-induced components. At equilibrium, real aggregate demand still equals income earned from production. Equilibrium is found again by substituting Y_E for E and Y in equation 4.18, with m replacing (c + d).

$$Y_{E_5} = \bar{A} + m Y_{E_5} \qquad\qquad Y_{E_5} = 500 + .8 Y_{E_5} = 2{,}500. \qquad\qquad \textbf{4.19}$$

To find the multiplier, we can either measure the amount of change in income resulting from any change in autonomous spending, or we can use the general rule that the multiplier is one over one minus the marginal propensity to spend. If a function has a constant slope, it is simplest to consider all autonomous spending and income as additions over a level of zero, or

$$k = \frac{\Delta Y}{\overline{\Delta A}} = \frac{1}{1-m} = \frac{2500}{500} = \frac{1}{1-.8} = 5.$$ **4.20**

Any increase in the marginal propensity to spend raises the multiplier, while a downward movement in m reduces the multiplier. Equilibrium depends on total desires to spend, including an autonomous and an income-induced component.

Taxes and Transfers as a Function of Income

Income may be shifted through autonomous changes in government spending or taxes. Of even more significance, however, are movements which come about because both tax collections and transfer payments are functions of income. The real aggregate demand curve shifts under the impact of additional induced-income effects. With a few exceptions, most tax revenues rise as the GNP grows. Income taxes are assessed against earnings. When personal income rises, the government's share swells. The income tax is progressive, with higher rates applied to higher brackets. Corporate income tax rates are generally flat, but profits rise and fall more than income. As a result, tax collections on profits fluctuate even more than others. Sales and liquor tax collections expand roughly with income. To some degree, social security, property, and gas tax collections move less than the GNP.

When the GNP grows, the share of transfer payments drops. With more jobs, fewer unemployment benefits are paid out; people delay retiring, with the result that social security payments do not rise as fast; fewer families are on welfare. Some government expenditures also fall—for example, programs to hire the unemployed will be cut back.

Let us consider a net tax and transfer function in which part of the collections and transfer payments are autonomous ($\overline{T}$) and part are a function (t) of income. In the numerical example, $\overline{T} =$ \$200 billion and $t = .25$, or the total tax function is now

$$\overline{T} + t(Y) = 200 + .25Y.$$

Taxes are subtracted from income earned to obtain disposable income at each income level:

$$YD = Y - \overline{T} - t(Y).$$ **4.21**

INCOME TAXES AND EQUILIBRIUM INCOME

The income tax function can be added to the consumption and investment functions to obtain a more general real aggregate demand curve. Taxes and transfers reduce the disposable income out of which spending decisions are made. When the income tax and government-expenditure functions are added to the previous functions of equation 4.18, the results are

$$E = \overline{C} + \overline{I} + \overline{G} + (c+d)(Y - \overline{T} - tY)$$

$$E = 300 + 200 + 400 + .80(Y - 200 - .25Y)$$

or

$$E = \overline{A} + (m)(Y - tY) \qquad E = 740 + .8(Y - .25Y) \qquad \textbf{4.22}$$

where

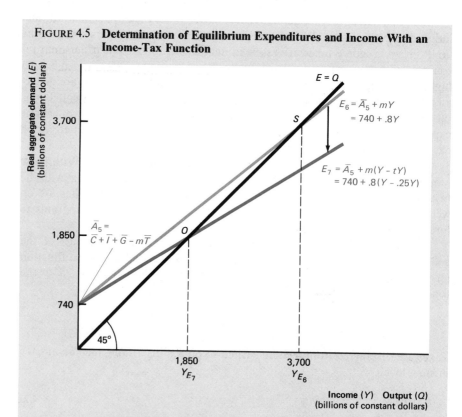

FIGURE 4.5   **Determination of Equilibrium Expenditures and Income With an Income-Tax Function**

Inclusion of an income-tax function (T = tY) rotates the real aggregate demand curve down to the right and reduces the multiplier and equilibrium expenditures. Any autonomous spending increase has a diminished impact. A reduction in income taxes will raise demand at all income levels.

$$\bar{A} = \bar{C} + \bar{I} + \bar{G} - m\bar{T} \qquad \bar{A} = 300 + 200 + 400 - 160 = 740.$$

Since equilibrium is where real aggregate demand equals income earned,

$$Y_E = \bar{A} + (m)(Y_E - tY_E) \qquad Y_E = 740 + .8Y_E - .2Y_E = 1,850. \quad \textbf{4.23}$$

Or, again, put in a form equivalent to the multiplier

$$Y_E = \frac{1}{1 - m + mt}\bar{A} \qquad Y_E = \frac{1}{.4}(740) = 1,850. \qquad\qquad \textbf{4.24}$$

The introduction of the income tax function reduces equilibrium income even though autonomous spending and the consumption and investment functions are unchanged. Why? Because the disposable income available for dividing between spending and saving is reduced by the amount collected in taxes. The desires to spend do not change, but they are applied to reduced levels of disposable income.

How this works is illustrated in Figure 4.5. The addition of an income tax shifts the desire to spend from line E_6 to E_7. The total desire-to-spend line rotates downward to the right. The gap between the two spending lines is wider as income rises. The logic of the rotation effect is quite evident: As the GNP grows, a tax rate proportional to income produces a steady increase in tax collections and larger amounts to be subtracted from disposable income. At zero income, while autonomous taxes and transfers exist (the assumed level is 200), collections from the rest of the tax function are zero $(.25(0) = 0)$. At a GNP of $1,850 billion, tax collections related to income are $.25(1,850)$ or $462.50 billion.

A TAX FUNCTION REDUCES THE MULTIPLIER

Observe that an induced tax function alters the government deficit in addition to reducing both the multiplier and the equilibrium level of income. The change in the multiplier is obvious when one compares that of equation 4.19, in which it is

$$k = \frac{1}{1 - m} \qquad k = \frac{1}{1 - .8} = 5$$

with that of equation 4.24, in which it is

$$k = \frac{1}{1 - m + mt} \qquad k = \frac{1}{1 - .8 + .8(.25)} = \frac{1}{1 - .6} = 2.5.$$

When the income tax function is added, the divisor in the equation for the multiplier increases, and the multiplier falls.[4] If the tax function is sizable, as it is in the United States, the multiplier is reduced by a large amount. The sensitivity of the economy to shocks is greatly lessened. Tax receipts are leakages from the income stream. When income starts to rise as a result of autonomous spending desires, leakages grow at a faster rate. Unless these added leakages are òffset by additional injections from either investment or government spending, they sharply lower equilibrium income. In Figure 4.5, equilibrium income prior to the introduction of the income tax function was $3,700 billion, with a deficit of $240 billion. After the desire-to-spend line shifts down because of induced taxes, equilibrium income is $1,850 billion. The government deficit $(G - T)$ has now become a surplus. Income taxes collected rise by $462 billion, more than offsetting the previous deficit. A major shift from government deficit to surplus can cause income to drop sharply. Total private and public saving must equal investment. If private desires to spend remain constant when the government surplus or saving increases, the necessary smaller amount of desired private saving will occur only at a sharply lower level of income.

4. Another minor and less obvious point which follows from equation 4.23 is that the multiplier, of the effect on GNP of a shift in the tax function (t), will depend on the level of income at the time that taxes are shifted. The income tax multiplier (kt) is

$$kt = \frac{-mY_E}{1 - m + mt} \qquad\qquad kt = \frac{-.8Y_E}{1 - .8 + .8(.25)} = -2Y_E. \qquad\qquad 4.25$$

This equation can most easily be derived by use of calculus. The level of income from equation 4.23 is

$$Y_E = \overline{A} + m(Y_E - tY_E) = \frac{\overline{A}}{1 - m + mt} \qquad\qquad \text{4.23 and 4.24}$$

By taking the derivative of Y_E with respect to t, we find

$$\frac{dY_E}{dt} = (\frac{\overline{A}}{1 - m + mt})(\frac{-m}{1 - m + mt}). \qquad\qquad 4.26$$

We note from equation 4.24 that this first term is equal to Y_E so, by substitution of equals, we find

$$kt = \frac{dY_E}{dt} = \frac{-mY_E}{1 - m + mt}. \qquad\qquad 4.27$$

The logic of the multiplier is easy to see. If income is $2,000 billion and taxes are lowered 5 percent, taxes will fall by $100 billion. If income is $3,000 billion, the same percentage decrease will lower taxes by $150 billion. The larger decrease will have a greater impact in determining the new equilibrium level of spending.

BALANCING THE BUDGET

The concept of the spending multiplier containing an endogenous function and its impact on the budget deficit throws light on two interesting questions related to balancing government budgets. During the Great Depression it was widely believed that taxes ought to be raised and government expenditures cut in order to balance the budget. But note the difficulty of removing a deficit when incomes are falling. Not only does a tax increase have a negative multiplier that leads to lower income, but because taxes are a function of income, raising taxes is likely to bring in less revenue than expected.

For example, the tax multiplier for equation 4.23 is

$$kT = \frac{-m}{1 - m + mt} \qquad kT = \frac{-.80}{1 - .80 + .8(.25)} = -2. \qquad \textbf{4.28}$$

What would happen if a new autonomous tax ($\Delta \overline{T}$) of $10 billion was voted and this tax multiplier of -2 was real? The tax increase would reduce GNP by $20 billion. But what would be the net increase in tax revenues? Instead or raising revenues by $10 billion, the total increase in tax collections would be less. Why? In addition to the initial autonomous tax increase of $10 billion, revenues depend on the amount collected through the income tax (t). When GNP falls as a result of higher autonomous taxes, income tax collections are reduced. If we neglect the effect on income of these smaller income tax collections, the fall in GNP will be $20 billion. The change in total revenues equals the change from both sources, or

$$\Delta T = \Delta \overline{T} + t\Delta Y \qquad \Delta T = 10 + .25(-20) = 5. \qquad \textbf{4.29}$$

The fall in income tax collections offsets part of the autonomous rise. If the tax also shifts the desire to produce and spend, the effect will be worse. Does this then suggest that a tax decrease can raise spending and increase total tax collections? As we shall see, the answer depends primarily on the supply curve and the inflationary process. It is one of the critical issues in the debate between so-called supply-side and traditional economists.

Expectations

Most economic decisions depend on how people feel about the future. Economic analysis has always been based on the idea that spending depends on *expectations,* which are beliefs or anticipations of the future values of a variable. In recent years, the part played by expectations in policy making has assumed critical importance.

Two aspects of expectations can be differentiated. On the one hand, most decisions are based on anticipations. For example, how much to save and how much to invest will be decided on the basis of expected incomes, prices, and

available credit. Similarly, the concept of nominal and real interest rates assumes that people anticipate certain price increases and factor them into rates
they accept. Decisions are based on expected real rates, not the nominal ones
quoted in the market.

On the other hand, a significant component of many theories is the possibility of an independent shift in expectations. Such shifts alter the autonomous
component $(\overline{A})$ or the slope of aggregate demand. Expectations are especially
important in explaining the inflationary process. Many models list a downward
shift in expected prices as a necessary condition for ending inflation. Business-
cycle theories also place considerable emphasis on shifts from optimism to
pessimism. History contains numerous examples of spending sprees which can
be explained only as outbursts of animal spirits or mass psychology. However,
in such instances it is difficult to interpret what happened as either rational or
irrational. Looking back at the behavior of the stock market in the late 1920s,
at the Florida land boom, at real estate speculation in 1972–78 or commodity
purchases in 1980, one is likely to conclude that expectations far surpassed any
semblance of reality. But what explains the fact that people were willing to buy
and hold these items? Without buyers, prices could not have climbed as they
did.

The problem arises because every decision can be justified by claiming
that it would not have been made if it were not rational. However, such an
approach is not operational. We need to know whether actions were based on
sound logic, whether the economy was swept by irrational waves of optimism or
pessimism, or whether markets were dominated by speculation. Large sums
can be made irrespective of whether markets are moving to or from equilibrium, provided that another buyer is found. Speculators make money as long
as they are not left holding the bag. Success can depend on the risky skill of
finding another "sucker," not on determining whether prices are too high or too
low.

HOW ARE EXPECTATIONS FORMED AND MEASURED?

The expectations on which spending depends are formed either on the basis of
past values of variables or of changes in the environment. In all cases they are
filtered through people's psychological reactions or opinions. How to estimate
current expectations and explain their formation is very controversial. Three
different approaches are used: (1) apply the concept of adaptive expectations,
(2) model them from the relevant economic theory (rational expectations), and
(3) take a survey.

Adaptive expectations are based on the idea that expected future values
depend upon some weighting of past values. Decision units form their expectations from past experience in accordance with some logical rules. They may,
for example, assume that income has been changing and believe it will continue
to shift along a related path.

An example of adaptive expectations can be found in estimates of how past income affects the expected lifetime income from which decisions to consume are made. Some models may show that expected disposable income is a weighted average of a limited number of past levels:[5]

$$YD^e = w_1 YD_0 + w_2 YD_{-1} + w_3 YD_{-2}$$

$$YD^e = .7 YD_0 + .2 YD_{-1} + .1 YD_{-2}. \qquad \textbf{4.30}$$

Equation 4.30 says that expected disposable income depends on disposable income of the current and past two periods, with most of the weight (.7) coming from current income. If $w_1 = 1$ and $w_2 = w_3 = 0$, the equation would indicate that expected and current income were the same ($YD^e = YD$).

Another example of adaptive expectations can be found in Milton Friedman's work on permanent income, discussed in Chapter 10. He makes the assumption that families base their expectations of the future on their income history. In doing so, the weights (w) they assign to past periods decline geometrically. In general form, this can be stated

$$YP^e = w YP_0 + w(1-w) YP_{-1} + w(1-w)^2 YP_{-2} \ldots w(1-w)^n YP_{-n}. \qquad \textbf{4.31}$$

Families give more weight to current and recent events than to those in the remote past. They adapt their expectations to their experiences.

By substituting numbers in equation 4.31 you can observe that if w is large—say, .8—most weight is assigned to recent events. In the example, current income would have a weight of .8; last period's of $.8(1-.8)$, or .16; two periods back would be $.8(1-.8)^2$, or .032; and so on. The weights add to 1 to obtain the average. On the other hand, if w is a small number—say, .2—you will find by similar calculations that current events play a much smaller part.

Rational expectations are based on the concept that anticipations "are essentially the same as the relevant economic theory."[6] It may be logical to form expectations adaptively if the economy is quite stable, but it would be foolish for economic agents to continue to act on past trends if the economy is exploding around them. If oil prices double, many other costs will rise. People realize this and act accordingly. They won't act as if gasoline prices would not jump.

Rational expectations theory says that individuals will use all information available to them at a reasonable cost in forming their expectations. No obvious profitable opportunity will remain unexploited; somebody will grab it and make a profit. The pressure of competition means that the market reflects both all information and its best estimate of how that information should be used in

5. Throughout this volume the superscript ^{e} is used to designate an expected value. The coefficient w measures the weight of the variable.

6. The definition and concept arise from the work of John F. Muth. For a detailed description of the concept and its use, see B. Kantor, "Rational Expectations and Economic Thought," *Journal of Economic Literature* 17 (December 1979): 1,422–41.

making decisions. Anticipations may turn out to be very wrong. Studies of financial markets show extremely large errors in the forecasts of future events made by the market. Rational expectations theory does not deny such errors; it simply asserts that anticipations and decisions are formulated by well-informed and rational people. Nonbelievers in the theory point out that many markets, and particularly consumption choices, seem not to follow economic logic. Changes occur slowly. Information is costly and not readily available to many decision makers.

Because of their importance in spending decisions, many *surveys of expectations* attempt to measure them directly. Much of the early work in this sphere was conducted by the Survey Research Center at the University of Michigan. Now other research and marketing organizations conduct such surveys at intervals of a week to a year or more. The surveys usually ask questions designed to discover how a household feels about the future. They may ask, "Do you expect that your income will rise, that prices will rise, that times will be better?" or "Do you plan to buy a house, a car, a major appliance?" They may also ask about changes in income or saving or similar events.

The answers to these questions are combined into an index using weights and limits on the values with the aim of correlating the resulting index with past

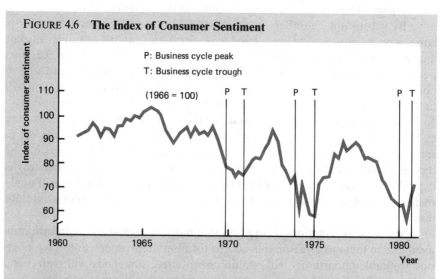

FIGURE 4.6   **The Index of Consumer Sentiment**

Expectations rise and fall with fluctuations in output, prices, and policies. They can cause or be the product of economic change. Surveys measure consumer reactions. The results are combined into an index of consumer sentiment.

SOURCE: University of Michigan, Survey Research Center (*P* and *T* are as designated by the National Bureau of Economic Research.)

changes in spending. Such indexes are used in an attempt to measure. the psychological or anticipatory inputs into spending. Figure 4.6 shows the movements in such an index, the index of consumer sentiment (ICS), from 1954 to 1980. The fluctuations are sizable, but they are obviously related to past recessions and drops in expenditures. Experience with such indexes reveals close relationships to events.

EXPECTATIONS AND SPENDING

The importance of expectations and the actions they cause in economic activity varies from time to time. An interesting example is the effect of expected inflation on spending. While it is often assumed that expectations of future price increases will lead to an increase in purchases, this need not happen. Instead, consumers who are uncertain about their future real income may want to save more. In particular, they may avoid purchases and contracts that call for large future payments. If they buy and assume debts on the strength of a hunch that their incomes and prices will rise, they may have to make considerable sacrifices if it turns out that they guessed wrong.

F. T. Juster, director of the University of Michigan's Survey Research Center, puts it this way,

> If it turns out that money income actually grows more rapidly than they had guessed, all they have lost is the opportunity to consume at somewhat more favorable prices. But losing a favorable consumption opportunity does not create the kind of uncomfortable and constrained financial situation faced by consumers who have made spending plans on the assumption of a ten percent money income increase and ended up with five percent instead.

Since 1974, the Michigan survey has periodically asked the following question:

> When prices go up some people buy things they need before prices go up further, while others react by trying to cut down on spending because they are worried about making ends meet. What do you do when prices go up?

About four or five times as many respondents answered that their reaction to inflation is to cut back on spending and increase saving as those who answered that they would spend more. Such reactions tended to limit inflationary spending. But the concept of expectations always threatens change. The longer inflationary experiences persist and the dimmer the memory of past depressions grows, the more likely it is that expectations will multiply expansionary forces in the consumption function.

RATIONAL EXPECTATIONS OR SPECULATIVE EXCESSES?

An example of how difficult it is to determine the rationality of expectations at any given time is the strong demand which appeared in the commodity markets in the last half of 1979 and the first quarter of 1980. Some facts are clear:

1. Worldwide inflation was rising as a result of extremely large increases in OPEC petroleum prices.
2. War fears were spreading through the Middle East.
3. Demand for gold, silver, diamonds, and all types of commodities reached a fever pitch.
4. The price of gold rose from $200 to $875 an ounce.
5. The price of silver went up from $6.50 an ounce in January 1979 to more than $50 in January 1980, or by more than 600 percent.
6. Most major grains rose in price by 20 to 40 percent in a few months.
7. The selling prices of copper and similar metals doubled.

The unprecedented silver price-rise was fueled by publicity given to an attempt by a few Texas and Arab billionaires to corner (control) the available silver supplies. Oil price-increases partially reflected uncertainties as to supply, due to the Iranian revolution.

The United States government and the Federal Reserve felt compelled to react to the market activity. They feared that the world could be faced with a self-fulfilling prophecy. Higher metal prices could lead to increased wage demands and to a speed-up of the inflationary process. They acted to raise interest rates, to make it harder to obtain credit, and imposed direct restrictions on some commodity market activities. By March 1980, less than two months after the height of activity:

1. Silver prices fell from $50 to $15 an ounce.
2. Gold prices were cut in half.
3. Grains sold at prices below those of the previous year.
4. Copper returned to near its initial range.

The unanswered question was whether these price reactions were based on rational expectations or speculative fever. Had the market correctly anticipated higher prices and then correctly shifted because of the Federal Reserve's policy? Or were the price movements primarily reflections of ill-advised speculative activity?

Many observers judged the moves to be primarily speculative. Prices reached could not be justified in terms of knowledge of supply and demand. To make the price increase rational, the rate of inflation would have had to shoot up far beyond levels previously experienced. It was believed that, as many times in the past, speculative fever had pushed prices well beyond reasonable expectations. As is usually the case, some early participants made a great deal of money, while others were left holding the bag. Still, the fact that sales were made at top prices indicated either that some believed they would continue to rise or that, at a minimum, other buyers would be found. Only time can tell how many, if any, of the moves made sense. (The reader might check current gold and silver prices to see what time seems to have shown.)

Summary

1. Aggregate demand plays a critical role in determining a nation's income and output. While disagreements exist over the size and importance of the coefficients applicable to individual variables, most economists concur as to the general shape of the aggregate demand schedule and the importance of monetary and fiscal policies.

2. When the government sector is added, it must be included in total injections and leakages. Thus, autonomous spending includes investment and government expenditures (plus that of households). Leakages from the circular flow can be caused by saving or by tax collections. The injections $(I + G)$ must equal the leakages $(S + T)$. Another way of putting it is that private investment (I) must equal saving plus a government surplus $[S + (T - G)]$ or minus a government deficit.

3. Any autonomous change in spending will induce income-related expenditures and a new equilibrium. When the model is expanded to include autonomous government expenditures, changes in $\overline{G}$ have effects parallel to changes in investment or other autonomous variables.

4. Increases in taxes lower the income from which spending decisions are made. A change in disposable income from a tax increase or decrease will impact on both consumption and saving in accordance with the economy's propensity to consume.

5. The autonomous spending change which is multiplied when taxes shift is not the amount of taxes collected, but the amount which would have been spent from an equal amount of income. Thus, the tax multiplier is $\frac{-c}{1-c}$. It is negative because a tax increase reduces income and spending. The marginal propensity to consume in the numerator tells how much of the change in disposable income will affect spending. The remainder will be saved.

6. The size of multipliers depends on all marginal propensities to spend (m). This means that marginal desires to invest from income must be included as well as those for consumption. When m increases, the multiplier is higher and the aggregate demand curve rotates up.

7. Taxes and transfers may also increase with income. When income-induced tax revenues increase, they reduce disposable income and the multiplier. A higher income tax-transfer schedule (t) rotates the aggregate demand curve downward.

8. Expectations influence the desire to spend (holding all other factors constant). Because expectations shift with psychological attitudes, they can cause rapid movements in spending.

9. Expectations may be formed adaptively to past events. In adaptive expectations, the weights applied to any prior period may change as new forces are felt in the economy.

10. Rational expectations are formulated in accordance with the processing of current information in whatever models are actually used by decision makers. Their values will depend on how decision makers think and on how they use available information.

11. It is difficult to judge what expectations are and whether they are rational. Surveys are of some help in observing how expectations shift.

Questions for Discussion and Review

1. Why, until recently, did macroeconomics concentrate on the factors influencing aggregate demand?

2. Consider an economy described by the following relations (quantities in billions of dollars):

$$C = 300 + .75YD$$
$$I = \bar{I} = 200$$
$$G = \bar{G} = 100$$
$$T = \bar{T} = 100$$

(a) What is the equilibrium level of income?
(b) What is the value of the government expenditures multiplier?
  What is the value of the investment multiplier?
(c) By how much would government expenditures have to be increased to raise equilibrium income to $3,000 billion?

3. Let d be the marginal propensity to invest in the investment equation,
$$I = 200 + dY.$$
Show how the multiplier will be different from the one you obtained in (2). The rest of the problem is the same. What is equilibrium income if $d = .05$? Why is it greater than, less than, or equal to the answer you got in (2)?

4. Assume the following values:

$$\bar{C} = 100$$
$$c = .8$$
$$t = .25$$
$$\bar{G} = 200$$
$$\bar{I} = 100$$
$$\bar{T} = 100$$

(a) Calculate equilibrium income when $C = \bar{C} + c(Y - \bar{T} - tY)$.
(b) Does $G + I = S + T$?
(c) Does $S = I$? How come?

5. Why was there inflation during World War II and the Vietnam War? Could it have been prevented?

6. In 1976 President Ford designed a tax and spending package to stimulate the econ-

omy. He asked Congress for a $20 billion tax cut along with a $20 billion cut in government expenditures. Would you expect this policy to do what it was designed for? Why or why not?

7. If there is no government sector, equilibrium is attained when $S = I$. With the addition of a government sector, $\overline{G}$ and $\overline{T}$, at equilibrium, which of the following are true?
   (a) G must equal T.
   (b) S must still equal I.
   (c) $S - I$ must equal $G - T$.
   (d) Inventory investment must be zero.
   (e) $I = S + (T - G)$.

8. Explain in your own words why the tax multiplier is always less than the spending multiplier.

9. What are some differences between adaptive and rational expectations?

References

Chandler, Lester V. *America's Greatest Depression, 1929-41.* New York: Harper & Row, 1970.

Gordon, R. A. *Economic Instability and Growth: The American Record.* New York: Harper & Row, 1974. Chapter 6.

Hicks, J. *The Crisis in Keynesian Economics.* New York: Basic Books, 1974.

Sargent, T. J., and N. Wallace. *Rational Expectations and the Theory of Economic Policy.* Federal Reserve Bank of Minneapolis, 1975.

Appendix 4.1   The Balanced-Budget Multiplier

Government actions may expand the GNP even though the deficit or surplus does not change. Because the spending and tax multipliers are not equal, a balanced expansion of government revenues and taxes will raise the equilibrium level by the amount that they rise. The multiplier of an increase in a balanced budget is 1.

Let us consider an increase in government spending and taxes of $400 billion. What will happen to spending and to the deficit if both expenditures and taxes are raised by this amount? The increase in the desire to spend from the autonomous change in government expenditures will be the amount $\Delta\overline{G}$ times the multiplier of equation 4.9, or

$$\Delta Y = k\Delta\overline{G} = \frac{1}{1-c}\Delta\overline{G} \qquad \Delta Y = \frac{1}{1-.75}(400) = 1,600. \qquad \textbf{4.32}$$

The decrease in the desire to spend will be the amount $\Delta\overline{T}$ times the tax multiplier of equation 4.16, or

$$\Delta Y = kT\Delta\overline{T} = \frac{-c}{1-c}\,\Delta\overline{T} \qquad \Delta Y = \frac{-.75}{1-.75}(400) = -1,200. \quad \textbf{4.33}$$

We can add the two changes together to get their joint effect. When we do, we find that since both government spending and taxes rose by $400 billion, the deficit does not change:

$$DEF = (\Delta\overline{G} - \Delta\overline{T}) \qquad DEF = 400 - 400 = 0. \qquad \textbf{4.34}$$

On the other hand, when the effect of the two changes on income is added, note that

$$\Delta Y = (k\Delta\overline{G} + kT\Delta\overline{T}) \qquad \Delta Y = 1,600 - 1,200 = 400. \qquad \textbf{4.35}$$

Or, as a result of the joint change, equilibrium rose by $400 billion.

This phenomenon reflects the balanced-budget multiplier. *The balanced-budget multiplier* (kBB) is defined as the change in equilibrium which results from the changes in government expenditures and revenues when both increase by the same amount. Thus

$$kBB = \frac{\Delta Y}{\Delta\overline{G}} = \frac{\Delta Y}{\Delta\overline{T}} \qquad kBB = \frac{400}{400} = 1. \qquad \textbf{4.36}$$

The balanced-budget multiplier is thus 1. Aggregate demand increases by exactly the amount of the increase in government spending. If you think income is low and we need more demand but you don't like the idea of a larger deficit, this is a good thing to know. If you want more national parks, dams, or government jobs but are afraid that any rise in aggregate demand will be inflationary, then even if you are willing to see taxes go up to pay for these things, the balanced-budget multiplier will inhibit your desire to raise government spending.

The fact that the balanced-budget multiplier is 1 can again be checked out by applying the spending multiplier to the autonomous increase in government expenditures and to the autonomous decrease in spending from the higher taxes. The total change in equilibrium spending equals the multiplied change from the increase in expenditures plus the multiplied change from the increase in taxes, or

$$\Delta Y = \frac{1}{1-c}\,\Delta\overline{G} + \frac{1}{1-c}(-c\,\Delta\overline{T})$$

$$\Delta Y = \frac{1}{1-.75}(400) + \frac{1}{1-.75}[-.75(400)] = 400. \qquad \textbf{4.37}$$

When the change in the budget is balanced, $\Delta \overline{G} = \Delta \overline{T}$; therefore $\Delta \overline{G}$ can be substituted in equation 4.37 for $\Delta \overline{T}$:

$$\Delta Y = \frac{1}{1 - c}\Delta \overline{G} + \frac{-c}{1 - c}\Delta \overline{G} \qquad \Delta Y = \frac{400}{1 - .75} - \frac{.75(400)}{1 - .75} = 400$$

and, collecting terms

$$\Delta Y = \frac{1 - c}{1 - c}\Delta \overline{G} \qquad \Delta Y = \frac{1 - .75}{1 - .75}(400) = 400. \qquad\qquad \textbf{4.38}$$

To find the balanced-budget multiplier, the change in total spending is divided through by the autonomous change which caused it:

$$kBB = \frac{\Delta Y}{\Delta \overline{G}} = \frac{1 - c}{1 - c}(\frac{\Delta \overline{G}}{\Delta \overline{G}}) = 1 \, .$$

4.39

$$kBB = \frac{\Delta Y}{\Delta \overline{G}} = \frac{1 - .75}{1 - .75}(\frac{400}{400}) = 1.$$

Multiplier analysis shows that if a gap exists between aggregate demand and potential output it can be reduced by the government's altering its expenditures. An increase in the government's surplus will reduce inflationary pressures, while an enlarged deficit will raise demand. Furthermore, the expansion in demand will be a multiple of the change in the deficit. Analysis based on the balanced-budget multiplier shows that an increase in government spending matched by an equal rise in taxes raises income and the total desire to spend by the exact amount of the autonomous change. Observe how large an increase in the size of the government's budget must be if an expansion occurs by the balanced-budget technique. The budget must grow by much more than when a deficit is run. Clearly, those who believe that most government spending is inefficient would not advocate such a large increase. Depending on their analysis of other effects of a deficit, they would either prefer not to attempt to close a gap between demand and potential output, or they would be willing to see a surplus reduced or perhaps, as a last resort, a deficit incurred.

5

Interest Rates and Equilibrium in the Real Goods Market

Changes in monetary policy and in market interest rates become headline news when interest rates rise or fall rapidly. Shifts in interest rates alter demand and the equilibrium of income and output. This chapter adds interest rates to the previous discussions of autonomous and income-induced spending. Movements in interest rates affect the desire to spend because they shift the relationships between the cost of an asset and the value of the income it is expected to yield in the future. Aggregate demand in each sector drops as real interest rates rise. Investment falls because the ownership of new capital goods is less profitable. Consumption declines in response to reduced household wealth. Government capital expenditures, particularly at state and local levels, are postponed because borrowing becomes more expensive. The relationship between interest rates and equilibrium income levels is described by **investment-saving** (*IS*) schedules. When the schedules are plotted with interest rates and income on the axis, such curves show all the joint equilibrium points of interest rates and income in the market for real goods and services. At each point on an *IS* curve, the economy's desires to buy and produce goods are equal. The curves slope down to the right with income increasing as interest rates fall. To understand why the curves take the position and shape they do, what causes them to shift, and how disequilibriums of an excess demand or excess supply of goods are removed, we examine in this chapter:

Interest rates and present values.
Interest-rate effects on the desire to spend.
The investment-saving schedule.
The slope and shifts in the $I - S$ curve.
Real and nominal interest rates.

The discussion of interest rates and equilibrium in the real goods market completes half of the model of the determination of income and output. Part 3 will develop the other half—that of equilibrium in the money market—and it will show how the two markets interact to determine the final relationships of aggregate demand, those between prices and output.

Interest Rates and Present Values

Changes in market interest rates affect the worth of assets by altering the present value of the future stream of income which an asset is expected to yield. The **present value** of an asset is the amount a purchaser must pay today to receive a future stream of income given a specified interest rate. Consider the case of John Solomon, a typical investor. In February 1975 he paid $1,000 for a $1,000 United States government bond due in 1993. When he bought the bond, market interest rates were 6.75 percent on United States government bonds of this maturity. The bond he purchased had coupons attached which gave him the right to collect $33.75, twice annually, on each February 15 and August 15. In addition, the government promised to pay him back $1,000 in principal on February 15, 1993.

In March 1980, Solomon needed cash, so he decided to sell his bond. He took the best offer he could find, but received only $650 for the bond which had cost him $1,000. Why had he lost so much money on a bond which he thought of as a riskless investment? The answer is that although he didn't need to worry about the government's defaulting, he had neglected the fact that changing interest rates alter the present value of future payments.

In March 1980, market interest rates for U.S. government bonds payable in 13 years rose to 13 percent. Since the government was selling new $1,000 bonds which paid $65 semiannually and had the same promise to repay principal as his older bond, anyone who paid him more than $650 for his bond with its $33.75 coupons would have lost money. In the financial market, offers to buy or sell an asset are based on the present value of future expected payments.

Appendix 5.1 explains how present values are calculated. To find the market value of a bond, each coupon and the promise to repay the principal at maturity are discounted back to the present. Thus (neglecting the fact that payments are in fact semiannual) we can ask what happens to the value of a $100 bond with coupons paying 7 percent interest annually and ten years to maturity if market interest rates rise from 7 to 10 percent. The first equation shows the value before and the second equation shows the approximate value after such a change, using the discount formula derived in the appendix (equation 5.17):

$$PV = 100 = \frac{7}{1.07} + \frac{7}{(1.07)^2} + \frac{7}{(1.07)^3} + \ldots + \frac{7}{(1.07)^{10}} + \frac{100}{(1.07)^{10}}$$

$$PV = 81 = \frac{7}{1.10} + \frac{7}{(1.10)^2} + \frac{7}{(1.10)^3} + \ldots + \frac{7}{(1.10)^{10}} + \frac{100}{(1.10)^{10}}$$

Such calculations are readily available in bond tables. Table 5.1, an example from a bond table, shows that the value of a bond with 7 percent coupons depends on what rates the market is paying for new borrowing and how far in the future the existing bond will mature.

TABLE 5.1   **A Sample Bond Table**

Market interest rates (percent per annum)	Value of a $100 7 percent bond (based on semi-annual coupons) with time to maturity of			
	5 years	10 years	15 years	20 years
4	$113.47	$124.53	$133.59	$141.03
6	104.27	107.44	109.80	111.56
7	100.00	100.00	100.00	100.00
8	95.94	93.20	91.35	90.10
10	88.42	81.31	76.94	74.26
14	75.42	62.92	56.57	53.34

The present value of a bond varies with the amount of interest it promises to pay (represented by its coupons), with its maturity (when the principal is due), and with current market interest rates. The bottom line of column 2 shows that $75.42 is the present value of a $100 bond which promises to pay 7 percent interest and with principal due in 5 years when market interest rates are 14 percent (column 1).

The table shows that how the value of a bond with a fixed coupon alters as market interest rates change depends on its time to maturity. If interest rates rise from 4 percent to 10 percent, owners of 7 percent 20-year bonds will find their wealth cut almost in half. Even though the change in interest rates would not alter the income of the bondholders, their wealth would be reduced.

Interest-Rate Effects on the Desire to Spend

The example of the bond table (Table 5.1) shows how the values of assets change with interest movements. Movements in asset values cause the aggregate demand curve to shift. When interest rates rise, investment falls. Some investments worth engaging in before interest rates rise are uneconomical to make afterward. Methods of analyzing the effect of interest rates on investment are detailed in Chapter 9. For now, we need know only that the desire to spend for investment declines with higher interest rates. Chapter 10 shows that the desire to consume also falls as interest rates rise. Families have less wealth and therefore tend to reduce their spending while higher receipts from interest payments may make saving, which now will yield more future consumption, a better deal.

THE SPENDING-INTEREST FUNCTION

How much the desire to spend at any income level will decline as interest rates rise depends on the spending responsiveness of the economy to interest rate movements. To complete our previous models of aggregate demand, we must include a coefficient (b) which measures the interest responsiveness of spending. It tells how much demand falls for each increase in interest rates.

We can illustrate the interest-rate effects assuming initially that they influence only investment. We use the notation r to represent **real interest rates**, while i represents **nominal interest rates** (see Chapter 8). The interest responsiveness adds a factor ($-br$) to the previous investment function (equation 4.17). When the changed investment function is combined with the spending function of the other sectors, we find a new equation for real aggregate demand

$$E = \overline{A} - br + m(Y - tY) \qquad E = 740 - 2{,}000r + .8(Y - .25Y) \qquad \textbf{5.1}$$

(E).[1] Equation 5.1 shows that the real aggregate demand curve reflects

The level of autonomous spending ($\overline{A}$).
The coefficient of interest responsiveness (b).
The level of interest rates (r).
The marginal propensity to spend (m) and to tax (t).

THE SPENDING-INCOME CURVES WITH INTEREST RATES

Figure 5.1 demonstrates how the inclusion of interest rates affects real aggregate demand curves. The parallel lines in the figure are expenditure curves

1. The new equation for E is derived by combining the spending functions of the individual sectors:

$$C = \overline{C} + c(Y - tY - \overline{T}) \qquad C = 300 + .75(Y - .25Y - 200) \qquad \textbf{5.2}$$

$$I = \overline{I} + d(Y - tY - \overline{T}) - br \qquad I = 200 + .05(Y - .25Y - 200) - 2{,}000r \qquad \textbf{5.3}$$

$$G = \overline{G} \qquad G = 400 \qquad \textbf{5.4}$$

$$T = tY + \overline{T} \qquad T = .25Y + 200. \qquad \textbf{5.5}$$

and with $m = c + d$

$$E = \overline{C} + \overline{I} + \overline{G} - m\overline{T} - br + m(Y - tY) \qquad \textbf{5.6}$$

$$E = 300 + 200 + 400 - (.8)200 - 2{,}000r + .8(Y - .25Y)$$

or, combining all autonomous forces and the propensities to spend

$$E = \overline{A} - br + m(Y - tY) \qquad E = 740 - 2{,}000r + .8(Y - .25Y) \qquad \textbf{5.1}$$

FIGURE 5.1   **Equilibrium Income and Interest Rates**

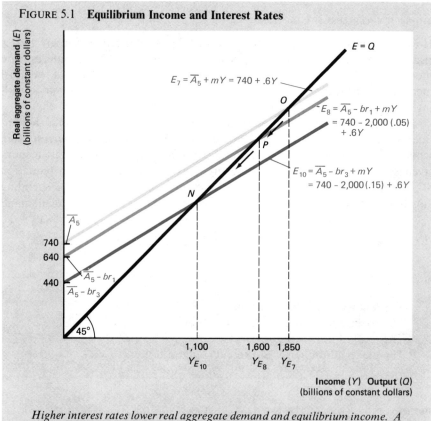

Higher interest rates lower real aggregate demand and equilibrium income. A rise in interest rates from zero (E$_7$) to 15 percent (E$_{10}$) lowers equilibrium spending from O to N.

(E). The interest rate (r) differs for each curve. The top line pictures a real aggregate demand curve without interest-rate effects. It is the same curve as E$_7$ in Figure 4.5. What happens when demand becomes responsive to interest rates? The intercept, or zero income demand, differs with the level of real interest rates. Thus the spending-income curve E$_8$ in the middle includes the term $-br_1 = -2,000(.05)$. It indicates real aggregate demand when real interest rates are 5 percent. At the intercept, demand is $640 billion: $\overline{A}_5 - br_1 = 740 - 2,000(.05)$. The bottom line measures planned expenditures at each income level when interest rates are 15 percent. Its intercept is $440 billion $[740 - 2,000(.15)]$.

Each real aggregate demand curve differs from every other one depending on the level of real interest rates. The curves are parallel because income changes induce identical amounts of additional planned expenditures along each line. The arrows show what happens to the desire to spend at a particular income level if interest rates fall. Demand shifts from one curve to the other. At point N on the 15 percent interest-rate curve, the desire to spend is $1,100 billion when income is $1,100 billion. If interest rates fall to 5 percent, the equilibrium desire to spend would shift up to point P, or to $1,600 billion.

THE EQUILIBRIUM OF SPENDING AND INCOME REVISITED

The inclusion of interest effects in real aggregate demand does not alter the methods of finding the equilibrium level of spending. Figure 5.1 shows the level of equilibrium shifting down from O to P to N as interest rates rise. In the same way, the general equation and the numerical example measure the magnitude of change. Thus, with interest rates at 5 percent, procedures similar to those of the last chapter indicate that equilibrium income is $1,600 billion at point P. At equilibrium, the economy desires to spend all it receives as income and to purchase all output, so Y_E substitutes for its equals, E or Q or Y. To simplify notation, the coefficient m is used to represent all factors in the marginal propensity to spend and tax. Thus $m \equiv (c + d) - (c + d)t$. This convention is followed for the rest of the volume. For the numerical examples, m is .6 and the value of interest-responsiveness is 2,000. With these assumptions,

$$Y_E = \overline{A} - br + mY_E \qquad\qquad Y_E = 740 - 2000r + .6Y_E \qquad\qquad \textbf{5.7}$$

Following previous solution procedures,

$$Y_E = \frac{1}{1-m}(\overline{A} - br) \qquad\qquad Y_E = \frac{1}{1-.6}(740 - 2,000r)$$

and since $k = \dfrac{1}{1-m}$,

$$Y_E = k\overline{A} - k(br) \qquad\qquad Y_E = 2.5(740) - 2.5[2,000(.05)] = 1,600. \qquad \textbf{5.8}$$

Equilibrium income equals the multiplier times the level of autonomous spending minus the multiplier times interest effects. If interest rates rise to 15 percent, the real aggregate demand curve shifts down (E_{10} in Figure 5.1). Equilibrium moves to point N, for which the numerical example indicates a value of $1,100 billion:

$$Y_E = k\overline{A} - k(br) \qquad\qquad Y_E = 2.5(740) - 2.5[2,000(.15)] = 1,100.$$

The movement from equilibrium N to P can be visualized. At all points to the left of an equilibrium, the desire to spend exceeds output and income. When interest rates fall from 15 to 5 percent, the desire-to-spend line shifts up from E_{10} to E_8. At the prior equilibrium output of $1,100 billion, unplanned disinvestment would occur because, with lower interest rates, spending exceeds output. Production and income expand until the new equilibrium is reached at point *P*.

The Investment-Saving Schedule

The variables given primary attention in the analysis of income determination vary with the state of the economy. In the 1930s, lack of adequate demand was the center of concern. Attention focused on government expenditures and transfers as variables which could inject additional demand into the system. Equally important were attempts to measure the multiplier, since induced increases in consumption and investment will accompany any autonomous increases. During wartime, attention shifted to taxation. Government purchases had to expand. As an anti-inflation measure, taxes could be raised to reduce disposable income and dampen some of the excess demand. In the late 1970s, the appeal for a balanced budget followed similar reasoning: Excess demand could be reduced if the government spent less and/or taxed more. In contrast, in the early 1960s, taxes had been reduced and the budget was unbalanced in order to raise an inadequate level of aggregate demand. Lower taxes leave more disposable income available from which sectors can make their spending decisions.

Beginning with the first work on income analysis, in addition to fiscal policy, monetary policy and interest rates have been of extreme concern. The analytical tools and framework were developed so that the effects of money on aggregate demand could be included. One of the techniques used has been to consider *investment-saving* (*IS*) curves. These curves show the levels of equilibrium demand for real goods which result from the interactions of interest rates and income. The *IS* schedule can be combined with interest and income relationships developed in money markets (liquidity-money, or *LM* curves) and with price factors in order to analyze movements in aggregate demand. The *IS* curve makes it possible to visualize the many factors which can alter the desire to spend. Its shape reflects the sensitivity of demand to interest rates and to the marginal propensity to spend. It shifts its position in response to fiscal policy, wealth, prices, expectations, and similar economic variables.

A DERIVATION OF THE *IS* CURVE

The relationship between *IS* curves and the income-spending–interest-rate schedules are shown in Figure 5.2. Given a set of spending desires, a separate spending level and an equilibrium of income exist for each level of interest rates. The spending desires are those of equation 5.8 which is the general form of the *IS* schedule.

A separate desire-to-spend line exists for each interest rate. When interest rates fall, as from 15 percent to 10 percent and 5 percent, each drop in interest

FIGURE 5.2   **Equilibrium in the Real Goods Market: The *IS* Curve**

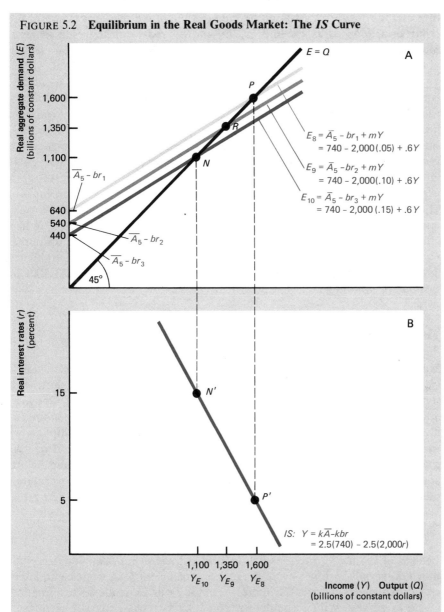

$$E_8 = \bar{A}_5 - br_1 + mY$$
$$= 740 - 2,000(.05) + .6Y$$

$$E_9 = \bar{A}_5 - br_2 + mY$$
$$= 740 - 2,000(.10) + .6Y$$

$$E_{10} = \bar{A}_5 - br_3 + mY$$
$$= 740 - 2,000(.15) + .6Y$$

IS: $Y = k\bar{A} - kbr$
$$= 2.5(740) - 2.5(2,000r)$$

Income (*Y*)   Output (*Q*)
(billions of constant dollars)

*In the top panel, equilibrium levels of output (Q) depend on desires to spend
(E) and real interest rates (r). With other spending factors unchanged, separate equilibriums of real aggregate demand and output (points N, R, P) exist
for each interest rate. All of the interest-output points of equilibrium in the
real goods market are plotted in the lower panel to form an IS curve.*

increases the desire to spend, raising the intercept of the spending curves or the points of $\overline{A} - br$. Thus, the lines E_8, E_9, and E_{10} represent desires to spend at interest rates of 5, 10, and 15 percent respectively. Changes in interest rates do not alter the slope of the lines; each parallels the others.

Panel A of Figure 5.2 contains the 45° line where desires to spend (E) equal incomes produced (Q). Income and spending desires are in equilibrium where each curve crosses the 45° line. These points provide the information needed to draw an IS curve. This is accomplished in panel B of Figure 5.2. Interest rates are measured on the vertical axis and equilibrium incomes on the horizontal. Each equilibrium point in panel A is plotted against its particular interest rate and income. Thus, points N and N' mark interest rates of 15 percent and income of $1,100 billion. Points P and P' show 5 percent and $1,600 billion. The line connecting these and all other possible equilibrium interest and income points from the IS equation forms the IS curve. When interest rates rise, the economy moves upward to the left along an IS curve. Even with the desire to spend constant, less will be purchased because, at higher interest rates, less investment and consumption takes place and this fall in spending is multiplied.[2]

The Slope and Shifts in the IS Curve

Many of the arguments over macroeconomic policies are based on divergent views as to the shape of IS curves and the factors causing them to shift. The slope of the IS curve tells how much income will change as a result of a move in interest rates. The slope depends on (1) the responsiveness of spending to interest rates—the coefficient b in the equations—and (2) the multiplier (k) which determines how the initial interest effects are multiplied. The way changes in these factors rotate the IS curve is pictured in Figures 5.3 and 5.4. In addition, a change in autonomous spending, such as an increase in government purchases, will shift the IS curve, but by equal amounts at all interest rates.

THE SLOPE OF THE IS CURVE

Panel A of Figure 5.3 presents two sets of real aggregate demand curves (E) which differ only with respect to the interest coefficient b. A decrease in interest-responsiveness changes the intercepts of the E curves and leads to a rotation of the IS curves. With a smaller interest-responsiveness, any rise in interest rates causes a smaller decline in real GNP.

For lines E_8 and E_{10}, which have interest rates of 5 and 15 percent, the value of b is 2,000. Lines E_{11} and E_{12} also have interest rates of 5 and 15 percent, but the value of b is 1,000. The intercepts show that when b is larger, a

2. Because the IS curve is an important tool, various techniques of explaining its development from sector-spending curves have been devised. Appendix 5.2 shows an alternative method of deriving the IS curve, known as the four-quadrant technique.

FIGURE 5.3   **A Change in Interest Responsiveness Rotates the *IS* Curve**

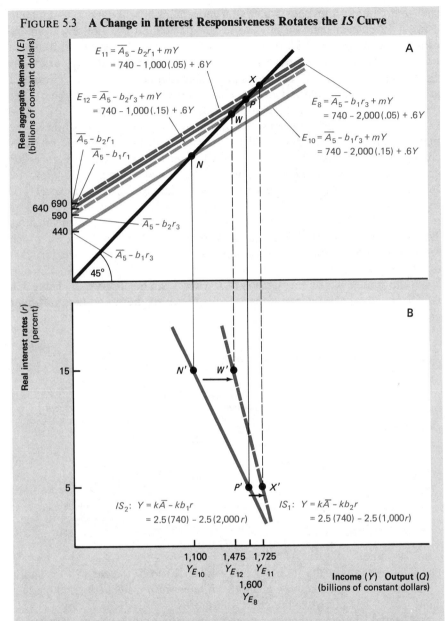

In the top panel, because they have a less negative interest response coefficient (b), the real aggregate demand curves E_{11} and E_{12} are closer together than E_8 and E_{10}. When the equilibriums of $E_{11}, E_{12},$ and all others with the same interest coefficient are plotted, the curve IS_1 is steeper. With a smaller coefficient (b), any interest movement leads to a smaller change in output (Q).

change in interest rates causes a greater movement in real aggregate demand. Thus, a 10 percent increase in r causes a \$200 billion drop of E_{10} from E_8, compared to a decline of \$100 billion for E_{12} from E_{11}. When the equilibrium points are transferred to panel B, the resulting curve (IS_2) rotates upward to the right compared to IS_1. To achieve a particular change in income as a result of an interest-rate movement, the change in interest rates will have to be greater the less sensitive the economy is to interest effects.

But the amount of response to any interest change also depends on the marginal propensity to spend and tax (the multiplier). When interest rates change, aggregate demand shifts, as shown in lines E_8 and E_{10} on Figures 5.3 and 5.4. How much equilibrium income changes depends on the initial impact, shown at the intercepts, and also on the size of the multiplier. In panel A of Figure 5.4, lines E_{13} and E_{14} rise more steeply because the multiplier is 3.33 rather than 2.5. Any interest change induces a larger movement in income. The result shown in panel B is again to rotate the IS curve. On IS_2, which results when the multiplier is larger, any interest change causes a greater reaction in output and income.

The joint effects on the position of IS curves can be observed in Table 5.2. All factors other than interest rates, interest-responsiveness, and the multiplier are held constant.

TABLE 5.2   **Levels of Equilibrium Income**

Interest-responsiveness coefficient (b)	Billions of constant dollars at interest rate of			
	15 percent		5 percent	
	Multipliers of		Multipliers of	
	2.5	3.33	2.5	3.33
1,000	1,475	1,967	1,725	2,300
2,000	1,100	1,467	1,600	2,133

How much a change in interest rates alters income depends on the multiplier and on the responsiveness of the economy to interest rates (coefficient b), shown in the first column 1.

The table shows that the interest change from 15 to 5 percent will lead to a larger increase in income with a greater interest-responsiveness (2,000). The multiplier of 3.33 increases the effect still more.

It should be clear that a change in interest rates does not alter an IS curve. When interest rates fall, the economy spends more. The change in interest rates causes a movement along a preexisting IS curve. In contrast, movements in either interest-responsiveness or the desire to spend change the coefficient parameters of the system; new IS curves result. Such movements are called **structural changes** in the system. They are the source of many of the

FIGURE 5.4   **Larger Multipliers Increase the Economy's Reactions to Interest Changes**

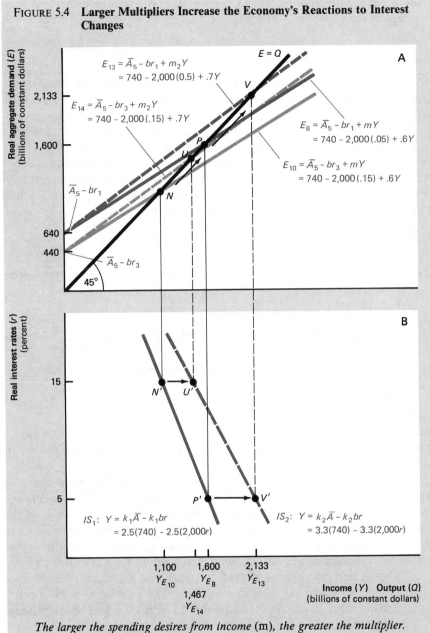

The larger the spending desires from income (m), the greater the multiplier. Consequently, each decrease in interest rates induces more spending compared to a real demand curve with a smaller multiplier. The curve IS_2 is flatter than IS_1. Income is less stable when interest rates shift.

problems encountered in attempts to find useful statistical models of the relationships in the economy.

Any shift in autonomous desires to spend will shift the position of the *IS* curve.
Government purchases ($\Delta \overline{G}$) or government taxes and transfers ($\Delta \overline{T}$) can shift.
Expectations or some other factors may also shift, causing autonomous move-
ments in consumption ($\Delta \overline{C}$) or investment ($\Delta \overline{I}$). Any or all of these factors can
combine to cause a particular shift in autonomous spending ($\Delta \overline{A}$). What is the
relationship between the size of the autonomous change and the movement of
the *IS* curve? We can compare the position of an *IS* curve at each interest level
before and after a movement in autonomous spending. Equation 5.9 and
Figure 5.2 show the *IS* curve in its most general form. Thus,

$$IS: Y = k\overline{A} - k(br) \qquad\qquad Y = 2.5(740) - 2.5(2{,}000r). \qquad\qquad \textbf{5.9}$$

If autonomous spending changes, the effect on the position of the curve will be

$$Y + \Delta Y = k(\overline{A} + \Delta \overline{A}) - k(br)$$

$$Y + \Delta Y = 2.5(740 + 100) - 2.5(2{,}000r) \qquad\qquad \textbf{5.10}$$

or, by subtraction of equation 5.9 from 5.10, the change is seen to be

$$\Delta Y = k(\Delta \overline{A}) \qquad\qquad \Delta Y = 2.5(100). \qquad\qquad \textbf{5.11}$$

Each equilibrium point of interest and income on the *IS* curve shifts not merely
by the increase in autonomous spending but by the increase times the multiplier. The shift is shown on Figure 5.5.

The panel A of the figure illustrates an increase in autonomous spending
which shifts each income-spending–interest-rate curve. The difference between
the darker and the lighter curves at the intercept shows the amount of the
autonomous moves. Note, however, the greater distance between the new and
old equilibriums. The equilibriums differ by the amount of both the autonomous and the income-induced spending. Each equilibrium is shifted by $k\Delta \overline{A}$.

When a new *IS* curve is plotted, in panel B of the figure, the distance
between the two curves at each interest rate is $k\Delta \overline{A}$. The new *IS* curve is
parallel to the previous one, but the equilibrium of income at each interest rate
is larger by the factor $k\Delta \overline{A}$.

At any time, recent shifts in demand may cause markets to depart from equilibrium. Examples of two such situations are found in Figure 5.6. The points
N' and Z' in panel B of the figure are at 15 percent interest rates. However N' is

FIGURE 5.5   **Changes in Autonomous Spending Shift the *IS* Curve**

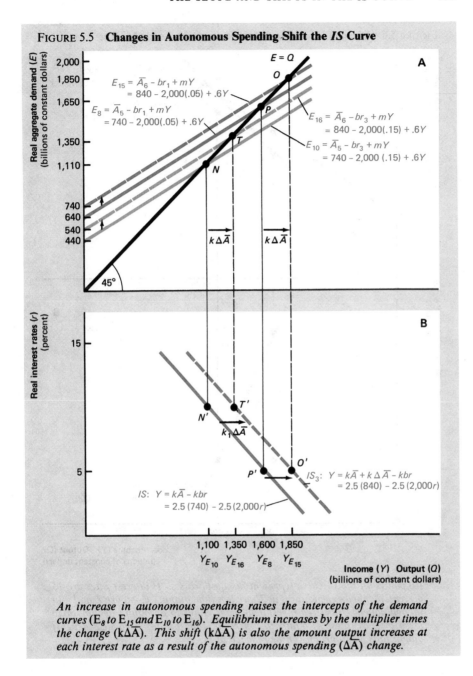

An increase in autonomous spending raises the intercepts of the demand curves (E_8 to E_{15} and E_{10} to E_{16}). Equilibrium increases by the multiplier times the change ($k\Delta\bar{A}$). This shift ($k\Delta\bar{A}$) is also the amount output increases at each interest rate as a result of the autonomous spending ($\Delta\bar{A}$) change.

on the *IS* curve, while Z' is off it to the right. What can be said about market conditions at point Z'? Follow the line from Z' up to the aggregate demand curve at 15 percent interest rate in panel **A** of the figure. Note that the demand at Z is less than the amount of output which is found on the 45° line at P. An

FIGURE 5.6   **Disequilibrium Conditions in the Real Goods Market**

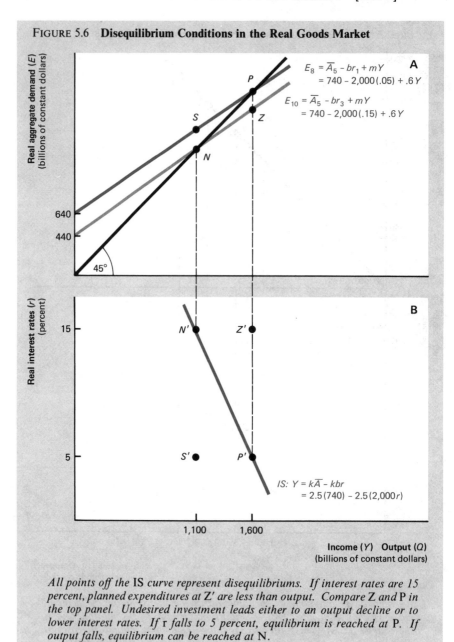

$$E_8 = \overline{A}_5 - br_1 + mY$$
$$= 740 - 2,000(.05) + .6Y$$

$$E_{10} = \overline{A}_5 - br_3 + mY$$
$$= 740 - 2,000(.15) + .6Y$$

$$IS: Y = k\overline{A} - kbr$$
$$= 2.5(740) - 2.5(2,000r)$$

Income (Y)   Output (Q)
(billions of constant dollars)

All points off the IS curve represent disequilibriums. If interest rates are 15 percent, planned expenditures at Z' are less than output. Compare Z and P in the top panel. Undesired investment leads either to an output decline or to lower interest rates. If r falls to 5 percent, equilibrium is reached at P. If output falls, equilibrium can be reached at N.

excess supply of goods is being produced and not sold. The disequilibrium can be cured by producers cutting back to rid themselves of their unwanted inventory or interest rates can fall. Output will drop until the excess supply vanishes at point N, or somewhat higher if interest rates fall.

In contrast, consider point S' with interest rates at 5 percent. The level of output is the same as at point N. But because of lower interest rates, demand is higher. An excess of demand for real goods exists. To move back to equilibrium, either interest rates must rise or output increase. Probably both types of movements will occur. The economy will return to equilibrium between points N and P on the 45° line. At that point, which represents an equilibrium in the real goods market, the economy will be on the IS curve. The excess demand will be gone.

Real and Nominal Interest Rates

In measuring the effect of interest rates on demand, it is necessary to differentiate carefully between nominal and real interest rates and between rates paid or received before and after taxes. The IS curves are drawn in terms of real interest rates, real income, and real output. Investors and consumers, to the extent of available information, consider real expected rates of return after taxes in making their decisions.

Nominal rates of return are ratios of income to principal uncorrected for either anticipated or actual changes in the purchasing power of the income or asset. Market rates of interest are quoted in nominal terms. *Real rates of return* are nominal rates corrected for changes in anticipated or actual inflation over the period during which a physical or financial asset is held. When taxes apply to income or capital gains, the nominal rates of return must be corrected for both price changes and taxes to obtain the real aftertax rate of return.

BORROW AND BUY

The inflation of the 1970s was accompanied by much talk of a new economic philosophy—"borrow and buy." The apparent logic behind the philosophy has been well expressed. In *Moneypower,* Benjamin and Herbert Stein (a past chairman of the Council of Economic Advisers) bring out the strong arguments behind the borrow-and-buy attitudes:[3]

> If the world were as it should be, people could work and save and come out ahead. In America, in our era, people who work and save are losing money every minute of every day. The world has become so convoluted and bizarre, in fact, that only those who take financial risks avoid the certainty of financial loss. Borrow for houses. Borrow for gold. Borrow for foreign currencies. But borrow, risky though it is, and you will make money.[3]

Similarly, Robert T. Parry, chief economist for Security Pacific National Bank of Los Angeles, summarized a widely held view:

> The lesson of the 1970s was that you came out ahead by borrowing, repaying with cheaper dollars, and using the proceeds of the loan to buy assets that would appreciate or would cost you more to buy tomorrow. That

3. Ben Stein with Herbert Stein, *Moneypower* (New York: Harper & Row, 1979), p. 194.

lesson was so well learned that we all underestimated how strong consumer spending would be, how strong the economy would be, and how strong inflation would be.[4]

These statements support the point that those who took chances on inflation's continuing or speeding up in the 1970s made large profits. If actual inflation increases faster than anticipated, those who follow the philosophy of borrow and buy can reap large sums. However, if prices rise at a slower rate than expected they can incur substantial losses and bankruptcy.

NEGATIVE REAL INTEREST RATES

The acceleration of purchases of real assets with borrowed funds came about because the tax system, together with inflation, created major advantages for ownership of real assets while penalizing ownership of traditional savings deposits. Income from savings accounts was both fully taxed and restricted by ceiling interest rates (Regulation Q). While bonds and other financial assets were not subject to ceilings, they were fully taxed and they carried considerable risk if inflation speeded up (as shown by the example at the start of the chapter). In contrast, inflationary returns from houses and many other durable goods were either not taxed or taxed at reduced rates. Furthermore, the cost of sums borrowed for their purchase was reduced by the fact that interest payments made on such loans can be deducted from taxable income, thus lowering the owners' taxes. Each dollar saved in this way brings about an equivalent reduction in the cost of a loan.

Table 5.3 illustrates why personal savings declined in the late 1970s while consumer purchases of durables and borrowings on mortgage and consumer debt rose rapidly. The table compares expected real aftertax rates of return from investments in houses with the returns from funds placed in thrift institutions' savings accounts. The table assumes expectations based on the previous year's price change. It shows why purchases of durables were logical up to a point. However, as the last chapter pointed out, near the end of the decade, expectations appeared to rise more rapidly, making it difficult to determine whether or not they were irrationally high.

The first half of the table shows the net aftertax anticipated interest rates on the purchase of a house. These rates, with their signs reversed, are also the expected rates of return from such investments in a house. In the table, the nominal interest rates are market rates as reported for the last month of the prior year. The aftertax rate assumes that the borrower's marginal tax bracket is 30 percent and that the deduction reduces taxes due on other income. The anticipated change in prices is the percent increase in housing prices over the previous twelve months. These figures will vary depending on the region of the country, the source of price estimates used, and the manner in which expectations are formed. However, differences from these sources would not alter the

---

4. *The Wall Street Journal,* April 3, 1980, p. 46.

TABLE 5.3 **Expected Real Aftertax Interest Rates**
(percent)

Period starting January 1	Purchase of houses				Purchase of savings deposits			
	Nominal mortgage interest rate		Expected percent change in house prices	Net aftertax real interest rate paid	Nominal saving interest rate		Expected percent change in CPI	Net aftertax real interest rate earned
	Before tax	After tax			Before tax	After tax		
1977	9.10	6.37	11.1	−4.73	5.25	3.68	4.8	−1.12
1978	9.09	6.36	13.1	−6.74	5.25	3.68	6.8	−3.12
1979	10.02	7.01	18.0	−10.99	5.25	3.68	9.0	−5.32
1980	11.65	8.16	16.3	−8.14	5.50	3.85	13.3	−9.45

SOURCE: *Federal Reserve Bulletin.*

Home buyers expect to profit by paying negative real interest rates (fourth column). Their aftertax interest payments (second column) were less than the expected increase in house prices (third column). Meanwhile, savers received negative real interest (eighth column). Their aftertax returns (sixth column) were less than inflation.

fact that most house purchasers expected negative real interest costs and very positive profits when buying houses in the 1970s.

In contrast, the second half of the table shows the expected rate of return from savings deposits. The anticipated prices are the percent change in the consumer price index over the previous 12 months. When interest receipts are corrected for tax payments and expected inflation, they are strongly negative.

The table makes clear how much larger was the anticipated return from holding real assets during this period. Borrowing to buy paid off because of negative real aftertax interest rates. Lenders lost; borrowers gained. Those owning the savings accounts should have anticipated a negative real value. People who retained savings accounts either failed to understand what was happening or were willing to accept negative returns because they put a high value on liquidity and safety, or they had no idea where else to put their money. The differences in returns explain the excess demand for houses and mortgages in this period and the reason housing prices shot up so much faster than the general price level.

What is not as obvious is that house purchasers were also taking much greater chances. Those who bought on the assumption that house prices would continue to accelerate more rapidly than other prices risked being proven wrong. The advantage of borrowing and buying continues only as long as prices rise as fast as anticipated. Yet this is unlikely to occur if anticipations are based primarily on past price increases. Housing prices rose because buyers realized what a good deal they were being offered by the tax break. When this information became built into market prices, the excess rate of housing price increases compared to the general price level would diminish. Actual price increases would be less than expected, leading to downward pressure. Outside shocks to demand would increase the risks of frustrated anticipations, with a likelihood of losses.

The considerations show how important it is to properly estimate real, not nominal, interest rates. The *IS* curve reflects an equilibrium of real interest rates and real income. To find where the economy will settle, we must next turn to the factors determining the relationship between money and interest rates.

Summary

1. When market interest rates change, they shift the value of all assets. Movements in interest rates alter the discount rates used in finding the present value of an asset's expected future income. Unchanged income flows discounted at new rates alter present values for each asset.

2. By shifting the value of investments and the wealth of households, changes in interest rates modify desires of the economy to spend. Higher interest rates lower investment, consumption, and state and local expenditures. Each interest rate determines a separate demand curve. The amount demand reacts to new rates depends on how responsive spending is to interest rates.

3. An equilibrium of output and the desire to spend for real goods exists for every interest and income level. A curve representing these points of equilibrium for goods plotted in an interest-income space is called an investment-saving, or *IS* curve.

4. The slopes of *IS* curves depend on the responsiveness of spending desires to interest rates and on the marginal propensities to spend and tax (the multiplier). A change in the structure of the economy results in different spending coefficients and a new *IS* curve.

5. A rise in interest rates causes the economy to move up to the left along an *IS* curve to a lower equilibrium level of income. The more interest-responsive is spending and the larger the multiplier, the more will income and output react to any change in interest rates.

6. Any change in an autonomous spending factor shifts the *IS* curve. Each new equilibrium income point at an interest level differs from the prior income point by the multiplier times the amount of shift in autonomous spending.

7. An economy off its *IS* curve is in a state of disequilibrium. If an excess supply of real goods exist, producers may correct the situation by cutting back on output. Depending on the situation in the money markets, discussed in the next two chapters, interest rates may also decline. A fall in r raises the demand for real goods and reduces the amount output must be cut back in order to bring about an equilibrium.

8. Similarly, an excess of demand for real goods may be met partially through an increase in output, or it may be reduced as a result of an increase in interest rates.

9. In analyzing the effects of interest rates on spending, one must differentiate between nominal and real rates. The *IS* curve is based on real, not nominal, rates. In the 1970s, when real aftertax rates of interest became negative, those who borrowed to buy profited handsomely. The expectation .of continued negative real rates raised the demand for houses and housing prices, as well as those for other durables. Risks increased that high expectations would not be fulfilled by actual events and that losses would occur.

10. Given an existing structure for the economy, the demand for goods and services, as well as the equilibrium level of income and output, depends on: (1) autonomous spending factors, including tastes, resources, government budgets, and levels of expectations; (2) marginal propensities to spend and tax (the multipliers); (3) the responsiveness of wealth and spending to interest rates; and (4) the actual interest rates developed in the economy through interactions between the markets for money and for goods.

Questions for Discussion and Review

1. Calculate the present value of a $100 note paying 8 percent at each of the next four years, with repayment due at the end of year 4, if market interest rates for such a note are 10 percent.

2. If investment depended on total income or output rather than on disposable income, how would equation 5.3 be changed? What effect would it have on the multiplier calculated from equation 5.7 when $Y_E = E$?

3. Consider an economy described by the following relations (quantities in billions of dollars):

$C = 300 + .75\,YD$
$I = 200 - 2{,}000r$
$G = \overline{G} = 400$
$T = \overline{T} = 100$
$r = 10\%$

   (a) What is the equation for the *IS* curve?
   (b) What is the equilibrium level of income?
   (c) Suppose the autonomous component of spending desires decreases by 300. What is the new equilibrium level of income?
   (d) Suppose the interest rate falls to 7 percent. What is the new equilibrium level of income?

4. Is it true that an increase in the interest rate will, all other things equal, shift the *IS* curve to the left?

5. (a) Fully explain why the size of the multiplier and the degree of interest-sensitivity of investment spending affect the slope of the *IS* curve. (b) During the Great

Depression of the 1930s, interest rates fell to very low levels without reviving investment spending. What light does this fact throw on the degree of interest elasticity of
aggregate demand?

Questions 6 and 7 refer to the following model:

$$Y = C + I + G$$
$$C = 50 + .5YD$$
$$YD = Y - .3Y$$
$$I = 200 - 1,500r + .1YD$$
$$\overline{G} = 400$$
$$t = .3$$

6. Write down the following:
   (a) The equation of the IS curve.
   (b) The autonomous component of the desire to spend.
   (c) The interest-determined component of the desire to spend.
   (d) The multiplier.

7. What additional information do you need in order to calculate the equilibrium level
   of income? Make an assumption about this, and calculate the resulting equilibrium
   level of income.

References

Ackley, G. *Macroeconomics: Theory and Policy.* New York: Macmillan, 1978. Chap-
    ter 11.

Fisher, I. *The Theory of Interest Rates.* New York: Macmillan, 1930.

Laidler, D. E. W. *The Demand for Money,* 2nd edition. New York: Dun-Donnelly,
    1977. Chapter 1.

Van Horne, J. C. *Financial Markets Rates and Flows.* Englewood Cliffs, N.J.: Pren-
    tice-Hall, 1978. Chapters 3 and 8.

APPENDIX 5.1   The Present Value of an Investment

Let us look at the logic (the mathematics of finance) by which the present value
of investments is calculated. We know that because of the time value of money,
no one would be willing to pay $3,000 today for a promise to get back $1,000 in
each of the next three years. Because money now in hand can earn interest,
$1,000 to be received next year is not worth as much as $1,000 today. The
amount that future promises are worth depends on how much interest can be
earned in the interim. If we knew we could invest current money at 10 percent
interest, we would pay only $909 today for next year's promised payout. Simi-
larly, for the $1,000 payable in two years, we would pay only $826, and for the
$1,000 payable in three years, we would pay a maximum of $751.

   While present values are normally found by either a computer, a hand calculator, or in a set of compound interest tables, it is quite useful and not too difficult to understand how present values are arrived at. Let us start by considering the mechanics of a savings account. We are all familiar with the idea that if a sum of money can be invested so as to yield a return, it will grow to a larger sum in the future. If $751 are put into a savings account that pays 10 percent interest compounded annually, how much will the account contain at the end of three years? Table 5.4 shows the figure at the end of three years to be $1,000. The initial amount of $751 is found in the top position of year 1. That year, $75 is earned, so that at the end of the year the account holds $826. The arrow shows this total invested at the start of the second year. With $83 earned in the second year, it becomes $909. This sum, invested for the third year plus the $91 earned, makes up the final total of $1,000.

TABLE 5.4   **Compound Interest and Present Values**
(dollars)

	Year 1	Year 2	Year 3
Beginning amount and present value (P_0)	751	→ 826	→ 909
Interest calculation $(1 + i)$	× ___1.10	× ___1.10	× ___1.10
Interest earned (i)	75.1	82.6	90.9
Beginning amount	751.0	826.0	909
Principal + interest $(P_0)(1 + i)^n$ or ending amount (P_n)	826.1	908.6	999.9

An initial principal of $751 invested for three years at 10 percent compound interest will grow to $1,000 (999.9). When the discount rate is 10 percent, the present value of $1,000 to be received in three years is $751 since that is the initial investment which will grow to $1,000 given the time period and compound interest rate [751 (1.10)³].

THE COMPOUND INTEREST FORMULA

From the table, it is fairly easy to derive the compound interest formula. Let us define the following terms:

P_0 = principal or beginning amount at time 0
i = interest rate or yield for one interest-earning period
n = number of interest-earning periods
P_n = principal value at end of n periods

If a person has $751 today and the bank will pay her 10 percent interest, she will have at the end of the year the principal at time 0 plus the interest earned; or, according to Table 5.4, her total sum at the end of year 1 is

$$P_1 = P_0 (1 + i).$$ 5.12

In the second year she will be lending the bank $826 and will again be receiving 10 percent interest. For the two years, the amount she deposited is compounded at 10 percent; or she will get $1.10 \times 1.10 = 1.21 \times$ her initial investment, or

$$P_2 = P_1 (1 + i) = P_0 (1 + i)(1 + i) = P_0 (1 + i)^2.$$ 5.13

At the end of three years, her principal will have increased by a factor of $1.10 \times 1.10 \times 1.10 = 1.331$, or

$$P_3 = P_2 (1 + i) = P_0 (1 + i)^3.$$ 5.14

In general we can apply the familiar compound interest formula, which says that the compound amount P_n at the end of any year, n, is found as

$$P_n = P_0 (1 + i)^n.$$ 5.15

If an investor has $751 in a savings account at 10 percent payable in 3 years, she will have

$$\$1{,}000 = \$751 (1 + .10)^3.$$

The values of $(1 + i)^n$, called the **compound interest factor**, are readily available in tables.

PRESENT-VALUE CALCULATIONS

Table 5.4 also enables us to calculate present values. The table indicates that we would have to invest $751 today to receive $1,000 three years from now. But recall that the definition of the present value of a future payment is the amount that would have to be invested today to grow to the future amount. This is what the table shows. The deposit of $751 is the present value of $1,000 to be received three years from now when the interest rate is 10 percent.

   Finding the present value, or **discounting,** is simply the reverse of compounding. Thus, to find present values, we can invert the previous relationships found in the compound interest formula (P_0 is the present value):

$$P_n = P_0(1 + i)^n \qquad\qquad \$1{,}000 = 751(1 + .10)^3$$

$$P_0 = \frac{P_n}{(1 + i)^n} \qquad\qquad \$751 = \frac{1{,}000}{1.131}.$$ 5.15

   To find the present value of a bond or any other investment that will return funds in the future, merely find the present value of each future receipt (R) and add them together to find the present value of the asset:

$$PV = \frac{R_1}{(1 + i)} + \frac{R_2}{(1 + i)^2} + \frac{R_3}{(1 + i)^3} + \ldots + \frac{R_n}{(1 + i)^n}.$$ 5.16

To see how this works, assume that, with market interest rates at 10 percent, a government note promises to pay $70 at the end of each of the next three years (let *COU* represent these coupons), and the principal (*PRI*) will be repaid in three years. Then the present value of the bond is:

$$PV = \frac{COU_1}{(1+i)} + \frac{COU_2}{(1+i)^2} + \frac{COU_3}{(1+i)^3} + \frac{PRI}{(1+i)^3} \qquad \textbf{5.17}$$

$$= \frac{70}{1.10} + \frac{70}{(1.10)^2} + \frac{70}{(1+.10)^3} + \frac{1,000}{(1+.10)^3}.$$

This is the same as

$$PV = .909(70) + .826(70) + .751(70) + .751(1,000) = 925$$

or, the present value of the bond is $925.

When market interest rates shift, the value of *i* used in discounting future income changes to reflect what the market charges. As a result, even though no alteration occurs in the promises to pay the individual coupons and principal, the present value—and therefore, what a note or bond sells for—does change.

Appendix 5.2   A Four-Quadrant Derivation of the *IS* Curve

Because of the importance of the *IS* curve, it is worthwhile to show how it relates to changes in interest rates and spending and saving desires through another technique as well. We can trace the effect of interest-rate changes on injections into the income stream and on equilibrium income by use of a four-quadrant diagram that equates injections (*I*) and leakages (*S*) at each interest level. This additional graphical derivation of the IS curve is demonstrated by Figure 5.7. Quadrant A plots the autonomous and interest-responsive factors ($\bar{A}$ and $-br$). These can be thought of as investment, or injections, to reflect all the autonomous and interest-responsive factors. Quadrant c plots leakages, or net income-induced movements [$S = (1-m)Y$]. These can be called saving. Quadrant B is the familiar 45° line. At each point on this line, investment equals saving.[5]

To see how the desire to spend and save interact with interest rates and income, select interest rates and see what equilibrium incomes result. Start with

5. The level of injections in panel A includes all autonomous expenditures reduced by interest effects. Thus, they include $\bar{I} + \bar{C} + \bar{G} - c\bar{T}$. The leakages in panel c include all income-induced saving and tax effects ($s + mt$) and do not include autonomous saving or taxes. However, to simplify the presentation, the total of autonomous factors in A are lumped together as *I* and called investment, and all income-induced factors in c are summed as *s* and called saving.

FIGURE 5.7   A Four-Quadrant Exposition of *IS* Relationships

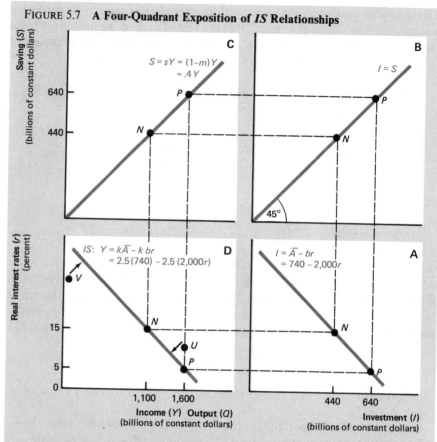

The curve in quadrant A shows at each r net levels of desired autonomous
expenditures reduced by interest effects. Lower interest rates raise the desires
to invest or consume. At equilibrium I = S, as in quadrant B. Quadrant C
shows the amount of income needed for each planned saving level. In D on the
IS curve, each point shows an equilibrium income-interest-rate level. The
square is complete. These interest rates determined the level of investment in
A and B, which are matched by the income-induced saving in C.

an interest rate measured on the lower vertical scale (quadrant A). Look at the
investment function. The intersection of an interest-rate line with the investment function tells the amount of autonomous and interest-responsive spending. Note that with interest rates at 15 percent (point N on the diagram),
investors will want to spend $440 billion, the amount read off the bottom scale.

Finding the amount of investment, we also know the equilibrium level of
saving because, at equilibrium, S = I. Follow the line from the desired level of
investment ($440 billion) at the selected interest rate (15) up to quadrant B. At
each investment amount on the 45° line, the equilibrium level of saving can be

read off the left-hand saving scale. At what income would this amount of saving be desired? Follow the line from the point on the 45° line to the left until it intersects the saving function. This shows the equilibrium level of income for the desired amount of saving and investment. The 15 percent interest points are marked N in each quadrant. It takes an equilibrium income of $1,100 billion to generate a saving of $440 billion. What would happen if initially income were $1,400 billion? People would want to save more than the $440 billion invested. Leakages would occur until income fell to $1,100 billion.

In the first three quadrants, we start with selected interest rates and find their equilibrium levels of income. Each interest-income value determines a point which can be plotted on the *IS* curve (quadrant D). These are found by continuing the line from the equilibrium saving-income point in quadrant c back to the *IS* quadrant (D). Each interest-income point is where the line from an equilibrium income point in quadrant c intersects an initial interest-rate line. In the numerical example, this is the point where the 15 percent interest line intersects the income level of $1,100 billion.

Every point on the *IS* curve can be developed in the same way. Check the line where interest rates are 5 percent to see how one arrives at the income of $1,600 billion. For each point, move from interest rates through the investment and saving functions to the desired level of income. These are the points marked *P*. Each specific interest rate determines an equilibrium level of real income, given the consumption and investment schedules.

Figure 5.7 shows why a rise in interest rates causes a drop in income. Higher interest rates reduce investment demand. To match this reduction at equilibrium, required saving falls. This smaller saving is compatible only with a lower income level. If people tried to save more than planned investment, income would fall. In the numerical example, when interest rates rise from 5 percent to 15 percent, the desired level of investment drops by $200 billion, and saving must fall by the same amount. Because of the multiplier, for the economy to reduce its desire to save by $200 billion, income must drop by $500 billion.

The figure also allows us to observe what a disequilibrium in the goods market looks like and to picture how it gets corrected. Look at point *U* in quadrant D. At this point, interest rates are 10 percent and income and output are $1,600 billion. That this is not an equilibrium can be ascertained by substituting these values in the *IS* equation 5.9:

$$Y = k\overline{A} - k(br) \qquad 1,600 \neq 2.5(740) - 2.5(2,000 \times .10) = 1,350. \quad \textbf{5.9}$$

The desire to spend when interest rates are 10 percent is only $1,350 billion, not $1,600 billion. Autonomous and interest-responsive spending, as shown in quadrant A, is only $540 billion. If production is $1,600 billion, undesired inventories will accumulate. Output must fall. This may cause interest rates to decline also. In any case, because the desire to save (leakages) exceeds the desire to invest (injections), the economy will move in the direction shown by the arrow from point *U* until it returns to equilibrium at a point on the *IS* curve.

At point V, injections are greater than leakages. Substitution in the IS equation will again show a disequilibrium; but in this case, the desire to spend will exceed output. The economy will expand until it again reaches equilibrium on the IS curve.

SHIFTS IN AUTONOMOUS SPENDING

The effect of an autonomous shift in the desire to spend can also be traced through by use of the four-quadrant diagram. How much will income increase if there is an autonomous shift in investment of $\Delta \overline{A}$ (assume $200 billion)? How will it affect the IS curve? Of course, the autonomous shift could be in $\overline{C}$, $\overline{I}$, or in $\overline{G}$ or $\overline{T}$. From the previous analysis and from the IS equation 5.9, we know that equilibrium income grows by any shift in autonomous expenditures times the multiplier.

An increase in autonomous spending ($\Delta \overline{A}$) will shift the injection (I) curve in panel 5.7A to the right by an equal amount at each interest rate. Thus if A increases by $200 billion, the desire to invest at 15 percent interest will now be $640 rather than $440 billion. It will be $840 billion if the interest level is 5 percent. The points marked P in panels B and C show the required amount of saving and income needed to match an injection of $640 billion into the spending stream. The point P in panel C shows that income must be $1,600 if $640 billion is to leak out in saving and taxes. When each altered income-leakage point is traced down to panel D, the result of the added spending desire ($\Delta \overline{A}$) is a new IS curve parallel to the previous one. At 15 percent interest, the total desire to spend has risen from $1,100 to $1,600, or by $500 billion as a result of the autonomous change in the desire to spend of $200 billion.

A similar increase of $500 billion occurs in the total desire to spend at each interest rate. The IS curve has shifted up, not merely by the autonomous increase, but by the autonomous increase times the multiplier. At each interest rate, equilibrium in this goods market has increased by $500 billion as a result of the multiplier times the autonomous change, $k\Delta \overline{A}$. Of course, the IS curves and the shifts in them derived from the four-quadrant diagram agree exactly with those derived from the slope-intercept form presented in the body of the chapter. They are both graphical presentations of a single IS equation.

Part 3

Equilibrium in the Money Market
and Determination of Aggregate
Demand

6

The Creation and Supply of Money

The model of the market for real goods developed thus far provides only a partial explanation of the determination of equilibrium of demand, income, and output. It shows that demand depends, among other factors, on interest rates, on wealth, on prices, and on expectations of their anticipated values; but it does not explain how these variables are set and how they move. To fill this gap, we here introduce and describe a market for money and other financial assets.

Changes in the supply of and demand for money shift the equilibrium of interest rates and income in the market for money. Important issues in this market center around the factors entering into the *demand for money,* which comprises the decisions of the public to hold wealth in the form of money rather than in other assets. In some ways, the term *demand for money* is misleading. What we are in fact seeking are estimates of such factors as how much income and interest rates will have to change if the money supply grows before people are willing to hold the additional money and not make further purchases.

To many economists, money is the most critical economic variable—it is the chief regulator of aggregate demand and prices. The model of the money market developed in this section shows how money demand and supply interact with interest rates and income. Equilibrium in the money market varies with both. The *liquidity-money function (LM)* represents all the possible combinations of real interest rates and real income that equate the demand for and the supply of real money. The *LM* curves then are combined with *IS* curves to complete the explanation of aggregate demand. Initially, the *IS-LM* interactions are limited to real values, but the addition of prices allows for the analysis of movements in nominal aggregate demand as well. The combined models explain the forces which cause demand to fluctuate. These fluctuations, or cycles, in business and economic activity in turn cause movements in output, employment, and prices.

The starting point for analyzing money is finding out what it is and how it is created. This chapter considers the following topics:

What is money?
Measuring the stock of money.
The Federal Reserve and the monetary process.
How commercial banks expand deposits and create money.
Control of the money stock.
Targeting monetary operations.
Other possible monetary targets.

In Chapter 7, we analyze the factors which determine the willingness of people to hold money and we trace the relationships between money and spending and equilibrium in the money market. Chapter 8 studies the interactions of the money and goods markets in determining aggregate demand, as well as the effects of prices on monetary equilibrium and spending.

What Is Money?

One of the few precepts of economics accepted almost unanimously is that the growth of money must be controlled because it plays so vital a role in the economy. Within the government, the Federal Reserve has been given responsibility for managing money. Not many contemporary observers are satisfied with the results. To see why and to be able to forecast future interest rates and prices, we need to understand what money is and the process by which it is created.

Money is an asset, a claim by individuals and firms against the government and financial institutions. Looked at from another point of view, money (an asset) is simultaneously a liability of those who owe the claims to the public. To follow the process by which money is created it is necessary to grasp what happens on both sides of financial balance sheets. When monetary authorities and banks increase their assets by buying additional securities or making new loans, they simultaneously increase their liabilities and, therefore, the amount of money.

In addition to knowing how money is created, we must be able to define and measure it. We talk about money all the time, but what do we actually mean? It is difficult to define money, as pointed out by Allan Meltzer, a prominent monetarist:

> Money is an ambiguous concept. The ambiguity arises from the use of the same concept—money—to denote an asset that is important for explaining

changes in the price level and an asset that renders a variety of "services" usually summarized by some undefined phrase.[1]

FOUR FUNCTIONS OF MONEY

Basically, money can be anything which people accept generally in exchange for all other goods. What is and has been used as money has varied widely over time. Nevertheless, the services or functions which money performs can' be categorized in four ways:

1. Money serves as a *unit or standard of value.* It is the unit in terms of which the values of goods and services are measured and expressed. We compare all other items to money to obtain a measure of their relative values.
2. Money acts as a *medium of exchange.* It is accepted by others in exchange for their goods and services. It is generalized purchasing power. With money, you can buy all other items. You don't have to worry that people may not want the particular goods and services you can offer; they'll take your money instead.
3. Money serves as a common *store of value.* It is a medium of exchange over time. If you accumulate a stock of money today, you will be able to use it for purchases in the future. While you might hold other stores of value instead, when you want to spend them, they will have to be converted into money.
4. Money functions as a *standard of deferred payments.* Many contracts for future payments are stated in terms of the current unit of account. Bonds, leases, mortgages contain promises to pay a certain number of dollars at intervals in the future.

These last two functions of money are the reason that inflations cause grave problems. By establishing money, society enters into an implied social contract between present purchasing power and the future. People are willing to hold assets denominated in dollars on the assumption that when they trade them sometime in the future, their value will not be too different. If this is no longer true, they will seek to hold other types of assets and the value of money will drop.

For working purposes, *money* can be defined as those liabilities of the government or of financial institutions which the public holds at a particular time in order to obtain the services or functions money performs. Money is created when the government or financial institutions issue liabilities which provide monetary services. What money is changes as the public alters its views as to whether and to what degree a particular liability can perform the desired functions. The key concept is that either an item can be used as a medium of exchange or it has sufficient liquidity for its owners to consider it so nearly equivalent to a medium of exchange that it influences their demand and

1. A. H. Meltzer, "Money, Intermediation, and Growth," *Journal of Economic Literature* 7 (March 1969) 39.

spending in the same way. *Liquidity* is the ability to turn an asset into a medium of exchange rapidly, with a minimum of transactions costs and danger of loss in capital value. The **supply of money** or the **money stock** consists of the units of liabilities held by the public that they consider yield monetary services. Measures of the money supply and its growth differ depending on how it is defined.

Measuring the Stock of Money

Because money performs a variety of functions and because a vast number of financial institutions issue liabilities which can serve the public as money, the measurement and control of the stock of money is a complex matter. The simplest measure, and one which the Federal Reserve can control accurately, is the **monetary base.** It consists of the monetary liabilities (or their asset equivalents) to the public of the country's monetary authority (the Federal Reserve and the Treasury) or, more simply, currency and reserves of banks at the Fed. This is also called M-0 (M-zero), or high-powered money. In 1981, M-0 stood at $160 billion. Of this amount, $117 billion consisted of currency held by the public and $43 billion were reserves held by depository institutions at the Federal Reserve System.

While some economists believe that the monetary base can be used as a measure of money and as the control variable for policy, the concept presents some analytical difficulties. Bank reserves are held by institutions. They are the base of their creation of money, but they are not used by the public as money. Furthermore, changes in the monetary base are dominated by movements in currency (paper money and coins), yet currency accounts for only about 10 percent of payments. Broader concepts are necessary to explain what money does and why. Table 6.1 contains five definitions of money adopted by the Federal Reserve in late 1979 after several years of work aimed at improving the analytical and statistical reliability of individual money measures.

Both definitions and money measures are frequently revised. This is necessary because the public modifies what it uses as money, or because analysts believe a new measure may offer a better insight into what money is and what it does. The altered definitions are advanced as means of establishing more stable relationships between measures of money and spending. An example is found in Table 6.1. Comparing the definitions in the table yields clues as to why discrepancies arise over how to measure money and why no measure is completely satisfactory. It also shows how definitions shift as new types of institutional liabilities are devised to provide monetary services.

The most common definition of money includes all liabilities of financial institutions and the government (assets of their household and business owners) that can be used as a medium of exchange. This concept has usually been labeled M-1, and it is measured as the total of currency, most deposits which can be transferred by check, and travelers checks. (It excludes deposits held by the U.S. government, depository and foreign official institutions, and other

TABLE 6.1   **Measures of Money and Liquid Assets**

Aggregate	Component	Amount in billions of dollars (not seasonally adjusted) January 1981	
M-1A		372.8	
	Currency		116.6
	Demand deposits*		256.2
M-1B		416.1	
	M-1A		372.8
	Other checkable deposits†		43.3
M-2		1,683.0	
	M-1B		416.1
	Overnight repurchase agreements (RPs) issued by commercial banks		27.8
	Overnight Eurodollar deposits held by U.S. nonbank residents at Caribbean branches of U.S. banks		5.1
	Money market mutual fund shares		80.1
	Savings deposits at all depositary institutions		379.2
	Small time deposits at all depositary institutions‡		777.1
	M-2 consolidation component§		−3.0
M-3		1,972.7	
	M-2		1,683.0
	Large time deposits at all depositary institutions‖		257.9
	Term RPs issued by commercial banks		25.6
	Term RPs issued by savings and loan associations		6.2
L		2,337.3	
	M-3		1,972.7
	Other Eurodollars of U.S. residents other than bank		34.5
	Bankers acceptances		27.6
	Commercial paper		97.1
	Savings bonds		80.0
	Liquid Treasury obligations		125.4

NOTE: Components of M-2, M-3, and L measures generally exclude amounts held by domestic depositary institutions, foreign commercial banks and official institutions, the U.S. government (including the Federal Reserve), and money-market mutual funds. Exceptions are bankers' acceptances and commercial paper for which data sources permit the removal only of amounts held by money-market mutual funds and, in the case of bankers' acceptances, amounts held by accepting banks, the Federal Reserve, and the Federal Home Loan Bank System.

* Net of demand deposits due to foreign commercial banks and official institutions.

† Includes negotiable orders of withdrawal (NOW), automated transfer services (ATS), and credit union share draft-balances and demand deposits at thrift institutions.

‡ Time deposits issued in denominations of less than $100,000.

§ In order to avoid double-counting of some deposits in M-2, those demand deposits owned by thrift institutions (a component of M-1B) which are estimated to be used for servicing their savings and small time deposit liabilities in M-2 are removed.

‖ Time deposits issued in denominations of $100,000 or more.

Each higher measure of money adds more classes of deposits to the previous one. Most additions have less liquidity, but the placements of others are based on the availability of current data.

minor categories.) The table shows *M*-1 ($416.1 billion) divided into *M*-1*A* plus additional components. The two together are labeled *M*-1*B*. This dual definition was an interim step used by the Federal Reserve to broaden the *M*-1 measure. Until the late 1970s, commercial banks had a virtual monopoly on furnishing the medium of exchange that supplements currency. When savings and loans and other thrift institutions began issuing checkable deposits and with the increased use of travelers checks, the methods of measuring *M*-1 had to be revised. While efforts were made to maintain comparability, it is necessary for some analytical purposes to differentiate between *M*-1*A* and *M*-1*B*, since each has been used in policy making.

In the table, *M*-1*A* consists of currency plus commercial bank **demand deposits**—deposits payable immediately and which can be transferred by check. In 1980 this category was reduced by subtracting out deposits held by foreign banks and institutions. At the same time, other checkable deposits were added to yield *M*-1*B*. In 1981 travelers checks were included because of their growing importance as a medium of exchange. Such additions and subtractions call attention to the somewhat arbitrary nature of the actions that must be taken in attempting to measure the analytical concept of money. In the table, *M*-1 does not include credit cards, which in most cases are a more satisfactory medium of exchange than a $100 bill or a personal check. Another major exclusion is that of most deposits denominated in U.S. dollars held at banks in other countries (Eurodollars). When we consider an open economy in Part 6, we shall find that these deposits can influence spending in the U.S. in a manner similar to those items now included in the *M*-1 measure of money.

Each higher order definition of money adds components to the preceding one. *M*-2 shows the greatest differences, in both size and concept. It is almost four times as large as *M*-1, and adds two separate types of accounts. The first group consists of repurchase agreements (RPs, which are overnight loans to banks, arranged in the form of sales and repurchases of bank assets to their customers), a minor share of Eurodollar deposits, and money-market mutual funds. These all are similar to other checkable deposits, and many economists feel that they should be included in *M*-1.

The second group, saving and small time deposits, is quite different. Before they can be used as a medium of exchange, they must first be converted into cash or checking deposits. While this requirement could be onerous, in fact it is usually simple; your bank or S and L (savings and loan association) will be happy to arrange for automatic transfers of savings accounts to demand deposits. Other accounts require only slightly more effort. Therefore, many owners of such deposits consider them to be as liquid as those payable on demand. Furthermore, they have the added benefit of paying interest to their owners, which is true of only some checkable deposits.

The final two measures, *M*-3 and *L,* add other assets whose liquidity is somewhat less. While they may be equivalent to the other forms of money for corporations and for the very wealthy, they are not for most individuals. However, since they are money equivalents for those who spend the most, these concepts may have impacts as important as those of the previous measures.

DIFFERENCES IN GROWTH RATES

Table 6.2 shows that the growth rate of money differs considerably depending on how money is defined. Even though higher numbered measures contain the lower ones, some growth rates may exceed others over the period of a year by as much as several hundred percent. For example, look at 1969–70, 1974–75, 1976–77, and the quarterly data. In some cases, even the direction of growth differs. Some measures show growth declining even as others show an acceleration. For example, the growth rate of M-1 increased in 1971–72 as well as in 1976–77, while the growth rate of M-2 declined in those periods. Was money acting to expand or to contract demand? Depending on which measure the Federal Reserve used as a guide, its actions in any given quarter could have been completely different. Not infrequently one money concept may be signaling the need to contract the money supply just when others are indicating that an expansion is called for.

When examining the economic outlook in May 1979, Allan Meltzer (ten years after his earlier statement quoted) wrote:

> Current monetary statistics may indicate the economy is headed toward a major recession, a mild recession, or perhaps no recession at all. The

TABLE 6.2   **Annual Rates of Monetary Growth**
                    (percent)

Year	M-1	M-2	M-3
1969	3.8	4.2	1.5
1970	4.8	5.8	8.9
1971	6.6	13.5	14.8
1972	8.5	12.9	14.0
1973	5.7	7.3	11.7
1974	4.7	6.0	8.7
1975	4.7	12.3	9.4
1976	5.5	13.7	11.4
1977	7.7	11.5	12.6
1978	7.4	8.4	11.3
1979	5.0	9.0	9.8
1980	5.0	9.8	9.9
Annual rates in quarter			
1980–1:Q1	4.8	7.2	7.8
1980–2:Q2	−3.9	5.5	5.7
1980–3:Q3	11.0	15.5	12.6
1980–4:Q4	8.4	9.3	12.3

SOURCE: Federal Reserve Bulletin.

Each measure of money grows at quite a different rate from the others. Variations are greater over short periods, but may be significantly different for several years.

numbers that could give more accurate information cannot be separated from available financial data.[2]

To those who consider money only one among many variables influencing the economy, such differences are to be expected. They do not believe that changes of 2 or 3 percent in money growth, particularly in quarterly periods, are either good measures of monetary policy or can be used to predict or control spending. Any quarter-to-quarter or even year-to-year movements in money require extensive analysis to be useful. Only occasionally can they be used by themselves to predict what will happen to demand or prices.

To those who believe that changes in money dominate economic activity, the facts that short-term fluctuations in money are large and that each definition of money differs in its rate of growth from all others are worrisome. If we cannot be sure what money is and how it is growing, how can it be controlled? If *M*-1 is rising while *M*-2 falls, should the Federal Reserve act to speed up or to curtail monetary expansion? Particularly if they lead to changes in expectations, any swings can create difficulties. To the extent that money measures are inadequate, movements in money are hard to diagnose and control.

Contrasted with those concerned over divergent short-term fluctuations of money measured in separate ways are others, like Milton Friedman, who have argued that differences in movements of various types of money are not likely to be significant. What does count are movements of money over longer periods and the assurance that it is being properly controlled. Stabilization of any one of the measures of money will achieve most of the benefits of good monetary policy. Over several years, money measures will move closer together. Losses due to inexact definitions and measures will be minor.

The Federal Reserve and the Monetary Process

Whichever measure or combination of measures is selected as the best guide to the money stock, the processes through which money is created and controlled are similar. Three main actors determine how much money is available for spending.

1. The Federal Reserve determines the monetary base, that is, the amount of high-powered money in existence.
2. Depository institutions, primarily commercial banks, issue deposits to the public in accordance with the amount of high-powered money made available to them, their legal requirements, and their profit and operating possibilities.
3. The public, in its turn, decides whether to hold currency, demand deposits, or other types of assets which function as money.

The interactions of these three determine the amount of money and its influence on spending. At one extreme, each dollar of currency uses a dollar of

2. *The Wall Street Journal,* 9 May 1979.

the monetary base; at the other, travelers checks and money-market funds require no specific use of reserves. In between, deposits vary in their use of the base depending on their type and location. Shifts in components of the money stock which use different amounts of the base can cause variations in monetary growth as large as those caused by changes in the amount of high-powered money.

THE MONETARY BASE IS THE FOUNDATION

The monetary base is the foundation of the monetary system. It is called high-powered money because it includes the reserves which institutions need to create additional money. Among other provisions under the Financial Institutions Deregulation Act of 1980, every institution that issues deposits against which checks can be written—including commercial banks, savings banks, saving and loan associations, and credit unions—must hold *required* or *legal reserves* equal to a percentage of each dollar of its deposits. The required percentage varies with the size of the institution and type of deposit. The reserve requirements can be met either by holding cash in the vault or by deposits in the Federal Reserve. (To avoid listing all institutions able to issue checkable deposits every time we refer to them, from here on we generally use the generic term *banks*.) A unique feature of high-powered money is that it consists of the debts of the government upon which no interest is paid. The monetary base can be created in unlimited amounts by printing currency (Federal Reserve notes) or by issuing deposits from the Federal Reserve to banks. When the Federal Reserve alters the amount of high-powered money, it sets in motion movements in the money supply, credit, and interest rates. Such actions are the heart of monetary policy. A change in the base alters either currency or the assets of banks which serve as their required reserves. While the public and banks can alter the relationship between the monetary base and money, the Federal Reserve can offset, with sufficient time, their actions by speeding up or slowing down the rate at which it adjusts the base.

THE COMPOSITION OF THE MONETARY BASE

The size of the monetary base depends almost entirely on the assets and liabilities of the Federal Reserve. Until 1914, the Treasury was the monetary authority. The passage of the Federal Reserve Act and the establishment of a central bank took the responsibility for monetary policy away from the Treasury. While it retains the right to issue coins and some currency and to buy and sell gold and foreign currencies, the results of the Treasury's actions on the base are minor. Its actions are among the many factors which the Federal Reserve considers when it decides whether and how to expand or contract its balance sheet.

Table 6.3 shows a combined balance sheet of the monetary authorities. One side lists the sources and the other the uses of the monetary base. Most important by far are the holdings of U.S. securities ($128.2 billion) purchased

TABLE 6.3   **Factors Influencing The Monetary Base, January 1981**
(billions of dollars)

Sources		Uses		
Federal Reserve credit		Reserves of banks		44.6
U.S. government securities	128.2	Deposits at Fed	31.8	
Loans (discounts)	1.4	Vault cash	12.8	
Float plus other Fed assets	13.1			
Subtotal Federal Reserve credit	142.7	Currency held by public		115.8
Treasury deposits at Fed	−3.2			
Gold stock, treasury currency, other	20.9			
Monetary base	160.4			
				160.4

SOURCE: Federal Reserve Bulletin.

The Federal Reserve controls the total size of the monetary base by open-market purchases or sales of securities. They add to or offset movements in all other categories to insure that bank reserves follow an agreed-upon path.

by the Fed in open-market operations. But there are other major sources. Member banks borrow (rediscount) from the Fed; their loans ($1.4 billion) are an asset of the Fed, and the credit to their account at the Fed becomes a source of reserves. Float, an important item, fluctuates a great deal on a day-to-day basis. Float arises when the Fed credits reserves to a bank which deposits a check for collection before the account of the paying bank is reduced. The Fed daily grants several billions of advance credit to banks in this form. When the volume of checks increases or bad weather delays collections, the amount of float can balloon. The three items—holdings of securities, loans, and float—equal outstanding Federal Reserve credit.

The Treasury issues gold certificates, coins, some forms of currency, and similar liabilities ($20.9 billion) primarily to the Federal Reserve, but in some cases directly to the public. As these shift, they alter the level of the monetary base. Most changes in Treasury issues reflect the gold it holds. In early periods, changes in the U.S. gold stock were a significant cause of movements in the monetary base. Until the 1960s, the expansion of the base was limited by the amount of gold held.

On the other hand, the Treasury also holds deposits at the Fed. These are Federal Reserve liabilities and should be shown, by accounting convention, on the right side of the balance sheet. But since they reduce rather than expand the base, for convenience they are shown as a negative entry on the left side of Table 6.3. Other minor assets of the Fed are also a base source.

Currency in the hands of the public ($115.8 billion) is by far the largest use of the base. The remainder of high-powered money serves as the reserves of member banks ($44.6 billion). Most of this latter category consists of deposits at the Fed, although vault cash in member banks is also counted as part of their reserves.

OPEN-MARKET OPERATIONS

Because most legal reserves must be held as deposits at the Federal Reserve, the Fed can modify the ability of banks to issue deposits by controlling the size of their accounts. The process of monetary expansion or contraction begins when the Federal Reserve increases (or decreases) the monetary base through its *open-market operations.* These operations consist of purchases (or sales) of government securities (and foreign currencies). When the Federal Reserve buys securities in the market, it pays for them with its own check (or newly printed currency). The checks are deposited at banks which, in turn, deposit them in their accounts at the Federal Reserve. The Fed has a new asset—the bond it bought—and a new liability—the deposit it owes the commercial bank. The transaction directly increases the reserves of banks.

Because reserves, as the base for an expansion of deposits, are the heart of the monetary system, most open-market operations aim at their control. The Fed daily estimates how reserves will be affected by changes in all factors (including seasonal fluctuations in the demand for currency) except its own security holdings. These other movements, called technical changes, cause fluctuations of billions of dollars a week in bank reserves. However, the Fed offsets them almost automatically by purchases or sales of securities. In fact, when we speak of open-market operations, we normally ignore those conducted for technical (also called defensive) reasons. Excluding the technical operations, an open-market purchase of government securities does at least three things:

1. By increasing demand for them, it raises the price and therefore lowers the interest rate on government securities.
2. It increases the reserves of banks, allowing them to expand their deposits, which they do through purchases of additional securities and making more loans.
3. It lowers the federal funds rate. The *federal funds rate* is the interest rate charged by financial institutions for lending reserves to each other, primarily on an overnight basis. It varies with the amount of excess reserves held by individual banks. The federal funds rate is one of the most sensitive and significant of all short-term interest rates.

Purchase of a security by the Fed immediately affects both the amount of bank reserves and short-term interest-rates. One of the disputed issues of monetary policy concerns whether the Fed should use reserves or a measure of money or a measure of interest rates as a target or variable to decide when to start and when to halt open-market operations.

How Commercial Banks Expand Deposits and Create Money

When the Federal Reserve enlarges the monetary base, why and how do banks increase their deposits and the money supply? The simple answer is that banks can raise their profits by utilizing their added reserves as a base upon which to expand their earning assets and liabilities. In normal circumstances, the more banks can expand their investments and loans, the better off they are.

THE SIMPLE DEPOSIT MULTIPLIER

The main restriction on the growth of deposits in the banking system is the **reserve requirement,** the amount of legal reserves that banks must hold. It is established by law and regulation as a specific percent of each type of deposit. Before the Monetary Control Act of 1980 (Public Law 96-221) was passed, Federal Reserve member banks were required to hold varying percentages of reserves against 12 categories of deposits, while nonmember deposit institutions had no required reserves at the Fed. The new law established the reserve requirements shown in Table 6.4. However, the law also provides an eight-year phase-in period. Until 1989 required reserves will continue to vary depending on whether an institution was a member or nonmember bank when the act was passed.

The total deposit expansion of banks is limited to a multiple of their increased reserves. The **deposit multiplier *(kD)*** is the ratio by which deposits

TABLE 6.4   **Reserve Requirements**
(percent)

Type of deposit and deposit interval	Final after phase-in	Range within which Federal Reserve can vary requirement[†]
Net transaction accounts*		
$0 to $25 million	3	———
Over $25 million	12	8–14
Nonpersonal time deposits by original maturity		
Less than four years	3	0–9
Four years and over	0	0–9
Eurocurrency liabilities		
All types	3	0–9
Supplementary reserves	0	0–4

  * Transaction accounts include all subject to payments to third parties.
  † The Federal Reserve can set other requirements for 180 days in emergencies.

Reserve requirements are being simplified and applied to all deposit institutions. The table shows the legal requirements that will be in place by 1989. A partial phasing-in takes place each year.

expand as a result of an increase in total bank reserves (ΔRT) due to an expansion of the monetary base. To understand the process of deposit expansion, we start with the simple deposit multiplier, which assumes that all reserves are used for demand deposits and deposits expand to the maximum. It is the inverse of the ratio of required reserves. Actual expansion of deposits depends on the degree to which growth in the base increases reserves and on the types of deposits issued.

Any increase in deposits (ΔD) raises the amount of required reserves. The maximum expansion or multiplication of deposits from an increase in the monetary base occurs when the added amount of reserves required equals the change in the total reserves (ΔRT). The amount of increase in required reserves (ΔRR) depends on the percent reserve requirement (rd) against each dollar of deposits. An increase of $500 billion in deposits requires $100 billion added reserves if the reserve requirement percentage is 20 percent.

$$\Delta RR = rd(\Delta D) \qquad \Delta RR = .2(500) \tag{6.1}$$
$$\Delta RR = 100.$$

Since, at a maximum expansion, the change in required reserves equals the change in the total reserves made available by the expansion of the monetary base, one can be substituted for the other in equation (6.1). The deposit multiplier (kD) will be the change in deposits over the change in added total reserves, or one over the percent reserve requirement:

$$kD = \frac{\Delta D}{\Delta RR} = \frac{\Delta D}{\Delta RT} = \frac{1}{rd} \qquad kD = \frac{500}{100} = \frac{500}{100} = \frac{1}{.2} = 5. \tag{6.2}$$

Thus, the 20 percent reserve requirement gives a deposit multiplier of 5.

THE PROCESS OF BANK DEPOSIT EXPANSION

An increase in the monetary base creates *excess reserves (RE)* in the hands of banks. These are reserves over and above the banks' legal or required reserves. To utilize them, the banks expand their deposits. When banks are again loaned up, the new reserves are no longer excess; they are supporting the added deposits. To see how this expansion comes about, let us look at a simplified balance sheet which shows added reserves and deposits for the banking system (Figure 6.1). Assume that the Federal Reserve buys an additional $100 million of government securities in the market. To pay for the bonds, the Fed issues $100 million of its own checks to government bond dealers. The dealers deposit these checks in their commercial bank-accounts. Their claims against the banks expand. To collect what is owed them, banks send the checks to the Fed for payment. The Fed credits the accounts of the banks on the Fed's books with the $100 million. The banks' deposits (reserves) at the Fed are increased by the full amount.

FIGURE 6.1   **Expansion of Deposits as a Result of Federal Reserve Open Market Operations**
(millions of dollars)

Federal Reserve				Commercial banks			
Assets		Liabilities		Assets		Liabilities	
U.S. government securities	100	Commercial bank deposits (reserves)	100	Deposits at Fed	100	Deposits	100
				Required reserves	20		
				Excess reserves	80		
				Total assets	100	Total liabilities	100

The Federal Reserve alters the monetary base and the deposits banks hold with it by purchasing securities in the open market. The economy must hold the expanded monetary base (the Fed's liabilities) in the form of either bank reserves or currency.

After the first round of events, Federal Reserve holdings of government securities have grown by $100 million. Its debts to member banks have expanded by the same amount. In the combined statement for commercial banks, note that this increase in their reserves at the Fed is an increase in their assets. Their additional assets are balanced by an increase in outstanding deposit liabilities of $100 million. Assume also that the percent of deposits which banks are required to maintain as reserves (their percent reserve-requirement) is 20 percent. Since the public's deposits are up by $100 million, the banks' required reserves are $20 million more; they have $80 million in excess reserves. This information is shown in Figure 6.1 by the boxed supplementary breakdown of the banks' reserves.

Since excess reserves yield no return, banks would prefer to replace them with earning assets. Assume that they decide to use the extra $80 million in reserves to buy bonds. They pay the public for the bonds with their checks. After the public has deposited these checks in their own banks and all have cleared through the Fed, the situation is that shown in Figure 6.2. The balance sheet of the Fed is not presented because it has not changed. The particular banks that hold reserves may switch, but the total assets and liabilities of the Fed stay constant until it undertakes its next open-market operation.

But what does Figure 6.2 show has happened to the commercial banks? Their balance sheets have grown. They now owe $180 million in deposits—the $100 million deposited in stage one plus the $80 million paid out to buy bonds at this second stage. Their assets include the $80 million in bonds and the $100 million owed them by the Fed. Now, however, their required reserves are $36 million (180 x .20) and their excess reserves have dropped to $64 million.

Since they still have excess reserves, the banks can again expand their assets. Suppose that they buy mortgages or make loans of that amount. The

FIGURE 6.2 **Expansion of Deposits**
(millions of dollars)

	Commercial banks		
Assets		**Liabilities**	
Bonds	80	Deposits	180
Deposits at Fed	100		
Required reserves	36		
Excess reserves	64		
Second stage Total assets	180	Total liabilities	180
Bonds	80	Deposits	244
Loans	64		
Deposits at Fed	100		
Required reserves	48.8		
Excess reserves	51.2		
Third stage Total assets	244	Total liabilities	244
Bonds	100	Deposits	292.8
Loans	92.8		
Deposits at Fed	100		
Required reserves	58.56		
Excess reserves	41.44		
Fourth stage Total assets	292.8	Total liabilities	292.8
Loans and Securities	400	Deposits	500
Deposits at Fed	100		
Required reserves	100		
Final stage Total assets	500	Total liabilities	500

*Banks which receive new reserves expand their assets and liabilities (deposits)
by making loans and purchasing securities. The maximum expansion of
deposits equals the increase in reserves (less any leakage into currency) times
the deposit multiplier (kD).*

situation after their new loans or purchases is shown as stage 3. Their deposits
are $244 million, their securities and loans are $144 million, and their reserves
remain at $100 million. But the split of this total between required and excess
reserves has changed. Required reserves are now $48.8 million, while $51.2
million are still excess. Stage 4 shows another expansion, leading to $292.8
million in deposits and $41.44 million in excess reserves. It is easy to see that
this process will come to an end only when all excess reserves have been
utilized. This is the final stage in Figure 6.2. Deposits have been expanded by
$500 million; loans and investments are $400 million higher. The reserves at
the Fed remain at $100 million, but all are now required; excess reserves have
all been used. Because required reserves are 20 percent, the deposit multiplier,
or the amount deposits expand for each dollar of additional reserves, is 5.

ONE BANK COMPARED TO MANY

In showing how an increase in the base leads to a multiple expansion of deposits in the banking system, we have avoided the question of whether an individual bank can create deposits over and above its own excess reserves. At any step, banks lend only the excess reserves they hold. But as shown in the figure (and in any elementary economics text), all banks acting together bring about the same expansion as if there were a single monopoly bank which could immediately create the $500 million in deposits for $100 million in added reserves. The example tells us nothing about how the expansion is distributed among individual banks. Which banks end up with more deposits depends on the competition among them and on the tastes of the public. The multiple expansion takes place and the fractional reserve system works because all banks are required to hold their legal reserves at the central bank. No leakages occur from the reserve base. All reserves are available to support the expansion of deposits. If leakages did occur, however, the Fed could offset them by defensive operations.

Control of the Money Stock

The monetary process depends on how much high-powered money (M-0) is created by the Federal Reserve, on how financial institutions utilize the monetary base to create liabilities, and on the degree to which the public treats the institutions' liabilities as money. If the Federal Reserve could control the money stock directly, many problems related to equilibrium in the market for money and financial assets would not arise. Unfortunately, the actual process is more complex. Control of the money supply is indirect. To understand how money is controlled, we must recognize that fluctuations occur in the *money multiplier (kM)*, which is the relationship between money and the monetary base.[3]

$$kM = \frac{M\text{-}1}{MB} \qquad\qquad \textbf{6.3}$$

In effect, three different forces are at work shifting the money multiplier:

1. The money supply consists of separate components, each with a different reserve requirement. For example, demand deposits in all banks are part of the money supply, but until 1989 reserve requirements will differ among

---

3. There will be a different money multiplier for each definition of money, since reserves vary by type of deposit. Thus: $\dfrac{M\text{-}1}{MB} \neq \dfrac{M\text{-}2}{MB}$. Appendix 6.1 contains a technical discussion of how and why changes in the growth rates of reserves differ from those of money.

classes of banks. When deposits move from one bank to another, the relationship between the base and *M*-1 will shift. Or, the public may decide to hold a smaller share of money in the form of currency and a larger share in demand deposits. When funds leave savings deposits to go to the money market, reserves that supported the savings deposits are freed. Demand deposits can expand. Because required reserves against demand deposits are higher than those against saving deposits, money supply *M*-1 grows, but money-supply *M*-2 contracts.

2. Banks may decide to hold more or fewer excess reserves. An increase in excess reserves lowers the money multiplier.

3. The public alters its concept of what it uses as money. It might add travelers' checks, credit cards, and bank repurchase-agreements (overnight loans to banks) to what it considers as money. Even though money as measured does not appear to change, the money which affects spending decisions does.

Most studies of the money supply have been concerned with changes of the first two types. During the 1930s and after World War II, excess reserves seemed to be a critical problem. The Fed feared that their large volume would interfere with control of money and credit and, therefore, that they threatened to cause inflation. However, since 1965, with improvements in money markets and higher nominal interest rates, net excess reserves have been uncommon.

INSTRUMENTS AND TARGETS

The Constitution grants Congress the right "to coin money [and] regulate the value thereof." For many purposes, this power has been delegated to the Federal Reserve. To control the amount of money, the Federal Reserve must

FIGURE 6.3   **Monetary Instruments and Targets**

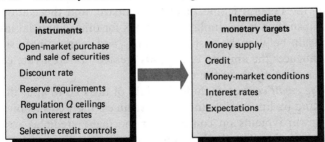

The Federal Reserve has direct control over its instruments but only partial control over its targets. It selects the targets it believes are most closely related to ultimate policy goals. The arrow shows targets altering in response to changed instrument. Which target is best and how closely it should be tracked remain unsettled issues.

determine what money is and measure it properly. A three-step process is involved: (1) A decision must be reached as to what constitutes money, (2) the Federal Reserve must set targets as to the desired amount of growth in money, (3) the Federal Reserve must operate through its instruments in such a way as to hit its targets.

Figure 6.3 illustrates the targets and instruments the Fed has available. *Monetary targets* consists of variables influenced by Federal Reserve actions which in turn have a direct effect on aggregate demand. The Fed selects targets in an attempt to measure the impact of its operations on spending. The arrow reflects the fact that the values of targets change when the Federal Reserve alters its instruments, although they are also affected by the reactions of the public and financial institutions.

Instruments include regulations and operations which the Federal Reserve controls. The chief instrument is *open-market operations,* which are used to alter Federal Reserve credit and the monetary base. The Fed engages in such operations almost daily. The remaining instruments are used only occasionally, and then usually for special purposes.

The Federal Reserve's *discount rate* is the interest it charges banks on money it loans to them. They borrow in order to obtain more reserves if they do not have enough to meet their reserve requirements. The discount rate gains its prominence because the Fed sometimes signals major policy changes by moving the rate. However, while it frequently makes the headlines, the influence of the discount rate on actual operations is slight. Borrowed reserves, which equal the loans to which the rate applies, rarely rise as high as 2 percent of the monetary base.

Another instrument is the right of the Fed to change *legal reserve requirements,* thereby altering the amount of reserves banks are required to hold behind deposits. A change in required reserves directly shifts the money multiplier.

Through *Regulation Q,* the Fed sets the maximum legal interest rates which member banks can pay on deposits. The Federal Deposit Insurance Corporation, the Federal Home Loan Bank Board, and the National Credit Union Administration have similar regulations for other financial institutions. The relationship between interest-rate ceilings and market interest rates significantly influences the amount of deposits created. Interest-rate ceilings are in the process of being phased out.

Selective credit controls include the right of the Fed to alter the terms or costs of lending by financial institutions. At times, the Fed has increased the minimum downpayments on consumer or mortgage credit as well as their repayment terms. In 1980, the Fed raised by 15 percent the cost of borrowed money used to fund additional extensions of consumer credit. This was done by requiring that if an institution's consumer credit exceeded the amount the lender had outstanding in a base period, non-interest-bearing reserves equal to 15 percent of the expansion had to be deposited at the Fed.

The Federal Reserve changes its operations and instruments in order to achieve, insofar as possible, agreed-upon monetary targets. As shown in the diagram, only one of the actual targets is the money supply. The other possible targets have been, and are, used because of the difficulties of agreeing on how to measure money.

AN OPERATIONAL DEFINITION OF MONEY

The Fed attempts to find a monetary target whose growth will have a predictable impact on aggregate demand. Growth in money should help to achieve the desired level of income and prices. However, an agreement is necessary as to the operational definition of the target which the Fed tries to hit. The difficulty of measuring and controlling money increases when people change their minds about what they use as money. Such shifts occur both because of technical developments among financial institutions and because innovations become profitable if money is tight. For monetary policy to control the money stock, a decision must first be made as to what assets are included in money; then a statistical measurement system must be devised. If all lists of assets which could be considered as money moved together, no problem would exist. But, as Table 6.2 made clear, they do not do so. Variations in growth using different specific definitions of money are as great as or greater than variations in the spending they influence.

Controlling a specific list of assets will be useful only if it is highly correlated in its movements with actual money—that which spending units consider in making their decisions. Another way of making the same point is to say that money is that which serves the public as such. Theories explain how money influences spending desires. What must be measured are those assets which affect spending through their monetary attributes. If for institutional or other reasons the list changes, so, in effect, does money. This view—that money is what money does—was well enunciated by Milton Friedman and Anna Schwartz:

> We conclude that the definition of money is to be sought not on the grounds of principle, but on grounds of usefulness in organizing our knowledge of economic relationships.... a definition that will enable us most readily and accurately to predict the consequences for important economic variables of a change in conditions of demand for or supply of money.[4]

Friedman and Schwartz propose that an operational definition of money be those liquid assets that maintain a "dependable and reproducible" relationship with national income. This concept, however, can cause severe difficulties in the control of money. When should the Fed change the measure of money it is using for policy purposes? Who should decide that what is money has shifted? How can the new measure of money be inserted into the spending and demand models in order to decide what is the proper amount of money to create?

4. M. Friedman and A. Schwartz, *Monetary Statistics of the United States* (New York: National Bureau of Economic Research, 1970), pp. 137–89.

Targeting Monetary Operations

Within the Federal Reserve, decisions are formulated by the Board of Governors and by the 12-member Federal Open Market Committee (FOMC), which consists of the seven members of the Reserve Board plus a rotating 5 of the 12 presidents of the Federal Reserve District Banks. The FOMC selects the path it would like the monetary targets to follow.

When the Fed changes its instruments by buying securities or changing reserve requirements, it cannot be sure how spending will be affected. The ultimate result depends on how the public and financial institutions translate the Fed's operations into changes in money and interest rates. It is not the Fed's holding of securities that primarily influences spending; it is how the public uses the base to change its monetary assets. Because the lags between the Fed's operations and changes in spending may be both erratic and long, if operations were conducted only in terms of spending, they might bring about a constant cycling, as actions to change reserves always undershoot or overshoot the long-run desired impact. By concentrating on targets or longer-run movements in money, greater stability can be introduced into the system. The best monetary target is the one through which the Federal Reserve can best achieve its ultimate objectives:

> Which total or totals best satisfy that requirement depends in turn on (1) how accurately the total can be measured; (2) how precisely, and at what costs, including unwanted side effects, the Fed can control the total; and (3) how closely and reliably changes in the total are related to the ultimate policy objective.[5]

THE SELECTION OF MONETARY AGGREGATES AS A TARGET

The Federal Reserve began in 1970 to plan its operations with the objective of controlling specifically the rate of growth of monetary aggregates.[6] This shift to a system of monetary targeting was reinforced by a joint resolution of Congress in 1975 and became law in the Federal Reserve Reform Act of 1977 (Public Law 95-188). Section 2A of that law states;

> The Board of Governors of the Federal Reserve System and the Federal Open Market Committee shall maintain long-run growth of the monetary and credit aggregates commensurate with the economy's long-run potential to increase production, so as to promote effectively the goals of maximum employment, stable prices, and moderate long-term interest rates. The Board of Governors shall consult with Congress at semi-annual hearings ... about the Board of Governors' and the Federal Open Market Committee's objectives and plans with respect to the ranges of growth or diminution of monetary and credit aggregates for the upcoming twelve months, taking account of past and prospective developments in production, employment, and prices. Nothing in this Act shall be interpreted to require

5. "Operating Guides in U.S. Monetary Policy: A Historical Review," *Federal Reserve Bulletin* (September 1979):686.

6. See S. J. Maisel, *Managing the Dollar* (New York: Norton, 1973), Chapter 10.

that such ranges of growth or diminution be achieved if the Board of Governors and the Federal Open Market Committee determine that they cannot or should not be achieved because of changing conditions.

The Humphrey-Hawkins Act of 1978 (Public Law 95-523) continues the emphasis on monetary targets but sets a somewhat conflicting goal. It requires biannual reports on how the 12-month target-tracks of monetary and credit aggregates relate to the "short-term goals set forth in the most recent *Economic Report of the President.*" Under the laws, the FOMC periodically picks a monetary target for the next year. For example, as the minutes of the FOMC meeting (the policy record) of February 2–3, 1981, show

> [t]he Committee adopted the following ranges for growth in monetary aggregates for the period from the fourth quarter of 1980 to the fourth quarter of 1981, abstracting from the impact of introduction of NOW accounts on a nationwide basis: M-$1A$, 3 to $5\frac{1}{2}$ percent; M-$1B$, $3\frac{1}{2}$ to 6 percent; M-2, 6 to 9 percent; and M-3, $6\frac{1}{2}$ to $9\frac{1}{2}$ percent. The associated range for bank credits is 6 to 9 percent.

These targets may be revised as new data on the economy and monetary growth are received.

This shift to a system of monetary targets was a major victory for those who felt that movements in money were the critical determinants of spending and prices. However, problems of implementing the new procedures have been so great that controversies remain nearly as acute as they were before the new techniques were adopted.

FEDERAL RESERVE OPERATIONS

Because the Federal Reserve controls only the monetary base and not the money supply, it must plan its operations with two objectives: (1) to determine the monetary base and (2) to influence or react to movements in the money multiplier. Appendix 6.1 shows that the money multiplier depends on the desires of banks to issue deposits and to hold excess reserves, and on the public's desires to hold currency or different types of deposits. Until 1979 the Fed attempted to control both the monetary base and the multiplier by shifting the federal funds rate. In 1979 it adopted a new technique under which, in order to control the monetary aggregates, it altered reserves available to banks on a daily and weekly basis.

How does the system work? The FOMC picks a monetary target for the year. It then meets monthly (or more often if necessary) to outline a strategy for hitting that target. In accordance with the committee's directives, purchases or sales are made by the manager of the open-market account in New York. The Board of Governors of the Federal Reserve System meets weekly (or more often) to check progress and to decide whether or not to use the other instruments as a supplement to open-market operations.

The strategy calls for altering reserves on a daily or weekly basis in order to control the monetary base and the monetary aggregates. The manager of the open-market account is instructed to buy or sell securities so that reserves follow the desired path. Because unexpected movements in the federal funds rate are likely to indicate something amiss, the manager is also instructed to buy or sell securities if rates move beyond a rather broad band—say 3 to 6 percent—even if this means that the amount of reserves being furnished is not on the specified track.

Variations in the growth rates of reserves, the monetary base, and money are expected. For example, Table 6.6 in the appendix shows that from September to December 1979, reserves grew at an annual rate of 13.8 percent, the monetary base by 8.1 percent, and M-1 at 3.1 percent. Such differences arise because of varying reserve requirements and changes in the public's desire to hold currency compared to deposits.

ARE OPERATIONS THE PROBLEM?

The Federal Reserve's system of guiding operations and selecting targets has always been controversial. However, it should be recognized that even before the current techniques were adopted, the Fed was relatively successful in hitting its annual targets. Figure 6.4 shows a typical development of the money supply related to selected targets. The straight solid lines are the original growth-rate targets for the money stock *(M-1A)* chosen by the FOMC at the beginning of the year (3.5 to 6.0 percent). The dotted lines represent a revision from 2.25 to 4.75 percent made in mid-year to reflect a movement from demand deposits to NOW accounts not included in M-1A. The weekly-average line shows how erratic short-period changes are. However, much of the short-term movements arise merely from noise (errors) in the data. The 13-week moving average is smoother.

In this period, the Fed was criticized severely for not maintaining the growth rate within the target lines. However, as is typical, growth for the year was close to the target. For the final quarter, M-1A had increased 5 percent, compared to a 4.75 percent maximum target. Moreover, as the figures shows, by December, growth was below the midpoint of the target. The Federal Reserve believes that too much attention is paid to reported weekly and monthly fluctuations in the money supply. A large amount of such changes is due to measurement problems. In addition, lags in monetary demand and spending mean that wide fluctuations in interest rates would result if the monetary base were altered more sharply. The Fed believes that such erratic movements in interest rates would cause more difficulty in achieving spending goals than do the sharp short-run monetary movements.[7]

It is important to recognize that neither the targets nor operating procedures are frozen. The FOMC meets monthly to establish new two-month ranges for money growth and to reconsider both the annual targets and opera-

7. Federal Reserve, *Report to Congress on Monetary Policy Objectives for 1981*, February 25-26, 1981.

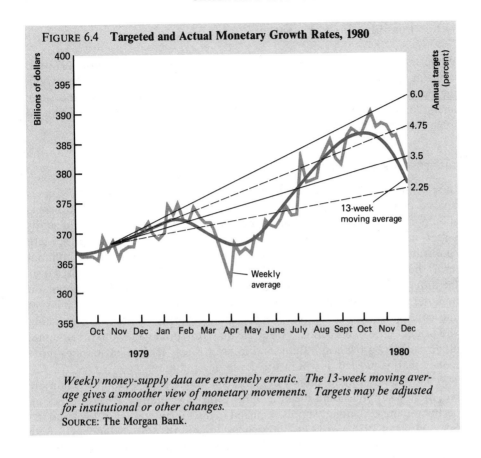

FIGURE 6.4   **Targeted and Actual Monetary Growth Rates, 1980**

Weekly money-supply data are extremely erratic. The 13-week moving average gives a smoother view of monetary movements. Targets may be adjusted for institutional or other changes.
SOURCE: The Morgan Bank.

tions. On the average of once during the year, the annual target has been adjusted slightly—usually one side of a range raised or lowered by half a percent. However, in November 1978, the entire goal was drastically shifted with the objective of raising interest rates to help support the exchange rate of the dollar. In October 1979, operating procedures were revamped, moving from the use of the federal funds rate to reserves as the day-to-day index of what was happening to the demand and supply of money. Such revisions in targets and operations come as a shock to the economy,but they should not be unexpected in an economic world that may undergo drastic changes. The controversies are really concerned with whether the targets chosen by the Federal Reserve are the best ones, whether the range selected is too large or too narrow, and the significance of the variations in the monthly and quarterly growth rates. To some, every squiggle in the line of growth is significant, even if it is later revised. To others, it is of minimal importance because the money which affects demand in any period is an average of past movements going back at least one or two years and because money is only one among many variables influencing demand.

Other Possible Monetary Targets

While the Federal Reserve was able to hit its targets in the period 1975–81, monetary policy was subject to tremendous criticism. No one was pleased with the performance of the economy. Inflation was too high; growth too slow; unemployment too high. Shouldn't the Federal Reserve have been able to solve these problems by creating money at the proper rate?

THE FEDERAL RESERVE'S DILEMMA

In selecting a proper monetary target, the Fed faces many difficulties. One is how to define and measure the money stock. Which of the many concepts should it use? Another question is whether the Federal Reserve should set its targets in terms of nominal or real growth. The instructions from Congress are confusing. Most monetarists are clear that targets should be set in nominal terms, but some other economists disagree strongly. The difficulty arises over the difference between the long and short run. The argument for targeting on nominal money is based on the belief that it is all the Fed can really measure and control. People determine the real money supply by adjusting spending and prices to the Fed's actions. Over the long run, prices adjust to the nominal money supply, growth in output, and interest rates. If the Fed supplies more money than is needed, it will insure continued inflation.

On the other hand, money demand is in real terms. Cutting back on the real money supply should mean a sharp drop in spending. Record-breaking declines in the real money supply occurred in the fourth quarter of 1974 and the first quarter of 1975 and 1979. Those who thought that the real money supply drove the economy feared that major contractions in spending would follow shortly. In fact, nominal demand continued to rise. Real demand rose rapidly in 1975 and slowly in 1979. The fact that demand did not contract means either that people changed what they were using as money or that their demand for money shifted. For these two reasons, some analysts feel that the Fed must supplement money with other intermediate targets.[8]

Keynes showed that interest rates play a critical role in investment and saving decisions. Changes in Fed operations affect interest rates and, therefore, the Fed could target its operations on them. A number of models show how changes in spending relate to movements in real interest rates. But for interest rates, as with the money supply, measurement problems interfere with theoretically attractive targets. Because the Fed cannot measure them, many feel that real interest rates are not a good target. In contrast, measuring changes in real money balances is not as dependent on expectations. Nominal money stock

8. The difficulty of picking a target is exacerbated by lack of agreement as to which is cause and which effect: Does more money cause more spending, or does more spending engender more money? See E. L. Feige and D. K. Pearce, "The Casual Causal Relationship between Money and Income: Some Caveats for Time Series Analysis," *The Review of Economics and Statistics* 61 (November 1979):521–33.

can be related to nominal spending, and both of these can be corrected to real terms by use of the same price index.

EXPECTATIONS AND CREDIT

Because measurements of real interest rates and money are difficult, other targets have been suggested and used. Two principal ones are expectations and credit availability. Both have had considerable theoretical support, and both have many advocates, especially in the Federal Reserve System. For example, the stringent monetary policies of 1979–81 were expressly stated to be an attempt to thwart the economy's inflationary expectations. Most analysts were convinced that the resulting drop in the real money stock and supply of credit would sharply curtail demand and bring about a recession or depression. Yet few observers—outside of labor and the real-estate industry—objected to the actions. Even those who in the past had advocated policies of steady growth in money applauded the Fed's action. They agreed that, given the inflationary situation, expectations rather than money was a proper target.

Those who advocate credit as a monetary target base their views on a different picture of demand than do those who choose the money supply. They emphasize the creation of demand which occurs when deposits are expanded and spending units are given a newly created ability to purchase. Such actions increase demand and income. In contrast, when credit is curtailed, demands cannot be financed, and output and income fall.

Those who emphasize money supply as a key target tend to believe that money's importance arises from its role as wealth and assets, which increase spending. Those who emphasize credit point out that it causes spending to shift directly because it increases the ability to make purchases. Deposits are created in order to be spent. When income expands, the new deposits may end up in the hands of unwilling holders. Until they can be spent, the holders are forced to save. Equilibrium will not be regained until income has expanded enough to make willing holders of the newly created deposits. In this view, the Fed's policies become effective primarily when they squeeze credit or, alternatively, expand it considerably. Growth in the money stock can fluctuate within several percentage points and still have only slight effects on demand. Monetary policy makes a difference primarily when money moves too far in either direction. Some of the most astute dealers in bonds and the money market based their actions on variants of the importance of credit theory. The Federal Reserve, in its policy directives and its reports to Congress, in fact does consider the growth rate of credit along with money as a target in determining operations.[9]

Both expectations and credit as targets have measurement problems as well. Indexes for expectations and availability are missing. Target values must be estimated from what is happening in the market. Which factors can analysts at the Fed measure best—expectations, availability, real interest rates, or nomi-

9. A. M. Wojnilower, "The Central Role of Credit Crunches in Recent Financial History," *Brookings Papers on Economic Activity* 80(2):277–340.

nal or real balances? Dedicated monetarists have no doubt as to the correct answer: Only the nominal money supply can be measured accurately.

MONETARY TARGETS, 1975-79

Some of the problems encountered by the Federal Reserve in following the monetary targets became evident in the period of expansion between the first quarter of 1975 and the end of 1979. This period can be characterized as one of inflation combined with expansions of real output which did not appear excessive. The inflation rate averaged over 6.5 percent during the period. The lowest rate of price increase was 4.7 percent in 1976. By 1979, prices were rising at an annual rate of over 10 percent. In contrast, in 1975 unemployment averaged 8.5 percent, while in the last year of the expansion, its rate was 5.8 percent.

The economic goals during this period were to slow the rate of inflation while closing the gap between potential and actual output. The gap was estimated to be well over $100 billion a year in 1975. In October–November 1978, another goal was introduced; action was taken to raise interest rates in order to halt the falling exchange rate for the dollar, which appeared to be approaching crisis levels. Foreign holders of dollars seemed to be dumping them out of fear that inflation was causing the value of the dollar to drop in comparison with other currencies they might buy. Government goals and policies remained somewhat equivocal because of a lack of agreement over the level of full employment and the optimum methods of fighting inflation, but one may conclude that from 1975 to 1978, the goals were to raise demand so that output would rise and unemployment fall. In mid-1978 the objective of policy was to slow growth in real output to 2 percent a year, while maintaining unemployment in the 6 to 6.5 percent range. It was assumed that if this amount of slack were maintained for several years, the inflation rate would gradually diminish.

POLICY TARGETS

Table 6.5 presents the annual targets for growth in M-1 and M-2 established by the FOMC at the start of each year. The table also shows the actual rates of growth for money in nominal and real (corrected by actual changes in the GNP deflator in the period) terms as well as for the nominal and real GNP. Observe that on the whole, the Fed succeeded in hitting its annual targets. In 1976 and 1979, the growth in M-2 was higher than targeted, but M-1 was in range. The opposite occurred in 1977. For the entire period, the growth in M-1 averaged about .5 percent above the midpoint of the target ranges.

What constituted money led to some debate, however. Should the Fed have been targeting on M-1 or M-2? For the period, M-2 grew 50 percent faster than M-1. However, in 1977 its rate was only 15 percent higher. In contrast, in 1976 it was 70 percent greater and in 1979 was again close to the average at 40 percent larger than M-1. Obviously, an analyst who believed in M-1 and who felt it was critical to control money quarter by quarter or even year by year during this period would come up with predictions quite different from those who followed *M*-2.

TABLE 6.5   **Monetary Targets and GNP Growth**
(percent)

Period Four quarters starting in	M-1*			M-2			GNP	
	Target	Actual		Target	Actual		Actual	
		Nominal	Real		Nominal	Real	Nominal	Real
1975:Q1	5–7	5.3	0.2	8.5–10.5	9.7	4.6	13.4	7.2
1976:Q1	4.5–7	6.25	1.0	7.5–10	11.0	6.75	9.5	4.1
1977:Q1	4.5–6.5	7.7	1.4	7–9.5	8.8	5.5	10.3	3.6
1978:Q1	4–6.5	4.9	−2.6	6.5–9	7.1	−0.4	13.7	4.7
1978:Q4	3–6	5.8	−3.3	5–8	8.3	−1.0	10.0	0.8

* The definitions of *M*-1 and *M*-2 are those in use prior to 1980.

Monetary targets are chosen to influence movements in the GNP. Although annual targets are hit quite well, the levels of real and nominal GNP frequently diverge from desired goals.

During the period, nominal interest rates were high by historical standards and rose to record heights. Real interest rates, before taxes, were in a normal range. As noted earlier real interest rates after taxes were probably negative. In any case, a belief arose that whatever targets were being followed were not succeeding in achieving the nation's goals. In mid-1979, inflation reached new highs. The dollar came under tremendous pressure. Gold prices were at record highs. There seemed to be a flight from money.

As a result, arguments were raised that neither the various measures of money nor those of interest rates were reflecting the underlying situation. Because expectations were that prices would continue to rise, it was argued that few were willing to hold money, and real interest rates were negative. The evidence was that credit availability remained high and borrowers were demanding all they could find.

In October 1979, the Fed seemed to agree with these arguments. It indicated that it had to reduce the real stock of money and raise nominal interest rates to new highs in order to dampen expectations and credit availability. Policy appeared to follow the views of those who had argued that other targets are as significant or that money measures are inexact and that measurement problems will always exist. Therefore, no single measure of money can be used. To understand how changes in the monetary base are affecting spending means taking into account changes in expectations, availability, interest rates, and the moneyness of different types of deposits. Use of information about all these factors leads to better decisions about the real money stock and the impact of monetary policy than does a single, unchanging measure of what must be an inherently oversimplified definition of money.

Summary

1. To explain the determination of demand and income, actions in the money markets must be combined with those for real goods. This chapter begins by explaining how money is created and controlled.

2. Money serves as a unit of account, a medium of exchange, a store of value, and a standard of deferred payments. To measure money, one must find which assets issued by the government and financial institutions can perform these functions and to what degree.

3. Money consists of currency and some portion of deposits and liquid assets which the public holds as a source of desired monetary services or as a supply of liquid assets which can be rapidly converted to purchasing power with a minimum cost or loss in value. Money defined as M-1 represents assets which can be used directly as a medium of exchange. The definitions M-2, M-3, and L add other assets which can serve some money functions. Because the public can shift what it uses as money among a large variety of assets, it is difficult to define or measure money exactly.

4. The amount of money created in a period depends on changes in the monetary base produced by the Federal Reserve and on the money multiplier determined by financial institutions and the public. Both what the public uses for money and the multiplier vary from period to period. If money can be measured properly, the Fed can, over a quarter or a half-year, alter the base so as to offset changes in the multiplier.

5. Banks and financial institutions can expand their deposits by increasing their assets through loans or purchases of securities. The ability of an individual bank to expand depends on the services and interest it pays depositors in competition with other institutions. The ability of the banking system to expand depends on its reserves (part of the monetary base) and the required reserve percentages behind each type of deposit, set by government regulation. In the absence of regulation, experience and estimates of possible reserve losses can determine what minimum reserves are safe.

6. The sources of the monetary base are primarily Federal Reserve holdings of securities and loans to banks (including float) plus Treasury holdings of gold and issues of currency, offset by Treasury and other noncommercial bank deposits at the Fed. The uses of the base are currency in circulation and bank deposits (reserves). The manager of the Fed's open-market account buys or sells government securities almost every day. Purchases and sales, under the direction of the Federal Open Market Committee, are made to control the

amount of bank reserves and the interest rate which banks charge each other for lending reserves overnight—the federal funds rate.

7. The Federal Reserve determines what daily operations to engage in by a procedure which aims at controlling the growth rate of a monetary target. Since 1970 this target has been a set of monetary aggregates. While monthly and quarterly movements in these variables have fluctuated above and below the desired ranges, the Fed has been able to hit its annual target rather well.

8. The lack of agreement on what is money, the independent movements of the separate money measures, and the divergence in theoretical opinions of what is important have led some observers to urge the Fed to use a broader list of targets. They would examine movements in money, interest rates, expectations, and credit availability and believe that the Fed should shift the range of money targets on the basis of the total information contained in all of these variables. Others disagree on the basis that money is the paramount factor in spending or that differences in money measures are comparatively unimportant over the long-run, or that the use of several related targets would reduce the accountability of the Fed for its actions. They urge that the Fed choose as a target a simple measure of money and stick with it.

Questions for Discussion and Review

1. Some countries have no legal reserve requirements. How would this affect monetary policy?

2. During the Russian civil war of 1918–20, czarist paper currency continued to circulate widely even after the czar's death, the dissolution of his government, and the disappearance of the country's gold reserves into Siberia. What insight does this incident give into the nature of money?

3. How does inflation affect the ability of money to perform the services associated with it?

4. What is meant by *liquidity?* What is the importance of this concept in defining the appropriate measure of the stock of money?

5. Define:
   a. Monetary base.
   b. Open-market operations.
   c. A technical change or adjustment.
   d. Federal funds rate.

6. If through an open-market operation $1 billion in new reserves is made available, and if the reserve requirement is 10 percent, what will be the increase in deposits?

7. Explain the apparent logic used in drawing up the five different measures (definitions) of money.

8. Why does the Fed use monetary targets—money, credit, etc.—instead of focusing directly on the impact of its instruments on aggregate demand?

9. What are the disadvantages of using rates of growth of the monetary aggregates as a target of monetary policy?

10. Discuss the problems the Fed faces in selecting a proper monetary target.

11. In what sense can the commercial banking system be said to "create money"?

12. What is the money multiplier, and what factors can cause it to vary? What are the implications of shifts in the money multiplier for the conduct of monetary policy?

13. What is the formula for the money multiplier in terms of the reserve and currency-deposit ratios? What is the effect on the money multiplier of a decline in the desire of the public to hold cash?

14. Suppose the money supply is $500 billion, currency held by the public is $50 billion, and reserves are $100 billion:
    a. What is the value of the money multiplier?
    b. If the monetary base and the ratio of deposits to reserves do not change while the amount of currency held by the public increases to $60 billion, what will be the value of the money supply?

References

Board of Governors of the Federal Reserve System. *The Federal Reserve System: Purposes and Functions,* 6th edition. Washington, D.C.: Government Printing Office 1974.

Cagan, P. "Financial Development and the Erosion of Monetary Controls." In *Contemporary Economic Problems, 1979,* edited by the American Enterprise Institute, pp. 117–52. Washington, D.C.: Government Printing Office 1979.

Duesenberry, J. S. *Money and Credit: Impact and Control,* 3rd edition. Englewood Cliffs, N.J.: Prentice-Hall, 1972.

Feige, E. L., and Pearce, D. K. "The Casual Causal Relationship between Money and Income: Some Caveats for Time Series Analysis." *Review of Economics and Statistics* 61 (November 1979):521–33.

Friedman, M., and Schwartz, A. *Monetary Statistics of the United States.* New York: National Bureau of Economic Research, 1970.

Laidler, D. E. W. *The Demand for Money,* 2nd edition. New York: Dunn-Donnelly, 1977.

Tobin, J. "Commercial Banks as Creators of Money." In *Banking and Monetary Studies,* edited by D. Carson. Homewood, Ill.: Irwin, 1963.

APPENDIX 6.1   The Money Multiplier

If the money multiplier (the relationship between changes in the monetary base and changes in a particular definition of money) were constant, the Federal

Reserve would have a much easier time controlling any definition of money which was picked as a target. Unfortunately, however, the money multiplier varies considerably. This is not obvious when one first looks at a table of multipliers. For example, the multiplier for *M-1A* in 1979 and 1980 moved between 2.33 and 2.46, which does not seem large. However, this is more than a 5 percent change in the multiplier, and 5 percent exceeds typical fluctuations in spending from its trend. Most observers would like to see far smaller fluctuations in money and spending.

In any quarter—or even a year—anywhere from 50 to 100 percent of the change in the money stock may be due to changes in the multiplier rather than in the monetary base. This does not create an insurmountable difficulty because, with time, the Federal Reserve can adjust the monetary base to offset any movements in the multiplier. It is, however, another in the chain of factors that cause some economists to distrust the money stock as the sole target for Federal Reserve action. They point out that the influence of money on spending, even with a proper target, will be affected by (a) noise or errors in measurement, (b) movements of the money multiplier, (c) changes in what the public uses for money, and (d) shifts in the demand for money.

SHIFTS IN THE MONEY MULTIPLIER

The Federal Reserve determines the monetary base *(MB)* by open-market operations. Each money multiplier, however, depends on how the banks and the public divide the base between currency and reserves, and what deposits financial institutions issue as a result of a change in their reserves. When the new reserve requirements for all deposit institutions are fully in place in 1989, the monetary base will have five uses:

1. Currency *(CU)*.
2. Reserves *(RR)* against transaction deposits *(DD)* in the money supply, set initially at 12 percent for deposits over $25 million and at 3 percent for those below $25 million.
3. Reserves against transaction deposits not in the money supply *(ODD)*; these are included with *DD* for reserve requirements.
4. Reserves against nonpersonal time deposits *(TD)*.
5. Excess reserves *(ER)*.

Each of these uses causes a difference in the money multiplier and in how much money results from a given increase in the monetary base. One cannot simply use a multiplier equation such as

$$kM \times MB = M\text{-}1 \qquad\qquad 6.3$$

to predict how much money will rise from a given increase in Federal Reserve operations. In some periods an addition of a billion dollars to the monetary base will lead to no expansion of the money supply for lags of one to several months. At other times, money may grow at a rate of 3 or 4 percent with no

FIGURE 6.5   **Changes in the Money Multipliers**
(compound annual rates)

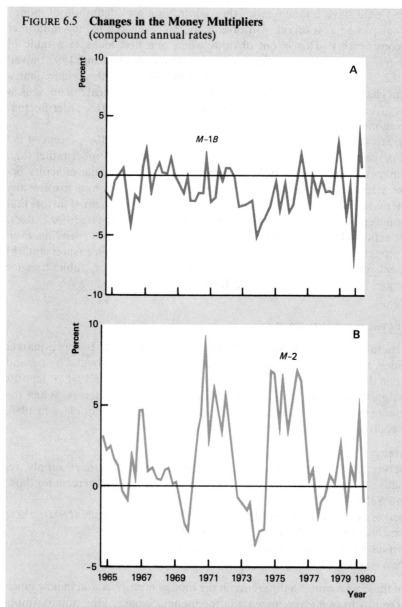

The chart records the quarter-to-quarter percent changes at annual rates in the money multipliers. The top shows the multiplier changes for M-1B

$$(\Delta kM\text{-}1B = \Delta\frac{M\text{-}1B}{MB}),$$ *and the bottom for* M-2 $$(\Delta kM_2 = \Delta\frac{M\text{-}2}{MB}).$$ *If not corrected for through adjustments in the monetary base, these movements can cause wide swings in the money supply.*

SOURCE: The Morgan Guaranty Survey (February 1981).

increase in the base. Figure 6.5 demonstrates the large quarter-to-quarter fluc-tuations in the money multiplier.

How these variations occur can be traced by separating the base and reserves into component parts. The monetary base consists of currency *(CU)* and total reserves *(RT)*:

$$MB = CU + RT. \qquad\qquad\qquad 6.4$$

The amount of deposits created from any given base depends both on the division of the base into its currency and reserve components and on how the financial system uses such reserves. The amount of deposits that can be created depends on the reserve requirements *(rd)* against demand deposits *(DD)* in-

TABLE 6.6   **Change in Reserves, Monetary Base, Money, and Money Components, September–December 1979**

	Growth rate in percent at annual rates
Member bank reserves	13.8
Monetary base	8.1
M-1	3.1
M-2	6.8
Currency	5.3

Use of monetary base	Percent of total	Approximate use of monetary base per dollar of M-1
Currency	42.0	1.00
Reserves	58.0	
Use of reserves		
Member bank demand deposits	8.0	0.14
Not in M-1	92.0	
Other demand deposits	19	(0.14)
Time and saving deposits	58	(0.03)
Excess reserves	15	1.00
In M-1 but not requiring reserves		
Nonmember bank deposits	2.1	0.00

The monetary base multiplier (kMB) differs for each definition of money because each component such as currency or member bank demand deposits has a different reserve requirement. The final column shows what percent of a dollar in the monetary base is used for each dollar change in a component. Thus each dollar increase in currency or excess reserves uses up a dollar of the base. In contrast, increases in other demand and time and savings deposits utilize part of the base even though they do not increase money measured as M-1.

cluded as money and also on those against foreign, interbank, and similar deposits *(ODD)* not included in the money supply as well as on the reserve requirement *(rt)* against nonpersonal time deposits *(TD)* and on the amount of excess reserves *(RE)*, those which do not lead to any deposits. Thus total reserves equal

$$RT = rdDD + rdODD + rtTD + RE. \qquad\qquad 6.5$$

The large variations in the growth rates for the monetary base, reserves, and money, shown in Table 6.6, are accounted for by the differences in reserves used by currency and those for each deposit component. The first column shows both growth rates and the actual use of the base in this period. Only 8 percent went to reserves against demand deposits. The second column shows how the expansion of the monetary base related to the growth in money. Note that in 1979 every dollar of added currency required one dollar of the base; every dollar in a demand deposit at a member bank required about 14 cents, while deposits at nonmember banks during this period required no use of the base at all. On the other hand, the base was used for reserves against some demand, time, and savings deposits not included in M-1. Finally, banks expanded excess reserves, which used up some of the added base without expanding money.

There is a different money multiplier for M-1, M-2, and M-3. Each depends on required reserve ratios and on how the public and financial institutions divide their holdings among currency and various categories of deposits. Roughly, a $1 expansion of currency uses the same amount of the base as an $8 expansion of demand deposits and a $33 growth of nonpersonal time deposits.

Money multipliers can be calculated with the simplifying assumption that the public desires to hold a constant ratio of currency and each type of deposit. For illustrative purposes, assume that the public wants to hold a fixed ratio of 30 percent of currency for each dollar of demand deposits. The ratio of currency to demand deposits $\left(\dfrac{CU}{DD}\right)$ can be defined as *cu*.

$$cu = \frac{CU}{DD}. \qquad\qquad 6.6$$

For the time being, assume that no other use exists for reserves except demand deposits, so that

$$RT = rdDD \qquad\qquad 6.7$$

and the amount of demand deposits is the reciprocal of the reserve requirement times the amount of reserves:

$$DD = \frac{1}{rd}RT.$$

These values can be substituted in equation (6.4), the division of the base into currency and total reserves. The numerical example assumes that the base is $124 billion, the currency ratio is .3, and the reserve requirement is .143.

$$MB = cuDD + rdDD \qquad\qquad 124 = .3DD + .143DD. \qquad\qquad \textbf{6.8}$$

Solving for demand deposits, we find

$$MB = (cu + rd)DD \qquad\qquad 124 = (.3 + .143)DD$$

or,

$$DD = \frac{1}{cu + rd}MB \qquad\qquad DD = \frac{124}{(.3 + .143)} = 280.$$

However, demand deposits make up only part of the money supply. The remainder is currency. Given the assumption that the public wants to hold a fixed percentage *(cu)* of currency compared to demand deposits, the composition of the base and the amount of money can be calculated. Thus, with money defined as currency plus demand deposits, we can derive by substitution the ratio of money to demand deposits:

$$M\text{-}1 = cuDD + DD \qquad\qquad\qquad\qquad\qquad \textbf{6.9}$$

or,

$$M\text{-}1 = DD(1 + cu) \qquad\qquad M\text{-}1 = (1 + .3)DD.$$

By substituting equation (6.8), which explains how much demand deposits result from a given monetary base, into the demand deposit component of equation (6.9), we arrive at the amount of money:

$$M\text{-}1 = \frac{1}{cu + rd}MB(1 + cu) \qquad M\text{-}1 = \frac{1}{.3 + .143}(124)(1 + .3) = 364. \;\; \textbf{6.10}$$

which consists of $280 billion of demand deposits and $84 billion of currency. Now we divide through equation 6.10 by MB to arrive at the definition of the money multiplier *(kM)*.

$$kM = \frac{M\text{-}1}{MB} = \frac{1 + cu}{cu + rd} \qquad\qquad kM = \frac{364}{124} = \frac{1 + .3}{.3 + .143} = 2.93. \qquad \textbf{6.3}$$

This says that the amount of money created from a given base depends on how much currency the public desires to hold relative to deposits, as well as on the reserve ratio.

The money multiplier will shift if the public alters the amount of currency it wants to hold compared to demand deposits, and if the reserve ratio changes. Furthermore, this simplified example does not include the possibilities of leakages into the other uses of reserves shown in equation (6.5). Shifts in such uses will alter the simplified money multiplier.

The ratio between currency and demand and other deposits will change with institutional factors (for example, credit cards), tastes, and interest rates. At higher interest rates, people will reduce their holdings of currency and demand deposits compared to time and savings deposits. The result is that, just as what people use for money varies with interest rates, so will the amount of money created from a given monetary base. Until the new reserve requirements are in place, the money multiplier will continue to be particularly difficult to predict. Differences in the amount of the monetary base needed for each factor included in a definition of money cause differing movements among the monetary base, reserves, and types of money.

7

The Demand For Money

The money supply has been a key factor in all major depressions and inflations because its movements cause aggregate demand to shift. Such shifts raise numerous questions. For instance, if control over the money supply were improved, would the instability of demand cease to be a problem? What does the demand for money look like? How does money influence spending? The theory of the demand for money offers a straightforward explanation of how spending reacts to the money supply. Demand for money depends on income, wealth, and interest rates. When a money demand factor shifts or the money supply changes, a disequilibrium develops. To restore equilibrium, spending for goods or services, for bonds, or for existing capital assets must change.

Equilibrium depends on the cost of holding money compared to other assets, on the services that money performs, and on the amount of money supplied to the market. If the money supply is increased, the demand for money either to hold as an asset or to be used in transactions must expand by the same amount. The added money will be held only if interest rates are lower or incomes are higher, or a combination of both types of movement overlap. A shift in money demand will cause similar readjustments to a new equilibrium. Such reactions are traced through the model of income determination by combining the demand for and supply of money into *liquidity-money (LM)* curves, which represent equilibrium positions in money markets. They show all equilibrium points between interest rates and real income. Changes in either the supply of or demand for money shift the *LM* curve. Through interactions with the market for real goods, a new equilibrium for income and spending is reached.

Some economists prefer to explain new levels of spending as a direct result of the added money supply without using the *IS-LM* model. In their view, a new equilibrium between money demand and a larger stock comes about because more money upsets the balance between the money services people want and those furnished by the enlarged stock. A return to balance requires more spending, which modifies prior levels of output, prices, and wealth. Demand stabilizes only when spending units conclude that their portfolios of assets are once again in equilibrium. This occurs when, as a result of movements in income, prices, assets, and interest rates, they are willing to hold the new level of money. In the process, they will also have raised "demand curves for current productive services, both for producing new capital goods and for purchasing current services. The monetary stimulus is spread in this way from the financial markets to the markets for goods and services."[1]

This chapter introduces money demand through a "standard" model in which money is held either to be used for transactions or as an asset. Each type of demand can be explained by a variety of theories. Growth in the transactions demand for money is roughly proportional to growth in income. If all money were used primarily for transactions, *velocity* (defined as income divided by the amount of money) would be stable. But adding money held as an asset to that used for transactions purposes causes velocities to vary. One of the analytical disagreements with respect to money demand centers on the probable stability of velocity.

In addition, modern analysis extends beyond the standard schedule to explain the demand for money as merely one aspect of a general model of portfolio (all holdings of assets) behavior. The demand for money and for purchasing goods or any other asset depends on a balancing of the relative costs and satisfactions from each. While the views of analysts as to the factors that can influence the demand-for-money balances have moved closer together, they still differ with respect to the emphasis they place on specific factors and their judgment as to the importance and the probable stability of each. Such differences underlie the topics discussed in this chapter:

Money and spending: Contrasting views.
The standard money demand schedule.
Theories of transactions or income demand for money.
Theories of assets demand for money.
Modern theories of money demand.
Money-market equilibrium.
Contrasting views as to the shape of the *LM* curve.
Empirical evidence on the *LM* curve.

Money and Spending: Constrasting Views

As an introduction to the demand for money, it is useful to examine some of the differences between the views of monetarists and neo-Keynesians as to the way

---

1. M. Friedman and A. Schwartz, "Money and Business Cycles," *Review of Economics and Statistics* 45 (February 1963): 60. This article gives an excellent description of how changes in the supply of money affect financial and real markets.

TABLE 7.1   **Views of Monetarists versus Neo-Keynesians**

Subject	Monetarists	Neo-Keynesians
Money supply	Measurable; Federal Reserve can control.	Hard to measure and control; private sector can neutralize Fed's actions.
Money demand	Stable.	Unstable.
Money demand responsiveness to i	None to small.	Large to infinite.
Velocity of money	Predictable.	Erratic.
Interest rates	Difficult to measure real interest rates. In classical theory, rates depend on saving and investing.	While measurement is a problem, it can be accomplished. Rates depend on money supply, liquidity preference, and spending.
Determination of interest rates	Expectations of spending units are significant.	The Federal Reserve.
Responsiveness of income to changes in money supply	Predictable.	May be slow; erratic.
Responsiveness of investment and consumption to interest rates	Responsive.	Reaction of I or C to r is critical, but their reactions may be insensitive.
Sectoral effects, such as on rate of investment or income distribution	Not important.	Significant and costly.
Effectiveness of monetary policy	High if stable; uncertain if shifting.	High if shifted sufficiently; uncertain if stable.
Effectiveness of fiscal policy	Destabilizing.	Stabilizing.
Effect of government deficit	Causes excess creation of money.	Need not affect money supply.

The table highlights critical issues in monetary policy. Few analysts hold the extreme views listed, but significant philosophical differences persist in the approach of economists to questions of money demand and supply.

in which the money market operates and what happens when the money supply shifts (Table 7.1). These contrasts provide a frame of reference as the theory of money demand is developed, indicating possible alternative pictures of how equilibrium develops in money markets. Key contrasts are found in the monetarist and neo-Keynesian estimates of the shape and stability of liquidity-money schedules and their interaction with investment-saving curves. When questions such as the following are asked, the two schools give answers which are quite far apart:

What are the key variables which influence the shapes of the *LM* and *IS* curves?

How responsive is demand to movements in money and interest rates?

How stable are demands in the private market?

Does the market contain self-correcting mechansisms which will automatically return it to full employment?

If instability worsens and output and employment are at an unsatisfactory level—too much inflation or recession—should the government act to try to improve the situation?

If operations are decided upon, should more emphasis be placed on monetary or on fiscal policy?

Many economists object to lists like that in Table 7.1 because they tend to overemphasize the differences between the two analytical schools. Few economists would agree with all the characterizations of either list. In fact, many feel that the divisions are out of date. With time and better information about the economy, more eclectic views of how money works and its importance have become common. As Chapter 1 pointed out, in place of a debate over money, other analytical factors have become far more significant in distinguishing views. Among these factors are concepts of how markets operate, how expectations are formed, how much importance to assign to the short or long run, what factors influence supply, and the likelihood and causes of disequilibrium. However, because the divisions are traditional and because there are certain advantages to drawing distinct contrasts, it is a useful shorthand to speak of monetarists and neo-Keynesians and to contrast the simple quantity theory with modern ones which ascribe movements in velocity and spending to changes in interest rates.

To understand what money is and what it does, consideration must be given to how interest rates react to changes in money and how spending reacts to interest rates. When the money supply moves, will the result be primarily an increase in demand or a drop in interest rates? This is equivalent to asking whether velocity will stay constant or shift. The table reveals conflicts in views over both money demand and supply, their stability, the ability to measure and control the amount available, and how money influences aggregate demand. Based on disagreements over these issues, the two analytical schools have tended to adopt differing positions as to government policy. On the strength of their belief that money demand is stable and that spending responds predictably to changes in the money supply, the monetarists emphasize control over money as the key governmental policy variable. Moreover, because they stress the importance of long-run trends and the inaccuracy of short-term observations as well as the basic stability of the private sector, monetarists hold that the money supply should grow in a steady and stable manner. It should not be allowed to vary with short-run movements of demand. The Fed should adopt a rule for steady growth of money and stick with it.

Neo-Keynesians also emphasize monetary policy, but they are more likely to believe that trying to maintain a stable money supply may aggravate instability. Both the demand for money and the demand for goods fluctuate. Furthermore, what the economy uses for money also undergoes changes. The Federal Reserve should not lock itself into a fixed growth rate or a single definition of money; it should take account of divergent trends among different money measures, credit, and interest rates. Government budgets and the multiplier are important, as are external shocks from abroad, strikes, and crop failures. Shifts in expectations of prices and profitability can overwhelm other factors. Failure to adjust the money supply as demand shifts can cause inflations, financial crises, and depressions. Complications arise in the use of stabilization policies, but programs capable of reacting to current needs and predicted problems are better than those which neglect such factors.

The Standard Money Demand Schedule

For purposes of exposition, it is helpful to divide the services rendered by (and therefore the demand for) money into two parts, one related to income and the other to interest rates. This division is carried out even though it is recognized that money provides many overlapping services. The same dollar may be held to meet current expenses, to pay for an emergency next week, and to be available to purchase an asset if a good buy comes along.[2] We use the term *transactions demand* to describe those elements of money demand related to the level of income. Those related to interest rates are called *assets demand*. According to this schema, the total demand for real money $\left(\dfrac{MD}{P}\right)$ consists of:

1. The *transactions* (or income) demand *(MY)*, which is the desire to hold real money balances as a medium of exchange for the purpose of buying goods, services, financial assets such as bonds, or physical assets. An advantage of holding money is that it can be used directly; you can buy what you want when you want it. If money is not a medium of exchange, it can be turned into one with a minimum of cost and inconvenience. A disadvantage is that there is a cost to holding money; you lose the interest or yield that you could gain from holding alternative assets. For convenience, only that money whose demand changes with the level of income is considered under the heading of transactions demand. Even though some transactions balances are influenced by interest rates, it is simpler analytically to treat these, plus

---

2. A word about notation: The nominal stock of money is *M*. Letters after *M* designate special features. *MS* is nominal money supply; *MD* is nominal money demand. Dividing through by the price level, *P*, gives real money supply $\left(\dfrac{MS}{P}\right)$ and real money demand $\left(\dfrac{MD}{P}\right)$. *MY* and *MA* refer to transactions and assets demand. They are in real terms.

all other balances which change with interest rates, as part of assets demand. Since the final demand for money reflects all income and interest effects, this artificial division does not affect the total results.

2. The **assets demand (MA)**, which is the desire to hold some portion of a portfolio of assets in the form of money balances because of the utility it provides in commanding future generalized purchasing power. Portfolios may include currency, demand deposits, time and saving deposits, bonds, common stocks, houses, or a variety of other assets. The assets demand is also called speculative, portfolio, or wealth demand.

The amount of any asset, including money, which people hold depends on what they expect to gain from it, based on their own tastes and their estimate of its convenience, liquidity, and expected yield. The utility of holding each type competes with that expected from every other asset adjusted for risk. The level of a decision maker's wealth sets a limit and defines a budget within which decisions to hold money must be made. Whether one holds money or some other asset depends on the relative cost of holding money and the satisfactions one receives from it. The price paid for holding currency and demand deposits is the interest *not* received. Other concepts of money require less sacrifice of interest, but there are compensating inconveniences and possible losses if the assets must be converted to a medium of exchange. The higher the potential costs of trading near-money for cash, whether because of inconvenience, risk of capital loss, or costs of trading assets, the smaller will be the loss from holding cash. When interest rates are high because of either real factors or expected inflation, holding cash is expensive. In contrast, if interest rates rise, it will be

FIGURE 7.1   **Changes in Money Supply Shift Incomes and Interest Rates**

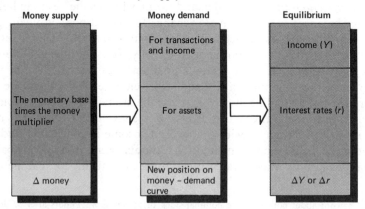

Added money must be used. Assets and transactions demands for money determine how much income and interest rates must move before money is held willingly.

more expensive to hold bonds or other assets with values that move opposite to interest rates than it would be to hold money, whose value will not fall as a result of an increase in interest rates.

The simple division of money into two parts dependent on income or interest rates applies to money supply as well as money demand. Some of the money stock fulfills a transactions need. The remainder (the total stock minus that used for transactions puposes) is available to be held as an asset. When the money supply increases, it will cause a new equilibrium in the money market. To the degree that income expands, the amount said to be held for transactions purposes will be higher. To the degree interest rates fall, more money will be held as an asset. These two uses together must completely absorb the added money (see Figure 7.1).

It must also be recognized that other factors in addition to income and interest play a part in determining the demand for money; when they shift, the two-sector demand schedule will change. Among these other factors, the impact of price changes, of expectations, and of wealth play a major part in various money demand theories. At appropriate times, they must be brought into the discussion. All are present in most of the modern eclectic models used for forecasting interest rates and the impact of money on income.

THE TRANSACTIONS DEMAND CURVES

Figure 7.2 shows transactions demand curves for money, drawn on the assumption that they are not influenced by interest. In Figure 7.2A, as income (measured on the horizontal axis) rises, the amount of money demanded (measured vertically) expands. The demand equation is assumed to be of the form:

$$MY = eY \qquad MY = .1\,Y = .1\,(1,600) = 160. \qquad \textbf{7.1}$$

The coefficient e indicates the sensitivity of money demand to changes in real income.

We can also express the demand for money as a function of interest rates. This transformation is accomplished by measuring the amount of money demanded on the horizontal axis and interest rates on the vertical. Let us take the amount of money demanded at one income level and check its values on the transformed diagram (Figure 7.2B). What does the demand for money look like when income is a given amount, say, $1,600 billion? Note that because the transactions demand is assumed not to depend on interest rates, the amount of money demanded—$160 billion— is the same at all interest rates. (The demand for money is completely interest-inelastic.) The demand curve is a straight vertical line. What happens when income rises, say to $2,000 billion? The demand curve shifts to the right. The amount of money desired rises to $200 billion. Again, it is the same amount at all interest levels, or its responsiveness to interest is zero.

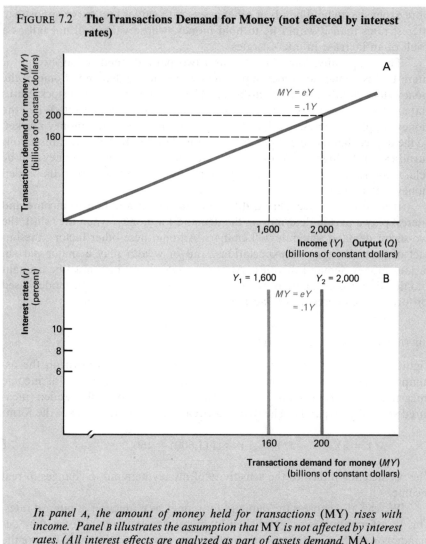

FIGURE 7.2   **The Transactions Demand for Money (not effected by interest rates)**

In panel A, the amount of money held for transactions (MY) rises with income. Panel B illustrates the assumption that MY is not affected by interest rates. (All interest effects are analyzed as part of assets demand, MA.)

THE ASSETS DEMAND CURVES

Figure 7.3 shows an assets demand curve for money. The amount of money which will be held drops as real interest rates *(r)* rise. Each higher rate means a greater sacrifice for not holding other assets; therefore, less money will be held. An equation showing this dependence on interest rates of demand for money to be held as an asset can be written as

$$MA = \overline{MA} - hr \qquad MA = 420 - 2{,}000r. \qquad\qquad 7.2$$

FIGURE 7.3   **The Assets Demand for Money**

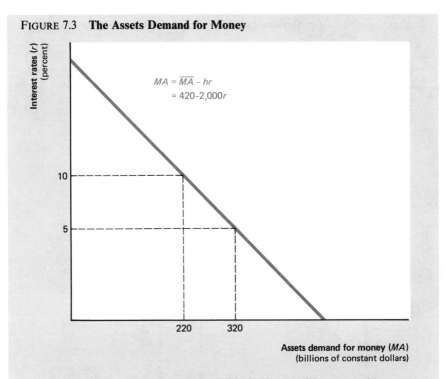

At lower interest rates, more money will be held in portfolios as an alternative investment (MA). *Higher interest rates on other assets raise both the opportunity cost and speculative risk of holding money.*

This shows an autonomous demand to hold money $(\overline{MA})$ plus a demand related to interest rates. The sensitivity of this demand to interest rates is expressed by the coefficient h. (If there were an unlimited demand at very low interest rates, a different functional representation would be required.)

THE COMBINED DEMAND CURVE FOR MONEY

The relationships expressed in equations 7.1 and 7.2 can be combined into a single demand-for-money equation. Thus, we have

$$\frac{MD}{P} = MY + MA. \qquad\qquad 7.3$$

By substitution

$$\frac{MD}{P} = eY + \overline{MA} - hr \qquad\qquad \frac{MD}{P} = .1Y + 420 - 2,000r \qquad 7.4$$

FIGURE 7.4   **The Total Demand for Money Depends on Both Interest Rates and Income**

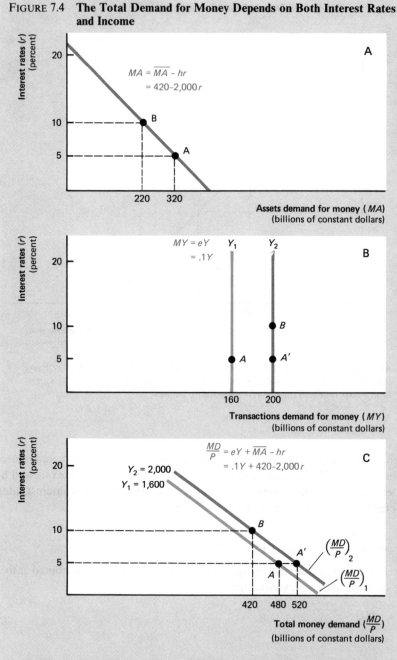

Total money demand declines with interest rates (assets demand declines); compare points A and B. Money demand increases with income (transactions demand rises). When income rises, a money demand curve shifts to the right; compare points A and A'.

At a specific real interest rate and level of real income, the demand for money can be calculated. Thus, if we assume an interest rate of 5 percent and an income of $1,600 billion, the demand for money is

$$\frac{MD}{P} = .1(1,600) + 420 - (2,000)(.5) = 480.$$

In Figure 7.4, the first curve (7.4A) expresses the asset demand shown in Figure 7.3. The second (7.4B) shows the income demand from Figure 7.2. The two are combined in the final panel (7.4C). When interest rates are 5 percent and income is $1,600 billion, the demand for money (at point A on all three panels) is $480 billion: transactions demand is $160 billion and that for assets is $320 billion. When interest rates are 5 percent and income is $2,000 billion, money demand rises to $520 billion (point A^1). Each income level has a separate interest-demand curve $\left(\frac{MD}{P}\right)_1, \left(\frac{MD}{P}\right)_2$. If interest rates rise to 10 percent and income is $2,000 billion, money demand drops to $420 billion (point B). The combined curves show how money demand varies with interest rates; as interest rates rise, less money is demanded. On this diagram, a change in the level of income (as from $1,600 to $2,000 billion) will cause a shift in the money-demand curve. So will any autonomous changes in the underlying demand for money to be used for transactions or to hold as an asset.

Theories of Transactions or Income Demand for Money

The previous section presented a standard model of the demand-for-money balances. A study of its development and some of the controversies surrounding it provides a useful tool for future analysis. We will begin by reviewing the two major positions.

Monetarists believe that a close relationship exists between changes in money and spending. If money expands, the economy will spend more, thereby raising demand, prices, and perhaps output in the short run. In this way, the desired relationship between money and income is reestablished. They see the demand for money as stable and interest-inelastic.

Neo-Keynesians, on the other hand, view money demand as both erratic and interest-sensitive. More money will increase spending and income, but it is not possible to predict how much income will rise by knowing only how much the money supply expands. Changes in spending depend on many other factors as well. Additional money may boost spending and output, or it may be used to meet assets demand. An expansion of money in one period may offset a slower growth of money in another. Over a long period, the average increase in money primarily will affect prices, but in the interim, changes in the money supply may have a very important influence on real output.

THE CLASSICAL QUANTITY THEORY

While recognizing differences between the long and the short run, quantity theorists emphasize the importance of changes in money to changes in prices. More modern versions of this theory agree with the Keynesians that in an intermediate period, one cannot predict how changes in spending will divide between prices and output. They also acknowledge that changes in interest rates can influence velocity, or the relationship between money, spending, and prices. But such variances are comparatively unimportant. In the long run, moreover, they predict that changes in money beyond those needed to accommodate a growth in real transactions will primarily change prices.

Early versions of the relationship between money and the level of spending go back to the eighteenth century. Modern analysis has built on the work of Irving Fisher of Yale, one of the foremost economists of the first quarter of this century, and that of the great English classicist, Alfred Marshall, who taught at Cambridge in the same period. Fisher made famous the equation of exchange (equation 7.5). This approach starts with the concept of velocity. The *velocity of the circulation of money* is the rate at which the nominal stock of money *(M)* changes hands per year to complete the sales transactions of the economy. Thus, if the stock of money is $400 billion and there are $4,000 billion worth of sales and purchases of goods, services, and assets made during the year, the annual transaction velocity is 10, or $\left(\dfrac{4000}{400}\right)$.

Fisher's equation of exchange is an identity:

$$MV \equiv PT \qquad 400 \times 10 \equiv 2 \times 2{,}000. \qquad\qquad \textbf{7.5}$$

The amount of money *(M)* times its velocity *(V)* is the flow of money purchases in a period. The identical money purchases can be looked upon as the nominal value of all goods and services sold. The nominal value is the quantity of transactions *(T)* times their prices *(P)*. Transactions requiring money include intermediate and final sales of goods and services as well as the transfer of existing assets, such as bonds or houses.

The equation of exchange and early quantity theories can be interpreted as somewhat mechanical versions of the relationship between money and spending as well as money and prices. Money was not valued for itself, but only as an input into the production spending process. Turnover depended on the institutional structure, which would evolve only slowly. The rate at which money turned over could be thought of as almost a mechanical process resulting in a relatively stable velocity. If more money was created, it would lead to increased spending. The growth of transactions in a period would equal the new stock of money times the velocity of circulation.

In the classical system, the equation of exchange turned into a theory of price determination. The potential ability of the economy to produce limits the number of physical transactions. Classicists were concerned primarily with analyzing a full-employment economy. If both velocity *(V)* and transactions *(T)* are basically stable, what happens when the amount of money increases? Since spending *(MV)* rises but physical transactions can't expand, prices must rise in the same proportion as the increase in money. The **crude quantity theory** states that the price level is proportional to the money supply. Any increase in money will raise prices equivalently.

THE CAMBRIDGE INCOME OR CASH-BALANCE APPROACH

The development of the quantity theory at Cambridge University moved away from emphasis on the stability of institutional factors and velocity to the development of a theory of money demand which could be used to explain why changes in either the demand for or supply of money altered the desire to spend. In this process, the Cambridge economists also shifted concern away from total transactions (which included not only income expenditures but also intermediate purchases of goods, financial transactions, and transfers) to those critical in the determination of income. The demand for cash balances can be explained by the need to hold money as a medium of exchange. The amount desired depends on the tastes of spending units. The demand for nominal money balances will vary inversely with the price level.

Spending or prices could change as a result either of movements in money or of changes in the desire to hold cash balances. In the Cambridge income equation, total transactions *(T)* are replaced by the physical amounts of goods and services *(Q)*–the real GNP. The measure of velocity *(V)* is replaced by a demand to hold cash balances *(K)* (not the multiplier). Average prices or the price level is still *(P)*.

$$M = KPQ \qquad 400 = \frac{1}{5} \times 2 \times 1{,}000. \qquad \textbf{7.6}$$

What determines the relationship between velocity and the amount of money that units desire to hold? In equilibrium, people will want to hold exactly the amount of money supplied. In fact, this is the key assumption of the quantity theory. The flow of spending, but of no other variable, increases until the economy is just willing to hold the stock of money. In equilibrium, the money demanded *(MD)* equals the amount of money *(M)* and can be substituted for it. To bring out the relationship between the Cambridge equation, the equation of exchange, and modern transactions-demand theory, we use only *Q* rather than considering all transactions *(T)*. Substituting money demand in equation 7.5, the equation of exchange, and output *(Q)* for transactions, we find

$$MD(V) = PQ \qquad\qquad 400 \times 5 = 2 \times 1{,}000 \qquad\qquad 7.7$$

and

$$MD = \frac{1}{V}PQ \qquad\qquad 400 = \frac{1}{5} \times 2 \times 1{,}000.$$

Thus, the equation of exchange is transformed from an identity into a demand schedule.

If we also insert the demand for money in place of the money stock in the Cambridge equation and compare equation 7.7 with 7.6, we find that $K = \frac{1}{V}$. The demand to hold money is the reciprocal of the velocity of circulation. The money demand for transactions purposes can be analyzed either through asking what are the institutional and psychological factors determining how much money people want to hold to match a specific money income or by asking what decides the rate at which money will turn over.

THE TRANSACTIONS DEMAND IN KEYNES

John Maynard Keynes was one of the foremost Cambridge economists. Although he rejected the crude quantity theory, some part of his views, especially with respect to the transactions demand, grew out of the Cambridge tradition. Keynes believed that new theories were needed because the classical economists erred in their failure to analyze what happened in an economy with less than full employment and also because they neglected important factors affecting the demand for money which helped determine income and interest rates.

Keynes used the term *liquidity preference* to categorize these factors. **Liquidity preference** is the schedule of the ratio of money balances to income and assets that an individual wishes to hold. Chapter 6 defined liquidity as the ability to turn an asset into a medium of exchange rapidly, with a minimum of transactions costs and danger of loss in capital value. Keynes used the term *liquidity* to emphasize that this key attribute predominated among the reasons for holding money in preference to other assets. He divided liquidity preference into three parts: (1) the transactions motive, (2) the precautionary motive, and (3) the speculative motive. The last forms one of the bases for current views about assets demand.

The transactions motive emphasizes primarily the need to hold money to bridge the gap between income and normal expenditures from it. The precautionary motive can be thought of as holding funds for a rainy day. Some expenditures may be abnormal. A person falls ill; bills may mount while income shrinks. A chance to get a rare bargain may appear; one's car may break down completely. Without cash, getting the money for such contingencies might be difficult. The possibility that such demands will arise at some unforeseen time leads people to hold money for precautionary reasons. Precautionary demand is reduced if other assets can readily be converted into cash. Thus a savings account may serve most precautionary needs; the effort needed to turn it into cash would not be onerous if it arose only occasionally.

MODERN TRANSACTIONS DEMAND

Modern views of the transactions demand build on the need for money to meet precautionary and transactions requirements.[3] Given potential needs for present and future payments, how much money should an individual or a firm hold? How should cash be managed? The answer is that the stock or amount of money demanded should follow rules similar to those derived for optimizing the holdings of all types of inventories.

The amount of inventories held should depend on the probable needs for a good, the losses if a good is not available at a given time, the cost of obtaining a good by converting it to and from other assets, and the losses in income from not holding other assets. When applied to money, the inventory approach says that the amount of real money balances demanded depends on the total number and value of money transactions that a firm or an individual expects to make in a period, the cost of converting money (brokerage charges) to interest-bearing assets, and the loss in interest, or the opportunity costs of holding money. In the inventory-theoretic approach, the amount of money demanded does not rise at the same rate as these other factors. In the simplest theory, demand varies with the square root of these factors, but more complex theories show demand rising or falling in accordance with higher-order roots.

The result of this approach, however, is to give a money-demand function which depends on both the level of transactions (or, when simplified, real income) and interest rates. In addition, the amount of money held may depend on the cost and ability to manage cash. As firms and individuals learn how to conserve cash, the demand for money will fall. No matter which of these approaches is followed, the demand for money changes as income varies. This is a critical point because the converse is also true, as Figure 7.1 and the analysis demonstrate: the levels of income and interest rates move with changes in the quantity of money. Many debates concern the possible reactions of income. Will it increase proportionately, rapidly, or only slightly when money expands? Will the increased money supply primarily influence output, prices, interest rates, or some other variable? As the money supply grows, one form of adjustment will be a growth in spending. How much will aggregate demand rise? Income will grow until that point where the spending sectors are willing to hold

3. W. J. Baumol, "The Transactions Demand for Cash: An Inventory Theoretic Approach," *Quarterly Journal of Economics* (November 1952):545–56 and J. Tobin, "The Interest Elasticity of Transactions Demand for Cash," *Review of Economics and Statistics* (August 1956):241–47.

the new money. When money expands, demand is equated to the new supply. The increase in the demand for money is brought about by either an increase in spending or a drop in interest rates, or both.

DIFFERENCES IN VELOCITY

If the demand for money depended only on the amount of income, the two would change at similar rates. The income velocity of money would be constant, or at least would change in a regular manner. On the other hand, if the transactions demand depends on interest rates or if there are significant demands related to other factors such as holding money as an asset, velocity will vary. To predict how spending will change when money shifts then requires a more complex theory. Let us picture how pressures to expand build up when the money supply grows. Assume nominal income to be $2,400 billion and the money supply to be $400 billion. Each spending unit holds a share of the stock of money which just matches its demand for money. It turns over its money at the average rate for the economy, six times a year. Now the money supply grows to $500 billion; each unit finds itself with 25 percent more money than before the increase.

What does the quantity theory predict, and how does it explain what happens? The additional money causes disequilibrium between money demand and supply. Something has to give. When will spending stop? When income has grown to the point where the relation of the money now held by a unit to its spending is the same as that before the money stock grew. At that point, velocity will return to its prior stable position, which was 6, with K equal to $\frac{1}{6}$. The increase in total spending will be equivalent to the increase in money, or 25 percent. Nominal GNP will grow to $3,000 billion. If real income and output are unchanged, the rise in prices will be proportional to the increase in money.

The crude quantity theory assumes that prices vary with money because the economy produces at full potential and velocity is relatively stable. We know that the first assumption is not always true; the economy has often had unemployed resources. When spending grows in such periods, some increases induce higher output, and only part goes into prices. What about the second assumption, the stability of velocity? Look at Figure 7.5, which pictures the level of velocity of M-$1B$ and M-2 from 1965 to 1980. From a study of the figure, would you say that velocity has been relatively stable? Note the steady rise in M-$1B$ and the sharp movements from quarter to quarter. The velocity of M-2, which includes interest-bearing time and savings deposits, has been more stable than M-$1B$. Between 1965 and 1980 the turnover of M-$1B$ grew from about 4.0 to 6.6. The shift in the velocity of M-2 went from a high of 1.67 in 1970 to a low of 1.53 in 1976 and back to another high of 1.67 in 1979.

What do these data tell us with respect to the crude quantity theory? If the theory were correct, any change in the money supply would be reflected in

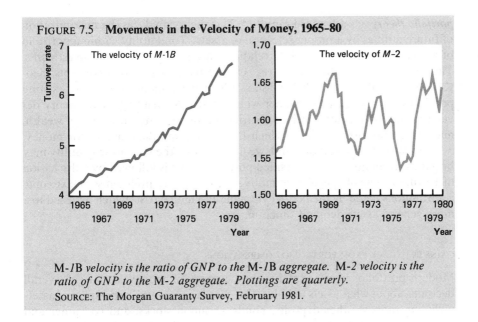

FIGURE 7.5   **Movements in the Velocity of Money, 1965–80**

M-*1B velocity is the ratio of GNP to the* M-*1B aggregate.* M-*2 velocity is the ratio of GNP to the* M-*2 aggregate. Plottings are quarterly.*
SOURCE: The Morgan Guaranty Survey, February 1981.

higher spending and prices. We would be able to predict a future level of spending by multiplying the expected amount of money by recent velocity. How good would such predictions be? In 1979, each difference of .1 in the velocity of M-1B, when multiplied by the stock of M-1B, would be equal to a change of over $35 billion in spending. Anyone trying to predict the GNP for the fourth quarter of 1979, even knowing accurately what the money stock would be in that period and assuming no change in velocity over the fourth quarter of 1978, would have missed the actual GNP by nearly $100 billion.

Most analysts agree that the crude quantity theory is incorrect. Velocity does change. Disagreement arises over the ability to predict velocity from a limited number of additional variables. Monetarists believe that spending increases are closely related to changes in money. Velocity will vary with the stage of the business cycle and with interest rates, but reactions of spending to changes in money are certain and predictable. Neo-Keynesians are less convinced; they believe that the demand for money and, therefore, the rate at which money turns over, are not only inconstant, but are also quite irregular, varying with interest rates, with expectations, with financial conditions, and with changes in financial institutions.

Theories of Assets Demand for Money

While income and transactions needs are important in explaining money demand, so are desires to hold money as an asset. Since the time of Keynes, *portfolio theory* has advanced rapidly.[4] This theory analyzes the maximization of future utilities by a proper selection of assets. Total utility within a portfolio of assets is enhanced by the interrelationships among individual investments. The whole is greater than its parts. On the basis of portfolio concepts, neo-Keynesians and monetarists have shown how, when money is created, existing portfolios are revised in a manner which increases spending. This theory develops additional factors, such as a variety of interest rates, the level of wealth, and inflationary expectations, which help determine the demand for money.

In examining assets demand, we first consider the reasons why utility may be gained from holding a diversified portfolio. This is followed by a discussion of Keynes's view of speculative motives and liquidity preference. Next come contributions made by the neo-Keynesians and monetarists which have led to a more general assets demand function.

GAINS IN UTILITY FROM PORTFOLIO COMBINATIONS

Modern portfolio theory explains the demand for money as part of overall decisions about what assets to hold. The economy contains a spectrum of assets including money, other deposits, bonds, common stocks, and consumer and business physical assets. Each class of assets differs from the others in the degree of liquidity, its expected rate of return, and in the risks that the actual return will fall short of expectations.

Demand deposits and currency are completely liquid and have a constant nominal capital value, but they pay little or no interest. Their real value drops with inflation. Savings deposits also have a guaranteed nominal value and they pay interest, although they are slightly less convenient to use as a medium of exchange. Bonds may promise higher yields, but both their real and nominal values fluctuate; their actual return can fall far below expectations. In about one-fourth of the past 40 years, the total nominal rate of return on long-term corporate bonds was negative. In other years, nominal earnings were offset by inflation, so that real returns were even more negative. Rates of return on common stocks fluctuate even more. Annual rates of total return of plus or minus 20 to 40 percent are not unusual. While most analysts believe that, over time, the returns from common stocks as a whole will be positive, during long stretches this has not been true. In the 1970s, houses had the highest rate of return, on average, of any major asset; but, again, their real yields have frequently been low or negative.

Because of uncertainty about future yields and because every asset can offer some unique utility, people diversify their portfolios. They don't concen-

4. J. Tobin, "Liquidity Preference as Behavior Towards Risk," *Review of Economic Studies* 25 (February 1958): 65–86; H. M. Markowitz, *Portfolio Selection: Efficient Diversification of Investments* (New York: Wiley, 1959, 1979); and W. F. Sharpe, "Capital Asset Prices, A Theory of Market Equilibrium Under Conditions of Risk," *Journal of Finance* 19 (September 1964): 325–42.

trate all their wealth in money or bonds or common stock. Most people dislike uncertainty and consequently avoid risking sizable changes in their wealth. Modern texts in finance and investment[5] show that, depending on their attitude toward risks, most people gain utility by holding diversified portfolios. It doesn't pay to put all your eggs in one basket.

What then happens when the amount of money grows? Every spending unit adjusts its portfolio. When the money stock expands, its price and the economy's wealth are affected. The marginal utility of money and its relative value fall, reducing its price compared to other goods. The total wealth of the economy expands as a result of the greater money stock. People's portfolios are in disequilibrium; they have to reshufle their assets holdings. The demand for money adjusts to the new money supply as a result of expansion in the demand for other assets, goods, and services. Equilibrium returns when the demand for money in terms of the interest rate (its opportunity cost) is once more in balance.

YIELDS FROM AN INVESTMENT

How is the best portfolio selected? Investing is far from a simple operation. Everyone would like to get the highest possible yield. Are you better off owning common stock, bonds, commodities, real estate, or money? What share of your assets should be held in each form? What will your yield or rate of return depend upon? When you buy a bond, you will be quoted its interest rate, which is also called its expected yield to maturity. But after holding the bond for a period, you may find that its actual yield differs greatly from what was quoted. In some sense, U.S. government bonds are as safe an investment as you can make, but in another way they are quite risky. In the first three months of 1980, long-term U.S. government bonds dropped by more than 20 percent in nominal value and by nearly 25 percent in real values.

Every time interest rates shift, the present value—and therefore the market selling price—of a bond changes. If the market price moves more than expected when the bond was bought, the actual rate of return differs from that anticipated. If the price level changes more than the buyer thought it would, the real rate of return will not equal expectations either. Table 7.2 shows the changes in market interest rates, both short-term (3 to 6 months) and long-term (25 to 30 years), which have occurred in the past. Short-term rates rose by more than 1,000 percent (from 2 to 23 percent) in 1920, and by more than 200 percent in 1980. In the period from 1977 to 1980, holders of long-term bonds lost more than half their capital. Because changes like these occur in values, investors will gain utility by holding a variety of diversified assets in their portfolios.

5. See, for example, W. F. Sharpe, *Investments* (Englewood Cliffs, N.J.: Prentice-Hall, 1978) and J. C. Van Horne, *Financial Management and Policy,* 5th edition (Englewood Cliffs, N.J.: Prentice-Hall, 1980).

TABLE 7.2   **The Behavior of Short and Long Yields during Selected Periods**

Period	Short-term rates			Long-term bonds	
	Yield at high (percent)	*Rise in percentage points*		*Yield at high (percent)*	*Price decline*
1904 to 1907	125	—		4.21	−19
1916 to 1920	23	+21.12		5.56	−35
1925 to 1929	20	+18.00		4.59	−4
1930 to 1932	5	+1.00		4.83	−12
1967 to 1970	8	+4.55		9.25	−41
1971 to 1974	10	+6.65		10.40	−31
1977 to 1980	18	+12.22		14.50	−53

SOURCE: Salomon Brothers.

In the first and third columns, the table shows how high short- and long-term interest rates rose in selected interest cycles. The second column reports the increase in percentage points over the previous low. The final column shows the percent decline in the price of bonds with 25 to 30 years to maturity due to the rise in rates from the previous low to the reported high.

SPECULATIVE MOTIVES AND LIQUIDITY PREFERENCE

Keynes used knowledge of fluctuations in bond prices to explain the speculative motive for holding money. He asked why anyone would hold money, which paid no interest, in preference to bonds or stocks, which do. His answer was the speculative motive. People hold cash because they are uncertain about future interest rates. If rates rise, cash will have been a better investment because capital losses will have been avoided. Holders of cash will be able to buy bonds at lower prices after interest rates rise than would have been possible before. Because they avoided a capital loss, their rate of return for money, even though it earns no interest, will exceed that from a bond which pays interest but suffers a capital loss exceeding the value of the coupon.

Keynes theorized that people's expectations about future rates depended on the level of the current rates. When interest rates are high, investors assign a greater probability to a future drop. At higher rates the probability of future capital gains appears enhanced. People are more willing to hold bonds than money because of a diminished fear of future losses. Thus, Keynes assumed that at higher interest rates, since people would prefer bonds, the speculative demand for money would be less than at lower rates. As rates fell and approached zero, there would be an almost unlimited demand for money (the liquidity trap). It would cost very little to hold cash, and people would feel that interest rates were more likely to rise in the future, leading to capital gains from not holding bonds. Low rates would set a floor under future losses.

The Keynesian speculative demand for money is illustrated in Figure 7.6. Interest rates are on the vertical axis and money demand on the horizontal. The curve graphs the relationship between the demand for money and interest

FIGURE 7.6   **The Keynesian Speculative Demand for Money and the Liquidity Trap**

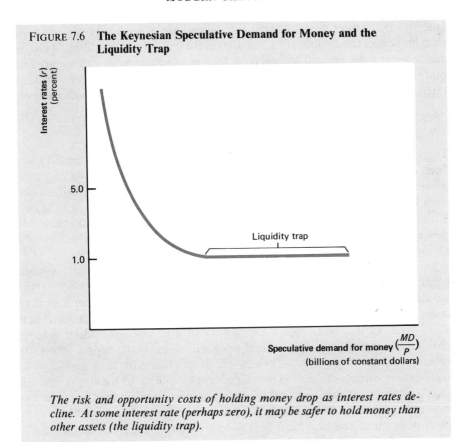

The risk and opportunity costs of holding money drop as interest rates decline. At some interest rate (perhaps zero), it may be safer to hold money than other assets (the liquidity trap).

rates, or the economy's liquidity preference. At high interest rates, less money is held because opportunity costs are higher and holding money rather than bonds loses chances for speculative gains from interest-rate declines. At lower interest rates, opportunity costs are less, possible losses from holding bonds increase, and the advantage of having money available to purchase other assets is greater. Finally, at the right of the diagram, the interest elasticity of the demand for money becomes infinite. The horizontal sector of the liquidity preference curve is called the *liquidity trap.* At this low interest rate, individuals would be willing to hold unlimited amounts of additional money. Increases in the money stock would not lower interest rates or increase spending. People would hold all added money as a speculation against future increases in interest rates.

Modern Theories of Money Demand

Controversies over the variables in the demand for money have died down. Most analysts now agree on the broader approach stemming from portfolio analysis. Differences center around the importance of each variable and how each influences the channels of transmission from money to spending. Income and interest rates are still the primary factors affecting money demand, but other variables contribute toward shifting the demand function derived from interest and income. These other factors must be included in current analysis.

THE NEO-KEYNESIANS

The validity of Keynes's explanation of the speculative demand for money has been challenged over time. He dealt in a two-sector market containing only money and bonds. Neo-Keynesians have shown, on the basis especially of the work of James Tobin of Yale, that it is necessary to include other asset choices. Savings deposits, for example, pay interest but have a fixed capital value. If one were uncertain about bond prices, would it not be preferable to hold savings deposits instead of money, which pays no interest?

Modern portfolio theory recognizes that spending units have a wide choice of assets. Few will choose to hold either all money or all bonds. Individual uncertainty does not lead to an either/or situation but rather to one of more or less. Every asset competes with all others, depending on its individual utility and relative cost. When the supply of any asset, including money, changes, its point of equilibrium and price will shift. If the supply grows, its marginal value compared to all others will drop. To return their portfolios to equilibrium, owners of an asset in excess supply will try to reduce its ratio in their portfolios. If the asset whose supply increases is money, they are less willing to hold it. But because the supply of money is assumed to be exogenously determined and because it cannot be used up, any increase in the supply of money or drop in its value cannot cause a lesser amount to be held. Instead, spending units will buy more of other assets. Financial institutions and other borrowers will find that it pays to issue new debt. In this process, the desired stock of capital grows; investment increases. Households may also prefer to buy more consumption goods and services. The change in individual portfolios brings about a new equilibrium in the money market following an increase in the money supply. It is achieved when marginal returns for all assets are again equal.

THE MONETARIST DEMAND FOR MONEY

Modern monetarists also build their money demand concept on the general idea that households and businesses divide their wealth among capital assets, including money, according to the services each renders. While they consider several broad factors that influence the demand for money, as is implied by the name—modern quantity theory—which is applied to their work, they stress the importance of money and spending. Milton Friedman, for example, does not try to delineate the specific channels through which money sways the economy. The effects are so pervasive that too much attention to details could cause us to miss the general picture.

Money, like other goods, is held for the utility it renders. Some of the factors analyzed by Keynes and the neo-Keynesians—the gap between income and spending, precautionary desires, portfolio, among other factors—certainly apply. But the demand for money can be more general. Money may also be demanded as a temporary store of value. For this and for historical reasons, Friedman used M-2, which includes time and savings deposits in banks, as his measure of money. The utility derived from money depends on the financial and payment systems. As with the earlier versions of the quantity theory, these systems, and therefore the demand for money, are assumed to change only gradually.

Decisions as to the size of money balances to hold are made within a budget constrained by wealth and income. Wealth includes human capital, but because this form of capital is hard to measure, Friedman uses permanent income as a proxy to estimate its value. Because human capital is not readily available for transfer into other assets, it will have a different impact on money demand than other forms of capital. Interest rates and expectations of inflation and changes in rates are also significant.

THE TOTAL DEMAND FOR MONEY

The modern versions of money demand can be summarized in a single model. Although it includes more variables, income and interest rates remain the most important. Equation 7.8 is a general form of the modern version of money demand:

$$MD = f(Y, i_a, i_b, W, P, EX).\qquad\textbf{7.8}$$

This equation shows in general form that the demand for money depends on a larger number of variables when portfolio considerations are included. The specific form of the coefficients varies from model to model. The variable of greatest concern remains income *(Y)*. The amount of money demanded rises with income, and spending increases as the money supply expands. Interest rates (i_a, i_b) enter because they partially determine the cost of holding money. The number of interest rates included varies with the size of the model. It is not uncommon to find six to ten interest variables in a full-scale model. Wealth *(W)* affects the size of the portfolio to be distributed among available assets. In larger models, wealth is subdivided into a number of categories. These are frequently related to the interest rates included. Thus, some models show bonds, savings deposits, common stock, short-term money-market investments, and physical assets separately. Prices *(P)* are included because of the distorting effect of changing prices on relative values of individual assets.[6]

Expectations *(Ex)* and uncertainty also play a key role. The cost of holding money and other assets depends on what happens to future interest

6. The assumption is frequently made that the function is homogeneous of degree one in prices, so that the demand for money becomes a demand for real money in terms of real balances. The function then contains the expected rate of inflation and not the price level.

rates and prices, as well as on the risks that arise from unfulfilled expectations. To explain how spending units divide their portfolios, we need to estimate what they believe will happen in the future. Furthermore, expectations are not always formed in the same way. To predict accurately, we would like to include observations on changing expectations and on the factors causing them to shift.

Money-Market Equilibrium

With an understanding of the forces shaping money demand and supply, we can bring the two together to see how equilibrium develops and how it may shift. To measure the effect of changes in money on spending, we must first see how the demand for and supply of money interact with interest rates and income. Equilibrium in the money market varies with both. The liquidity-money *(LM)* function was defined as all the possible combinations of interest and income where the demand for real money $\left(\dfrac{MD}{P}\right)$ and the supply of real money $\left(\dfrac{MS}{P}\right)$ are equal.

Equation 7.4 showed that the total demand for money is

$$\frac{MD}{P} = eY + \overline{MA} - hr \qquad\qquad \frac{MD}{P} = .1Y + 420 - 2,000r \qquad\qquad 7.4$$

and with interest rates at 5 percent and income of $1,600 billion

$$\frac{MD}{P} = .1(1,600) + 420 - 2,000(.05) = 480.$$

While Chapter 6 showed that the supply of money could vary with the interest rate, let us assume that, by a feedback or some similar process, the Fed succeeds in controlling the money supply so that the supply of money is exogenous at any level determined by the Fed. In money-market equilibrium, the demand for and supply of money are equal. Thus the supply of money $\left(\dfrac{MS}{P}\right)$ can be substituted for the demand $\left(\dfrac{MD}{P}\right)$ in equation 7.4 to yield the *LM* equation. With a given supply of money, the relationship between interest rates and income depends on the money-demand function. If a more complicated money-supply function is used, it would be substituted for the exogenous value in the equation. The liquidity-money *(LM)* equation is:

$$\frac{MS}{P} = \frac{MD}{P} = eY + \overline{MA} - hr \qquad\qquad \frac{MS}{P} = .1Y + 420 - 2,000r. \quad 7.9$$

Solving equation 7.9 for interest rates, the *LM* equation is

$$r = \frac{1}{h}\left(eY + \overline{MA} - \frac{MS}{P}\right) \qquad r = \frac{1}{2,000}\left(0.1\,Y + 420 - \frac{MS}{P}\right), \qquad \textbf{7.10}$$

and with a money supply of $480 and real income of $1,600 billion,

$$r = \frac{1}{2,000}[.1(1,600) + 420 - 480] = .05.$$

We note that the relationships to income depend on the transactions-demand coèfficient *(e)*, the assets demand coefficient *(h)*, any autonomous money-demand factors $(\overline{MA})$, and the money supply $\left(\dfrac{MS}{P}\right)$.

DERIVATION OF THE *LM* CURVE

Liquidity-money schedules can be found by means of the *LM* equation. Curves showing *LM* equilibriums can also be derived by combining real-balance demand curves with money-supply curves. The curves $\left(\dfrac{MD}{P}\right)_1 \left(\dfrac{MD}{P}\right)_2$ in Figure 7.7A are sections of the money-demand curves derived in Figure 7.4c from the model of assets and income demands. Each curve shows, for a given level of income, the amount of money demanded at any interest rate. On each income curve, more money is demanded at lower interest rates. For a specific interest rate, the amount of money used rises as we move from any income level to a higher one.

The vertical line shows a particular supply of money. It is drawn vertically on the assumption that the Federal Reserve determines the money supply and that it will adjust the monetary base, if necessary, to retain a certain supply of money irrespective of interest-rate movements. Money supply is completely inelastic with respect to interest rates.

An equilibrium exists at each point where the money-supply curve intersects a money-demand curve. Each equilibrium level of interest and income is plotted in Figure 7.7B. Thus *A'* and *B'* correspond to points *A* and *B* in Figure 7.7A. The line connecting all such points is the *LM* curve. It slopes up to the right. At the left, income is low, so small transactions balances are required; most of the money stock is available for assets purposes. Low interest rates mean that people will be willing to hold the available money in their portfolios. As the curve rises to the right because income is higher, more money is required for transactions. It becomes available because higher interest rates, also reflected in the rising curve, make it more expensive to hold money as an asset.

Using the *LM* equation and the numerical example, we see that at point *A* in Figure 7.7, an equilibrium of 5 percent interest with income of $1,600 billion results when the money supply is $480 billion. At point *B*, the money supply has

FIGURE 7.7   **The Derivation of the Liquidity-Money Curve**

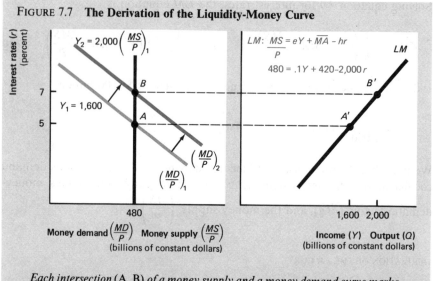

Each intersection (A, B) of a money supply and a money demand curve marks an equilibrium in the money market. The points of equilibrium for the money demand curve at each income level (Y₁, Y₂) with a single real money stock form an LM curve as pictured in panel B.

not changed and the money market is in equilibrium at 7 percent interest with an income of $2,000 billion. If we go back to equations 7.1 and 7.2, what has happened becomes clearer. A fixed money stock of $480 billion must be divided between transactions and assets uses. At point A', the income use [$eY =$ .1(1,600)] is $160 billion, and the assets use [$\overline{MA} - hr = 420 - 2,000 (.5) =$ 320] is $320 billion. An income of $2,000 billion at point B' requires $200 for transactions purposes. As the result of a rise in interest rates to 7 percent, assets holdings fall to $280 billion. The money market remains in equilibrium.

THE SLOPE OF THE *LM* CURVE

The *LM* curves illustrate reactions of equilibrium to movements in the demand for and supply of money. The slope of the curve shows how much interest rates must rise (the response of demand to r is negative) to release enough money from assets demand to fund additional income. What determines the slope of the curve? Look again at equation 7.10 and Figure 7.7. Note that each equilibrium point depends (1) on how much money people want to hold as an asset at each interest rate, or the responsiveness of assets demand for money to interest rates *(h)*; (2) on the responsiveness of money demand to income *(e)*; and (3) on the responsiveness of money supply to interest rates.

This illustration assumes that the money is determined by the Fed and does not respond to interest rates. Other models show that, with higher interest rates, a monetary base of a given size will yield a larger supply of money. This occurs because banks and the public economize by holding less currency and excess reserves the higher are interest rates. $\left(\dfrac{MS}{P}\right)$ will show more supply at higher interest rates. If you draw such a money-supply function in Figure 7.7 rising to the right, you will find that it results in a flatter LM curve. The more effective interest rates are in creating money from a given base, the less they will rise as income expands.

The effects of changes in responsiveness to income and interest rates can be illustrated by the numerical example and can be pictured on the diagrams. According to the numbers in equation 7.10, an increase in income of $100 billion will absorb an added $10 billion in money. With a constant money supply, how high interest rates will have to rise to release this amount from assets demand depends on h, its interest-responsiveness. In the example, with h equal to 2,000, interest rates rise by .5 percent (.005) for each $100 billion change in income. It can readily be seen that the larger e becomes, the greater will be the amount of transactions balances required for a given increase in income. A still larger e results in an LM curve with a steeper slope. On the other hand, if assets demand were more responsive (if h were larger), any amount needed for transactions balances would be released from money held as an asset, with a smaller increase in interest rates.

The effect of an increased interest-responsiveness is to rotate the LM curve downward to the right. Just as with the IS curves, we can think of any changes in the coefficients which reflect the responsiveness of money demand or supply to interest rates as a change in the structure of the economy or as autonomous movements in demand. The slopes of the LM and IS curves affect the way in which spending responds to other variables.

Every LM curve represents a fixed quantity of money. But note that as one moves up the curve, the levels of income and interest rates rise. What is happening to velocity? Since a higher income is being divided by the same real money supply, velocity is rising.

$$\text{Velocity } (V) = \frac{Y}{\dfrac{MS}{P}}. \hspace{3cm} 7.11$$

From the LM equation and the figure, we note that in the numerical example, the velocity at 5 percent interest is 3.33 $\left(V = \dfrac{1,600}{480}\right)$. At a 7 percent interest rate, velocity is 4.17 $\left(V = \dfrac{2,000}{480}\right)$. According to the standard or portfolio model, as interest rates rise, velocity rises.

SHIFTS IN THE *LM* CURVE

What shifts the *LM* curve? The curve will shift if the money supply changes, as shown in Figure 7.8. $\left(\dfrac{MS}{P}\right), \left(\dfrac{MD}{P}\right)_1$ and $\left(\dfrac{MD}{P}\right)_2$ are the money-demand and -supply ($480 billion) curves found in the preceding figure. Assume that the Fed increases the money supply by $40 billion, to $\left(\dfrac{MS}{P}\right)_2$. The result is an entirely new set of equilibrium points. The new equilibrium points, *C* and *D*, are mapped onto Figure 7.8B. The new *LM* curve is represented by *LM*$_2$, drawn through them.

Compare points *B'* and *D'*, which are at the same income. None of the extra money is required for transactions purposes. To absorb the excess, interest rates must drop sufficiently to make people willing to hold the added money as an asset. The distance between the *LM* curves at each income level depends on the coefficient of interest-responsiveness *(h)*. Similarly, we can compare points *A'* and *D'*, which have identical interest rates. All of the excess money

FIGURE 7.8   **Shifts in the Liquidity-Money (*LM*) Curve**

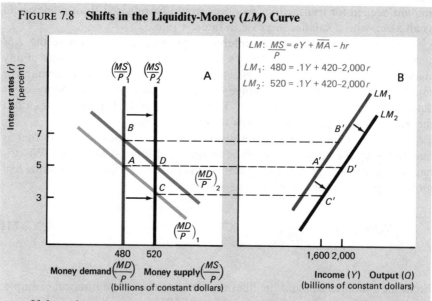

If the real money stock changes, all equilibrium points in panel A will shift. The new equilibrium points form a new curve, LM$_2$, dependent on the altered money supply $\left(\dfrac{MS}{P}\right)_2$. The slopes of the LM curves reflect the sensitivity of money demand to real interest rates (h). How much the LM curve shifts at each interest rate when real money alters depends on the desire to hold money for transactions purposes (e).

must be absorbed by higher transactions demand. At any interest rate, the horizontal distance thê *LM* curve shifts depends on the coefficient *e*, which determines how much added money will be absorbed in transactions balances for every dollar of added income. The numerical example and equation 7.10 show at *A'* an equilibrium of 5 percent interest with income of $1,600 billion. Point *D'* represents an interest rate of 5 percent with an income of $2,000 billion. With interest rates constant, the increase of $40 billion in money raises income by $400 billion ($e = .1$). With income constant, the added $40 billion would reduce interest rates by 2 percent ($h = 2,000$), found by comparing points *A'* and *C'*.

DISEQUILIBRIUM IN THE MONEY MARKETS

The *LM* schedule can be used to answer questions as to what happens if the money markets move into temporary disequilibriums. For example, note the points in Figure 7.9 (which repeats curve *LM*₁ from Figure 7.8). Point *D* is not

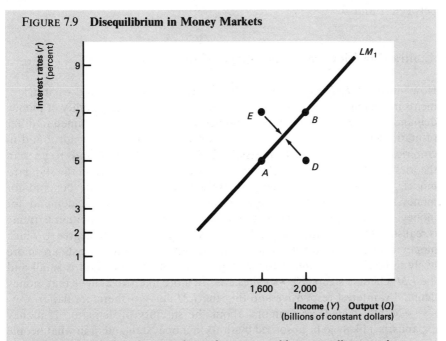

FIGURE 7.9   **Disequilibrium in Money Markets**

The money stock and money demands are in equilibrium at all points along the curve LM₁. *At point* D, *money demand is in excess (supply short), while at* E *money supply would be in excess (demand short). At* D, *decision makers striving for equilibrium will sell assets and make fewer purchases of goods and services. Interest rates rise and/or output will fall. At* E, *they purchase more assets and goods and services.*

on the *LM* curve. It is a disequilibrium point which could be maintained only if more money were created. At *D* the same amount of money is required for assets purposes as at point *A*; but since income is higher at *D*, the need for transactions balances is greater. The two needs cannot be met, so an excess demand for money exists. How does the economy adjust to remove the disequilibriums? If the money supply is not modified, changes must occur in income or in the interest rates. From point *D*, the excess demand for money would be reduced by interest rates rising and income falling until the economy moved back to an equilibrium position on the *LM* curve somewhere between points *A* and *B*. On the other hand, if the Fed desired to maintain the income level of *D*, it could increase the money supply. This would shift the economy to a new *LM* curve, as LM_2 in Figure 7.8, which would go through *D*.

At point *E*, since the money stock would support only the equilibriums on LM_1, interest rates must be too high or income too low to absorb all real balances. An excess supply of money exists. For the economy to remain at *E*, the Fed would have to remove the excess supply, shifting the economy to a new *LM* curve which passes through *E*. Otherwise, as people spend the money they do not want to hold, by purchasing bonds or other assets or current output, interest rates will drop and income rise, moving the economy to some point between *A* and *B*.

Contrasting Views as to the Shape of the *LM* Curve

How much the *LM* curve is shifted by an increase in money and what movements in aggregate demand result depend on the shape and stability of money demand. At one time, monetarists and neo-Keynesians were assumed to differ primarily with respect to their positions on these topics. While not found in empirical studies of post-Depression *LM* curves, classical and Keynesian theories point to two possible elasticities which differ entirely from the standard model. A naïve quantity theory shows a completely inelastic demand for money. A naïve Keynesian view shows a completely elastic demand for money. Modern quantity theorists and Keynesians agree that neither extreme is realistic. However, they may still differ over estimates of the degree to which money changes will affect spending or interest rates. Monetarists are more likely to hold that the interest-responsiveness of money demand is small and the *LM* schedule steep. Neo-Keynesians are more likely to believe that money demand is interest-responsive and that the *LM* curve is therefore flatter.

Closely related are opinions about the stability of demand. If money expands, is it likely to be absorbed by shifts in money demand or in what people use as money? Neo-Keynesians consider both types of shifts probable; monetarists think that both are unlikely.

Finally, monetarists put greater emphasis on the divergence of movements in real and nominal interest rates. The Federal Reserve's control over real interest rates is very diffuse. It depends on what spending units believe will happen to prices, not on the simple relationships observed in the *LM* curve.

THE CLASSICAL AND LIQUIDITY-TRAP SECTORS OF THE *LM* CURVE

This chapter has pictured three possible shapes for money demand. Most common is the standard schedule, in which the demand for money varies with other interest rates and the level of income. When interest rates rise, they reduce the assets demand to hold real money balances. How this works was pictured in Figure 7.4A. A second form of the demand for money was seen in the classical or quantity theory. In this version, the demand for money does not depend at all on interest rates; it is completely interest-inelastic. This occurs if the asset demand for money is missing. Demand for money depends only on income. The result is the vertical money-demand curves shown in Figure 7.2B.

In contrast, an extreme view—called Keynesian but never held by Keynes—shows the demand for money becoming completely elastic after real interest rates fall to a minimum level. This is the liquidity-trap portion of Figure 7.6. Under this assumption, when interest rates are very low, people prefer to hold money for assets purposes. If more money were created, spending would not be influenced because people would be willing to hold it for speculative purposes. Until the point at which money demand becomes infinite with respect to interest rates, every increase in money acts to lower interest rates for each income level. However, after interest rates reach this minimum, all additional money is held as an asset. A larger money stock does not reduce interest rates any further; they remain stuck at the level reached prior to the money expansion. If an increase in the desire to spend depends on a lower interest rate, greater spending will not be forthcoming.[7]

While the specific analysis of how the shape of *LM* curves influences the effectiveness of monetary and fiscal policy is delayed until Chapter 8, the conclusions can be summarized easily. If the demand curve for money is vertical—the classical case—an increase in the money supply will have a maximum effect on income. None of the added money is absorbed by assets demand; it can all support an expansion of output. If the demand curve for money is horizontal—the liquidity trap—added money will not cause interest rates to fall or income to expand. All of the new money is absorbed for assets purposes at the existing interest rates.

When money demand is vertical, the *LM* curves are also vertical. An increase in the money supply shifts the *LM* curve to the right by an amount equal to the change in money times its income velocity. (Equation 7.11 indi-

---

7. The three versions can be thought of as unique views of the value of assets demand in equation 7.4:

$$\frac{MD}{P} = eY + \overline{MA} - hr. \qquad\qquad \textbf{7.4}$$

In the quantity theory, the value of assets demand ($\overline{MA} - hr$) is zero. In the liquidity trap, the value of h is infinite. In the standard version, it falls between the two extremes. Chapter 8 analyzes these contrasts in more detail.

cates that $\Delta Y = \left(\dfrac{\Delta MS}{P}\right)_1 V$; if the assets demand is zero, then $V = \dfrac{1}{e}$.) Where money demand is horizontal—the liquidity trap—an equivalent horizontal sector exists on the LM curve. An increase in the money supply will not shift the LM curve down. For example, if demand for money is infinite at or below 1 percent, added money does not lower the LM curve below this level. Interest rates will not fall because all additional money will be absorbed by assets demand. If a decline in interest rates were needed to raise spending, it would not come about. Interest rates are at a minimum in the liquidity trap.

Empirical Evidence on the LM Curve

Since both the shape and the stability of the LM curve are important for analysis, it is worth looking at some empirical data on the demand for money relative to interest rates. How well does the demand for money fit the alternative theories? Questions concern the responsiveness of interest rates to money and of spending to interest rates. A demand for money insensitive to interest rates supports the quantity theory. If money demand is inelastic, monetary policies will rule the roost and fiscal policy will be ineffective. Questions of stability in the models are also significant.[8] If the models are accurate and do not shift for extraneous reasons or because of omitted variables, we should be able to predict what will happen to aggregate demand and interest rates when the money supply is changed.

Instability of the LM function can occur for many reasons. Shifts may take place in the institutional structure of financial institutions as well as in what people use for money. Tastes may change; random events may disrupt relationships; important variables may be missing from the estimated functions. Movements of the omitted variables can lead to sharp shifts in estimated demand relationships.

THE SHAPE OF MONEY DEMAND

Early debates over the possible shape of the demand curve for money waned as a result of numerous empirical studies of the relationships. The standard model, shown in equation 7.4 and in Figure 7.4, has been explored many times.[9] Most studies show that the income elasticity of money demand is between .5 and 1.0. Every 1 percent increase in current-dollar income raises the demand for M from .5 to 1.0 percent. Since the price elasticity is assumed to be 1, nominal money demand rises at the same rate as price indexes. Although not

8. C. F. Laidler, *The Demand for Money: Theories and Evidence,* 2nd edition (New York: Dun-Donnelley, 1977), pp. 30–35 and 119–20.

9. For a list of studies and results, see Laidler, *The Demand for Money,* and J. T. Boorman, "The Evidence on the Demand for Money" in T. M. Havrilesky and J. T. Boorman, *Current Issues in Monetary Theory and Policy* 2nd ed. (Arlington Heights, Ill.: AHM Publishing Co., 1980.)

in complete accord, these studies also show that the money demand is neither completely elastic nor inelastic with respect to interest rates. The actual estimates of interest elasticities vary depending on whether a study uses bonds or short-term rates to measure the level of interest, and whether it uses $M1$ or $M2$. The range of results for major studies is

	Interest elasticity
$M1$ with long-term rates	−.7 to −.9
$M2$ with long-term rates	−.4 to −.6
$M1$ and $M2$ with short-term rates	−.1 to −.4

The money supply is measured in real terms, but interest rates are in nominal terms because of the uncertainty of how to find real interest-rates. This means that part of the measured elasticities may reflect the effect of anticipated inflation. However, for most of the period used in fitting these studies, this effect would be minor.

THE STABILITY OF MONEY DEMAND

Until 1975, many observers believed that empirical studies showed the demand for money to be stable. Econometric models were able to explain the demand for real money with a minimum number of variables, such as those used in the standard model. For example, a well-known model by Stephan Goldfeld showed that the real demand for money could be explained by movements in real income (Q), nominal interest rates on time deposits (i_{TD}) and on commercial paper (i_{CP}), and on the money stock of the previous period $\left(\dfrac{MS}{P}\right)_{-1}$.[10]

According to such models, taking into account the lagged effects of changes in the demand for money in prior periods, every 1 percent change in real income caused money demand to rise about .55 percent. A 1 percent rise in nominal interest increased money demand about .19 percent. Lags were estimated to be comparatively short. In the first quarter, about 40 percent of the effect of changes in income and interest would be felt. By the end of the two quarters, about two-thirds of their impact would have occurred.

However, when the period covered by such studies included 1974 through 1978, the same variables were no longer able to explain the money demand. Changes in income and interest rates no longer had a logical or statistically significant impact on money demand. Adding 10 quarters to the previous 85

10. As an example, see G. Garcia and S. Pak, "Some Clues in the Case of the Missing Money," *American Economic Review* 69(May 1979):330–34, which gives the following equation based on data from 1952:Q2 to 1973:Q4:

$$\frac{M}{P} = .179Q - .042i_{TD} - .018i_{CP} + .676\left(\frac{M1}{P}\right)_{-1}. \qquad \textbf{7.12}$$

produced an empirical model which reduced the impact of income and interest rates on real money demand by over 90 percent in the year after these variables change.

The result of an apparent shift in the demand for money is demonstrated in Table 7.3. This table shows how far the initial equation missed in predicting the demand for money during this period. The final two columns report the cumulative error in predictions by the model (such as equation 7.12) from 1974 to 1978. From 1970 through the fourth quarter of 1974, the total error was less than $5 billion. The model was doing very well. Then it disintegrated. By the end of 1978, errors had cumulated to $53 billion. The shortfall in estimated demand was 14.7 percent of the total. From 1970 through the middle of 1974, the average error in predicting money demand was only .2 percent, while the root-mean-square error was 1.6 percent. (Roughly one-third of the errors would be expected to be, and were, larger than this amount.) From mid-1974 through the end of 1978, however, the average quarterly error jumped to 2.9 percent, and the root-mean-square error rose to 3.8 percent.

TABLE 7.3   **Errors in Prediction of Demand for Money (M1)**
(billions of dollars)

Period	Actual money stock	Error in prediction	Percentage error
1974:Q4	282	5	1.8
1975:Q4	295	20	6.8
1976:Q4	312	40	12.8
1977:Q4	337	47	13.9
1978:Q4	361	53	14.7

Money demand can shift. The first column shows the actual money supply. The second column lists the additional amount that standard money-demand models estimate should have been demanded on the basis of actual interest rates and income in each year. The third column shows the percentage shortfall of actual compared to that estimated.

These errors were a blow to many who had chosen money because of its prior stability as the best policy variable for the economy. One of the key empirical supports for preferring monetary to fiscal policy or a more eclectic view evaporated. Many new studies were undertaken in an effort to explain what had happened during the period. On the whole, it was found that the demand for currency had not shifted greatly but that for demand deposits had. Most of the errors seemed to arise in the demand of nonfinancial businesses for working balances, not in that of households.[11]

11. Other examples of possible shifts in money demand are described in P. Temin, *Did Monetary Forces Cause the Great Depression?* (New York: Norton, 1976), pp. 121–37, and H. Vane and J. Thompson, *Monetarism, Theory, Evidence, and Policy* (New York: Wiley, 1979), pp. 45–46.

WHAT DOES THE FAILURE OF THE MODEL MEAN?

While the shift in demand was great, many monetarists remained convinced from their theoretical reasoning that the demand for money was stable. They attributed the failure of the model primarily to institutional changes in the payments mechanism and to regulations such as those forbidding interest on demand deposits and limiting rates on other deposits. Some new elements, such as NOW accounts, money-market funds, and repurchase agreements, did develop into money. More changes are probable in the future as electronic funds transfer systems become more common and speed up the velocity of transactions.[12]

Some believed that the problems experienced could be lessened simply by improving the model, which failed to reflect the full complexity of modern portfolio theory. While it did follow the modern quantity theory, perhaps more variables, and in a different form, were needed to account for changes in the financial structure. Another suggestion was that the definition of money be changed. Because spending units were substituting other kinds of balances for demand deposits, these other types ought to be included in money measurement. Some change in the structure of the financial system had taken place; past relationships had altered. Therefore, the traditional definition of money in this period was a poor indicator for policy.

Perhaps reform of the regulatory system would help the situation. However, Phillip Cagan, one of the foremost scholars of the problem, is not optimistic. He concludes that

> Although changes in the payments system will erode monetary controls during the transition, it might be thought that the erosion will eventually end when a new system is fully established and further changes occur slowly. At that time the relationship between some new definition of transactions balances and aggregate expenditures might be identified as a reasonably accurate basis for the implementation of monetary policy. Although this is possible, there are reasons for doubt, and the developments now under way provide little room for complacency about the dangers to monetary policy.[13]

Nonmonetarists pointed to the failure of the model as proof of their view that either the demand for money includes many more variables than either the modern quantity theory or the standard model shows, and therefore it is subject to shifts and instability, or that what is money changes endogenously as a result of the pressures of higher interest rates and new financial needs.

Some of the breakdown in the model was due to shifts in money demand caused by inflation, government regulation, and high interest rates. The model failed to include expectations, which might have been undergoing rapid

12. For a complete discussion of this matter, see P. Cagan, "Financial Development and the Erosion of Monetary Controls" in American Enterprise Institute, *Contemporary Economic Problems 1979* (Washington: AEI, 1979), pp. 117–52.

13. P. Cagan, "Financial Development and the Erosion of Monetary Controls," p. 140.

changes. It also lacked a variable reflecting the impact of wealth. The probable change in what the economy uses as money occurred because every time monetary policy begins to pinch in a free market, new types of money develop. Changes in the institutional structure are almost a necessity. The use of money as a control variable leads to a shift in the economic structure in response to maneuvers of those in the market to avoid the impact of policy. This is one of the reasons that the nonmonetarists feel it would be a mistake to pick a single variable and limit policy to its control. Shifts in the structure, such as occurred in 1974, can lead to major policy errors. These can be avoided by accepting a more eclectic view based on more careful observations of what is happening to various possible measures of money as well as to interest rates.

Summary

1. Many debates over policy center around different assumptions as to the shape and stability of the curve reflecting equilibrium in the money market—the liquidity-money *(LM)* curve, which shows the interest-income points at which money demand and supply are in equilibrium.

2. A standard model of money demand shows total demand depending on a transactions demand related to the level of income and on an assets demand related to the level of interest rates.

3. The crude quantity theory, as expressed in Fisher's equation of exchange and the Cambridge cash-balance equation, assumes that the level of spending will rise in proportion to any change in money. Since resources would be fully employed, output would not increase with spending; additional money would merely raise prices.

4. Keynes analyzed more completely the transactions demand for money and also pointed out that money would be held for speculative or assets purposes. Changes in spending would not be proportional to increases in money. Returns on a portfolio consisting of money will differ from one of bonds, depending on what happens to interest rates. The amount of money held for both transactions and speculative demand will rise as interest rates fall, and vice versa. Furthermore, if there are unemployed resources, an increase in demand can raise output rather than prices.

5. Modern theories of the demand for money expand on the previous analysis. Money is one asset among many in a portfolio. It serves as a medium of exchange and its demand is related to income. In addition, money may be an attractive or an undesirable asset compared to other portfolio possibilities. Its demand depends on interest rates, wealth, prices, and expectations. The relationship between money and spending depends on how money demand is influenced by these other factors.

6. While modern monetarists agree that other factors enter into the de-

mand for money, they believe either that these are not significant or that their impact can be accurately predicted, especially over the long run. Changes in money remain the dominant factor driving changes in spending. Even if errors are made in concentrating on money as the chief policy-control variable, errors will be smaller than would be the case using an eclectic approach.

7. Neo-Keynesians emphasize other demand factors and the potential instability of the demand for and shifts in the money stock as people adjust their views of money. Forecasting and control over spending and prices require knowledge of many variables in addition to changes in the money supply.

8. The liquidity-money *(LM)* curve can be derived by combining schedules for the money supply with the income and assets demand for money. The curve slopes upward to the right. A given money supply must be split, with reduced demand for money as an asset resulting from higher interest rates releasing money to be used for transactions balances.

9. Changes in the money supply shift the position of the *LM* curve. An increase in the money stock allows more spending at each interest rate.. A decrease in the desire to hold money has a similar effect.

10. Two potentially interesting segments of the *LM* curve are the extremes, which might be either interest-inelastic or completely elastic. If such segments exist, they would change the relationship between money and spending from that set forth in the standard model. However, most post-Depression empirical models of money demand indicate that neither of these situations is likely.

11. For many years, empirical estimates of the demand for money using income and interest rates as the main variables were quite accurate. The explanatory powers were high, and the coefficients appeared stable. But after 1974, the models became erratic; predictions became poor. Institutional changes occurred. Disagreement exists as to whether the standard theory is wrong and more variables must be included to get better predictions, or whether what the economy uses as money changed, and the change was not reflected in the equations.

Questions for Discussion and Review

1. What is the opportunity cost of holding money?

2. Distinguish between the transactions demand and the assets demand for money.

3. Contrast the monetarist and post-Keynesian views on the demand for money. Why is a knowledge of the degree of stability of the demand for money important for the implementation of monetary policy?

4. Why does the crude quantity theory state that the price level is proportional to the money supply?

5. Why in the Cambridge version of the quantity theory is the demand to hold money the reciprocal of the velocity of circulation?

6. What were the three motives for holding money identified by Keynes?

7. Discuss the portfolio and inventory theory approaches to the demand for money.

8. Suppose Mr. A buys a bond for $100 in December 1979 which promises to pay interest of 10 percent per year and to repay principal (of $100) at the end of five years. If in December 1980 the interest rate on this type of bond rises to 15 percent, for how much will Mr. A be able to sell his bond? Supposing he does sell, what was the actual yield on the bond during the year Mr. A held it?

9. How has modern analysis altered Keynes's conception of the speculative demand for money?

10. Identify and briefly give the significance of each variable which enters into the modern total-demand-for-money equation.

11. What factors determine the slope of the *LM* curve?

12. Under what circumstances might an economy find itself on the liquidity-trap section of an *LM* curve?

13. What factors cause the *LM* curve to shift?

References

Baumol, W. J. "The Transactions Demand for Cash: An Inventory Theoretic Approach." *Quarterly Journal of Economics* 66 (November 1952):545–56.

Boorman, J. T. "The Evidence on the Demand for Money." In *Current Issues in Monetary Theory and Policy*, 2nd edition, edited by T. M. Havrilesky and J. T. Boorman. Arlington Heights, Ill.: AHM Publishing Co., 1980.

Friedman, M. "A Theoretical Framework for Monetary Analysis." *Journal of Political Economy* 78 (March/April 1970):193–238.

Goldfeld, S. "The Case of the Missing Money." *Brookings Papers on Economic Activity* (1976): 683–730.

Hicks, Sir John. *The Crisis in Keynesian Economics.* New York: Basic Books, 1974.

Leijonhufvud, A. *On Keynesian Economics and the Economics of Keynes.* New York: Oxford University Press, 1968.

Temin, P. *Did Monetary Forces Cause the Great Depression?* New York: Norton, 1976.

Tobin, J. "The Interest-Elasticity of Transactions Demand for Cash." *Review of Economics and Statistics* (August 1956):241–47.

Tobin, J. "Liquidity Preference as Behavior Toward Risk." *Review of Economic Studies* 25 (February 1958):65–86.

Vane, H., and J. Thompson. *Monetarism, Theory, Evidence, and Policy.* New York: Wiley, 1979.

8

Aggregate Demand: Equilibrium of Money, the Desire to Spend, and Prices

The models of equilibrium in the money and goods markets which we have developed thus far are building blocks in the more complete system needed to explain why aggregate demand fluctuates and creates inflationary and deflationary pressures. Combining the *IS-LM* curves can illustrate why real income and the demand for output move. However, this model is not complete enough to explain the many problems that arise in an actual economy plagued by inflation and supply problems.

Demand analysis developed in an attempt to find the causes of depressions and inflations. Until the 1930s, it was generally believed that the economy contained sufficient self-correcting mechanisms to return by itself to positions of relative price stability and full employment. Today, because of the experience of recessions, depressions, inflations, and stagflations, fewer believe that an unguided economy will automatically regain a desirable level of output and price stability. Major debates recur both over what policy actions should be taken and over the extent to which policies should be used. For instance, is it necessary to alter government spending and taxes or will movements in the money supply suffice to bring about a desirable goal? Once policies are decided upon, further questions arise about whether policy variables should be changed aggressively or general policies formulated and followed steadily, with only minor changes in direction.

Some of these issues revolve around the shape and stability of the variables determining real demand and their reactions to movements in monetary and fiscal policies. The first part of this chapter discusses equilibrium points on the *LM* and *IS* curves and how these points are influenced by the shapes of each curve and by disturbances that cause the curves to shift. The second part of the chapter removes the restriction on the macroeconomic model, maintained since Chapter 3, that prices are constant (fixed) with all analysis in real terms. If prices are flexible, and not constant, they become an additional influence on the level of spending, causing the *IS-LM* equilibrium to shift. Such shifts have traditionally been analyzed primarily through the direct effects of changes in prices on the real money supply. In recent years, however, more emphasis has been placed on the effect of changes in money on expectations of future prices and on nominal interest rates. Such considerations are included in the discussion of the flexible price model. Price movements influence aggregate demand through their effects on the nominal money supply and wealth. Therefore, prices and movements in nominal values must be combined with real factors. Only when real and nominal values are combined and their effects on the *IS* and *LM* curves are measured, can movements in aggregate demand be completely analyzed.

To analyze some of these issues, this chapter first examines forces determining equilibrium values for output and real interest rates. It then introduces price movements, showing how they affect aggregate demand and market interest rates. Some of the topics considered in this development include:

> The equilibrium of real demand.
> Gaps between real aggregate demand and output at full employment.
> Monetary policy and the *LM* and *IS* curves.
> Fiscal policy and the *LM* curve.
> The multiplier also depends on interest rates.
> Changes in the price level and aggregate demand.
> Price expectations, aggregate demand, and interest rates.
> Fluctuations in money, credit, interest rates, and aggregate demand.

The Equilibrium of Real Demand

Chapters 3, 4, and 5 explained how each sector's desires to save and spend could be combined into an investment saving *(IS)* schedule. Chapters 6 and 7 similarly described how the demand for and supply of money could be combined to form a liquidity-money *(LM)* schedule. While the *IS* and *LM* schedules separately yield valuable information about the real goods and money markets, neither schedule alone determines real demand. Both the *IS* and *LM* curves and equations contain two unknowns *(Y* and *r)*. To determine the level of demand, the two curves (and their equations) must be combined. Such a juncture is accomplished in Figure 8.1. This diagram repeats the *IS* curve developed in equations 5.8 and 5.9 and presented in Figure 5.2 and the *LM* curve from equation 7.10 and Figure 7.7.

The diagram shows the only point *(A)* where interest rates and income levels yield an equilibrium for both the goods market (the *IS* curve) and the money market (the *LM* curve). At point *A*, with *r* at 5 percent and a real

FIGURE 8.1   **Equilibrium in the Goods and Money Markets**

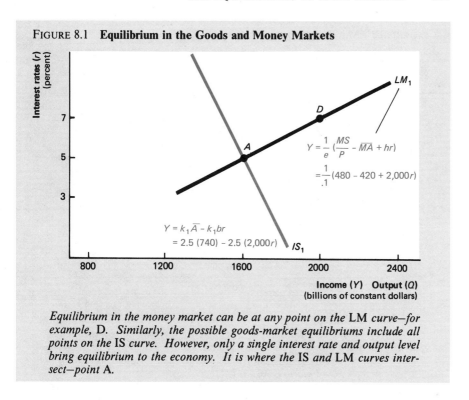

Equilibrium in the money market can be at any point on the LM curve—for example, D. Similarly, the possible goods-market equilibriums include all points on the IS curve. However, only a single interest rate and output level bring equilibrium to the economy. It is where the IS and LM curves intersect—point A.

income and output of $1,600 billion, all spending units will be in balance. A real desire to spend exactly equals output and income. A balance also exists in portfolios between the desire to hold money and the real money supply.

A SHIFT TO A NEW EQUILIBRIUM

The *IS-LM* diagram enables us to analyze what happens to the equilibrium of output and interest rates when some variable—for example, a new technology or a decreased desire to save—shifts the *IS* curve or when an increase in the money supply or drop in money demand shifts *LM*. The IS_2 line in Figure 8.2 illustrates an increase in the desire to spend. Assume an increase in autonomous spending of $\Delta \overline{A}$ ($160 billion).Where is the economy's new equilibrium? The *simple multiplier* (k_1) shows how much spending would change as a result of an autonomous shift in the *IS* curve *if* the effect of interest rates on demand were zero, or if interest rates remained constant. However, output and income do not end up at point *B*, the increase indicated by multiplying the autonomous change in spending $(\Delta \overline{A})$ by the simple multiplier (k_1). Instead, the economy settles at point *C*. This is because initially the new demand is met by an unplanned decrease in inventories or by a larger backlog of orders. In either case, firms expand output. As activity increases, so does the money demanded for transactions purposes. To shift part of the money supply from assets to transactions purposes, interest rates must rise. As interest rates climb, the

FIGURE 8.2   **Movements to Equilibrium**

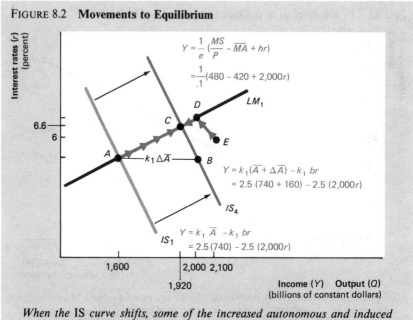

When the IS curve shifts, some of the increased autonomous and induced desires to spend are offset by higher interest rates. The supply of money is insufficient for the economy to stay at B; the demand for goods is too low at D. At point C, both markets regain balance.

interest-responsive effect ($-br$) in the goods market depresses the demand arising from the expansion of autonomous spending. At point C, the new equilibrium results from the sum of the changes in autonomous spending, induced spending, and demand reduced by higher real interest rates ($\Delta Y = k_1(\Delta \overline{A} - b\Delta r)$).

What if the flow of new orders caused an overoptimism on the part of businesses and they mistakenly increased output to point E? The analysis of Figures 5.6 and 7.9 showed how such a disequilibrium situation would affect the individual goods and money markets. A point below the LM curve signals an excess demand for money. The combined needs for transactions and assets are greater than the money supply. Decision units adjust their portfolios by selling bonds or other assets. Interest rates rise until the money market comes into equilibrium somewhere on the LM curve (shown in the diagram as point D).

Note, however, that the goods market is not in equilibrium at either point E or D. An excess of goods exists. Demand is below output. To bring the goods market into equilibrium and sell their excess inventories, businessmen will cut production. Income will fall, as will the transàctions demand for money. Money is freed for assets purposes, and interest rates drop. The economy moves down the LM curve until it reaches the stable equilibrium point C. At this lower income, the desire to save is less than on an IS curve which would go through D, while a reduced r leads to a greater desire to invest.

THE *IS-LM* EQUILIBRIUM EQUATIONS

The fact that point A in Figure 8.2 is an equilibrium point and the others are not can be proved by solving the goods and money market equations simultaneously, either in the general algebraic or specific numerical example. The *IS* equation is

$$Y = k_1(\overline{A}) - k_1(br) \qquad\qquad Y = 2.5(740) - 2.5(2,000r) \qquad \textbf{8.1}$$

and that for the money market is

$$Y = \frac{1}{e}\left(\frac{MS}{P} - \overline{MA} + hr\right) \qquad\qquad Y = \frac{1}{.1}(480 - 420 + 2,000r). \qquad \textbf{8.2}$$

When the *IS* and *LM* equations are solved simultaneously, the market is found to be in equilibrium at A, with levels of real income and interest of \$1,600 billion and 5 percent.[1]

The IS_4 line depicts the effects of an assumed increase in autonomous spending of \$160 billion. Using the equations, we find that equilibrium income increases by \$320 billion to \$1,920 billion, and interest rates are at 6.6 percent (point C). The actual multiplier derived from the combination of the two markets is 2.0, compared to the simple multiplier of 2.5 in the goods market (shown by equation 8.1) alone. Rising interest rates needed to bring the money market into equilibrium reduce the demand for investment goods. The equations also show why points D and E are disequilibriums. For example, at point D the interest rate is 7 percent and income is \$2,000 billion. When inserted in equation 8.2, these figures do show an equilibrium in the money market. The increase in output from \$1,600 billion to \$2,000 billion raises transactions demand by \$40 billion, while the higher interest rates reduce assets demand by an identical amount. But when the numbers are substituted in equation 8.1, a disequilibrium results. At the new level, while output would rise to \$2,000 billion, the desire to spend would drop to \$1,900 billion as a result of the higher

1. Using the information from equations (8.1) and (8.2), they are solved as:

$$Y = \frac{k_1\left(b\dfrac{MS}{P} - b\overline{MA} + h\overline{A}\right)}{k_1 eb + h} \qquad Y = \frac{2.5[2,000(480) - 2,000(420) + 2,000(740)]}{2.5(.1)2,000 + 2,000} = 1,600 \quad \textbf{8.3}$$

$$r = \frac{k_1\overline{A} - \dfrac{\dfrac{MS}{P}}{e} + \dfrac{\overline{MA}}{e}}{\dfrac{h}{e} + k_1 b} \qquad r = \frac{2.5(740) - \dfrac{480}{.1} + \dfrac{420}{.1}}{\dfrac{2,000}{.1} + 2.5(2,000)} = .05. \qquad\qquad \textbf{8.4}$$

Appendix 8.1 illustrates in more detail the algebraic relationships within the *IS-LM* curves as well as the derivation of the numerical example.

interest rates. It is this shortfall of spending compared to output that causes a contraction back to equilibrium point *C*.

Gaps between Real Aggregate Demand and Output at Full Employment

The analysis of real demand has been based thus far on a model with constant prices. Changes in production are assumed to respond fully to changes in the desire to spend. Output rises or falls to match all movements in demand without any effect on the price level. But this is an artificial abstraction; it is unlikely that demand can change without affecting prices. When demand shifts, it will open a gap between the level of spending and that necessary to maintain output at a full-employment level. This gap, in turn is likely to cause price movements.

Even though the first part of this chapter continues to use the fixed-price model, the concept of gaps makes clear why movements in demand are of such concern. By definition, the full-employment level of output (Q^*) is where the level of demand and actual output exerts no upward or downward pressure on prices. This concept is pictured in panel B of Figure 8.3. At point *B*, the *IS-LM* equilibrium of demand is exactly on the full-employment line (Q^*). There is no pressure for prices to change. The number of unemployed is the minimum number (the natural rate) needed to keep inflation from accelerating or decelerating.

In contrast, in panel A at point *A*, equilibrium demand falls to the left of the line of output at full employment. In panel A, demand in the goods market is less than in panel B, with equilibrium at a lower level of output and interest rates. The economy produces at less than potential output. Demand to the left of full-employment output means that firms have excess capacity and labor is unemployed, causing a ***deflationary gap;*** some pressures will be felt for prices to decline. This model, however, contains no information as to how fast or how much prices will react to the deflationary gap. In fact, no price data appear on the figure. While excess unemployment will put pressure on prices, the analysis of how much must await the introduction of the concepts of aggregate supply in Chapter 12.

Panel C pictures a situation opposite to the first. In this case, a movement of the *IS* curve up to the right leads to an equilibrium with the *LM* curve at point *C*, with higher interest rates and equilibrium output to the right of the line of output at full employment. Since output cannot meet demand, an ***inflationary gap*** arises. It is assumed that prices will rise, but again, by how much and how fast can be predicted only when aggregate supply and demand are combined.

Policy debates center on possible gaps between equilibrium real output and potential output at full employment—the gap between A and B and B and C. Will the economy self-adjust to remove the gap, or should monetary or fiscal policies attempt to shift the IS-LM *equilibrium to a point on Q*?*

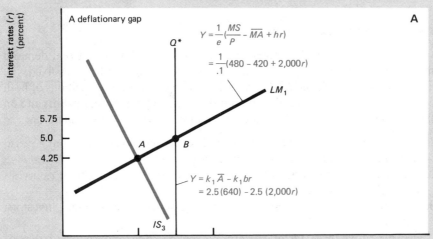

FIGURE 8.3   **Equilibrium of Real Demand Not at Full-Employment Output**

A deflationary gap

$$Y = \frac{1}{e}(\frac{MS}{P} - \overline{MA} + hr)$$

$$= \frac{1}{.1}(480 - 420 + 2{,}000r)$$

LM_1

$$Y = k_1\overline{A} - k_1 br$$
$$= 2.5(640) - 2.5(2{,}000r)$$

IS_3

A

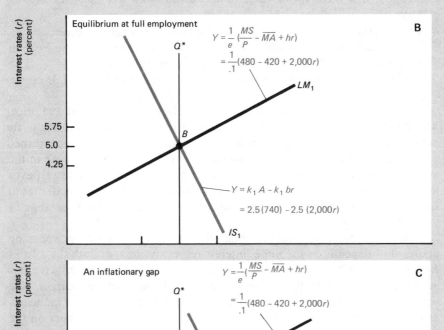

Equilibrium at full employment

$$Y = \frac{1}{e}(\frac{MS}{P} - \overline{MA} + hr)$$

$$= \frac{1}{.1}(480 - 420 + 2{,}000r)$$

LM_1

$$Y = k_1 A - k_1 br$$

$$= 2.5(740) - 2.5(2{,}000r)$$

IS_1

B

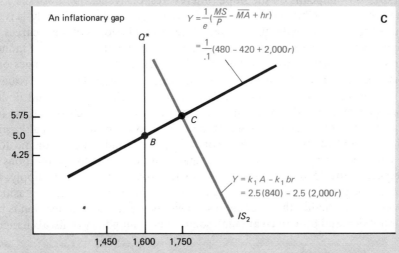

An inflationary gap

$$Y = \frac{1}{e}(\frac{MS}{P} - \overline{MA} + hr)$$

$$= \frac{1}{.1}(480 - 420 + 2{,}000r)$$

$$Y = k_1 A - k_1 br$$
$$= 2.5(840) - 2.5(2{,}000r)$$

IS_2

C

1,450   1,600   1,750

Income (Y)   Output (Q)
(billions of constant dollars)

FORCES ALTERING DEMAND EQUILIBRIUM

Given a particular level of potential output, the equilibrium of real demand
may cause inflationary gaps or excess unemployment. With prices fixed, the
amount of demand at the *IS-LM* equilibrium depends on the positions of both
curves. How demand alters depends on the degree to which either shifts and on
their slopes. In other words, equilibrium and the size of gaps depend on:

1. The autonomous desire to spend $(\overline{A})$ of consumers, businesses, and government (and the foreign sector in an enlarged model).
2. The marginal propensities to spend, *m* (including consumption, *c;* investment, *d;* and tax functions, *t*).
3. The interest-responsiveness *(b)* of spending desires of consumers, investors,
   and the government.
   (These first three factors determine the position and shape of the *IS*
   curve.)
4. The demand for money *(MD)* for transactions and assets purposes.
5. The nominal supply of money *(MS)*, determined primarily by the Federal
   Reserve, but also by the public and financial institutions.
   (These latter two factors govern the position and shape of the *LM* curve.)

While, as the second half of this chapter shows, actual output and prices
also depend on how demand reacts to price movements and on aggregate
supply, much of the analysis of inflations, recessions, and growth is concerned
with the forces determining real aggregate demand. Disturbances arise in the
amount of output demanded as a result of movements in any of the five types of
factors determining the *IS-LM* equilibrium. In other words, private desires to
save, spend, or to hold money may shift, and so may government spending or
the money supply.

Where income and output settle when the money supply or spending
desires shift depends on the slope (interest-responsiveness) of both the *IS* and
LM curves. As Chapter 7 pointed out, the history of demand analysis is characterized by ongoing discussions about the probable slopes of these curves. The
significance of these debates lies in the fact that the effectiveness of monetary
and fiscal policy, as well as the stability of aggregate demand, hinges on the
manner in which interest rates affect spending. Knowledge of the issues underlying these controversies reveals the forces leading to over- and underex-
pansions of demand. In recent years, the importance attached to these issues
has diminished as emphasis has turned more to expectations, wealth, supply
shocks, political pressures and economic policy, and other dynamic forces.
Furthermore, experience has shown that some of the extreme positions with
respect to the *IS* or *LM* curves are not realistic. If the money supply, fiscal
policy, or private desires shift, the economy will respond. Leaving aside the
question of whether the ultimate results will be desirable, if a decision is made
to shift demand by a given amount, some level of monetary or fiscal change can

accomplish the task. There is less agreement, however, over the degree to which demand can be controlled by smaller movements in either money or fiscal policy.[2]

To understand these issues, we will first examine the relationships between the results of changes in monetary policy and the slopes of the *LM* and *IS* curves, and then see why the results of shifts in fiscal policy depend upon similar factors.

Monetary Policy and the *LM* and *IS* Curves

Monetary policy consists of changes in money and credit. The results of policy depend on the size of the change and on how the economy reacts to it. If the Federal Reserve decides to alter the money supply, how will aggregate demand be affected? When more money is created, equilibrium in the money market is disturbed. At the same time, the amount of real balances (a form of wealth) will shift. This section shows how the *IS-LM* diagrams can be used to analyze the impact of shifts in the money market. Later sections consider the effects which are due to such changes in real balances.

THE SHAPE OF THE *LM* CURVE

What happens to demand when the money supply increases? As demonstrated in Figure 8.4, given a fixed *IS* curve, the amount the money supply expands demand depends on the slope of the *LM* curves, which depend on the demand for money. In all three examples, the real money supply $\left(\Delta \dfrac{MS}{P}\right)$ increases by the same amount ($20 billion). Panel A shows the special case of the crude quantity theory. The demand for money is completely unresponsive to interest rates. The *LM* curves are vertical. After the money supply expands, the new level of demand equals the additional money times its velocity. Assets demand is zero, and therefore velocity is constant and equal to the reciprocal of the transactions demand for money $\left(V = \dfrac{1}{e}\right)$. The *IS* curve does not affect the level of spending; it merely determines interest rates.

Panel B depicts the standard case. The slope of the *LM* curve depends on both an income and an assets demand for money. When the money supply increases, the *LM* curve shifts. Initially, an excess of money causes bonds or other assets to be purchased. Interest rates fall to point *B*. Now, however, an excess demand for goods exists. The desire to invest exceeds saving. Businesses must expand production to meet the additional demand for goods. Output grows until equilibrium is regained at *C*.[3] Part of the additional money funds a growth in output, part a decline in interest notes.

2. See M. Friedman and W. Heller, *Monetary vs. Fiscal Policy* (New York: Norton, 1969).

3. For a more complete discussion of the equations and the numerical example, consult Appendix 8.1.

FIGURE 8.4   **The Effect on Income and Interest Rates of a Change in the Money Supply**

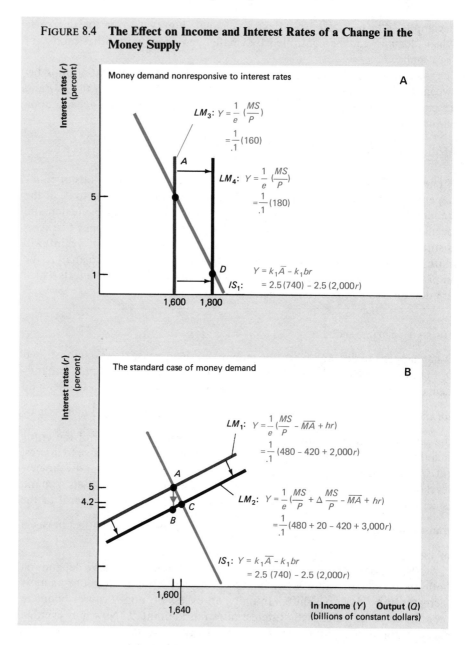

When a liquidity trap exists (panel c), the demand for money is perfectly (infinitely) elastic with respect to interest rates. An increase in money has no noticeable effect on the *LM* curve; it remains horizontal. All increases in money are absorbed in assets demand; none expands spending. Interest rates do not fall. Neither investment nor consumption increases. Additional money is ineffective in changing demand. After the money stock grows, the *LM* curve and equilibrium income remain exactly as they were.

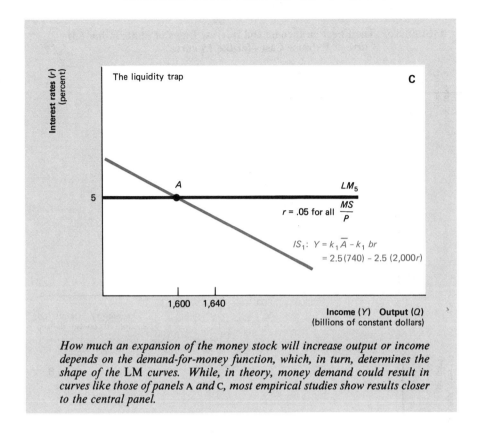

The liquidity trap

C

$IS_1: Y = k_1 \overline{A} - k_1 br$
$= 2.5(740) - 2.5(2,000r)$

How much an expansion of the money stock will increase output or income depends on the demand-for-money function, which, in turn, determines the shape of the LM *curves. While, in theory, money demand could result in curves like those of panels* A *and* C, *most empirical studies show results closer to the central panel.*

THE SHAPE OF THE *IS* CURVE

If either fiscal or monetary policy changes, equilibrium income depends, as has been noted, on the slopes of both the *LM* and the *IS* curves. If the *IS* curve is very responsive to interest rates, spending will increase more than if it is only slightly responsive. The two polar cases of Figure 8.5 demonstrate these relationships.

In panel A, the responsiveness of spending to interest rates is zero (complete inelasticity); the *IS* curve is vertical. Under such circumstances, what happens when the money supply increases? The LM_2 curve represents a shift due to an increase in real money. Immediately following the growth in money, the economy, which remains at *A*, is in disequilibrium. An excess supply of money exists with the economy above the new *LM* curve. As a result, people buy bonds or other securities in order to readjust their portfolios to the new money supply. Interest rates drop, but spending does not respond (because the *b* coefficient in the *IS* curve is zero). Instead, interest rates decline until all the added money is absorbed into assets uses.

Panel B illustrates the opposite extreme. In this case, the *IS* curve is completely responsive to changes in interest rates; it is perfectly (infinitely) interest-elastic. Even the slightest drop in interest rates means that all added

FIGURE 8.5   **The Effect on Income and Interest Rates of Shifts in the *LM* Curve at Extreme Cases for the *IS* curve**

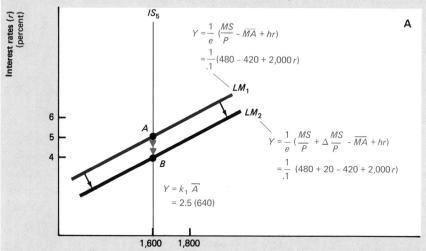

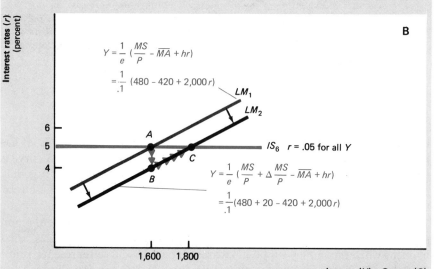

The shape of the IS *curve depends on how spending responds to interest-rate changes. In panel* A, *spending is the same at all interest rates. More money and a reduction in rates has no effect on real demand or output. In* B, *since the slightest decline in rates causes an unlimited increase in spending, all added money can go for transactions purposes; any initial drop in interest rates and absorption of money by assets demand is reversed.*

money goes to increase spending. Income expands by the new money times its income velocity. In the figure, new money spent initially for bonds or other financial assets causes the economy to move to point *B* on the shifted curve, LM_2. With lower interest rates, the demand for goods rises. Consumption, investment, and output increase. The economy expands to point *C*, where the excess demand for goods has been removed.

Since, in actuality, neither extreme of the *IS* curve is likely to exist, the effect of any change in the money supply will depend on the *IS* slope. Figure 8.4B illustrated an *IS* curve between the extremes. The closer the economy's actual *IS* curve is to vertical, the less will a given change in the money supply affect income and output. The less responsive spending is to interest rates, the greater must be the drop in interest rates to achieve any desired expansion of demand. But when interest rates fall sharply, more money is held for assets purposes. The amount available for transactions purposes and for higher demand is reduced. In contrast, if the *IS* curve is very responsive to interest changes, interest rates need not fall far for assets uses will absorb only a small amount of added money; most will go to support expanded spending.

Fiscal Policy and the *LM* Curve

Under certain circumstances monetary policy may not be able to shift equilibrium demand rapidly enough, and there is fear of higher interest rates and their impacts on growth and income distribution. In such a case, the government may attempt to use fiscal policy—its purchases of goods and services, taxes, or transfers—to close a deflationary gap. What happens when the government shifts the level of demand in the real goods market (the *IS* curve) depends, as in the case of monetary policy, on the interest-responsiveness of the *LM* and *IS* curves.

Assume that a deflationary gap exists and that the government desires to increase demand so that a new equilibrium would arise at or closer to full-employment output (Q^*).[4] The previous section demonstrated how monetary policy could shift the *LM* curve to accomplish this goal. The next section shows how price changes can also shift demand. But now, we ask how much added expenditure or reduction in taxes would be needed to shift equilibrium enough to close the gap. What happens if the government shifts the *IS* curve to the right by increasing expenditures or lowering taxes by an increment of autonomous spending ($\Delta \overline{A}$) of $100 billion is illustrated by Figure 8.6. (Numerical examples can be worked out with the equations in Appendix 8.1; the results can be found in Table 8.2)

---

4. For the present, we assume that the increased output could be produced without a price change. Tertiary effects of government expenditures or tax changes and the problems of financing the deficit, to be discussed in Chapter 11, are also not taken into account at this point.

FIGURE 8.6   **The Effectiveness of Fiscal Policy Depends on Money-Market Equilibriums**

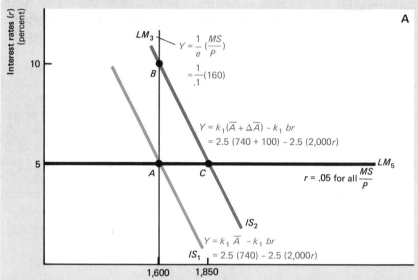

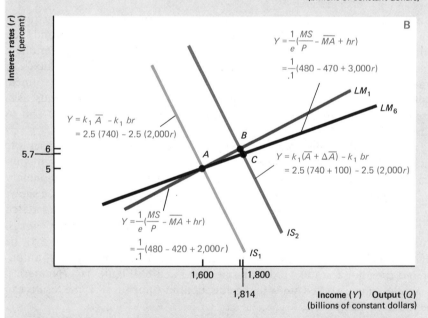

When an IS curve shifts, the slope of the LM curve determines how much output increases (the actual multiplier). Panel A presents extreme cases. On LM$_3$, a failure to release transactions balances halts any added spending; on LM$_5$, balances are fully available. Panel B shows more realistic cases; portfolio adjustments allow more spending.

Changes in the money supply were seen to yield opposing results on income if the demand for money has extreme interest reactions. *LM* curves that are either completely responsive or nonresponsive to interest rates also mean that shifts in the *IS* curve will yield opposing results. The effect on fiscal policy of zero or infinite elasticities in the *LM* curves is pictured in Figure 8.6A. In this example, when the government increases spending, the *IS* curve shifts from IS_1 to IS_2. On the diagram, LM_3 is a vertical curve (a completely inelastic demand for money), and LM_5 a horizontal, or completely elastic, curve.

When the *LM* curve is vertical (the classical assumption), increased government expenditures have no impact on total demand. No money is used for assets purposes. With a constant money supply, spending cannot expand. Velocity remains fixed. The crude quantity theory applies. When government expenditures $(\overline{G})$ increase, the point of equilibrium moves from *A* to *B*. Interest rates rise, but income does not. The higher $\overline{G}$ merely replaces private spending. A substitution occurs as higher interest rates reduce the desire of the private sector to spend. The higher $\overline{G}$ completely crowds out a similar volume of investment or consumption.

A horizontal *LM* curve (the liquidity trap) gives exactly opposite results. Large excess supplies of money are held for assets purposes. When the government increases demand, this money can be used to fund the added transactions. The economy moves from point *A* to point *C* in Figure 8.6A. Interest rates do not rise. Demand is augmented by the full multiplied effect of the rise in government expenditures.

Neither of the extreme versions of the *LM* curve is realistic. The demand for money reacts (and not infinitely) to a change in interest rates. Neither the simple nor a zero multiplier applies. Instead, the reaction of demand to a shift in the *IS* curve follows that illustrated in Figure 8.6B. The change in spending desires raises output and income. Higher transactions balances are released from assets uses only through higher interest rates, which reduce investment and consumption desires. The final multiplier falls between zero and the simple multiplier, depending on the interest-responsiveness of the two curves.

In Figure 8.6B, the same shift in the *IS* curve occurs as in the previous panel. It also pictures two *LM* curves. LM_1 is steeper and LM_6 flatter. On LM_1 interest need not increase much to release money from assets use. Note that if LM_6 prevails, the increase in demand measured by the distance between points *A* and *C* will be greater than the move to point *B*. With a flatter *LM* curve, an outside shock causes a more drastic reaction in demand. With a steeper *LM* curve, more of the impact from the *IS* shift is absorbed in a rise in interest rates.

Why does the effect of a change in government expenditures depend on the interest-responsiveness of money and spending? The answer is found in the concept of **crowding-out,** which is the process through which private demand is diminished by an increase in public spending. While crowding-out can occur in several ways, this section considers only reductions in the multiplier dependent on the *IS-LM* relationships. When the *IS* curve shifts to the right, a new equilibrium with the *LM* curve results. Interest rates rise because people holding money as an asset will release it for transactions purposes only if their costs of holding it rise. Higher interest rates, in turn, crowd out interest-sensitive investment and consumption. These reductions offset part of the expanded government spending. The actual multiplier is smaller than the simple one. With complete crowding-out—a vertical *LM* curve—the multiplier would be zero. Public spending would merely replace private spending. On the other hand, with a flat *LM* curve, the simple multiplier would apply.

The interest-responsiveness of the two curves also, of course, determines the effectiveness of a shift in monetary policy. As noted in Chapter 7, many monetarists believe that the interest-elasticity of the demand for money is low and that the responsiveness of spending to changes in money is predictable. Because *LM* curves are steep, most of each addition to the money stock will cause spending to rise, with only a minor part of it used for assets purposes. Neo-Keynesians are not as certain. They worry that a specific increase in money may go primarily to meet a shifting assets demand. Interest rates will fall slightly, but not enough to insure an increase in spending. The responsiveness of spending to interest rates may be low. Most of an increase in money may go to decreasing velocity (a greater desire to hold money). For these reasons, they feel it is necessary to observe what is happening to interest rates and to the desire to invest rather than focusing all attention on measures of the money supply.

The Multiplier Also Depends on Interest Rates

The manner in which interest-responsiveness affects the results of changes in the money supply and of shifts in spending desires is summarized in Table 8.1.

TABLE 8.1   **Changes in Money and Spending**

	Effect on aggregate demand	
	If spending is more responsive to r	*If money demand is more responsive to* r
The *LM* curve is	—	flatter
The *IS* curve is	flatter	—
Changes in money have	more effect	less effect
Changes in autonomous desires to spend have	less effect	more effect

Flatter LM *curves mean that (a) added money primarily goes to meet assets demand rather than expanding output, and (b) an* IS *shift has a large actual multiplier because interest effects are minor. Flatter* IS *curves mean that (a)* LM *shifts primarily influence output, not interest rates, and (b) the actual multiplier is less than on a steeper* IS *curve.*

The flatter the *LM* function and the steeper the *IS* curve, the less will be the change in income for any given increase in money and shift in the *LM* curve. At the extremes, if an addition to the money stock fails to lower interest rates, it will not increase equilibrium desires to spend. If desires to spend for real goods are not responsive to interest rates, even an ability to achieve lower rates will not result in higher spending.

A NUMERICAL EXAMPLE OF CROWDING OUT

Figures 8.6 and 8.7 diagram and Table 8.2 presents a numerical example illustrating four possible reactions to a shift of the *IS* curve from added $\overline{G}$. The illustrations in the table are based on the standard model and the numerical examples detailed in Appendix 8.1. Each column assumes that government expenditures on goods and services increase autonomously by $100 billion. Figure 8.6A showed that with a vertical *LM* curve (if money demand failed to respond to interest rates at all), crowding out would be complete. On the other hand, if money demand were completely interest-elastic (the *LM* curve were flat), no crowding-out would occur; the simple multiplier would apply. The other figures showed that in more typical cases, the amount of crowding-out depends on both the interest-responsiveness of spending and money demand.

  A fourth possibility affecting crowding-out exists. Called **accommodative monetary policy,** it describes the situation when the Federal Reserve shifts the

TABLE 8.2 **Effect of the Shape of *LM* and Its Curves on the Multiplier**
(billions of 1972 dollars)

	Completely inelastic demand for money	*Completely elastic demand for money*	*Standard* LM *model*	*Expanded money supply*
1. Change in $\overline{G}(\Delta \overline{A})$	100	100	100	100
2. Change in expenditures from simple multiplier $k_1(\Delta \overline{A})$	250	250	250	250
3. Interest effects on expenditures $k_1(-b\Delta r)$	-250	0	-50	0
4. Total change in expenditures (lines 2 + 3)	0	250	200	250
5. Actual Multiplier $k_2 = \dfrac{\Delta Y}{\Delta \overline{G}}$	0	$\dfrac{250}{100} = 2.5$	$\dfrac{200}{100} = 2$	$\dfrac{250}{100} = 2.5$
6. Δ in interest rates	$+5\%$	0	$+1\%$	0

> *How far the actual multiplier falls below the simple one depends on interest effects (line 3). These are zero if the demand for money is completely elastic (column 2) or if it is completely accommodated (column 4). In columns 1 and 3, rising interest rates work to hold down the increase in actual spending.*

FIGURE 8.7   **Accommodative Monetary Policy**

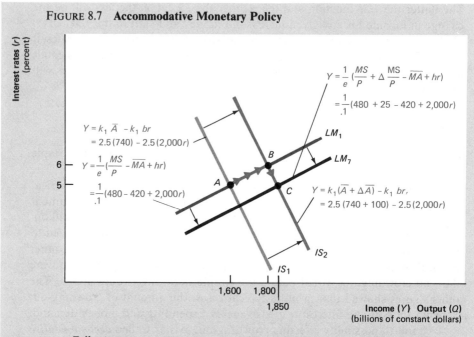

Following an increase in government expenditures (IS_1 to IS_2), the actual increase in output—the horizontal distance from the old to a new equilibrium—depends on the slope of the LM curve. Rising interest rates hold spending down. However, by furnishing enough reserves to hold interest rates (r) constant, the Federal Reserve can accommodate the full multiplier. The economy moves to C rather than to B.

money supply sufficiently to the right so that interest rates either do not rise or rise less than would otherwise be the case. The extra transactions balances needed for higher incomes are supplied by the Fed. Interest rates do not have to rise to free them from money held as an asset. In Figure 8.7, increased government spending shifts the economy to curve IS_2. If the money supply does not change, equilibrium is at point B (shown in the third column of Table 8.2). However, if the Fed expands the money supply and shifts the economy to LM_2, the equilibrium will be at C (the fourth column in the table) instead of at B. As a result, the increase in spending is equal to the initial simple multiplier.

In Table 8.2, the first column represents the case of the completely inelastic demand for money. The increase in autonomous spending which shifts the IS curve only raises interest rates. They rise high enough so that the interest-responsive effects ($-b\Delta r$) on I and C exactly offset the increase in G. Their demand falls by the amount G rises. Crowding-out is complete; income does not change. The second column presents the opposite extreme. With a completely elastic LM curve, the IS shift causes no increase in interest rates. The entire expansion in $\overline{G}(\Delta\overline{A})$ is multiplied. Fiscal policy is completely effective in increasing demand by $k_1\Delta\overline{A}$. The third column is the standard model. Both an assets and a transactions demand for money exist. When an autonomous shift in spending occurs, interest rates go up. Some of the autonomous move is offset as a result of interest-reduced spending $(-b\Delta r)$. In this case, interest rates rise by 1 percent. $(-b\Delta r)$ equals \$20 billion, which, multiplied to give $k_1(b\Delta r)$, causes a \$50 billion drop in consumption and investment. This offsets part of the change induced by the policy move, so that aggregate demand increases only \$200 billion. The actual multiplier $\left(\dfrac{\Delta Y}{\Delta\overline{G}}\right)$ is 2. Finally, the fourth column illustrates action by the Federal Reserve to hold interest rates constant by offsetting the impact of the added government borrowing. With additions to the money supply sufficient to meet additional transactions demand, interest rates need not rise. No change occurs in $(-b\Delta r)$. The full increase in government expenditures is multiplied by an unchanged multiplier. The Fed supports the full fiscal change through an accommodative increase in money.

How the Federal Reserve reacts should depend on national goals and the amount of demand assumed to be optimum at any period. If national policy calls for expanded total demand to increase employment and output, the Fed is likely to pursue an accommodative policy along with an increased deficit. If, however, government expenditures and deficits are growing when aggregate supply is already tight, the Fed may not only fail to accommodate the move, but may instead shift the *LM* curve to the left. This is a logical policy for wartime, when the aim is to force some resources out of the private sector and into war industries. Such a policy was followed during the Korean and Vietnam Wars, but unfortunately not in earlier wars.

Empirical estimates have been made of what actually happens when the *IS* curve is shifted. Economists ask how much smaller the actual multiplier will be, compared to the simple multiplier, as a result of crowding-out. They obtain their answers from simulations based on the *LM* functions derived from standard money demand theory. Some economists distrust the estimates because they depend for their validity on the stability of the demand for money, which they question. In the short run—say, a year or two—the effect of crowding-out is a good deal less than in the long run. This is a typical example of lags between a shift in a variable and its initial and final impact on demand. In the short run, the movement along the *LM* curve and the need to free money from assets uses is estimated to crowd out from 7 to 15 percent of the expected effect of the simple multiplier. In the long run, the lost efficiency rises to between 20 and 50 percent, depending on what money demand function is used.[5] If these estimates are correct, the example found in the third column of Table 8.2 would lie in the middle of the range.

5. B. M. Friedman, "Crowding Out or Crowding In: The Economic Consequences of Financing Government Deficits," National Bureau of Economic Research, Working Paper No. 284, October 1978.

Changes in the Price Level and Aggregate Demand

Our discussion thus far has described how demand was determined in the markets for *real* goods and *real* money under the assumption that all prices remained fixed even if a deflationary or inflationary gap existed. In other words, movements in variables altered the equilibrium level of real income and output without affecting prices. Many past debates among economists emphasized two special cases of this fixed-price model—that of the horizontal *LM* curve (Figure 8.4c) and the vertical *IS* curve (Figure 8.5A) because, under these conditions, changes in the money supply would fail to shift demand. As a result, if equilibrium demand was either higher or lower than potential output, active fiscal policy would be required to achieve a noninflationary full-employment situation. While these special cases appear unlikely to occur, views still differ as to how closely markets resemble either extreme and, therefore, on the extent to which movements in the money supply are likely to result in changes in output or interest rates.

To continue the analysis of why and how demand moves in the economy, we now drop the assumption that prices are fixed. We turn to a model in which prices are flexible and adjust in response to either inflationary or deflationary gaps. We ask what is the relationship between the overall price level and the demand for real output when prices are *not* constant. We also examine a related question concerning the real values of a nominal money supply. How do changes in real money balances affect the demand for output? Do price changes open another path to insure that full employment will be reached? Finally, with flexible prices, movements in the nominal money supply can alter expectations of future prices and therefore can directly influence nominal interest rates. In recent years, this direct impact of expectations on nominal interest rates has been the center of active discussions over Federal Reserve policy and the channels through which changes in money influence output and prices.

THE AGGREGATE DEMAND CURVE

Decisions to buy, sell, and borrow are made in markets whose prices are quoted in current (nominal) dollars. To relate these actual markets to the fixed-price model, the concept has been developed of an aggregate demand curve whose shape and position depends on both the forces in the real goods and money market and on prices. An **aggregate demand curve** or **function (AD)** expresses the relationship between real outputs and levels of prices (Chapter 1, Figure 1.9). Each change in the overall price level alters the value of a given nominal money stock and therefore provides different *LM* and *IS* curves and a new equilibrium of output and real interest rates. Examining an *AD* curve, as in panel B of Figure 8.8, we note a larger demand for output as prices decrease. Price movements shift the *IS* and *LM* curves by altering the real money supply, wealth, and expectations so that these forces must be added in analysis to those altering demand in real terms.

FIGURE 8.8   **An Aggregate Demand Curve Reflects Shifts in *LM* Curves in Response to Changes in Real Money Balances**

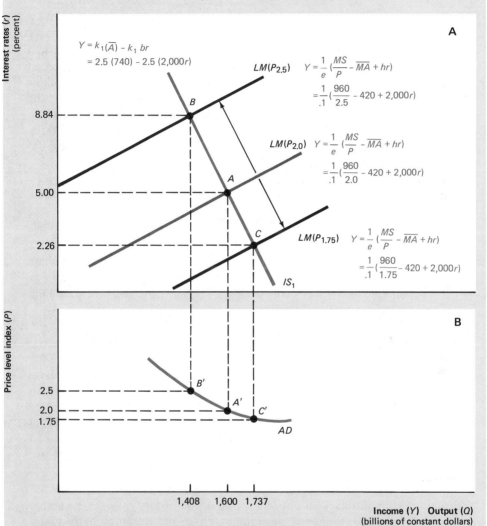

The nominal money stock is constant. However, since real balances vary with prices, related to each price level are a real money stock, an LM curve, and an equilibrium demand for output (as shown in panel A). The AD curve in panel B plots the equilibrium of output demand for each level of prices.

Every time a fixed nominal quantity of money is divided by a new price level, the quantity of real money changes. Lower prices raise real money balances and lower interest rates. The AD curve plots the equilibrium real demands from each of these real money stocks against its related price level. A trillion current dollars equal the same number of real dollars if the price level is 1.0. They will equal only half as many real dollars ($500 billion) if the price level arises to 2.0. The *AD* curve reflects the results of the *IS-LM* shifts arising from such price movements.

CHANGES IN THE REAL MONEY SUPPLY AND THE *LM* CURVE

Each new price level leads to a different *LM* curve. Each *LM* curve results in a new equilibrium level of real demand. These relationships are demonstrated in Figure 8.8. Panel A contains three *LM* curves. Each is identical to the others (real demand and the nominal amount of money are unchanged) except for the price level. Each line on the figure is identified with the price index which determines its real money supply. In other words, $P_{2.5}$, $P_{2.0}$, $P_{1.75}$ reflect three readings of the price index. (Such price indexes are usually multiplied by 100 to put them in percent terms.)

Look at the line marked $P_{2.0}$ (this is the *LM* curve found in Figure 8.1). The real money supply equals $480 billion. Since *P* equals 2, nominal money $\left(P \times \dfrac{MS}{P} \right)$ is $960 billion. The interaction of *LM* $(P_{2.0})$ with the *IS* curve gives an equilibrium, point *A*, of $1,600 billion in real expenditures at a 5 percent interest rate. This equilibrium of $P_{2.0}$ and $1,600 billion is real income in point *A'* on the *AD* curve in the lower half of the diagram.

What happens when prices rise, as to $P_{2.5}$? The price increase lowers the real money supply ($\dfrac{960}{2.5} = 384$). Figure 8.8A shows the *LM* curve shifts to the left. A new spending equilibrium results at point *B*. Solving the *IS-LM* equations 8.1 and 8.2, we find in the numerical example real expenditures of $1,408 billion and a real interest rate of 8.84 percent. This is point *B'* on the *AD* curve. Similarly, a fall in prices to 1.75 raises the real money supply to $548.6 billion and results in an increase in income to $1,737 billion and a lowered interest rate of 2.26 percent; this too can be traced out with the *IS-LM* diagrams and equations. Note that this *AD* curve is considerably different from one obtained merely by multiplying the $1,600 billion of equilibrium income by the different price levels.

The fact that flexible prices can shift the *LM* curve and increase the demand for output plays an important role in the history of macroeconomic theory. It is the basis for one of the arguments as to why it is improbable that a prolonged period of inadequate demand could withstand an aggressive monetary policy that kept the money supply growing. Suppose that in Figure 8.8 the full-employment level of output is at point *A*, but because of some autonomous factor, the *IS-LM* curves are in an equilibrium at point *B*. Is there any danger that the economy will remain stuck at the less-than-full-employment point? To those who believe in flexible prices and wages, the answer is no. Because an excess of labor and supply exists, wages and prices will start to drop. (The reasons are explained in Part 5.) What happens when prices fall? The price effects shown in the top part of Figure 8.8 cause the *LM* curves to shift down and the *IS* curves to shift up. As a result of the lower prices, a new equilibrium of demand occurs at point A, the full-employment level. Excess supply causes prices to fall; falling prices raise the real money supply and the desire to spend; the *IS-LM* curves shift until they reach the point of full-employment equilibrium.

CHANGES IN REAL BALANCES AND THE *IS* CURVE

A second influence of changes in prices on demand is through their impact on wealth and therefore on the desires of consumers and investors to spend. Movements in wealth shift the position of the *IS* curve. When prices fall, the real money supply $\left(\dfrac{MS}{P}\right)$ rises which means wealth has increased. Both consumers and investors expand their spending. The expansionary effect of an increase in the real money supply (real balances) is often called the ***Pigou effect,*** after the distinguished English economist A. C. Pigou, who pointed out as part of the debate over Keynes's *General Theory* that with flexible prices, declines in the overall price level would shift the consumption function up and therefore would eventually lead to full employment. Further developments in the analysis of prices and real balances show that they may influence expectations of future prices, the burden of the public debt, and the distribution of income between debtors and creditors. Their overall impact, consequently, is more complex than their initial effects. These and similar points are taken up in greater detail in later chapters.

The consequences of the Pigou or real-balance effect is that an increase in the nominal money supply shifts the *IS* curve to the right. Equivalently, a fall in the price level with a constant nominal money supply also raises the real money stock and shifts the *IS* curve to the right. Because a larger real money supply increases wealth, and therefore desires to consume and invest, changes in money cause real demand to become more responsive to price movements. In other words, the additional impact of prices through real-balance effects on the desires to spend (the *IS* curve) augment the impact through the assets demand for money (the *LM* curve).

THE SLOPE OF THE AGGREGATE DEMAND CURVE

The AD curve shows that as prices rise, the quantity of real goods and services demanded will fall. Underlying each AD curve are a given nominal money supply and fixed desires to spend and hold real money. Falling prices raise the real value of a fixed nominal money supply. People will hold more real money only at lower interest rates. The lower interest rates and expanded real money stock raise the demand for output and equilibrium nominal income.

An analysis of why the AD curve slopes down to the right gives an insight as to what the steepness of the curve, the responsiveness of demand changes to price movements, depends on. When the price level changes, the real money supply moves proportionately. An increase in the real money supply results in a shift of the *LM* curve to the right. Earlier sections showed that the amount of the shift depends on how responsive the demand for money is to interest rates. If all the added money is absorbed in speculative balances, the *LM* curve does not shift, and there is no impact on aggregate demand through this channel. The Pigou effect shows that the *IS* curve will also shift to the right. How much will depend on the effect of real balances on spending.

In addition to the magnitude of shifts, the amount demand increases as a result of more real money depends on the slopes of the *LM* and *IS* curves. They reflect the way in which the real desire to spend reacts to changes in interest rates. The flatter the slope of the *IS* curve (see Figure 8.6), the more aggregate demand will grow with a given increase in real money. The flatter *IS* curve reflects either a greater spending responsiveness to interest rates or a larger multiplier.

SHIFTS IN THE POSITION OF AGGREGATE DEMAND

Inflations and recessions result from shifts in the position of the *AD* curve relative to the aggregate supply (*AS*) curve. Some shifts are due to internal or external forces in the private economy, some to changes in monetary or fiscal policy. Critical issues include the degree to which private shifts are likely to occur and, if they do, whether a desirable level of real income and output is more likely to be achieved with or without an active change in government policy.

To see how policies can shift the *AD* curve, let us consider a situation in which an external shock has moved aggregate demand to the left so that the equilibrium of *AD* and *AS* is well below the level of full employment. The previous section shows that, under such circumstances, movements down the *AD* curve due to falling prices could bring the economy back to full employment. (Chapter 12 also shows that falling prices could cause the *AS* curve to shift toward a full-employment equilibrium.) But what if the response of demand to price changes is very inelastic? Falling prices cause people to expect further price cuts and so they postpone spending; or perhaps the lack of employment causes them to save more. Another possibility is that prices and wages are really inflexible. They stick at their prior levels and decline slowly or not at all, even when excess demand is high. Many economists believe that a combination of such factors occurred in the 1930s. In the Great Depression, prices fell somewhat, but not enough to raise aggregate demand to the full-employment level. The number out of work remained large.

Such possibilities are shown by the AD_1 line in Figure 8.9B. The curve is so inelastic that no drop in prices will be sufficient to move demand to the full-employment level (Q^*). Or one can imagine that prices have been falling, but so slowly that they have only reached point *B*. After several years, aggregate demand is still far from adequate to insure full-employment output. At this point, many might suggest that monetary policy be used to shift the *AD* curve enough to bring about a new equilibrium at full employment. How

FIGURE 8.9   **Inelastic Demand Curves and the Effect of Increased Money**

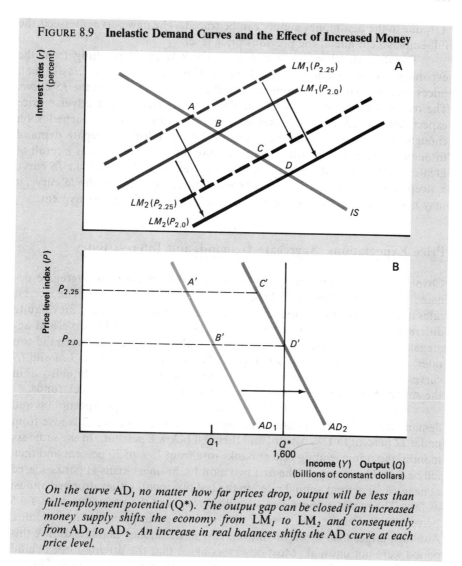

On the curve AD_1 no matter how far prices drop, output will be less than full-employment potential (Q^*). The output gap can be closed if an increased money supply shifts the economy from LM_1 to LM_2 and consequently from AD_1 to AD_2. An increase in real balances shifts the AD curve at each price level.

would this work? Assume that the money stock is increased. The top panel of Figure 8.9 shows a shift from $LM_1(P_2)$ to $LM_2(P_2)$. The increase in nominal money raises the real money supply. More money will be held only at the lower interest rates and higher income shown at point D. The new curve $LM_2(P_2)$ has the same price level as before. The higher income and same price in a new AD point, that marked D' in the lower part of the figure.

The effect of the addition to the money supply can be analyzed at each of the price levels shown on the AD curve. Thus, the points A and C mark the old and new income levels at the price level 2.5. In the same way, the entire shift to

AD_2 due to the new money supply can be traced. The new curve intersects the full-employment line at the previous price level.

The diagram shows only a shift in the LM curve resulting from the expanded nominal money stock. However, if money is increased faster than prices rise, real balances (additional wealth) will also be shifting the IS curve. The real-balance effects show that if slow price movements or adverse price expectations mean that a desirable equilibrium will not be reached soon enough, the price effects can be strengthened by shifting aggregate demand through added money. Furthermore, because the IS curve shifts as a result of greater real balances, the ineffectiveness of monetary policy when the IS curve is steep may be overcome. To the degree that more wealth shifts the IS curve, it may not be necessary to use fiscal policy to bring about full employment.

Price Expectations, Aggregate Demand, and Interest Rates

Changes in money and interest rates are key determinants of aggregate demand. Yet the relationships between the two are far from simple. The interest rates quoted daily in the paper are market or nominal rates. They move quite differently from the real rates which help determine the LM curve and aggregate demand. Price expectations shift and alter the spread between the two rates. Other dynamic money and credit relationships also shift the LM and IS curves. Executives may fear a shift in the economy's demand for liquidity or in the supply of money; they may then rush to borrow or to pay back funds.

The first six months of 1980 witnessed a massive shift in expectations and demand for credit. The interest rate on three-month Treasury bills rose from under 12 percent to 15½ percent and then fell below 8 percent. In the same six months, the prime lending rate at banks rose from 15¼ to 20 percent and then fell back to 11 percent. In the first two months, business loans at banks soared at nearly a 30 percent annual rate. In the last two months, they dropped almost as fast. The monetary base rose steadily throughout the period at about a 6.5 percent rate. Output fell steadily and rapidly during the last five months. Although larger than most, the movements in the money markets during this period were not unusual. Most observers agree that the driving force behind the shifts in demand and prices for money was primarily expectational as the market changed its mind about the near-term prospects for output, prices, and Federal Reserve policy.

THE MONEY SUPPLY AND MARKET INTEREST RATES

Chapters 2 and 5 showed divergent movements in real and nominal values resulting from changes in price expectations. Such movements can cause real and nominal interest rates to spread apart. The result may be an unexpected change in market (nominal) interest rates when the money supply grows. An increase in the money stock may raise, not lower, market interest rates. Final real demand will also be affected. To see how this works, recall that nominal interest rates (i) equal real interest rates (r) plus expected price changes ($\dot{P}^e$).

$$i = r + (\dot{P}^e).^6 \qquad\qquad 8.5$$

A change in anticipated prices will alter market interest rates and aggregate demand.

The top half of Figure 8.10 presents an IS-LM curve similar to previous ones except that interest rates are in nominal, not real, terms. At the start of a period, equilibrium is at point A, where the curves $LM_1(P_{2.0})$ and $IS_1(P_{2.0})$ intersect. Now assume that the money supply grows. The effect is similar to that illustrated in Figure 8.4B. More money increases liquidity and lowers both real and nominal interest rates. The markets are in disequilibrium at point B. Businesses then expand output until a temporary equilibrium is reached at point C, where the original curve, IS_1, and the shifted curve, LM_2, join.

How this affects aggregate demand is shown in the bottom panel. The increase in the money supply shifts the aggregate demand curve. The new equilibrium of the IS-LM curves yields a point on the new curve, AD_2. Since prices have not changed, the points A' and C' show that more money has caused the desire to purchase real output at the same price level (2.0) to increase. But these curves ignore the possible effects of more money on the price level. What if, because of either past experience or rational expectations, borrowers and lenders assume that the additional money will raise prices? Both spenders and lenders calculate the change they expect in prices and, therefore, in the real rather than the nominal interest rates. Since each nominal interest rate is recognized to have a lower real rate, this has the effect of shifting the LM and IS curves to the right. If people believe prices will rise by 2.5 percent, or to a new price level of 2.05, then each nominal interest rate has related to it a real interest rate which is lower by 2.5 percent. A 7.5 percent nominal rate is equal to a 5.0 percent real rate, and people will be as willing to borrow at this rate as they were at 5 percent expecting no new price level.

If this were the only effect of prices, the IS and LM curves would shift by equivalent amounts. A new equilibrium would be reached at higher nominal but equivalent real rates. But other factors come into play. The rising prices alter the real money supply. As noted in Figure 8.8, the IS and LM curves shift for these reasons also. As a result of all these forces, new IS and LM curves arise. They are designated by the new price level, 2.05. The final equilibrium depends on the relative shifts of the IS and LM curves. In the figure, at D, the

---

6. The dot over a variable indicates that it is a measure of the growth rate per period or the percentage rate of change in the variable:

$$\dot{P} = \frac{\Delta P}{P} \text{ or } \frac{\left(\dfrac{dP}{dt}\right)}{P}.$$

FIGURE 8.10   **An Increase in the Money Stock May Raise Nominal Interest Rates**

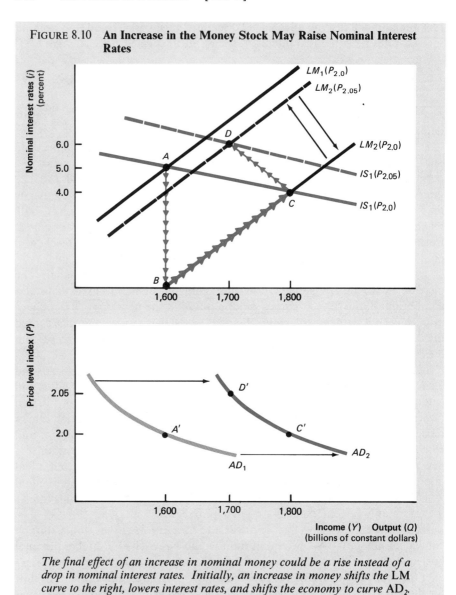

The final effect of an increase in nominal money could be a rise instead of a drop in nominal interest rates. Initially, an increase in money shifts the LM curve to the right, lowers interest rates, and shifts the economy to curve AD₂. However, higher prices and expectations can raise nominal rates even above their initial value, moving the economy to D′ on AD₂.

new equilibrium, both real income and nominal interest rates are higher than before the money supply expanded. The changing expectations and rising prices have caused a move up the *AD* curve to point *D′*. Higher incomes and higher expected prices more than offset the initial reduction in nominal interest rates brought about by the additional money.

Fluctuations in Money, Credit, Interest Rates, and Demand

While an *IS* curve shows that interest rates are expected to be low when output is high and vice versa, actual data reveal exactly the opposite; high output and high interest rates go together, as do low ones. Does this mean that the theory is wrong? No; but it does mean that care must be taken to differentiate between a static model, which takes up one relationship at a time, and the economy in which numerous variables shift simultaneously. Many factors in addition to price expectations alter aggregate demand. Shifts in the demand for money and in its availability cause far larger swings in interest rates than would be predicted merely from movements in the money supply. Such swings are closely related to fluctuations in output and prices. Demand in the flexible price model is far more complex than in the simple one.

THE PATTERN OF MONETARY AND INCOME MOVEMENTS

The GNP, investment, borrowing, money, and interest rates frequently rise and fall together. When credit expands, shifts in the desire to spend occur primarily in the markets for durable goods. Physical assets become more desirable. Wealth increases. Financing becomes more available. Investment in plant and equipment, inventories, housing, and automobiles expands rapidly. The demand for durable goods grows faster than the demand for services. Heightened expectations of higher income or prices make spending even more desirable.

Very sharp increases in rates occur just prior to recessions. Usually, one or more of five separate factors are at work: (1) The real demand for money increases as a result of upward movements in income. (2) The Federal Reserve reduces the rate of growth in the money supply. (3) More rapid price changes raise price expectations and widen the gap between the nominal and real rates. (4) Interest rate regulations and other institutional factors cause large-scale disintermediation and shortages of funds in some markets. (5) Liquidity in both the financial and nonfinancial sectors evaporates rapidly. As a result, the equilibrium of the *IS-LM* curves shift down to the left leading to a fall in real output. The degree to which prices and nominal interest rates drop depends partly on expectations and partly on the process relating price changes to movements in aggregate demand and supply.

These factors, added to lags and other dynamic forces, provide partial explanations of why the economy experiences such wide fluctuations in interest rates, lending, and output. Among the theories which explain how movements in money are transmitted to changes in aggregate demand, some economists emphasize the availability of credit, the large impact of shifting expectations, and liquidity squeezes. A comparison of the explanations in the standard model of how money affects aggregate demand with the elaborations offered by these other views of possible channels can broaden one's understanding of monetary fluctuations and their real impacts.

THE PATHWAY FROM MONEY TO SPENDING

In equilibrium, portfolios and the prices of financial assets, real assets, and money are balanced. The value of money depends on how many dollars must be paid for other assets. If more money is created, a disequilibrium develops. Supply exceeds demands. To clear the market, the price (value) of money must fall. All other prices rise equivalently. Close substitutes for money will feel the price effect first. New money appears first as a demand for government securities. It then spreads out. Soon bond prices rise and interest rates fall; demand and prices for physical assets and consumer services increase. Equilibrium is restored when purchases and prices have risen enough so that all are willing to hold the added money.

The Federal Reserve can determine the amount of nominal money, but spending units determine its real value. When the supply of nominal money increases, if spending units retain their preexisting demand for real balances, they will be unwilling to hold these additions to their money balances. They will spend until higher prices shrink the real value of their nominal money back to its prior equilibrium.

When an increase in money raises bond prices and lowers interest rates, the lower rates bring about more investment. If the demand for investment is $150 billion at a real interest rate of five percent, it might increase to $175 billion at a four percent rate. More money means larger portfolios. With more money, people's net worth rises. With greater wealth, they will increase consumption and investment. The wealth effect removes the threat of a liquidity trap. The economy cannot stall on dead center providing money is increased sufficiently.

These forces cause a shift to the right in the *LM* and *IS* curves and a similar shift in aggregate demand, which will lead to more output. However, if the increased demand leads to higher prices, some of the effect of the money will be dissipated. The real money supply will fall, or at least increase at a slower rate than the desire to spend. Market interest rates shoot up. Some businesses and consumers decide it is no longer profitable to borrow money to invest. Lenders may curtail loans because they fear that liquidity is drying up or that incomes may not rise fast enough to insure repayments of both the higher nominal interest rates and the loan principal.

THE AVAILABILITY OF CREDIT: DISINTERMEDIATION AND RATIONING

Some economists believe that the availability of credit is more important than changes in its price. Limited availability plays a key role in bringing expansions to an end. The number of houses or automobiles households buy is strongly influenced by whether or not they can get credit. Many people might be eager to borrow to buy, on the theory that inflation causes real interest rates to be negative. But lenders require high enough incomes so that loans can be repaid from current take-home pay, not future expected profits. People cannot borrow as much as they would like. Credit is rationed; that is, the amount demanded at current interest rates exceeds what lenders will supply. For institutional or legal reasons, rates do not rise. Fluctuations in housing production are a clear example. At times, builders find it impossible to obtain credit even though they would be willing to pay higher rates. The government may also impose credit restrictions, as it did in 1980.

To some, credit rationing is an anomaly. In a "perfect" market, all factors, including credit, are rationed by price. In an "imperfect" market, however, other forces may allocate funds. Among the most important are usury laws and the government ceiling on maximum interest rates—the so-called Regulation Q. The refusal of credit to sound potential borrowers at prices they would be willing to pay is a sign of credit rationing. Because of the usury laws or fear of public reaction if the market charges all it will bear, thrift institutions, for example, may post an interest rate on mortgages—say 12 percent—at which the loans demanded exceed the banks' willingness to lend. Techniques are introduced to ration would-be borrowers. Some customers may be refused because they have not been depositors in the past; or the percentage required in downpayments may be raised; or the maturity of loans shortened. Such actions remove from the queue seeking funds borrowers who would willingly pay the posted rate. Spending drops because the customers can't obtain loans.

The importance of credit rationing has been magnified because the Federal Reserve, through Regulation Q, and the other financial regulators through related regulations, set maximum interest rates on different classes of deposits. When market rates rise above the regulated ones, savers take money out of institutions and lend directly to final borrowers. This process is called **disintermediation.** The rate of growth in the money supply slows. Borrowers who cannot get loans curtail their spending. Some analysts believe that such market disruptions are critical in the process by which monetary changes reduce spending. Moreover, they believe that reducing credit availability may be a useful supplement to higher rates for purposes of monetary stabilization. They fear that a large number of bankruptcies and bank failures may follow extreme interest rate shifts. Without credit rationing, the magnitude of fluctuations in short-term interest rates would increase, and many firms not prepared for such market shifts would fail. Others argue that the market would adjust rapidly to any type of movement and believe that such fears are unwarranted.

EXPECTATIONS

Shifting expectations of future prices and interest rates may also alter aggregate demand. While potentially one of the key ways through which changes in money affect spending, this effect is one of the hardest to document empirically. All agree that disequilibrium in the money market can cause a shift in future outlooks. Some observers, especially believers in rational expectations, feel that all spending reacts rapidly to a monetary disequilibrium. They argue that monetary policy ought to be based primarily on theories of how it influences expectations. Believers in the impact of expectations have been especially critical of sharp, short-run swings in the money supply. Even though such swings might not be large enough by themselves to cause changes in the *IS-LM* equilibrium and spending, they could have a substantial impact if they cause rational decision makers to alter their expectations of Federal Reserve policy and of future prices and interest rates.

Others argue that little is known about how expectations are formed rationally. What information the market uses and how it is used are uncertain. They doubt that transient factors such as random movements in the money supply are likely to be significant. The man in the street doesn't even know what the money supply is, let alone what has been happening to it. People do change their willingness to hold money at any market interest rate and their spending habits, but reactions may be slow. Expectations change in reaction to movements in prices, wages, and interest rates, not to the money supply alone.

LIQUIDITY SQUEEZES

Expectations can also cause sudden shifts in liquidity. The *financial instability hypothesis* explains movements from shifts in money to liquidity to spending. Analysis based on financial instability was a major factor in Keynes's own view of business cycles. Some neo-Keynesians argue that this hypothesis explains a main way in which changes in money affect the economy.[7] Critical shifts in spending result from instability in the capacity of firms to borrow. When money is being created at a normal pace, firms can borrow because the future looks bright. Good expectations and low interest rates cause a drop in the rate used to discount future cash flows. Capital values of firms increase; expectations of a continued adequate supply of funds together with profitable investment opportunities cause higher investment. Then, either because the demand for funds to support expanding incomes begins to exceed supply or because the supply of money is curtailed, interest rates start to climb. Higher discount rates cause balance sheets of corporations to deteriorate. They can no longer spend as they did. The equilibrium of the *IS-LM* curves shifts to the left. At the new point, the demand for real output is less.

The normal workings of the market can thus create rapid shifts in the ability of financial institutions to lend and of corporations to borrow and spend. Because in prosperous periods there is a tendency to disregard the need for liquidity, when the situation alters, the market changes dramatically. Unless the government steps in through the Federal Reserve or other means of lending, a financial crisis develops. Bankruptcies become widespread; spending is sharply curtailed. Such events have been typical of past cycles.

Although financial crises moderated in the period after World War II, doubt has been expressed by some observers as to whether the government will be able to bring about such moderation in the future. They believe that because of the danger of financial crises, any attempt to tie the hands of the

7. See H. P. Minsky, "An 'Economics of Keynes' Perspective on Money," in S. Weintraub, ed., *Modern Economic Thought* (Philadelphia: University of Pennsylvania Press, 1977).

Federal Reserve in its ability to create money when necessary may aggravate future instability.

Summary

1. Some economists argue that the economy contains significant self-correcting mechanisms. Left to itself, with money furnished at a proper rate, the resulting equilibrium of spending will be at full employment with stable prices. Others believe that internal stabilizing forces are weak. To achieve desirable levels of output and prices requires discretionary action.

2. The schedules for equilibrium in the goods market (*IS*) and in the money market (*LM*) can be combined to solve for an equilibrium of real desires to spend. Given the underlying functional relationships, each equilibrium level of spending and income relates to a particular level of interest rates.

3. When the money supply changes, the shape of money demand determines the shift in the *LM* curve. While extreme cases of money demand, either nonresponsive or completely responsive to interest rates, could theoretically occur, normally some money will go for transactions and the remainder for assets purposes. In the same way, it is possible but not likely that the slopes of the *IS* curves can be either completely responsive or nonresponsive to interest rates.

4. How equilibrium demand reacts to changes in the money supply or the shifts in autonomous spending (including fiscal policy) depends on the interest-responsiveness (steepness) of the *LM-IS* curves. The flatter the *LM* curve, the less will be the effect of any change in the money supply. The flatter the *IS* curve, the greater will be the effect of a change in money. The opposite reactions occur with respect to fiscal policy.

5. Many monetarists believe that the demand for money is relatively steep (interest-inelastic), that spending reacts strongly to changes in money, and that the demand for money is stable. They therefore hold that spending can be maintained at desirable levels if monetary policy is conducted properly.

6. Neo-Keynesians agree that money affects spending. However, they emphasize the instability of the demand for goods, of the demand for money, and of velocity. In depressions and recessions as well as in booms, spending—dominated by expectations—may react only weakly to nominal monetary moves. Achieving a desirable demand may require large shifts in money and fiscal policy.

7. Because spending declines as real interest rates rise, and because money is needed for additional transactions, the actual multiplier of any autonomous increase in spending will be less than the simple multiplier. How much less depends on the interest-responsiveness of the *IS* and *LM* curves. Neo-Keynesians believe that crowding-out will not be great, particularly in

recessions. Furthermore, crowding-out can be offset by an accommodative monetary policy.

8. Much of the analysis of expenditure changes is done in terms of real desires to spend and to hold real money. However, changes in the price level affect real money and wealth. This means that one cannot merely multiply changes in real demand by movements in the price level to obtain estimates of movements in nominal aggregate demand. Price changes shift the *IS-LM* equilibrium.

9. The shape of the aggregate demand curve shows how the demand for output varies with the price level. The shape depends on how price movements alter the *IS-LM* equilibriums. The *AD* curve moves in response to any forces shifting the *IS* or *LM* curves.

10. Market (nominal) interest rates depend on both real rates and expected prices. When money increases, more liquidity lowers both real and market interest rates. Soon, however, market rates are pulled up by demand for transactions balances required at higher incomes and by borrowers and lenders who incorporate expected price changes in their demands.

11. Sharp cyclical variations occur in the amount of money demanded, in credit, in interest rates, and in investment or purchases of durable goods. Expanding output or a decrease in monetary growth can raise interest rates. Higher interest costs, restricted credit, or diminished liquidity and borrowing ability may cause aggregate demand to shift down sharply.

12. Money, nominal interest rates, and nominal and real demand tend to fluctuate more or less together. Shifting expectations and credit availability play an important role in the relationship between money and interest rates. They are causes of the fluctuations in demand.

Questions for Discussion and Review

1. Consider the following model:

$$Y = C + I + G$$
$$C = 100 + .5YD$$
$$YD = Y - .34Y - 10$$
$$I = 200 - 2{,}000r + .17Y$$

$$G = 300$$
$$MY = .2Y$$
$$MA = 400 - 1{,}500r$$
$$\frac{MS}{P} = 500 \quad \text{with } P = 1$$

a) Write down the equations for the *IS* and *LM* curves.
b) Calculate the equilibrium levels of income and the interest rate.
c) Suppose the price level doubles and *MS* increases by 316. What are the new equilibrium levels of income and the interest rate?
d) Suppose the autonomous component of consumption spending increases by 100. By how much will the *IS* curve shift? What will be the new equilibrium levels of income and the interest rate?

2. Discuss the significance of the interest-responsiveness of the *IS* and *LM* curves.
3. What are the channels through which a change in the money supply can affect spending?
4. Why is it not possible for the Federal Reserve to determine the real value of money? What is the significance of this for monetary policy?

5. Why do shifts in the desire to spend as a result of a monetary expansion occur primarily in the market for durable goods?
6. Why do we tend to observe sharp increases in interest rates prior to recessions?
7. Define the following:
   a) Credit rationing. c) Regulation Q.
   b) Disintermediation. d) Financial instability hypothesis.
8. What problems can arise from an attempt to control economic fluctuations primarily through the use of monetary policy?
9. If government spending is increased by $50 billion, with a simple multiplier of 2, the *IS* curve will shift right by $100 billion. If monetary policy is unchanged, explain in detail why the change in equilibrium income will be less than $100 billion.
10. What does the aggregate demand curve represent? Would an increase in the nominal money supply result in a shift of the aggregate demand curve or in a movement along it?

References

Carlson, K. M., and R. W. Spencer. "Crowding Out and Its Critics." Federal Reserve Bank of St. Louis, *Review* (December 1975).

Hicks, J. R. "Mr. Keynes and the 'Classics': A Suggested Interpretation." *Econometrica* (April 1937): 147–59.

Katona, G. "Atttitudes toward Fiscal and Monetary Policy." Reprinted in W. E. Mitchell *et al.*, eds., *Readings in Macroeconomics: Current Policy Issues.* New York: McGraw-Hill, 1974.

Pigou, A. C. "The Classical Stationary State." *Economic Journal* 53 (December 1943): 345–51.

Spencer, R. W. "Channels of Monetary Influence: A Survey." Federal Reserve Bank of St. Louis, *Review* (November 1974): 8–26.

Stein, J. L., ed. *Monetarism.* New York: North Holland, 1976.

APPENDIX 8.1   Algebraic Relations within the *IS-LM* Model

Equilibrium income and output result from the meshing of desires to spend and to hold money. The model developed in Chapters 3 through 8 enables us to see how equilibrium in the economy develops out of the interactions of these functional relationships.

EQUILIBRIUM IN THE GOODS MARKET-THE *IS* FUNCTION

The goods market, which is the real sector of the economy, can be described by four functional relationships and one identity giving an equilibrium condition:

$C = \overline{C} + c(Y - t(Y) - \overline{T})$	$C = 300 + .75(Y - .25(Y) - 200)$	**8.6**
$I = \overline{I} - br + d(Y - t(Y) - \overline{T})$	$I = 200 - 2{,}000r + .05(Y - .25Y - 200)$	**8.7**
$G = \overline{G}$	$\overline{G} = 400$	**8.8**
$T = \overline{T} + t(Y)$	$T = 200 + .25(Y).$	**8.9**

The equilibrium condition is

$$Y_E = C + I + G \qquad\qquad\qquad\qquad\qquad\qquad\qquad\qquad \textbf{8.10}$$

The autonomous factors, $\overline{C} - c\overline{T} + \overline{I} - d\overline{T} + \overline{G}$ are combined into $\overline{A}$, and m replaces $(c + d) + (c + d)t$ to represent all factors in the marginal propensity to spend and tax. Thus, as shown by equation 5.8, the equilibrium condition can be written as

$$Y_E = \overline{A} - br + mY_E \qquad\qquad\qquad Y_E = 740 - 2{,}000r + .6\,Y_E. \qquad \textbf{8.11}$$

By solving equations 8.6–8.10, we find the IS function, which is

$$Y_E = \frac{\overline{A}}{1 - m} - \frac{br}{1 - m} \qquad\qquad Y = \frac{740}{1 - .6} - \frac{2{,}000r}{1 - .6}. \qquad \textbf{8.12}$$

We define the simple multiplier as that which excludes all interest effects, or

$$k_1 = \frac{\Delta Y}{\Delta \overline{A}} = \frac{1}{1 - m} \qquad\qquad k_1 = \frac{1}{1 - .6} = 2.5. \qquad \textbf{8.13}$$

Substituting in equation 8.12, we derive a more useful form of the IS function:

$$Y = k_1\overline{A} - k_1(br) \qquad\qquad\qquad Y = 2.5(740) - 2.5(2{,}000r). \qquad \textbf{8.14}$$

EQUILIBRIUM IN THE MONEY MARKET–THE LM FUNCTION

The monetary sector of the economy is described by two functional relationships and an equilibrium condition. The real demand for money or liquidity preference function combines transactions and assets demand:

$$\frac{MD}{P} = eY + \overline{MA} - hr \qquad\qquad \frac{MD}{P} = .1Y + 420 - 2{,}000r. \qquad \textbf{8.15}$$

The money supply is assumed autonomous:

$$\frac{MS}{P} = \frac{\overline{MS}}{P} \qquad\qquad\qquad \frac{MS}{P} = 480. \qquad \textbf{8.16}$$

The equilibrium condition is

$$\frac{MS}{P} = \frac{MD}{P} \qquad \text{or} \qquad \frac{MS}{P} = eY + \overline{MA} - hr. \qquad \textbf{8.17}$$

By solving equations 8.15 through 8.17 for Y, the LM function is found:

$$Y = \frac{1}{e}\left(\frac{MS}{P} - \overline{MA} + hr\right) \qquad Y = \frac{1}{.1}(480 - 420 + 2{,}000r) \qquad \textbf{8.18}$$

or, solving for interest rates:

$$r = \frac{e}{h}(Y) - \frac{1}{h}\left(\frac{MS}{P} - \overline{MA}\right) \qquad r = \frac{.1}{2,000}Y - \frac{1}{2,000}(480 - 420). \qquad \textbf{8.19}$$

EQUILIBRIUM OF INCOME AND INTEREST RATES

We solve the *IS* and *LM* functions (equations 8.14 and 8.19) simultaneously to obtain the equilibrium levels for income (*Y*) and interest rates (*r*). The equation for *Y* is

$$Y = \left(\frac{1}{\frac{1}{k_1} + \frac{be}{h}}\right)\overline{A} + \left[\frac{1}{\frac{1}{k_1} + \frac{be}{h}}\left(\frac{b}{h}\right)\right]\left(\frac{MS}{P} - \overline{MA}\right) \qquad \textbf{8.20}$$

$$Y = \frac{1}{\frac{1}{2.5} + \frac{2000(.1)}{2000}}(740) + \left[\frac{1}{\frac{1}{2.5} + \frac{2000(.1)}{2000}}\left(\frac{2000}{2000}\right)\right](480 - 420)$$

$$Y = 1,600.$$

To obtain the equation in this form, first substitute the value of *r* from equation 8.19 in equation 8.14, to obtain

$$Y = k_1\overline{A} - k_1 b\left[\frac{e}{h}(Y) - \frac{1}{h}\left(\frac{MS}{P} - \overline{MA}\right)\right].$$

Next, add $\dfrac{k_1 be}{h}\left(Y\right)$ to each side, resulting in

$$Y + \frac{k_1 be}{h}(Y) = k_1\overline{A} + \frac{k_1 b}{h}\left(\frac{MS}{P} - \overline{MA}\right).$$

Divide through by k_1 and factor out the *Y*:

$$Y\left(\frac{1}{k_1} + \frac{be}{h}\right) = \overline{A} + \frac{b}{h}\left(\frac{MS}{P} - \overline{MA}\right).$$

Both sides are then divided by the multiplier of *Y* (which we define as k_2), resulting in equation 8.20.

The solution for *r* is found from the *IS* and *LM* equations (8.14 and 8.19) in a similar manner:

$$r = \left(\frac{ek_1}{h + ek_1 b}\right)\overline{A} - \left(\frac{1}{h + ek_1 b}\right)\left(\frac{MS}{P} - \overline{MA}\right)$$

$$r = \frac{(.1)(2.5)}{2,000 + .1(2.5)2,000}(740) - \frac{1}{2,000 + .1(2.5)2,000}(480 - 420)$$

$$r = .05. \tag{8.21}$$

The term multiplying r is found to be $\left(\dfrac{h + ek_1 b}{h}\right)$.

The equations show that equilibrium income rises with autonomous desires to spend $(\overline{A})$ and with increases in the stock of real money $\left(\dfrac{MS}{P}\right)$. It falls with an increase in the autonomous demand to hold money $(\overline{MA})$. Interest rates rise with autonomous spending and desires to hold money, and fall as the money stock increases. The equilibrium solution for the numerical examples shows an income of $1,600 billion of constant dollars with a real interest rate of 5 percent.

MULTIPLIER EFFECTS ON INCOME AND INTEREST RATES

Equations 8.20 and 8.21 can be used to measure the effects on income and interest rates of changes in autonomous spending, the money supply, and the autonomous demand for money. Movements in each cause multiplied effects, the size of which depends on the spending and interest-responsiveness of the economy.

From equation 8.20, the following equations for income multipliers can be derived. The simple multiplier is

$$\frac{\Delta Y}{\Delta \overline{A}} = k_1 = \frac{1}{1 - m} \qquad k_1 = \frac{1}{1 - .6} = 2.5. \tag{8.13}$$

When interest rates are included, the actual multiplier is

$$\frac{\Delta Y}{\Delta \overline{A}} = k_2 = \frac{1}{\dfrac{l}{k_1} + \dfrac{be}{h}} \qquad k_2 = \frac{1}{\dfrac{1}{2.5} + \dfrac{2,000(.1)}{2,000}} = \frac{1}{.5} = 2. \tag{8.22}$$

The crude or transactions multiplier of money is

$$\frac{\Delta Y}{\left(\Delta\dfrac{MS}{P}\right)} = k_3 = \frac{1}{e} \qquad k_3 = \frac{1}{.1} = 10. \tag{8.23}$$

When assets demand is included, the actual income multiplier for money is

$$\frac{\Delta Y}{\left(\Delta\dfrac{MS}{P}\right)} = k_4 = \frac{b}{h\left(\dfrac{1}{k_1} + \dfrac{be}{h}\right)} = \frac{b}{h\left(\dfrac{1}{k_2}\right)} = \frac{bk_2}{h}$$

$$k_4 = \frac{2,000(2)}{2,000} = 2. \tag{8.24}$$

Equation 8.13 is the simple multiplier (k_1) neglecting interest rate effects. When interest-rate effects are included, the actual multiplier (k_2) is smaller by an amount dependent on the term $\dfrac{be}{h}$ [equation (8.22)].

In equation 8.23, the transactions multiplier of money follows from the crude quantity theory. Velocity is the reciprocal of the coefficient of the transactions demand, and it is constant. When the assets demand is included, velocity and the income multiplier of the change in the money stock decline. How much the actual multiplier (k_4) drops depends on the interest-responsiveness of spending and money demand, the term $\dfrac{b}{h}$.

Equation 8.21 shows the effect on interest rates of a change in autonomous spending or the money supply. From it, one can derive interest-rate (in contrast to income) multipliers:

$$\frac{\Delta r}{\Delta \overline{A}} = k_5 = \frac{ek_1}{h + ek_1 b} \qquad k_5 = \frac{.1(2.5)}{2,000 + .1(2.5)2,000} = \frac{.25}{2,500} = .0001 \cdot \qquad \textbf{8.25}$$

$$\frac{\Delta r}{\left(\dfrac{\Delta MS}{P}\right)} = k_6 = -\frac{1}{h + ek_1 b} \qquad k_6 = -\frac{1}{2,000 + .1(2.5)2,000} \qquad \textbf{8.26}$$

$$= \frac{-1}{2,500} = -.0004.$$

Autonomous spending raises interest rates by an amount k_5 which depends on the simple multiplier, the demand for transactions balances, and the interest-responsiveness of spending, and money demand. The same variables influence k_6—the money-supply interest-rate multiplier. In the numerical example, a billion-dollar increase in autonomous spending raises interest rates by .01 percent. A billion-dollar increase in the real money stock reduces interest rates by .04 percent. The two basic equations show that the multiplier of an autonomous change in the demand for money ($\overline{MA}$) equals that of a movement in the money stock, but its sign is reversed. Its impact is equal but opposite.

AGGREGATE DEMAND

The previous multipliers are in real terms. To find multipliers in nominal terms, the effects of changes in prices and expected prices must be included. As the body of the chapter showed, changes in prices alter the real money stock. Therefore, such movements can be analyzed simply as changes in real money. The discussion also brought out, however, that an additional effect on spending—through real balances—must be added to get a fuller picture. Wealth shifts the *IS* curve. Furthermore, the total impact will also depend on how new money or altered spending desires influence expected prices.

THE IMPACTS OF FISCAL AND MONETARY POLICY ON SPENDING EQUILIBRIUMS

The equations in the appendix can be compared to the figures in the chapter to underscore the situations in which monetary and fiscal policy will be more or less effective in altering aggregate demand. What influences makes the actual multiplier (k_2) larger and therefore render fiscal policy more effective? Equation 8.22 shows that the multiplier depends on k_1 and the term $\dfrac{be}{h}$. Therefore:

1. The size of the multiplier depends on the economy's propensity to spend and tax (c,d,t or m). The greater the desire to spend and the less to save or tax, the larger the multiplier.
2. The less responsive spending is to interest rates (the smaller is b and the steeper the IS curve), the larger the fiscal multiplier will be. When spending grows, higher interest rates mean less money needs to be held as an asset; more is available for transactions.
3. The greater is the transactions demand for money (e is larger), the less effective fiscal policy will be. Any autonomous shift in spending will drive interest rates higher.
4. The greater the interest-responsiveness of the demand for money (h is larger, the LM curve is flatter), the more effective fiscal policy will be. Less money will be absorbed in assets demand.
5. As a special case, if the demand for money is completely elastic (h is infinite) or if the Federal Reserve holds interest rates constant, fiscal policy will have its maximum effect; the simple multiplier will apply.
6. At the opposite extreme, if the assets demand for money (h) is zero (money demand is completely insensitive to interest rates), fiscal policy will be utterly ineffective. A change in G will raise interest rates, not income.

The equations can also be studied to see what makes monetary policy more or less effective. Equation 8.24 shows that, under normal circumstances, the amount income increases as a result of a larger money stock depends on the income multiplier (k_2), the responsiveness of spending to interest rates (b), and the responsiveness of assets demand to interest rates (h).

1. Monetary policy is more effective the smaller the interest-responsiveness of money demand (h). When money grows, more can go for transactions balances and less will be used as an asset. The larger is h, the less effective is monetary policy.
2. As a special case, if h is infinite (the liquidity trap), monetary policy is useless.
3. At the opposite extreme, if h is zero, only monetary policy will work. Income will grow as the reciprocal of transactions demand $\left(\dfrac{1}{e}\right)$. Spending will expand by the amount of new money times velocity.
4. The greater the interest-responsiveness of spending (b), the more effective monetary policy will be. A small change in money will lead to more spending.
5. As a special case, if spending is completely insensitive to interest rates (b is zero and the IS curve is vertical), the income multiplier of money is zero and monetary policy is useless.

Part 4

Instability in Spending

9

Investment Spending and Capital Goods

The model of aggregate demand shows that there are many possible sources of instability in the economy. Investors, consumers, borrowers, and lenders change their desires to spend, save, and hold money. The government alters its spending and taxing. The Federal Reserve allows more or less money to be created. Economic and financial institutions develop new technologies. The movements of the economy brought about by shifts in spending and money are not simply random. Economic history is replete with fluctuations in which the economy expands and contracts in a series of wavelike movements. Why does aggregate demand appear to move in cycles? What causes spending to fluctuate?

Each sector of the economy shifts its spending as a result of new values for the variables in its demand function. But instead of leading to random movements, the interactions of the economy's response mechanism turn such shifts into a pattern of regular fluctuations. More production means more income, leading to higher demand and still more output. More money or increased investment demand can cause nominal interest rates to soar. This chapter takes up in more detail the forces influencing investment spending, Chapter 10 discusses consumption, and Chapter 11 examines the government's spending and taxing.

In studying past movements, we have noted that the production of investment goods fluctuates far more than output in the other sectors. Why is this so? Why do new housing starts fall by 50 percent or more? Why are most recessions accompanied by sharp declines in inventory investment? Capital investment in plant and equipment is vital for future growth and increased productivity; yet at times it becomes stagnant. This chapter examines the response of investment to movements in interest rates and output. Changes in output magnify capital demands because adding a dollar of output requires several additional dollars of capital investment. Rising interest rates reduce the returns from purchasing capital goods. If expected profits fall too far, investment will grind to a halt. Investment decisions and production take time. How fast output can increase depends on capital utilization and the costs and availability of financing. Some of the dynamic factors which create instability in investment spending include:

> Business cycles.
> Fluctuations in demand.
> The importance of investment.
> The investment decision.
> Output and investment.
> Stock-adjustment models—the flexible accelerator.
> Models of inventory investment.
> Interest rates and investment.
> Investment in residential construction.

Any of these forces can lead to an upward or downward cycling of output. In this chapter, we first examine the record of past fluctuations and then analyze the way in which these various factors cause investment demand to vary.

Business Cycles

Throughout United States history, the economy has oscillated between prosperity and depression. Most measures of the economy show expansions followed by declines, prosperity succeeded by recessions or crashes. Variations in economic activity have been large. Production income and most other measures of economic activity show repeated expansions and contractions. Because the rises and falls follow each other and appear to be related, the term *business cycle* has been applied to the fluctuations of the economy which recur in a regular manner. Figure 9.1 depicts an idealized version of the relationships during a cycle. As illustrated for analytical purposes, business cycles are frequently divided into four phases. The lowest point of a recession or depression is called the *trough* (or upturn). It is followed by the *expansion* period, during which output and business activity grow. The *peak* (downturn) marks the highest point of activity in a cycle. It encompasses the downturn into the *contraction,* or period of recession and falling output. A contraction ends in a trough or upturn. As the figure shows, one cycle leads into another.

The National Bureau of Economic Research (NBER) has traced the expansions and contractions in United States economic activity back to 1854. Table 9.1 lists the periods of business-cycle expansions and contractions as

FIGURE 9.1   **The Phases of the Business Cycle**

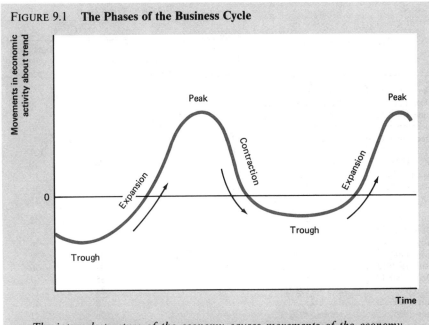

The internal structure of the economy causes movements of the economy which have related characteristics. Expansions come to a peak, followed by contractions which reach a trough leading to the next expansion. However, cycles in economic activity do not follow an exact path; each cycle has a somewhat different amplitude and duration.

defined and measured by the NBER. The first column gives the approximate dates of the troughs; the second column dates the peaks. Agreement is lacking as to whether what follows any given peak should be called a depression or a recession, since the difference between a recession and a depression depends on the observer's view of its severity. The old saw, "A recession is when you lose your job; a depression is when I lose mine" is probably as good a definition as any. In any case the NBER uses the neutral term *contraction*.

The third and fourth columns measure the amount of time between each successive trough and peak. For example, the figure 65 (in column 3) on the line with March 1879 indicates that the economy was in a contraction from October 1873 to March 1879, a period of 65 months. The table then shows that the economy expanded for 36 months until March 1882. While an expanding economy is better off than one in which a contraction persists, a period of expansion is not necessarily prosperous. For example, the economy advanced from March 1933 to May 1937, but in 1937 real output was still less than it had been eight years earlier in 1929. During the 50 months of this long expansion, unemployment averaged over 20 percent, clearly neither a prosperous nor even

TABLE 9.1 **Business Cycle Expansions and Contractions in the United States, 1854–80**

Business cycle reference dates		Contraction (trough from previous peak)	Expansion (trough to peak)	Cycle	
				Trough from previous trough	*Peak from previous peak*
Trough	*Peak*				
December 1854....	June 1857.............	....	30	....	....
December 1858....	October 1860	18	22	48	40
June 1861............	April 1865............	8	46	30	54
December 1867....	June 1869.............	32	18	78	50
December 1870....	October 1873	18	34	36	52
March 1879.........	March 1882..........	65	36	99	101
May 1885..............	March 1887..........	38	22	74	60
April 1888	July 1890..............	13	27	35	40
May 1891	January 1893	10	20	37	30
June 1894.............	December 1895 ...	17	18	37	35
June 1897.............	June 1899.............	18	24	36	42
December 1900....	September 1902...	18	21	42	39
August 1904.........	May 1907	23	33	44	56
June 1908.............	January 1910	13	19	46	32
January 1912........	January 1913	24	12	43	36
December 1914....	August 1918.........	23	44	35	67
March 1919.........	January 1920	7	10	51	17
July 1921.............	May 1923	18	22	28	40
July 1924.............	October 1926	14	27	36	41
November 1927...	August 1929.........	13	21	40	34
March 1933.........	May 1937	43	50	64	93
June 1938.............	February 1945	13	80	63	93
October 1945	November 1948...	8	37	88	45
October 1949	July 1953..............	11	45	48	56
May 1954.............	August 1957.........	10	39	55	49
April 1958	April 1960............	8	24	47	32
February 1961	December 1969 ...	10	106	34	116
November 1970...	November 1973...	11	36	117	47
March 1975.........	January 1980	16	58	52	74
Average, all cycles:					
1854–1980 (28 cycles)........................		19	34*	52	53
1854–1919 (16 cycles)........................		22	27	48	49†
1919–45 (6 cycles).............................		18	35	53	53
1945–80 (6 cycles).............................		11	49‡	59	‽60
Average, peacetime cycles:					
1854–1980 (23 cycles)........................		20	28§	46	47
1854–1919 (14 cycles)........................		22	24	46	47‖
1919–45 (5 cycles).............................		20	26	46	45
1945–80 (4 cycles).............................		11	39#	45	49#

NOTE: Underscored figures are the wartime expansions (Civil War, World Wars I and II, Korean War, and Vietnam War), the postwar contractions, and the full cycles that include the wartime expansions.

* 29 cycles. † 15 cycles. ‡ 7 cycles.
§ 24 cycles. ‖ 13 cycles. # 5 cycles.

SOURCE: National Bureau of Economic Research, Inc. and U.S. Department of Commerce.

The information on the left shows the month and year of the peak and trough of each business cycle. The four columns to the right show the number of months that each contraction, expansion, or full cycle lasted. The averages at the bottom indicate that since World War II the length of expansions has grown while contractions have been shorter.

FIGURE 9.2 **Changes in the Growth Rate of Real Gross National Product, 1901–80**

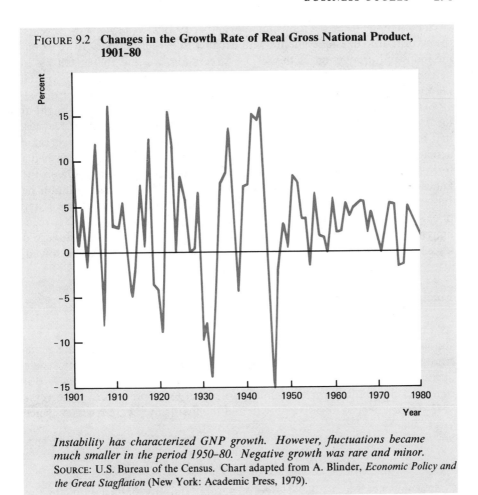

Instability has characterized GNP growth. However, fluctuations became much smaller in the period 1950–80. Negative growth was rare and minor.
SOURCE: U.S. Bureau of the Census. Chart adapted from A. Blinder, *Economic Policy and the Great Stagflation* (New York: Academic Press, 1979).

a satisfactory situation. At the peak of the recovery in 1937, unemployment was still above 10 percent.

Figure 9.2 shows the actual percentage increases and decreases in the GNP between 1901 and 1980. It and Table 9.1 seem to indicate a historical lessening in the severity of contractions. Since World War II, output in the economy appears to have been doing better. For example, prior to World War I, contractions averaged 22 months for the 14 cycles—nearly as long as the 24 months of expansions. Between the two world wars, even with the Great Depression, contractions averaged 20 months compared to expansions of 26 months. Since 1945 a dramatic change has occurred. Contractions have been relatively short. Even excluding the decade of the 1960s (during which there were the shortest contractions in the period after World War II) expansions have been more than three times as long as contractions.

The evidence is similar with respect to changes in output. Figure 9.2 shows much smaller declines in real output in the post-World-War-II period.

Even though the recession following November 1973 was the worst in 30 years, the cyclical drop did not compare with declines in earlier periods. If we examine industrial production in the 1973–74 recession, we find that it fell by 20 percent, compared to roughly 50 percent in 1907, 33 percent in 1920, and 60 percent in 1929. Similarly the general stability of employment has improved.

But has the greater stability of output and employment been bought at the expense of inflation? Ever since the recognition, with the work of Keynes, that the government could reduce and, if desired, halt declines in aggregate demand, questions have been raised as to whether Keynesians had unleashed a force (like the Sorcerer's Apprentice) that they could not control. Given the knowledge that depressions need not occur, could demand and inflation be turned off? Is there a fundamental contradiction between full employment and price stability? Does a long period without depressions build inflationary reactions and processes into the economy? While this dilemma has been discussed since the early 1950s, sharp disagreements persist as to whether it can be solved.

Fluctuations in Demand

As Figure 9.2 shows, from 1959 to 1969, the economy grew in every year, although at varying rates. During this long period of prosperity, some economists thought that the business cycle was a thing of the past that severe fluctuations had been eliminated by the use of fiscal and monetary policy. But rumors of the business cycle's demise turned out to be premature. The years 1973–74 experienced negative growth and the first truly severe recession since World War II.

CAUSES OF INSTABILITY

Contrasting views as to the degree of natural stability or instability in the economy lie at the heart of the dispute among economists about how to explain, forecast, and offer policy prescriptions for the economy. Does instability arise primarily from forces within the private sector where most spending decisions are made or does it result principally from swings in government-controlled variables—the money supply, government expenditures, and taxes. To neo-Keynesians, theory borne out by history shows that it is due to an underlying lack of stability in the structure of the economy. In contrast, monetarists ascribe most of the fluctuations to errors in public policy; in their view, fluctuations occur when the government misuses either monetary or fiscal policy.

Previous chapters developed the basic theory needed to explain fluctuations. The equilibrium of aggregate demand (AD) results from interactions of the investment-saving (IS) and liquidity-money (LM) curves and the way the curves are affected by price changes. The level of aggregate demand fluctuates because of shifts in the underlying schedules which then are either absorbed or multiplied as a result of the structure of the economy. Independent originating forces shift the desire to spend. Changed expectations, innovations and new investment opportunities, export demand, foreign curtailment of energy or other resources, wars or a sharp increase in government expenditures or taxes—all are examples of initiating forces.

The disturbances arising from such shocks may be enhanced or dampened. How the economy reacts to shifts in spending schedules depends on its structure or *response mechanism.* An example of this mechanism is spending induced by income changes, such as the multiplier. Related reactions come from induced movements in interest rates and prices. The timing and magnitude of shocks and the response mechanism determine whether fluctuations grow larger and last longer or whether they dampen down. Some variables take on new values as a result of both shocks and the structural relations. Expectations, inventories, and wealth shift exogenously, but the system's framework causes them to follow similar paths from one cycle to the next.

INITIATING FORCES

The economy is subject to many shocks and shifts in both autonomous spending and in the propensities to consume and to invest. These shocks trigger fluctuations. Among the key factors causing spending to change are the following:

1. While the desire to spend tends to be stable, it also exhibits sudden bursts of spending and at other times near panic and unwillingness to buy even the greatest bargains. At times, ownership of capital goods, property, and all types of assets promise a bright and prosperous future. People can't wait to spend. At other periods, gloom and doom prevail; goods can hardly be given away.
2. Similar fluctuations appear in the demand for money and credit. Lenders can't keep pace with the clamor for funds. Debt and credit financed purchases surge. Then times change; liquidity crises take over. Lenders have a hard time obtaining money. Pressures from creditors and bankruptcies hold spending down. Inventories pile up; production and income are cut.
3. While in highly industrialized societies nature plays a much smaller role than in the past, natural disasters still take their toll. Crops fail; hurricanes and earthquakes cause devastation. For instance, worldwide crop failures in 1972–73 were a major initiating force of unsatisfied demand and inflation.
4. Technological change and innovations do not follow a smooth path. Demands for new investment swell and then sag, as major new industries grow and then mature. An example is the tire industry, once a major demander of capital; because tires now last much longer than they used to, investment in this industry has steadily declined.
5. In the 1970s, as in prior periods, external pressures were highly destabilizing. The oil exporting nations curtailed supplies to raise prices. Other shortages of natural resources developed. Production innovations abroad

dealt heavy blows to large domestic industries such as autos and the manufacture of TVs and radios.
6. Wars and defense spending have been among the most critical sources of
   instability. Demand in these cases is not governed by existing income, but
   by the nation's perceived needs and the ability of governments to borrow
   and print money.
7. The rules of the game change. Ecology, conservation, cancer scares, health,
   urban decay, poverty becomes matters of intense public interest. Both public and private spending habits are altered by new legislation.

INHERENT STABILITY

While most economists agree that factors such as those listed above can shock
demand, they do not concur as to the size and significance of the shocks. Are
the shocks likely to be large or small? More important, how will the economy
react to them? The structure of the economy may absorb shocks, dampen them
and offer a self-correcting mechanism, or it may amplify them, leading to major
swings in demand and to inflation, unemployment, or both.

To classicists and new classicists (including most monetarists), the answer
is clear. The existence of self-correcting forces, particularly price adjustments,
real asset balances, and changing interest rates, will insure that a shock will be
followed by a return to a noninflationary level of demand sufficient to generate
jobs for all who really want to work. These beliefs are based on an economy
which is primarily competitive and in which markets are rational. Spending
units adjust rapidly to external shocks and new circumstances. Good private
forecasts of supply and demand remove unwanted capacity and pockets of
unemployment. An interplay of flexible prices and wages signals necessary
changes to the market, which adjusts to an optimum equilibrium.

In this view, the chief danger to the economy arises from government
interference and improper policies. The government mistakenly alters demand
by its fiscal policies or by not properly managing the money supply. It runs
large deficits and lowers incentives by high taxes, tariffs, exchange and commodity stabilization programs, failing to act against unions and oligopolistic
corporations, and by poor regulatory action. If the government would stop
tinkering with the economy and would, instead, balance the budget and adhere
to prescribed monetary rules, the problem of instability would disappear.
While fluctuations would occur, their costs in lost jobs, output, and inefficiencies would be far lower under a system of prescribed monetary and fiscal rules
for demand management than under one based on discretionary changes in
policies.

A CONSTRASTING VIEW

Eclectic and neo-Keynesian economists find this view utopian and unrealistic.
Their reading of history and economic theory shows little relationship between

such an artificial model and the economic, social, and political structure that exists today. These observers emphasize factors such as the multiplier; fluctuations in capital investments; and inventory cycles in stocks of goods, houses, consumer durables, and producers' equipment, which may amplify shocks into major fluctuations. In addition to induced cycles, instability is aggravated by "animal spirits"—sharp changes in moods and expectations—and by financial markets in which demands for credit and interest rates tend to outrun their initial pressures. The simple market model cannot explain what happens because it fails to take into account how markets operate. Adjustments take time. Decisions must be made, prices set, orders placed; investment, production, and distribution must be undertaken. Each of these lags can lead to cycling and to instability.

These economists see little evidence that the performance of the market accords with the idealized theories. Information is costly, hard to come by, and often inadequate. The record of market behavior as a forecaster of future events is inferior. At times, speculation is rampant and destabilizing. Money illusion leads to errors. Far from being flexible, prices and wages are sticky and move as a result of past momentum; they are not good estimates of the future. A large share of prices and wages reflects contracts, utility rate-setting, established custom or habit; they are not arrived at in the auction markets of competitive theory.

Furthermore, many economists tend to believe that it is naïve to expect that a democracy can follow prescribed rules for fiscal and monetary policy. What people want and the political pressures they bring to bear are in a constant state of flux. Large corporations and powerful unions set prices and wages and influence government policies in their favor. Pollution, health, poor nutrition, conservation, energy, poverty, old age, and unemployment are all problems which lead to political actions in the economic sphere. Consider, for example, the social security programs, by far the largest and fastest growing government expense. No country has abolished or greatly weakened social security; yet it makes up the bulk of the government taxes and benefits which are constantly attacked as welfare.

Economists holding these opinions conclude that, as a result of both the economic and political structure, the government will continue to influence aggregate demand. It therefore becomes necessary to insure that it uses its discretion as well as is humanly and politically possible. The need for flexible government policies cannot be ignored. Wages and prices in an industrialized society cannot act as they would in a Robinson Crusoe economy.

A PHYSICAL MODEL OF FLUCTUATIONS

The interaction of initiating forces and the economy's response mechanisms are frequently likened to the movements of a rocking chair which has received a series of random or deliberate shoves. Any number of shoves (initiating forces) from the outside may set the chair rocking. Once it starts, the distance through which it rocks and the time until it reverses direction depend both on the force of the shove and the way in which the rockers were built—its response mechanism. If the chair is pushed hard enough in the middle of a movement, its direction can be reversed before it would normally start back (as a fuel crisis near the start of a recovery may abort that recovery). On the other hand, further pressure can cause the chair to continue in the same direction even though the built-in forces are working to reverse it. World War II and the Vietnam War extended expansions, which might otherwise have been expected to reverse, to lengths of 80 and 106 months—three to four times the average duration of expansions. If the outside forces are strong enough, they can knock the chair off its rocker in either direction—a hyperinflation or a political explosion like that which brought Hitler to power in Germany.

Because the size and number of shocks varies greatly, economic fluctuations do not follow a regular path or pattern over time. But the response mechanism—the shape of the rockers—remains significant nevertheless. Once an expansion or contraction of demand is under way, many elements combine to reinforce the movement. The mechanics of financial markets, the multiplier, inventories, price movements, and expectations all tend to push demand in the same direction. But after pushing together for a while, the strength of the elements tends to dissipate. On the other hand, it must not be taken as inevitable that because an expansion has been going on for a long period it must weaken and come to an end. Outside forces, such as government expenditures or a burst of exports, can offset declining demand in the private sector. Confidence may then build anew, counteracting a deterioration in prices or profits. While internal forces in the economy may be self-reversing, expansions have no fixed or necessary end. The actual path of the economy depends on the interplay of decisions to spend or not to spend by the private sectors, or international events, and on government policies.

THE IMPORTANCE OF INVESTMENT

The investment sector is the most dynamic in the economy. Movements in investments spread their influence to production and sales through the multiplier. Large swings in investment spending dominate movements in both aggregate demand and supply. Every recession witnesses sharp cutbacks in investment. In the Great Depression, the level of real investment fell to below 15 percent of its prior peak. Industries like steel, lumber, and construction ground almost to a halt. Cities dependent on the production of investment goods suffered far more than those with balanced economies. Typically, in the post-World-War-II period, the drop in investment accounted for all of the total decline in real GNP between the top and bottom of every recession.

As important as its effect on demand, however, is investment's influence on aggregate supply. **Real investment spending** is the process of increasing or maintaining the physical capital—factories, machinery, oil pipelines, etc.—of the economy. Replacing, expanding, and modernizing the capital stock may speed up increases in productivity. Added investment can remove bottlenecks or capacity constraints. It can bring about innovations in goods and processes, better working conditions, and greater protection from environmental pollution, occupational hazards, and product deficiencies. Many believe that a downturn in investment incentives, primarily due to inflation, uncertainties, and higher real taxes, led to the poor economic performance of the 1970s.

Levels of investment in structures have a major effect on how we live and on our urban and suburban environments. Buildings make up more than two-thirds of our capital stock, with over 40 percent consisting of housing alone. To many Americans, the good life is intimately related to their housing. Fluctuations in construction give rise to important economic and political issues because the income, wealth, and jobs of so many are tied to real estate sales, lending, and production.

THE INSTABILITY OF INVESTMENT

Table 9.2 pictures the relationship between investment and the GNP in a typical economic fluctuation. The expansion which had begun in 1970 reached its peak in the fourth quarter of 1973. Investment spending on plant, equip-

TABLE 9.2   **A Comparison of Changes in Investment and the Gross National Product in a Recession**

(in billions of constant 1972 dollars, SAAR)

	Private investment				Gross national product	Cumulative change	
Quarter	Plant and equipment	Residential construction	Inventory investment	Total private investment		GNP	Invest-ment
1973:Q4	133.9	54.3	24.4	212.6	1,240.9	—	—
1974:Q1	133.5	49.9	11.4	194.8	1,230.4	− 10.5	− 17.8
Q2	131.6	47.0	9.4	187.9	1,220.8	− 20.1	− 24.7
Q3	127.3	43.9	5.1	176.2	1,212.9	− 28.0	− 36.4
Q4	121.8	39.3	8.0	169.1	1,191.7	− 49.2	− 43.4
1975:Q1	116.6	36.3	− 20.0	133.0	1,169.8	− 71.1	− 79.6
Q2	112.0	36.9	− 18.0	130.9	1,188.2	− 52.7	− 81.7
Q3	111.0	39.3	2.9	153.1	1,220.7	− 20.2	− 59.5
Q4	111.3	42.6	− 4.6	149.2	1,229.8	− 11.1	− 63.4

SOURCE: U.S. Department of Commerce.

The first through fourth columns show typical reactions of private investment and its components in a recession. Their movements can be compared with total output (GNP in constant dollars). In every quarter except one, the cumulative decline in investment exceeded that for the entire GNP. The other sectors as a whole expanded slightly.

ment, and inventories was at an all-time high. Residential construction, however, had retreated somewhat from an artificial peak created by record
government subsidies in 1972, as part of the Nixon reelection campaign.

A downturn in investment spending, especially for inventories, ended the
expansion. Compare the last two columns in Table 9.2, which show cumulative
movements in the GNP and in investment. In most of the recession, the drop in
investment alone was greater than that of total GNP. All spending of the other
sectors together held about even. The total decline in output in the worst
recession since the 1930s was not as large as the drop in investment spending.
In the spring of 1975, changes in housing and inventory expenditures became a
plus factor marking the start of a new expansion. When investment expenditures stopped falling, the economy could once again expand. The upswing was
unusual, however, because investment expenditures were slow in returning to
their previous peak. Businesses were extremely cautious about expanding their
investments in plant and in inventories. The failure of investment to take off
slowed the entire economy.

Figure 9.3 demonstrates the instability of investment spending. It charts
fluctuations in real gross private domestic investment. Each recession witnessed a major drop in investment. In the recession of 1973–75, it fell by more
than one-third. When investment is high, the economy booms; when it is low,
total output is depressed.

WHAT CAUSES THE INSTABILITY IN INVESTMENT?

The fluctuations in investment depicted in Figure 9.3, although sizable, are not
exceptional. They are in fact not as large or as sharp as those in many prewar
periods. It seems that investment instability is built into the economy. But
why? Fluctuations follow from the way in which investment decisions are
made, from the dominant role of financing in investment, from amplified reactions to shifts in output, and from huge swings in inventories which reflect a
concentration of unplanned accumulations and disinvestments.

Decisions to invest depend upon *expected* profitability. Before tying up
money in physical capital, investors must expect that the rate of return will
exceed current interest rates on borrowing or lending. Since investment is the
process of expanding or replacing capital, firms and households must estimate
whether expected profits will or will not increase if they make a specific investment expenditure. Many factors influence the success or failure of an investment. Income depends on both the amount and prices of future sales.
Expenses include payments for wages, energy, and other production costs, and
also interest rates, depreciation, and taxes. A new machine may cut costs. A
new store may boost sales. Pollution control measures allow plants to keep
operating. At the time investment decisions must be made, none of these
factors is known with certainty. They must be projected for periods of up to 20
years or more into the future. Several natural aspects of this investment process
cause fluctuations.

FIGURE 9.3   **Gross Private Domestic Investment**

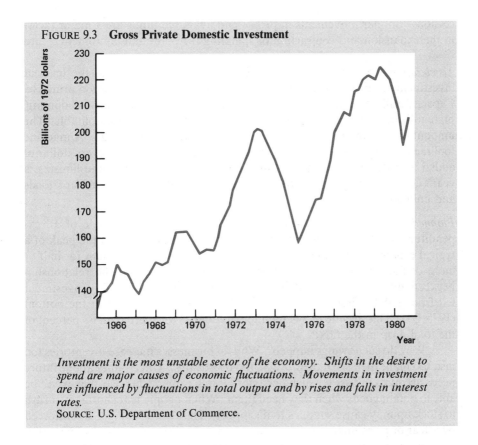

*Investment is the most unstable sector of the economy. Shifts in the desire to
spend are major causes of economic fluctuations. Movements in investment
are influenced by fluctuations in total output and by rises and falls in interest
rates.*
SOURCE: U.S. Department of Commerce.

Expectations.   The decision to spend depends on projections. Wide swings in
expectations from high optimism to sharp declines in confidence are not only
possible, but common.

Postponability.   Because investment goods are durable, new purchases can be
postponed without disturbing production of consumer goods.

Financing.   Because of their size and durability, most investments must be
financed by borrowing. The ability to get money and the interest rates which
must be paid undergo wide fluctuations. Internal sources of funds are also
volatile. Profits swing more and dividend payments vary less than output. As a
result, business saving cycles up and down. Traditional accounting methods
mean that profits are overstated in inflations. This leads to higher taxes, a
further reduction of business saving, and a decline in investment. The impact
of financing is especially evident in the housing market. Shifts in the cost and
availability of mortgage money create tremendous swings in construction expenditures. Downturns in housing starts are a leading indicator of future re-

cessions. Similar movements in profits and available funds are a major factor in the expansion and contraction of spending for plant and equipment.

Acceleration.   The relationship between changes in output and the level of investment required to produce that output is called the acceleration principle. Capacity utilization goes through wide swings. When the economy is booming, high utilization rates make new investments both necessary and profitable. The amount of investment required per unit of added output is large. A machine tool factory may have to make an added investment of $10 for every dollar of added output; an electric utility, far more. In both inventories and housing, a year's current investment will be only a small percent of the total stock of goods and units available.

Planned and Unplanned Inventory Investment.   The most volatile of all expenditures in the GNP are those for business inventories. From the peak of a typical expansion to the bottom of the next recession, they account for half or more of the total drop in investment and output. Look at the relationship between inventories and GNP in Table 9.2; it is typical. Inventory investment fell from $24.4 billion at the peak (1973:Q4) to $-20.0 billion at the bottom (1975:Q1). This decline of $44.4 billion accounted for more than 62 percent of the total drop in the GNP.

Why do such swings happen? Why do businesses increase inventories too fast, too high; then slash their orders too drastically? Uncertainty about future needs accounts in part for such behavior. Purchasing agents fear they won't be able to obtain goods when they need them. When people fear shortages, a rush to stock up may cause supplies to disappear. The fear of outages is reinforced by a fear of price increases. As demand grows, prices tend to rise. Increasing stock on hand can lead to an inventory profit if prices go up. But when the recession comes, prices may drop and it becomes costly to hold excess stocks.

As important as deliberate increases may be, unplanned inventory accumulations are much more serious. Sometimes they originate in technical problems of coordinating sales, orders, and production. Inventories are where adjustments take place when errors are made elsewhere. An unexpected decline in final demand means that goods produced won't be sold. When Chrysler got into trouble and asked for government aid in 1979, it was partially because of the high costs of holding cars produced but not sold. To get out from under these costs, they had to slash prices. A shift from planned to unplanned inventory investment is reflected in Table 9.2. At the peak in the fourth quarter of 1973, inventory investment was unusually large. Probably a good deal of it was unplanned and undesired. Businesses then had to cut back production, both because lower output required less inventories and because they hoped to rid themselves of some unwanted prior investment. During a period of inventory cutback, sales exceed output; income and jobs from production are curtailed.

The Investment Decision

To see why these forces cause instability in spending and output, we must examine investment decisions in more detail. Such decisions are in two parts: (1) Businesses must decide how much physical capital they need; what additions to plant and equipment will be desirable. (2) When desired capital exceeds that on hand, orders must be placed before investment goods are produced, and the production against these orders takes time. In any period, only part of the total gap between actual and desired capital will be met through new investment. Suppose a salesman calls on an auto parts producer and offers a new milling machine at a cost of $100,000. What factors must the firm consider in determining whether it ought to buy the new equipment?

Expected Income or Net Revenues. Most important are the firm's expectations of net income which the added machine will produce. The profitability of capital ordered today can be calculated by comparing the known supply cost of an item to the present value of its expected net revenue, which in turn depends on the physical quantity of goods the firm believes it will sell, the prices it expects to receive, and its costs of production. Note the importance of expectations. Current high demand is significant primarily if it portends good sales in the future. The demand for capital can shift as a result of changes in expected prices as well as of output. Many gas and oil wells were drilled in the late 1970s, for instance, on the correct assumption that rising prices would make wells that were marginal at 1970 prices bonanzas in the 1980s. Depending on the speed of change and on expectations, movements in projected income can be large. Keynes, who was a most acute observer, felt that shifting expectations were critical in creating investment instability. At times corporate executives seem to be depressed and pay little attention to good news; at other times they become euphoric and expand faster than their needs really call for.

In addition to predicting its future revenues, a firm must estimate the expected costs of operating a new machine. What will happen to its labor, energy, and material costs as a result of purchasing new capital? It is net revenue after costs that a firm must consider. Capital may be purchased because of fear of high future costs. A backhoe to replace five laborers may not be profitable if wages are $5 an hour, but may yield a high return if labor's wages escalate to $10 an hour. If a machine will last ten years, the decision to buy it must consider the degree to which it will be used, the prices at which its product will be sold, and the wages, energy, and other costs saved over the period.

Taxes may also play a prominent role. Incentives may be granted to make certain investments more profitable. Again, it is the net revenue after taxes that the firm must use in its calculations.

Financing costs. The decision to invest in physical capital means either that money must be borrowed or that alternative investments must be forgone. If the firm must borrow to buy and its friendly banker charges 14 percent for financing the purchase, this rate will enter into its calculations of expected profitability. On the other hand, if the firm and its owners hold excess funds and their best alternative investment yields 10 percent, this is a rate which will affect their financing. The theory of corporate finance shows how the firm can calculate its actual financing costs, given its equity, debt, and tax situation.

The Demand for Capital. Projecting its expected net revenues and costs of financing, the firm can decide whether or not it should buy a capital item. If the firm finds that future net income discounted by financing costs yields a present value which exceeds the purchase price of the equipment, an investment will be profitable. Another way of calculating profitability is to find out whether an investment's expected marginal revenue product exceeds its user cost of capital.

OUTPUT AND INTEREST RATES

While the variables influencing investment expenditures are numerous and complex, output and interest rates are the two major factors in the investment decision: (1) Increases in output signal expected future sales and the need for additional capacity to produce more goods and services. (2) Changes in interest rates alter the cost of funds and, frequently, the availability of financing. These, in turn, shift the amount of capital goods used in the production process. Interest rates influence the value of future revenues by altering the discount rates used by firms in their planning.

The simple relationships between output, interest rates, and investment must, however, be augmented in order to make them reflect more closely the actual investment process. In more complex models (often called flexible-accelerator or stock-adjustment models), the relationship between output and investment demand is expanded to include (1) the degree of capacity utilization, (2) the need for replacements, (3) changes in expectations, (4) the rate at which firms want to close the gap between desired and actual capital, (5) the time it takes to order new equipment and produce it, and (6) the costs and availability of financing.

Similarly, a model in which the profitability of an investment is determined by the relationship between its rate of return and the costs of financing it may be expanded to take into account (1) different production possibilities, (2) the costs of wages and materials, (3) the effect of inflation and taxes on the costs of using capital, and (4) other costs of financing in addition to simple interest rates.

Figure 9.4 outlines some of these forces which influence expenditures. (Note that unfamiliar terms used in the table will be defined and explained in the remainder of this chapter.) Changes in output and interest rates act to alter the desired level of capital. When output (Q) increases, more capital is needed to maintain the capital-output ratio. Changes in output affect expected sales

FIGURE 9.4   **The Forces Influencing Investment**

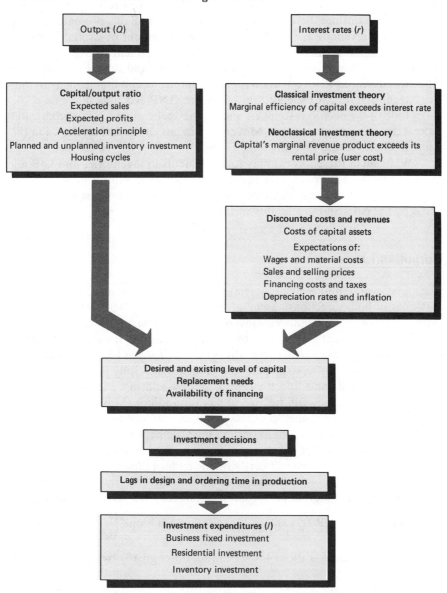

To different degrees, all investment expenditures respond to movements in output and interest rates. The boxes show that these variables influence the desired capital stock. In response to a need for additional physical capital (provided financing is available) firms decide to invest in more physical assets. Because goods must be ordered and produced, investment expenditures (I) lag behind investment decisions. The length of these lags varies with the production process and with available production capacity.

and profits. Fluctuations in desired capital also occur because of the acceleration principle and inventory and housing cycles. Interest rate (r) movements
alter the relationships between costs of financing and the present value of
expected net revenues and therefore the desired amount of capital. The lag
between changes in desired capital and actual investment may be long and
irregular. The size of the gap between the desired and actual capital stock
influences decisions to invest, as do replacement needs and financing availability. Actual investment expenditures (I) in the GNP accounts depend on the
magnitude of the decisions to invest and on the speed at which the production
process can turn out new orders. Movements in any of the factors shown in the
figure influence actual investment.

While all of these forces apply to investments in inventories and housing
as well as to those for plant and equipment, changes in output play the most
prominent role in the case of inventories, while housing appears to be dominated by the costs and availability of financing.

Output and Investment

Fluctuations in output are closely related to fluctuations in investment. Caus-
ality goes in both directions. Some of the expansion in the GNP arises from
autonomous or interest-induced movements in investment. Some of the fluctuations in investment are induced by changes in output. If output is to grow,
more capital goods are needed. Investment is the process of expanding capital.
Furthermore, as sales rise, so do potential profits. With rising profits, firms have
more internal funds and find it easier to borrow still more if they so desire.
Lenders judge that they will be able to pay for additional investments.

Let us see how changes in expected output can lead to a desire for more
capital. For the present, we shall consider the ratio between capital and output
to be fixed, leaving to later sections qualifications needed to account for the fact
that the capital-output ratio will vary with the costs of inputs and financing and
with lags in adjustment—the flexible accelerator. Table 9.3 shows the total real
capital stock and real output for the United States in 1975. Dividing the capital
stock (K) by the GNP (Q) shows a capital-output ratio $\left(\dfrac{K}{Q}\right)$ for the entire
economy. The $\dfrac{K}{Q}$ ratio is about 4.5. The ratios differ greatly by commodity and
services. Haircuts and shoeshines have a ratio under 1. The reported ratio for
housing is about 13.

Private investment, moreover, is only a fraction of total capital. The total
stock includes consumer and government capital; expenditures in these categories show up as consumption and government expenditures rather than as
investment. Gross private investment is roughly 4 percent a year of the capital

TABLE 9.3   **Capital-Output Ratio and Gross Capital Stock of Reproducible Tangible Assets in the United States in 1975**

(billions of 1972 dollars)

Type of Capital		*Capital-Output Ratio*
Private		
Equipment	806	Capital $(K) = 5,390$
Nonresidential structures	896	
Housing	1,443	GNP $(Q)\ \ = 1,202$
Inventories	290	$\dfrac{K}{Q} = \dfrac{5,390}{1,202} = 4.5$
Consumers	954	
Governments	1,001	
Total	5,390	

SOURCE: A. H. Young and J. C. Musgrave, "Estimation of Capital Stock in the United States," U.S. Department of Commerce.

Calculating the capital-output ratio for the entire economy conceals about as much as it reveals because the ratio of capital to output differs so greatly among types of capital.

stock to which it is related. Many believe this ratio is too small and creates a need for active policies to increase its supply.

A technical relationship exists between capital and output, which requires large increases in investment to allow small expansions of output. To obtain services from a durable item we must invest large amounts now, only a small percent of which will yield present services, while most will return future services. If a machine releases 4 percent of its services each year, we must invest 25 times as much now as we receive in any year. Services will then continue to flow from this capital over the next 25 years. To look at it another way, the economy at any time has a large stock of equipment which satisfies most of current demand. Normal investment requires the replacement of a small percentage of the stock. However, if more services are required from the capital, a large investment is needed. If only 4 percent of the stock is being replaced each year, a 4 percent increase in final demand will require capital that will last 25 years and will raise investment requirements by 100 percent. Investment doubles even though the total amount of capital and the services it renders go up by only 4 percent. This principle applies to construction, to equipment, to inventories, and to durable consumer goods in exactly the same way. The way in which these technological relationships work out is characterized by the capital-output ratio and the acceleration principle.

THE CAPITAL-OUTPUT RATIO

Let us look first at the relationship between capital and output. As Table 9.3 shows, to produce a dollar of real output takes several dollars of invested capital. The amount of capital in the economy is K. The level of output is the GNP, or Q. The capital-output ratio needed for production is $\dfrac{K}{Q}$. With a fixed capital-output ratio, how much additional investment is necessary to produce a new level of output? The answer depends on the increase in desired output and on the capital-output ratio. For example, what if Acme Tool Company projects a permanent increase in its sales (Q) of pliers from $100,000 to $105,000? If the capital-output ratio $\left(\dfrac{K}{Q}\right)$ is 5, to change its level of output and sales by $5,000 it must increase its capital stock by an additional investment of $25,000.

If K is the new amount of physical capital and net investment (I) is the expenditure on capital goods which expands the stock of capital (K_{-1}) of the previous period, then

$$I = (K - K_{-1}). \tag{9.1}$$

The amount of capital desired depends on the level of output times the capital-output ratio in each period, or

$$K_{-1} = \frac{K}{Q}(Q_{-1}) \qquad K_{-1} = 5(100,000) \tag{9.2}$$

and

$$K = \frac{K}{Q}(Q) \qquad K = 5(105,000). \tag{9.3}$$

The difference in output in each period determines the required change in the capital stock:

$$(K - K_{-1}) = \frac{K}{Q}(Q - Q_{-1}) \qquad (K - K_{-1}) = 5(105,000 - 100,000) = 25,000. \tag{9.4}$$

This difference also equals the desired level of investment, which therefore can be expressed in several ways:

$$I = (K - K_{-1}) = \Delta K \qquad I = (525,000 - 500,000) = 25,000$$

or

$$I = \frac{K}{Q}(Q - Q_{-1}) = \frac{K}{Q}(\Delta Q) \qquad I = 5(105,000 - 100,000) = \tag{9.5}$$

$$5(5,000) = 25,000.$$

All these equations say that knowing how much capital is required to produce a dollar of output ($5 in this example), we can estimate the amount of added capital and investment needed to increase output. An increase of $5,000 in output requires that the level of capital be raised by $25,000. Net investment expenditures must equal the amount needed to increase capital.

THE ACCELERATION PRINCIPLE

The simple relationship between income and investment becomes more complex when we allow for replacement and for the fact that if capital is not being fully utilized, output can grow without added investment. The **acceleration principle** has been defined as the relationship between the *changes* in sales or output and the *level* of investment. Expanding demand for final goods can induce a highly magnified or accelerated requirement for investment goods, but it can also lead to periods in which no investment at all is needed.

Table 9.4 shows a simplified arithmetical example of this principle. Suppose that a knitting mill requires $5 of capital equipment for every $1 of sales $\left(\dfrac{K}{Q} = 5\right)$. In the table, line 1 shows a balanced situation: the firm's sales are $100,000; its capital (total stock of goods) is $500,000, and one-twentieth, or $25,000 worth, of its equipment wears out and requires replacement every year.

In the second year, the firm's sales increase by $5,000. This 5 percent rise in final sales means that the total necessary capital equipment must increase by a similar percentage, or to a stock of $525,000. The addition to capital stock of $25,000 plus the normal replacement demand of $25,000 gives a $50,000 gross investment requirement in this second year. A 5 percent increase in income has induced a 100 percent increase in investment.

TABLE 9.4   **The Acceleration Principle**
(thousands of dollars)

Period	Annual Sales (Y)	Required stock of capital (K)	New investment required	Replacement investment (DEP)	Total investment (I)
1	100	500	—	25	25
2	105	525	25	25	50
3	115	575	50	25	75
4	120	600	25	25	50
5	115	575	(−25)	25	0

Changes in the required stock of capital are assumed to depend directly on the capital-output ratio and annual sales. Total investment depends on the level of replacements and the amount of additional capital needed which is determined by the changes in sales and required capital.

In the third year, sales grew another $10,000. Required capital is now $575,000. Demand for new investment rises to $50,000 which, when added to normal replacement, makes $75,000 of gross investment. (For ease of calculation, it is assumed that the replacement total does not increase until after the additional stock of capital has been in use 20 years.) The fourth year's figures are most disconcerting. Sales rise $5,000, or more than 4 percent, but required investment drops. A decline in the *rate* at which sales increase suffices to cause a drop in the absolute amount of investment, despite the fact that sales did rise.

In the fifth year still another relationship emerges. Final sales drop back to $115,000. Only $575,000 stock of capital is required, which is the amount available. This is the stock at the beginning of the year of $600,000 less the $25,000 of machines wearing out. No investment at all is required. Because of the excess capacity, the firm need not even replace the old machines. Note, too, that in periods 3 and 5, sales were the same, yet total investment in period 3 set a record, whereas in period 5 it was zero.

Acceleration depends on the basic technological relationship expressed in the capital-output ratio. It is a factor which causes investment demand to rise with income, and it can lead to great instability. Examining investment decisions in more detail, however, we find other factors, especially in the process of ordering and producing investment goods, which tend to iron out some of these simple reactions. Investment does depend on income, but the relationship takes the form of a more flexible acceleration principle.

Stock-Adjustment Models—The Flexible Accelerator

Changes in desired capital explain only some of the fluctuations in investment. While changes in investment follow shifts in desires, conformity between their movements may be erratic. Both for firms and for the economy, delays occur between the time added capital is desired and investment goods are produced. Investment takes time. Desires for capital must be translated into decisions to invest; financing must be arranged; orders must be placed; production started and completed. The movement from desires to investment leads to the concept of **stock-adjustment** or **flexible-accelerator** models, in which the gap between desired and actual capital is only partially filled by investment in each period.

Equation 9.6 presents a general form of a stock-adjustment model. The amount of investment varies in proportion to the gap between desired and actual capital and the need for replacement of the capital stock. The equation for investment demand is

$$I = \lambda (K_d - K_{-1}) + \delta K_{-1}. \tag{9.6}$$

This equation says that in any period, if the amount of desired capital (K_d) increases, investment will go up, but only a fraction (lambda) of the gap between desired and actual capital will be filled in the current period. The time structure of the investment process may differ among classes of investments. Another way of looking at the relationship is to say that current investment is a weighted average of past changes in desired capital and gaps from the actual level. The final item in equation 9.6, δK_{-1}, indicates that the amount of gross investment also depends on the need for replacements. This is a fraction (δ) of the level of capital.

THE LAG BETWEEN CHANGES IN DESIRED CAPITAL AND INVESTMENT

When the level of desired capital (K_d) goes up because of changes in the amount of output, expectations of higher future sales, or increased profitability, it may take a considerable time for investment expenditures to rise. One of the pertinent factors is the size of the gap. How much the desire for capital has risen compared with the existing stock affects the rate at which investment grows. Also important are the physical processes through which capital goods are ordered, the rate at which industry can increase production, and the general availability of funds. For example, at the start of the 1980s the automobile industry had a major recognized need for new equipment to turn out more fuel-efficient cars. However, desired investment was spread over several years. The introduction of full lines of modern models was delayed because of shortages of both credit and capacity among suppliers of the tools and equipment needed to produce the new models.

For most investment expenditures, the lag between changes in capital desires and production is long. After businesses become convinced that an increase in demand is permanent, they must decide what item of plant or equipment to order. They must allocate necessary funds in the capital budget of the firm and arrange the financing. The plans for the goods they want must be worked out on the drawing board; orders must be placed, and production embarked upon. Even after installation, there may be a considerable period of modification before full production is achieved. Studies show that it takes from one to two years after demand increases before investment expenditures reach their peak. The average length of an investment expenditure is between two and three years. Expenditures are still being made as long as six or seven years after the demand to raise the capital stock is first perceived. Because demand works its way through the firm in a slow and complex manner, orders and production will adapt more smoothly to changes in demand than the simplified acceleration principle shows. Changes in income and output are smoothed out.

Lags are also altered by the degree of capacity utilization. The accelerator model showed that the timing of replacements and of expansion needs was quite different, depending on whether a firm was producing at or below full capacity. Because unused capacity is expensive, most executives report that they don't try to beat inflation by ordering investment goods before they are sure of their need. Still, several recent bursts of investment expenditures can be explained primarily as anticipating higher future prices.

The level of capacity utilization affects costs and the ability to obtain deliveries. If all firms increase their investment orders together, costs rise and deliveries are delayed. The supply price of capital goes up, and some investments take too long. Firms that undertake too much may find themselves with half-finished plants, a situation that can lead to sizable cost overruns compared to initial cost estimates.

Replacement Needs. It is hard to differentiate between the factors altering the lags in net investment and those causing changes in the rate of replacements. Replacement needs are usually shown as a percent of the existing capital stock. In fact, replacements also vary with output. If production is near capacity, it will pay to use older, less efficient equipment. Whether or not a replacement is necessary also depends on factors similar to those influencing desired capital, such as the level of expected output, costs, and financing availability.

Models of Inventory Investment

Closely related to the general acceleration principle are models of inventory investment, which show that cycles in inventory investment are likely to occur as a result of the physical relationships between sales, production, and inventories. It has already been noted that inventory fluctuations are frequently the largest of all.[1]

In the simplest inventory models, the level of desired inventories (INV_d) is assumed to be some ratio to expected sales (Y^e). For example, assume that f, the desired ratio, is .5:

$$INV_d = f(Y^e)   INV_d = .5(Y^e). \qquad \textbf{9.7}$$

The level of production (Q) is set so as to equal the amount of expected sales plus any planned inventory investment or disinvestment. Planned inventory investment equals the difference between the desired level of inventory and the actual level, $[f(Y^e) - INV_{-1}]$, where actual is the amount in inventory at the end of the previous period. Production equals expected sales plus planned inventory investment, or

$$Q = Y^e + [f(Y^e) - INV_{-1}]. \qquad \textbf{9.8}$$

1. The basic theory is presented in L. A. Metzler, "The Nature and Stability of Inventory Cycles," *Review of Economic Statistics,* 23 (August 1941): 113–129. See also P. G. Darling and M. C. Lovell, "Factors Influencing Investment in Inventories," Chapter 4 in J. S. Duesenberry *et al.,* eds., *The Brookings Quarterly Econometric Model of the United States* (Chicago: Rand-McNally, 1965), and B. Bosworth, "Analyzing Inventory Investment," *Brookings Papers on Economic Activity,* 2 (1970): 207–27.

Inventories act as a buffer stock. If sales exceed expectations, there will be an unplanned decrease in inventories. If sales fall below expectations, unwanted accumulations will occur. Thus the level of inventory investment (ΔINV) in a given year equals planned inventory investment plus or minus the difference between expected and actual sales, or

$$\Delta INV = Y^e - Y_a + [f(Y^e) - INV_{-1}]. \qquad \textbf{9.9}$$

When plans are made for the next production period, they again will equal expected sales plus any adjustments desired in inventories.

Because inventories form a buffer stock, investment in them can be extremely erratic. Table 9.5 shows why this is so. The model underlying the table is that of equation 9.9. The first two columns list the amount produced for expected sale plus the desired change in inventories. Their sum equals total production (Q) shown in the third column. Actual sales (Y_a) in a period are shown in the fourth column. The difference between output and actual sales is inventory investment, the fifth column. The division of this change in inventory between planned and unplanned is shown in the sixth and seventh columns. The final column shows total inventories. They change by the amount of inventory investment or disinvestment.

In each period, expected sales are set equal to the previous period's sales (Y_{-1}). Planned inventory investment equals the difference between one-half of this period's expected sales and the amount on hand at the end of the previous period (the eighth column). Production (Q) equals expected sales plus planned inventory investment. Thus production is 1,000 in period 2 and 1,250 in period 3. In period 2, sales increase by an unexpected $100 million, causing

TABLE 9.5   **A Simplified Model of Inventory Fluctuations**
(millions of constant 1972 dollars)

Time	Production (Q)			Sales	Inventory investment			Total
	For sale+ Y^e (1)	For inventories= $+.5Y^e - INV_{-1} =$ (2)	Total Q (3)	$- Y$ (4)	Total $=$ ΔINV (5)	Unplanned+ (6)	Planned $0.5Y^e - INV_1$ (7)	Inventories (8)
1	1,000	0	1,000	1,000	0	0	0	500
2	1,000	0	1,000	1,100	−100	−100	0	400
3	1,100	150	1,250	1,200	50	−100	150	450
4	1,200	150	1,350	1,300	50	−100	150	500
5	1,300	150	1,450	1,350	100	−50	150	600
6	1,350	75	1,425	1,300	125	50	75	725
7	1,300	−75	1,225	1,275	−50	25	−75	675

Production equals expected sales plus planned inventory investment. Actual total inventory investment equals the difference between production and actual sales. Unplanned inventory investment is the difference between planned and actual inventory investment.

an unplanned drop in inventories of this amount. For period 3, production is set to equal expected sales (those of period 2—$1,100 million) plus the amount of investment ($150 million) needed to bring inventories up to their desired level (.5 times expected sales of 1,100 less the 400 in inventory). But as a result of higher income, sales expand again. In period 3, while $150 million in planned investment is made, the extra sales result in an unplanned drop of $100 million, so net inventory investment is only $50 million (150 planned minus 100 = 50). An even sharper shift occurs between periods 6 and 7. In period 6, the sum of planned and unplanned inventory investment is at a record high. This situation leads to planned disinvestment and the greatest change in ΔINV. The amount of investment in inventories falls by $175 million (from + 125 to − 50).

A shortage of capacity may be of special significance in inventory investments. If production is limited, inventories may be drawn down unwillingly. At one point in a boom, a high proportion of sales may be met from the stock of goods on hand. Near the end of an expansion, inventory investment grows as firms produce more in order to raise inventories back to desired levels. Then investment in inventories may accelerate as sales drop and unwanted stocks begin to accumulate. Most peaks in production are marked by such inventory movements. Production is not cut back as fast as sales. Later, these unwanted inventories are sold off, causing output to decline even more than final demand. Expenditures on inventory investments are cut at the same time as sales of final goods drop. The two together have a magnified multiplier.

Because the shifts in planned investment and output are so large, most empirical models assume that firms will plan to go only part way in adjusting desired inventories to meet changes in sales, and they will fill only part of the gap between actual and desired inventories. Barry Bosworth presents as a typical model[2]

$$\Delta INV_o = .11 Y_o + .26 Y_{-1} - .33 INV_{-1}. \qquad \textbf{9.10}$$

This equation states that inventory investment in this quarter rises with the sales of this quarter and the last quarter. Investment decreases if inventories at the start of the period are high, and rises if they are low.

A relationship between output and investment is one of the foundations of the multiplier. The larger the amount of investment induced by income changes, the larger the multiplier. However, because acceleration relates investment spending to changes and not to the level of output and because the accelerator is flexible, the economy's multiplier is more complex than that of the earlier model. Investment shoots up faster than a simple model predicts. Furthermore, it may turn down even if income continues to expand, simply as a result of a slowdown in the rate of growth of income.

---

2. B. Bosworth, "Analyzing Inventory Investment," p. 212. The equation is for inventories of durable goods held by retailers and wholesalers.

Interest Rates and Investment

The simple model shows the desire to spend (the *IS* curve) falling with interest rates. Monetary policy exerts critical impacts on investment. When the money supply grows less than its demand, nominal and real interest rates rise; financing availability contracts; expectations of future sales fall. Chapter 5 showed how the value of assets changes when interest rates shift. The concepts of discounting and present value add insights into investment decisions and the shape of the *IS* curve. Because of the need to discount future receipts by today's rates, when interest rates rise, the present value of an investment with a certain expected income flow falls. Some purchases of capital goods which would have been profitable at the lower interest rates no longer promise a competitive return. Fewer capital goods will be bought; investment expenditures will decrease.

In formulating their investment decisions, businesses can follow either of two basic and nearly equivalent methods. The same procedures allow the selection of one or several from among competing investments.

1. Given the current capital cost of an investment and its expected future costs and revenues, the firm calculates the **net present value** of the stream of future payments and receipts based on the interest rate the firm must pay for its funds. If the net present value is positive, the investment will be profitable. If the firm's funds are limited, it should invest first in those items with the highest net present values.
2. Alternatively, the firm can calculate the **internal rate of return** (the marginal efficiency of capital) for each proposed investment. This is the rate at which a present value would have to grow to equal a specified future value. It will then be profitable to invest in all items with an internal rate of return exceeding the cost of funds to the firm. Again, if funds are limited, the firm should buy those items with the highest rates of return first.[3]

For an example of how interest rates affect investments, let us posit the following situation. A firm is offered some new stamping machines at a cost of $100,000. The machines will wear out and be worth nothing at the end of three years. The cost of money to the firm, or its interest rate, is 10 percent a year during this period. The firm makes the following calculations: Cost of machines $100,000; salvage value at end of year 3 is zero; cost of money (*i*) is 10 percent.

3. For those familiar with the literature on finance, it will be obvious that this section does not discuss the fine points of the differences between the use of present values and the internal rate of return in accepting or rejecting investments; nor is account taken of the difference in risks and the necessary adjustments to a certainty equivalent return resulting from greater or lesser degrees of uncertainty. It is well-known that in a few special cases these two rules will not give identical rankings for individual projects. Those interested in these problems may consult a basic book on finance. They are discussed in considerable detail in S. J. Maisel and S. Roulac, *Real Estate Investment and Finance* (New York: McGraw-Hill, 1976), Chapters 5, 17, and Part VI.

	Year 1	Year 2	Year 3
Gross revenues	$120,000	$120,000	$120,000
Materials, labor, etc.	70,000	70,000	70,000
Net revenue	$ 50,000	$ 50,000	$ 50,000

The firm believes that it can earn $50,000 a year in net revenues. Given the cost of money (the interest rate) of 10 percent, is the investment worthwhile?

PRESENT VALUE OF INVESTMENT

To find whether or not such an investment will be profitable, a firm can compare the present value of the expected net revenue from a purchase with the cost of the equipment. The present value formula shows how expected future revenues ($R = 50,000$) in this case can be discounted by the cost of funds (i) to obtain the present value of an asset (PV), or

$$PV = \frac{R_1}{(1 + i)} + \frac{R_2}{(1 + i)^2} + \frac{R_3}{(1 + i)^3} \qquad \textbf{9.11}$$

$$= \frac{50,000}{1.10} + \frac{50,000}{(1.10)^2} + \frac{50,000}{(1.10)^3}$$

$$= .909(50,000) + .826(50,000) + .751(50,000)$$

$$PV = 124,300.$$

The present value can then be compared to the cost of the item. With a present value of $124,300 and a cost ($COS$) of $100,000, the comparison shows

$$PV > COS \qquad 124,300 > 100,000.$$

The investment will be profitable because the present value of the receipts exceeds the capital cost. The same results are obtained by considering both the capital cost and the revenues in the same equation to obtain an estimate of the net present value (NPV).

$$NPV = (-COS) + \frac{R_1}{(1 + i)} + \frac{R_2}{(1 + i)^2} + \frac{R_3}{(1 + i)^3}$$

$$NPV = (-100,000) + .909(50,000) + .826(50,000) + .751(50,000)$$

$$NPV = \$24,300.$$

This proposed investment has a net present value of $24,300, which must be compared to other possible alternatives.

THE INTERNAL RATE OF RETURN ON AN INVESTMENT

The second, and closely related, method of finding whether an investment will pay off is to compare its internal rate of return to the cost of funds. An investment will be profitable when its internal rate of return (Ir) exceeds its cost of funds (i). We can compare the two techniques by continuing with the example of the machines. The information about capital cost, expected revenues, and interest rates is identical in both cases. In the first, the data were used to solve for the net present value of the proposal. The investment is made if the net present value is positive or larger than for other potential investments. In this second case, the same data are used to find the internal rate of return (Ir) rather than the NPV. The investment is made if Ir exceeds the interest rate.

The reverse of the present value process asks, "If one knows the cost of an asset, what rate of discount (internal rate of return) is needed to. make the present value of the future income flow equal to the cost?" More formally, the *internal rate of return* is that rate at which the present value of all future positive inflows is equal to the present value of all negative outflows. This is usually simplified to assume that the only outflow is the capital expenditure. In practice, however, a machine may break down or undergo other periods when its out-of-pocket costs exceed its revenues. Periods of negative flows are especially prevalent in the case of buildings.

The formula for finding present values, knowing the interest or discount rate and the future revenues, was given as

$$PV = \frac{R_1}{(1 + i)} + \frac{R_2}{(1 + i)^2} + \frac{R_3}{(1 + i)^3}. \qquad \textbf{9.11}$$

This can be turned into an equation for finding internal rates of return. Let COS be the capital cost or known present value (PV) of a machine. Substitute the unknown internal rate of return (Ir) into the equation instead of the interest rate (i), and solve the equation. For a specific example, use the case of the machines with net revenues of $50,000 for each of 3 years. However, for ease of calculation, let us assume that their capital cost is $124,300. Then:

$$COS = \frac{R_1}{(1 + Ir)} + \frac{R_2}{(1 + Ir)^2} + \frac{R_3}{(1 + Ir)^3} + \ldots + \frac{R_n}{(1 + Ir)^n}.$$

$$\$124,300 = \frac{50,000}{(1 + Ir)} + \frac{50,000}{(1 + Ir)^2} + \frac{50,000}{(1 + Ir)^3} + \ldots + \frac{0}{(1 + Ir)^n}$$

Answer: $Ir = .10$.

Unfortunately, if we didn't have the previous example, or if we had used the capital cost of $100,000, finding the exact value of Ir would be difficult. The easiest and most common way of finding Ir is to use a computer or calculator with an internal rate of return package. In this particular problem, because all the flows are equal, the value of Ir can be found without too much trouble by the use of interest rate tables that give the present value of an annuity.

MARGINAL EFFICIENCY OF CAPITAL

The *marginal efficiency of capital* (*MEC*) for an asset is its internal rate of return, or the rate of discount, which equates the present value of the asset's expected net revenues with its supply price or capital cost. Thus in the previous example, 10 percent is the rate of discount which equates $50,000 of expected revenue for each of the following three years with a capital asset that has a current cost of $124,300. It is the marginal efficiency of capital for that particular asset. It would be profitable for the firm to buy the asset if the interest rate or financial cost of the funds it had to use was under 10 percent.

An individual firm can rate its potential investments by their *MEC*s. Such a rating is presented graphically in Figure 9.5. Potential investments with the highest expected marginal efficiency appear at the left. For the first $50,000 of investments the firm might expect a rate of return of 26 percent. The firm then lists the investments with the next lower rates of return, and so on. The

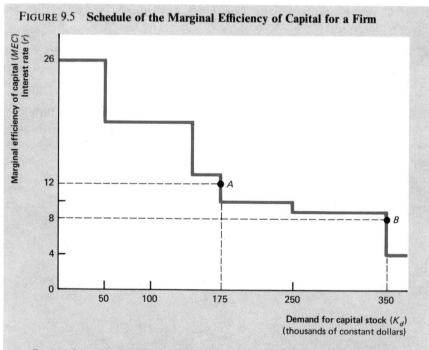

FIGURE 9.5   **Schedule of the Marginal Efficiency of Capital for a Firm**

Potential purchases of physical capital are ranked according to their marginal efficiency (internal rate of return) with those having the highest rate on the left. It pays to invest in a capital asset if its marginal efficiency exceeds the interest rate that must be paid to fund its purchase. For example, if interest rates are at 12 percent, all assets to the left of A have a higher rate of return and will be profitable investments.

lower the *MEC*, the more numerous are the potential investments, measured as the horizontal distance from the origin.

The figure can be used also to determine the amount of capital the firm would want invested at various given interest rates. How much capital would the firm want if the interest rate (its cost of funds) was 12 percent? Point *A* on the figure shows that the firm would want $175,000 of capital goods if the cost of funds was 12 percent. This amount of goods has an *MEC* which exceeds the interest rate (*r*). If it could obtain $350,000 at 8 percent interest (point *B*), it would invest that amount. The firm's cost of funds determines a cutoff point dividing profitable (all to the left) from nonprofitable investments. Each potential investment to the left of the cutoff has an *MEC* which exceeds the firm's cost of funds (*r*). A clear relationship exists between interest rates and the optimum amount of capital a firm would like to invest in at any time. This desired capital is one of the key variables determining the investment schedule. The movements in the desired capital stock as interest rates shift are major factors influencing the investment–interest-rate function.

It is often assumed that the marginal efficiency of capital curves for all individual firms can be added to obtain a similar curve for the economy. This is not quite accurate. In the process of aggregation, the possibility of new firms, of new products, and of foreign competition must be taken into account. The supply and demand prices that each firm expects in drawing up its own marginal efficiency of capital may be altered.

Abstracting from these problems, a marginal efficiency of capital curve for the economy will resemble Figure 9.5, but the demand for capital stock will apply to the entire business sector. It will be in billions, not thousands, of constant dollars. When the real interest rate declines, the desired stock of capital (K_d) will rise. A gap will open between the desired and the actual stock $(K_d - K_{-1})$. The previous discussion showed that when this gap widens, the rate of investment goes up. However, the increase in the current period will be far less than the gap. How fast investment expands depends on the lags in planning, production, and financing.

THE NEOCLASSICAL INVESTMENT THEORY

The present value and the internal rate or return formulations of the desired stock of capital, while correct, fail to show explicitly several significant forces. For example, firms can alter costs by substituting capital, labor, energy, or materials for each other. The traditional models also fail to bring out the importance of inflation and of differing tax rates and subsidies. In an effort to correct for several of these factors, Dale Jorgenson and others have reexamined classical theory and presented it in a form called the **neoclassical investment theory**. In this theory, too, capital is desired if the present value of its expected revenues exceeds its costs. However, the calculations explicitly include possible changes in production possibilities—the production function—as well as in expected prices and taxes.

A firm's desired capital (K_d) is proportional to the ratio of the value of output (PQ) from an investment to the rental price of capital services (PRC).[4] This can be written as

$$K_d = \pounds \frac{PQ}{PRC},$$ 9.12

where $\pounds$ depends on the production function. This is another way of saying that a firm invests to the point where the marginal product of a unit of capital exceeds the rental price (user cost) of its services. This formulation makes clear that expected sales or revenues (PQ) remain a critical factor in the investment decision. Equally important are the production methods used and the costs of other inputs which determine the degree to which capital is substituted for or complements other factors. More detailed analysis shows the importance of the factors which influence the cost of using capital.

THE RENTAL PRICE OF CAPITAL SERVICES

The net present value of an investment depends on its purchase price and on the discounted net income it produces in each future period. When demand for output expands, a firm must decide whether the change is temporary or permanent. It must then weigh the benefits expected to be gained from a new investment which will add production capacity against the cost of using the increased capital.

The Cost of Physical Capital. One of the key costs of production is the physical capital used up to obtain the revenue of a period. This cost depends on the price of investment goods and their rate of depreciation. If the price of investment goods falls compared to revenues, firms will increase their demand for capital. To be profitable and stay in business, a firm must be able to get back the amount invested in an asset plus enough earnings to cover the cost of borrowing. Depreciation is an allowance for the amount of physical capital

---

4. There are numerous methods of formulating the rental price of capital services. A simple form shows

$$PRC = \frac{PK(r + DEP)(1 - TI)}{(1 - TP)} - \dot{P}K^e.$$ 9.13

This says that PRC depends on the price and expected change in the price of capital (PK and PK^e), real financing costs (r), the depreciation rate (DEP), corporate profits tax rates (TP), and the net investment tax credit (TI). For a more detailed discussion of this and the current state of investment models, see G. Ackley, *Macroeconomics: Theory and Policy* (New York: Macmillan, 1978), Chapter 18; D. W. Jorgenson, "Econometric Studies of Investment Behavior: A Survey," *Journal of Economic Literature* 9(December 1971): 1,111–47; L. R. Klein and R. Eisner, "Issues in Econometric Studies of Investment Behavior," *Journal of Economic Literature* 12(March 1974): 43–50; and R. Eisner, "Econometric Studies of Investment Behavior," *Economic Inquiry* 12(March 1974): 91–104.

used up during a period. If the rate of real depreciation declines, the cost of using a capital asset will fall.

Financial Costs.   In many financial theories of investment, the desire to invest depends either on the cost (interest rate) of financing or on its availability. Finding the rate to use for determining the potential profitability of a capital investment is more complex than just looking in the paper to see what has been happening to interest rates. For instance, firms must be concerned with their own costs of capital, which differ from market rates depending on individual risks and on taxes.

The literature of finance contains many debates about whether financial markets are efficient enough to permit firms to borrow all they want at market rates adjusted only for their own individual risks. Capital theory in finance offers two conflicting views. In one, named for Franco Modigliani of MIT and Merton Miller of the University of Chicago, the cost of capital is independent of the financial structure of the firm and of dividend policy. In the more traditional view, a firm's cost of financing depends on its debt-equity ratio (the amount of borrowing compared to the owner's capital). In either case, the discount rate used by a firm has to take account of uncertainties in its future cash flows as well as of the cost of raising money. A nationally known company in Fortune magazine's top 500 can get funds more cheaply than a small firm in a local market. Actual discount factors used by firms are a good deal higher than risk-free market interest rates such as those on government bonds.

Inflation.   In addition to impacting revenues, the expected rate of inflation influences the price of capital services in several ways. The rate of depreciation may actually turn into appreciation for a period if prices of new equipment, factories, and buildings rise rapidly. Such potential changes must be taken into account. The expected rate of inflation also affects nominal and real interest rates. Because expected prices for individual goods may vary around the average and because taxes are based on changes in book value, not real values, inflation also complicates the calculation of user costs. It is possible, as we saw in the case of housing, for real interest rates to become negative. Inflation may make it profitable to borrow and invest. On the other hand, because inflation may cause an understatement of costs for tax purposes, it may lead to higher real taxes and lower profits.

Taxes.   Whether welcomed or not, governments are partners with firms in their investment results. Investors pay taxes on profits to governments. In making decisions, they must compare their aftertax returns from one investment to aftertax returns from another. Taxes interact with interest rates and depreciation. Since interest paid out is a deduction from income for corporate profits tax purposes, and dividends or undistributed profits are not, the cost of capital is distorted. Some investments are made more profitable by differential tax treatments that increase their aftertax returns. For example, in the case of housing, some oil and gas wells, and farms, tax shelters are important. The investment tax credit returns 10 percent of the amount invested in some capital.[5] Other forms of capital are allowed more rapid depreciation. Most of these special tax treatments aim at increasing either total investment or that in particular spheres.

Changes in how taxes are assessed and in their levels alter the rental price of capital. When these costs decline, more investment takes place. Tax laws shift the desired level of investment. Some influence the overall level of K_d; some affect the timing of investment expenditures, and others influence the type of goods bought. Some economists believe that the use of historical cost accounting and the failure to adjust the tax base of capital to reflect inflation have been major impediments to additional investment. They consider the interaction of the tax system with inflation to be a significant explanation of the fall in productivity. The failure of the tax system to adjust for inflation raises the price of capital services and reduces internal sources of financing.

THE REDUCED IMPORTANCE OF INTEREST MOVEMENTS

The inclusion of high depreciation rates, uncertainties, and costs of financing in the calculation of the present values of future income reduces the significance of movements in real interest rates. Because revenue to be received after a few years has a very low present value, higher rates for capital services reduce the horizon over which estimates must be made. When depreciation and uncertainty are large, analysts assign less importance to interest rates as a determinant of income. For equipment lasting only a few years, the magnitude of depreciation may far outweigh interest effects. Suppose a machine will last three years and a firm expects to earn 15 percent on its capital. The revenues, before depreciation is subtracted, must exceed 48 percent a year (15 percent interest plus 33 percent depreciation). Suppose now that because market interest rates are rising, the firm sets its earnings goal at 20 percent plus depreciation. The needed revenues would rise only from 48 percent to 53 percent, or by about 10 percent.

In contrast, an apartment house might have a depreciation rate of only 3 percent, using a life of $33\frac{1}{3}$ years. Its net cost of funds from mortgage and equity together might be 10 percent. It would need net revenues of 13 percent to cover depreciation and financing charges. If a credit squeeze caused its cost of money to rise to 15 percent, it would have to earn 18 percent. It would have to increase its revenues by nearly 40 percent. Given the difference between a needed increase in revenues of 40 percent versus 10 percent, one would expect interest rate changes to have a much greater impact on the demand for apartment houses than for short-lived machines; and they do.

THE AVAILABILITY OF FINANCING

In addition to the rental price of capital services, the availability of internal

---

5. The government grants a credit against other taxes equal to 10 percent of certain types of capital expenditure.

funds and the ability to borrow have a significant impact on investment. The amount of inventories firms can carry must be reduced if their bankers demand that loans be repaid. Firms often find themselves unable to finance investments that look profitable but cannot be made because of limited equity capital and traditional ratios of debt to capital required by lenders. When money grows tighter they may have to forego opportunities they would normally welcome.

In boom periods, interest rates rise and availability shrinks. The liquidity of borrowers and lenders deteriorates. Risks increase. While the expected revenues from an investment may rise, its present value may not grow because of higher discount rates. Even if investors want to purchase added capital, they may find no willing lenders. It is difficult to separate the availability of financing from its cost. Most firms could obtain some loans if they were willing to pay much higher rates. Loan sharks still exist. However, risks to the owners and managers of the firm rise as the percent borrowed increases.

Much attention has been paid to the difference between internal sources of funds (depreciation allowances and undistributed profits) and external sources—those which must be borrowed. Some analysts assume that firms will make investments with a lower marginal efficiency of capital if internal funds are available. As with interest rates, it is hard to separate movements in profits from availability. Do firms invest more because their profits are higher or because, with higher profits, they have more internal funds? Initially, as profits increase, more internal funds are available. Balance sheets improve and external financing can be arranged. As expansions continue, however, liquidity deteriorates even though profits stay high. Interest rates rise; less financing is available. If to this factor are added the critical swings in funds for construction and home purchases, a high probability for investment instability is apparent.

Investment in Residential Construction

One of the clearest examples of the stock-adjustment–flexible-accelerator process at work can be found in the demand for residential construction expenditure. In the Great Depression, housing starts fell to only 10 percent of their previous peak. The drop from a cyclical peak in 1972 and in 1978 to the following low was over 50 percent. Figure 9.6 illustrates the extreme instability of housing starts. All three of the major influences on investment—financing, acceleration, and lags—affect residential construction. Changes in relative prices and real income influence the amount spent for houses but these factors have less effect on the number of starts.[6]

6. For detailed examination of the cause of housing fluctuations, see S. J. Maisel, "Non-Business Construction," Chapter 6 in J. S. Duesenberry et al., eds., The Brookings Quarterly Econometric Model of the United States (Chicago: Rand-McNally, 1965), and S. J. Maisel, "The Effects of Monetary Policy on Expenditures in Specific Sectors of the Economy," Journal of Political Economy 76(4): part 2, 496–514, and references therein.

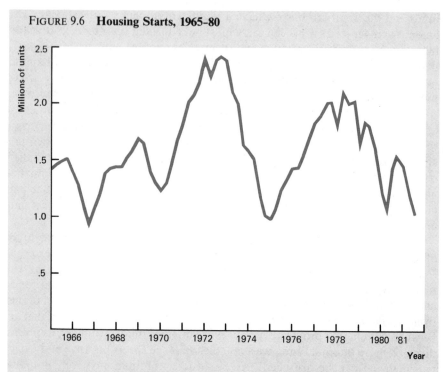

FIGURE 9.6   **Housing Starts, 1965–80**

Fluctuations in housing production (starts of new units are shown in the figure) exceed those of most other spending categories. Inventories of vacant units can be occupied, allowing a temporary postponement of new building. Increases in interest costs reduce investment desires when families cannot meet required monthly payments. Financing becomes harder to obtain as lenders find other loans more profitable than mortgages.

FINANCING AND HOUSING CONSTRUCTION

Housing has traditionally been the sector of the economy most influenced by changes in interest rates and credit availability. When interest rates rise and credit becomes tight, housing starts and expenditures decline. When money becomes tighter, two paths lead to a curtailment of starts: (1) Greater demand for funds by businesses and households raises the cost of borrowing on mortgages fairly quickly. This directly lowers the profitability of construction to builders, and also decreases the demand of final purchasers for units. (2) The availability of money to both builders and buyers is reduced. Savers shift their money out of deposits to direct market investments, causing a drop in the funds available to the main mortgage lenders. In addition, many financial institutions lower the relative share of the funds they desire to place in mortgages.

The degree to which each type of spending is affected when credit tightens depends on the proportion of purchases made with credit, the amount of credit required per unit of expenditure, the ability or willingness to absorb higher interest rates, the institutional character of the market, and the degree to which traditional lenders are influenced by policy changes. Housing ranks high in sensitivity to monetary changes on all these counts. About 95 percent of new single-family housing is sold with the benefit of long-term financing. In 1978 the amount of mortgage loans made on houses was about 200 percent of residential construction in the year. Thrift institutions are the main source of housing money, together with commercial banks (for which mortgage lending is a much smaller share of the total) and, in recent years, government agencies.

Depending on the particular year and the model used to estimate impacts, changes in financing account for between 40 and 90 percent of the movements in new housing starts. Recognition of the importance of financing has led to the establishment of a variety of government agencies and programs whose purpose is to improve the functioning of the mortgage market in order to temper the impact on housing of movements in financial markets. However, some analysts believe that their net impact has been destabilizing.

Other reasons why housing production varies so much are related to the acceleration principle and the inventory cycle. The ratio of capital to output in housing is high. To obtain a month's housing services, a large capital investment must be made. With 90 million houses, starts of 1,800,000 a year mean that the demand for additional space is only 2 percent of the existing stock. What if demand in a year rose to 3 percent? New starts would accelerate to 2,700,000—an increase in production of 50 percent. Fluctuations of nearly this magnitude are not uncommon.

At the same time, large planned and unplanned movements occur in the inventory of vacant houses—those available for occupancy or under construction. At any time, over 7 million vacant units are present in the nation's housing inventory. What would happen if new starts during a year dropped from 1.8 million to 1 million? The housing inventory that year would fall from 7 to 6.2 million vacant units. Shortages and problems would arise in some areas, but the needs of almost everyone wanting to occupy a house would still be met. Contrast that to what would happen if bread production fell by 40 percent; after two or three days, shortages would be keenly felt. Housing production can fluctuate so much without great hardships to users because increases and decreases in inventories can absorb the movements in production far more readily.

STOCK-ADJUSTMENT LAGS

As with other types of investment, lags occur between changes in inventories, in financing, and in housing starts. A further delay of six months to a year occurs between the time a dwelling is started and final production. A number of complex empirical models have been built in attempts to provide better explanations of housing fluctuations. The main differences between them lie in the amount of disaggregation and methods of fitting. The basic variables have steadfastly retained their significance as explanations of how the market works.

Equation 9.14, an early version of such models, contains the main analytical points.[7]

$$HS = -463.1 - .2988 \sum_{-1}^{-3} Int + .0102 \sum_{-1}^{-3} FIN$$

$$-.0821\,VA_{-2} + .5414\,HS_{-1} - .3313\,HS_{-3} \qquad\qquad \textbf{9.14}$$

$$+.8098 \sum_{-1}^{-3} \frac{R}{C} + .0380\,YDH.$$

$$R^2 = .86.$$

The first line shows the financial variables. Housing starts (HS) fall when interest rates (Int) rise and increase when financial institutions have more deposits (FIN) available for mortgage lending. The second line is the accelerator; starts fall when vacancies (VA) rise and in response to inventories of units in production ($HS_{-1} - HS_{-3}$). The third line shows starts rising if rents go up relative to housing costs $\left(\dfrac{R}{C}\right)$ and with disposable household income (YDH).

The lags are significant. What happens to the financial, cost, and production variables over the three previous quarters affects current starts. Vacancy effects lag two quarters and income one quarter. Since expenditures in the GNP lag behind starts another six months, the total lag between a change in interest rates or financial conditions and output expenditures is a minimum of three months and an average of over a year, while some impacts take over two years before they affect the GNP.

ESTIMATED IMPACTS

Table 9.6 shows the estimated impacts of various variables on the number of housing starts. In the year following the fourth quarter of 1965, the rate of new private housing starts dropped by 584,000, or nearly 40 percent. In this period, mortgage interest rates rose more than 100 basis points, or by 20 percent of their initial level. The three quarter lagged average flow of funds fell by about 35 percent. According to the model, these financial factors caused 268,000 of the drop in starts. The high inventories at the beginning of the period accounted for 192,000 units of the decline. Relative prices and income had a minor impact. The model fails to account for about 20 percent of the drop. Later models fit over a longer period attribute most of this residual to financial factors.

---

7. S. J. Maisel, "The Effects of Monetary Policy on Expenditures in Specific Sectors of the Economy," *Journal of Political Economy* 76(4): part 2, 496–514, Table 5, Equation 5. The sigmas (Σ) represent the value of the factors for the quarters indicated (-1 to -3); they are added together to form the variable in the equation.

In 1969, the downturn started with a completely changed inventory situation. After the previous fall, the level of inventories had failed to return to a normal level. Because they were low, they had a positive impact on production. There was a need for planned inventory investment. The movements in interest rates and financing were similar in the two periods, with the same impact on starts. The beginning of the inflation in housing costs meant a larger negative influence from them in the second period. The model does not do as well in explaining 1969 as it does for 1966. Later models tend to diminish the effect of inventories in 1969. They attribute the total drop in starts to changes in financing and relative prices.

TABLE 9.6 **The Contributions of Variables to the Decline in Housing Starts in 1966 and 1969**

(at seasonally adjusted annual rates)

Variables	From 1965:Q4 to 1966:Q4	From 1968:Q4 to 1969:Q4
Financial	− 268,000	− 252,000
Inventories	− 192,000	+ 112,000
Relative prices	− 12,000	− 40,000
Estimated change	− 472,000	− 180,000
Actual change	− 584,000	− 272,000

Based on a 1970 study by James Burnham.

Fluctuations in housing starts primarily reflect movements in the financial variables (interest rates and mortgage availability) and in the inventory of unoccupied houses.

While they differ with respect to specific variables and weights assigned to each, the many models for all types of investment resemble those for housing. Movements depend on lagged financial and output variables with occasional special factors arising from relative prices or capacity utilization which can cause expenditures to differ from underlying demand. The interaction of uncertainties, shifting expectations, financing, capacity constraints on production, and similar factors in the stock-adjustment model all contribute to the instability of investment expenditures and the difficulty of predicting them. The fact that stocks adjust with a lag and the diminished importance of interest rates would seem to decrease the likelihood of instability in comparison with the simple income-interest-investment function. On the other hand, the greater importance of expectations, the larger role of financing, the heightened importance of capacity utilization on prices, and the greater potential for acceleration in inventories and housing all work in the opposite direction.

Summary

1. The concept of business cycles enables us to describe the recurrent fluctuations in economic activity which mark the history of industrial societies.

The economy expands and contracts in response to initiating forces which shift the desire to spend and to borrow (the *IS-LM* curves). From one cycle to the next, patterns of change have a degree of similarity as a result of the manner in which spending shocks are absorbed by the economy's response mechanism.

2. Investment expenditures tend to be unstable. Their demand is derived from changes in final spending. This leads to acceleration and deceleration in expenditures. Because of durability, additions to capital can be postponed without curtailing current production. Expectations, which shift rapidly, are important in decisions. Since the services and income from new capital will be received in the future, their present value depends on the rate of discount. Such rates also undergo wide fluctuations. Since many investments require financing with borrowed money, the level of expenditures will be strongly influenced by the availability of financing.

3. Firms invest when expected profits exceed their costs of funds. A desire to increase capital depends on the present value of expected net revenues compared to the price of a new capital purchase. How much an addition to capital will increase revenues depends on how much output will be sold, on what prices will prevail, and on the costs or saving of inputs to be used with the equipment. Demand rises with the GNP, as do profits and available funds. The rate at which expected revenues will be discounted to arrive at their present values depends on a firm's financing costs.

4. The acceleration principle shows that investments in equipment, plant, inventories, and housing depend on the rate of change in output or the demand for services from capital goods. While the fluctuations in investment due to movements in demand are in fact somewhat subdued compared to those illustrated by simple models, they constitute one of the most unstable forces of the economy.

5. In stock-adjustment–flexible-accelerator models, investment expenditures vary with the gap between the desired and actual capital stock. Lags exist between increases in the gap and investment expenditures. The amount of expenditures in any period depends on a weighted average of past gaps. In addition, however, the rate at which desires to invest are filled depends on technological factors in ordering and production and on capacity utilization. Gross investment includes the replacement of existing capital. The rate of replacement can vary in relation to the same factors that cause the level of desired capital to shift and cause the rate of expenditures to be flexible.

6. Inventory investments are among the most volatile of all, rising and falling with production and expected sales. They may also be built up in fear of shortages and to beat price rises. Many movements occur simply because inventories are the buffer between production and unexpected changes in sales. After an unplanned rise or fall, the rate of inventory investment must shift to return stocks of goods to their desired level.

7. To be profitable, an investment must have a positive net present value or, equivalently, an internal rate of return (marginal efficiency of capital) that exceeds the firm's cost of funds. To calculate profitability, investors must know the supply price of a capital good, estimate its expected net revenues, and then discount these to find the net present value of the asset.

8. The neoclassical theory of investment shows more explicitly that desired capital will vary with changes in production possibilities, costs of inputs, and other factors, such as inflation and taxes, which influence the rental price of capital services (user costs). A firm will desire a capital investment if its net marginal product exceeds its user costs.

9. Almost every estimate is influenced by expectations, or how decision makers feel about the future. At times, purchasers of capital goods seem to be propelled upward by high spirits. They place orders at a rapid rate. At other times, they are completely pessimistic. They ignore all good news. Keynes and many others believe that such shifts in expectations may account for a good deal of the instability in investments.

10. The housing market and models of residential construction serve as good examples of how movements in interest and output change desired investment. In housing, financial factors—both interest rates and availability—have caused most shifts. However, the relationship between services demanded and the stock or inventory of dwellings also influences production. Firms must plan their expenditures. Production must be ordered. Actual output must take place. As a result, the level of spending in the GNP changes only after a considerable interval following movements in the variables which cause investment to shift.

Questions for Discussion and Review

1. Discuss the role of expectations in the decision to invest.

2. Why are inventories the most volatile component of investment?

3. Suppose a new machine has a capital cost of $20,000 and will yield a net revenue of $20,000 in each of the next two years, after which its scrap value will be zero.
   (a) Calculate the net present value of an investment in the machine if the firm faces an interest rate of 10 percent.
   (b) Calculate the internal rate of return.

4. Suppose that sales are currently 2 million, the capital-output ratio is 5, and depreciation is 5 percent of existing capital stock. If sales rise by 300,000, what will gross investment be?

5. Why does expanding demand for final goods lead to a magnified increase in the demand for investment goods?

6. What is meant by the "flexible accelerator"?

7. Discuss the problems involved in estimating the rental price of capital services.

8. It is sometimes urged that investment spending be spurred by allowing businessmen to depreciate or "write off" their investments more quickly. Evaluate this proposal in light of the model presented in this chapter.

9. Discuss the differing conclusions about the instability of investment spending resulting from the simple accelerator and stock-adjustment models.

10. What types of governmental programs might be effective in moderating the severe fluctuations in residential construction?

11. "If investment spending were observed to increase during a period of rising interest rates, this means that the marginal efficiency of capital must be positively sloped." Do you agree?

References

Bischoff, C. W. "Business Investment in the 1970's: A Comparison of Models." *Brookings Papers on Economic Activity* 1(1971).

Bosworth, B. "Analyzing Inventory Investment." *Brookings Papers on Economic Activity* 2(1970): 207–27.

Darling, P. G. and M. C. Lovell. "Factors Influencing Investment in Inventories," Chapter 4 in J. S. Duesenberry *et al.*, eds., *The Brookings Quarterly Econometric Model of the United States.* Chicago: Rand-McNally, 1965.

Jorgenson, D. W. "Econometric Studies of Investment Behavior: A Survey." *Journal of Economic Literature* 9(December 1971): 1,111–47.

Keynes, J. M. *The General Theory of Employment, Interest, and Money.* New York: Harcourt, Brace & World, originally published in 1936, Chapter 12.

Maisel, S. J. "Non-Business Construction," Chapter 6 in J. S. Duesenberry *et al.*, eds., *The Brookings Quarterly Econometric Model of the United States.* Chicago: Rand-McNally, 1965.

Metzler, L. A. "The Nature and Stability of Inventory Cycles," *Review of Economic Statistics* 23(August 1941): 113–29.

Samuelson, P. A., "Interaction Between the Multiplier Analysis and the Principle of Acceleration." *Review of Economic Statistics* 21(May 1939): 75–78.

10

Influences on the Level of Consumption

Unlike investment spending, consumption spending tends to be orderly, rising and falling primarily in response to disposable income. It is less likely to initiate fluctuations in output. As a rule, movements in investment or in government or foreign spending alter income levels and induce (the multiplier) related movements in consumption. The consumption sector is not entirely passive, however. Some types of expenditures, such as those for consumer durables or luxuries, shift in response to nonincome forces, such as inflationary expectations, consumer credit, and changes in interest rates. For instance, a precipitous drop in automobile sales, reacting to such pressures, was a key factor causing output to decline in 1980.

Since consumption purchases bulk large in the total GNP, even small fluctuations can be significant. By 1981 consumption expenditures exceeded $1.9 trillion and accounted for well over 60 percent of the GNP. Cyclical movements are especially important in some large industries supplying consumer goods and services, such as automobiles, airlines, travel, and recreation. Knowledge of the factors governing consumption plays a large role in the analysis of both the long- and short-run effects of changing fiscal policies. Alterations in tax rates can influence consumption spending by affecting disposable income. When taxes are raised, reduced income will lead to less spending, but the amount and timing of changes in spending and saving can be particularly important.

The simplified consumption function showed spending to be dependent on the marginal propensity to consume and on disposable income. This chapter examines additional factors which improve understanding of the consumption function and explain why it shifts. They include differences between consumption and income as measured in the GNP accounts and the concepts families use in making spending decisions and the need to include time or lags in decisions. When individuals and families make decisions to save or spend, they look beyond today to consider available resources over some longer horizon. This means that interest rates and net accumulated assets affect future income and therefore influence consumption.

The United States has a lower level of personal saving and investment than most other industrial nations. If more money were saved and invested, income and growth would be raised. Many policies designed to increase supply emphasize saving and capital formation. Among policies advocated as means of increasing saving are higher interest rates and lower taxes on wealth. To evaluate the impact of such policy changes, models and theories are required which take into account the effects of additional variables.

Earlier chapters described changes in expectations, interest rates, and wealth. This chapter brings them together in more dynamic models to explain how they influence the consumption function. In the light of historical movements in the consumption function, a number of variables are added to help explain how consumption expenditures are determined. The topics taken up are as follows:

> A historical consumption function.
> The relationship between income and consumption.
> The permanent-income hypothesis.
> Temporary tax changes and consumption.
> Consumption and wealth and population.
> Wealth or net worth influences consumption.
> Saving and interest rates.
> Consumption and price changes.
> The depressed consumer, 1973–75.

An emphasis on the effect of the additional factors on spending and saving differentiates modern analysis of aggregate demand from early versions of the consumption function.

A Historical Consumption Function

Historical relationships between real consumption and real personal disposable income are depicted in Figure 10.1. Each dot marks the disposable income and consumption expenditures in a particular year. Consumption is measured on the vertical and income on the horizontal axis, both in 1972 dollars. The line expresses the statistical relationship between these two variables found by regression. The actual regression covering the years 1947–80 is

$$C = 8.25 + .90YD \qquad R^2 = .999.$$

FIGURE 10.1   **The Consumption Function, United States, 1947–80**

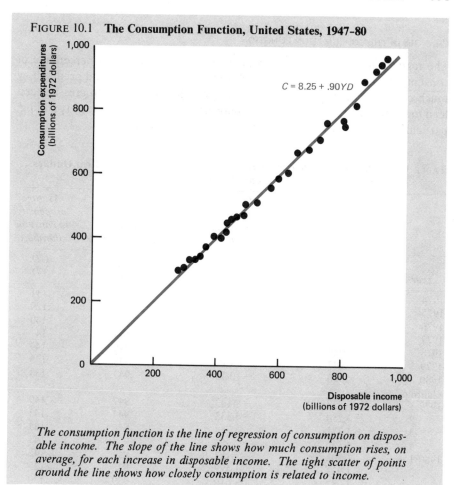

*The consumption function is the line of regression of consumption on dispos-
able income. The slope of the line shows how much consumption rises, on
average, for each increase in disposable income. The tight scatter of points
around the line shows how closely consumption is related to income.*

Autonomous consumption is \$8.25 billion. For every dollar increase in real
personal disposable income (YD), consumption (C) rises about 90 cents.

Because Figure 10.1 is based on historical data, the regression equation
reflects many other influences on consumption in addition to income. For
instance, in some years, automobile sales included in consumption were affected by strikes or by shortages of credit; these influences have not been
removed from the regression. Still, despite the effects of these extraneous
factors on the underlying schedules, the final relationships based on annual
data are close. Furthermore, similar relationships have been found in most
countries as well as in this country over long periods. On the basis of observations such as those contained in Figure 10.1 and the regression, economists
developed the concept of consumption functions.

CHANGES IN THE CONSUMPTION FUNCTION

The regression of consumption on income accounts for a high percentage of consumption in any year. However, if used by itself to explain and predict how much consumption expenditures and saving will change, the regression can lead to sizable errors. The differences between marginal and average spending, particularly on a quarterly basis, are evident from Table 10.1.

TABLE 10.1   **Marginal and Average Propensities to Consume: Total Real Outlays and Purchases of Consumer Durable Goods**

Year	Marginal propensity to consume $\dfrac{\Delta C}{\Delta YD}$	Marginal propensity to consume durables $\dfrac{\Delta CD}{\Delta YD}$	Average propensity to consume $\dfrac{C}{YD}$	Average propensity to consume durables $\dfrac{CD}{YD}$
1974	.739	1.304	.915	.131
1975	.862	− .023	.914	.129
1976	1.415	.440	.931	.140
1977	1.302	.364	.944	.147
1978	1.029	.189	.948	.149
1979	.947	.010	.948	.145
1980	.200	− 1.833	.943	.133
Quarter				
1979:1	.338	− .143	.947	.149
2	− 1.250	− 4.333	.944	.143
3	1.272	.284	.946	.144
4	4.350	− .350	.953	.143
1980:1	.303	− .182	.951	.142
2	1.931	1.477	.938	.125
3	1.057	.610	.939	.130

Source: U.S. Department of Commerce.

The first and second columns show how much marginal propensities to consume shift from year to year and quarter to quarter, especially for consumer durables. These changes are the result of movements in other variables and of lags. The final two columns demonstrate that the average relationship between consumption and income is far more regular, although the movements in durables are sufficient to create significant losses in income.

First, note the last two columns, which show average propensities to consume. Over the seven years of the table, average real consumption outlays ranged between 91.4 and 94.8 percent of disposable income. (As a corollary, saving varied between 5.2 and 8.6 percent, or by more than 65 percent.) A naïve prediction that the ratio of consumption to income would not change from year to year would do a fairly good job, but the table, which is typical of nonwar periods, shows that predictions from the simple consumption function could err by as much as $20 billion.

Movements in the marginal propensity to consume are much larger. The annual *mpc* ranges from .200 to 1.415. On a quarterly basis, and especially for durables, movements are quite irregular. Quarterly marginal propensities to consume in just seven quarters of 1979 and 1980 range from -1.25 to 4.35. In four of the quarters, the direction of change for durables was opposite to that for disposable income. Clearly, factors other than income alone seem to affect spending. The simple theory of consumption must be expanded to explain both such short-run differences and also how changes in the economic environment are likely to alter consumption and saving.

The Relationship between Income and Consumption

The knowledge that the largest share of changes in consumption expenditures results from movements in disposable income does not, by itself, suffice to answer several important questions. If income changes, by how much will consumption respond? Do all income shifts have the same impact on spending? What other factors are at work?

CONSUMER INVESTMENTS

Personal outlays, as listed in the National Income and Product Accounts, include expenditures on all consumer goods plus personal interest payments. These differ considerably from households' actual consumption of goods and services. The income accounts show as consumption expenditures all household purchases of automobiles, furniture, and other consumer durables. But from the point of view of a family, these are actually investments. Their current level of consumption is not based on these purchases, but rather on the services or satisfactions derived from them. Inventories of future services may be built up and then drawn down. Family expenditures on durables thus fluctuate far more than actual consumption. The sharp variation in reported expenditures on durables does not mean that consumption or satisfaction fluctuates to the same degree.

Models of consumption are of two types. One explains current consumption of services, of nondurables, and of services from durables—as developed in consumption theory—by subtracting recorded consumption expenditures on durables from the accounts and substituting for them estimates of depreciation and a yield on the total stock of durable goods held by consumers. Consumption in this type of model is more stable. The second type of model explains-consumption expenditures as recorded in the GNP, including the full value of all consumer durables even though an automobile may yield its services over the next ten years. This type of model is also needed because the level of consumption expenditures determines income. In a year like 1978, households invested (purchased) about $300 billion in durable goods, including newly constructed houses. Their net investment after depreciation was about $120 billion, split evenly between houses and consumer durables. When the amount of current consumer purchases changes, it can have a major effect on output and income, even if households' consumption of goods and services remains about the same. Models that analyze variations in the flow of goods and services must be adjusted and other variables included if they are to be used for forecasts or explanations of changes in the GNP accounts.

THE ABSOLUTE-INCOME HYPOTHESIS

The empirical consumption functions of Figure 10.1 and Figure 10.2 as well are examples of the ***absolute-income hypothesis,*** which states that consumption depends on the level of current disposable income. This hypothesis was popularized by Keynes, who wrote, "The fundamental psychological law . . . is that men are disposed, as a rule and on the average, to increase their consumption as their income increases, but not by as much as the increase in their income."[1] This says, in other words, that real consumption rises with income and that the marginal propensity to consume is less than one. Studies of how aggregate income and spending change from year to year as well as one-time surveys of household expenditures bear out the fact that as income rises, both consumption and saving increase. As families acquire more income, the pressures to spend all of it diminish. They will already have met basic needs for food, clothing, and shelter. Discretionary funds are available to use for commodities and services beyond essentials.

One probable use of this discretionary income is to start saving. The consumption curve in Figure 10.2 shows how, on average, Americans at different income levels divided their funds between consumption and saving in 1972–73.[2] At higher incomes, families spent more on consumption, but their spending as a percentage of income dropped. Their savings increased at a faster rate than income grew. Literally thousands of budget studies over the past hundred years reveal this type of relationship. When a sample of families is taken at one time, on average, the higher the income, the smaller the percentage of income spent. In almost all surveys, the marginal propensity to consume falls as incomes rise. As family incomes go up, the average and marginal propensities to save rise.

1. J. M. Keynes, *The General Theory of Employment, Interest and Money* (New York: Harcourt, Brace), p. 96.

2. The chart is based on the U.S. Consumer Expenditure Interview Survey conducted by the Bureau of Labor Statistics as part of the process of finding proper weights for the consumer price index.

FIGURE 10.2   **The Consumption Function, Survey of Consumer Expenditures, 1972-73**

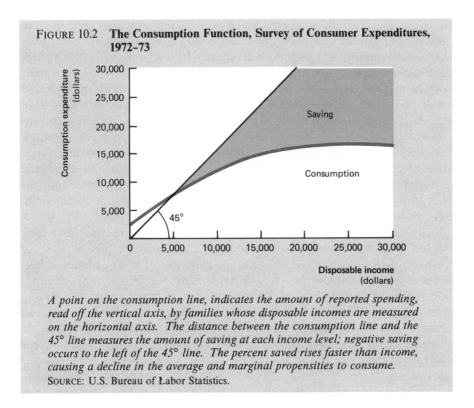

A point on the consumption line, indicates the amount of reported spending, read off the vertical axis, by families whose disposable incomes are measured on the horizontal axis. The distance between the consumption line and the 45° line measures the amount of saving at each income level; negative saving occurs to the left of the 45° line. The percent saved rises faster than income, causing a decline in the average and marginal propensities to consume.
SOURCE: U.S. Bureau of Labor Statistics.

A falling *mpc* means that if a nation becomes wealthier and every family has a higher income, the average rate of saving in the country should rise. But this has not in fact happened. Saving as a percentage of income has remained fairly constant. This failure of the nation's saving function to follow the path of the household surveys has been one spur to the development of more complete consumption functions. Another has been the recognition that the simple absolute-income hypothesis conflicted with some other generalizations which could be developed from the theory of consumption. An expanded consumption function can explain some of the discrepancies between the absolute income hypothesis and the facts. It is a warning against making policy decisions based on an oversimplified model.

CONSUMPTION BASED ON LIFETIME RESOURCES

Two closely related and more complex theories—the permanent-income and the life-cycle hypotheses—emphasize the importance of **lifetime resources** in determining consumption. Families decide the pattern of future saving and consumption recognizing that they can utilize income and assets either for current satisfactions or to increase resources and possible future consumption. The current expenditures of a family are the result of a long-term plan which enables it to obtain the highest level of satisfaction over its entire lifetime (including any desire to leave bequests at death). Families will not necessarily change consumption with variations in income. Instead, they will estimate how current movements affect their entire earnings horizon.

In making such plans, families must estimate both future income and needs. Wages and salaries usually rise to a point and then drop with advancing age. Higher education and training will add to their human capital and increase future income. Retirement marks the end of most labor earnings. Whether or not families can save for future needs depends on how much they are earning in relation to current needs. They may accumulate funds to be used in case of sickness or loss of jobs. Many families manage to save some funds but then go into debt to pay for their children's education. Later they save again to have income in retirement.

In addition to income from labor, families receive returns from their wealth. They may own physical assets—a car, a house, a plot of land—or financial assets—bonds, common stocks, or bank deposits. The ability to borrow and to lend or to invest in physical assets alters the time path of consumption and makes interest rates a significant factor in determining consumption spending. The existence of assets, loans, and interest means that borrowers can consume more at present, but less later on; for lenders, the opposite is true. In planning lifetime spending and saving, it is the present value of future income and future consumption that should be optimized. Because the distant future is uncertain and a great deal of effort is required to get information about it, families may give most weight to the immediate future and consider only a few basic long-range needs, such as education and retirement. They weigh opportunities and costs only roughly because they are unwilling or unable to make exact calculations. They may also find that while, in theory, current income should not limit their consumption because they can borrow against the future, it may prove impossible to do so. You may be sure that you will have a job and a high income in the future, but you may have trouble finding a creditor who shares your confidence enough to lend you the amount you want.

The Permanent-Income Hypothesis

One early proponent of the concept of lifetime resources and the need to broaden the consumption function was Milton Friedman. Because of his emphasis on the need to differentiate between permanent (expected lifetime) earnings and those temporary or transitory earnings received or reported in a period, this concept has been called the *permanent-income hypothesis.* The level of consumption of a household depends not on its current or absolute income, but rather on its permanent income—that which it expects to earn from work and wealth over its lifetime.

Friedman uses the term *permanent income* (*YP*) to represent the expected flow of income from the stock of human and nonhuman wealth. The planned consumption from this expected flow of income is called **permanent consumption** (*CP*). In any period, measured income for a family may differ from its long-run expectations, either because the reporting period is short or because of some special circumstances. Someone may have been temporarily laid off or received a bonus. The relationships between measured (*YM*), transitory (*YT*), and permanent (*YP*) income are

$$YM = YP + YT \qquad\qquad\qquad \textbf{10.1}$$
$$CM = CP + CT. \qquad\qquad\qquad \textbf{10.2}$$

Measured income (*YM*) is the sum of permanent income (*YP*) and transitory income (*YT*), which may be positive or negative. Similarly, measured consumption (*CM*) equals permanent consumption (*CP*) plus transitory consumption (*CT*). However, the critical relationship is that between permanent income and permanent consumption:

$$CP = \overline{C} + cYP. \qquad\qquad\qquad \textbf{10.3}$$

This equation represents the permanent-income hypothesis. The level of permanent or planned consumption is a function of the level of income flow from work and wealth. In Friedman's model autonomous consumption, $\overline{C}$, is zero.

The declines in the average and marginal propensities to consume observed in expenditure surveys such as Figure 10.2 are explained by this hypothesis as the result of aggregation. The reported expenditures of families reflect decisions based on their permanent income, while their reported income may include a positive or negative transitory component in addition to their permanent income. When a consumer survey, such as those underlying many consumption functions, is conducted, it reflects the spending decisions of a broad spectrum of families. A number will have experienced sickness or unemployment. Others may have received a sudden "windfall"—an unexpected or temporary increase in income. Some will be retired and living off past accumulations of wealth. Others will be saving for old age. The specific ratio spent or saved in a quarter or a year for the economy represents an average based on the numbers of people falling into each of these groups in that particular period. The aggregate consumption function will shift simply because of different numbers in each class of consumer, even though no family changes its own spending decisions.

The way in which shifting weights can alter the aggregate function is illustrated in Table 10.2. It shows 30 families, classified in the table by their employment experience and in the second column by their income earned in the past year. However, some additional information not normally found in a survey is available. Each of the families has expected lifetime earnings of

TABLE 10.2   **The Effect of Changes in Transitory Income on the Average Propensity to Consume**

| Employ-ment status | Reported income | Permanent consump-tion | Year A | | | Year B | | |
			Number in class	Total income	Total consump-tion	Number in class	Total income	Total consump-tion
Lost job	10,000	18,400	5	50,000	92,000	6	60,000	110,400
Average work	20,000	18,400	20	400,000	368,000	22	440,000	404,800
Big bonus	30,000	18,400	5	150,000	92,000	2	60,000	36,800
			30	600,000	552,000	30	560,000	552,000

$$\text{Average propensity to consume} \qquad \frac{Year\ A}{} \qquad \frac{Year\ B}{}$$
$$\qquad\qquad \frac{552,000}{600,000} = .92 \qquad \frac{552,000}{560,000} = .99$$

All families are assumed to have a permanent income of $20,000 and to consume $18,400, or 92 percent. A lost job results in a serious transitory drop in income and, because consumption continues to be based on permanent income, a high propensity to consume with negative saving. Recipients of bonuses act in the opposite way. The reported propensity to consume for the whole shifts with the numbers losing or receiving transitory incomes—year A compared to year B.

$20,000 a year. Each has an average propensity to consume of .92 from that income. Consequently, as shown in the third column, each will consume $18,400 a year, no matter what its temporary income is.

The year A is quite prosperous. As in a normal year, 5 families report decreased income due to part-time employment; 20 report they are earning at their expected lifetime rate, and 5 report high bonuses or overtime. All consume at a rate based on their expected lifetime income and consumption, or 92 percent. The fifth and sixth columns are arrived at by multiplying the number in a class (the fourth column) by each one's earnings and expenditures. They show total income of $600,000 and total consumption of $552,000. Since families with high incomes exactly offset those with temporarily low incomes, the APC of the economy represents each family's and the economy's desired long-term average of 92 percent.

In the year B income falls. More families lose jobs; fewer earn bonuses. The recession causes total income to drop to $560,000. But because families are able to maintain their lifetime consumption rate, even though those in the lowest bracket must dissave, the APC of the economy rises to .99. While the two years show a rise in the economy's APC as income falls, we recognize that the reported difference between the two years is due to an aggregation bias. Every year families consume the same amount of their expected lifetime earnings, but the economy's consumption function appears to shift because of the temporary recession.

TRANSITORY INCOME

Friedman introduced the concepts of transitory income (YT) and consumption (CT) to explain how consumption decisions are made. The theory also explains the biases of the surveys. It is easy to see that the time period over which income and consumption are measured will influence the relationships among observations. A person who receives a monthly paycheck will show little or no income if the survey asks "How much income did you receive this week?" and it is not a payroll week. If she reports her consumption, the average propensity to consume will be extremely high (perhaps infinite). While people do concentrate some of their spending near payday, most is spread throughout the month. Some people have lumpier income flows. An industrial real estate broker may make as few as two or three large sales a year. He doesn't stop eating in between. People do try to plan over a longer horizon than from payday to payday.

A survey of income and consumption shows that those families with negative transitory incomes ($-YT$) will report a measured income (YM) below normal. If they can, however, they will maintain their level of consumption expenditures (CP). Consequently their average propensity to consume will be higher than normal:

$$\frac{CP}{YP + (-YT)} > \frac{CP}{YP}.$$

If they have positive transitory incomes, the opposite will be true. They will report income higher than normal and a lower than normal APC. Note that even though all families have an identical consumption function from permanent income, if Table 10.2 is plotted, the result will resemble Figure 10.2. Low-income families who have lost their jobs and have negative transitory incomes report an average propensity to consume above one. High-income families are those who receive positive transitory income and they have a lower APC. The consumption line fitted to the average of each group falls (the mpc declines) as incomes rise.[3]

WINDFALL AND TEMPORARY INCREASES IN INCOME

The contrasts between the absolute- and the permanent-income hypotheses become significant in the analysis of a temporary or windfall increase in income. Will it be spent, and how fast? The analysis is complicated by the

3. It is not immediately obvious why those with negative transitory incomes should be those with lower incomes. If a Rockefeller's income falls below normal it would still be in the highest income class. But this is not true on average. More people will have moved into the higher income brackets through positive transitory income. A larger proportion in lower measured income brackets will be there because of negative transitory income.

existence of lags—the delay in making decisions—and by investments in consumer durables—the difference between consumption expenditures and use of services. Even though a family might not raise its planned consumption if it receives a thousand dollar windfall, the enhanced ability to meet downpayment requirements might lead to the purchase (expenditure and investment) of a car.

If people act rationally, shouldn't they make their consumption plans over a longer time period and disregard temporary windfalls? This is certainly the lesson of general consumption theory. But the theory tells us nothing about how long families would actually take to work out their return to equilibrium. Some argue for only a short lag. Many families don't save; they spend all they get, so their spending lags their earnings only slightly. Another argument is that while people wouldn't spend a large increase in income known to be temporary, if it is not large and if it appears in their pay check as a drop in withholding, they don't bother to determine whether or not the increase is temporary. As a result, they spend it quickly. Still others state that while they believe people make the necessary calculations, the adjustment period for current income changes may be comparatively short. The adaptation to what is considered permanent may be so fast that most current changes will influence spending over a short number of years. Those who argue the contrary believe that families have a longer horizon. They point out that many families do budget over a longer period and are unlikely to expand spending because of a temporary increase. Added income will go into saving and only gradually will it be felt in spending.

Empirical studies do show some increase in spending from temporary income, but they disagree on how much. If the increase in income is large, a smaller percentage will be spent currently. If the windfall is small, the percentage spent in the near period may be high. Questions of how families handle temporary increases in income dominate the arguments over the impact of temporary changes in taxes.

Temporary Tax Changes and Consumption

No one doubts that if the disposable income of consumers is reduced by a permanent tax increase, demand will fall. But can demand be curtailed by a temporary increase? Similarly, a permanent drop in taxes, by raising disposable income, will lead to more consumption. But what if, when taxes are lowered, the action is claimed to be temporary? Will people simply allow their rate of saving to rise, maintaining their long-run level of consumption? The impact of a temporary tax change depends on the degree to which households can and do alter saving rather than spending.[4]

4. For analysis of this matter, see R. Eisner, "Fiscal and Monetary Policy Reconsidered," *American Economic Review* 59(December 1969); A. M. Okun, "Personal Tax Surcharge and Consumer Demand," *Brookings Papers on Economic Activity* 1(1971); W. L. Springer, "Did the

THE TEMPORARY TAX INCREASE OF 1968-70

Many countries alter tax rates to shift spending away from periods of excess demand. The United States did so after considerable resistance in 1968. As the war in Vietnam expanded and inflationary demand grew, a bitter political battle was waged to enact a temporary tax increase for the purpose of offsetting some of the war-induced consumption demand. In January 1967, President Johnson proposed a tax increase. As in World War II, neither liberal nor conservative congressmen were willing to vote the increase. Finally, as a result of heightened speculation in gold, foreign pressure on the dollar, and fear of a money crunch, Congress voted in June 1968 a 10 percent surcharge against corporate and personal income taxes, together with a limit on nondefense spending. People calculated their income taxes according to existing laws and schedules; then they had to pay 110 percent of what would have been their previous liability. The surcharge on federal personal income tax, which was originally to extend from April 1968 to June 30, 1969, was extended through the first half of 1970. Increased payroll withholding began on July 15, 1968.

Whether the tax increase in fact decreased spending or not is still subject to argument and is an issue which is likely to be brought up every time a tax change is suggested to fight either inflation or recession. Robert Eisner was an early proponent of the view that the tax surcharge was doomed to failure. In December 1969 he stated:

> The basic economic error of those who saw in the 10 percent income tax surcharge an adequate measure against inflation may be charged to failure to take into account the implications of the permanent income hypothesis, both for consumption and, in correlative fashion, for business investment. Dealing in terms of equilibrium or permanent income, an increase in tax withdrawals of some ten or eleven billion dollars per year may be expected to have a very substantial depressant effect on aggregate demand, in the order of perhaps $8 billion on consumption alone. But the tax increase legislated in the surcharge did not represent a corresponding reduction in *permanent* aftertax income. It did clearly represent a reduction, in itself, in *current* or measured aftertax income for roughly a twelve-month period.[5]

According to the permanent-income hypothesis, the tax surcharge, because it was temporary, would have little effect on expected income or wealth; it would merely cause a transitory fall. On the basis of rough estimates of the magnitudes involved, Eisner guessed that the surcharge would depress consumption by less than $3 billion current dollars.

1968 Surcharge Really Work?" *American Economic Review* 65(September 1975); A. M. Okun and W. L. Springer, "Did the 1968 Surcharge Really Work, Comment and Reply," *American Economic Review* 68(March 1977); F. Modigliani and C. Steindl, "Is a Tax Rebate an Effective Tool for Stabilization Policy?" *Brookings Papers on Economic Activity* 1(1977).

5. R. Eisner, "Fiscal and Monetary Policy Reconsidered," p. 898.

Many believe that Eisner hit the nail right on the head. In the year prior to the tax increase, saving had been unusually high. It averaged 7.5 percent of disposable income, compared to a more normal rate of under 6 percent for the decade. In the first year of the surcharge, the rate of saving slumped to below 6 percent. It then climbed rapidly above normal levels for the second year. People seemed to be following the permanent-income hypothesis. When they recognized a temporary cut in income, they reduced saving, not consumption.

One of the foremost advocates of the temporary tax increase to pay for the war was Arthur Okun, chairman of the Council of Economic Advisers when the surcharge was passed. He disagrees with what many consider the conventional wisdom. He points out that because consumption lags behind income, a slower rate of growth in income always causes a temporary drop in the saving rate, which rises as income accelerates. This phenomenon, which has nothing to do with transitory or permanent income, can explain the drop in saving during the first year of the surcharge. In Okun's view, even if the permanent-income hypothesis is correct it is unlikely to apply to small, barely noticeable income changes. In 1968, while the surcharge was sizable in aggregate, its impact on most families was slight. The surcharge reduced the income of an average family about $2 a week—an amount insufficient to cause a replanning of expected lifetime income and consumption. It would mean, however, that families would find themselves with small deficits at the end of the month unless they cut out some consumption.

PREDICTIONS OF SPENDING

Okun suggests that a better test than the saving rate is to measure the gap between what the economy did and the predictions that policy makers had available during the period the tax was under consideration. Table 10.3 displays information of this kind. The table reports the result of simulations of four econometric models used to measure what changes in consumption were expected and what actually happened. Similar simulations were conducted in advance of the tax increase.

The first column contains an estimate of the amount by which tax collections reduced disposable income as a result of the surcharge. In the first four half-year periods, tax collections rose by a total of 12 billion constant 1958 dollars. According to the models, lowering disposable income by this amount should have reduced consumption over the same period by $6.6 billion (the second plus the fifth column). Two-thirds of the reduction would be expected in expenditures for nondurable goods and services, (second column) and one-third for durables (fifth column). In the models, both tax collection and impacts on consumption lag the change in the law. In the first half-year, the decrease in expenditures for goods and services is only half that of the second.

What actually happened to spending? Look at the figures for the total of both years in the table. Consumption of nondurables and services dropped

TABLE 10.3   **Estimated Impact of 1968 Tax Surcharge on Consumption
Expenditures: Decrease in Expenditures Compared to Models without
Tax Increase**

(billions of 1958 dollars)
Seasonally Adjusted Annual Rates

Period (half years)	Tax increase effect	Nondurables and services			Durables		
		Expected	Actual	Error (A − E)	Expected	Actual	Error (A − E)
1968:Q2	$− 5.5	$− 1.4	$− 2.9	$− 1.5	$− 1.1	$+ 2.3*	$ 3.4
1969:Q1	− ·8.8	− 2.7	− 3.8	− 1.1	− 1.7	+ 2.6*	4.3
1969:Q2	− 5.8	− 2.5	− 4.0	− 1.5	− 1.1	− 0.1	1.0
1970:Q1	− 3.9	− 2.2	− 3.8	− 1.6	− 0.5	+ 0.2*	0.7
Total	−12.0	−4.4	−7.2	−2.8	−2.2	+2.5*	4.7

* Increase above models.

SOURCE: A. M. Okun, "The Personal Tax Surcharge and Business Demand," *Brookings Papers on Economic Activity* 1(1971). Based on an average of simulations from models of: Data Resources Inc., University of Michigan Research Seminar in Quantitative Analysis; U.S. Department of Commerce, Office of Business Economics; and the Wharton-University of Pennsylvania.

> *The second and fifth columns show expected effects of higher taxes on spending. Econometric models are used to estimate how much the loss in disposable income (first column) will curtail demand. The third and sixth columns picture changes in actual expenditures. The fourth column shows that spending on nondurables and services fell more than expected, while the seventh column shows that durable expenditures exceeded expectations. In fact, the tax increase did not appear to reduce spending on durables.*

more than anticipated. Spending on durables did not fall at all; in fact, purchases of durables went up faster at first than was projected assuming no surcharge. Total consumption was expected to fall by $6.6 billion. It actually fell $4.7 billion (the third plus sixth column). Looking at each model in turn, Okun concludes that the effectiveness of the surcharge was about 70 percent of what was forecast. In all cases, the record for durables was dismal; for other goods and services, it was good.

As in many empirical tests, the answer is not clear-cut. Alan Blinder examined Okun's study and other previous ones, while including later data.[6] He concentrated on a temporary cut in taxes to raise spending—the opposite of the Okun study. He estimated that about 50 percent of a permanent cut in taxes would be effective in raising consumption in its first year, and over 80 percent by the end of the second year. In contrast, a temporary tax cut or rebate

6. A. S. Blinder, *Economic Policy and the Great Stagflation* (New York: Academic Press, 1979), pp. 155–65.

would be only about 40 to 60 percent as effective as a permanent cut in the first year. But by the end of the second year, the temporary and permanent cuts showed similar effects. Thus, he concluded that a temporary tax cut would certainly raise spending in its first year, and it would be fully as effective as a permanent change by the end of the second year. However, because of the differences in timing, it would be less useful (possibly even harmful) if the need for added demand was concentrated in the first year after taxes were cut.

Consumption and Wealth and Population

Advocates of the permanent-income hypothesis estimate expected permanent income directly from past income. Wealth is not measured independently, since it is difficult to do so. Expected permanent income may or may not be adjusted for current movements in interest rates. This technique, in effect, deemphasizes current movements in wealth; their impact is felt only when they are reported in income. There are no direct asset effects on spending.

THE LIFE-CYCLE HYPOTHESIS

Another form of the theory of consumption based on lifetime resources is the *life-cycle hypothesis,* originally introduced by Franco Modigliani, R. E. Brumberg, and A. Ando. As in the permanent-income hypothesis, a family's current expenditures are considered to be part of its lifetime plan to spend in a manner that will provide maximum satisfaction or utility. A family's consumption is not based on current income alone; rather, it takes into account both current and expected future income from working and from property. Expanding influences other than current income on consumption in this way causes at least two significant alterations in the simple consumption function:

1. How much wealth a family owns will influence its consumption. If you have property, you can use income from it for current consumption and it is less necessary to save. Furthermore, changes in interest rates and expectations cause wide fluctuations in the value of financial assets, especially of common stock. As a result, movements in interest rates and stock prices alter wealth and cause the amount consumed from current income to shift.
2. The need to save also varies with age. Young families have few assets and many wants. They can look forward to higher future wages. It makes sense for them to go into debt now rather than save. At the opposite extreme, retired people have no wage income. To maintain their standard of living, they are likely to dissave. Thus consumption and saving are a function of the population in particular age groups, and the nation's consumption function will vary with the number in each age group. Furthermore biases can arise in consumption functions estimated from surveys if they fail to correct for the varying numbers in each age bracket.

Wealth or Net Worth Influences Consumption

Wealth yields current income to be spent or saved. A family that already holds assets need not save as much to cover future needs. Thus a family's net worth should affect both its expected lifetime income and its ability to spend more than current income. When wealth shifts, even if the desire to spend from a given lifetime income remains constant, the consumption function will alter. The life-cycle hypothesis expresses the consumption function as

$$C = \overline{C} + c_1 YD^e + c_2 W. \qquad \qquad \textbf{10.4}$$

Current consumption depends on an autonomous factor ($\overline{C}$), on expected disposable income (YD^e), and on wealth (W). Because future income is not worth as much as present income, money expected in the future must be discounted in measuring its impact on current spending.

The inclusion of expected income in the function leads to a variety of factors which can be included in studies for particular purposes. Many models of automobile demand, for example, exclude transfer payments from disposable income, on the theory that changes in social security or unemployment benefits are not likely to have much impact on the sales of new cars. The models may also include different forms of wealth in addition to that represented by wages and salaries. Nonhuman wealth consists of money; other kinds of financial claims such as bonds and savings deposits; equities, either in the form of holdings of common stock or directly through ownership of noncorporate plant and equipment; and investments in consumer durable goods such as cars, furniture, and houses. Families also have liabilities such as installment and mortgage debt. The difference between a family's assets and liabilities represent its net worth. These differences in the form of wealth cause a variety of reactions when interest rates and prices change.

The Stock of Durable Goods. The ownership of physical assets may delay or hasten purchases of additional durables. Experience shows that at certain times consumers rapidly step up their purchases of houses, automobiles, or other durables. This affects the expenditures of the following periods. More goods in use means some additional depreciation and, therefore, a need for more replacements. But this effect can be overwhelmed by the fact that something bought or built today means that less needs to be bought tomorrow. When purchases of durables rise above their normal rate of growth, the following period is likely to experience a drop in purchases. Such cycles are very evident in the housing and automobile markets. In other words, fluctuations in expenditures can result from cycles in the stock of durable goods held by families.

The Stock Market. Prices of common stocks are far more volatile than those of other assets. They move inversely to interest rates and fluctuate widely as the market constantly reevaluates risks and potential earnings. Stock prices are quoted daily in the press. People know if their capital has gone up or down.

TABLE 10.4   **Debt Owed by Household Sector**
(billions of dollars)

End of year	Mortgages	Consumer credit	Other	Total
1976	541	248	110	899
1977	634	289	122	1,045
1978	738	340	132	1,210
1979	852	382	146	1,380
1980	935	385	169	1,489

SOURCE: Federal Reserve Balance Sheets for U.S. Economy, June 1980; Flow of Funds, Feb. 1981

Households increased their borrowing rapidly in response to inflation. The virtual failure of consumer credit to expand in 1980 was both a cause and a result of the recession.

This may influence their spending. Some recent empirical studies show stock prices as having a significant impact on consumption.

Consumer Debts.   Another factor that can influence spending is the amount owed by families. A high percentage of houses and a sizable share of other durables are bought on credit. At any time, consumers owe 80 percent or more of their expected next year's income on mortgages, installment, and other credit. As a group, households commit from 20 to 25 percent of this year's income to repay past debts. When credit is expanding, some consumers, by going into debt, will be spending more than their incomes. Their saving will be negative. Moreover, as the level of outstanding debt grows, payments must increase to repay both interest and principal on the outstanding loan. When this occurs, less income is available to make current purchases.

Table 10.4 shows how rapidly consumer debts expanded in the late 1970s. A "borrow and buy" philosophy seemed to have swept the country. At the start of 1981, consumers owed $590 billion more than they had four years previously. Consumers' debts jumped from 71.5 to 78 percent of their disposable income. Since interest rates rose between 20 and 100 percent, depending on the item, the amount consumers had to pay as a share of income shot up even faster. This rapid increase in consumer debt appeared to many to be a chief factor in accelerating the inflation. It was one of the features of the economy that led to the imposition of controls by the Federal Reserve over additional extension of consumer credit in March 1980 and to the small expansion of consumer credit in 1980. It was one of the factors causing consumers to spend less—particularly on automobiles—in 1980 and 1981.

THE INFLUENCE OF THE POPULATION'S AGE DISTRIBUTION

The life-cycle hypothesis demonstrates that, because it affects a family's income, assets, and needs, age has a decided impact on the consumption function. The average consumption function and the marginal propensity to consume will, therefore, be influenced by the age distribution of a country. When growth in a population slows down or speeds up (as it did in the post-World-War-II baby boom), the numbers in specific age groups change from decade to decade, and not in a consistent manner. Currently there is a bulge in the young adult group, aged 25 to 35. The resulting population pyramid, with large differences in age brackets, can cause shifts in the consumption function because of the differences in spending and saving over the life cycle of a family.

When a family is young, its income is usually lower than what it will earn later on. Young families also have a critical need to accumulate capital in the form of household goods, cars, and housing. They must build up the family's human capital through education, a major investment for the future. Consequently, most families can accumulate few, if any, financial assets until children leave home. After the children are gone, incomes are usually at their highest. The need to save is also greater because the family must accumulate assets looking toward retirement. After retirement, current incomes drop off sharply, and most families dissave at a rapid rate.

Figure 10.3 shows an idealized curve reflecting the lifetime relationship between income and consumption. Incomes rise until the middle or late 50s,

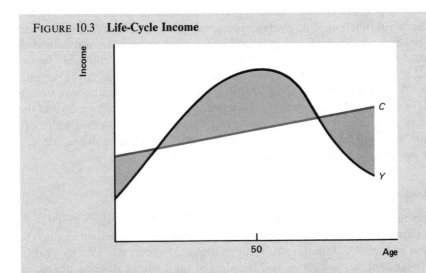

FIGURE 10.3   **Life-Cycle Income**

On average, family incomes rise until middle age and then decline. Both the young and the elderly dissave, as shown by the relationship between the income line (Y) and the consumption line (C). Saving (color) and dissaving (gray) smooth the stream of consumption compared with income and increase utility over a life cycle.

and then decline, on average. The figure also shows a consumption line and periods of saving and dissaving. The consumption line rises steadily on the assumption that, with productivity increases, the general level of income and consumption will continue to grow. In their youth, families consume more than their incomes, a condition made possible by going into debt. Borrowing on mortgages is a prime example. At older ages, families maintain their consumption by selling assets, or dissaving. Their consumption level may fall because income plus dissaving may be inadequate for spending at previous rates.

Table 10.5A shows how both income and consumption actually were related to age in the Bureau of Labor Statistics Consumer Expenditure Survey of 1972–73. The average consumption function differs with both age and income. The young and the old have a high average propensity to consume. The middle-aged have lower average propensities to consume. Why does average consumption correlate with age? Low-income people—predominantly the young and the old—have high propensities to consume. High-income people are the middle-aged, who have low *APCs*. Because of the correlation between age and income and age and saving, there is a correlation between income and saving, giving the survey a biased result (as was illustrated in Figure 10.2 which is based on the same survey).

Table 10.5B, an idealized example of two age-income surveys taken at different times, shows again how aggregation biases arise in measuring the consumption function. The average propensity to consume drops from .92 to .87—not because the relationship between consumption and disposable income has changed, but merely because the number in each class has changed. Just as in Table 10.2, a decrease appears to occur because a change in the weights causes the average for the total to shift. The degree to which consumption changes with population depends on the shifting weights of each group and the differences in their consumption patterns. This means that demography can explain what happens over long periods far better than over a decade or less, since age groups do not vary much in the short run.

AN EMPIRICAL EXAMPLE OF INCOME AND WEALTH EFFECTS

Numerous empirical consumption functions of the lifetime resources type have been estimated, usually with movements in spending lagging behind changes in income and wealth. Equation 10.4, for example, has been modeled by Franco Modigliani and his associates and the staff of the Federal Reserve Board. A reestimate can be found in an article by Frederic Mishkin.[7] His empirical regression equation, equivalent to 10.4, is

$$C = .659\,YD + .112\,W \qquad R^2 = .994 \qquad SE = .007249. \qquad \textbf{10.5}$$

7. F. S. Mishkin, "What Depressed the Consumer: The Household Balance Sheet and the 1973–75 Recession," *Brookings Papers on Economic Activity* 1(1977): 129.

TABLE 10.5   **The Effect of Changes in Percentage in Age Classes on the Average Propensity to Consume**

(A)

Age of head	Reported mean income (YD) 1972 (dollars)	Average consumption 1972 (dollars)	Average propensity to consume 1972
14–24	$5,773	$5,916	1.025
25–34	9,969	8,504	0.853
35–44	12,114	10,168	0.839
45–54	13,069	10,192	0.780
55–64	10,277	7,785	0.758
65 and over	5,764	4,754	0.835

SOURCE: U.S. Bureau of Labor Statistics, Consumer Expenditure Survey, 1972–73.

(B)
Assumed Changes in Number in Class

			Year A			Year B		
Age of head	Reported income	Consumption	Number in class	Total income	Total consumption	Number in class	Total income	Total consumption
Under 30	10,000	10,000	10	100,000	100,000	4	40,000	40,000
30 to 70	20,000	16,000	10	200,000	160,000	16	300,000	256,000
Over 70	8,000	9,000	10	80,000	90,000	10	80,000	90,000
Total			30	380,000	350,000	30	440,000	386,000

$$\text{Average propensity to consume} \quad \frac{\text{Year A}}{} \quad \frac{350,000}{380,000} = .92 \qquad \frac{\text{Year B}}{} \quad \frac{386,000}{440,000} = .87$$

The final column in part A of the table shows that reported average propensities to consume vary with the age of the household head. Part B demonstrates how, even though the propensity to consume of families for each age group, as shown in the first and second columns, remains constant, a shifting age distribution can alter the reported average propensity to consume for the population (from .92 to .87).

The equation is in constant 1958 dollars based on data from 1954: Q1 to 1972: Q4. As the next paragraphs explain, it includes lags.

Disposable Income.   What is the relationship between real disposable income and real future consumption? According to the equation from Mishkin, at equilibrium, per capita consumer expenditures (C) equal .659 of per capita disposable income, a much smaller coefficient than in simple models of the absolute income type. Equally important, the effects of income changes are felt over the next three years. Thus, in Mishkin's equation, the effect of income (C_Y)

on consumption depends on the current and previous 11 quarters:

$$C_Y = .085\,YD_o + .082\,YD_{-1} + .078\,YD_{-2} + .074\,YD_{-3} + .069\,YD_{-4}$$
$$+ .063\,YD_{-5} + .056\,YD_{-6} + .048\,YD_{-7} + .040\,YD_{-8} + .031\,YD_{-9}$$
$$+ .022\,YD_{-10} + .011\,YD_{-11}. \qquad \textbf{10.6}$$

The marginal propensity to consume out of current income (YD_o) shown by the coefficient is only .085. By the end of a year, consumption has increased by .319 of the change to a new level of income. By the end of 12 quarters, the *mpc* is .659 (the total of the coefficients on YD found by the regression).

Consumption is defined to include real expenditures on nondurables and services, but it includes only the estimated use of services (rental value) of consumers' durables, not actual expenditures as recorded in the GNP. Because spending on durables reacts faster to income changes than does the current flow of services, the impact of a change in income on the GNP would be somewhat faster. For instance, auto sales vary more with income than do the miles driven.

Wealth. Changes in wealth affect current expenditures more rapidly. The model includes two measures of wealth—real per capita holdings of common stock (STK) and real per capita nonstock net worth ($NSNW$). The regression model shows the wealth effect (C_W) on consumption as

$$C_W = .056\,NSNW_o + .017\,STK_o + .013\,STK_{-1} + .010\,STK_{-2}$$
$$+ .007\,STK_{-3} + .005\,STK_{-4} + .003\,STK_{-5} + .001\,STK_{-6}. \qquad \textbf{10.7}$$

According to equation 10.7, a one-dollar rise in real nonstock net worth leads to an increase of $5\frac{1}{2}$ cents in consumption in the same time period. Since families had roughly three to four dollars of nonstock net worth for every dollar of consumption expenditures, changes in net worth could have substantial impacts. Families' holdings of common stocks were about one-fourth as large as other forms of wealth. The impact of a change in a dollar of wealth due to stock changes is assumed equal to that for other assets, but the effect is spread over the current and next six quarters. Wealth affects more than a quarter of expenditure. Higher income, whether permanent or transitory, has a rather delayed impact.

While the age structure is not included directly, the use of per capita data partially corrects for some population effects. The considerable lags and the importance of wealth mean that consumption, as in similar permanent-income models, reacts only slowly to movements in transitory income.

Saving and Interest Rates

Classical economists believed that real interest rates were a significant variable affecting consumption. Interest determined how much consumption a person would receive in the future as a reward for abstaining in the present. Since interest rates were the price paid for saving, as they rose people would save more. In fact, however, a more complete analysis of the relationship between interest rates and consumption shows that the classical price (or substitution) effect is only one of at least four ways in which interest rates influence spending and saving. To understand the full impact of interest rates, let us assume that in a quarter, real interest rates rise from 2 percent to 5 percent. How should this affect the level of consumption? Let us discuss each of four possible effects in turn.

Substitution Effects.   The substitution effect on spending is clearest. If we are paid more for doing something, we will step up our effort in that direction. When the amount paid for saving goes up, the cost of current consumption rises. We should be willing to substitute more future consumption for current consumption, spending less now. If tastes remain the same, more satisfaction is obtained by substituting future expenditures for present ones.

Income Effects.   When interest rates rise, each dollar saved will yield a higher future income. Investing a thousand dollars at 5 percent rather than at 2 percent increases real annual income from $20 to $50. This might be expected to increase savings, so that families can benefit from this higher income. But that need not be the case. The desire to save in order to accumulate a given future income for retirement or similar purposes is another possible motive.

Assume that a person wants to retire with an income of $15,000 a year and leave the principal intact for his heirs. If real interest rates are 2 percent, he must accumulate $750,000 in savings to realize a real future income of $15,000 a year. If interest rates rise to 5 percent and there is no change in goal, only $300,000 need be accumulated instead of $750,000. Furthermore, if saving takes place through insurance or some other plan which accumulates the earned interest, the necessary saving will drop still faster. If $1,000 a year is placed in an account that accumulates interest at 2 percent, at the end of 25 years the account will total $32,000, while it will total $48,000 at 5 percent interest. Roughly, when interest rates rise from 2 percent to 5 percent, only about one-quarter as much must be saved to get a return of $15,000 after 25 years. If, instead, the goal were an annuity of $15,000 a year with nothing left to heirs, given the interest rate rise of the example, an even more dramatic decrease in the need to save would occur.

A third income factor can also be at work. When interest rates rise, people who have more wealth will receive higher incomes. At higher interest rates, income shifts from debtors to creditors. How this will affect saving depends on the marginal propensity to consume and the marginal propensity to save of the two groups.

When these various income possibilities are factored into the analysis, we see why it is not obvious whether a change in interest rates will lead to more or less saving. Among other factors, the effect will differ from period to period depending on age distribution and that of existing wealth.

Wealth Effects.   Of all their varied effects, the impact of interest rate changes on the wealth of the owners of assets may be the most important. When interest rates rise, people who hold assets with current yields that are fixed, or nearly so, will be poorer. If interest rates drop, their wealth will rise. The first section of Chapter 5 showed how prices of existing bonds and other assets change in response to interest movements. In the first quarter of 1980, the value of bonds with five years or more to maturity dropped about 20 percent. For this and related reasons, common stock prices fell nearly as much. As shown in the life-cycle model, effects of this kind are significant. The stock market may well influence spending. When stock prices are high, people are willing to spend more; when they fall, people will spend less. The rise in interest rates lowers both bond prices and the value of stocks with a given and expected dividend. Their market price drops; spending declines.

Credit Effects.   Finally, many people need to borrow. They find it impossible to save, no matter what interest rates prevail. They must borrow either to meet current consumption needs or to buy a car or a house. A rise in interest rates forces them to pay more for their loans. Therefore, they are less likely to spend. This is especially true if there is a related drop in the availability of consumer credit.

Because demand is so closely tied to available credit, consumer-credit controls have been imposed periodically—for instance, during World War II, the Korean War, and in 1980. The earlier regulations limited the amount that could be borrowed to buy consumer durable goods by raising required down-payments and reducing the number of months over which the loan had to be repaid. With higher required monthly payments, fewer goods could be bought. In 1980, the controls raised the marginal cost of funds to lenders and thereby increased the rates they charged.

On the whole, such regulations have not met with much favor. They appear to affect primarily those in lower brackets who are forced to buy on credit, while they favor families who have already accumulated enough wealth to buy what they want by drawing down existing financial assets. In addition, the number of lenders on consumer credit is so high—several hundred thousand—that the regulations are hard to police. Most economists feel that controls over consumer credit are not an equitable or efficient type of control.

EMPIRICAL STUDIES OF SAVING AND INTEREST

Theory cannot predict with any surety whether higher interest yields will increase personal saving or not. Some channels lead to higher saving and lower consumption, while others have the reverse effect. Results depend on the magnitudes of opposing influences. Despite the many uncertainties, the subject is at the heart of important political and policy debates for a number of reasons. One path to increase productivity is through greater capital investment. One path to greater investment may be more saving. Normally, higher interest rates would make investment less attractive, even if they raised saving. But reducing taxes on saving or providing subsidies can raise yields to savers without increasing costs to borrowers. What do the studies show about the possibility of increasing saving and thus investment by lowering taxes on interest?

A well-developed permanent-income-type model shows spending going up as interest rates rise. Higher permanent interest income leads to more consumption spending. Studies which treat property income show similar effects; as interest rates rise, the income from assets grows, and consumption goes up.[8] Wealth models tend to give the opposite results. Impacts depend primarily on the relative magnitude of the changes made by interest rates on income, wealth, and the cost of using houses and automobiles. Higher rates raise disposable income, lower the value of financial assets and common stocks, and raise the cost of using fixed assets. As the cases which follow demonstrate, such models can show large adverse impacts on the level of spending as interest rates rise.

Another group of studies, aimed primarily at estimating saving functions, finds that higher interest rates increase saving and lower consumption. Such studies, based on early work by Hendrik Houthakker and Lester Taylor, have been replicated by F. T. Juster and Paul Wachtel. They find a positive relationship between interest rates and saving, but the effects are weak and only marginally significant.[9]

Michael Boskin has attempted to measure directly the effects of interest changes on consumption, using annual data from 1929 to 1969. He finds that increases in interest yields reduce consumption and raise saving.[10] Because the Boskin study is frequently cited as showing the advantages of shifting taxes away from saving and to consumption, attempts have been made to replicate it and to examine it in more detail. E. P. Howrey and Saul Hymans, after studying Boskin's results and other similar relationships in detail, conclude that higher interest rates are not likely to increase loanable-fund saving. They and many others conclude that the data needed to arrive at a clear conclusion are not available. While higher yields may raise saving, at the present time neither theory nor empirical work can prove or disprove this belief. Whether consumption should be taxed rather than saving appears more likely to be argued and decided on political than economic grounds.[11]

Consumption and Price Changes

Interest rates are a price for saving, but other prices change as well. How should consumption and saving react to price changes and inflation? In de-

8. See W. L. Springer, "Did the 1968 Surcharge Really Work?" and F. Modigliani and C. Steindel, "Is a Tax Rebate an Effective Tool for Stabilization Policy?"

9. H. S. Houthakker and L. Taylor, *Consumer Demand in the United States, 1929–1970, Analysis and Projections,* 2nd edition (Harvard University Press, 1970); L. Taylor, "Saving out of Different Types of Income," *Brookings Papers on Economic Activity* 2(1971): 383–407; F. T. Juster and P. Wachtel, "A Note on Inflation and the Saving Rate," *Brookings Papers on Economic Activity* 3(1972): 765–78; F. T. Juster, "A Tax Cut Might Not Do Much for Savings," *Fortune* (June 29, 1981): 25–26.

10. M. J. Boskin, "Taxation, Saving, and the Rate of Interest," *Journal of Political Economy* 86(April 1978): S3–S27.

11. E. P. Howrey and S. H. Hymans, "The Measurement and Determination of Loanable Funds Saving," *Brookings Papers on Economic Activity* 3(1978).

mand theory for individual goods, prices play a major role. If the price of steak rises, we eat more spaghetti. But a rise in general prices does not alter the relative prices of consumption, saving, and income. In fact, because all depend on the same price index, their relative prices move together. No simple theoretical relationship exists between aggregate price changes and the amount of consumption. Most empirical studies do not find price movements to be significant variables altering consumption.

Yet when price movements become large and irregular, some effect on spending appears likely. All prices do not move together. Receipts of income and purchases made from it do not occur simultaneously. Differences in timing of price movements can affect spending and saving.

As noted in Chapter 8, the **real-balance** or *Pigou effect* shows that a change in the price level, through its impact on the real value of money alters wealth and therefore spending. When prices as a whole change, one major asset has a price which must react in the opposite direction. This good includes money and other dollar-denominated assets. If the consumer price index falls, the purchasing power of a dollar rises. The real value of money and government debt owned by families will rise if prices fall. As prices drop, households possess added wealth. (The effect is exactly the same as that of a fall in interest rates.) With increased wealth, households spend more from a given income. The opposite also applies. In inflation, rising prices diminish the value of monetary assets. The real balance effect says that inflation will lower the wealth of households and decrease expenditures.

Another possible path by which price changes can increase consumption and lower saving is through *money illusion,* which causes economic units to act illogically through failure to perceive fully how the expansion or shrinkage of the value of money really affects them. If prices rise 15 percent, disposable income will probably rise about the same degree. Nominal income has gone up, but real income has not. A family may raise consumption because it fails to recognize that its larger paycheck does not mean that its real income has increased. If it does so, it is said to be suffering from money illusion. In a period of rising prices, such action can lead to an upward shift in the consumption function.

The belief that prices will be higher in the future and, therefore, that one can beat inflation by buying now is another way in which price changes can affect spending. If you need a car and believe its price will rise from $5,000 to $6,000 in two months, it is clearly to your advantage to buy it without delay and beat the price rise. But if most people felt this way, why wouldn't prices rise immediately? Any opportunities to buy before prices rise mean that the market is not working properly. In most cases, someone buying to beat the market is either pitting his judgment against the market or taking advantage of some flaw in the market.

Buying to beat a price rise and borrowing to buy, discussed earlier, are merely two examples of how consumption can be affected by expectations. While in the late 1970s fears of higher prices seem to have sparked more consumption from a given income and lowered saving, at other times such apprehensions have led to lower spending. If families fear that inflation will cut their real income so much that they will be unable to buy necessities, expectations of price increases can reduce demand. In any case, expectational impacts on spending increase instability. Buyers may be strongly influenced by waves of optimism or pessimism, resulting in fluctuations of consumption, output, and income.

The Depressed Consumer, 1973–75[12]

In choosing among competing consumption functions, one must take all with a grain of salt. We cannot accept literally the numbers spewed out by computers. The statistical difficulties of choosing among different relationships mean that a good deal of uncertainty remains. Nevertheless, simulation studies are valuable. They take a particular view of the economy and tell how changes in policy or outside events may have influenced it. Those who accept a certain theory gain a rough estimate of what did happen. This holds true even though everyone recognizes that the numbers emanating from the model are subject to all kinds of qualification.

The recession of 1973–75 was the most serious since the Great Depression of 1929–33. The cyclical expansion which began in 1971 reached its peak in the last quarter of 1973. The economy then experienced its sharpest postwar slump. There are many opinions as to why this drop occurred. Among the possible causes were the OPEC oil embargo, inflation, and excess investment in housing, inventories, and plant and equipment. Consumer spending failed to grow at its normal pace.

In a study of this experience, Frederic Mishkin analyzed the extent to which the failure of consumption to grow was due to a decrease in household wealth, marked by a decline in real balances and a sharp drop in the stock market. Mishkin sets out to measure the impact of these financial changes. He asks how much of the direct drop (excluding the multiplier) and later failure to grow of expenditures on consumer durables and nondurables, services, and new single-family homes can be attributed to the decline in the stock market and other household assets.

Figure 10.4 shows the real net worth of households in 1972–75. In the previous decade, household wealth had expanded on average by more than 5 percent a year. Mishkin uses the gap between what households would normally have had and what they actually owned in estimating how wealth influenced consumption. According to the figure, the sharpest drop in wealth occurred in stock market assets, which declined nearly 50 percent in real terms. Stock market prices fell even as double-digit inflation reduced the real values of the

---

12. Based on F. S. Mishkin, "What Depressed the Consumer: The Household Balance Sheet and the 1973–75 Recession."

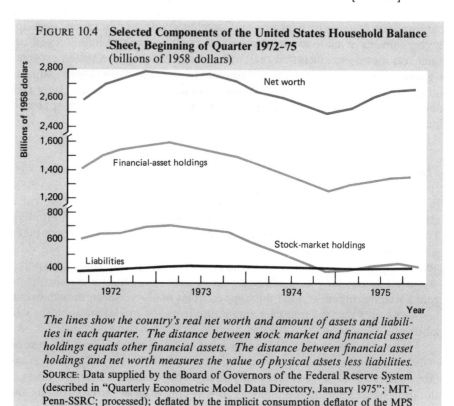

FIGURE 10.4   **Selected Components of the United States Household Balance Sheet, Beginning of Quarter 1972–75**
(billions of 1958 dollars)

The lines show the country's real net worth and amount of assets and liabilities in each quarter. The distance between stock market and financial asset holdings equals other financial assets. The distance between financial asset holdings and net worth measures the value of physical assets less liabilities.
SOURCE: Data supplied by the Board of Governors of the Federal Reserve System (described in "Quarterly Econometric Model Data Directory, January 1975"; MIT-Penn-SSRC; processed); deflated by the implicit consumption deflator of the MPS model.

quotations. Other financial assets grew slightly in real terms, but at well below their trend rate. Rising interest rates and sharp inflation kept real growth to a minimum. The value of physical assets expanded slightly, but their real growth was also less than normal. One factor did improve the situation of households; their debts could be paid off in cheaper dollars. Real household liabilities, which must be subtracted from their assets to get their net worth, fell. However, because households as a whole are net creditors, not debtors, inflation substantially decreased their net worth.

CONSUMPTION AND THE DECLINE IN REAL WEALTH

Mishkin asks what consumption expenditures would have been had wealth continued to grow according to its past trends. He contrasts the actual level of household real financial assets, the physical stock of single-family houses and consumer durables, the value of common stock, and the real value of consumer liabilities with their trend rates of growth. Given the gap between actual and trend, how much were consumption expenditures affected? Table 10.6 presents the results. The first three columns show the model's estimates of the amount

TABLE 10.6   **Partial Effects of Household Balance Sheets on Aggregate Demand**
(billions of 1958 dollars)

Year and quarter	Type of assets and effect on demand				Decrease in consumption expenditures by type	
	Net financial liabilities	Net worth less stocks	Common stock	Total	Nondurable and services	Durables
1973:Q1	−1.4	−1.3	−0.6	−3.3	−1.4	−1.9
Q2	−1.6	−2.1	−3.1	−6.8	−2.4	−4.4
Q3	−1.0	−0.5	−7.3	−8.8	−1.8	−7.0
Q4	0.0	−2.3	−12.3	−14.6	−4.7	−10.1
1974:Q1	3.1	−5.3	−18.4	−20.6	−9.1	−11.5
Q2	7.2	−6.6	−24.7	−24.1	−11.9	−12.2
Q3	11.1	−7.4	−32.3	−28.6	−15.1	−13.5
Q4	14.2	−8.6	−40.6	−35.0	−18.8	−16.2
1975:Q1	16.0	−8.6	−45.0	−37.6	−21.1	−16.5
Q2	17.2	−7.6	−44.2	−34.6	−20.9	−13.7
Q3	18.2	−6.6	−41.6	−30.0	−20.6	−9.4

SOURCE: F. S. Mishkin "What Depressed the Consumer?" *Brookings Papers on Economic Activity* 1 (1977): Tables 5, 6, 8.

The first four columns present estimates from a life-cycle model of the effect on demand of actual movements in households' assets and liabilities. The assets in a period are subtracted from an estimate of what their values would have been if growth had continued on trend. The difference times the models' coefficients shows how much demand was reduced by the smaller growth or a decline in the asset. The final two columns divide the decrease in demand by type of consumer good or service.

each gap affected spending. Most of the failure to grow is attributed to the slump in stock prices. Their impact begins slowly because their effects are felt only with a lag. By the end of 1974, however, according to the model, the fall in stock prices led consumers to reduce their annual rate of spending by 40 billion 1958 dollars. Stock prices started up in 1975, but because of lags and inflation, their negative influence in the third quarter of 1975 was still above the end of 1974. The failure of other household assets to expand in real terms at their trend rate also reduced spending, but their influence was far less.

In contrast, the falling weight of debt liabilities pushed spending higher. Initially, families were paying slightly more than normal on their debts, but inflation reduced the burden even as consumers decreased the rate at which they borrowed. By the beginning of 1975, the reduction in real liabilities was a major expansionary force.

The fourth column shows the total effect of these three separate factors. The difference between potential and actual spending widened steadily until the first quarter of 1975, the low point of the recession. In the spring of 1975 the household asset position began to push demand up again. The burden of debts had lightened. Stocks of physical assets were below normal. Stock prices were climbing. The improving financial position of consumers helped to turn the recession around.

The final two columns show the divergent impact of wealth on expenditures on durable goods in contrast to nondurables and services. Durable expenditures make up less than 20 percent of the total; yet in the first year, the decrease in the demand for them is twice as great as that of the other 80 percent. The total wealth effect reduces spending on consumers' nondurables and services by less than .5 percent at the maximum. However, a small influence applied to a large magnitude does add up. By mid-1974, even though the loss for nondurables was less than .5 percent, their effect exceeded that of durable expenditures, which were about 12 percent below normal.

Professor Mishkin's model has been criticized as overemphasizing the impact of stock prices on wealth, in contrast to the views of others that stock prices primarily affected confidence and expectations. His critics believe that consumer spending was below normal because of a fall in both wealth and confidence. However, this thesis is not confirmed by further analysis. When a direct measure of confidence through a survey of expectations is added to the model, it has only minor effects. The analysis in this model shows a strong influence of wealth on consumption. Real balances fell early in the recession and could have been one of the initiating causes of the decline. At the bottom of the slump, the model estimates that even though consumption of nondurables and services was close to its pre-slump level, the direct effect of smaller household balances, by reducing their expansion and cutting purchases of durables and houses, may have accounted for between one-third and one-half of the total gap between demand and full potential.

Summary

1. Historical consumption functions, based on a simple relationship over time between consumption and disposable income, can explain a large share of movements in consumption. However, in short periods, the simple marginal and average propensities to consume are not stable. Furthermore, surveys of consumption and income show both the *mpc*s and the *APC*s declining as income grows, but such declines have not occurred as the nation's income has expanded.

2. In order to improve both explanations and predictions, more complex theories of consumption have been developed. They include income changes, population, wealth, interest rates, prices, and expectations as possible variables influencing consumption.

3. The absolute-income hypothesis states that real consumption rises with real income, the marginal propensity to consume is less than one, and the average proportion of income saved will rise as the income of the country increases.

4. The life-cycle and permanent-income hypotheses explain a weaker relationship between current income and spending. Families plan their expenditures on the basis of their expected future income and on interest earned on savings. Income is earned from labor and from wealth as well. People may not spend income increases believed to be temporary. They will reestimate their future income on the basis of events and make their consumption decisions accordingly.

5. The permanent-income hypothesis offers an explanation of why consumer surveys show the percentage saved rising with income, contrary to the experience of the economy over time. The survey data include some families who report a low saving rate because their incomes are temporarily reduced, but they continue to spend in proportion to their permanent income. Other families report higher incomes due to high transitory income and high saving rates because they do not spend their temporary increases in income.

6. The life-cycle hypothesis offers a separate explanation of the divergence between the *mpc* in survey and in time-series data. Some families, both young and old, have low saving rates because they need to draw on assets or go into debt to maintain a spending level close to their average income over their lifetimes. Others have high saving rates because they are at a high income stage in the life cycle and must accumulate resources for retirement. Since consumption rises and saving falls with wealth, the continued expansion of the nation's wealth can also explain why the national saving rate has not risen. A richer nation can spend more on consumption at every level of income.

7. Changes in wealth can be sudden as a result of inflation, interest movements, and swings in the stock market's evaluation of the future. A surge in purchases of consumer durable assets and a sharp increase in consumer debt in addition to movements in net financial worth are all likely to influence consumption expenditures, particularly on durable goods.

8. A rise in the yield on savings increases the relative price of current consumption. People will gain utility by substituting future consumption (saving) for current spending. A rise in yields increases income gained from an annuity or a saving package. Goals set in terms of a specific future income can be met with less saving. On the other hand, interest increases may cause capital losses, thereby lowering wealth. Higher interest rates decrease borrowing and, therefore, spending. Since these effects of higher rates conflict with each other, theory cannot predict whether or not saving will increase. Empirical tests also give ambiguous results.

9. In theory, a general rise in prices should not influence consumption, since the prices of goods and services rise together with income. The desire to buy a certain quantity of real goods from a specific real income should not be altered by changes in the price index used to deflate both sides. Furthermore, in perfect markets, opportunities to beat price rises should disappear rapidly, since everyone would bid prices up to take advantage of any profitable oppor-

tunities. But markets have imperfections. The prices of money and fixed-price assets move opposite to price indexes. Some prices and incomes may lag. As a result, price movements may influence spending.

Questions for Discussion and Review

1. Discuss the reasons for incorporating variables other than income into the consumption function.

2. Distinguish personal outlays from consumption expenditures.

3. Is it true that the permanent income hypothesis predicts that the *mpc* out of transitory income will be very high?

4. Evaluate the following policy proposal: The incipient recession should be attacked by a one-time rebate of $150 to every household.

5. What is meant by "permanent income"? What is the argument in favor of its being the proper definition of income as a variable in the consumption function?

6. Consider an economy where the ratio of permanent consumption to permanent income is .9 for every person. If in year one, Mr. A, who considers his permanent income to be $20,000, takes a one-time 10 percent pay cut, what would his observed APC be? How would your answer change if the pay cut were permanent?

7. Explain how the following affect current consumption expenditures:
   (a) The stock of durable goods
   (b) Stock market values
   (c) Consumer credit

8. If just consumption were taxed rather than all of income, would you expect saving to increase?

9. Suppose we have a consumption function of the type given in equation 10.4:

$$C = 300 + .7YD^e + .05W,$$

where YD^e is formed by:

$$YD^e = .7YD + .2YD_{-1} + .1YD_{-2}$$

$$YD_{-1} = YD_{-2} = YD = \$2,000 \text{ billion}$$

and $W = \$5,000$ billion.
If both wealth and taxes are increased permanently by $15 billion, what will consumption be after three years?

References

Ando, A., and F. Modigliani. "The 'Life Cycle' Hypothesis of Saving: Aggregate Implications and Tests." *American Economic Review* 53(March 1963): 55–84.

Boskin, M. J. "Taxation, Saving, and the Rate of Interest." *Journal of Political Economy* 86(April 1978): S3–S27.

Duesenberry, J. S. *Income, Saving, and the Theory of Consumer Behavior*. Cambridge: Harvard University Press, 1949.

Eisner, R. "Fiscal and Monetary Policy Reconsidered." *American Economic Review* 59(December 1969): 897–905.

Friedman, M. *A Theory of the Consumption Function*. Princeton: Princeton University Press, 1957.

Howrey, E. P., and S. H. Hymans, "The Measurement and Determination of Loanable Funds Saving." *Brookings Papers on Economic Activity* 3(1978).

Mishkin, F. S. "What Depressed the Consumer: The Household Balance Sheet and the 1973–75 Recession." *Brookings Papers on Economic Activity* 1(1977).

Modigliani, F. "The Life Cycle Hypothesis Twenty Years Later," in N. Parkin, ed., *Contemporary Issues in Economics*. Manchester: University of Manchester Press, 1975.

Modigliani, F., and R. E. Brumberg, "Utility Analysis and the Consumption Function: An Interpretation of Cross-Section Data," in K. K. Kurihara, ed., *Post-Keynesian Economics*. Rutgers, N.J.: Rutgers University Press, 1954, pp. 388–436.

Tobin, J. "Relative Income, Absolute Income, and Saving," in *Money, Trade, and Economic Growth: Essays in Honor of John Williams*. New York: MacMillan, 1951, pp. 135–56.

11

The Government Budget

In 1981, President Reagan proposed and Congress adopted the most revolutionary change in fiscal policy since Franklin D. Roosevelt proposed the New Deal in 1933. The new policy was heralded as a complete break from the demand-oriented policies of the past. The government budget for 1982 was reduced by $37 billion, and further cuts were promised so that by 1984, the government would be spending $130 billion less per year than it would have spent had previous trends continued. At the same time, taxes on individuals, businesses, and estates were slashed. In 1984 scheduled revenues (under the $4,097 billion GNP assumed for that year) would be $150 billion less than would have been collected under previous legislation. After 1984, as major provisions of the tax act continued to phase in, the reductions in taxes would be even larger.

This new fiscal policy primarily reflected a desire to reduce the role of government, but it also broke sharply with the past in two major ways: (1) It testified to the dominance in the administration of the new classicists. Inflation would be fought mainly by supply-side economics and by a reduction in expectations of future price increases. (2) It contrasted with the growing popular view (particularly deeply imbedded in conservative thought) that a balanced budget was essential for ending inflation. Major emphasis was placed on the idea that the government's impact on the economy extended far beyond its effects on aggregate demand. The size of the government and the rate of taxation also influenced aggregate supply and expectations of inflation. Inefficiency in government wasted resources. Lowered incentives curtailed desires to work and to invest. The Reagan fiscal policy aimed at removing the government's harmful effects. The private economy would be unleashed to expand potential output at a rapid rate. Increased supply would slow inflation. Rational expectations would lead to fewer price and wage increases.

Part 5 analyzes the supply-side aspects of the fiscal policy revolution, while Part 7 takes up possible overall impacts. This chapter examines only the effect of the government on aggregate demand. It enumerates the expanded federal expenditures that built up the pressures for reduced taxes. It describes additional ways by which government expenditures influence total spending. It takes up in more detail the issues of a balanced budget.

Although the ending of budget deficits was a key component of President Reagan's election campaign, its importance was downplayed in the new program. The new legislation assumed that the advantages of sharp tax cuts would offset any disadvantages from a delay in balancing the budget. The administration projected a balanced budget for 1984, but most budget analysts doubted that it would be achieved. This decision to accept further deficits conflicted with the clamor for a balanced budget which rose steadily through the 1970s from the public, the press, and both political parties. Because the average voter believed that eliminating budget deficits was a necessary condition for ending inflation, President Reagan had to use a great deal of personal persuasion before his new approach was accepted.

Even though the delay in balancing the budget ran counter to popular demands, the new program came closer to the views of most economists. The great majority of analysts did not share the conviction that a balanced budget was essential to curing the nation's economic distress. While agreeing that cuts in government spending and taxing could be useful, most economists were far less concerned than the public with the issue of a balanced budget. They were aware of the degree to which specific deficits or surpluses and apparent balances can vary depending on what accounting conventions are used. More important, economists saw that both the feasibility and the desirability of a balanced budget depended not only on the government's own decisions to spend and tax, but also on what was happening in the economy. Because of necessary interactions with other spending decisions, a large surplus or a large deficit might be preferable at times to a balance in the government's accounts.

What are some of the underlying causes of conflicting views as to the desirability of keeping the budget balanced? One crucial factor is the recognition that actual government expenditures, revenues, and deficits depend on both discretionary (autonomous) legislation that sets spending and tax limits and on the income-induced changes that come about when the GNP grows at faster or slower rates. Governments enact appropriation and tax revenue bills, but how much is spent and collected depends on the spending, output, and employment decisions of the rest of the economy. Other basic differences arise in the analysis of how helpful or harmful proposed spending and tax changes will turn out to be.

Chapter 4 analyzed some of the direct effects of government spending and taxing. It stressed the need to differentiate government purchases of goods and services which are part of production demand from expenditures for transfer payments which influence the GNP only indirectly by altering disposable income. It brought out the role of the multiplier in the total effect of government purchases (G), taxes (T and t), and transfers (TR). It also made clear that the simple multiplier declines when income-induced revenues are included in the total marginal propensity to spend (m) from personal income. Continuing the multiplier analysis, Chapter 8 showed that the simple multiplier had to be adjusted to take into account any impacts on spending caused by changes in interest rates in response to altered budgets.

Now we need to analyze other indirect effects of the budget on aggregate demand. (Impacts on aggregate supply are discussed in Chapters 14 and 15.) Government spending and taxing exert influence on efficiency, expectations, the demand and supply of money and credit, and the level of spending and saving. Of particular importance are issues related to the need to finance budget deficits. Do increases in government borrowing crowd out private investment? Do they lead to inflationary increases in the money supply? Does the existence of a large public debt reduce saving? These and related questions are analyzed through the following topics:

> The drive for a reduced and balanced budget.
> The total effects of fiscal policy.
> Income-induced changes in government revenues and expenditures.
> Financing the deficit and creation of excess money.
> The influence of the public debt on spending and saving.
> No simple answers.

The Drive for a Reduced and Balanced Budget

The demand that deficits be ended conformed to what appeared to be one of the most firmly held opinions of the average American: namely, that the budget should be balanced—if not every year, at least over some longer-range period. Americans have traditionally feared an unbalanced budget. People know they are worse off when they owe large debts and are better off when they are debt-free. A generalization from private debt experience is applied to the government. Borrowing money by this generation is believed to be unfair to future generations who will have to repay the debt, or at least pay interest on it. This firmly held view was greatly reinforced by the fact that inflation worsened simultaneously with a rise in government spending. Many were convinced that because resources were wasted through government inefficiency, output and real income would grow if the government's share of spending fell. Rising government expenditures occurred along with a proliferation of government regulations in the areas of pollution, plant safety, and energy, accompanied by falling productivity—a situation due, it was claimed, to the ineptness of the government's programs.

GOVERNMENT'S SHARE OF SPENDING

An examination of expenditures and deficits in the 1960s and 1970s reveals why the budget has become such a widespread preoccupation. Table 11.1 shows that expenditures and deficits, both in absolute dollars and in percent of GNP, rose to record levels for nonwar years. Under both political parties, large, persistent deficits became a fact of life.

TABLE 11.1 **Federal Government Expenditures and Deficits**

Calendar year	Billions of dollars		Percent of GNP	
	Expenditures	Deficits*	Expenditures	Deficits*
1962	110.4	−4.2	19.5	−0.7
1963	114.2	0.3	19.1	0.0
1964	118.2	−3.3	18.5	−0.5
1965	123.8	0.5	17.9	0.1
1966	143.6	−1.8	19.0	−0.2
1967	163.7	−13.2	20.5	−1.7
1968	180.6	−5.8	20.7	−0.7
1969	188.4	8.4	20.0	0.9
1970	204.2	−12.4	20.6	−1.2
1971	220.6	−22.0	20.5	−2.0
1972	244.7	−16.8	20.6	−1.4
1973	264.8	−5.6	20.0	−0.4
1974	299.3	−11.5	20.9	−0.8
1975	356.8	−69.3	23.0	−4.5
1976	384.8	−53.1	22.4	−3.1
1977	421.5	−46.4	22.0	−2.4
1978	460.7	−29.2	21.4	−1.4
1979	509.2	−14.8	21.1	−0.6
1980	601.3	−62.3	22.9	−2.4
1981(e)	683.0	−47.0	23.0	−1.6
1982(e)	724.0	−33.0	22.0	−1.0

* A minus number indicates a deficit. (e) estimated from July 1981 budget message.
SOURCE: U.S. Department of Commerce, National Income and Product Accounts.

The first two columns show actual federal expenditures and deficits; the third and fourth columns relate them to the GNP. While current dollar expenditures grew steadily, their percent of the GNP reached a high in 1975, when incomes were reduced by the "Great Recession." Lower output also accounts for some of the increase relative to 1980 GNP.

Not only did government expenditures grow rapidly, they also became a larger share of economic activity, as shown by the information presented in Figure 11.1. The two color segments represent the percent of total production of goods and services purchased by federal, state, and local governments. The solid color segments show federal government purchases as a share of the GNP, while the lighter areas reflect the share of states and localities. Several points stand out. While most discussions center on the federal budget, its share of goods and services actually reached a peak in 1967 and then fell steadily until 1979. Meanwhile, state and local purchases rose until 1975, when their share peaked also. The combined share of government purchases of goods and services peaked in 1968 at 22.8 percent, and then declined. Note, however, that

FIGURE 11.1   **The Relationship Between Government Expenditures and the GNP**

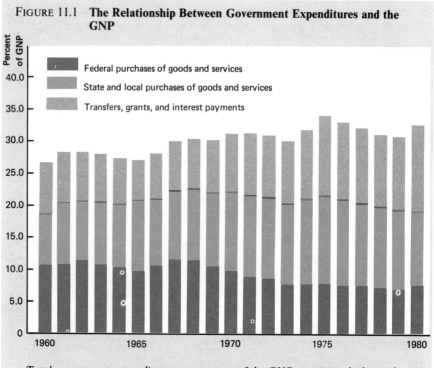

Total government expenditures as a percent of the GNP rose irregularly until 1975, then dropped, but rose again in the recession of 1980. The share of federal government purchases—the solid color segments—dropped rather steadily following the Vietnam War build-up. The share of state and local purchases—the lighter color segments—peaked in 1975. Any trend in the share of transfer payments—the gray segments—is hard to judge since they fluctuate with recessions and interest rates.
SOURCE: President's Economic Report, 1981.

the government's share, as is typical, rose in the recession periods of 1970, 1974, and 1980.

It is probable that if government purchases were the only government expenditures, pressures to reduce the budget would not be as strong. In recent years, however, transfer and interest payments have also grown rapidly. The gray segments show their relationship to the GNP. (Recall that expenditures for transfers such as social security payments are not included in the GNP but instead offset taxes by raising the recipients' disposable incomes.) The height of the three segments together shows the relationship of total government expenditures to the GNP. The figure reveals a steady growth to 1975, similar to movements in total federal expenditures as reported in the third column of Table 11.1. The share of government transfers and interest has steadily grown. From 7.1 percent in 1960, this spending increased to 11.5 percent in 1978 and

1979 and rose to 12.2 percent as a result of the 1980 recession. While federal purchases of goods and services as a share of the GNP declined fairly steadily after 1967, total federal expenditures continued to grow as social security payments rose and as the central government paid for an increasing share of local expenditures through grants and transfers. In 1960, federal transfers, grants, and interest payments made up 7.8 percent of the GNP, while they were 15.3 percent in 1980. Even though it did not directly use productive resources, this increase in federal spending was certainly a key factor leading to the demand for budget cuts.

CONTROLLING GOVERNMENT SIZE AND INEFFICIENCY

Because this growing GNP share for the government was accompanied by rising inflation and falling productivity, a sharp reaction against the size of the government occurred. It was widely felt that the economy would improve if the budget had to be balanced every year except during wars, depressions, or similar emergencies. By 1980 many had become convinced that governments were too large and expensive. People believed that their tax payments exceeded the benefits they received. The difference was lost to government inefficiency and to an oversized bureaucracy. Distaste grew for government programs which redistributed income to the needy or, in the view of many, to the not-so-needy. Even those who benefited from the government's programs seemed to feel that other, less worthy individuals should have their government incomes cut.

Americans have traditionally distrusted the government and have held a low opinion of its efficiency. Government decisions as to how and where to spend are made by politicians and bureaucrats, a fact which many feel virtually guarantees poor results. The choices of decision makers are made with a view to improving their own lot rather than the public welfare. In this view, politicians will always spend more and tax less in order to get reelected. Bureaucrats will respond to special interests by designing programs which politicians adopt in order to gain votes, even if it is at the expense of the general public. Closely related to concern over the size of the government and its inefficiencies is the belief held by some that taxation had reached such a high level that normal incentives to work and to invest were reduced (an issue that is discussed as part of supply-side economics in Part 5).

BUDGET DEFICITS AND INFLATION

Key political support for a balanced budget came from those who believed that federal deficits were a major cause of inflation. In contrast, most economists agree that no simple relationship exists between a federal deficit and inflation. Large increases in government spending do raise aggregate demand. If they occur when demand is excessive or if they move demand above potential output, they cause prices to rise. But in the last half of the 1970s, the size of federal deficits was small compared to inflation. Deficits moved down as inflation speeded up. In 1975, total government (including state and local) deficits were 4.2 percent of the GNP. They then fell year by year to 2.1, 1.0, and 0 before becoming a small surplus in 1979. Meanwhile, consumer prices rose at rates of 7.0, 4.8, 6.8, 9.0 percent, to reach 13.3 percent in 1979. In 1980, inflation and deficits rose together, but this was primarily the result of a recession which reduced government revenues.

Neo-Keynesians and monetarists agree that during this period, the relationship between inflation and the budget deficit was weak or nonexistent. For example, Robert Solow, a prominent neo-Keynesian, wrote,

> The first simple story about inflation is that its underlying cause is deficit spending by the federal government. In that case, the way to fix things up is simply to balance the federal budget. . . .The story is wrong. You may favor big government or small government for other reasons, but the facts speak against the theory that the balanced budget is the key factor in ending our current inflation. To see that, you have only to look at recent history.[1]

In the same vein, Karl Brunner, one of the most prominent originators of monetarism, has written,

> A persistent reduction in the budget deficit would certainly yield major benefits for our economy. The direct effect on inflation is however a negligible component of these benefits. Neither Keynesian nor monetarist analysis implies any significant impact on the ongoing *rates* of inflation. The encouragement to capital accumulation in the private sector seems the major gain obtained from a lower deficit. It reduces "crowding out" and shifts, over the longer horizon, the public's portfolio balance towards investments representing productive resources. The higher level of real growth associated with the expanded productive facilities raises over time our welfare but lowers the inflation rate by a negligible margin.[2]

If the deficit adds to inflation, it must be either because it is necessarily accompanied by an increase in the money supply, because it raises wealth, or because of its psychological impact. These possibilities will be discussed more fully in analyzing the public debt, but the conclusions can be summarized.

Some economists have argued that deficits cannot raise demand because of crowding out, or because the psychological effect of a larger public debt is to lower the desire to spend. These have been the key arguments against the use of fiscal policy for the purpose of raising demand. For the same reason, monetarists have stated that increases in debt could not raise demand unless they brought about an expansion in the money supply. If the debt has caused inflation, it is because deficits have led the Federal Reserve to increase money. The year-to-year relationships between deficits, inflation, and the money sup-

1. Robert M. Solow, "All Simple Stories About Inflation are Wrong," *The Executive,* July 1980 (extracted in the *The Washington Post,* May 18, 1980).

2. K. Brunner, "The Commitment to Permanent Inflation," in *Alternative Policies to Combat Inflation* (St. Louis, Missouri: Washington University, Center for the Study of American Business), January 1979, Working Paper No. 40.

ply are not close. The Fed states that it does not increase money to help the Treasury sell debt. Deficits tend to occur when interest rates are falling. When money and deficits grow together, it is usually because the country is trying to fight a recession.

A neglected possibility is that a larger debt does increase spending because it boosts the public's image of its net worth and wealth. Appendix 11.1 shows that if decision units neglect the present value of future taxes as a liability in their economic balance sheets (and most believe they do), they will feel richer when the public debt grows. Higher estimated wealth leads to more spending and less saving. Neo-Keynesians believe that to measure the total impact of government fiscal policies, the wealth effects of deficits must be added to the direct impact through autonomous and induced spending. They believe that, together, they cause significant increases in aggregate demand. If they raise demand when supply is limited, they can lead to price increases and inflation. If demand is inadequate, they will raise output and employment.

Everyone agrees that, as with other issues constantly in the news, the size of the debt and changes in it can have an important psychological effect on aggregate demand. But whether the effect is positive or negative is not certain. Furthermore, the sign may change. For many years those who opposed an active use of fiscal policy argued that government expenditures did not increase spending. The private sectors would recognize the dangers of the debt and would therefore cut back their own desires to spend by as much as or more than government spending expanded. Recently they have reversed their stand; government expenditures are said to raise demand by even more than the naïve multiplier. Fear of a huge debt causes people to rush out and buy goods now in order to avoid future losses due to inflation.

On the whole, however, most economists probably agreed with Milton Friedman when he wrote, "Government deficits can and sometimes do contribute to inflation. However, the relation between deficits and inflation is far looser than is widely believed. Moreover, the major harm that deficits do is to foster irresponsible government spending. . . .The political appeal of a 'balanced budget' has often been counterproductive."[3]

It was this point of view that seemed to dominate President Reagan's approach to cutting government expenditures. The key thrust was to reduce irresponsible government spending; the issue of a balanced budget was of only secondary importance. Expenditures were slashed in order to reduce the role of the government. Taxes were cut to increase incentives to save and invest and to stimulate the capacity for production. The president estimated that the joint effects would be to continue sizable budget deficits for several years at a level well above those proposed by President Carter. Even though the projected deficits could have been eliminated if the large expenditure cuts had been accompanied by a somewhat smaller tax cut, this path was rejected. The strategy adopted depended on stimulating expansion and growth rather than on a

---

3. M. Friedman, *Newsweek,* February 23, 1981, p. 70.

balanced budget. Over the longer run, it was assumed that pressures against unbalanced budgets and against higher taxes would prevent future votes to increase expenditures.

It was recognized that the program entailed considerable risks. Larger budget deficits would place added burdens on monetary policy. The following discussion also shows why most economists believe that the deficits would raise aggregate demand. Therefore, the success of the adopted program depended on supply expanding faster than demand and on a reduction in inflationary expectations. When the new program was passed by Congress, Republican Senator Hóward Baker, the Senate majority leader and one of the men most influential in its adoption, said, "What we are doing is really a riverboat gamble. We are gambling that this new economics will work—and it will, in my judgment."[4]

The Total Effects of Fiscal Policy

In recent years, debates over the size of government, efficiency, and inflation have tended to supplant prior arguments over whether a policy to shift expenditures and taxes is likely to bring about a more desirable level of aggregate demand. Government expenditures and taxation are large. Most inflations have been triggered, though not sustained, by government expenditures, especially those for wars. Since the actions of the government affect income, shouldn't it be concerned about its impact when it passes the budget? If aggregate demand is inflationary, shouldn't the government raise taxes to reduce spending, even if it means running a considerable budget surplus? If aggregate demand is low and unemployment high, shouldn't the government try to raise demand, even if it means running a deficit?

In a depressed economy, fiscal policy can raise spending desires with only minor real costs. Since the passage of the Full Employment Act of 1946, government policy has been based on the need to consider the impact of its budget on total demand. Discretionary changes have been made in the budget for the purpose of mitigating instability brought on by war or by shifts in private demand. The Office of Management and Budget (OMB) in the Executive Office of the President and the Congressional Budget Office (CBO) have analysts charged with predicting how a new budget will affect the economy. The levels of expenditures, of taxes, and the surplus or deficit recommended by the president and approved by Congress take into account the impact of the budget on total spending and the national welfare. In determining action, the government must consider both the impact of private income and demand on the government's surplus or deficit and that of the government's expenditures and taxes on private spending. Two separate factors determine the impact of

---

4. *The New York Times,* August 3, 1981, p. 19

fiscal policy on aggregate demand:

1. The government makes autonomous (exogenous) changes in its budgets. These government decisions interact with the other spending and saving sectors to determine the *IS* curve. Changes in spending appropriations and tax laws cause autonomous shifts in expenditures and taxes. Through the multiplier, such movements generate additional changes in the other sectors.
2. The government's budget results depend on the level of income as well as on discretionary action. Laws and appropriations set the government spending and tax functions, but they cannot, by themselves, determine the budget surplus or deficit. The amount actually collected and spent varies with the level of the GNP. Whether or not the government's budget is balanced will be mutually determined by the spending decisions of all sectors. But among the key factors establishing this equilibrium income are the government's marginal propensities to spend and to tax.

An increase in the government surplus or deficit can result from either a shift in the tax and appropriations levels or a shift in income. To analyze the impacts of the government's fiscal decisions, the cause of the surplus or deficit must be differentiated.

THE ULTIMATE EFFECTS OF POLICIES

Thus far in this volume, the models of both monetary and fiscal policies have dealt primarily with their initial impacts. They assumed no subsequent effects, such as a shift in the desire to spend of other decision makers. They also neglected possible consequences arising from either the necessary financing of deficits or the funds received in periods of surpluses. Such simplified analysis neglects some of the thorniest questions. Will—and if so, by how much— changes in the budget affect other variables such as interest rates and prices, as well as the spending decisions of other groups? Government actions can shift private desires to spend. An electric power plant built by the government may displace one by a private utility. A new national park may create a demand for hotels and marinas. How the budget affects expectations remains unclear. Will business and consumers cut back spending because of a government deficit, or will they buy more to meet the increase in demand and potential inflation? This analysis also neglects the effect of taxes and government competition for resources. These forces are analyzed in Part 5. This chapter continues to consider only the impact of the budget on aggregate demand.

The concept of rational expectations makes clear the possibility that expectations may reshape the entire response structure of the economy. The private sectors may change their spending in unexpected ways when activist policies are adopted. Forecasters have often failed to anticipate actions that businesses and consumers take to protect themselves from adverse government policies or to profit from favorable ones.

Figure 11.2 contrasts the initial and secondary effects of changes in monetary or fiscal policies with their final effects. The inner box shows the policy

FIGURE 11.2   **Monetary and Fiscal Influence on Aggregate Demand**

Possible actions change:

	Fiscal policy		Monetary policy	Financing deficit
Action	Government expenditures (ΔG)	Taxes (ΔT and Δt) and transfers (ΔTR)	Monetary base (ΔMB) Qualitative regulations	Government debt ($\Delta DEBT$)
Period of Result:	Results in changes in:			
Primary	Autonomous spending ($\Delta \bar{A}$)	Disposable income (ΔYD)	Money stock (M) Interest rates (i) Credit Money multiplier (kM) Expectations	Monetary base (MB) Public debt
Secondary	Income by amount of multiplier	Income by amount of tax multiplier	Desire to spend $\Delta \bar{I}$, $\Delta \bar{C}, c, d$ Income by change in A or r, multiplied	Money stock or interest rates Wealth
Tertiary	Fiscal policy effects on: Private spending Incentives Share of government in decisions Capital formation		Money stock effects depend on shapes of LM and IS curves and on effect of real balances on spending	Money stock effects as under monetary policy Public debt effects on real balances, on spending, and on expectations

The total effects of fiscal and monetary policy are more complex than simple multiplier theory. In addition to the primary and secondary (multiplier) effects on demand, the figure lists possible tertiary influences on private spending decisions. It also shows that fiscal policy includes the influences on spending of movements in government debt.

effects already discussed. The government alters its fiscal policies by shifting expenditures (ΔG), transfer payments (ΔTR), or taxes (ΔT and Δt). These changes in the government schedules induce changes in total income through the multiplier. Monetary policy primarily shifts the monetary base, resulting in movements in the stock of money, interest rates, credit availability, and expectations. These, in turn, change autonomous and induced desires to spend, while interest rate movements bring about new equilibrium income levels.

But stopping at the analysis within the inner box of Figure 11.2 fails to account for other influences. The increase in aggregate demand cannot be measured solely by the initial expenditure times the multiplier. The tertiary effects, through methods of financing, expectations, incentives, and productive efficiency, must also be considered in evaluating any proposed policy change.

The volume of possibilities makes clear why the size of the deficit or the level of government expenditures alone is not a good index of policy effects. Purchases of goods and services differ in their impact from transfer payments. Some analysts find defense expenditures to be especially inflationary because they use scarce resources and add nothing to capital or to output available for private consumption. In contrast, many conservative politicians tend to favor much larger defense expenditures while inveighing against welfare payments as disincentives to work. All agree that how money is raised affects the desire to spend, save, and work.

The effect of fiscal policies through necessarily related movements in the public debt may be as important as tertiary effects through changes in spending desires. The final column of Figure 11.2 recognizes that a government deficit must be financed. The gap between expenditures and taxes must exactly equal changes in the monetary base plus movements in the public debt in private hands. A deficit or surplus affects the money supply, private wealth, and interest rates. As a result, the total consequences of a change in fiscal policy depend on how a deficit is financed. If, when a deficit occurs, the Federal Reserve increases the money supply, any shift in the *IS* curve results in a different equilibrium from that reached if the money supply is held constant. To what extent, if at all, government expenditures crowd out private spending depends on the shape of the *LM* curve and on Federal Reserve actions. Accommodative and nonaccommodative monetary policies were illustrated in Table 8.2.

But the deficit also raises the outstanding public debt. Many people are uneasy about the larger debt. Does it create a burden for the future? How will it affect aggregate demand? If the debt lowers expectations, it may reduce spending. But if households assume that their net worth is greater or that future inflation is more probable, it may increase expenditures. (Refer to Appendix 11.1 to see how the larger public debt can increase private estimates of net worth.)

Income-Induced Changes in Government Revenues and Expenditures

Governments make discretionary changes in their budgets by passing appropriation and tax bills. But legislation only establishes tax schedules and authority for and entitlements to government payments. How much is actually collected or spent depends also on the GNP and, therefore, on shifts in the *IS-LM* equilibrium and price movements. Fluctuations in income induce movements in taxes, transfers, and other expenditures, altering projected revenues, expenditures, and budget surpluses or deficits.

Fiscal policies must be based on an analysis of such changes. (1) Induced movements cause the size of budget surpluses or deficits to vary. (2) The automatic adjustments to demand which occur as the GNP moves must be anticipated. (3) In expansions, increasing revenues may cause such sizable leakages from the circular flow as to make it unlikely that total demand will equal the full-employment GNP. (4) In recessions, induced effects may make it virtually impossible to balance the budget even if everyone agreed that such a policy was desirable.

AUTOMATIC STABILIZERS

Induced changes in government revenues and expenditures leading to movements in the surplus or deficit are called **automatic stabilizers.** The government
budget acts as a counterbalance to shifts in private spending. If demand declines, taxes fall and transfers increase. The government automatically offsets
some of the decline in private sector demand. If demand rises, so will net taxes.
This leakage to taxes and a government surplus leads to a smaller rise in
spending and a lower equilibrium income than would otherwise occur. With-
ou tany discretionary action, public demand tends to rise when private demand
is falling and to fall when private demand rises.

Table 11.2, which shows movements in the government surplus arising
from changes in the GNP, illustrates automatic stabilizers. Net taxes after
transfers depend on income, while expenditures are autonomous. The government surplus (SUR) or deficit equals taxes (T) minus purchases of goods and
services (G).

$$SUR = T - G. \qquad\qquad 11.1$$

Given the assumption that taxes and transfers are related to income, the
amount of the surplus will change with the GNP.

$$SUR = \overline{T} + t(Y) - G \qquad SUR = 200 + .25(Y) - 400. \qquad 11.2$$

Table 11.2 is based on this relationship.

TABLE 11.2 **Changes in Government Revenues and Surpluses Induced by Income
Movements**

(billions of dollars)

Income	Taxes and transfers	Government purchases	Surplus	
			Regular	Full Employment
(Y)	$[\overline{T} + t(Y)]$	(G)	(T − G)	(T* − G)
1,350	538	400	138	200
1,600	600	400	200	200
1,850	662	400	262	200

Full employment level (Y^*) is 1,600.
$T^* = \overline{T} + t(Y^*) = 200 + .25(1,600) = 600.$

*The second column pictures net taxes and transfers rising in response to the
assumed tax-transfer function as income (first column) grows. If government
purchases remain constant, budget surpluses (fourth column) also rise with
income. The full-employment surplus (fifth column) reports what the surplus
would be at a full-employment income of $1,600 billion; it does not change
with income.*

For the moment, disregard the final column of the table. The first four columns show net taxes rising as income increases. More GNP means higher tax collections and lower transfers, as unemployment and similar benefits fall. If expenditures are not changed by discretionary action, the government surplus (fourth column) will rise steadily. In the example, it rises from $138 to $262 billion. If, initially, the budget is in deficit, rising tax collections will bring about a surplus.

An income-tax system in which rates do not change (they are not indexed) can cause tax receipts to rise rapidly. Rates in the federal tax and transfer system in the 1970s were so constructed that if no action had been taken, revenues would have risen at about 1.4 times the rate of change in the GNP. Some estimates show that the automatic government stabilizers equaled about one-third of the movement in induced private demand. If investment fell by $1 billion, consumption would have been expected to drop by a similar $1 billion if no automatic stabilizer existed. But because of lower taxes and higher transfers induced by the drop in income, consumption fell by only $0.65 billion. Similar but opposite reactions occur when private demand rises. The 1981 tax cuts sharply reduced the income elasticity of the tax system. The inauguration of indexing in 1985 aims at bringing it still closer to unity.

THE FULL-EMPLOYMENT BUDGET

Because budget deficits or surpluses can arise either as a result of discretionary action or of income-induced changes, one cannot tell merely by examining the actual deficit or surplus which causal factors were at work. For example, Table 11.1 reveals that the largest budget deficits in history occurred in 1975 and 1976 under President Ford, who was known throughout his career as a strong advocate of a balanced budget. Does the record indicate a sharp dichotomy between his speeches and actions? Not necessarily; what happened was the result both of the government's actions and the economy's performance. In an attempt to separate discretionary from automatic budget reactions, the Council of Economic Advisers in the 1960s introduced the concept of the full-employment (now high-employment) budget.[5] The hope was that if voters understood that a deficit was due to a shortfall of GNP rather than to policy, they would be less worried. If people knew that a balanced budget was possible only at undesirably low income levels, there would be less pressure to balance the budget. For various reasons, the hoped-for results were not attained.

The *full-employment budget* shows the surplus or deficit that would result from the budget's appropriation and tax schedules if the economy were at full employment. It excludes both decreases in revenue receipts and increased expenditures due to the cyclical behavior of output and employment. In Table 11.2, for example, both the columns showing tax receipts and the regular surplus show that when income increases, revenues rise. A rise in income from $1,350 to $1,850 billion causes revenues to grow from $538 to $662 and the

---

5. See Council of Economic Advisers, *Annual Report,* January 1962, pp. 78–81.

surplus from $138 to $262 billion, given the assumed schedules, even though the government makes no change in its tax and expenditure schedules.

In contrast to this change in revenues, the full-employment budget asks how large would revenues and expenditures be at full employment even though, in fact, income is not at this level. The middle row shows that there would be a surplus of $200 billion at full employment. This amount therefore appears as the full-employment budget results for all income levels in the final column. Because actual income and that assumed at full employment differ, the real and full-employment budget surpluses, as shown in the last two columns, are not the same. Comparing the final two columns, note that if income were $1,350 billion and $250 billion below full employment, the surplus would be $62 billion (200–138) less than at full employment.

Information similar to that of the table is contained in Figure 11.3. The slanted colored line shows the level of government deficit or surplus at each

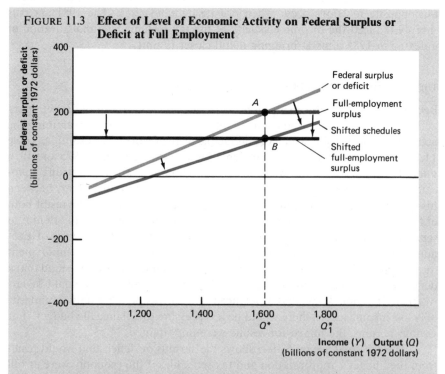

FIGURE 11.3   **Effect of Level of Economic Activity on Federal Surplus or Deficit at Full Employment**

The flat lines show that the full-employment surplus is independent of the actual level of income. Expected revenues and expenditures at a point of full employment determine the amount of the full-employment surplus which is the same at all income levels. Actual surpluses vary with income and output in accordance with the slope of the tax function. Legislation reducing taxes or raising spending shifts the expected surplus at each income as well as the full-employment surplus, illustrated by the darker lines at point B.

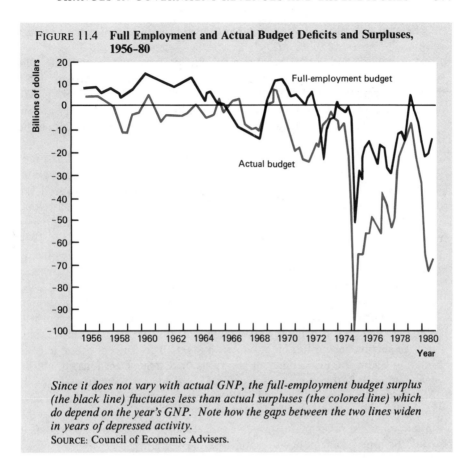

FIGURE 11.4   **Full Employment and Actual Budget Deficits and Surpluses, 1956–80**

Since it does not vary with actual GNP, the full-employment budget surplus (the black line) fluctuates less than actual surpluses (the colored line) which do depend on the year's GNP. Note how the gaps between the two lines widen in years of depressed activity.
SOURCE: Council of Economic Advisers.

level of income, based on the assumed budget function of the numerical example. Surpluses grow steadily as real income and output go up. In contrast, the flat line shows the surplus of the full-employment budget. Full employment (Q^*) is at $1,600 billion. At that level the budget would show a surplus of $200 billion (point *A*). This is the full-employment budget surplus. This same amount is shown at each income level. The difference between the two lines reveals the effect of income on the government budget. When demand is higher than potential output (Q^*), the actual budget will show a larger surplus than the full-employment one. To the left of the line of potential output, the opposite occurs. A reduction in taxes or higher spending appropriations would increase the expected deficit or reduce the surplus at each income level and also results in a new estimate of the full-employment surplus, as shown by the darker lines and point *B*. How this works in practice is shown in Figure 11.4, which gives both the actual budget surplus or deficit and the full-employment surplus or deficit for each quarter from 1973 to 1980. Note the increase in the full-employment surplus in 1974. Did this help to cause the recession of 1975 and the resulting record actual deficit?

Several difficulties are encountered in using the full-employment budget concept:

1. Many voters (and many congressmen) find it hard to understand. The original budget for 1981 showed a large full-employment surplus and a small projected actual deficit arising from a recession. Yet, even though the government was proposing to reduce demand through discretionary action, the public was deemed to want a still tighter policy in order to move the actual budget into surplus.

2. The full-employment budget depends for its accuracy on correct assumptions about the level of potential output at which it is measured. Changes in estimates of what output would be at full employment have caused the estimated full-employment surplus to differ from that based on the original estimates by as much as $25 billion. For example, in 1976 the *Economic Report of the President* estimated that the full-employment surplus in 1974 was $25.4 billion. The 1979 report estimated it at $2.6 billion, while outside observers found a full-employment deficit of over $15 billion.

3. More troublesome, some observers seem to assume that a proper fiscal policy requires the full-employment budget to be in balance, even though they recognize that if income is below full potential, the actual budget will show a deficit. But to achieve full employment without inflation may require a large surplus in the full-employment budget. The concept alone tells us nothing about the desirability of a surplus or deficit. Decisions should be made in terms of the economy's aggregate demand and aggregate supply. If private demands are high, a full-employment surplus and government saving may be best. A mere balance in the full-employment budget may be inflationary. In other periods, such as the 1930s, a full-employment deficit could be a necessary policy to achieve full potential.

THE MAGNITUDES OF INDUCED CHANGES IN REVENUES

The major impacts of many of today's spending and tax decisions fall, not on this year's or even next year's budget, but on budgets far into the future. In an effort to minimize undesirable future effects, the administration and the Congressional Budget Office (CBO) try to project the effects of current laws at least five years into the future.

To show how large the induced effects in the budget can be and also to show how they change as a result of the government's discretionary action, we can compare estimates of potential growth in federal government revenues and expenditures. Figure 11.5 displays estimates made in late 1977 by the CBO of what revenues and outlays would have been *if* the laws in effect in 1978 had not been revised and *if* real and current-dollar incomes and unemployment had followed the projections. It should be understood that these estimates are not expected to resemble actual results. They form a baseline against which to measure proposed legislative action. They show how much revenues and spending would amount to in future years under the policies in effect at the time the estimates are made, assuming that the economy attains a full-employment

FIGURE 11.5   **Growth of Government Expenditures and Revenues as a Result of Growth in the GNP**

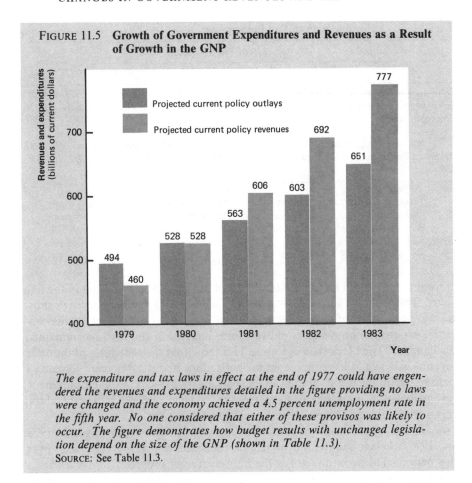

The expenditure and tax laws in effect at the end of 1977 could have engendered the revenues and expenditures detailed in the figure providing no laws were changed and the economy achieved a 4.5 percent unemployment rate in the fifth year. No one considered that either of these provisos was likely to occur. The figure demonstrates how budget results with unchanged legislation depend on the size of the GNP (shown in Table 11.3).
SOURCE: See Table 11.3.

equilibrium. Contrary to the assumptions, policies are expected to be changed, while actual forecasts may indicate that full-employment will not be reached.

Actual results will differ because (1) new laws will be passed; discretionary action will cause outlays and revenues to diverge from those prevailing when the estimates were made; and (2) the projections of the economy will not be exact. The actual level of income and unemployment will cause revenues and outlays to differ from those which would have occurred under the estimated conditions. Nevertheless, such estimates clearly demonstrate how significant are income-induced movements. Under the procedures on which the figure is based, the laws are assumed to be frozen. All movements result either from income changes or from existing laws; in other words, they are induced.

The projections of government revenues and expenditures shown in the bars in Figure 11.5 are based on the movements in the economy shown in Table 11.3. They assume that the GNP would have to rise at the rate of about 10.5 percent a year to reach full employment. More than half of this increase would come from inflationary price hikes. According to the projections, GNP in

TABLE 11.3   **A Possible Path to Full Employment**

	Fiscal years				
	1979	1980	1981	1982	1983
GNP in billions of current dollars	2,274	2,519	2,783	3,079	3,387
GNP in billions of 1972 dollars	1,451	1,520	1,593	1,670	1,736
Unemployment	6.3%	5.8%	5.3%	4.8%	4.5%

SOURCE: Congressional Budget Office, *Five-Year Budget Projections Fiscal 1979–1983, Technical Background* (U.S. Government Printing Office, January 1978), pp. 125, 132, 133, 135, 139.

To estimate future revenues and expenditures, one must project the GNP in current and constant dollars and unemployment. In the table, the first two years' data are based on actual forecasts. The last three trace one possible path toward full employment. These estimates are the basis for the budget projections in Figure 11.5 and Table 11.4.

current dollars could have risen from $2,274 billion to $3,337 billion in the five years. This is shown across the top row of Table 11.3. The following rows show related projections of growth in output and unemployment. Under this projected expansion, how fast would revenues increase if the tax laws remained unchanged? The black bars in Figure 11.5 show that the schedules of the 1978 revenue acts would have increased tax collections about 1.4 percent for each 1 percent rise in the GNP. If the GNP expanded 49 percent to full employment, revenues would jump nearly 69 percent, to a level of $777 billion. Federal revenues would be 22.9 percent of projected GNP.

Two separate factors in the tax system cause such a rapid surge. In 1972 and 1977, the law was changed to increase scheduled social security taxes over this period. The second factor is the high degree of progressivity (taxes are a greater percentage of higher incomes) in the individual income-tax schedule. Both types of taxes automatically work to swell revenues. They are stabilizing forces which tend to hold down aggregate demand.

In contrast to the rapid growth in revenues, existing programs called for a slower growth in expenditures. Projected expenditures would reach $651 billion, a rate of increase half that of tax collections. Without policy changes, spending would have grown at .65 percent for each 1 percent increase in the GNP. The projections include no new programs or expansions of existing ones. Why, then, would expenditures rise? Most of the increase would merely offset inflation. The projections assume that government salaries, pensions, social security payments, and purchases of goods and services would all move up with the cost of living. In addition, population growth would boost expenditures for items such as social security and medicare.

FISCAL DRAG

Was it likely that a rapid increase in the federal government surplus, as pictured in Figure 11.5, would occur? No such surpluses have developed in the past.

Why not? Two constraints, one political and one economic, seem to be at work. Politically, any sizable surplus generates strong pressures to cut taxes and increase spending. Every predicted surplus generates political forces which alter the policies underlying the automatic surplus. The projections assuming no discretionary change do not hold in practice.

The economic arguments against such surpluses may be even stronger. If the government revenue function led to a large surplus, equilibrium income would be less than potential. Government savings are leakages from the circular flow. By restricting the growth of the GNP, such leakages could make the enhanced tax collections and surpluses impossible. The process whereby leakages from the income stream through government revenues increase faster than outlays is called *fiscal drag.*

Figure 11.6 illustrates the problem of fiscal drag. The initial column for

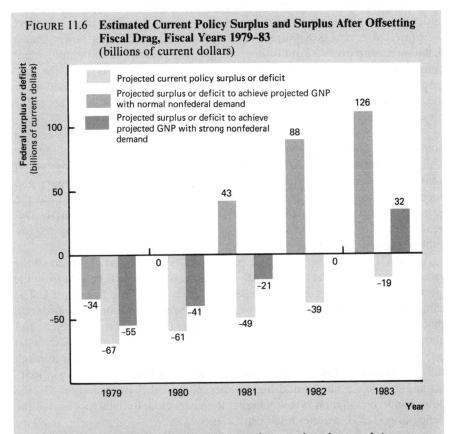

FIGURE 11.6   **Estimated Current Policy Surplus and Surplus After Offsetting Fiscal Drag, Fiscal Years 1979–83**
(billions of current dollars)

The amount of fiscal drag in the 1977 expenditure and tax laws made impossible the achievement of the surpluses shown in the first columns for each year. For income to grow as indicated in Table 11.3, legislation would have to reduce the fiscal drag. The second and third columns assume such action. With strong private demand, full employment would be reached with larger government surpluses—the third column—than if private demand were weak.
SOURCE: See Table 11.3.

each year shows projected deficits or surpluses, as calculated from the data presented in Figure 11.5. Note how rapidly the surpluses grow. The next two columns answer the question: What budget levels would be necessary to fill the gap between aggregate demand and potential output? The columns depict budget amounts necessary to achieve full potential. They differ only in their assumptions as to private demand. The difference between the first column and either the second or third is a measure of fiscal drag. If the government retained its initial tax and spending schedules, income would never in fact rise to the full-employment level. To offset fiscal drag and to match aggregate demand to potential, the government must alter current policies and programs. If the projections underlying the figure were correct, to achieve the required surpluses or deficits, the government would have to lower taxes or raise expenditures compared to the current policies underlying the first column.

Note that fiscal drag creates a catch-22 situation. The budget projected under present policies may be economically impossible. The effort to collect the projected revenues withdraws so much private purchasing power that a deflationary gap opens. Equilibrium income drops below the full-employment path. GNP is not high enough to generate the revenues. To reach the full-employment level by 1983, either expenditures would have to be stepped up or the tax schedule shifted down. Neither action nor inaction can bring about the projected surpluses.

The differences between the second and third columns bring out a related point. The higher the private sector's desire to spend, the smaller is the gap which the government must close. Note how this shows up in the estimate. If nonfederal demand is strong, an inflationary rather than a deflationary gap opens up. The government would have to run a sizable surplus to hold the economy's desire to spend within the noninflationary output potential. Depending on the demands of the other sectors, good fiscal policies may require either deficits or surpluses.

Table 11.4 presents the actual budget results for the first two years of the estimates, to see how they compared. (Readers can fill in further data from the latest *Economic Report of the President* or from *Economic Indicators*.) The actual figures for fiscal 1979 are surprisingly close to the estimates, considering that the estimates were made almost a year before the start of the fiscal year and almost two years before it ended. The data for fiscal 1980 are more nearly what one might expect. While the estimates were based on a path needed to reach full employment in 1983, the economy actually experienced a recession in 1980, leading to a lower output and higher unemployment than projected. On the other hand, the inflation rate was higher than expected. Both factors caused the deficit to go far above the initial estimates.

AUTOMATIC CHANGES IN INCOME AND A REQUIRED BALANCED BUDGET

Because government revenues and outlays depend on the size of the GNP,

TABLE 11.4   **Comparison of 1977 Congressional Budget Office (CBO) Projection to Actual**

(fiscal years)

	1979		1980	
	Estimated	*Actual*	*Estimated*	*Actual*
GNP current dollars	2,274	2,307	2,519	2,567
GNP 1972 dollars	1,451	1,428	1,520	1,482
Unemployment	6.3%	5.8%	5.8%	6.8%
Outlays dollars	494	494	528	580
Revenues dollars	460	466	528	520
Deficit dollars	− 34	− 28	0	− 60

(All dollar outlays are in billions.)

SOURCE: Congressional Budget Office, *Five-Year Budget Projections Fiscal 1979–83, Technical Background* (U.S. Government Printing Office, January 1978), Tables 50 and A.1, and *Economic Report of the President,* 1981.

The first and third columns report the CBO's 1977 estimates; the second and fourth columns give actual results. Inflation, and therefore current-dollar expenditures, rose faster than projected. A shortfall in output also tended to widen the deficit in 1980.

estimates of the deficit or surplus under a given set of appropriations and tax laws can vary widely. In the debate over the desirability of a balanced budget, one issue of concern is whose estimates should be used in determining whether the proposed budget is balanced or not, and what to do if forecasts turn out to be wrong.

A recent example of this difficulty arose in the discussions of the 1980 budget in the midst of the debate over a constitutional amendment to require that the budget be balanced. In its initial proposal for the 1980 fiscal year budget, the administration projected a deficit of $29 billion. The Congressional Budget Office, analyzing the same proposals, disagreed. They announced that in their view, enacting the proposed budget would result in a deficit of $40 billion.

What caused the difference in the projected budget deficits? The two estimates differed only because they did not agree on the future course of the economy, although they did seem to agree on how the economy affects the government's budget. The CBO was more pessimistic than the administration; it estimated that a decrease in demand from fiscal policy and the drop in the money supply would raise unemployment. The rate of inflation would fall from its near record levels, but only slightly. Their estimates of the tax and transfer functions were close. According to the CBO, in 1980 a 1 percent rise in unemployment would increase the government's deficit by $20 billion a year. A step-up in the rate of inflation of 1 percent would reduce the deficit by $3 billion a year.

The CBO projection of unemployment for fiscal 1980 was .7 percent above that of the administration, and their assumed inflation rate was .8 percent higher. Application of the conflicting CBO and administration forecasts to the same basic revenue schedules resulted in sizable differences in estimates of how large the deficit would be. An unemployment rate higher by .7 percent (that of the CBO) causes a reduction in revenues of $14 billion below the administration's projections. Inflation higher by .8 percent would raise revenues by $2.4 billion. If the CBO were correct in both projections, the deficit would be $11.6 billion above that estimated by the Carter administration. (Chapter 19 details a similar divergence in estimates between the CBO and the Reagan administration.)

In this and similar cases, explaining the difference is often not difficult; more critical is determining which estimate is more nearly correct. In fact, as shown by Table 11.4, neither turned out to be correct. The level of output was lower and the level of unemployment was higher than either estimate had predicted. As a result, the income-induced change in revenues and transfer payments caused a still larger deficit than predicted. Despite the fact that actions were taken to reduce both outlays and the deficit, the path of the economy led to an increase in the deficit. The point of the example, however, is not which was the better projection or that both were wrong, but rather that whether or not a budget is balanced depends on income-induced effects in addition to discretionary action. Legislation passed in a given year with respect to taxes and appropriations is only a starting point for next year's budget. Whether the government actually runs a surplus or a deficit also depends on aggregate demand and the level of the GNP.

Financing the Deficit and Creation of Excess Money

The government alters spending through its purchases, transfers, and taxes. It exerts further influences on demand through changes in fiscal policy which increase or decrease the size of the public debt. When the government runs a deficit, the shortfall must be financed. A deficit is not something that can be spent; funds must be raised to cover all payments. If expenditures exceed revenues, money to cover the difference must be borrowed. The public debt must be increased. A *government budget constraint* requires that all expenditures be financed by taxing or borrowing. It is similar to that which applies to individuals.

Major differences exist, however, between a government's and an individual's budget constraint. If you are broke and try to borrow, you may not find a friendly or even an unfriendly lender. If governments cannot sell their debt to others, they can sell it to their central banks. The banks can always get enough money to purchase the debt by expanding the monetary base, through issuing either more bank reserves or more currency. Whether increases in the debt do or do not influence the money supply is a key issue of fiscal policy. In most countries, the issuing of currency and the actions of the central banks are controlled directly by the government. In the United States, the Federal Reserve has been granted a great deal of independence, primarily so that changes in the money supply will not be influenced by Treasury debt sales. Some observers believe, however, that at times the separation has not been complete enough.

A second key concern is whether the size of the debt causes undesired changes in demand. When it issues bonds, the government raises its liabilities to the public. The size of the public debt is greater. What will be the effect of the larger public debt on spending? The mere existence of the debt might cause people to spend more and save less. In addition, the debt requires interest payments—a not inconsequential budget item. A larger debt means higher taxes, which affect decisions to work and save.

SELLING BONDS TO THE FEDERAL RESERVE

Throughout the world, a favorite way for governments to finance their deficits is to have the central bank pick up the tab. It seems easy; the government can lower its future interest payments and taxes by increasing the monetary base, which pays no interest. In many countries, governments simply send the bonds over to the central bank and get back currency and bank deposits. Direct transactions of this type are, except in emergencies, illegal in the United States. If the Treasury wants to obtain interest-free loans, it has to convince the Federal Open Market Committee to buy the bonds in the market. The Fed then collects interest from the Treasury with one hand but transfers most of it back to the Treasury, as a form of franchise tax, with the other.

The criteria used by the Federal Reserve in deciding whether or not to buy government bonds are closely related to the issues of crowding out and accommodative monetary policy, discussed earlier. They are illustrated in Figure 11.7. Suppose the economy is in equilibrium at point A and then an increase in defense expenditures (G) causes a shift to curve IS_2. Assume that the government does not raise taxes to fund the added spending, but rather pays for some of it through the higher income-induced tax collections and the remainder by selling bonds. The new equilibrium of income and output is at point B, where IS_2 intersects the existing curve LM_1.

At point B, the additional government spending has crowded out some expansion of private investment and consumption. The actual multiplier falls short of the simple multiplier because of the interest effect ($-br$) on private spending. The sale of government bonds and a higher transactions demand for money raise interest rates. Fewer private bonds will be sold. Some investment will be delayed because it will not be profitable at the higher interest rates or because financing is harder to get. To the degree that the desire to save rises with interest rates, consumption is reduced.

FIGURE 11.7   **Monetary Policy's Responses to Increases in the Public Debt**

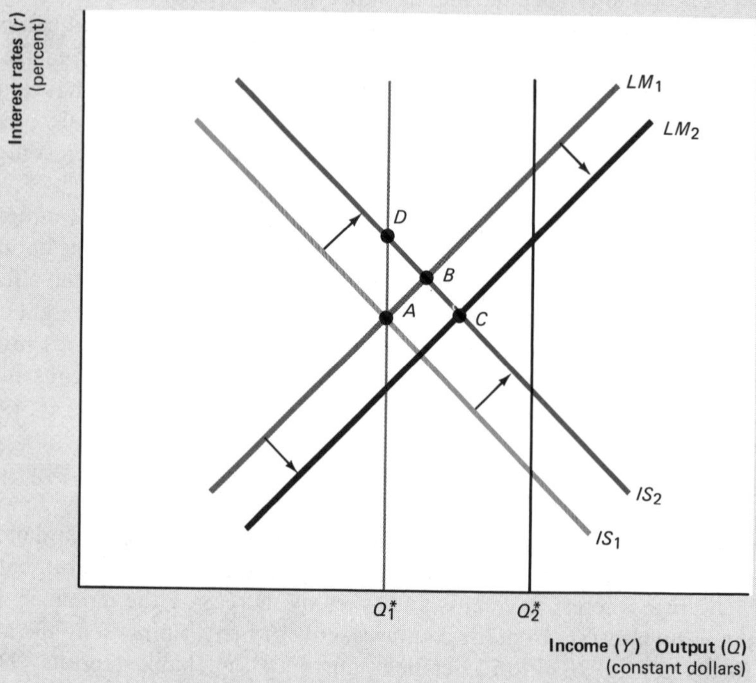

Increased fiscal expenditures shift the IS curve, increasing the deficit. If the Federal Reserve does not change the money supply growth rate, higher inter-est rates will reduce investment and consumption growth. The Fed can ac-commodate the increase through a shift to LM₂. What it does should depend on whether the gap between the new equilibrium output level and that at full employment is positive or negative.

In such a situation, what is a logical policy for the Federal Reserve? The answer depends on the relationship of the new equilibrium (B) to the full-employment level of output. If the economy is underemployed, with the full-employment level at Q^*_2, the nation's goals and related monetary targets could call for a continued expansion of the money supply. The Fed would buy some additional bonds, expanding the monetary base and thereby shifting the econ-omy to curve LM_2. With such a policy, interest rates would not rise, since an expansion of money would fully accommodate the increase in government spending, bringing about a new equilibrium at point C. Such action accompa-nied the Kennedy-Johnson tax reduction act of 1964, the objective of which was to expand demand in order to raise the economy to the full-employment level.

In contrast, if the full-employment level was Q^*_1, all of the additional demand created by the shift in the IS curve would be inflationary. The Fed might decide to reduce the rate of growth in the money supply by buying fewer bonds. The *LM* curve would shift to the left, perhaps reaching equilibrium at point *D*. Such a policy was followed in 1966 in response to the initial Vietnam War spending. When the economy is already at full employment, either potential output must expand or private spending will be crowded out to make way for the increased government demand. Most economists assume that a policy to reduce demand by monetary or fiscal actions is preferable to crowding out through an inflationary price increase. Policy requires either a more restrictive monetary stance or, alternatively, taxes could be raised, shifting the *IS* curve back to its original position and to the equilibrium at *A*. While the higher-tax–lower-interest-rate policy with equilibrium at *A* has advantages over the lower-tax–higher-interest-rate equilibrium at *D*, particularly for the Federal Reserve, it has been harder to achieve politically.

HAVE DEFICITS INCREASED THE MONETARY BASE?

It is easy to see the problems that arise when the monetary base is expanded to cover deficits. The government creates high-powered money, which becomes the base for a multiple expansion. This added money raises spending. When demand grows faster than production, prices rise. Too many dollars are chasing too few goods. This process underlies most of the world's inflations. Hyperinflations, like those in Germany, Hungary, and China, typically resulted from expansion of the monetary base at an accelerating pace to pay for wars or postwar reparations.

Some economists believe that this situation is at the root of the United State's inflation as well. If they are asked how deficits could raise prices in the face of unemployment and excess production capacity, as was the case in the 1970s, they answer, "because the Fed buys too many bonds and thereby expands the money supply." In the opinion of those who believe that the government cannot increase demand because it crowds out private demand, the expansion of the monetary base is the chief explanation of inflation.

Even though the Fed cannot buy bonds directly from the Treasury, does it in fact step up its market purchases when the Treasury is selling? Treasury sales raise interest rates. Will this cause the Fed to buy some of these bonds with high-powered money? During World War II and at some other periods, the Federal Reserve did in fact react by increasing open-market operations. Some of the deficits were funded through high-powered money. The Federal Reserve and the Treasury engaged in a running debate over this issue between the end of World War II and 1951. The debate was ended by the "Accord of March 1951," in which it was agreed that monetary policy would no longer concern itself primarily with the financing costs of the debt. The dangers of allowing decisions with respect to the proper supply of money to be dominated by the desire of the government to pay low interest rates is now well recognized.

Since the 1951 accord, the Federal Reserve has not been constrained by considerations of interest costs to the Teasury. Monetary policy has been conducted primarily with a concern for how changes in the money supply are expected to affect aggregate demand. While a rise in the debt, because it increases demand in financial markets, does influence Fed action, the criteria for decisions are based on what is good for the economy, not on what it costs the Treasury. It is now recognized that the Treasury can well afford to pay market interest rates.

The data presented in Table 11.5 show changes in the amount of the federal debt held by the Federal Reserve during each five-year period from 1951–80 as well as the cumulative federal deficits (national income basis) and the changes in the level of the GNP over each period. From 1951 to 1970, when deficits were relatively small, the Fed's purchases of government securities exceeded the deficits. The Fed needed to expand the monetary base, and to do so, it bought bonds from the public.

TABLE 11.5   **Relationship of Federal Deficits, Change in GNP, and Federal Reserve Holdings of Federal Debt**
(billions of dollars)

	Increase in Federal Debt at Federal Reserve	Federal Deficit	Δ in GNP
1951–55	4.3	5.9	113
1956–60	3.2	0	107
1961–65	11.9	10.5	105
1966–70	24.7	25.0	302
1971–75	30.6	125.2	557
1976–80	33.0	205.7	1,079

SOURCE: U.S. Treasury; deficit and GNP from National Income and Products Accounts.

The Federal Reserve purchases Federal debt in the open market to increase the monetary base. For 1951–70 the Fed purchased over 100 percent of the deficits. In 1971–80, the Fed purchased 19 percent of the increase in the debt; the actual amount was only slightly above that for the previous five years although the GNP grew nearly three times as fast.

But what about the 1970s, when the deficit exploded? Between 1971 and 1975, deficits totaled $125.2 billion, or 5 times as much as in the previous 5 years. The increase in the GNP almost doubled. The Fed increased its purchases of government securities by one-quarter. The share of Fed purchases of the deficit dropped from over 100 percent in the previous 20 years to about 25 percent. But look at the last 5 years. During the period of large deficits and large changes in the GNP, the Fed expanded its purchases of government bonds only slightly—less by far than the amount of increase in either of the other categories. A comparison of the federal deficits and Federal Reserve credit year by year shows no obvious relationship. In many years, they moved in opposite directions.

The Fed believes that it bends over backward to make certain it does not increase the money supply to fund the Treasury debt. It recognizes that the government can adequately pay for whatever money it needs; it can't go broke.

Critics of the Fed are skeptical, however; they believe that as a result of larger deficits, the Fed has expanded the money supply more than it otherwise would. This debate is related to the question of proper intermediate monetary targets. Until 1980, the Fed based its targets on production and employment as well as on prices. If demand fell below full potential, the Fed tended to increase the real money supply, even if this meant that nominal money was expanding at a rate faster than real output.

Critics feel that the Fed does not determine policy on the basis of the nation's goals, but on an interest-rate target. They assume that if the deficit were not large, the Federal Reserve would not increase the nominal money supply. They feel that the inflationary increases in money are not caused directly by expansion of the debt, but occur because the Federal Reserve decision process is wrong; it reacts improperly to what happens in financial markets when the Treasury borrows. They believe that because Treasury sales of bonds raise interest rates, the Fed in fact does increase the money supply more than necessary in an effort to hold interest rates down. But David Meiselman, one of the earliest proponents of monetarist theories and over the years one of the Fed's severest critics, disagrees. He states: "The evidence is that, from 1960 to 1980, there was no significant relationship between changes in money supply and the national debt."[6]

In a detailed discussion of the total impacts of budget deficits, with particular reference to the money supply, the following conclusions were reached by Herbert Stein, a recognized conservative expert on fiscal and budget policy who was chairman of President Nixon's Council of Economic Advisers and is now a senior fellow of the American Enterprise Institute:

> A stable deficit, even if large, is probably not inflationary, and increases in a deficit, or reductions of a surplus, are probably not inflationary if they come at a time of slack in the economy. However, large increases of a deficit, coming at the wrong time, may be inflationary, largely but perhaps not entirely because of their effect on the money supply. But this effect on the money supply does not seem to be an inevitable consequence of the deficit and might be corrected without eliminating the deficit. Moreover, as is frequently the case, the increasing deficit is an instrument deliberately chosen to bring about an economic expansion that the government, the public, and possibly the monetary authority all want, preventing the deficit will not prevent the economic expansion and its inflationary consequences.[7]

The Influence of the Public Debt on Spending and Saving

Another independent influence of the public debt is through its impact on decisions to spend and save. Since Franklin Roosevelt's New Deal, most

---

6. D. I. Meiselman, *The Wall Street Journal,* July 21, 1981, p. 26.
7. H. Stein, "Balancing the Budget," in *Contemporary Economic Problems,* W. Fellner, Project Director (Washington: American Enterprise Institute, 1979), p. 192.

changes in fiscal policies have been accompanied by heated arguments over the effects of the existence of a larger debt on aggregate demand. New Deal spending on public works was attacked on the grounds that the debt increases required to finance them would so undermine confidence that private spending would decline by more than government expenditures rose. There would be a reverse multiplier. Some current new classicists also believe that the public debt has a contractionary impact. The debt is a burden that requires higher taxes to meet interest payments. When issued, the debt raises interest rates and lowers private investment and, therefore, future output, while its size reduces confidence and spending.

In contrast, many economists are convinced that the larger the public debt, the higher will be spending. As noted in Appendix 11.1, a sizable component of household and business balance sheets consists of their claims against the government. The existence of the debt increases households' ability—and probably their desires—to spend. In addition, people have been conditioned to assume that a large debt is inflationary, with the result that they spend more and save less. The degree to which a debt is inflationary depends on how people shift their spending desires in response to its creation and on whether or not it leads the Federal Reserve to create more money.

THE DEBT AND SAVING

Does a large public debt reduce private saving and increase spending? Although reasoning in different ways, most economists would probably agree at the present time that it does. At other times the conclusion might be the opposite. The points at issue are pictured in Figure 11.8. The line IS_1 is that which would apply if only a small debt existed. Why should desires to spend move merely because the public debt has grown? Specifically, the privately held U.S. government debt rose from $217 billion in 1970 to $616 billion in 1980. (State and local debt added over $110 billion more.) Is this increase a significant factor explaining a lower househould saving rate? Did it result in the replacement of IS_1 by IS_2? Those who believe that, instead, it caused a shift to IS_3 must explain the reduction in saving which occurred as either temporary or due to other causes.

The previous chapter showed that consumption rises with wealth. If people have more assets, they consume more. Do people act wealthier when the public debt grows? The nation's balance sheet in Appendix 11.1 shows that $820 billion of the net worth of households consists of claims against the government, represented by the monetary base or securities. (Most claims are not direct; they are in the form of bank deposits, insurance, or equities backed by corporate holding of the debt.) Believers in rational expectations would answer that these holdings should not influence spending; rational people would recognize that the debt will cause higher future taxes. They would set up a liability (explicitly or implicitly) on their balance sheets equal to the present value of the future taxes necessary to meet payments on the debt. As a result, they would

FIGURE 11.8   **The Effect of the Debt on the *IS* Curve**

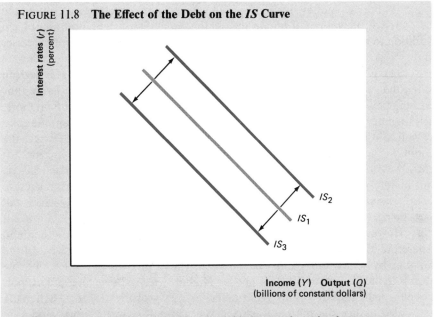

The existence of a larger public debt is likely to reduce the desire to save, leading to IS₂ in contrast to IS₁ with higher demand at each real interest rate. However, if the larger debt reduced confidence and increased desires for more saving, a shift down to the left, such as to IS₃, would be possible.

reduce their estimates of their net worth by an amount equal to the debt and would feel no wealthier. Few people seem to be that rational. Most probably look at their present assets and their rate of growth and increase their spending when they expand as the result of the creation of more public debt.

How the debt influences confidence and expectations is still more difficult to evaluate. Twenty years ago most economists probably believed that the debt either had a neutral or a slightly contractionary overall effect. Now, they might guess that so many families have been sensitized to believe that a positive relationship exists between debt and inflation that they tend to spend now and save less in order to beat inflation.

PRIVATE AND PUBLIC DEBT

Private and public debts are basically different. If you owe money to someone, you must sacrifice income or resources to meet payments of interest and principal. Incurring this debt may have improved your situation by enabling you to own a house or a car or to finish college, but it still hurts to meet the payments. Your bank or other lender is likely to insist that you pay off most of your debt before they will lend you more. Even though when you (or General Motors or

AT & T) borrow money it is to improve your economic well-being, you would be better off if you could obtain the same goods without going into debt. In addition to requiring repayment, debts carry a threat of bankruptcy or foreclosure.

The government's situation is quite different. No resources are used up when the government makes debt payments. It taxes Mary to pay Paul. Purchasing power is transferred, not consumed. Mary can buy less and Paul more, but together their ability to spend is unchanged. Any loss arises from the costs of collecting the taxes and the effect on Mary's incentives. Otherwise, the country is not worse off. Furthermore, the government cannot go bankrupt. It can always create money to pay off its debts. Usually it does not pay off its debt, but merely rolls it over. Few people want to raise taxes enough to retire the debt, realizing the bad effects that higher taxes would have on incentives and well-being.

However, it is necessary to use tax money to pay the interest on the debt. Therefore, one rough measure of the bad effects of the debt is its size and the amount by which taxes must be raised to make interest payments. People worry about the size of the debt per se. Higher taxes reduce work and output. People spend time trying to avoid taxes, or they work less hard. Higher tax rates also reduce the marginal efficiency of capital, raise the price of capital services, and reduce investment.

Between 1945 and 1970, the amount of federal debt in private hands fell, and then returned to its previous level. Over those 25 years, there was no increase in the privately held debt. Snce the economy grew, the ratio of the debt to the GNP fell from over 100 percent to about 20 percent. The 1970s saw a sharp reversal of this trend. In that decade, the amount of debt in private hands rose nearly 200 percent, or somewhat faster than the GNP grew. Perhaps more important, interest payments by the federal government rose steeply. As a share of the GNP, such payments in 1980 were higher than in either 1945 or 1970. While the size of the debt was probably less of a problem than it was at the end of World War II, the large deficits of the 1970s meant that progress in easing the burden had reversed.

THE COST TO FUTURE GENERATIONS

Everyone in college now should be concerned about whether a larger debt means a greater burden for them in the future. Will future generations have to work harder because the country has gone into debt? The question cannot be answered with certainty, but it is probable that the consequences of continuing to expand the debt at a rate comparable to that of the 1970s will not be serious. (The following analysis is concerned only with the size of the debt, not with any excess of demand engendered by the spending creating the deficit.)

Some have claimed that since the debt is both owed and owned, total wealth does not change. We owe the debt to each other. While income is transferred, the total is unchanged. This argument neglects the possible costs of the transfers. It also ignores the fact that about 20 percent of the debt is in foreign hands. If debt is held abroad, future generations will have to export goods and services to pay for it, thus cutting into the share of current production available at home. This seems to be a clear burden for the future. Why, then, do so many countries finance current expenditures by borrowing abroad? Because if the loan increases productive capacity, coming generations will have more income available domestically even after making interest and principal payments abroad. The percentage of output available for home use will be less, but it will come out of a larger pie. Similar actions form the basis for most creation of private debt. U.S. Steel finds that it pays to borrow even though, because of interest, future payments will far exceed the amount borrowed Much of our foreign debt merely reflects transfers of government bonds by private multinational companies and individuals to purchase real assets abroad. This burden of the debt is paid for by the earnings on the private assets.

Excluding the problems of taxes and transfers and the foreign debt, the principal way in which future generations can suffer is if they inherit a smaller capital stock because of the government spending. During wars, resources are transferred to the defense effort. Consumption and investment are curtailed. When the war ends the country is poorer. Because its capital stock is diminished, future output will be lower. To rebuild its wealth, the country will have to save a higher percentage of its reduced income. People will be worse off.

What about a peacetime deficit? Will it also leave the country poorer? If unused resources exist, a larger deficit can raise real output directly and indirectly through the multiplier. The deficit may augment physical and human capital; the country may be more prosperous, both because the higher government spending increases jobs and income and because the end of the period is marked by greater wealth. Shifts in the aggregate supply curve to the right will allow higher output and lower costs in the future. But the opposite is also possible. If the government makes inefficient use of resources that would have been more productive elsewhere, output may be reduced. Higher interest rates mean less investment. The net effect of a greater governmental use of resources and higher interest rates may be a diminished capital stock. Because future production will be reduced, future generations will be less well off.

No Simple Answers

Government spending, taxing, and debt financing are complex. To the degree that the government is wasting money, the national well-being is enhanced every time government efficiency is improved. To the degree that the government furnishes services that the private economy could better provide or ones whose costs outstrip their benefits, the country will be better off if they are abolished or reduced. In addition to questions of waste, there are numerous issues of income distribution. The larger the government budget, the higher are taxes; the more possible it is for the tax system to be unfair, and the more likely it is to alter economic activities. (These issues will be taken up in Part 5, under the topic of supply-side economics.)

Except to the degree that they limit the size of governmental expenditures, rules mandating a balanced budget receive far less support. As the prior discussion shows, government decisions alone do not determine whether the budget is in balance in any year. Tax collections and transfer payments depend on the spending desires of other decision units as well as on the government's budget. The size of the deficit varies with the marginal amounts of taxes and transfers induced by changes in income levels.

Economists also stress that a budget surplus may be useful or harmful, depending on the actions of the other sectors. If private demand plus that of the government exceeds potential output, the economy will be better off if the budget is in surplus. If aggregate demand is too low, a deficit may be best. The recognition that the good or harm of deficits is related to what is happening in the economy and is not an absolute good or evil leads to the concept of *functional finance.* This term encompasses the idea that the government's budget should be set so as to promote the most desirable level of aggregate demand, whether this requires a series of deficits or surpluses or a combination of both. In formulating the budget, however, it must be recognized that government expenditures and taxes exert other complex influences on incentives, investment, and income distribution which may far surpass the effects of deficits.

In determining the influence of the budget on demand, one cannot look only at the surface effects. Deficits must be financed, and surpluses mean that the government has funds which can be used to repay debt and probably increase the total level of saving in the economy. In contrast, a large public debt may reduce saving. Because these relationships are complex and because they vary from period to period, depending on private and foreign demand and production, any simple rules, such as balancing the budget every year, are likely to prove unworkable. To quote again from Herbert Stein's article on a balanced budget:

> Large and untimely increases in the deficit complicate the problem of avoiding inflation.
> Other things equal, productivity will grow more rapidly if the budget is in surplus on the average than if the budget is in deficit on the average.
> Expenditures will rise less rapidly if the decision to spend requires a decision to tax, just as they would rise less rapidly if the decision to spend entailed any other penalty for the decision maker, but the spending-taxing link does not assure optimum expenditure decisions or even necessarily lean in that direction.
> Even if faster growth of the economy and slower growth of expenditures are both accepted as desirable—and these are matters of preference— these conclusions do not require annual balancing of the budget.[8]

8. H. Stein, "Balancing the Budget," in *Contemporary Economic Problems,* W. Fellner, Project Director (Washington: American Enterprise Institute, 1979), p. 192.

Summary

1. The size of government taxes and expenditures has become a key political and economic issue. Government expenditures and taxes can decrease output and redistribute income. Too much demand arising from the government can cause prices to rise. However, the size of government demand in the last half of the 1970s does not provide a good explanation for continued inflation.

2. The greatest disagreements are over whether deficits and increases in the debt raise or lower aggregate demand. Some economists have emphasized the deflationary psychological impacts of a larger deficit and debt; others claim that such effects are more likely to be inflationary. The direct effect of the government's sales of debt is to raise interest rates, thereby lowering private investment and exerting an uncertain effect on the desire to save. In contrast, the wealth and portfolio effects of a larger debt increase private demand.

3. Movements of government spending and taxing play a significant role in determining the equilibrium level of aggregate demand. The government's impacts on aggregate demand may follow from autonomous decisions to shift its expenditures and tax schedules, but they may also follow from induced variations in revenues and expenditures as income changes.

4. Whether or not a budget is balanced depends both on autonomous changes in expenditure and tax schedules and on the induced impacts from income movements. One cannot estimate what a government surplus or deficit will be without a forecast of the nominal GNP.

5. The effects of induced revenues are labeled automatic stabilizers or fiscal drag. Because tax revenues rise with income, exerting an automatic damper, equilibrium desires to spend shift less rapidly than might be anticipated from autonomous and induced changes in investment and consumption.

6. The full-employment budget estimates what the deficit or surplus would be from existing tax and spending schedules if the economy were at full potential output. Actual deficits or surpluses depend on actual income.

7. Any shift in fiscal policy, except for equal changes in outlays and revenues, must change deficits or surpluses and the public debt. For this reason, the impacts of debt movements must be consolidated with the expected effects of naïve fiscal policy.

8. The Federal Reserve can fund the debt by purchasing government bonds and enlarging the monetary base. Any expansion of the base beyond that needed to match a desired growth in aggregate demand will lead to an unwanted increase in spending and to price rises. The Fed states that its policy is based on what it considers to be the best level of aggregate demand. Its actons are not influenced by larger or smaller deficits. Its critics disagree.

9. Government expenditures can crowd out private spending by raising prices or absorbing savings while reducing private investment through higher interest rates. The amount of crowding out depends on the shape of the *IS* and *LM* curves and on whether they shift as a result of larger portfolios.

10. A larger public debt may influence demand in a variety of ways. The larger debt does not require a reduction in investment and consumption to pay for it. Payments on the debt are transfers made with funds raised through taxing or additional borrowing. The debt can be a burden if it requires payments to foreigners or if the need to collect taxes lowers incentives or reduces aggregate demand below the optimum.

11. Future income and output will be lower if the capital stock was reduced when the deficits were incurred. On the other hand, expenditures funded by the debt could also lead to an increase in investment and capital. The ability to run a deficit probably increases government expenditures to some extent and defers taxes.

Questions for Discussion and Review

1. What arguments would you employ in favor of a proposed constitutional amendment requiring that the federal budget be balanced every year? What arguments would you use to oppose such an amendment?

2. Describe functional finance and the logic behind it. Would you favor it as a national policy? Why, or why not?

3. Examine Table 11.1 and Figure 11.1. If they were your only source of information, would you find it easy or hard to explain the drive for a cut in government expenditures? What would your conclusions be?

4. Figure 11.2 gives abbreviated indications of some of the relationships between fiscal and monetary policy and demand. Explain in your own words the influences you would expect from the factors not included within the inner box.

5. Explain how the full-employment budget works and what its relationship is to automatic stabilizers and fiscal drag.

6. The government's budget function consists of
$$T = \overline{T} + t(Y) \quad \text{where } \overline{T} = \$200 \text{ billion}$$
and
$$t = .2$$
$$G = \overline{G} \quad \text{where} \quad \overline{G} = \$750 \text{ billion}$$

(a) If the level of income at full employment is $3,000 billion, what is the full-employment surplus or deficit?

(b) If the level of potential output (full employment) grew to $3,500 billion, what would be the full-employment surplus or deficit?

(c) Given the assumptions of *b*, what would be the effect of reducing the marginal rate of income taxes by 20 percent?

7. Explain why fiscal drag introduces a dilemma into the process of balancing the budget.

8. Look in a current *Survey of Current Business* or the *Economic Report of the President* and compare the projections in Figure 11.6 with what actually occurred. What seem to be the major factors causing discrepancies? The data in Table 11.3 should be part of your explanation.

9. If the Federal Reserve sets its targets completely in terms of a constant growth rate in the money supply, how would the economy's fiscal multipliers be affected?

10. Relate the argument of the influence of the public debt on aggregate demand to the real balance (Pigou) effect discussed in Chapters 8 and 10.

11. Do you think the greatly increased size of the public debt is a burden on future generations?

References

Andersen, L. C., and J. L. Jordan. "Monetary and Fiscal Actions: A Test of their Relative Importance in Economic Stabilization." Federal Reserve Bank of St. Louis, *Review,* November 1968.

Barro, R. J. "Are Government Bonds Net Wealth?." *Journal of Political Economy* (December 1974).

Blinder, A. S., and R. M. Solow. "Analytical Foundations of Fiscal Policy" in *The Economics of Public Finance.* Washington: Brookings Institution, 1974.

Brown, E. C. "Fiscal Policy in the '30s." *American Economic Review* (December 1950).

Musgrave, R., and P. Musgrave. *Public Finance in Theory and Practice,* 3rd edition. New York: McGraw-Hill, 1980.

Stein, H. "Balancing the Budget" in *Contemporary Economic Problems.* Washington: American Enterprise Institute, 1979.

APPENDIX 11.1   Wealth, Net Worth, and Liquidity

One of the critical differences between current and earlier macroeconomic theory is the much greater emphasis now placed on the effects of changing portfolios and wealth. How much wealth households and businesses own has significant impacts on spending and interest rates. Consumption and saving depend on wealth as well as on income. Interest rates are partially determined by movements in wealth and portfolios. Some theories of how money influences spending trace the effect through greater wealth. In addition, spending is influenced by liquidity, the holding of assets in a form readily available and transferable into money at a minimum cost. Much of household wealth is held in the form of liquid claims against financial institutions.

What do we mean by wealth? In its broadest sense, a **nation's wealth** is equal to its store of knowledge, of physical goods, and of net claims against foreigners available to produce or purchase goods and services. However, conceptual and measurement problems are created in trying to measure the impact on spending of human capital, of government capital, and, in a different way, of foreign claims.

Human capital is extremely important in production and investment. But human capital is hard to measure; it does not appear in the GNP accounts or in most compilations of national wealth. Government capital, in forms such as the Tennessee Valley Authority, the highway system, or nuclear aircraft carriers, clearly raises our productive and defense capacities. To expand their public infrastructure or their weapons, countries must curtail private investment and consumption. A country with large stocks of government capital can spend more on private goods. Government goods ought to be included in wealth, but decisions as to what government goods to purchase are not made in the normal market. Government spending is determined by factors other than its impact on production and income. For these and other reasons government investment, though it may form a significant share of total wealth, does not appear in the GNP or in most measures of national wealth. Net claims against foreigners are conceptually far simpler. If a country has a net foreign debt, some output must be used to meet payments on it. In contrast, if Americans own factories and mines abroad, their net profits can be used to increase our standard of living. Net foreign claims are included in a country's wealth, but discussion of them is delayed until Chapter 16. (They are excluded from Table 11.6 merely to simplify its presentation.)

As a result of the various measurement problems, it is common, for statistical convenience rather than theory, to restrict measures of wealth to the market value of all private (nonhuman) economic goods which go into the production of goods and services. This total is closely related to the concept of **private net worth,** or the sum of privately owned assets minus private total liabilities. This sum may not exactly equal private wealth, depending on how claims against the government are treated.

ECONOMIC BALANCE SHEETS

A general picture of the form in which households hold their wealth as well as a measure of how much they hold is presented in Table 11.6. Households hold: physical assets—mainly houses and consumer durables; equities—primarily common stock; and financial claims—concentrated in deposits and insurance and pension rights plus money and minor holdings of financial instruments. Over time, households have sharply decreased the share of their assets held in the form of market instruments; they prefer to save through financial intermediaries, thereby gaining liquidity, flexibility, and a reduction in risk. The liabilities of households consist principally of mortgages plus installment and other consumer debt.

The assets of nonfinancial businesses are principally plant, equipment, and inventories. They possess a small amount of financial assets—merely enough to insure their liquidity. The claims against them are mainly common stock, although they do borrow enough to fund about a third of their assets.

Financial businesses are primarily banks, savings and loan institutions, mutual savings banks, insurance companies, and pension funds plus several other smaller entities. They collect household savings and lend them to the other groups through market and miscellaneous channels, mainly commercial-type loans, bonds and notes, mortgages, and consumer loans.

NET WORTH

The net worth of the economy equals its total assets minus its total liabilities. We can see what net worth consists of when the assets and liabilities of all sectors are summed. Look at the last three columns in Table 11.6. Note that with the exception of three items—physical assets, U.S. government debt, and the monetary base—all assets and liabilities net out. Financial claims change the form in which spending units hold their wealth, but not their net worth. For example, a family might buy three houses. Or, it could use its funds to own one house, a deposit in a bank backed by a mortgage, and an insurance policy backed by a mortgage. In the latter case, the family's net worth consists of the one direct and two indirect claims against the three houses. The net worth of the owners of the other two houses consists only of their equity in the houses, namely, their physical value less any mortgages owed. The existence of inter-mediaries and of deposits and mortgages may make investment in houses and saving easier, but their instruments are not an addition to wealth. The amount owed to some spending units is exactly offset by the amount others own. Financial intermediaries change only the form, not the amount of wealth. This is shown by the column totals. Most of the capital used in financial institutions (their net worth) pays for the physical assets they own. They lend out a small amount of their own capital, but most of their loans depend on their ability to borrow. They alter the form, but not the amount of lending and borrowing. This does, however, alter desires to spend.

For both financial and nonfinancial businesses, net worth is the gap between what they own and what they owe. This is also the equity in them held by households. Households show an equivalent asset—equities. To the extent that businesses do not distribute their profits, whether from normal income or from capital gains and losses, their net worth grows. Simultaneously, households who own the businesses show an increase in the value of their equities. The large share of investment financed by borrowing is reflected by the degree to which the physical assets of businesses exceed their net worth or equity owned by households.

The difference between the assets and liabilities of households is their net worth also. This exactly equals the sum of the final column—the total of all net assets; namely, physical goods, the privately held U.S. government debt, and the monetary base. Households hold some wealth directly and some through their residual ownership of business assets.

TABLE 11.6   **United States Net Wealth and Net Worth in 1979, by Sector**
(billions of dollars)

Item	Households		Nonfinancial businesses		Financial institutions		Total		Net worth
	Assets	Liabilities	Assets	Liabilities	Assets	Liabilities	Assets	Liabilities	
Claims on financial institutions	2,250	—	190	—	120	2,560	2,560	2,560	0
Market and miscellaneous instruments	380	1,380	620	1,690	2,660	590	3,660	3,660	0
Equities	3,610	—	—	3,490	180	300	3,790	3,790	0
Monetary base	50	—	40	—	70	—	160	0	160
Government debt (federal state and local)	250	—	100	—	310	—	660	0	660
Physical assets	3,280	—	4,230	—	110	—	7,620	0	7,620
Total	9,820	1,380	5,180	5,180	3,450	3,450	18,450	10,010	8,440
Net worth	8,440								

Figures are only approximate.
Based on Federal Reserve Flow of Funds Balance Sheets for the United States Economy.

Wealth consists of the physical assets available to produce goods and services. Households own all assets either directly or through their equity and debt claims against corporations. Their ownership of the monetary base and other government debt increases their net worth. How this affects spending depends on the way they treat government capital and liabilities for future taxes.

Net Worth Equals Past Savings

What is the connection between the net worth of households and past investment and saving? Net worth is the present sum of two past flows:

1. Current holdings of physical assets equal all past net investment plus any capital gains or losses, including that in land. Such capital changes are the difference between net investment and the current value of discounted future income from the assets.
2. The cumulative total of all past net government deficits equals the privately held U.S. government debt. This includes that which pays interest and that which does not (the monetary base).

The sum of past investments plus holdings of U.S. government debt exactly equals past accumulations of private savings, including capital gains.

Private domestic nonhuman *net wealth,* in constrast, is the nation's store of private physical goods available to produce goods and services. Note that this definition of wealth differs from the nation's net worth as measured in Table 11.6 because it does not include the amount owed by the government to the private sector as part of wealth.

Some economists believe that private decision makers base their calculations on this net wealth, rather than on private net worth. Their net wealth is less than their net worth by the size of their future liabilities to make payments through taxes for the public debt. Which operational definition—net worth or net wealth—makes most sense in attempting to analyze desires to spend? Do people spend in accordance with their net worth, or do they calculate their net wealth by correcting their net worth to reflect their share of the government debt for which they are liable?[9]

But most analysts reject this concept. In their view, the share of future taxes which a person will pay that is used to meet the interest on the debt is small and uncertain. Even the most rational economic man is not likely to calculate its present value and take it into account when making spending decisions. Money in the bank or in a savings account, which are claims against the public debt, thus is counted as wealth without any correction factor.

9. Note that because government wealth is excluded from Table 11.6, the wealth of households is really larger than indicated. A good deal of government debt went to pay for real capital—such things as aircraft carriers, tanks, highways, and dams. The only part of the public debt that does not represent real wealth is that part which exceeds the value of public capital.

Part 5

Aggregate Supply and Demand:
Causes and Costs of Inflation

12

Aggregate Supply and Equilibrium with Aggregate Demand

During the 1970s the primary focus of macroeconomics changed from forecasting and controlling aggregate demand to explaining prices and halting inflation. In everyday parlance, the term *inflation* has been used in two related ways. It has been defined as any increase in the general price level. More recently, however, the term *inflation* has been employed to describe a persistent rise in the general price level. This volume assumes the latter definition. The inflation process can be started by demand-pull or supply shocks; a continuation of such pressures adds to or subtracts from the inflation. It is the sustained character of inflation which creates the most difficult problems. Once started, an inflation develops a basic or underlying rate of price increases which seems almost to take on a life of its own.

The 1981 restructuring of economic policies by the Reagan administration, while drastic, was accepted because the measures promised a possible end to inflation. They enacted several of the anti-inflationary policies described here in Part 5. It was expected that improved government credibility would reduce inflationary expectations so that private decision makers would accept smaller increases in nominal wages and prices. Growth of both potential and actual output would be stimulated by the application of *supply-side economics.* This term has been used to describe policies aimed at shifting the aggregate supply curve down to the right by expanding factor inputs while speeding up the growth of productivity. Incentives to work and to invest would be increased. Regulations restricting output would be removed. Lower taxes and government expenditures would enhance the productive efficiency of the economy.

To understand how the 1981 program developed and how the policies were selected to carry it out from the wide variety available, we must examine the important issues that make up the macroeconomics of supply as well as those which can explain how inflation starts and how it can continue. President Reagan described his program as a major turnaround of the economic policy prevailing for the past 50 years and the largest-ever cut in domestic spending and tax programs. An understanding of the issues raised by these actions is necessary for analyzing the debates which are likely to continue over the best anti-inflationary and antirecessionary policies.

Discussions of the macroeconomics of supply and the causes of inflation treat a number of critical issues. Why in some periods do excesses of demand or pressures on costs lead to a one-time rise in prices, while in other periods similar forces result in a steady or persistent increase in prices—an inflation? How can prices continue to rise even after growth in output slows, production falls well below potential output, and the level of unemployment is excessive? How can inflation be halted? What factors can speed up the growth in potential output in order to raise real incomes and reduce the costs of fighting inflation?

The four chapters in Part 5 undertake to answer such questions by examining price changes, inflation, and aggregate supply. Although there is some overlap, each chapter takes up separate aspects of these issues. Chapter 12 deals with the forces that cause one-time movements in prices and real output. Chapter 13 takes up the pressures that lead to inflation. Chapter 14 explores some of the losses to the economy due to a failure to slow inflation as well as policies to fight inflation and their potential costs. Chapter 15 is concerned with actions to increase supply and speed up growth in real output.

PRICES AND SUPPLY-DEMAND EQUILIBRIUM

Price movements result from the interactions of aggregate demand and supply. Earlier chapters have shown how equilibrium demand is determined and the forces causing disturbances in it. Now we examine factors influencing the shape of the aggregate supply curve and causing it to shift. We find that costs of production determine the price levels at which the economy supplies specific quantities of real output. Wages and other forms of labor compensation make up the largest share of these charges, but in the short run the costs of other factor inputs, such as energy or raw materials, can also be important.

This chapter also shows that the equilibrium of aggregate demand and supply can be disturbed either by fluctuations in demand or by movements (shocks) in supply. In the short run, a shift in the AD-AS equilibrium results in movements of both prices and output. In the long run, it is often assumed that the economy cannot operate for long periods above full employment without suffering a steady increase in wages and prices. As a corollary, a long enough period of underemployment will result in their decline. To the extent that this assumption holds, prices will be stable only on the line of potential output. Thus the long-run aggregate supply curve can be thought of as a vertical line from the point of full-employment output. However, it must be recognized that because of short-run fluctuations in demand and supply, only rarely does output need to be on the long-run curve and, in addition, how much potential output grows partially depends on the levels of output achieved in the short run.

STATIC AND DYNAMIC MODELS

The models of aggregate supply described in this chapter are *static* models. They tell us why a disturbance leads to a higher price level, the type of forces that move prices, and the new point of equilibrium. But because static models do not include relationships over time, they cannot explain the inflationary processes that cause a persistent rise in prices. After static models reach a new equilibrium, prices will rise again only in response to another disturbance. A *dynamic* model is needed to analyze why the economy experiences high continuing rates of inflation—a model that contains lags and shows how movements in one period are influenced by those of a previous period. In inflations, forces must be at work moving aggregate supply and demand curves period after period. Chapter 13 shows how the individual price movements described in this chapter turn into an unbroken inflation. The topics that explain the aggregate supply curve and the *AS-AD* equilibrium include:

> An overview of price history.
> Aggregate supply curve with flexible wages and prices.
> Aggregate supply curve with less flexible wages and prices.
> Other forces shaping short-run aggregate supply curves.
> Equilibrium of aggregate supply and demand.
> The long-run aggregate supply curve.

An Overview of Price History

As Chapter 1 showed, inflation is not a new phenomenon, either in the United States or in the world. Figure 12.1 illustrates the record of the United States in this respect. It charts the movements of wholesale (now called producer) prices from 1780 to 1980. Long-run trends in prices are measured at the wholesale level because only this index is available for much of the period. While movements differ somewhat among the major price indexes—producers', the GNP deflator, and the CPI—the general picture of inflation over time is similar no matter which index is used.

The past has seen many periods of rapidly rising prices, mainly related to excess demand aggravated by wars. However, after each such period, the trend reversed and prices fell. Wars brought inflation; postwar depressions forced prices back to prior levels. In 1939, wholesale prices were lower than they had

FIGURE 12.1   **Movements in the Level of Wholesale prices, 1780–1980 (1910–14 = 100)**

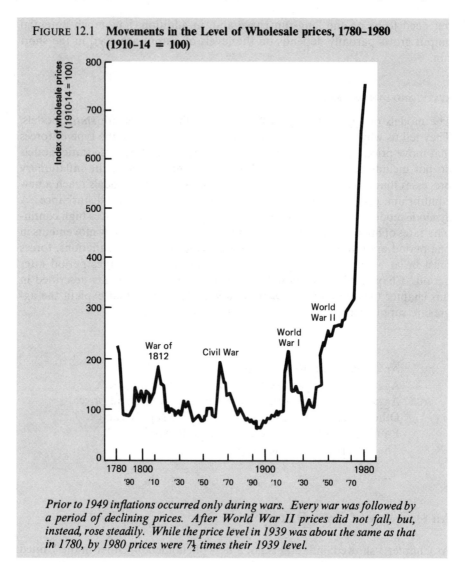

Prior to 1949 inflations occurred only during wars. Every war was followed by a period of declining prices. After World War II prices did not fall, but, instead, rose steadily. While the price level in 1939 was about the same as that in 1780, by 1980 prices were 7½ times their 1939 level.

been in 1800. It was not illogical for observers in 1949, looking back, to place a high probability on the idea that the price level would once again return to previous averages. But after World War II, no reversal in prices took place. Instead, prices have increased steadily since 1949. What has changed? A crucial development appears to be that prices have not fallen in recessions as they did in earlier periods. This shift probably reflects the fact that more active antirecessionary policies in the postwar period have markedly reduced the duration of recessions.

PRICE MOVEMENTS IN EXPANSIONS AND RECESSIONS

Table 12.1 shows movements of wholesale prices over past business cycles. Examining the 12 cycles between 1891 and 1933, we see that prices fell about as much as they rose. At the end of the period, prices differed only slightly from their initial level. In these 42 years, the wholesale price index rose about 15 percent. However, this reported increase was probably less than the upward bias in the index resulting from its failure to incorporate quality improvements. In contrast, during the 9 business cycles between 1933 and 1980, the index rose by well over 560 percent. A 1980 dollar would buy only about a sixth as much as a 1933 dollar.

Much of this change can be explained by the greater stability of the economy. Recessions have been shorter and not as deep. Between 1891 and 1933, the economy was in recession for almost as many months as it was expanding. In contrast, from 1933 to 1980, the months of expansion outnum-

TABLE 12.1   **Wholesale Price Changes during Business Cycles, 1891–1980**

Business cycles		Rates of price change (percent per year)		Total change (in percent)		
Period	Number	Expansions	Recessions	Expansions	Recessions	Full cycle*
May 1891– December 1900	3	2.6	−3.8	14.4	−18.5	−3.3
December 1900– January 1912	3	5.2	−2.7	33.1	−14.1	18.2
January 1912– July 1921	3	16.7	−14.1	123.3	−72.0	56.0
July 1921– March 1933	3	2.1	−9.7	12.6	−69.6	−57.2
March 1933– June 1938	1	9.0	−10.1	45.8	−11.5	30.6
June 1938– October 1949	2	7.3	−3.6	85.8	−5.9	77.3
October 1949– February 1961	3	1.4	2.6	19.7	1.5	21.2
February 1961– July 1980	3	4.5	11.9	76.4	33.9	100.6

* Percentages for full cycles is only an approximate sum of the two preceding columns.
SOURCE: P. Cagan, *Persistent Inflation* (New York: Columbia Univ. Press, 1979), p. 8.

The third column lists average yearly rates of price changes in expansion and the fourth column those in recessions during the business cycles in the periods of the first column. The right-hand three columns sum up growth and decline for all expansions and contractions in a given period. Note the failure of prices to fall in recessions after 1949.

bered those of recession by a ratio of more than 5 to 1. During most of the postwar recessions, while declines occurred in the rate of growth, actual decreases in production were relatively small. The Great Recession of 1973–75 was an exception, but it was characterized by a particularly virulent inflation.

Whether because the recessions were shorter or because output did not drop as steeply, in every recession since 1949 prices continued to rise. In contrast, in all except one of the recessions between 1891 and 1945, prices fell. In several postwar cases, the rate of inflation slowed, but even slowing did not occur in every recession. Note from the table that the rate at which prices moved up per month in the post-World-War-II expansions was not greater than in earlier periods. The upward price movements simply continued for longer intervals. Even if somewhat slower rates prevail, if they continue for longer periods, the economy ends up at a higher price level. At the same time, the failure of upward movements in prices to reverse during the periods of recession brought about a drop in purchasing power. The greater use of policies to curtail the extent of postwar recessions is one key explanation of the failure of prices to fall back as they did in earlier times. But the accelerating rate of inflation in the 1970s seems to require other explanations as well.

DEMAND, OUTPUT, AND PRICES

Shifts in equilibrium desire to spend are major forces influencing price movements. An increase in aggregate demand may induce a rise in both output and prices. Successful efforts to halt recessions or inflations require knowledge of how the economy reacts to moves in nominal spending. But knowledge of what happens to prices and output cannot be gained by looking at demand alone. While the existence of potential inflationary or deflationary gaps-can be found by comparing the levels of demand and full-employment output, explaining how much or how fast prices and output respond requires more complex analysis. The fluctuating relationships between demand, output, and inflation are illustrated in Figure 12.2. Each column shows year-to-year percentage changes in current-dollar, or nominal, GNP. The bottom section shows changes in real output. The distance between nominal GNP and real output (the shaded area) measures the rate of inflation in each year. Compare years such as 1971, 1974, 1975, and 1976. In each of the first three years, aggregate demand expanded by almost similar amounts; yet the growth rates of prices and output differed greatly. In 1971 and 1976 price movements were similar, but increases in real output differed by 60 percent. Similar apparent anomalies are found throughout the figure. In fact, a superficial look at the figure, without taking into account any of the factors behind the movements, might lead one to judge that whenever aggregate demand declines, output falls while prices rise even faster. This is exactly the opposite of the results one might expect.

A necessary relationship exists between the three movements. Recall that the level of aggregate demand, or the GNP, is merely the amount of output times the price level:

FIGURE 12.2 **Changes in Nominal and Real GNP**

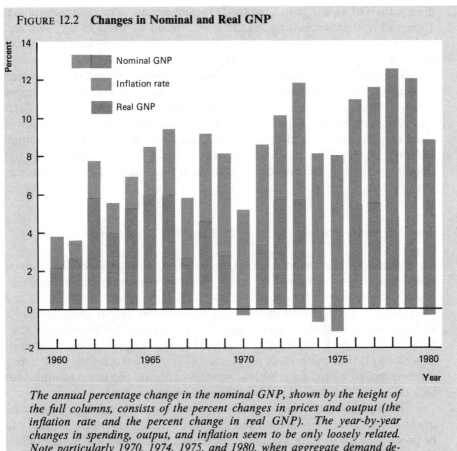

The annual percentage change in the nominal GNP, shown by the height of the full columns, consists of the percent changes in prices and output (the inflation rate and the percent change in real GNP). The year-by-year changes in spending, output, and inflation seem to be only loosely related. Note particularly 1970, 1974, 1975, and 1980, when aggregate demand declined, leading to actual drops in output, while inflation continued at record rates.
SOURCE: Economic Report of the President, 1981.

$$GNP = AD = P \cdot Q. \hspace{4cm} \textbf{12.1}$$

Moreover, the percentage rate of change in the GNP equals the percentage rate of change in prices plus the percentage rate of change in output.[1] Thus the relationship is

$$\dot{AD} = \dot{P} + \dot{Q}. \hspace{4cm} \textbf{12.2}$$

Changes in aggregate demand can also be measured (as was demonstrated by

---

1. As noted previously, a dot over a letter or symbol is used to indicate the growth rate in that variable.

the equation of exchange in Chapter 7) by movements in monetary spending. Thus, rather than explaining spending as a result of shifts in any demand variable, some believe that changes in money are the primary causes of movements in spending, prices, and output.

In either case, to explain fully what happens when demand shifts, we need to understand supply conditions as well. What shapes aggregate supply curves? What causes their positions to shift? How do the interactions of *AD* and *AS* determine new equilibriums? If labor, capital, or raw materials are in short supply, more of added GNP will accrue to prices and less to output. Moreover, an equilibrium of *AS* and *AD* may not last. Whether prices will stabilize or, instead, increase depends on other forces in the price-income-output structure.

The Aggregate Supply Curve with Flexible Wages and Prices

An understanding of supply curves begins with an analysis of the costs of production. Movements in prices and output reflect the conditions under which goods and services are produced and supplied. How much firms produce and what they charge depend on their costs. Firms increase output when demand is sufficient to enable them to make a profit over and above their costs of production. They cut back when further output becomes unprofitable. Their costs depend on (1) their methods of production, (2) on how much they have to pay for their inputs—labor, materials, the services of capital goods, taxes, and other factors—and (3) on the output they obtain from these inputs.

Their **production function** expresses the technical relationship between the quantities of various inputs used and the maximum amount of output that can be produced with them in a period. Equation 12.3 presents a general production function in which output (Q) depends on inputs of labor (N), of capital (K), and of raw materials (MR).

$$Q = f(N,K,MR). \qquad \textbf{12.3}$$

How much output can be achieved from any set of inputs depends on knowledge, technology, and similar forces which determine productivity.

Costs of production change with the length of the period analyzed. It is common to assume that, in the short run, the amount of capital and the prices of materials and of wages are fixed, but that the amount of labor can vary (workers may be asked to put in overtime). In slightly longer periods, input prices and wages may alter in response to increased demand. Over still longer periods, the amount of capital and methods of production shift. A study of how the amount and costs of labor are determined forms a logical introduction to the forces shaping and shifting aggregate supply. Wages are by far the largest cost in production. Wages and salaries make up over three-quarters of national income.

THE NEOCLASSICAL ASSUMPTIONS

It is useful to begin the analysis of aggregate supply by seeing what such curves look like under a set of simplified assumptions and then comparing them with those which result when the assumptions are relaxed. The neoclassical model provides a set of simplified conditions. The battle following Keynes's attack on the classical system led to a more careful examination of the market conditions implied in macroeconomic analysis. One result was a more complete formulation of the neoclassical assumptions, the basis for the simplified part of classical and neoclassical analysis.

These assumptions include a market with flexible prices that adjust instantaneously. Prices are determined by perfect competition among firms and workers; they have no influence over their own prices and wages. The participants in the market possess full information about demand and supply, prices and wages. These assumptions yield a market with full employment and with wages which adjust as the supply of and demand for labor shift. The flexible prices form a self-correcting mechanism to remove deflationary or inflationary gaps in aggregate demand. In such a market, individuals decide how much to work by comparing the real wages they are offered with the value of their leisure time. Employers hire additional hours of work as long as they profit from the extra (marginal) unit produced. It pays to produce until wages and other variable costs equal the revenue yielded by the last unit of product.

But the actual economy differs considerably from one operating under assumed conditions of pure, perfect competition. For a variety of possible reasons—transactions and information costs, oligopoly, uncertainty, fixed costs, faulty expectations, money illusion—wages and prices become sticky. As a result, the amount produced and labor employed may be more or less than would be the case at equilibrium in perfectly competitive markets. In the actual economy, initial adjustments occur primarily through movements in output and employment; prices adjust slowly. When markets adjust by movements in quantities sold rather than by prices, even though there are still sellers who would like to sell at the prevailing price or workers who would like to work at the going wage, it is said that the **markets fail to clear.**

THE DEMAND FOR LABOR

In the market of neoclassical theory, units of labor and product are standard, and no firm or union can influence the market price. More important, knowledge is free and completely available. Job mobility is nearly instantaneous. As a result, all firms pay a uniform going wage and obtain all the labor they want at that wage. If such conditions actually existed, what would determine how much labor a firm wants? A firm would pay for more hours of work as long as the additional units produced could be sold profitably. Profitability depends on how much labor it takes to produce the marginal unit, on the wages that must be paid, and on the unit's selling price. The quantity of labor required per unit depends on the firm's production function.

Since capital and the other factors in the production function are assumed to be fixed, changes in output depend only on labor. While technical problems arise in assuming that what applies to a firm or worker applies to the economy as a whole, it is common to move from reasoning about an individual firm to an aggregate production function with an aggregate demand for and supply of labor, while noting the existence of possible complications. Thus Figure 12.3A is an assumed short-run production function for the economy. It shows that the amount of output (Q) depends on the number of hours of labor worked (N). Readers may recognize that the shape of the production function reflects the law of diminishing returns with respect to labor inputs. A movement up the curve to the right indicates that more and more units of labor are being added to a constant amount of other factors. As a result, each extra unit of labor has fewer fixed inputs to work with than the previous one has. More laborers are using a fixed amount of equipment; instead of one man per shovel, there may be five, ten, then twelve. The functional relationship shows that while total output continues to rise, the extra output from each added worker is not as great as the extra output contributed by the previous one.

MARGINAL WAGES PAID EQUAL MARGINAL REVENUES EARNED

As the output produced by an added unit of labor grows smaller, the wages paid for producing that unit must also diminish. Think in terms of an average firm. It can profitably hire labor as long as the revenues from an extra unit just cover the wages paid to produce it. Equation 12.4 shows the equilibrium conditions: Marginal costs—the money wages (W) paid—must equal marginal revenues— the marginal product of that unit of labor (MPL) times the price (P) at which the output sells.

$$W = P \cdot MPL. \tag{12.4}$$

Alternatively, this can be stated as the real wage paid $\left(\dfrac{W}{P}\right)$ for an extra unit of labor must equal its marginal product:

$$\frac{W}{P} = MPL. \tag{12.5}$$

This relationship allows one to draw a demand curve for labor (ND), as shown in Figure 12.3B. Choose a point, A, on the production function in Figure 12.3A. The slope $\left(\dfrac{\Delta Q}{\Delta N}\right)$, or derivative of the function, at that point measures the marginal productivity of labor. Equation 12.5 shows that the MPL equals the real wage that will be paid for that amount of labor. The MPL or real wage for

FIGURE 12.3   **The Production Function and the Demand for Labor**

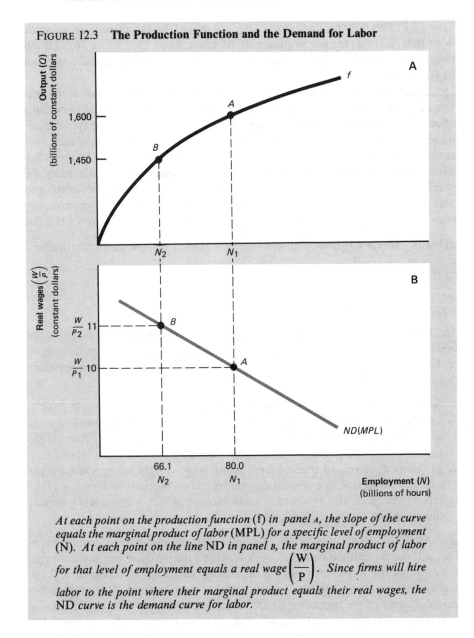

At each point on the production function (f) in panel A, the slope of the curve equals the marginal product of labor (MPL) for a specific level of employment (N). At each point on the line ND in panel B, the marginal product of labor for that level of employment equals a real wage $\left(\dfrac{W}{P}\right)$. Since firms will hire labor to the point where their marginal product equals their real wages, the ND curve is the demand curve for labor.

each added unit of labor is shown in Figure 12.3B. Look at the relationship at point A, where the labor supply is N_1. At this point the *MPL* is smaller than that from an additional unit of labor at point B, where fewer hours are being worked with the same equipment. Appendix 12.1 contains a numerical example used to obtain the numbers on Figure 12.3. Under its assumptions, for output to rise from $1,455 billion to $1,600 billion, the hours worked must rise from 66.1 to 80 billion. The effect of adding more labor to a fixed capital stock is to reduce the marginal productivity of labor from $11, when 66.1 billion hours turn out $1,455 billion of product, to $10 when 80 billion hours turn out $1,600 billion.

The demand curve for labor (*ND*) in Figure 12.3B shows that if the real wage decreases, as in the move from *B* to *A*, the number of hours of work firms offer (labor demanded) will increase. Why? Because when it pays a lower wage, the firm can afford to hire more units of labor, even though each suc-ceeding unit turns out less product and brings in less revenue. On the other hand, when real wages rise, as from *A* to *B*, if firms tried to maintain the previous hours of work, they would lose money on every unit of labor employed between *A* and *B*, and eventually they would go broke. If real wages were to rise from $10 to $11, firms would reduce their labor demand to N_2 (66.1 billions of hours). If real wages are reduced to $\dfrac{W}{P_1}$ ($10), they will increase their demand to N_1 (80 billion).

EQUILIBRIUM OF LABOR DEMAND AND SUPPLY

To find the amount of labor which will actually be employed, we must know the other blade of the scissors—how much labor the population will supply at each real wage rate. The shape of the labor supply curve is affected by two opposing factors:

1. As rates of pay rise, some people will want to work more hours; it pays to sacrifice leisure if you can augment your income. Although hours of work are fixed by tradition or technology in many jobs, high pay may cause people to moonlight and persuade other family members to enter the labor force.
2. In contrast, increased income from rising wages might make some people decide to work less, or even cause some secondary workers to drop out of the labor force. Families can earn as much income as they want in less time and thus may opt for more leisure.

Observers are uncertain as to which effect predominates. When wages rise, will the diminished desire to work resulting from higher income outweigh the effect of the higher price being offered for each unit of labor, or will the higher rates win out? Figure 12.4 adds a labor supply curve (*NS*) to the labor demand curve of the preceding figure. It shows the supply of labor increasing somewhat with higher real wages. The equilibrium point, where the labor demand and supply curves meet, determines the amount of employment and the level of real wages. This equilibrium point is *A*. When wages are above equilibrium—say at *B*—households want to supply more work than firms want to hire. The distance between *B* and *C* shows an excess of labor. The market is in disequilibrium. In a perfect market, disequilibrium would cause those wanting jobs to offer to work for less. As real wages fall, excess labor supply shrinks by a movement down the supply curve, even as demand increases by a

FIGURE 12.4   **The Demand for and Supply of Labor**

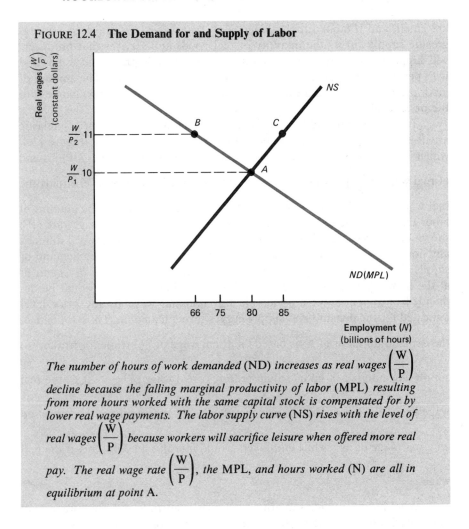

The number of hours of work demanded (ND) increases as real wages $\left(\dfrac{W}{P}\right)$ decline because the falling marginal productivity of labor (MPL) resulting from more hours worked with the same capital stock is compensated for by lower real wage payments. The labor supply curve (NS) rises with the level of real wages $\left(\dfrac{W}{P}\right)$ because workers will sacrifice leisure when offered more real pay. The real wage rate $\left(\dfrac{W}{P}\right)$, the MPL, and hours worked (N) are all in equilibrium at point A.

movement to the right on the demand curve. Finally, equilibrium is reestablished at point *A*.

We have defined the point where labor supply and demand are in equilibrium at a noninflationary wage rate as the ***point of full employment.*** At this point some natural level of unemployment exists, made up of the minimum number of workers in the process of seeking new jobs at the prevailing wage rate. All factors which shift the demand or supply curves for labor alter the level of full employment. Over time, the point of full employment has fluctuated by 1 or 2 percent.

FULL EMPLOYMENT AND THE SUPPLY CURVE WITH FLEXIBILITY

If producers hire labor up to the point where their marginal revenues and costs are equal, and if labor supply depends on real wages, we can derive an ag-gregate supply curve—the quantity of real goods and services that producers will supply at each price level. In a model with flexible prices and wages and with perfect knowledge, the aggregate supply curve is vertical. The amount of labor producers hire and the amount of output they furnish do not change with the price level.

The forces that lead to a supply curve which is completely price-inelastic are illustrated in Figure 12.5. Look at Figure 12.5A. In contrast to Figure 12.4, which it resembles, the vertical axis now measures nominal wages (W) instead of real wages $\left(\dfrac{W}{P}\right)$. A nominal wage rate divided by a price level equals the real wage rate. The lines labeled $ND(P_1)$ and $NS(P_1)$ indicate the amount of labor that would be demanded and supplied at each nominal wage rate (W) shown on the vertical axis when the price level is P_1. Real wages will differ at any nominal wage level depending on the price designation of the demand or supply curve going through a point. For example, consider points B, C, and B' at the nominal wage of W_2. To find how many hours of work would be de-manded or supplied, we must divide this nominal wage by the price level indicated for the demand and supply curves through a point. Thus at point B, the demand for labor of N_2 is based on a real wage of $\dfrac{W_2}{P_1}$ while for workers to supply this number of hours would require a real wage of $\dfrac{W_2}{P_3}$. At C, the real wage is $\dfrac{W_2}{P_2}$ for labor demand and supply. At B' the supply offered is based on a real wage of $\dfrac{W_2}{P_1}$, while employers would hire this amount only if the real wage is $\dfrac{W_2}{P_3}$.

What happens when the price level rises from P_1 to P_2? Real wages will fall at each nominal wage rate. As a result, when prices rise, labor demand falls and the supply offered increases at each money wage rate (W). For example, when prices rise from P_1 to P_2 because real wages have dropped, the demand for labor at nominal wages of W_2 rises from B to C, while the number of hours of work offered at the reduced real wage rate declines from B' to C. The fact that labor demand at each nominal wage rate (W) shifts every time the price level changes is shown on Figure 12.5A by the set of curves labeled $ND(P_1)$, $ND(P_2)$, and $ND(P_3)$. The decline in the number of hours offered at the nominal wage of W_2 when prices rise from P_1 to P_2 to P_3 is shown by the shifts from $NS(P_1)$ to $NS(P_2)$ to $NS(P_3)$ and by the points B', C, and B.

In this classical real-wage model, the market sees through and adjusts instantaneously to all price movements. The amount of labor demanded and supplied depends on real, not nominal, wages. Consequently, changes in the general price level do not affect the real labor market equilibrium since both the

FIGURE 12.5   **An Aggregate Supply Curve with Flexible Prices and Wages**

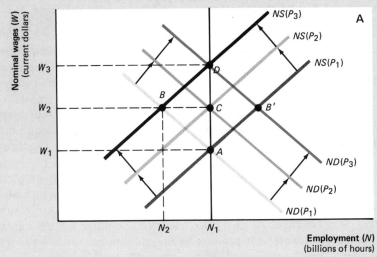

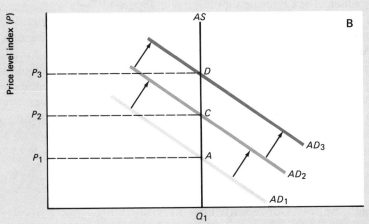

In panel A, at each nominal wage (W) an increase in prices from P_1 to P_2 to
P_3 lowers real wages $\left(\dfrac{W}{P}\right)$. Consequently, a price increase shifts the curves
for labor demand to the right and for labor supply to the left since at each
nominal wage the lowered real wage means that employers can hire more and
workers will offer fewer hours. Such shifts are illustrated by the curves NDP_1,
NDP_2, NDP_3, and NSP_1, NSP_2, and NSP_3. Since the price changes do not
alter the equilibrium of real wages and the MPL, employment (N) is the same
at each price level, as shown by the equilibrium points A, C, and D. When
employment does not change, neither does output (Q). The result shown in
panel B is an aggregate supply curve (AS) not affected by price (P) changes.

demand and supply of labor shift by identical amounts. At each of the equilibrium points A, C, and D, real wages $\dfrac{W_1}{P_1}$, $\dfrac{W_2}{P_2}$, and $\dfrac{W_3}{P_3}$ are the same, as is the amount of labor demanded and supplied.[2]

Since, with a given production function, each number of hours worked yields a specific output, the equilibrium employment levels can be used to specify the economy's aggregate supply curve. Figure 12.5B shows the aggregate supply curve (AS) which results from the neoclassical assumptions. It relates the amount of output on the horizontal axis to each price level shown on the vertical axis. The level of output for each of the labor-price equilibrium points in Figure 12.5A is calculated and plotted against the price levels in the second panel. In this case, changes in prices have no effect on the level of employment (N_1). The assumption of flexible prices, wages, and competition assures that a shift in the price level causes identical movements in both demand for and supply of labor. Nominal wages and prices adjust rapidly, so that real wages do not change. At each price level firms continue to offer the same amount of hours of work and produce at the same point on the production function. Since the hours worked do not move, the level of output does not change either. The aggregate supply curve in Figure 12.5B shows the amount of output which will be produced at each price level. It is the quantity of output that results when employment is at N_1 with a given production function.

An economy with a vertical supply curve has other significant properties. Shifts in aggregate demand will not alter the level of output or employment; they can only change prices. This is illustrated by the aggregate demand curves in Figure 12.5B. When demand rises, as depicted by the movement from AD_1 to AD_2 to AD_3, the equilibrium of aggregate demand and supply shifts from point A to point C to point D. Greater demand raises prices. Nominal wages go up, but real wages remain constant. Labor equilibrium, the point of full employment, and the amount of output do not change.

Aggregate Supply Curve with Less Flexible Wages and Prices

While many believe that a vertical aggregate supply curve represents long-run behavior, in short periods—which may extend over several years—aggregate supply appears in fact to be shaped so that both output and prices rise together. Business cycles are characterized by sharp shifts in output and jobs, not in prices alone. Furthermore, Table 12.1 and Figure 12.2 showed that, at times, when aggregate demand declined, prices continued to rise even as output fell. In all cases, when demand rose, both prices and output increased. Thus, in the short run, the aggregate supply curve does not appear to be vertical.

---

2. The appendix to this chapter derives these relationships by an alternative set of diagrams and presents a numerical example showing how the production function, labor demand and supply, real and nominal wages, and output are related.

THE EFFECT OF LAGS AND IMPERFECT KNOWLEDGE

Many suggestions have been offered as to why supply and prices react as they do rather than in the completely price-inelastic manner shown in Figure 12.5 B. Because in reality prices and wages lack complete flexibility, because knowledge and information are imperfect, and because of adjustment lags, markets fail to clear. There are many reasons offered for the lack of flexibility, the uncertainty, and the delayed movements of prices:

1. Uncertainties and incorrect judgments arise over what is happening as well as what is likely to happen in the price sphere. Wages and prices set in error lead to incorrect levels of output.
2. Workers suffer from money illusion; they confuse nominal and real wages. As a result, they offer more labor than they would if they realized that their real wages were falling.
3. At other times, workers fail to reduce their nominal wages and thus remain unemployed because of wage demands which are too high.
4. Even were wages cut, dynamic instability can lead to a continuing decline in demand and output. Demand falls because of expectations about future prices and because of the difficulty of reducing debt in a period of declining prices.

All of these factors reflect the fact that, for better or for worse, the markets around us are not perfect. Frictions abound. Many types of jobs, labor, and products have unique features. It costs money to search for and find new jobs. People migrate only slowly from one area to another. It takes time for information to spread. Many prices and wages are sticky. The markets where many wages and prices are set may be called **contract markets** in contrast to **auction markets,** like those for wheat or common stocks, in which prices adjust almost instantaneously to changes in supply and demand. Firms and employees form erroneous expectations of future prices and demand. As a result of some or all of these factors, markets can be in disequilibrium.[3] At times, some people who would like to work at the existing real wage rate cannot find jobs. The demand for labor is less than the supply. At other times, such as in 1967 and 1973, demand for labor outruns the normal full-employment level. The economy enters into an inflationary process. Higher supply prices are required to meet the excess demand.

SHORT-RUN EQUILIBRIUM OR DISEQUILIBRIUM

The effect on supply curves of a lack of flexibility, of uncertainty, and of

---

3. For a description of these processes, see E. S. Phelps, *Inflation Policy and Unemployment Theory* (New York: Norton, 1972), Chapters 1 and 2; A. M. Okun, "Inflation: Its Mechanics and Welfare Costs," *Brookings Papers on Economic Activity* 2(1975): 352; and R. M. Solow, "Alternative Approaches to Macroeconomic Theory: A Partial View," *Canadian Journal of Economics,* 12(August 1979): 339–54.

FIGURE 12.6   **The Aggregate Supply Curve with Sticky Wages and Prices**

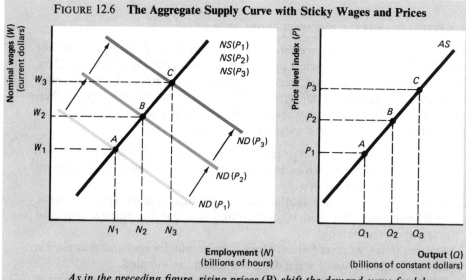

As in the preceding figure, rising prices (P) shift the demand curve for labor
(ND) to the right at each nominal wage (W). However, if labor offers to work
in response to nominal, not real, wages, price increases do not shift the labor
supply curve (NS). Its labels show that it is the same for all price levels. The
equilibrium of hours worked and nominal wages moves from A to B to C
because higher prices mean lower wages and an opportunity for firms to use
more hours of work even with a declining MPL. More employment means
more output. Panel B shows an aggregate supply curve (AS) in which output
rises in response to higher prices.

delayed reactions is illustrated in Figure 12.6A. The initial labor supply and
demand situation here is the same as in Figures 12.4 and 12.5. Point A reflects
an equilibrium of demand and supply with the price level at P_1. Employers
continue to operate as in the previous case. When prices rise, they recognize
that real wages $\left(\dfrac{W}{P}\right)$ are lower at each nominal wage (W) level. With no
change in production capabilities and a lower real wage, the marginal cost of
additional hours of work drops. Consequently, at each nominal wage rate,
firms will purchase more work to increase output. Thus, in Figure 12.6A, when
prices rise from P_1 to P_2 to P_3, the demand for labor shifts up to the right. At a
nominal wage such as W_1, real wages fall as prices rise, from $\dfrac{W_1}{P_1}$ to $\dfrac{W_1}{P_2}$ to $\dfrac{W_1}{P_3}$,
the hours firms will hire grows as shown by the W_1 level on $ND(P_1)$, $ND(P_2)$,
and $ND(P_3)$.

However, in this figure labor is assumed to respond to price changes in a
different way. Because workers focus on nominal instead of on real wages, they

do not shift their supply curve in response to price movements. Thus a single labor supply curve applies at all price levels. It is therefore labeled $NS(P_1)$, $NS(P_2)$, and $NS(P_3)$ to show that labor supply depends only on nominal, not on real wages and that it does not respond to movements in prices.

The equilibrium points of A, B, and C show the consequences of the lack of wage flexibility in the labor market. Firms can afford to increase hours of work (even though the marginal productivity of labor declines) because they pay lower real wages as prices rise. They want to use N_2 billion hours when real wages are $\dfrac{W_2}{P_2}$, and N_3 with real wages of $\dfrac{W_3}{P_3}$. The unchanged labor supply curve indicates that workers are willing to supply these extra hours even though real wages are less. Panel 12.6B displays the aggregate supply curve (AS) related to these equilibrium points. Every increase in hours worked results in a higher output level. The AS curve plots each higher output against its related price level.

If prices fall, the failure of labor supply to shift leads to a decline in employment and output. If money wages are rigid and cannot move down because of contracts or other reasons, real wages rise as prices decline. Employers will reduce their demand at each nominal wage. Workers will be laid off and output will decrease. The labor market will fail to clear at prevailing nominal wages.

In practice, neither completely flexible nor inflexible wages are found in labor markets. Nominal wages adjust to price movements, but with decided lags. Nominal wages (except those with cost of living escalators) do not move rapidly, since they are restrained by actual or implied contracts lasting one to three years. While union contracts cover only a minority of labor, similar factors influence wage-setting in other markets. When contracts are renegotiated or wages are set in nonunion firms, what has been happening to other wages and prices plays a greater role in the new wage rates than does the state of demand or unemployment. A company which tried to move its wages or working conditions up or down frequently would soon find itself unionized. Even during a recession, carpenters can bargain on the basis of the last contract gained by plumbers or neighboring carpenters rather than on unemployment statistics. Government wages are set as much through political bargaining as by supply and demand.

Economists assign varying weights to the factors that have been advanced to explain why prices and wages do not move in accordance with the simplified assumptions and why markets fail to clear. Some stress errors or uncertainties; some, contracts; some, costs of adjustment; some, poor information; and some, other factors. All, however, agree that wages do not move at the same rate as prices, as they are assumed to do in the neoclassical case. It is this failure of labor demand and supply to move together that underlies any explanation of the short-run nonvertical supply curve.

Other Forces Shaping Short-Run Aggregate Supply Curves

The lags in real wage rates behind price movements provide an important clue as to why prices and output move together. However, the story is not yet complete. First of all, wages make up only part of production costs. The reactions to increased demand of the prices of raw materials and the pricing policies of firms tend to reinforce the shape of the short-run supply curve produced by uncertainties in the labor market. Secondly, we have not considered the long run. The short-run curve is shaped by lags and imperfections. With time, these should disappear. What does, in fact, happen over the longer run when prices, wages, and production costs have time to adjust completely? The long-run supply curve appears to be vertical, for reasons similar to those shaping the short-run curve in a perfect market.

However, as is highlighted by the great interest in supply-side economics, the amount of future output is not fixed. It depends on what happens in the succession of short runs that make up the long run. The level of capital investment, labor skills, and technology available in the future are all influenced by levels of demand, output, interest rates, and inflation in the interim.

PRICES OF COMMODITY INPUTS AND PROFIT MARGINS

The discussion up to this point has related the shape of the aggregate supply curve to the marginal product of labor and to the differences between nominal and real wages as prices alter. To obtain a still more realistic picture of supply, however, account must be taken of the fact that the costs of materials and the margins of firms over costs also vary with output. In theory, except for imported and raw materials, commodity prices depend only on the value added by labor and capital. Since materials are intermediate products, their costs can be assigned to their capital and labor components. In fact, however, in the short run prices of many raw commodities—food, lumber, oil, metals—respond more to demand forces than to their labor and capital costs. When output expands, their prices rise quite rapidly. Firms must add these higher costs to their prices.

Among other factors that contribute toward higher costs is the fact that many input markets are not of the auction, or purely competitive, type. Some firms—for example, those selling farm and forest products and minerals—set their prices in a nearly competitive sphere; but because of transactions costs, regulations, oligopolistic competition, and similar factors, others operate in markets far removed from perfect competition. These markets are described as contract or customer markets, or markets with administered prices. While prices in the wheat market, for example, may change minute by minute, IBM alters the prices of its computers no more often than once or twice a year. Regulated rates, such as those for telephones, also move only at long intervals.

The difference between reactions of prices and wages in imperfect markets and those in perfect markets plays an important role in explaining the

FIGURE 12.7   **The Short-Run Aggregate Supply Curve**

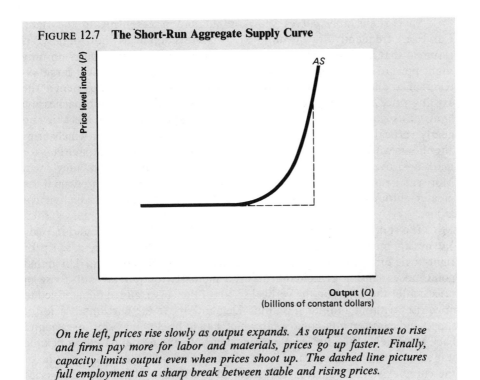

On the left, prices rise slowly as output expands. As output continues to rise and firms pay more for labor and materials, prices go up faster. Finally, capacity limits output even when prices shoot up. The dashed line pictures full employment as a sharp break between stable and rising prices.

reactions of prices and output. When demand grows, firms may find it possible to raise their profits even as costs rise by expanding their price margins over their costs. Furthermore, as output expands, capacity constraints come into play. Capital can expand only slowly. Whole industries, such as steel or railroads, may become bottlenecks as they reach their capacity limits. If aggregate output is to grow, substitute materials or services must be found, usually at higher prices. Crude materials, lumber, and similar products, the supply of which can grow only slowly if at all, experience rapid price rises. The net effect of all these different situations yields a short-run supply curve like that pictured in Figure 12.7.

THE STYLIZED SHAPE OF AGGREGATE SUPPLY

Figure 12.7 shows a stylized version of short-run supply curves. At the start of a period, the costs of the factor inputs determine the location of the supply curve. Given these costs, the short-run curve describes the reaction of firms to changes in demand. It reflects the movements in the price level necessary to permit firms to supply each amount of production.

Short-run supply curves show output and prices rising to the right. Curves are frequently drawn with the left-hand section nearly horizontal. It is assumed that, at first, firms can supply sizable increases in output with only slight upward movements in prices. Such elastic conditions reflect large excesses of labor and capital in the economy that would accept employment at the existing price level. At the right-hand side, as the economy approaches the limits of its capacity, the curves become almost completely price inelastic and nearly vertical. Such short-run supply curves reflect the way in which firms alter hours worked, the prices paid for materials, and their pricing margins (or mark-ups) over costs. Firms profit by raising the hours of work they offer. More can be produced and sold at higher prices, or higher margins, even if the greater output is accompanied by a decline in the marginal productivity of labor.

The short-run supply curve in Figure 12.7 resembles that found in early Keynesian models. As shown on the chart by the dotted line, a sharp or right-angle turn was often pictured as the point of full employment. Up to that point, an expansion of demand induced increased output without a rise in prices; after the angle, on the vertical sector of the curve, added demand led to price rises without additional output. Demand above the horizontal sector of supply indicated an inflationary gap which had to be closed by shifting demand back to the left of the full-employment point. In the model based on flexible wages and prices, in contrast to the Keynesian one, only the vertical section of the curve existed; all increases in demand are completely absorbed in price rises.

THE CURVE MAY BE ASYMMETRICAL

If demand falls, however, producers who have established prices are likely to cut their output before their prices. Fewer units will be offered than shown on Figure 12.7. Whether because wage payments are rigid, because changing prices is expensive and may threaten a price war, because firms may believe that the drop in demand is temporary, or because of adjustment lags, firms have difficulty cutting both costs and prices. Some prices may decline, especially in competitive spheres, but for the economy as a whole, reductions in the price level (or in the rate of price increases) tend to lag (as shown in Table 12.1 and Figure 12.2) far behind declines in output.

AN EXAMPLE OF A CONTRACT MARKET

The housing industry provides an example of how some of these factors intertwine. Prices rise rapidly when more units are under construction. Builders experience shortages of lumber, pipe, and other materials; they pay more for imported commodities; their normal discounts disappear, and delays occur while time is spent locating new supplies and waiting for postponed deliveries. Even though nominal wages may not rise, extra amounts will be paid for overtime work. Bonuses will be awarded to the better workers to prevent them from going elsewhere; new workers hired will be less skilled but will nonetheless receive prevailing wages. All of these factors raise costs. At the same time, builders are able to widen their profit margins. For example, a typical housing supply curve might show that if output is 1,600,000 units per year, the price of a house would be $60,000. This would consist of $50,000 paid out for land, materials, and labor plus a 20 percent mark-up which builders earn over their cost. To supply 2,000,000 units, prices might rise to $75,000 on average. Land, materials, and labor would cost $60,000 and the mark-up would rise to 25 percent.

Equilibrium of Aggregate Supply and Demand

As mentioned earlier in the chapter, models of aggregate demand do not provide sufficient information to analyze actual spending when the desire to spend shifts. The nominal aggregate demand curve relates price levels and purchases of real goods, but where the economy ends up also depends on the aggregate supply curve. In the short-run static model, price-output equilibrium can shift either because of changes in the desire to spend (the *IS-LM* equilibrium) or because of shifts in the aggregate supply curve. The new equilibrium depends on the size of the initiating shift and the shapes of the two curves. While the division is artificial and difficult to maintain in analysis, the term **demand-pull** is often applied to forces that cause price increases by shifting aggregate demand curves to the right. Prices and wages rise as output expands. In contrast, the term **supply shock** (or previously, **cost-push**) applies to forces that cause price increases by shifting the aggregate supply curve to the left. Prices and wages rise and output contracts. Favorable supply shocks (for instance, a good harvest) are also possible; they cause the *AS* curve to shift to the right, with a consequent decline in prices and increased output.

A SHIFT IN AGGREGATE DEMAND

What happens when aggregate demand shifts as a result of a movement in one of the *IS-LM* variables? Take as an example an increase in the money supply. One of the best known descriptions of inflation is "too much money chasing too few goods." Let us see what this statement means. Suppose that, to end a recession, the Federal Reserve increases the money supply by a fixed amount. Will a new equilibrium of demand and supply result, and if so, where? What is the process which follows the creation of more money?

The disequilibrium in the money market brought about by the additional money causes the *LM* curve to shift down to the right. Interest rates fall. The desire to spend (AD) shifts right also. There is a movement up the supply curve to higher prices and output. As a result of the change in prices, the real money supply declines somewhat. The LM curve shifts back to a point somewhere between its original position and the level that would obtain if prices had not risen.

Such a scenario, in which more nominal money raises prices and output, is illustrated in Figure 12.8. In the bottom panel, an increase in the nominal money supply causes the initial curve $LM_1(P_1)$ to shift to $LM_2(P_1)$. A new equilibrium of output occurs at point B. This increase in the demand for output from Q_1 to Q_2 occurs at the same price level, (P_1). The added money causes a higher demand for output at each possible price level. As illustrated in the top panel, an increase in the nominal money supply shifts the economy from curve AD_1 to AD_2 (as explained in Figure 8.9A). The shape of the supply curve shows that prices must rise if production is to expand. Higher prices (P_2) reduce the real money supply $\left(\dfrac{MS}{P_2}\right)$; the LM curve shifts to $LM_3(P_2)$. A new equilibrium of the IS-LM curves is reached at point C. Because only prices have changed and not the nominal money supply or other demand factors, the curve AD_2 does not shift (it already encompasses price movements). The point C is an equilibrium point for both current dollar demand and supply (panel A) and the real goods and money markets (panel B). As the figure shows, both the AD-AS curves and the IS-LM curves are in equilibrium at C, unlike the disequilibrium at B which led to the price and output readjustments.

The process can be traced through by use of a numerical example as well. Suppose that the economy starts at an equilibrium (point A in Figure 12.8) with output of $1,600 billion, prices at 100 percent, a real money supply of $480 billion, and real interest rates at 5 percent. Now the nominal money supply expands to $550 billion. The figure shows that the additional money shifts the market to LM_2.[4] With prices unchanged, the new level of output would be $1,940 billion, as shown at point B.

However, prices do not remain constant. The AS curve shows that prices must rise to supply this new demand. The new equilibrium of AD and AS is at point C, where the price level has risen to 110 percent. The rise in prices causes real money balances to drop to $500 billion $\left(\dfrac{MS}{P_2} = \dfrac{550}{1.1}\right)$. The nominal money increase from $480 to $550 billion has raised the real money supply only to $500 billion. The equilibrium level of spending is now $1,640 billion, with a price level of 110 percent. Real interest rates are at 4.2 percent.[5]

---

4. Chapter 8 showed that more money would shift both the LM and IS curves, but for simplicity, this example abstracts from the effects in the goods market.

5. These results are obtained from the numerical example when the new real money supply

$$\text{of 500 is substituted for the previous } \frac{MS}{P} \text{ of 480.}$$

FIGURE 12.8   **Equilibrium of Aggregate Demand and Aggregate Supply Depends on the Underlying Variables**

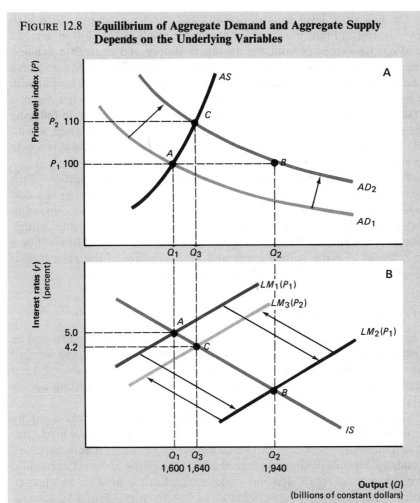

An increase in the money supply causes a shift from curve LM_1 to LM_2, resulting also in a shift from AD_1 to AD_2. Demand for real goods and services is in equilibrium at point B. However, the supply curve (AS) shows that this output can be met only at higher prices following an upward movement along AD_2 and AS. Prices rising to P_2 lower the real money supply, causing a shift to LM_3. At point C the markets for real goods (IS) and money (LM) are in equilibrium, as are aggregate supply and demand (AS-AD).

IS: $Y = k_1\overline{A} - k_1 br$	$Y = 2.5(740) - 2.5(2,000)r$	**12.6**
LM: $Y = \dfrac{1}{e}\left(\dfrac{MS}{P} - \overline{MA} + hr\right)$	$Y = 10(500 - 420 + 2,000r)$	**12.7**
	$Y = 1,640 \quad r = .042.$	

Compare this result to equations 8.1 and 8.2 where $\dfrac{MS}{P} = \dfrac{480}{1}$ rather than $\dfrac{550}{1.1}$.

The new price level equates demand and short-run supply. How high prices must rise and how much output grows as a result of any shift in demand depend on the shapes of both the aggregate supply and aggregate demand curves. If production costs are not responsive to output changes, the AS curve will be flat and most of added demand will be met by increased output with only slight increases in prices. (The opposite is also true; with such a curve, it will take large drops in demand and output to have much impact in reducing prices.) If the cost situation pushes prices up, however, real balances are altered. The amount by which demand is reduced depends on how it reacts to price increases, as shown by the shape of the AD curve.

The stability of the short-run equilibrium is also a critical question. Such stability depends on whether the suppliers of inputs are satisfied at the new price level. Is the level of real wages such as to equate supply and demand in the labor market? If, as often happens, real incomes are not in equilibrium, production costs and the short-run supply curve will shift. The result will be a quite different long-run supply curve and a new picture of the price-output trade-off compared with that exhibited in the short-run analysis.

A SHIFT IN AGGREGATE SUPPLY

The analysis used to trace the effects of shifts in aggregate demand can also be applied to analysis of the supply shocks in the short run. Such shocks were all too common in the 1970s. To mention but a few, energy prices soared; crop failures around the world caused wheat prices to skyrocket; building unions won large wage raises which spread throughout the economy.

Figure 12.9 represents a supply shock that shifts the aggregate supply curve to the left. This causes fewer goods to be supplied at any price level. But what determines the new equilibrium of output and prices? Where the economy ends up depends on the size of the shock, on the shape of the AS curve, and on the shape of aggregate demand as determined in the product and money markets. When the supply curve in Figure 12.9 shifts from AS_1 to AS_2, demand exceeds the amount the economy will supply at the initial price level. To close the gap, prices begin to rise. A move up the demand curve from A to B takes place. How much real spending drops depends on the relationships between prices, interest rates, and the desire to spend which determine the shape of the AD curve. Changes in the equilibrium will also depend on whether policy actions are taken to offset the fall in output by increasing nominal demand.

When prices rise, if the money supply is held constant, the situation is similar to that of the demand-pull example illustrated by the shift from LM_2 to LM_3 in Figure 12.8. As a result of a lower real money supply, a new IS-LM and a new AD-AS equilibrium come into existence. In Figure 12.9, the new equilibriums occur at point B. The flatter the aggregate demand curve (the more responsive spending is to prices), the more will an increase in costs result in a decline in output. The flatness of the AD curve depends on how the IS and LM curves shift as real money is reduced, and on how responsive spending is to

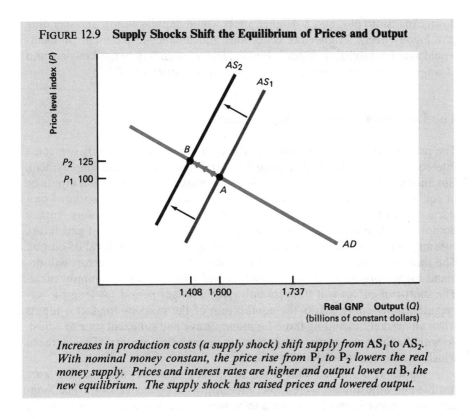

FIGURE 12.9   **Supply Shocks Shift the Equilibrium of Prices and Output**

Increases in production costs (a supply shock) shift supply from AS₁ to AS₂. With nominal money constant, the price rise from P₁ to P₂ lowers the real money supply. Prices and interest rates are higher and output lower at B, the new equilibrium. The supply shock has raised prices and lowered output.

interest rates. If a large move in spending is required to balance the decrease in real money, the *AD* curve will be quite flat.

A STABLE EQUILIBRIUM

In the case of both demand-pull and cost-push price rises, the fact that the disequilibrium is expected to end in a new stable position follows traditional analysis. Neither monetarists nor Keynesians gave much thought to a dynamic inflationary process. Both had models with assumptions that insured that an increase in demand would lead to a one-time rise in prices, not to inflation. In the monetarists' model, each higher price requires an increase in money. Inflation cannot develop simply from one, or even several cases of excess demand. Inflations require a steady and growing expansion of the money supply. As soon as the money supply stabilizes, prices stabilize as well.

In the Keynesian model, increases in money are not necessary for prices to go up. Velocity can increase instead. An inflationary gap could be caused by a shift in the investment or consumption functions, or in the demand for money. However, price increases would tend to be self-limiting; without added money, velocity would reach a maximum. Interest rates would rise, holding down expansions of C and I. Higher prices would depress wealth and spending (the Pigou effect). Higher tax collections and balance-of-payment problems would also be stabilizing factors. Finally, lags of spending behind income and of wages behind prices would assure the end of a price spiral.[6]

The Long-Run Aggregate Supply Curve

The previous discussion showed that short-run demand and supply can come into equilibrium with a higher price level and more output and employment. But another critical question arises: Will the markets for production inputs be in equilibrium? If the short-run equilibrium is to continue, the factors of production must readjust their underlying demand and supply situations. If they do not alter their real desires for work and leisure and for present and future consumption, some factors will be overemployed at the new level of output. The short-run equilibrium will not be stable. The production factors will demand higher prices. Costs of production will rise, shifting the supply curve. The short-run curves will stabilize only over a longer period. A long-run aggregate supply curve marks the equilibrium of the markets for factor inputs when all markets, including those for money, have had sufficient time to adjust. As with the short-run curves, the concept is an analytical artifact. The degree to which equilibrium is achieved is uncertain.

Figure 12.5 showed that when the prices of inputs and outputs were flexible and adjustments were rapid, the supply curve was vertical. The long-run supply curve is usually assumed to be vertical, since over a longer period of time, all costs will adjust to their underlying supply-demand conditions. Neither labor nor capital will sell their services for less than their real worth. In the long run, prices are therefore neutral. The level of output will be determined by the technical ability of the economy to produce (the production function) and the underlying forces of demand and supply in the factor input markets. The level of production will be the same irrespective of the price level.

MOVEMENTS TO LONG-RUN EQUILIBRIUM

Figure 12.10 shows how the economy moves from the situation in the short run, when changes in demand influence both prices and output, to the long run in which changes in demand primarily influence the price level. In Figure 12.10, an increase in aggregate demand from AD_1 to AD_2 brings about a new equilibrium at point C with the aggregate supply curve AS_1. Firms meet the increase in demand by hiring more work, paying more for materials, and perhaps raising their profit margins. But the equilibrium at point C is only temporary. The

---

6. A. M. Okun, "Inflation: Its Mechanics and Welfare Costs," *Brookings Papers on Economic Activity* 2(1975): 352.

FIGURE 12.10   **Long-Run Aggregate Supply**

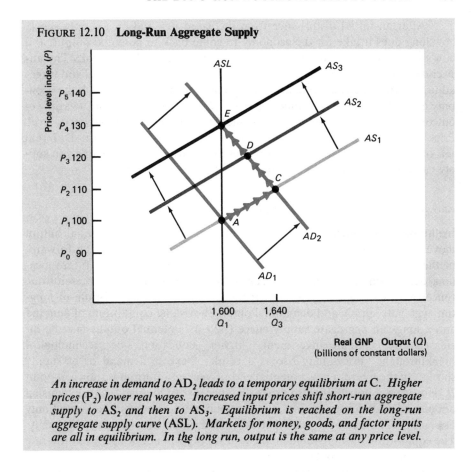

An increase in demand to AD₂ *leads to a temporary equilibrium at* C. *Higher prices* (P₂) *lower real wages. Increased input prices shift short-run aggregate supply to* AS₂ *and then to* AS₃. *Equilibrium is reached on the long-run aggregate supply curve* (ASL). *Markets for money, goods, and factor inputs are all in equilibrium. In the long run, output is the same at any price level.*

market for labor and other input will not be in equilibrium. Workers will not be receiving the real wage that equates with their desires for leisure. As a result, suppliers will demand higher wages and revenues to compensate for their drop in real income. Firms find their costs of production rising.

The AS_1 curve shifts to AS_2. A new temporary equilibrium again comes into existence at point D. But the economy is still overemployed and underpaid. Again production factors raise their costs, shifting supply to AS_3. As higher prices cause real balances to fall and bring about a move up the aggregate demand curve, firms cut back on output and employment. Finally point E is reached, with a price level of 130. At this point, short-run demand and supply are again in equilibrium and no further pressures for change are felt. In the markets for the factors of production, supply and demand are also in equilibrium. Labor and other factors are satisfied with their real income. There is no tendency to cut back or to expand. Output is at full employment and the economy is on the long-run supply curve (ASL).

After an initial disturbance from increased demand or a supply shock, how long does it take for the economy to come back to potential output, and how much additional output and employment occur in the interim? The answer depends on how good information is and on how rapidly prices and wages adjust. If knowledge is available quickly and adjustments are rapid, the economy might move to point E almost at once. With poor information, a variety of outcomes is possible. Output could oscillate around the full-employment level. Price rises could first accelerate and then slow down, or vice versa. Different sets of assumptions lead to alternative results. Furthermore, the long-run supply curve toward which the economy heads is not a fixed point.

GROWTH IN OUTPUT AND PRICE MOVEMENTS

In the course of time, the position of full employment and potential output moves as a result of the dynamic events in the economy. Looking forward, neither price nor output levels have yet been determined. Their future locations depend on events that will occur in the future. Figure 12.11 presents one conceivable sequence of year-to-year movements in the equilibrium of long-run aggregate supply and demand. Point A shows one equilibrium of demand and a long-run aggregate supply curve (ASL_1). Potential output may be increased by capital investment, higher education, or technological breakthroughs. Prices may rise as a result of excess demand or of supply shocks. In the figure, a new potential end-of-year equilibrium is shown at point B. However, a possibility also exists that, because of an inadequate expansion of demand and adjustment lags, the year-end equilibrium will be located only at point F. The economy will experience unemployment and unused capacity The equilibrium of short-run demand and supply will not be at the natural rate of unemployment (or potential output).

Equally uncertain are still later rates of growth in both productive capacity and prices. The figure illustrates various possibilities through its uneven year-to-year movements in both the price level and potential output. Dynamic developments depend on what happens in the interim. What policies will be developed to expand or contract demand? Will more or less active supply-side policies be adopted? How will the private economy and the rest of the world react to events?

Figure 12.11 demonstrates that even though the long-run curve is drawn as vertical, the economy's potential output does vary with movements in short-run demand. In the long run, when demand and supply can adjust fully to altered conditions, the level of output depends on the economy's ability to produce and on the quantities of capital, labor, and imported materials that are available as inputs to the production process. The level of prices depends on the dynamic changes that have occurred in the interim. Growth in potential output depends on increases in available production inputs—capital, labor, and natural resources—and on improvements in productivity. These growth factors are likely to be enhanced by high levels of demand. Labor skills and human

FIGURE 12.11   **Potential and Actual Output and Prices Grow Unevenly**

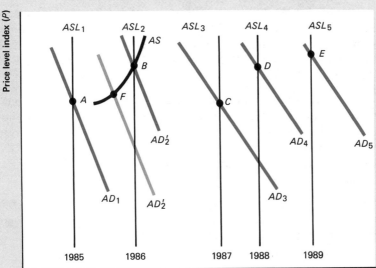

*The uneven year-to-year movements in the long-run aggregate supply curves
(ASL) and the erratic movements in the equilibrium of AD-AS (points A to
F) call attention to the fact that growth in long-run aggregate supply depends
on what happens to aggregate demand and output in the interim. The trend
rate of growth in potential output is not independent of demand, price, and
output movements even though, for ease of exposition, it is common to picture
(as in Figure 12.10) the long-run curve as not dependent on prices.*

capital will be greater. Investment will be higher, enlarging the capital stock
and encompassing the latest technological innovations.

Even though the actual growth in potential output varies considerably as
demand and investment expand and contract, it is common in macroeconomic
analysis to assume that equilibrium supply and demand grow steadily along a
long-term trend path. Potential output expands as the labor force and capital
increase and productivity improves. Fluctuations in demand and output occur
as deviations from such a growth path. To the extent that output expands,
additional money and demand do not lead to higher prices, but merely fund the
larger real GNP. Analysis of shifts in demand and supply are primarily centered on deviations around longer-run trends. Most figures and tables implicitly adjust for normal growth. This volume follows such a convention. When
we speak of movements in AS and AD, it is assumed that the movements are
adjusted for normal growth. In contrast to the assumptions, however, the
actual path of growth is not likely to be smooth. One of the key issues at the
start of the 1980s was how to get back to a more rapid growth path.

Summary

1. Until after World War II, the history of price movements is one of price increases and inflations followed by price declines and deflations. Since 1940, however, periods of rising incomes have been longer and recessions shorter. Prices have risen steadily, with only occasional periods when the rate of inflation has slowed.

2. The levels of prices and output are determined by interactions of the aggregate demand and aggregate supply curves. Static models show how new price levels arise as a result of disturbances in the equilibrium of either demand or supply. To explain persistent inflation, however, one must have dynamic models that describe the process of consistent movements from one price level to another.

3. The aggregate supply curve starts from the concept of the production function. Costs of output depend on prices of labor, capital, and materials. Firms produce to the point where marginal product from an input equals the marginal revenue from its output.

4. In markets with perfect information and flexibility of adjustments, the supply of labor and other inputs will balance with demand. The level of demand (that for labor, for example) is set where real wage payments equal labor's marginal productivity. At the full-employment level (the natural rate of unemployment), the labor market is in equilibrium, with all who want work at the prevailing wage able to find it. After allowance is made for frictional and similar unemployment, with perfect information and flexibility the aggregate supply curve would be vertical at the point of full employment.

5. Markets fail to clear because of frictions, transactions and information costs, and lags in adjustments. As a result, changes in demand may influence output and unemployment as well as prices and wages. Material costs and profit margins vary with demand, as do wages and employment.

6. When aggregate demand or supply shifts, a new equilibrium results. The amount by which output or prices respond depends on the shapes of the *AS* and *AD* curves, on how responsive output is to changes in prices, and on how demand is influenced by shifts in real money balances. While some new short-run equilibriums may be stable, others may include within themselves pressures which will lead to dynamic movements to new positions.

7. The long-run aggregate supply curve pictures a period during which the markets for all production inputs adjust to their underlying demand-supply situations. The long-run curve depicts a situation in which the economy adjusts to real rather than nominal factors; therefore, prices do not influence supply.

8. How much output is actually produced, its growth rate, and the price level over the long run depend on the dynamic forces of the short run which affect both demand and supply. The output level in 1990 depends on how

capital and labor and productivity grow before then, and on aggregate demand at that time.

Questions for Discussion and Review

1. Compare the movement of prices in pre- and post-1950 contractions and expansions.

2. What is meant by a market failing to clear? What changes in the post-World-War-II economy may have contributed to making this phenomenon more common?

3. Why do firms tend during a recession to cut output and employment rather than wages and profits?

4. Describe the several forces which shape the short-run aggregate supply curve.

5. Why have aggregate supply curves become the object of so much attention from economists in recent years?

6. (a) Why are employers willing to hire workers up to the point where the wage rate equals the marginal revenue product of labor?
   (b) What factors determine whether an increase in the real wage rate will call forth an increase in the amount of labor supplied?

7. What conditions would have to prevail in the economy for the short-run aggregate supply curve to be vertical?

8. If firms believe they will be unable to sell everything they produce, how will their demand for labor be affected? What are the implications for the aggregate supply curve?

9. What are the primary forces causing the short-run aggregate supply curve to shift?

10. In what direction would the following changes initially cause the aggregate demand curve to shift?
    (a) An increase in the money supply.
    (b) An increase in government spending.
    (c) An increase in the demand for money.
    (d) An increase in tax rates.
    (e) An increase in the desire to save.

11. For what purposes would you want to use the concept of
    (a) the short-run rather than the long-run supply curve?
    (b) the long-run rather than the short-run curve?

References

Eckstein, O., ed. *The Econometrics of Price Determination.* Washington, D.C.: Board of Governors of the Federal Reserve System, 1972.

Gordon, R. J. "Recent Developments in the Theory of Inflation and Unemployment." *Journal of Monetary Economics* 2(1976): 185–219.

Mansfield, E. *Microeconomics: Theory and Applications,* 4th edition. New York: Norton, 1982, Chapter 13.

Okun, A. M. "Inflation: Its Mechanics and Welfare Costs." *Brookings Papers on Economic Activity* 2(1975): 351–90.

Phelps, E. S. et al. *Microeconomic Foundations of Employment and Inflation Theory.* New York: Norton, 1972.

Rees, A. *The Economics of Work and Pay,* 2nd edition. New York: Harper & Row, 1979.

Solow, R. M. "Alternative Approaches to Macroeconomic Theory: A Partial View." *Canadian Journal of Economics* 12(August 1979): 339–54.

Taylor, J. B. "Recent Developments in the Theory of Stabilization Policy" in *Stabilization Policy* (April 1980). (Published by the Center for the Study of American Enterprise, St. Louis, Mo.)

APPENDIX 12.1   Labor Supply and Demand

Pages 413 to 420 and Figure 12.5 show the relationship between labor demand and supply, wages, prices, employment, and output. These same relationships can be illustrated by a four-quadrant diagram which combines the production function, the labor market, and the relationship between real and nominal wages. It demonstrates again a vertical aggregate supply curve at full employment. Figure 12.12 pictures these interactions, showing graphically how a labor market with perfect information and flexibility would operate. Quadrants c and b are the production function and labor supply and demand curves of Figures 12.3 and 12.4, except that their axes have been transformed. Employment is now on the vertical axis; output and real wages are on the horizontal. Quadrant d has a vertical line drawn at the level of full-employment output. This level of full-employment output reflects the output and employment level of point A on the production function (quadrant c). In turn, this point is determined by the number who want to work at the equilibrium supply and demand for labor pictured at point A in quadrant b.

Quadrant a shows a series of curves, each of which reflects a separate nominal wage rate (W). The real wage rate differs at each point on these curves as a result of the interaction of the nominal wage with each separate price level. At every point, the real wage rate can be found by dividing the nominal wage by the price level at that point. The real wage is the same at every A point $\left(\dfrac{W_1}{P_1} = \dfrac{W_2}{P_2} = \dfrac{W_3}{P_3}\right)$. This real wage is the full-employment wage rate, for when it prevails, the desire to work exactly equals the demand for labor. At full employment, the real wage rate demanded by the labor force to furnish a given supply exactly equals the marginal product of labor determined by the existing production function. Note that under these conditions, the aggregate supply curve in quadrant d is vertical; the quantity of output supplied is the same at every price level. Of course, since GNP equals price times quantity, even with real output fixed, nominal output increases every time the price level rises.

FIGURE 12.12   **The Equilibrium of Nominal and Real Wages with the Marginal Product of Labor**

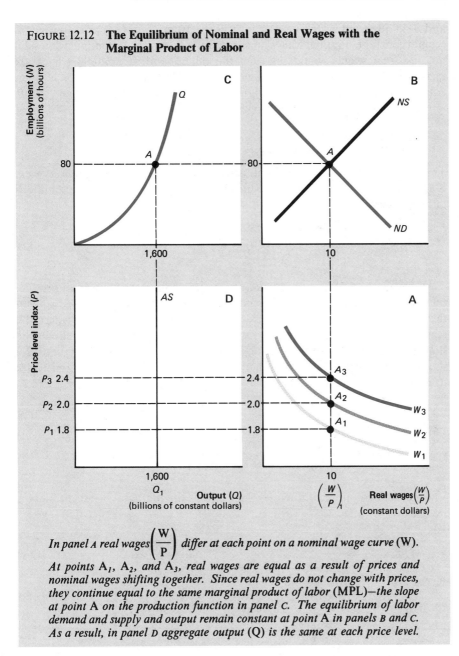

In panel A real wages $\left(\dfrac{W}{P}\right)$ differ at each point on a nominal wage curve (W). At points A_1, A_2, and A_3, real wages are equal as a result of prices and nominal wages shifting together. Since real wages do not change with prices, they continue equal to the same marginal product of labor (MPL)—the slope at point A on the production function in panel C. The equilibrium of labor demand and supply and output remain constant at point A in panels B and C. As a result, in panel D aggregate output (Q) is the same at each price level.

What happens when either prices or nominal wages rise? Since the level of real wages and output is determined by real factors, it is not affected by a change in prices. When prices rise, the real wage remains constant as the result of an equivalent rise in nominal wages. If nominal wages rise first, the consistency is obtained through an equivalent price rise. To see this, look at points A_1

and A_2 in quadrant A. Imagine that prices rise from A_1 to A_2. For real wages to remain constant, nominal wages must rise from W_1 to W_2. If nominal wages did not rise, real wages would fall. On the other hand, if nominal wages are increased from W_2 to W_3, note again that to maintain real wages at their equilibrium value, prices must also rise. In this case they must go from P_2 to P_3 in order to maintain equal real wages at A_2 and A_3.

A NUMERICAL EXAMPLE OF EQUILIBRIUM

This action and reaction can be illustrated by a numerical example as well. Start with a labor supply curve in which the amount of labor offered (in billions of hours) depends on real wages:

$$NS = \overline{N} + n\frac{W}{P} \qquad NS = 70 + 1\frac{W}{P}. \qquad \textbf{12.8}$$

The economy has a production function in which the amount of product (in billions of constant dollars) depends on the number of hours worked. Given this function, the amount of labor demanded will rise to the point where the real wage equals the marginal product of labor. The MPL, in turn, equals the slope (first derivative) of the production function at any point. Equation 12.9 shows the production function with a constant supply of capital (K), and 12.10, its derivative, or the demand for labor.

$$Q = K\sqrt{N} \qquad\qquad Q = 178.9\sqrt{N} \qquad \textbf{12.9}$$

$$ND = MPL = \frac{dQ}{dN} = \frac{K}{2\sqrt{N}} \qquad ND = \frac{89.45}{\sqrt{N}}. \qquad \textbf{12.10}$$

Since, at real equilibrium, the real wage equals the marginal product of labor, we have

$$MPL = \frac{W}{P} = \frac{K}{2\sqrt{N}} \qquad\qquad \frac{W}{P} = \frac{89.45}{\sqrt{N}} \qquad \textbf{12.11}$$

or

$$ND = N = \left(\frac{K}{2\frac{W}{P}}\right)^2 \qquad N = \left(\frac{89.45}{\frac{W}{P}}\right)^2. \qquad \textbf{12.12}$$

These are the equations for the supply (12.8) and demand (12.12) schedules for labor. At equilibrium they are equal and measure the level of work at full employment. Assume that at full employment people want to work 80 billion hours. (A substitution of this amount of labor in equation 12.9, the production function, shows that real output will be $1,600 billion.) By solving the equation for supply and demand, we find that at full employment, equilibrium exists at a real wage rate of $10 an hour. When $NS = ND = 80$,

$$NS = \overline{N} + n\frac{W}{P} \qquad\qquad 80 = 70 + 1\frac{W}{P}$$

$$ND = \left(\frac{K}{2\dfrac{W}{P}}\right)^2 \qquad\qquad 80 = \left(\frac{89.45}{\dfrac{W}{P}}\right)^2$$

$$\frac{W}{P} = 10.$$

Note that when the full-employment wage rate $\left(\dfrac{W}{P}\right)$ is $10, if the price level is 2, as at point A_2 on the nominal wage curve, the nominal wage (W) is $20. What happens if prices fall, say to 1.8, as at point A_1? We see from equations 12.8 and 12.12 that for the labor market to stay in equilibrium, the real wage must remain at $10. This means that as prices fall, nominal wages must drop also, in this case to $18 $\left(\dfrac{W}{P} = \dfrac{18}{1.8}\right)$. Similarly, if nominal wages rise to $24, the labor force will be fully employed only if the price index rises to 2.4, point A_3 on the diagram.

13

Inflation, Demand, and Output

While shifts in aggregate demand and supply bring about a new price-output equilibrium, one-time price changes like those analyzed in Chapter 12 do not adequately explain inflation. In those examples, demand-pull and cost-push impulses raise the price level, but the time span is too short to encompass cost increases for labor and other factors of production and to initiate cumulative price movements. One-shot increases in demand result only in a new equilibrium with a higher price level. In contrast, inflations require continuous expansions of aggregate demand. Where do such continuous expansions come from? While price movements raise the amounts paid for labor, capital, and materials and thereby expand the circular flow of income and demand, a steady growth of aggregate demand requires equal increases in monetary spending (MV). An explanation of inflation must therefore make clear why the growth rate of monetary spending stays high enough to allow the persistent expansion of demand and prices. Why does demand continue to grow?

This chapter develops a dynamic model of inflation. While the Phillips curve shows how excess demand can result in steady wage increases, its analysis does not yield satisfactory explanations of inflation. Many economists doubt that the trade-offs between inflation and unemployment shown on Phillips curves are possible. And even if they do exist, there are questions as to whether they are likely to be ephemeral or significant over extended periods. Modern models of inflation contain several other features: (1) Most important, expanded models show how past price increases engender dynamic inflationary forces based on either the inertial momentum built up in the price-wage structure or on expectations of future prices. (2) Current theories also explicitly model the concept of supply shocks. (3) Because time is critical in analysis, broader theories also deal with the relationship between short- and long-run curves.

In the theory of inflation, as in that of income determination, disagreements over the flexibility of prices and wages, the formation of expectations, the significance of the short and long run, and the role of money cause economists to hold conflicting views as to optimum policies. Some believe inflation to be primarily a monetary phenomenon that can be ended quite rapidly by a proper control of the money supply. Others emphasize the importance in inflation of the economy's price-wage structure. While inflation could be ended by sufficient monetary restraint, they conclude that the result would be a sharp drop in output, high interest rates, and possible financial difficulties. High costs in lost output, bankruptcies, and unemployment would be inevitable if worthwhile declines in the inflation rate were to be achieved over a short period.

Many observers believe that the failure to end inflation in the 1970s and early 1980s reflected an apparent willingness on the part of the public (or at least of the government) to put up with inflation in order to avoid the costs of ending it. Others felt that the failure merely reflected errors in judgment by policy makers. In any event, 1981 introduced a new administration committed to stronger anti-inflationary policies. The results may provide a testing ground for some new policies and their cost benefits. This chapter supplies the necessary background for analyzing inflation and anti-inflationary policies. It includes:

Wage and price Phillips curves.
Short-run Phillips curves and aggregate supply.
Inflation curves of aggregate supply with price inertia and inflationary expectations.
Long-run inflation curves and the natural rate of unemployment.
Natural-rate hypothesis: acceleration and deceleration.
Aggregate demand and inflation.
Supply shocks.
Rationalists and structuralists.
Inflation, recessions, and monetary growth.
Estimates of demand, shock, and core inflation.

Wage and Price Phillips Curves

An early contribution to the theory of inflation was the Phillips curve. While the initial model underlying Phillips curves showed the connection between unemployment and wage movements, it has now been broadened to include the analysis of prices and the ratio of actual to potential output. In other words, this curve expresses the relationship between *the rate of increase* in wages and a measure of the under- or overutilization of the economy's productive capacity. Although lacking an explanation of the connection between past and current price changes, Phillips curves can readily be related to the static models of price determination. They represent a series of persistent shifts in short-run aggregate supply curves, thus serving as a springboard to the development of true dynamic price models which include lags.

Phillips curves derive their name from a famous article by A. W. Phillips in which he estimated a relationship between the annual average rate of unemployment and the annual percentage change in nominal wages over almost a hundred years of British history.[1] Many other empirical studies have produced evidence of similar relationships. However, no firm theory has been advanced to explain the curve. James Tobin has called it "an empirical generalization in search of a theory." Those who believe in the curve seem to assume that, depending on the level of demand, both producers and labor can demand higher prices and wages.

Figure 13.1 shows an empirical Phillips curve for the United States economy compared to data covering the years 1955 through 1969 (black dots). While exceptions appear, the cluster of these dots around the line is quite close. The curve shows that when unemployment stood at 7 percent, inflation was about zero. Unemployment at 2 percent would be related to extremely high rates of price increase. The curve appears to chart a trade-off between output and price changes. High demand and output cause unemployment to fall below the natural rate. Such a situation is accompanied by a high rate of inflation. On the other hand, when demand is below the full-employment level, excess capacity holds price increases in check.

But notice the colored dots on the figure. They chart similar data for the years 1970 through 1980. They present quite a different picture. Looking at them, one might conclude either that no regular relationship exists between capacity utilization and price changes or that any regularities have shifted over time. In other words, the dots either could represent points on a series of short-run curves rather than those on a single curve or they could indicate the absence of a relationship.

WAGES AND UNEMPLOYMENT

One possible explanation for the shape of the curve as determined by Phillips and others is that the rate at which nominal wages change depends on the excess or surplus demand for labor. The rate of unemployment measures the amount of the excess. A shortage of labor is likely to be accompanied by an increase in wages. On the other hand, the larger the number seeking work unsuccessfully, the harder it is for labor to raise wages. The relationship between unemployment and changes in wages is not constant. As unemployment falls, further reductions of equal size lead to an accelerating rate of wage boosts. Fewer and fewer workers are available to fill jobs. To raise output, an

1. A. W. Phillips, "The Relationships between Unemployment and the Rate of Change in Money Wage Rates in the United Kingdom, 1861–1957," *Economica* 25(1958): 283–99.

FIGURE 13.1   **An Empirical Phillips Curve**

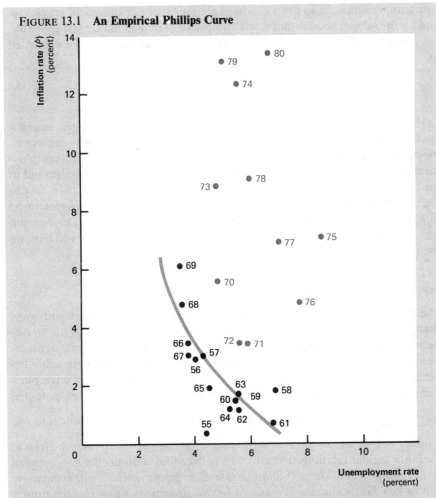

The dots show the amount of unemployment and inflation in each year. The line of regression tracing the relationships over time between the rates of inflation and unemployment is a Phillips curve. The curve fits well for the period 1955–69. The much higher dots after 1969 show either that the relationship has shifted or that it is not a good explanation of inflation.
SOURCE: Economic Report of the President, 1981.

employer will be forced to hire those already at work. A faster increase in wages will be needed to obtain additional hours of work. Identical increases in demand result in ever-larger increases in wages and smaller additions to hours worked. Because of these relationships, Phillips curves appear to be convex, as shown in Figure 13.1. In the opposite direction, as unemployment rises, wages are likely to be sticky. For the numerous reasons discussed previously, declines in wages are not likely to be as rapid as increases. The percentage of workers tied semipermanently to firms becomes a larger share of those still employed, and for the sake of good future relationships, wage reductions are less probable.

In general terms, the effect of unemployment on wages can be expressed as

$$\dot{W} = \overline{W} + l(U^* - U) \qquad\qquad 13.1$$

In this equation, $\dot{W}$, the percentage rate of change in nominal wages, equals a constant ($\overline{W}$) plus a relationship expressed by the coefficient l between unemployment at the full-employment level (U^*) and the actual rate of unemployment (U). The rate of change in wages depends on excess or slack demand in the labor market. Excess unemployment puts a downward pressure on wages. On the other hand, if the number seeking jobs falls below full employment, as in wartime or in other periods of excess demand, wages increase at a more rapid pace. The larger is l, the more effect labor-market tightness or ease will have on the rate of wage change.

PRICE-OUTPUT CURVES: OKUN'S LAW

The Phillips curve expresses a relationship between employment and wage changes. However, of greater interest for macroeconomic analysis are movements in output and prices. The same concepts apply when output replaces unemployment and prices replace wages. Such a substitution is possible because prices are dominated by wage movements and each rate of unemployment (U) has an associated capacity utilization rate—actual over potential output $\left(\dfrac{Q}{Q^*}\right)$. One can shift between a chart measuring unemployment to one utilizing output simply by altering the scale. **Okun's law** is the name given to the fairly regular relationship that exists between lost output (the gap between actual and potential output) and the rate of unemployment.[2] Either measure tells us how far production is above or below capacity and how much output is being lost as a result of inadequate demand. Since excess capacity is being related to excess unemployment, the sign on unemployment is opposite to that in equation 13.1.

Okun's law takes the form of

$$\frac{Q^* - Q}{Q^*} = f(U - U^*), \qquad\qquad 13.2$$

where $\dfrac{Q^* - Q}{Q^*}$ is the gap between potential and actual output and where ($U - U^*$) is the percent of excess unemployment. The coefficient f indicates the functional relationship. The actual relationship from 1974 to 1980 is displayed

---

2. Arthur Okun first called attention to this regularity in an article, "Potential GNP: Its Movement and Significance," *Proceedings of the Business and Economic Statistics Section of the American Statistical Association*, 1962.

in Table 13.1. On average during this period, an excess rate of unemployment of 1 percent was related to a 2.0 percent loss in output below potential. In prior periods, losses in output ran about 3 percent for every 1 percent excess unemployment. The 3.4 percent excess in unemployment in 1975 meant a loss for the year estimated at 86.7 billion constant 1972 dollars.

Prices and wages move together, but not necessarily by identical amounts. To the degree productivity $(\dot{PR})$ improves, increases in nominal wage rates $(\dot{W})$ can exceed those of prices $(\dot{P})$. When more units of output are turned out for each hour worked, the cost per unit drops as the wage rate is spread over a larger number of units. If wages remain constant, costs of output and prices can decline. If prices remain constant, wages can rise. These relationships are expressed in the following equation:

$$\dot{P} = \dot{W} - \dot{PR}. \tag{13.3}$$

The rate of increase in prices equals the rate of increase in wages less that of productivity.

Equations 13.2 and 13.3 can be substituted in equation 13.1 to obtain a Phillips curve in terms of prices and output. The equation equivalent to 13.1 is:

$$\dot{P} = q\left(\frac{Q - Q^*}{Q^*}\right) - \dot{PR}. \tag{13.4}$$

The inflation rate $\dot{P}$ increases in accordance with the coefficient q to the degree

TABLE 13.1   **The Relationship between Excess Unemployment and the GNP Gap**

Year	Actual rate of unemployment minus rate at full employment $(U - U^*)$ (percent)	Gap between potential and actual output over potential $\left(\dfrac{Q^* - Q}{Q^*}\right)$ (percent)	Loss in real GNP (billions of constant 1972 dollars)
1974	0.6	2.3	29.5
1975	3.4	6.6	86.7
1976	2.6	4.7	64.7
1977	1.9	2.8	39.7
1978	0.9	1.5	22.4
1979	0.7	1.4	21.6
1980	2.0	4.4	67.8

SOURCE: Economic Report of the President, 1981, p. 181.

The first column shows the level of excess unemployment. The second and third columns are estimates of the gap in real GNP, the first in percentages, the second in constant 1972 dollars.

that actual output (Q) exceeds full-employment output (Q^*), and it is reduced by the rate of increase in productivity ($\dot{PR}$). The smaller is q, the flatter will the curve be and the less effect will output have on prices.

Short-Run Phillips Curves and Aggregate Supply

The price-output Phillips curve can be used as a first step in examining the relationship between static and dynamic models. On a static aggregate supply curve, each point shows the relationship between output and the *level* of prices. In contrast, on a Phillips-type price-output curve, each point shows the relationship between the ratio of output to potential and the *percentage rate of growth* in prices. With a constant ratio of actual to potential output, the price level may expand steadily.

PHILLIPS CURVES SHOW CONSTANT RATES OF INCREASE IN PRICES

The relationship between a particular type of moving equilibrium of aggregate demand and supply and a Phillips curve is shown by Figure 13.2. On this diagram, panel 13.2A pictures a shift in aggregate demand from AD_1 to AD_2 along an aggregate supply curve. The equilibrium of AD and AS moves from point A to point B. The ratio of actual to potential output $\left(\dfrac{Q}{Q^*}\right)$ rises from 100 to 102 percent. Unemployment falls from 5.5 to 4.83 percent. Higher demand results in a price increase to 100.6, or .6 percent ($100.6 - 100$). For reasons to be explored shortly, such an equilibrium may not be stable; the aggregate demand and supply curves both shift upward to AD_3 and AS_2, and a new equilibrium is reached at point C. With the capacity utilization rate remaining at 102 percent, prices rise again by .6 percent ($101.2 - 100.6$). Now suppose that another shift in AD and AS occurs and the economy moves to point D (the lines are omitted). Output remains at 102, while prices rise again by .6 percent ($101.8 - 101.2$).

The complex information which is presented so awkwardly in Figure 13.2A can be depicted more simply, as in Figure 13.2B, by changing the vertical scale to one measuring percentage rates of change in prices rather than price levels. In this figure, point X summarizes the information contained in the movements from point B to C to D. Output above potential at 102 causes a steady rise in prices ($\dot{P}$) of .6 percent. Similarly, output at 104 and unemployment of 4.17 percent lead to an inflation rate ($\dot{P}$) of 1.2 percent. The line connecting the points in Figure 13.2B is a short-run Phillips price-output curve. The curve is a representation of equation 13.4. The horizontal axis of figure 13.2B is labeled in such a way as to bring out the idea that either output $\left(\dfrac{Q}{Q^*}\right)$ or

FIGURE 13.2   **Short-Run Aggregate Supply and Phillips Curves**

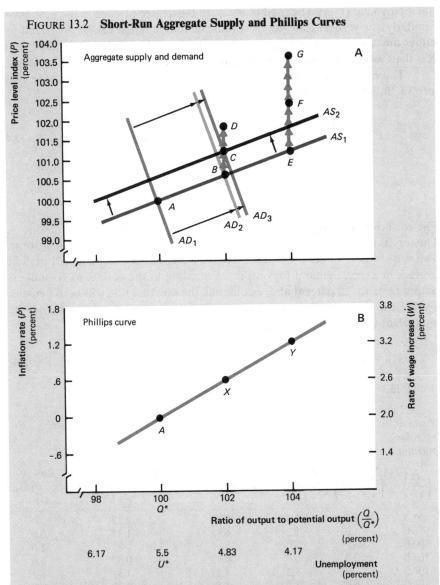

Aggregate supply curves relate output and price levels; Phillips curves relate output and inflation rates. In panel A, a shift in demand to AD_2 causes equilibrium to rise from point A to point B. Prices increase in response to output above potential. A continuation of excess output at 102 percent causes a series of shifts in both AD and AS to an equilibrium at C and then at D. Output above potential causes a steady rate of price increases (.6 percent per period). This series of price rises is summarized by a single point X in panel B. Point X represents a relationship between output at 102 percent of potential and an inflation rate of .6 percent. Similarly, point Y shows that an output level of 104 percent causes prices to rise at a rate of 1.2 percent, the same information shown more awkwardly by points E, F, and G in panel A.

unemployment (U) can be used to measure the degree of slack in the economy. Similarly, the vertical scales in 13.2B indicate that inflation can be measured by either the rate of price or wage increase. On the curve, prices rise by 2 percent less than wages on the assumption that all productivity gains accrue to wages.

The numerical example for equation 13.4 and the curve underlying Figure 13.2B, holding $\dot{PR}$ constant, is

$$\dot{P} = q\left(\frac{Q - Q^*}{Q^*}\right) \qquad \dot{P} = .3\left(\frac{Q}{Q^*} - 1\right) \qquad \text{13.4}$$

$$\dot{P} = .3\left(\frac{102}{100} - 1\right) = .006.$$

The coefficient relating inflation to the utilization of production potential is .3. The results must be multiplied by 100 to express the rate of inflation in percent. The size of q determines the steepness of the curve and the response of inflation to slack or excess demand for output. According to the equations, as long as output remains 2.0 percent above potential, the inflation rate will be .6 percent. Table 13.2 shows other examples from this price-output equation and the equivalent unemployment-wage changes.

TABLE 13.2   **Rates of Price and Wage Changes and Capacity Utilization**
(percent)

Ratio of actual to potential output $\left(\dfrac{Q}{Q^*}\right)$	Excess output $\left(\dfrac{Q}{Q^*} - 1\right)$	Rate of inflation $(\dot{P})$	Rate of unemployment (U)	Rate of excess employment $(U^* - U)$	Rate of wage change $(\dot{W})$
93.3	−6.7	−2.0	7.72	−2.22	0
96.0	−4.0	−1.2	6.83	−1.33	0.8
100.0	0	0	5.50	0	2.0
102.0	2.0	0.6	4.83	0.67	2.6
104.0	4.0	1.2	4.17	1.33	3.2
106.0	6.0	1.8	3.50	2.00	3.8

The rate of inflation is assumed to equal 0.3 times the ratio of excess output in percent ($\dot{P} = .3\left[\dfrac{Q}{Q^*} - 1\right]$). Wages change at .9 times the percent by which unemployment (U) falls below full employment (U*) and by an additional 2 percent to match the expected improvement in productivity ($\dot{W} = .9$ [5.5 − U] + 2). Price changes equal wage increases minus this 2 percent.

FIGURE 13.3   **The Expectations-Augmented Inflation Curve**

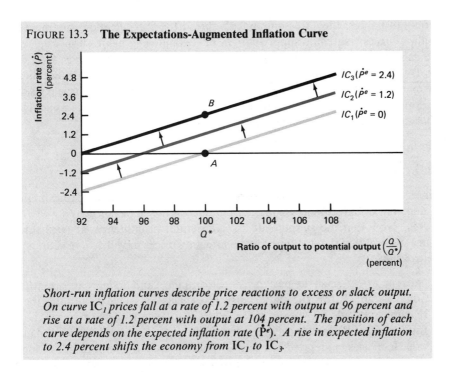

Short-run inflation curves describe price reactions to excess or slack output.
On curve IC$_1$ prices fall at a rate of 1.2 percent with output at 96 percent and
rise at a rate of 1.2 percent with output at 104 percent. The position of each
curve depends on the expected inflation rate ($\dot{P}e$). A rise in expected inflation
to 2.4 percent shifts the economy from IC$_1$ to IC$_3$.

Inflation Curves of Aggregate Supply with Price Inertia and Inflationary Expectations

Modern theoretical developments bring out other factors that influence the rate
of inflation in addition to the simple Phillips relationship. Among the most
important of these additions are the inclusion of terms for dynamic price effects
and for supply-side disturbances. When such factors are included, a more
complete model of inflationary price determination becomes

$$\dot{P} = q\left(\frac{Q}{Q^*} - 1\right) + p(\dot{P}e) + PM - \dot{P}R.$$ **13.5**

This equation adds to the simpler Phillips equation (13.4) the extremely important dynamic impact on the inflation rate of expected price changes ($\dot{P}e$) as
well as movements in material prices (PM) or other supply factors.

An example of what curves based on equation 13.5 look like appears in
Figure 13.3. When these curves are plotted, as with previous models containing
more than two variables, they result in a set of curves rather than in a single
one. The basic shape is the same as the price-output Phillips curve of Figure
13.2B, but a separate curve exists for each change in any of the other variables.
Since they are still in the process of development, such curves have been given a

variety of names; they are sometimes referred to as expectations-augmented Phillips curves, aggregate supply curves, or dynamic aggregate supply curves. We call them **inflation curves of aggregate supply** or **inflation curves** (*IC*) for short. Occasionally we also use the other terms in order to make clear that these are merely different names for the same concept. Each inflation curve consists of a price-output Phillips curve that has attached to it, explicitly or implicitly a label showing the level of expectations existing when it is drawn.

THE DYNAMIC FACTORS IN INFLATION

When macroeconomics was concerned principally with analyzing determinants of demand, disagreements frequently focused on the slopes of the *IS* and *LM* curves. Now that the supply side is given equal prominence, at least three issues surrounding the dynamic factors affecting prices have become centers of controversy.

1. Current prices react to past price performance and to new information. Some theories stress the importance of expectations in determining these reactions. People set wages or prices in accordance with their views about future prices. If they expect prices to fall, wage demands will be reduced and price increases moderated. In contrast, others stress the importance of inertia, or the wage-price structure, as a dynamic force. A momentum builds up from past price increases. Workers and firms demand higher wages or prices in an effort to catch up with past losses in their standard of living. Since their real income is already reduced, they will lower demands only slightly in response to altered expectations.

2. The speed with which the economy adjusts to past prices or to new information is uncertain. Some believers in expectations emphasize that rational decision makers will adjust immediately to new useful information. They are forced to do so by competition. Lags can be expensive. In contrast, many studies find that expectations can be modeled as a gradual adaptation to price history. Those who reject expectations and stress the significance of the structure believe that adjustments, especially reductions in inflation, will take a long time.

3. The analysis of long-run, as opposed to short-run, dynamic inflation curves resembles that of static supply curves. Since the economy has time to adjust, long-run inflation curves should be vertical. The effect of prices on the level of output should disappear except to the degree that the dynamic process influences the level of potential output. But to many, this exception is critical. Long recessions or depressions cause large losses in output and reduced capital and labor skills that may never be regained. On the other hand, inflations may bring about policy-imposed restraints on demand and a slow-down in productivity gains. Both views concur that the position of the long-run curve and the amount of output depend on what happens to demand in the interim.

EXPECTATIONS-AUGMENTED INFLATION CURVES

The introduction of the dynamic variable $\dot{P}e$ into the price determination model resulted from a recognition that the Phillips curve was an incomplete description of reality because it failed to include the reactions of price and wage setters to past price movements. According to the Phillips curve, a possible favorable trade-off exists between unemployment and inflation. Policy makers could choose a point on the curve which would yield higher output paid for by only a small amount of inflation. For example, if Table 13.2 were factual, the fourth line shows it possible for the economy to achieve output 2 percent above potential at a cost of an annual inflation rate of .6 percent. Many might feel that such a rate of price increase would be worth tolerating in order to raise every family's real income by $400 a year.

However, such favorable trade-offs are unlikely. They exist only as long as labor fails to adjust nominal wages to new price levels. Output is higher because real wages are below equilibrium. As soon as workers realize this, they are likely to demand a cost-of-living adjustment (COLA). Costs would rise and the aggregate supply curve would shift. The fight by some to regain lost income and efforts by others to anticipate price increases could lead to a dynamic process of price-wage and wage-price spirals.

To find out what happens in the process of adjustment, we must examine the dynamic term $p(\dot{P}e)$ in the price determination equation. When the entire price equation is analyzed, it appears that there is not one single short-run price-output relationship, such as that in equations 13.2 and 13.3, but rather a different one for each imbedded price trend or expected level of prices. Future prices and outputs depend on how decision makers react to the past perform-ance of wage and price movements.

Table 13.3 presents a simplified numerical example of how short-run inflation curves will shift when the dynamic price term is included in the price equation. The table is based on a dynamic price equation of

$$\dot{P} = q\left(\frac{Q}{Q^*} - 1\right) + p(\dot{P}e) \quad \dot{P} = .3\left(\frac{Q}{Q^*} - 1\right) + 1P_{-1}. \qquad \textbf{13.6}$$

Here the inflation rate $(\dot{P})$ is considered to depend on the deviations of output from normal $\left(\frac{Q}{Q^*} - 1\right)$ and on the persistence factor $p(\dot{P}e)$. It assumes the simplest model of lags and formation of expectations.[3] The coefficient p is 1 and this period's expected inflation equals last period's actual inflation rate $(\dot{P}e = \dot{P}_{-1})$. In each period the inflation rate depends on both the output ratio

3. See E. M. Gramlich, "Macro Policy Responses to Price Shocks," *Brookings Papers on Economic Activity* 1(1979): 125–66. As an example, Gramlich shows on page 134 the rate of wage increase $(\dot{W})$ dependent on unemployment and partly on prior changes in prices $(\dot{P})$ to account for

TABLE 13.3 **Inflation and the Position of Short-Run Inflation Curves Depend on Prior Price Changes**

| Period | Expected inflation rate $(\dot{P}_{-1})$ | Ratio of output to potential (percent) (unemployment rate in parentheses) | | | Illustrated in Figure 13.3 by curve |
		96.0 (6.83)	100 (5.50)	104.0 (4.17)	
		Rate of inflation (percent)			
1	0	−1.2	0	1.2	IC_1
2	1.2	0	1.2	2.4	IC_2
3	2.4	1.2	2.4	3.6	IC_3
4	3.6	2.4	3.6	4.8	—

In a period, the rate of inflation depends both on the ratio of output to potential and on the dynamic expected rate of inflation. In this example, the expected rate of inflation equals the actual rate of the previous period. The numerical equation which the table illustrates is:

$$\dot{P} = .3\left(\frac{Q}{Q^*} - 1\right) + \dot{P}_{-1}$$

in which the excess or slack output is expressed as a percent; when the ratio of output to potential is 96 percent, the slack in output is − 4.0 percent.

and prior inflation rates. The table also shows in parenthesis the unemployment rate related to each output ratio.

These simplified examples are charted in Figure 13.3. Note that each curve is labeled with an expected rate of inflation. On each short-run inflation curve (IC), excess or slack demand leads to similar movements in the rate of inflation. However, the position of each curve differs in accordance with its level of expected inflation. The higher the value of $\dot{P}^e$, the higher the curve. Thus, on the lowest curve, the expected rate of price increase is zero; on the next it is 1.2 percent, and on the top, 2.4 percent. Because the values at each output level are augmented by the amount of expected price movement, these are called expectations-augmented inflation or Phillips curves.

In the debate over inertia versus expectations, both the size of the coefficient p and how the term $\dot{P}^e$ is determined play a prominent part. If p is small, the weight of expectations on current price changes will be small. Many theories emphasize that p may change in response to a learning process. Closely related to the size of p is the issue of what the term $\dot{P}^e$ really represents. Does it arise from rational or adaptive expectations or from inertia? The

expectations as well as on prior changes in wages to account for inertia or catch-up:

$$\dot{W} = -.394 + 6.895 U^{-1} + .3198 \dot{P}_{-1} + .4041 \dot{W}_{-1} + .1374 W_{-2}$$

$R^2 = .834$ Standard error $= .675$.

models of rational expectations show the possibility that policies may influence prices almost immediately. The inertia models indicate that policies to reduce the $\dot{P}^e$ term are likely to take a long time to be effective.

SUPPLY ECONOMICS

The final two items (PM and $\dot{P}R$) in equation 13.5, the model of inflationary price determination, show that the rate of inflation is also affected by factors on the aggregate-supply side. They will shift the basic Phillips-type curve in the same way as do changes in price expectations. In the 1980s, arguments over the potential importance of shifts in supply have taken their place beside dynamic price responses as key areas of macroeconomic interest. The explanations of the factors influencing aggregate supply showed the variety of changes which could shift the curve and alter price-output relationships. Prices of imports and of natural resources (energy, food) may rise; profit margins may expand; production taxes may go up. Every such shift can lead to higher costs and prices. Favorable shocks that reduce costs are also possible, but they have been rare.

A single increase in supply costs will raise prices and temporarily shift the inflation curve upward. A series of shocks, such as the OPEC oil price increases, may hold the curve at a new higher level. As important as the direct impact of such changes, however, will be their influence on the dynamic price term ($\dot{P}^e$) and on spending. If the supply shocks raise the inflation rate, methods of reducing supply-induced price increases do not differ greatly from those used to reduce excess demand.

The final term ($\dot{P}R$) encompasses both growth in productivity and other factors which influence potential output. Added production inputs turning out a greater supply with fewer hours of work exert a downward pressure on prices. Productivity increases reduce the rate of inflation for any amount of slack or excess in output. Chapter 15 analyzes in more detail the forces of supply and ways of increasing potential output. More goods per unit of input mean either that prices need not rise as fast or that wages can rise faster. While in the past, most productivity gains have raised incomes rather than reducing prices, the opposite is possible. In addition, cyclical movements in output cause short-term swings in productivity, but such short-run fluctuations appear to have minor effects on prices compared with the effect of the underlying productivity trend.

Long-Run Inflation Curves and the Natural Rate of Unemployment

Before considering the interactions of dynamic inflation and demand curves, let us examine the relationship between short- and long-run inflation curves. Such relationships are connected to the concept of the natural rate of unemployment. Figure 13.4 contains the same set of short-run inflation curves as the preceding figure. The economy is in equilibrium at point A, with full employment and no inflation. What would happen if aggregate demand were increased by monetary or fiscal policy enough to raise the level of output to, say, 108 percent of potential? The figure shows a movement along the short-run inflation curve (IC_1) to point B.

LONG-RUN INFLATION CURVES

The diagram shows that an increase in employment and real income is accompanied by a rise in the inflation rate of 2.4 percent. According to the assumptions of the model, an 8 percent rise in real income becomes possible at the cost of this 2.4 percent a year inflation. If such a trade-off were feasible, it might be welcome. However, most observers believe such trade-offs are unlikely. For the economy to stay at B, people must be willing to accept higher prices without adjusting their own wage or price demands. The value of $p(\dot{P}^e)$ must be zero. Any trade-off between output and inflation can exist only as long as the economy fails to adjust costs to prior prices.

Instead of staying on an existing short-run inflation curve, the economy will move over time from one short-run curve to another until it reaches the long-run inflation curve (ICL). Current analysis points to such a curve's being vertical. The logic follows the same general reasoning that applies to why the long-run aggregate supply curve becomes vertical when the effects of lags and imperfections have disappeared. In the long run, the amount of work offered and accepted, as well as employment and output, will be at the point of full employment. Changes in prices or inflation will not alter this output point except to the degree that demand and inflation affect capital and productivity. The **long-run inflation curve** (ICL) represents all points of long-run dynamic equilibrium. Output is at the full-employment level at each point, demand and the rate of inflation are expanding at the same pace. The expected rate of inflation equals the actual. As shown on the figure, the long-run inflation rate (ICL) is a vertical line drawn from the point of full employment and of potential output (Q^*).

When the economy moves out along the short-run inflation curve (IC_1) in Figure 13.4 to point B, a dynamic process gets under way. Both output and prices rise. The costs of production increase. Workers bargain for a cost-of-living raise to recoup the drop in their real wages. Utilities and other regulated industries apply for and receive the right to raise prices. Anticipating inflation, lenders demand higher interest rates. Expected prices rise and the economy shifts to a new short-run inflation curve (IC_2).

Appendix 13.1 as well as later examples show that the path to a new equilibrium is complex, depending on the lags in supply adjustments and on what is happening to demand. Figure 13.4 is a simplified schematic presentation. It shows the economy moving from B to point C on the line $\dot{P}^e = 1.2$. But now with higher costs, unless demand expands again, purchases of output

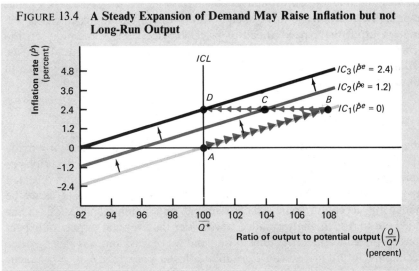

FIGURE 13.4   **A Steady Expansion of Demand May Raise Inflation but not Long-Run Output**

When aggregate demand expands, the AD-AS equilibrium moves from A to B along inflation curve IC₁. The higher inflation rates lead to higher expected prices (P^e), causing inflation curves to shift to IC₂ and IC₃. More of spending pays for price increases, reducing the amount available for output. Equilibrium moves from B to C to D. If aggregate demand (AD) expands at the rate of inflation, point D can continue as a long-run equilibrium. It is an intersection of a short-run inflation curve (IC₃) with the long-run inflation curve (ICL).

decline. Higher prices absorb some spending. The output ratio continues to fall until it again reaches the full-employment line of Q^*. As long as demand continues to grow at a 2.4 percent rate, a new dynamic equilibrium will be maintained at point D. Here, both the current rate of inflation and the expected rate of inflation (shown by the designation $\dot{P}^e = 2.4$ on the short-run IC_3 curve) are equal.

Since output is at the full-employment level for every point on the long-run inflation curve (ICL), all are potentially stable. No pressure arises from the output-price mechanism to alter the inflation rate. In contrast, all points on either side of the curve are unstable. To the right of the line, factors are overemployed. Because inputs are not receiving a real return sufficient to compensate them for their effort, production costs shift up. Depending on what happens to demand, such pressures lead to increases in the inflation rate and/or to the cutting back of output toward the line of full employment. If the economy is in the area to the left of the line, the reverse situation prevails; prices fall and/or output rises.

Because of lags in adjustment, the path by which the economy reacts to an upward movement in the expansion rate of demand can be extremely complex.

Each reaction time and adjustment coefficient for expectations leads to a separate path. In addition, both the speed of adjustment and the coefficients will change. Output may speed ahead of prices or vice versa, depending on the specific adjustment relationships. In this process of adjustment, it should be noted that the situation is dynamically stable at point D only because demand continues to increase at the rate of inflation.

THE NATURAL RATE HYPOTHESIS: ACCELERATION AND DECELERATION

In the late 1960s, both Milton Friedman and E. S. Phelps independently made the point that trade-offs between output and inflation could exist only as long as people failed to take into account all past price increases.[4] They both objected to the view that the Phillips curve showed that additional output could be obtained by accepting some excess demand and potential inflation. They pointed out that such analysis failed to consider the eventual impact of expectations on price increases. As long as demand was excess and was raising price expectations, future prices would go up at a faster pace.

The only level that will stop the inflation rate from rising or falling is the natural rate of unemployment; that is, the long-run equilibrium of dynamic supply and demand. At the natural rate, the economy is on the long-run inflation curve. The key condition is that the economy's expectations are correct with respect to the behavior of prices and wages. At the natural-rate equilibrium, the existing rate of inflation will not change.

The example of Figure 13.4 can be expanded to show the acceleration or deceleration of inflation that occurs when the economy is not in dynamic equilibrium. If increases in demand sufficient to maintain the economy at an over-full-employment position occur continuously, the inflation rate rises steadily. This causes acceleration. If the level of demand falls constantly, a deceleration in inflation occurs at first, followed by an actual deflation.

When demand grows at a steady rate, the result is a new stable rate of inflation. The processes by which changes in the rate at which demand increases cause inflation to advance and recede are pictured in Figure 13.5. As in the previous example, excess demand moves the economy out along the IC_1 curve ($\dot{P}^e = 0$). Again, higher prices cause the economy to shift to a new inflation curve with $\dot{P}^e = 1.2$. In this case, however, the movement back to the long-run curve as pictured in Figure 13.4 does not occur because the growth rate of demand ($A\dot{D}$) accelerates. To maintain a higher level of output, demand must grow at a constantly faster rate.

The actual division of new demand between output and inflation depends on the adjustment processes for production, prices, and price expectations. In the figure, the movements are shown in a simplified form. The rate of inflation

4. M. Friedman, "The Role of Monetary Policy," *American Economic Review* 58(March 1968): 7–11 and E. S. Phelps, "Phillips Curves: Expectations of Inflation and Optimal Unemployment over Time," *Econometrica* 34(August 1967): 254–81.

and the expected rate of inflation rise at the same pace as the growth in demand. Output remains at a constant level above its potential. In each new period, wages rise sufficiently to compensate for prior declines in real income. Nothing holds back the rush to make up for previous price increases. The economy follows the arrows up, with prices rising at an accelerated pace. The steady growth in demand and inflationary expectations as a result of previous price increases causes a constant rise in the rate of inflation. This process by which wages rise sufficiently to offset price increases and prices rise to compensate for higher wages is frequently called a *wage-price spiral.*

The area to the left of the natural rate of unemployment in Figure 13.5 is no more stable than that to the right. Suppose a policy decision is made to end inflation. Demand is furnished sufficient only to maintain output below potential. The economy moves down a short-run inflation curve (IC_4), as to point G in the figure. Now the rate of inflation is less than expected. Wages and prices are adjusted downward. The rate at which demand grows is reduced every time the rate of inflation drops. The economy moves to one lower IC curve after another. Inflation decelerates.

If demand remains slack and prices are sufficiently flexible, disinflation

FIGURE 13.5   **The Rate of Expansion of Aggregate Demand Determines the Acceleration or Deceleration of Inflation**

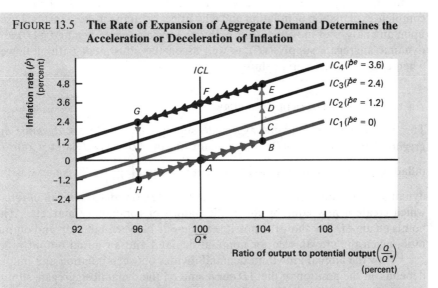

An increase in the growth rate of aggregate demand (AD) raises the equilibrium to B. Higher prices raise price expectations, causing a shift to IC_2. If the rate of growth in AD does not increase, equilibrium will return at ICL as illustrated in Figure 13.4. To maintain output at a level of 104 percent, AD must grow at the same rate as price expectations, causing an acceleration of inflation from point B to point E and upward. If the rate of increase in demand remains constant or declines, output will drop. To maintain output below potential if price expectations are falling, the growth rate of AD and prices must decelerate steadily from point G to H.

will be followed by deflation (a persistent fall in prices). To halt the decline in prices, the economy must generate enough demand to purchase all potential output. A stable equilibrium can prevail at the juncture of the natural rate of unemployment with the short-run inflation curve for which the inertia and expectations term are zero. This is point A in Figure 13.5.

Aggregate Demand and Inflation

Disturbances of the dynamic supply curve (IC) provide only half an explanation for movements in inflation. For prices to continue to rise, any shift in the inflation curve must be matched by an equivalent increase in the growth rate of demand. If the growth rate of aggregate demand remains constant when the short-run inflation curve shifts upward, any price increase would of necessity be accompanied by a drop in output. Less production would put a downward pressure on inflation. With sufficient time and price flexibility, if the growth rate for demand remained constant, the economy would return to the position it held on the long-run inflation curve prior to the supply disturbance. Both the neoclassical and Keynesian analyses show that inflation is possible only if accompanied by a simultaneous increase in the growth rate of demand. A complete explanation of inflation and why prices continue to rise must be based upon an analysis of movements in both dynamic aggregate demand ($\dot{A}D$) and dynamic aggregate supply (IC) as well as on the adustment paths followed when either of these curves shifts.

THE DYNAMIC AGGREGATE DEMAND CURVE

The counterparts of dynamic aggregate supply curves (IC) are **dynamic aggregate demand curves** ($\dot{A}D$). Each point on an $\dot{A}D$ curve relates a rate of inflation ($\dot{P}$) to a ratio of actual to potential output $\left(\dfrac{Q}{Q^*}\right)$. This curve is the dynamic twin of the static demand curve. Like AD, it shifts as a result of forces which create a new equilibrium in the money or commodity markets.[5] The points on an $\dot{A}D$ line show the possible trade-offs between inflation and output ratio, given the growth rate for nominal demand and an initial output ratio.

How the annual growth in demand divides between inflation and output depends on the position of the $\dot{A}D$ curve and on the dynamic aggregate supply curve (IC). In Figure 13.6, all along the curve $\dot{A}D_1$ aggregate demand

5. As noted in Chapter 12, if potential output is growing, aggregate demand must grow at the same pace or a deflationary situation will arise. In the analysis of dynamic equilibriums, as in the static ones, it is usual to consider the deviations from the growth trend separately from the trend. Thus, the zero $\dot{A}D$ curve contains a sufficient increase in demand, even though it is labeled zero, to allow for normal growth. Such trend movements are understood as imbedded in both the static and dynamic aggregate demand and supply curves. The specific analysis does not call attention to this steady expansion and the fact, as shown in Figure 12.11, that the AD-AS equilibrium is constantly shifting.

is growing at a constant rate of 2 percent a year. At point A, the economy is in equilibrium with inflation at a 2 percent rate and output at 100 percent of potential. Depending on the rate of capacity utilization in the previous period, this growth rate of $\dot{A}D$ could also support an economy at point C with a 4 percent rate of inflation, provided that the ratio of actual to potential output was 98 percent. Similarly, D is a possible trade-off, with zero inflation and actual output at 102 percent of potential.

However, while points A, C, and D are all compatible with a 2 percent per year rate of increase in aggregate demand, only point A could be a long-run equilibrium. In the other two cases, pressures for change would exist because the economy, as shown in the figure, would not be on its long-run inflation curve (ICL). The pressures for change can be observed by referring back to equation 12.2, which showed that the growth rate of aggregate demand ($\dot{A}D$) could be divided between the rate of inflation and the growth rate of output:

$$\dot{A}D = \dot{P} + \dot{Q}. \qquad\qquad 12.2$$

In short or intermediate periods, actual output (Q) can shift much faster than potential output (Q^*) can grow. Consequently, growth in output may lead to slack or to an excess use of capacity. This change in capacity utilization gives

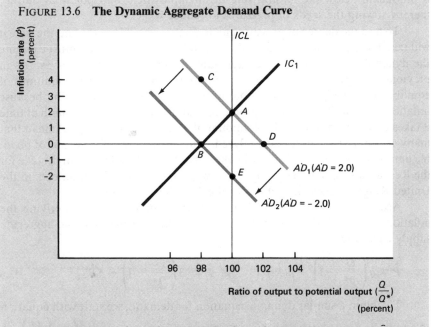

FIGURE 13.6 **The Dynamic Aggregate Demand Curve**

Static aggregate demand curves (AD) have dynamic counterparts. On a dynamic aggregate demand curve (ÀD), the rate of inflation (P̀) is related to the ratio of output to potential. The basic positions of ÀD curves result from the equilibriums formed by the interactions of IS and LM.

rise to price and wage movements, as shown in equation 13.6. When the economy is over- or underemployed, equilibrium can only be temporary. The existence of slack or excess capacity causes movements in the inflation rate, a new trade-off of aggregate demand, and alterations in expected inflation.

MODELING DYNAMIC INFLATION EQUILIBRIUM

Why positions above or below the natural rate of unemployment mean only temporary equilibriums and the complex dynamic paths which the economy may follow to a stable equilibrium can be demonstrated by picturing a shift in dynamic aggregate demand. Suppose that a restrictive fiscal or monetary policy was put in place or that consumers or investors decreased their spending desires, reducing the growth rate of aggregate demand to minus 2 percent. Such a shift is illustrated by the line AD_2 in Figure 13.6. According to this curve, with demand declining at a rate of 2 percent a year, a possible equilibrium could be reached at point B with an inflation rate of zero and capacity utilization of 98 percent, or at other points such as E, with prices falling at an annual rate of 2 percent and output at 100 percent of potential. The figure shows that if the curve IC_1 prevailed, a temporary resting place would be reached at B. However, the equilibrium will not be stable because the economy is producing below the natural rate of unemployment and potential output, thereby sowing the seeds of pressures to reduce wages.

To find the degree of pressure and to picture possible paths and the time it will take for the economy to get back to a stable equilibrium, we must examine the dynamic interactions of the aggregate demand and supply curves. As in previous examples, it is possible to compare the initial and final conditions of equilibrium while ignoring questions of time and dynamic paths. But because inflation is primarily a dynamic problem, a failure to consider the length of time it takes to reach stability and the amount of excess slack created will mean that many critical issues cannot be analyzed. The importance of time and of possible output losses were made clear by the debates over how long it might take for the Reagan anti-inflationary policies to work and by similar arguments in the United Kingdom over the actions of the Thatcher government.

According to equation 13.6, the forces in the economy underlying the inflation rate which determine the shape and shifts in the dynamic aggregate supply curve are

$$\dot{P} = q\left(\frac{Q}{Q^*} - 1\right) + p(\dot{P}_e) \qquad \dot{P} = .3\left(\frac{Q}{Q^*} - 1\right) - 1\dot{P}_{-1}. \qquad \textbf{13.6}$$

To obtain a similar dynamic equation for demand, we start with equation 12.2 but substitute a change in the ratio of output to potential $\left\{\frac{Q}{Q^*} - \left(\frac{Q}{Q^*}\right)_{-1}\right\}$ for the growth rate of output (Q^*). This substitution is necessary because it is the change in the amount of slack or excess use of potential that influences prices, not merely the growth rate of output (Q^*). How the increase in aggregate demand splits between inflation and capacity utilization depends on the previous level of utilization $\left(\dfrac{Q}{Q^*}\right)_{-1}$. When the change in the ratio of output to potential is substituted for the growth rate in output, equation 12.2 becomes

$$\dot{A}D = \dot{P} + \left\{\frac{Q}{Q^*} - \left(\frac{Q}{Q^*}\right)_{-1}\right\}.$$ 13.7

The equations 13.6 and 13.7 together form a dynamic two-equation model which describes the path taken to a new equilibrium in response to the dynamic interactions of aggregate demand and supply. Equation 13.7 shows that a shift in the rate of growth in demand (as that to $\dot{A}D_2$ in Figure 13.6) leads to a new rate of inflation and capacity utilization. Movements in the output ratio result in changes in actual and in expected inflation, causing the IC curve to shift. Movements in expectations and the dynamic supply curve lead to new junctures with the $\dot{A}D$ curve. Further shifts through a series of temporary equilibriums between inflation and the output ratio continue until the economy finally attains a long-run equilibrium.

The actual path and how long it takes to reach equilibrium depend on

TABLE 13.4   **The Reaction of Inflation and Output to an Increase in the Rate of Growth of Aggregate Demand**
(percent)

Period	Rate of inflation $(\dot{P})$	Excess or slack output $\left(\dfrac{Q}{Q^*} - 1\right)$
0	0	0
1	0.6	1.8
2	1.5	2.7
3	2.4	2.7
4	3.1	2.0
5	3.4	1.0
6	3.4	0
7	3.2	−0.8
.	.	.
.	.	.
.	.	.
Equilibrium	2.4	0

An increase in the growth rate of aggregate demand (AD) *of 2.4 percent raises output above potential and increases the inflation rate. With the growth rate of demand constant at this new level, the dynamic model (equations 13.6 and 13.7) shows inflation and output rising for several periods. Eventually, however, the absorption of demand by excess inflation is so great that output starts to fall. At equilibrium (point A in Figure 13.7), the new rate of inflation and growth of demand are equal. Output is back at the natural rate of unemployment.*

what happens to the rate of growth in demand ($\dot{AD}$) and on the values of the coefficients q and p in equation 13.6. Depending on these coefficients and the time lags between shifts, the economy may move fairly rapidly to a new stable situation, or the path can be quite tortuous. The remainder of this chapter as well as following ones demonstrate some of the dynamic possibilities and the arguments they engender with respect to anti-inflation policies. Table 13.4 shows what happens when the rate of growth in $\dot{AD}$ increases from zero to 2.4 percent and the numerical coefficients of equation 13.6 apply. The final equilibrium moves to an inflation rate of 2.4 percent, as was also indicated on Figure 13.4. In the process, however, the inflation rate rises as high as 3.4 percent, while output goes as high as 102.7 percent of potential and as low as 99.2 percent.

The data in the table are obtained from the dynamic model of equations 13.6 and 13.7 combined. Appendix 13.1 shows how the equations fit together and the calculations underlying the table. Since the numerical results depend on the assumed coefficients, they should not be given undue weight. However, the fact that the dynamic path can be cyclical, that time is extremely significant before equilibrium is reached, and that inflation may overshoot the change in demand while increases in output may be negative are all warnings that must be taken into account in analyzing the actual paths of inflation and its reaction to policy changes. Other assumptions yield still more diverse results.

Supply Shocks

Not all inflationary pressures arise from excess demand. In recent years the U.S. economy has undergone a major series of supply shocks. OPEC raised energy prices. Crop failures and other shortages caused a sharp upswing in food prices. Movements in exchange rates raised the prices of imported goods and materials. During the 1970s the government raised social security taxes and the minimum wage, causing exogenous increases in wage costs. These and similar forces increased the relative prices of particular sectors of the economy compared with the average price level, causing aggregate supply curves to shift upward. The immediate impact of such shifts is to raise prices and lower output. Moreover, such shocks can set off a further chain of events. Production functions may shift as a result of the cost increases. Productivity and growth in potential output fall. Higher costs cause movements to higher expectations-augmented inflation curves. The new costs can thus become imbedded in the core rate of inflation.

Not all supply changes need have negative effects, however. Supply-side economics emphasizes the possibility of shifting supply curves down by increasing incentives, particularly through the tax system. When such shifts occur, the results also depend on how expectations and aggregate demand react. The ability to shift supply to the right is analyzed in Chapter 15. When the shocks are favorable, in general, the following analysis of the effect of adverse supply shocks can be reversed.

SUPPLY SHOCKS REDUCE REAL INCOME

When exogenous increases occur in the prices of raw materials such as oil, the amount of potential output which can be produced by a given labor force declines. Energy is an input, along with capital and labor, into the production process. If costs of energy rise, some labor and capital are substituted for it. The marginal product of each falls. At the same time, the costs of imported materials go up in real terms. More goods must be transferred abroad for each unit used in production. The rise in the price of energy acts like a tax by foreign suppliers on American consumers.

One result, then, of supply shocks is to cause real incomes to grow more slowly, or even to decline. Because of the need to substitute labor and capital for energy, productivity declines and retards the growth of potential output. In addition, as with any tax, taxpayers have less income to buy other goods. The slower growth of real GNP in the 1970s was a key factor leading to distrust of the government and a demand for lower taxes.

THE POLICY DILEMMA

When the supply curve shifts upward, policy makers are faced with difficult choices. Should they attempt to alter the rate of growth in aggregate demand in such a way as to offset the drop in output? Or should they act so as to reduce the rate of price increase? Or should they do nothing, allowing both output to decline and prices to increase? Let us examine these alternatives in a simplified form. Figure 13.7 illustrates three possible paths for aggregate demand policy to take when the economy receives a supply shock. (Again, this example abstracts from dynamic interactions.) Figure 13.7 shows an economy in equilibrium at point *A*, with output at the full-employment level and no inflation. Now a single supply shock raises costs by 2 percent and shifts the economy from IC_1 to IC_2 in accordance with equation 13.5. The figure illustrates three possible policy responses prior to consideration of lags.

A ***do-nothing or neutral policy*** would maintain a zero growth rate for dynamic aggregate demand. The economy would remain on $\dot{A}D_1$. If the nominal GNP remains constant but prices rise, the amount of real goods purchased must fall. The economy moves to point *B*, reflecting the increased costs and the decline of output. How the economy next moves from this position depends on the specific coefficients for the lagged expectations-inertia term and on the rate at which output reacts to spending.

An ***accommodating policy*** would furnish sufficient aggregate demand to move equilibrium back to the full-employment level. This full-employment output, however, will be reduced compared with the pre-shock trend because of the productivity decline and higher payments to foreign suppliers. An accommodating policy means that nominal GNP grows by enough to allow potential output to be purchased even at higher prices. A shift in aggregate demand to $\dot{A}D_2$ occurs. The economy is in a new equilibrium at full employment, but with a higher inflation rate.

FIGURE 13.7   **After a Supply Shock, Prices and Output Depend on Dynamic Aggregate Demand**

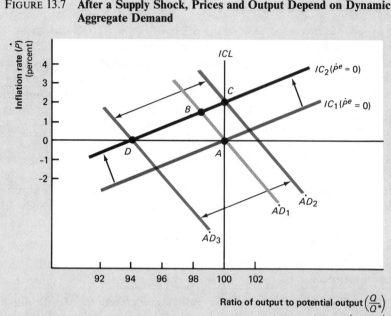

A supply shock shifts the economy from IC$_1$ *to* IC$_2$. *If the rate of change in aggregate demand* (A$\dot{D}_1$) *remains constant, the new equilibrium is* B, *with lowered output and higher inflation. An accommodating policy increases the growth rate of demand to* A$\dot{D}_2$, *returning output to potential but increasing inflation still more. An extinguishing policy reduces demand to* A$\dot{D}_3$. *Where the economy moves from points* B, C, *and* D *and how long it takes to return to* A *depend on the dynamic interactions of demand growth, output, and price expectations.*

A third so-called ***extinguishing policy*** would lower AD enough to prevent a rise in the general price level. To secure such results, demand would have to be curtailed, and output would drop by a good deal more than under the neutral policy. Under the assumptions of the numerical example in Appendix 13.1 the initial drop in output is four times as great as with a neutral policy. It is shown by the line $A\dot{D}_3$ and the new equilibrium at D.

While simplified, these choices are similar to those policy makers actually faced during the 1970s. Suggestions as to which policies should be selected followed closely the views economists held as to the role of money, expectations, and price-wage rigidity. Those convinced that the economy would adjust readily to the money supply wanted the growth rate of aggregate demand limited to an amount adequate to handle the trend of real output. Under this policy, if inflation did not decline, output would be curtailed. Those who believed that adjustments would occur mainly through avoidable declines in output preferred to see nominal spending expand at a rate close to the underlying core inflation rate. Neither policy was followed consistently; both were adopted, but in separate periods. The results were the deep recession of 1974–75 and the small one of 1980, but also a steady increase in the inflation rate and a great deal of economic stagnation.

DYNAMIC RESPONSES

The actual effects of supply shocks on the economy are far more complex than shown in Figure 13.7 because the interaction of supply and demand under dynamic conditions depends on a variety of factors. The most important of these are (1) the size of the shock, (2) whether it is a single shot or repeated, (3) how price changes and output are related (the slopes of inflation curves), (4) how expectations $(\dot{P}^e)$ react to prior price changes, and (5) the degree to which the rate of change in demand $(\dot{A}D)$ is adjusted to accommodate higher costs.

Let us consider some possible dynamic situations which develop under the simple assumptions of the two-equation model. What happens under a neutral or do-nothing policy after the economy reaches point B in Figure 13.7? The first three columns of Table 13.5 show one possible adjustment path.

TABLE 13.5   **The Reaction of Output and Inflation to a Single Supply Shock**

Period	Nonaccommodating demand $(\dot{A}D = 0)$			Accommodating demand $(\dot{A}D = 2.0)$		
	Percentage rate of change in		Percentage output gap	Percentage rate of change in		Percentage output gap
	Inflation $(\dot{P})$	Expected inflation $(\dot{P}^e)$	$\left(\dfrac{Q}{Q^*}-1\right)$	Inflation $(\dot{P})$	Expected inflation $(\dot{P}^e)$	$\left(\dfrac{Q}{Q^*}-1\right)$
0	0	0	0	0	0	0
1	1.50	0	−1.50	2.0	0	0
2	0.75	0	−2.25	2.0	2.0	0
3	0	0.75	−2.25	2.0	2.0	0
4	−0.56	0	−1.69	2.0	2.0	0
5	−0.84	−0.56	−0.85	2.0	2.0	0
6	−0.84	−0.84	−0.01	2.0	2.0	0
7	−0.63	−0.84	−0.62	2.0	2.0	0
.	.	.	.	.	.	.
.	.	.	.	.	.	.
Equilibrium	0	0	0	2.0	2.0	0

A supply shock $(\Delta \dot{P}M)$ of 2.0 percent occurs in Period 1. If demand is nonaccommodating $(\dot{A}D = 0)$, the slope of the PC curve determines how much prices increase and output falls. The dynamic model (equations 13.6 and 13.7) determines future paths. Equilibrium is reached when no further change occurs in inflation—when $\dot{P} = \dot{P}^e$. In the last three columns, inflation is accommodated by an increase in $\dot{A}D$ of 2.0 percent. Output does not fall. The economy moves immediately to its new equilibrium with higher inflation.

Holding nominal GNP growth constant means that any change in inflation ($\dot{P}$) must be equal and opposite to the change in output $\left(\dfrac{Q}{Q^*}\right)$ (see equation 13.7).

Given the assumed shape of the inflation curve, the figure and the second row of Table 13.5 show that inflation would rise by 1.5 percent and the output ratio would fall by the same amount. The slack in output gradually squeezes the initial increase in costs and prices out of the economy. Column 3 shows output falling and then gradually returning to the full-employment level. The economy at first overshoots equilibrium, but the interactions of the output gap and expected inflation cause demand to circle back to equilibrium. The type of path indicated in the table is illustrated by the dotted line in Figure 13.8, which moves from B back to A. Recall, however, that A will be on a new growth path for potential output, not the pre-shock route.

Columns 4 to 6 of Table 13.5 show the path taken if an accommodating policy is followed and the dynamic aggregate demand curve ($\dot{A}D$) is shifted up

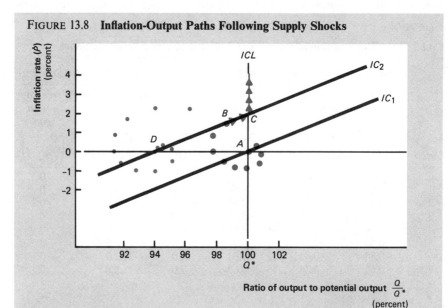

FIGURE 13.8   **Inflation-Output Paths Following Supply Shocks**

A series of supply shocks can bring about an accelerated inflation if matched by a faster growth in demand. The economy would follow the path B, C, and upward. If the rate of growth in demand remains neutral—constant—the economy would follow a path like that shown by the dots connecting points B and A. A series of shocks would tend to raise the inflation rate and decrease output. The dots connecting B and D show a possible extinguishing policy under such conditions.

TABLE 13.6   **The Reaction of Output and Inflation to a Series of Supply Shocks**

| Period | Nonaccommodating demand ($\dot{AD} = 0$) | | | Accommodating demand ($\dot{AD} = 2.0$) | | |
| | Percentage rate of change in | | Percentage output gap $\left(\dfrac{Q}{Q^*} - 1\right)$ | Percentage rate of change in | | Percentage output gap $\left(\dfrac{Q}{Q^*} - 1\right)$ |
	Inflation ($\dot{P}$)	Expected inflation ($\dot{P}^e$)		Inflation ($\dot{P}$)	Expected inflation ($\dot{P}^e$)	
0	0	0	0	0	0	0
1	1.50	0	− 1.50	2.00	0	0
2	2.25	1.50	− 3.75	4.00	2.00	0
3	2.25	2.25	− 6.00	6.00	4.00	0
4	1.69	2.25	− 7.69	8.00	6.00	0
5	0.85	1.69	− 8.54	10.00	8.00	0
6	0	0.85	− 8.54	12.00	10.00	0
.	.	.	.	.	.	.
.	.	.	.	.	.	.
.	.	.	.	.	.	.
Equili-brium	0	0	− 6.00	∞	∞	0

Supply shocks cause production costs to rise at the same rate (2.0 percent) in each period. If dynamic demand does not increase, inflation rates reach a peak and then decline under pressure from unused potential output. Output 6 percent below potential holds the inflation rate at an equilibrium of zero, even though production costs continue to rise. If an attempt is made to accommodate the steady increase in costs (columns 4 to 6), output does not fall, but inflation increases steadily as inflationary expectations move up from one period to the next.

immediately by 2 percent. The table shows that the rate of inflation rises by 2 percent and that the economy moves immediately to the new full-employment level.

Instead of a single shock that causes prices to rise, the pressure on costs could be continuous over a considerable period. Such a situation would cause the inflation curve to shift anew each period. When a series of shocks occurs, a strategy of controlling demand to extinguish any further pressures requires a larger drop in output. With a steady upward pressure from the cost side, the lagged expectational term causes the rate of inflation to rise and then to fall back toward zero in diminishing swings. The second set of dots in Figure 13.8, which move from A to D, and the first three columns of Table 13.6 show the reaction path to this extinguishing policy under the assumptions of the two-equation model. However, point D will not constitute a long-run equilibrium. At that point the economy is producing well below potential. With time, excess supply should shift the IC curves back so that output returns to the full-employment level. How long this will take depends on how sticky prices are.

A policy of full accommodation, on the other hand, aims at furnishing enough demand following a supply shock to permit the economy to remain at full employment. The rate of increase in aggregate demand must equal that of the rate of inflation. If the increase in costs is persistent, the inflation rate will accelerate steadily. Higher production costs (PM) in each period are matched by increases in the growth rate of aggregate demand $(\dot{AD})$. In each subsequent period the economy continues to produce at the reduced level of full potential. Higher costs and prices raise inflationary expectations, and they are matched by further increases in $\dot{AD}$. The model contains no necessary stopping point for the acceleration of inflation. Columns 4 to 6 and the arrows heading straight up at the level of full potential in Figure 13.8 illustrate such a situation.

Rationalists and Structuralists

In the 1950s and 1960s, monetarists and neo-Keynesians held contrasting views as to how aggregate demand reacted to monetary and fiscal policy. In the 1970s and 1980s, similar disputes arose over how output and inflation react to changes in demand, to excess capacity, and to government policies. Fundamental disagreements existed over how responsive the economy is likely to be to slack demand—the coefficient q in equation 13.5—and over how fast expectations—the term $p(\dot{P}^e)$—are likely to be affected by new information. The term *structuralists* has been applied to those who believe that the reactions of the economy to excess capacity are likely to be slow because inflation rates depend primarily on the wage-price structure. The name *rationalists* has been given to those who emphasize the importance of rational expectations and credibility in determining the economy's response. Other related methods of classification result in similar though somewhat different groupings. Of importance are views as to the degree to which markets clear—that is, how significant contracts and competition are in determining price movements. Other divisions result from the differing approaches of the new classicists, neo-Keynesians, and monetarists.[6]

Rationalists tend to believe that when consistent anti-inflationary policies convince the private economy that the government really means what it says, expectations and the rate of inflation will drop rapidly. In this view, actual adjustments are slow largely because government policies are wrong or uncertain. Inflation persists despite excess supply because spending units believe that anti-inflation policies will not last. Inflation expectations remain high for rational reasons. If people became convinced that policies would not cause excess demand, they would adjust their expectations and halt inflation. Once everyone recognizes that inflationary pressures have been contained and will

6. A detailed review of these issues can be found in John B. Taylor, "Recent Developments in the Theory of Stabilization Policy," in Center for the Study of American Business, *Stabilization Policies: Lessons for the Seventies and Implications for the Eighties,* Working Paper No. 53, April 1980, pp. 1–40.

not burst out again, the fight is won. The economy can return to full employment. Future bursts of excess demand and cost-pushes must be guarded against, but a successful demonstration that inflation can be halted will make it easier to devise effective future policies.

Structuralists tend to believe that inflation persists because of the institutional structure of our price-wage system. When aggregate demand increases less than inflation, real output falls, but inflation declines at a much slower pace. An unfavorable trade-off between output losses and inflation is probable. Short-run inflation curves are comparatively flat. These observers point to the complex decentralized system within which wages and prices are established in the United States. On the basis of studies of recent recessions, they estimate the trade-off as a drop in inflation of only .3 percent for each year in which unemployment is 1 percent above its natural rate.

INFORMATION, CREDIBILITY, AND RATIONAL EXPECTATIONS

One foundation for the views of the rationalists can be seen in the works of William Fellner who has been foremost among those who emphasize the *credibility hypothesis.* This theory argues that the expected future behavior of policy makers significantly influences both inflationary expectations and the lessons the market draws from demand slack. If demand management develops a credible policy of consistent disinflation, price decelerations speed up. Any amount of slack causes a much greater decline in inflation if people believe that future policies will not be more accommodative.

Closely related to the concepts of credibility are ideas derived from the theory of rational expectations discussed in Chapter 4. In information models based on rational expectations, the market departs from equilibrium because producers and labor confuse nominal and real changes in prices and wages. When workers are offered higher nominal wages, they restrict their job-seeking and their leisure. Unemployment drops; output rises. But if prices are higher by the time they are ready to spend their wages, they find their real wages lower than they expected. After being fooled a few times by the difference between nominal and real wages, they catch on. Their estimates of future real wages and prices become more accurate. They no longer make the mistake of offering additional work and allowing output to expand. They base bargains on expected real incomes.

Mistakes do continue to be made, however, because information is often inadequate and hard to process. When demand declines, output rather than prices may fall because producers and workers cannot tell why their demand has shifted. They misjudge the proper amount of output and labor to offer. More problems arise because lags prior to adjustment may be both long and variable. Both the rational expectations and credibility hypotheses recognize delays due to the difficulty of determining whether new policies are permanent or temporary, but both conclude that inflation primarily results from expectations and that a policy which successfully alters expectations can end inflation rapidly.

STRUCTURAL LAGS IN WAGES AND PRICES

In contrast to views based primarily on expectations, the structuralists emphasize the inertia in wage and price setting which causes inflation to continue even when demand is slack. Robert Solow, for example, has pointed out that between 1972 and 1980 the rate of increase in hourly compensation in private business remained within a narrow band despite the occurrence of a major recession in 1974–75 and a minor one in 1980. The rates of increase in compensation (in percent) were

1973	8.2	1977	7.9
1974	9.2	1978	8.5
1975	10.0	1979	9.4
1976	8.8	1980	10.2

Note that the rate of growth in wages rose through both recessions.

When demand shifts, rigidities in the wage and price structure may force the burden of adjustment onto output and unemployment. According to this view, a large amount of unemployment can be attributed to the failure of markets to clear. Traditional wage bargaining leaves little room for individual wage and price setting. Information and transactions costs mean that wages and prices are set over large sectors of the economy. The amount of production and employment adjusts to these prices, not to a true equilibrium of demand and supply.[7]

Such rigidities arise because explicit or implicit contracts make frequent price changes expensive and inefficient. Prices and wages are not set at a single time, but at irregular intervals. Staggered contracts contribute to the persistence of inflation. Because some groups would be caught with a loss of real income if the inertia term $(\dot{P}^c)$ dropped suddenly, such downward shifts are unlikely. Even with slack demand, those whose prices or wages are based on the price level of several periods back will fight to catch up. The result is persistence of the pressures to continue along a path of rising prices.

Prices are determined by the impact of actual past price changes on wages and the resulting impact of wage changes on the prices quoted by firms rather than primarily by expectational factors. Wages and prices continue to rise because of lags inherent in the institutional structure. Because of faulty information, transactions costs, and uncertainty, it is efficient for those in the market to establish contracts that last for extended periods. Changes in prices and wages due to recontracting occur only at fairly long intervals. At all times, some

7. Federal Reserve Bank of Boston, *After the Phillips Curve: Persistence of Inflation and High Unemployment*, Conference Series No. 19, June 1978 and P. Cagan, *Persistent Inflation*, (New York: Columbia University Press, 1979), p. 245.

contracts are being renegotiated. Current wage increases are based on both past and expected price movements. Most prices are administered by firms which tend to use some kind of standard mark-up over cost. Margins do change with demand, but not frequently. General Motors sets prices only once or a few times a year. In doing so, they look both backward at what has been happening to wages and prices and ahead to anticipated demand and costs.

To picture the constant reaction of prices to past events, assume that the average labor contract lasts two years. It provides for an agreed-upon wage. How well or poorly the worker does—that is, what average level of real wages he earns—depends on how the contract was negotiated. Because of uncertainty about future prices, many contracts include indexing to the cost of living, or automatic adjustments. In any case, no matter how good or bad the previous results, those negotiating a new contract will insist on a full catch-up. Assume that one-eighth of wage contracts are renegotiated in each quarter of a two-year period, and that prices rise at the rate of 8 percent a year, or 16 percent for the period. Wages are raised to cover changes in the cost of living. New contracts call for a 16 percent rise in wage rates. Thus, in any quarter, one-eighth of all workers receive a 16 percent increase in their wages; average wages rise at a rate of 2 percent a quarter. If prices are now set to reflect fully these wage increases, they will also rise at a rate of 2 percent a quarter, or 8 percent a year. If this rate of inflation is ratified by the monetary system, a long-run equilibrium can exist.

But won't inflation end if demand drops? The answer is, not necessarily. Even if demand falls somewhat, those whose contracts come up for renewal will still demand a 16 percent wage increase to catch up with the cost of living. Because firms believe that cost of living increases are fair, or because of union demands, they may well grant wage increases of the full amount, even if at the same time they are in the process of laying off workers because of lower demand. How rapidly wage fixing reacts to market demand is a demonstrable fact. Most studies show that decreases in demand have some, but only delayed, impacts on wage rates.

A MODEL OF THE CONFLICTING VIEWS

The differences between these views are illustrated in Figure 13.9. Initially, the economy is at point *A,* with full employment and an inflation rate of 10 percent. How much reduction in demand growth will it take and how long will output have to remain below potential for the economy to move to point *D,* an equilibrium with full employment and no inflation? The rate of growth is slowed steadily. For example, the Federal Reserve announced in 1980 that it would bring the growth of the money supply down to a noninflationary rate over the next three or four years.

The IC_1 curve and the corresponding dots in Figure 13.9 show one possible dynamic path, based on the assumption that inflation is primarily a problem of rigidity in the wage structure. The flatness of the curve reflects a low re-

FIGURE 13.9   **Fast or Slow Reactions to Decreased Demand**

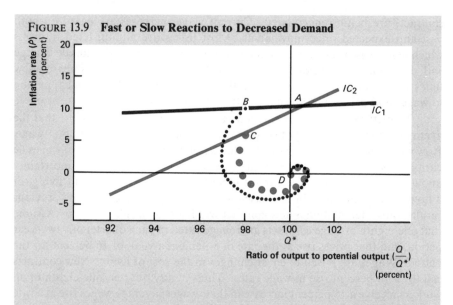

How fast slack in output reduces inflation depends on the slope of the inflation curve and on the lags in the price adjustment process. Aggregate demand (AD) is reduced so that output falls to 98 percent of potential. If the slope of IC_1 is flat and inertia is great, the economy might follow a path such as that from B to D. Period-to-period adjustments are small; the time to eradicate inflation is long, and output losses are large. The path from C to D indicates a more significant and rapid reaction of inflation to slack in output.

sponsiveness coefficient (q). It requires a large drop in output to reduce the inflation rate by much. The closeness of the dots reveals a considerable lag from the initial decrease in inflation to future ones, together with small impacts. Either the coefficient p is small or it takes a long time for past changes to influence $\dot{P}^e$. Under this set of assumptions, ending inflation requires a large number of periods—perhaps 40 quarters.

In contrast, the IC_2 curve and its corresponding dots show a much greater responsiveness of inflation to slack in output. Because q is larger, the initial drop in the inflation rate is substantial. Furthermore, because of a larger p or because $\dot{P}^e$ responds more rapidly, the lags in future downward movements are much smaller. According to the illustration, the economy goes down to point D in only 12 periods.

Inflation, Recession, and Monetary Growth

Closely related to the question of whether the views of the rationalists or those of the structuralists more accurately describe the economy is a continuing dispute over how much the money supply should grow when slack exists in the economy but prices are still rising rapidly. Most economists agree that inflation cannot continue without a growth in money. However, at any time, they are likely to disagree over what growth rate is proper. For example, in 1977–79 aggregate demand expanded at an annual rate of 11.7 percent; real output grew at 4.5 percent a year; the inflation rate was 7.2 percent; and unemployment averaged 6.3 percent. There was a consensus that, even with unemployment above the natural rate, monetary policy should be used to slow the growth rate of demand. But how much cut back was necessary and proper? If only enough money were to be furnished to fund a normal growth in real GNP, how fast should that level be reached? Should the Federal Reserve be concerned with the height reached by nominal or real interest rates and the level of unemployment? What weight should it give to its duty to coordinate policy with Congress and the executive? Arguments over proper policies resembled those often faced by monetary authorities—for instance, over what to do about the supply shock in 1973–75.

A restrictive enough monetary policy can always end inflation because the counterpart of an inflationary increase in spending must be an expansion in money or its velocity. Monetary spending and inflation are tied together by the equation of exchange. Nominal GNP is identical both to the price level times real output and to the amount of money times its velocity:

$$GNP = AD = PQ = MV. \qquad \textbf{13.8}$$

When this equation is expressed in terms of rates of change, we find that the growth rate of aggregate demand equals both the percentage rate of change in inflation and output and the growth rate of money plus that of its velocity:

$$\dot{AD} = \dot{P} + \dot{Q} = \dot{M} + \dot{V}. \qquad \textbf{13.9}$$

Demand (and inflation) can grow only to the extent that monetary spending expands. For inflation to continue, either money (M) or velocity (V) must be increasing constantly. Since growth in velocity encounters institutional constraints, a good part of any persistent inflation must depend on the continuous creation of money.

THE MONETARY VALIDATION OF INFLATION

Because growth in nominal GNP must be accompanied by an equivalent expansion of money or its velocity, many conclude that inflation is due mainly to errors committed by the Federal Reserve in creating too much money. As a corollary, they see tight limits on the growth in the nominal money stock as the cure for inflation. *Validation* is the process whereby the money supply grows at a rate sufficient to allow aggregate demand to match the upward spiral of the supply curve. Money becomes available to ratify higher price levels. Differing explanations as to why validation occurs have led to bitter disputes between monetarists, the Federal Reserve, and nonmonetarists.

The point of view of the monetarists has been expressed in the words of Milton Friedman: "There is one and only one basic cause of inflation, too high a rate of growth in the quantity of money. . . . There is one and only one basic cure for inflation, slowing monetary growth.[8] Monetarists and new classicists tend to assume that if money growth is slowed, inflation will drop quite rapidly without large losses in output. In emphasizing rational expectations, price flexibility, and the ability of the financial system to adjust rapidly, they describe an economy in which most monetary-induced declines in spending result in price reductions, not drops in output.

THE PROBLEM OF NONVALIDATION

In contrast to the monetarists, many economists view validation, or the monetary accommodation of basic forces in the economy, as a logical reaction to events not subject to control by the Federal Reserve. If OPEC raises prices or governments tighten certain regulations or unions win large wage gains, the dynamic aggregate supply curve shifts up to the left. If the money supply does not grow, employment and output will drop sharply, accompanied by only a slow decline in prices.

At any given time, a judgment as to how much to curtail demand through monetary policy depends on the expected consequences of slowing the economy. It is up to the nation to choose whether to risk the dangers of price increases or to accept the consequences of reduced output. If national policy does not wish to risk the costs of a slower rate of demand growth, the Fed must supply the necessary money. This point has been made by James Tobin:

> This dilemma has repeatedly faced the Federal Reserve and other central banks as well as the executive and legislative officials who make budget policy. Shall they provide the money to support normal economic growth at inherited inflation rates over which they have precious little immediate control, or shall they deny the economy that money, provoke additional unemployment, slowdown, and recession, and count hopefully on stagflation gradually to bring inflation down to more tolerable levels? Whenever they choose the first alternative, they could be accused of causing, or at least ratifying, inflation. But they are not responsible for the features of democratic, capitalist societies that bias noncommunist economies toward inflation and produce the recurrent dilemma. Their critics, monetarists and others, are unfair and misleading when they imply that the continuation of inflation is simply a reflection of obtuse stupidity by policy makers, of conceptual and operational errors which could be corrected at no cost to the economy.[9]

If past price changes have been accommodated monetarily, a rate of inflation will continue from one period to the next. The increases that are too

8. M. Friedman, *Newsweek,* October 3, 1977, p. 84.
9. J. Tobin, "Monetary Policy and the Control of Credit," in A. T. Sommers, ed., *Answer to Inflation and Recession: Economic Policies for a Modern Society* (New York: The Conference Board, 1975), p. 12.

expensive to reduce are called the underlying, or core inflation rate. The **core,** or **basic, inflation rate** measures the underlying trend, or persistence factor, in the price determination process. Following a price rise due to excess demand or to supply shocks, some price increases become imbedded in the short-run inflation curve. An equilibrium with a core rate of inflation above zero is pictured in columns 3 to 6 of Table 13.5 and at point A in Figure 13.6. If monetary spending and aggregate demand grow at the same rate as do expected and actual inflation, the short-run inflation curve (IC), the long-run inflation curve (ICL), and the dynamic demand curve ($\dot{AD}$) can be in equilibrium at a rate of inflation that differs from zero.

Some monetarists object to the concept of a core inflation rate above zero. They point out that if the economy is willing to bear the costs of a reduction in the growth rate of money, after some losses in output which they believe will either be small or worth suffering, the economy will return to a zero inflation rate. The debate over whether or not the concept of a core or underlying imbedded rate makes sense is part of the argument over how quickly growth in money can be reduced and inflation not be validated, given the realities of the economic and political structures. Halting inflation is a dynamic process that depends on the rapidity with which price increases react to slack in output and on the ensuing decline in the expectations term.

Estimates of Demand, Shock, and Core Inflation

Differences of opinion with respect to the cause of inflation and the rigidity of the wage-price structure influence the way in which economists interpret data. If the Federal Reserve furnished money primarily to accommodate other forces in the economy, one can visualize these other factors as the main cause of inflation leading to an increase in the underlying or core rate. But if excess expansion of the money supply is the major cause, the concept of a core rate does not make much sense.

A model based on the belief that inflation is caused by demand-pull or supply shocks which then raise the core rate was constructed by Otto Eckstein for the U.S. Congress Joint Economic Committee, using the model of Data Resources, Inc.[10] He then used this model to measure the forces that brought about inflation in the 1960s and 1970s. According to this model:

1. Demand inflation occurs when unemployment drops below the full-employment rate and manufacturing capacity is overutilized.
2. Shock inflation results from excess relative price increases in farm products and fuels and from declines in the exchange value of the dollar, as well as from increases in social security taxes and minimum wages.
3. Core inflation is caused by wage and price catch-ups and shifts in expecta-

---

10. U.S. Congress, Joint Economic Committee 96:2, *Tax Policy and Core Inflation,* Joint Committee Print (Washington: Government Printing Office, 1980).

tions. These pressures raise wages and capital costs to an extent that exceeds improvements in productivity.

THE STEADY INCREASE IN CORE INFLATION

Figure 13.10 illustrates the strength of demand and supply pressures and the steady increase in core inflation. During the first half of the 1960s, demand was below normal and supply costs were level. The underlying inflation rate fell below 1 percent, primarily because productivity improved at a faster than normal rate. In the mid-1960s the Vietnam War raised demand. Unemployment below the natural rate, together with an excess use of capacity, started prices upward. Small shocks from food and fuel price increases as well as in the minimum wage rate also put pressure on prices. Costs of both capital and labor rose in response to the price increases. Measures of price expectations remained quite low. At the end of the 1960s, the core underlying inflation rate was 3.5 percent, about where it had begun the decade.

The first half of the 1970s witnessed a series of major supply shocks. Farm prices shot up; OPEC began to raise oil prices; the exchange value of the dollar

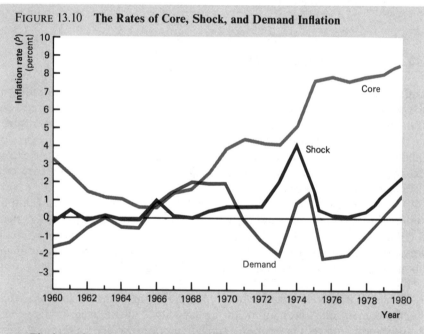

FIGURE 13.10   **The Rates of Core, Shock, and Demand Inflation**

The lines show the year-by-year movements in demand and shock inflation. The core rate of inflation, also shown, is influenced by them but it depends also on inertia and price expectations. It responded to prior price movements as well as to current excess or slack demand and favorable or unfavorable supply shocks.

fell; social security taxes rose. In 1974 the supply inflation rate was 3.8 percent. During most of this period, demand was weak, except for 1974–1975 when policies were adopted to end the recession. However, even without excess demand, wage and capital costs rose steadily in response to growing inflationary expectations and a slowdown in productivity improvement. In the last half of the decade, demand remained weak until 1979, but increases in farm and fuel prices and in the minimum wage, plus declining exchange rates, again shocked the system upward. The core underlying inflation rate experienced most of its climb in 1974 and 1975, but it continued high and rose again toward the end of the decade.

Although other models use alternative techniques and differ in detail from those shown in the chart, most of them arrive at similar movements.[11] Core inflation fell from 1960 to the start of the Vietnam War. It then rose until mid-1971, when it was halted temporarily by President Nixon's imposition of wage and price controls. Their removal plus a series of supply shocks boosted the underlying rate in 1974 and 1975. Although slack demand succeeded in stabilizing the rate for a period, at the end of the decade supply shocks were stronger than weak demand. The core rate continued to rise even through the recession of 1980, as inflationary expectations soared. By 1981 the underlying inflation rate was between 9 and 10 percent.

THE RELATION OF INFLATION TO SPENDING

Table 13.7 compares the model's estimates of inflation to movements in total spending and to monetary growth. It shows the average growth rates for the components of Figure 13.10 for the periods 1960 through 1980, as well as a comparison of inflation with the growth in nominal GNP divided into its monetary spending and price-output components.

The table illustrates how the inflation picture differs depending on one's point of view. For example, monetarists would disagree strongly with the breakdown of inflationary pressures presented in the table, since they attribute almost the entire change in the core rate and in inflationary expectations to the creation of too much money by the Federal Reserve.

According to the top half of the table, demand was excess primarily in the period 1965–70 (although it also averaged about .8 percent above its noninflationary level in 1979). This excess demand gave a small impetus to core inflation, but most of the rise in core inflation is attributed to supply shocks, particularly the food-energy price increases in 1973–74 plus housing and interest rates in 1978–80. Such forces speeded the rise in labor compensation, and labor costs increased even more on a comparative basis because rising compensation was not offset by improvements in productivity.

11. For example, see J. L. Scadding, "Estimating the Underlying Inflation Rate," Federal Reserve Bank of San Francisco, *Economic Review* (Spring 1979), 7–18.

TABLE 13.7   **Demand-Pull, Supply Shock, and Core Inflation Rates, 1960–80**
(percent per year)

Factors influencing inflation	1960–65	1965–70	1970–75	1975–80
Demand-pull	−0.3	1.5	−0.4	−1.1
Supply shock	0.0	0.3	1.9	1.5
Core inflation	1.5	2.0	5.4	8.1
Total growth in nominal and monetary spending (G$\dot{N}$P)	6.3	7.3	9.2	10.8
Growth in money ($\dot{M}$)	3.1	5.1	6.1	6.0
Change in velocity ($\dot{V}$)	3.2	2.2	3.1	4.8
Inflation rate ($\dot{P}$)	1.6	4.2	6.9	7.4
Growth in output ($\dot{Q}$)	4.7	3.1	2.3	3.4

SOURCES: O. Eckstein, "Tax Policy and Core Inflation" and Federal Reserve Bank of St. Louis.

> *The top section contains estimates from the DRI model of the factors at work in the inflationary process. The bottom section shows the division of the rate of change in aggregate demand (nominal GNP) into its price-output and monetary spending components. $G\dot{N}P = A\dot{D} = \dot{P} + \dot{Q} = \dot{M} + \dot{V}$. (Because of timing and measurement differences, divisions of inflation into its components do not add up to the total change in prices on a year-to-year basis, although they do so for the period as a whole.)*

The bottom half of the table shows a steady increase in nominal GNP and a doubling of the rate of growth in the money supply between 1960–65 and the 1970s. This greater money supply accompanied a speed-up in inflation. To those who believe that the relationship between money and inflation is close, this fact indicated that money was causing inflation. To others, the relationship was weak and was to be expected, given the poor growth in output even with the enlarged money stock. While growth in money doubled between the first and last periods, inflation more than quadrupled. The difference was accounted for by a decline in the growth of output and an increase in money velocity. Inflationary increases in wages and prices reflected past excess demand and supply shocks. When money growth was slowed most of the reduction in the growth of aggregate demand led to a fall in output rather than inflation. With production well below potential, money was furnished to avoid additional output losses.

The next two chapters continue the analysis of inflation. They consider its costs, how inflation relates to supply economics, and the policies available to bring inflation under control.

Summary

1. Inflation, defined as a persistent increase in price levels, requires continuous upward shifts in the levels of aggregate demand and aggregate supply.

2. Studies which led to Phillips curves showed a relationship between the rates of unemployment and inflation. Okun's law allows such relationships to be translated into price-output or inflation curves (IC). Later data and analysis questioned both the logic behind such trade-offs and the possible stability of such relationships.

3. Inflation curves, augmented by the concept that a separate curve exists for each value of the dynamic price variable $\dot{P}^e$ and for shifts in supply costs ($\dot{PM}$) and productivity ($\dot{PR}$) can be used to analyze dynamic relationships between demand, supply shocks, and inflation.

4. A stable rate of inflation can occur when the expected and actual rates of inflation are equal and aggregate demand expands at the same rate. The line drawn through such equilibrium points forms a long-run inflation curve. The level of unemployment at this line is the natural rate of unemployment.

5. In theory, at levels of output to the right or left of the natural rate, the economy should experience accelerating or decelerating inflation. In fact, lags in adjustment and other institutional factors can allow higher rates of output for considerable periods without an acceleration of inflation or a continued inflation even with slack demand and excess unemployment.

6. Dynamic aggregate demand curves ($\dot{A}D$) relate inflation and the ratio of actual to potential output. Their shapes and positions depend on (1) movements in the underlying static AD curves based on changes in the money and real goods markets, and (2) continued expansions in monetary spending required to fund the dynamic upward spirals in the AS and AD curves.

7. Supply shocks are felt when external forces raise the costs of production and lower potential output. What happens to output and the inflation rate following a supply shock depends on changes in demand. While some drop in output is inevitable, an accommodative demand policy will result in a smaller loss of output and a higher rate of inflation. At the opposite extreme, if the rate of increase in demand is reduced so that the rate of inflation declines to its initial rate all of the shock will be absorbed by a fall in output.

8. Differing views as to how fast prices and wages react to slack demand lie behind many disputes over anti-inflationary policy. Rationalists believe that a credible policy will cause inflationary expectations and the inflation rate to fall rapidly. Structuralists hold that the structure of the price-wage system results in a strong upward momentum which means that imbedded price-wage trends absorb most increases in demand. Slack demand is likely to lower output rapidly and inflation slowly.

9. Any increase in the rate of spending ($\dot{A}D$) must be matched by equivalent rises in either the growth rate of money or its velocity. Economists disagree strongly over whether or not the growth of the money supply should be allowed to expand to validate part of inflationary price rises.

Questions for Discussion and Review

1. Can stagflation be consistent with a simple Phillips curve that shows zero inflation when unemployment is 5.5 percent?

2. Explain why the expected rate of inflation affects the position of expectations-augmented inflation curves.

3. Why does the rate of increase in demand have to equal the inflation rate if the inflation rate is to be stable?

4. What is the relationship between an aggregate supply curve and a Phillips curve?

5. Is the statement "Inflation is always and everywhere a monetary phenomenon" true (a) in the short run? (b) in the long run?

6. Explain why the rate of output seems more responsive to changes in aggregate demand than does the rate of inflation. Over what period do you believe this would be true?

7. Explain why supply shocks lower the level of potential output.

8. If you were president, would you support a Federal Reserve policy of negative growth in the real money supply? Why or why not?

9. How does the rate of improvement in productivity affect the inflation rate?

10. Using equations 13.10 and 13.11 (in Appendix 13.1) and their numerical examples, show how a supply shock that raised costs by 2 percent in periods 1 and 2 and then returned to zero would affect output and prices if:
    (a) No growth occurred in the rate of increase in demand.
    (b) An accommodative policy were followed aimed at maintaining the level of output as close as possible to full potential.

References

Cagan, P. *Persistent Inflation.* New York: Columbia University Press, 1979.

Eckstein, O., ed. *The Econometrics of Price Determination.* Washington, D.C.: Board of Governors of the Federal Reserve System, 1972.

Fellner, W. "The Valid Core of Rationality Hypotheses in the Theory of Expectations. *Journal of Money, Credit and Banking* 12(November 1980): 763–87.

Friedman, M. "The Role of Monetary Policy." *American Economic Review* 56(March 1968):1-17.

Gramlich, E. "Macro Policy Responses to Price Shocks," *Brookings Papers on Economic Activity* 1(1979): 125–66.

Okun, A. "The Invisible Handshake and the Inflationary Process." *Challenge* (January/February 1980), 5–12.

Perry, G. "Slowing the Wage-Price Spiral." *Brookings Papers on Economic Activity* 2(1978): 259–91.

Phelps, E. *Inflation Policy and Unemployment Theory.* New York: Norton, 1972.

Solow, R. "All Simple Stories about Inflation are Wrong." *The Washington Post,* May 18, 1980.

Stein, J. L. "The Acceleration of Inflation." *Journal of Post Keynsian Economics* (Fall, 1979): 26–42.

APPENDIX 13.1   A Mathematical and Numerical Model of Shifts in Dynamic Demand

To avoid the complexities encountered in attempting to chart movements over time in a dynamic model, the discussions of shifts in dynamic aggregate demand curves and in inflation curves are based on a simplified picture of how the two interact. While not necessary for an understanding of the basic relationships, examination of the more complex model shows the degree to which actual levels of inflation and output depend on how the economy adjusts to new situations. When demand or supply shifts, the path to a new equilibrium may, in fact, be quite devious. Rates of inflation and added output may over- or undershoot the equilibrium toward which the economy is moving. Unless carefully analyzed, current observations may give a false picture of the underlying situation.

The equations underlying the model were given in the body of the chapter as

$$\dot{P} = q\left(\frac{Q}{Q^*} - 1\right) + p(\dot{P}e) \qquad\qquad \dot{P} = .3\left(\frac{Q}{Q^*} - 1\right) + 1(\dot{P}_{-1}) \qquad \text{13.6}$$

and

$$\dot{A}D = \dot{P} + \left\{\frac{Q}{Q^*} - \left(\frac{Q}{Q^*}\right)_{-1}\right\}, \qquad\qquad\qquad\qquad \text{13.7}$$

where the rate of price change $\dot{P}$ depends on the amount of excess or slack output $\left(\frac{Q}{Q^*} - 1\right)$ and on the previous history of prices $(\dot{P}_{-i})$. In the numerical example, expected inflation rates are set equal to the last period's rate of inflation $(\dot{P}e = \dot{P}_{-1})$. Coefficients are .3 for the response of prices to excess supply (in percent) and 1.0 for the expected rate of inflation. In the second equation, the rate of increase in dynamic aggregate demand $(\dot{A}D)$ approximately equals the rate of increase in inflation plus the change in the ratio of output to potential between the current and the previous period $\frac{Q}{Q^*} - \left(\frac{Q}{Q^*}\right)_{-1}$.

These two equations can be combined to yield a two-equation model that allows us to trace the path by which a shift in the rate of changes in demand $(\dot{A}D)$ finally brings about a new equilibrium.

$$\dot{P} = \frac{1}{1+q}(\dot{P}_{-1}) + \frac{q}{1+q}\left\{\left(\frac{Q}{Q^*}\right)_{-1} - 1 + \dot{A}D\right\}$$

$$\dot{P} = .75\dot{P}_{-1} + .25\left\{\left(\frac{Q}{Q^*}\right)_{-1} - 1 + \dot{A}D\right\}. \qquad \textbf{13.10}$$

$$\frac{Q}{Q^*} = \dot{A}D - \dot{P} + \left(\frac{Q}{Q^*}\right)_{-1}. \qquad \textbf{13.11}$$

The derivation of equation 13.10 starts with the equation for the expectations-augmented IS curve, 13.6. It is assumed that a period's inflationary expectations term ($\dot{P}^e$) is equal to the previous period's inflation rate. Therefore, $\dot{P}_{-1}$ can be substituted for ($\dot{P}^e$). The value of p is assumed to be one in the model. The term for the current output ratio from equation 13.11 and the term for the assumed inflationary expectations are substituted in equation 13.6 to give

$$\dot{P} = q\left\{\dot{A}D - \dot{P} + \left(\frac{Q}{Q^*}\right)_{-1} - 1\right\} + \dot{P}_{-1}. \qquad \textbf{13.12}$$

To obtain equation 13.10, this is simplified by factoring out $\dot{P}$ from the right side, resulting in the term $\dfrac{1}{1+q}$. For the numerical example, q is assumed to be $\frac{1}{3}$. The result is a dynamic two-equation model in which current inflation and output depend on current aggregate demand and the rates of inflation and output of the previous period. According to this model, if a new level of dynamic demand ($\dot{A}D$) is inserted into equation 13.10 along with the levels of inflation ($\dot{P}_{-1}$) and rate of output to potential ($\frac{Q}{Q^*}$)$_{-1}$ of the previous period, the estimated inflation rate for the current period ($\dot{P}$) results. The level of dynamic demand and this estimated inflation rate ($\dot{A}D - \dot{P}$) are then inserted in equation 13.11 to find the amount by which this period's output will differ from that of the previous period.

Table 13.4 is repeated as Table 13.8. It shows the results of substituting in the model. It assumes for period zero an economy in equilibrium with a zero growth rate for both inflation and $\dot{A}D$ and a ratio of actual to potential output of 100 percent. Now some force—a higher rate of government spending, or lower taxes, or a more rapidly growing money supply—raises dynamic demand ($\dot{A}D$) up to a rate of 2.4 percent. Inserting the data on $\dot{P}_{-1}$, $\left(\frac{Q}{Q^*}\right)_{-1}$, the constant 1 and $\dot{A}D$, all in percent in equation 13.10 results in:

Period 1 (13.10) $\dot{P} = .75(0) + .25(100 - 100 + 2.4)$ $\dot{P} = .6.$

TABLE 13.8   **The Reaction of Inflation and Output to an Increase in the Rate of Growth of Aggregate Demand**
(percent)

Period	Rate of inflation $(\dot{P})$	Excess or slack output $\left(\dfrac{Q}{Q^*} - 1\right)$
0	0	0
1	0.6	1.8
2	1.5	2.7
3	2.4	2.7
4	3.1	2.0
5	3.4	1.0
6	3.4	0
7	3.2	−0.8
.	.	.
.	.	.
.	.	.
Equilibrium	2.4	0

An increase in the growth rate of aggregate demand ($\dot{AD}$) of 2.4 percent raises output above potential and increases the inflation rate. With the growth rate of demand constant at this new level, the dynamic model (equations 13.10 and 13.11) shows inflation and output rising for several periods. Eventually, however, the absorption of demand by excess inflation is so great that output starts to fall. At equilibrium (point D in Figure 13.4), the new rate of inflation and growth of demand are equal. Output is back at the natural rate of unemployment.

The information for $\dot{P}$ is now substituted in the demand-price-output equation, which gives

Period 1 (13.11) $\dfrac{Q}{Q^*} = 2.4 - .6 + 100$ $\dfrac{Q}{Q^*} = 101.8.$

Output rises to 101.8 percent of potential. These data are recorded in the period 1 line of Table 13.8.

The information from period 1 is inserted into equations 13.10 and 13.11 to find the expected inflation and output rates for period 2:

Period 2 (13.10) $\dot{P} = .75(.6) + .25(101.8 - 100 + 2.4)$ $\dot{P} = 1.5$

Period 2 (13.11) $\dfrac{Q}{Q^*} = 2.4 - 1.5 + 101.8$ $\dfrac{Q}{Q^*} = 102.7.$

The rest of Table 13.8 except for the last line, is derived in the same way. Under the assumptions of this model, after an initial slow start, inflation rises above its equilibrium and output falls below potential for a period. It would be wrong, however, to emphasize the particular path to equilibrium followed in this numerical example. It depends directly on the coefficients inserted in the model. What is important is that the dynamic model shows that not only the final outcome but also the path of the adjustment can exert a significant economic impact.

The last line in the table shows the final equilibrium. By definition, at equilibrium the amount inflation and output changes will be the same as in the previous period: $\dot{P} = \dot{P}_{-1}$ and $\dfrac{Q}{Q^*} = \left(\dfrac{Q}{Q^*}\right)_{-1}$. Such knowledge is used to find the equilibrium and to check that the final line is correct.

The model can be expanded to include production costs (PM) in order to solve for the supply shocks in Tables 13.5 and 13.6. These were included in the initial price equation, 13.5. Their action, like that of the expected rate of inflation, raises the current level of inflation. When they are added to equation 13.10, the more complete equation is

$$\dot{P} = \frac{1}{1+q}(\dot{P}_{-1} + PM) + \frac{q}{1+q}\left\{\left(\frac{Q}{Q^*}\right)_{-1} - 1 + \dot{A}D\right\} \tag{13.13}$$

$$\dot{P} = .75(\dot{P}_{-1} + PM) + .25\left\{\left(\frac{Q}{Q^*}\right)_{-1} - 1 + \dot{A}D\right\}.$$

Equation 13.11 remains the same in the two-equation model with production costs:

$$\frac{Q}{Q^*} = \dot{A}D - \dot{P} + \left(\frac{Q}{Q^*}\right)_{-1}. \tag{13.11}$$

14

Controlling Inflation

Surveys of American public opinion confirm that most people view inflation as the number one problem of the United States and, indeed, of the world. The costs of inflation are high, although economists differ as to just how high they are. Inflationary costs arise principally from institutional factors in the economy and from market imperfections. In an economy in which the private and public sectors possess good information, foresight, flexible rules and contracts, and low transactions costs, all firms and individuals would be able to adjust efficiently to correct expectations of future prices. In such an economy, since everyone would wisely prepare for what was going to happen, inflations would not have serious consequences. Minor inefficiencies would occur, but on the whole, an economy operating according to the rules of a simplified model with competitive, efficient markets could adjust well to inflation.

The neoclassical model is based on such an economy, in which prices do not directly influence the level of real output or real income. Inflation becomes a problem primarily to the degree that the economy deviates from a purely competitive model with good information and flexible adjustments. It is mainly because price movements are not accurately anticipated and because markets do not adjust readily that inflation causes problems. The specific reasons that inflations are costly fall into four general categories: (1) Inflations require waste effort to avoid losses from price movements. (2) Inflations reduce output and lower standards of living. (3) Inflations lead to arbitrary redistributions of income and wealth. (4) The strain of staying abreast of inflation, uncertainty about the future, and anger over real or imagined losses in income lead to severe psychological costs.

The second half of this chapter and Chapter 15 examine some of the methods proposed to bring inflation to a halt. Inflations can be ended through proper management of aggregate demand, through policies to increase output, and through changes in the price-wage structure. Opinions as to which policies would be the most effective are highly correlated with theories of how the price-wage mechanism works. In this chapter, analysis of the costs of inflation and methods of ending it are considered under the following topics:

Fully anticipated inflation and deadweight losses.
Reduced output and income.
Redistribution of income by inflation.
Psychological costs.
The fight against inflation.
Demand management.
Removing government costs and obstacles.
Incomes policies.

Fully Anticipated Inflation and Deadweight Losses

The most significant costs of inflation arise because markets fail fully to anticipate future price changes. If markets predicted future prices correctly, most of
the costs and distortions due to inflation would not occur. There would be some
losses, however, primarily because it would be difficult to pay an inflation
premium on currency and because of the costs involved in adjusting to prices
that changed frequently. Extra efforts required to avoid losses from holding
currency and to make price adjustments are *deadweight costs,* or true social costs
due to having a unit of exchange the value of which is not constant and which
therefore does not adequately serve its purpose.

Comparing a market which does correctly anticipate inflation with the
actual economy shows how inflations engender deadweight losses. It also enables us to see that most of the harm in inflations is caused by the fact that some
prices adjust readily to anticipated price increases while others do not. It is not
the actual existence of inflation, but the uneven and uncertain adjustments that
cause most of the problems. However, since most prices do adjust to some
extent to anticipations, it is necessary to be aware of this fact in planning. Major
errors are caused by failure to recognize the difference between real and nominal prices and costs.

One way to imagine an economy that is fully adapted to anticipated
inflation is to assume that in such an economy all contracts, whether made in
the past or entered into for the future, are fully adjusted for inflation through
indexing. *Indexing* is the linking of payments (wages, taxes, interest, rents) to
changes in a price index for the purpose of maintaining their real or constant-
dollar value. For example, an indexed bond would promise $3 in interest and
the repayment of $100, both with a constant purchasing power. If a price index
rose by 10 percent, the amount in current dollars paid at the end of a year on
the bond would be $113.30 (103 $\times$ 1.10), equivalent to the promised $103 of
constant purchasing power. Because the tax system would also be indexed,
income taxes would be assessed against the real income of $3 rather than the
nominal income of $13.30 received. People who borrowed $100 and paid back
$113.30 instead of the expected $103 would find they were no worse off because
their wages or other sources of income would have risen by the same 10 percent.

Such an economy is pictured in the first three columns of Table 14.1. The only item in the table whose price does not rise at the inflation rate is the dollar. Its price is fixed at one, no matter whether other prices are rising or falling. It earns no interest and therefore cannot adjust through this channel. Anyone who holds currency or a noninterest-bearing checking account will lose purchasing power in an inflation. A $100 bill held through a year in which prices rise 10 percent will command 10 percent fewer goods at the end. As a result, in an inflation people would try to avoid holding currency or deposits because of their falling purchasing power. They would devote extra time and effort to shifting funds to indexed assets, going to the bank more frequently and being caught more often with insufficient cash to make desired purchases. These extra expenditures of time are called "shoe-leather costs" because of the need for more trips to the bank. All such extra efforts are deadweight costs.

While it is estimated that actual shoe-leather losses for the economy are small—well under a billion dollars a year—another type of deadweight loss is "menu costs." These are costs arising out of the effort required to change prices in contract markets to keep up with inflation. (In auction markets, prices constantly change.) In most businesses, however, someone has to write new menus, issue new catalogs and price lists, check the change in the price index to see what interest to pay, and so on. In a rapid inflation, such tasks can be extremely onerous. In mild inflations, prices may be altered less frequently. They jump ahead and then lag behind. Few attempts are made to keep them always current.

On the whole, inflations would engender only minor costs if all contracts, payments, accounting, taxes, and similar sums were constantly adjusted. Because people's incomes from all sources as well as all expenditures and values of capital assets and debts would be calculated in real constant-dollar terms, the

TABLE 14.1   **Effects of Indexing and Anticipations**

Item	Prices in a perfectly anticipated inflation			Prices when inflation is not correctly anticipated		
	Year 1	Year 2	Percent change	Year 1	Year 2	Percent change
The price level	100	110	10	100	110	10
Meat	2.00	2.20	10	2.00	2.10	5
Gasoline	1.00	1.10	10	1.00	1.20	20
Wages	6.00	6.60	10	6.00	6.60	10
Pension	300	330	10	300	303	1
Note and interest	103	113	10	103	103	0
Indexed tax	20	22	10	20	22	10
A dollar	1.00	1.00	0	1.00	1.00	0

In the first three columns, all prices, incomes, and asset values except for the dollar move together. The last three columns are a better representation of reality. While average prices rise by the same 10 percent, some sectors gain and some lose. The value of wealth—all assets—may fall.

effects of inflation would be slight. However, errors are constantly made in estimates of anticipated price changes and our economy is only partially indexed. Unexpected events cause inflation rates to surpass or undershoot expectations. The last three columns of Table 14.1 present a more typical situation. Decision makers cannot fully anticipate future prices and wages. Even if they could, many individuals would not be able to adjust their incomes and assets to expected price changes. People are limited in their ability to borrow. Few assets have values which change in close conformity to prices. Wages and salaries tend to adjust with a lag. This is true of taxes as well. When the price level goes up 10 percent, some prices will rise faster, and others not at all. It is the failure of prices to anticipate inflation and the ensuing distortions that add the costs of lost output, income redistributions, and psychological losses to the deadweight costs.

Reduced Output and Income

Inflations distort pricing, planning, and investment decisions. The economy produces less output and suffers a diminished standard of living. While proof is difficult, many economists blame the slower growth of productivity and potential output during the 1970s on the speed-up of inflation. Why does inflation reduce output and living standards? Production and investment are lowered because changes in the value of money cause poor decisions to be made. Prices set and investments made on the basis of historical costs are unrealistic because they do not conform to changes in real values. Uncertainty spreads; long-term commitments are avoided. Improperly calculated interest and discount rates bias investment decisions.

Problems arise in the rate at which institutions adjust to inflation. Particular difficulties are encountered in altering taxes and government regulations. To make matters worse, the demand for action to deal with inflation may lead to ill-conceived responses. Controls may be imposed improperly; needed programs may be curtailed. Political compromises that took years to work out may come unglued.

FAILURE OF MONEY AS A UNIT OF ACCOUNT

Major losses in output occur because economic institutions find it hard to adjust to fluctuating prices. The dollar serves as a unit of account, enabling managers to plan for current and future production and families to shift their consumption patterns over time by saving, borrowing, and lending. When the purchasing power of the unit of account fluctuates, it throws out improper signals. Poorer decisions will be made. Saving and investment will decline. Output and income will suffer.

Both pricing and investment become far more difficult if the unit of account is shifting. Firms find that recovering historical costs will not enable them to replace goods. Anyone contracting for future deliveries or issuing price lists has to guess at future prices and costs. The farther into the future, the more likely it is that unanticipated events and errors will occur. Horizons are shortened, leading to less productive techniques. It may seem safer to invest in diamonds or collectibles than in productive equipment. One of the problems encountered in substituting coal for oil—a measure urged in the United States in the late 1970s to help reduce oil imports—was the reluctance of potential users, suppliers, and transportation firms to enter into long-term contracts. Without such contracts, planning of plants could not be accomplished. Indexes allowing costs to move with prices are a partial, but not an efficient, substitute for long-term contracts.

When prices go up, contracts and accounting systems fail to differentiate between receipts which are returns of real income and those obtained to offset changes in purchasing power. For example, a 15 percent interest rate on a mortgage may reflect a 5 percent real return plus 10 percent to offset a drop in purchasing power. Even if the existence of an inflationary offset is recognized, it is no easier for a family to meet the higher annual payments. Before their income has had a chance to rise, they must contract to pay much larger amounts which are based on inflationary expectations, not current income. Lenders hesitate to make such loans, with the result that there are fewer purchases and less investment.

Through uncertainty, through expenditure of time and efforts to avoid its costs, through increasing the cost of information, through reducing the incentives to save and work, inflation cuts output. Clear examples of such costs are found in periods of hyperinflation. In post-World-War-II Germany, it was far more profitable for a miner to search for an egg or a piece of fruit than to dig coal. Stores and factories hoarded inventories as a protection against further inflation. Production dropped steadily. When the mark was revalued and price stability was established, production shot up.

DISTORTIONS FROM THE TAX AND REGULATORY SYSTEM

Other important failures to adjust to future prices are found in the tax and financial regulatory systems. Inflation distorts rates of taxation and regulated interest-rate ceilings. Tax rates stated in nominal terms cause the real burden of the tax system to increase when inflation raises nominal income. Chapter 11 showed how, under our tax system, rising incomes rapidly boosted federal government revenues. As a corollary, higher nominal incomes due to inflation alone mean that individuals pay more real taxes, and therefore their real incomes fall. As people move into higher income brackets, the percent paid in taxes moves up even though real income does not. How this happens is demonstrated in Table 14.2. In the tax brackets between $5,000 and $50,000 shown in the table, a 20 percent increase in prices and nominal income raises tax payments by 30 to 70 percent. Aftertax nominal income rises by less than inflation. Real income, after tax payments, is reduced compared to the pre-

TABLE 14.2   **Real Taxes May Increase in Inflations: Before and After a 20 Percent Price Increase**

(dollars)

Income		Tax		Nominal income aftertax		Real income aftertax		Loss in real income
Before	After	Before	After	Before	After	Before	After	
5,000	6,000	254	427	4,746	5,573	4,746	4,644	102
25,000	30,000	5,952	7,962	19,048	22,038	19,048	18,365	683
50,000	60,000	18,067	23,943	31,933	36,057	31,933	30,047	1,886

The table shows the taxes paid by a single person on the adjusted gross incomes in the first and second columns at 1980 tax rates. Inflations raise nominal income, pushing people into higher tax brackets. At each level, even though real before-tax earnings remain constant, real aftertax incomes fall because a higher percentage is paid in taxes.

inflation period. Such a drop in aftertax real incomes dampens incentives to work and raises incentives to search for tax avoidance methods.

Table 5.3 showed the large impacts the tax system made on the profitability of holding real assets or debts when nominal and real interest rates differ. Inflation lowers the real return on bonds and other nominal assets at the same time that it reduces the real costs of being in debt. As with individuals, inflation also raises the taxes corporations pay. Depreciation is charged against historical (book) costs, which are lower than real or replacement costs. Capital costs to firms are higher, and available funds are scarcer. Businesses make fewer investments, and those they make are of shorter duration. Price increases raise the nominal values of common stock and other assets. If these are sold, even though no increase in real values has occurred, capital gains taxes must be paid. Again, the level of investment falls. A "lock-in" may develop in existing stock holdings; people prefer to hang onto older investments in order to avoid having to pay taxes on their purely nominal gains.

One aim of the Economic Recovery Act of 1981 was to reduce the tax impact of inflation. Rates were lowered, particularly those on capital gains and corporate profits. Firms were allowed an acceleration of allowable depreciation deductions. Perhaps more significant was the agreement that after 1985, personal income-tax brackets would be indexed to halt inflationary bracket creep as in Table 14.2. Indexing provides that the bracket at which a tax rate applies moves up with the consumer or other price index. Thus under 1984 rates the average tax on a single person's income of $20,000 would be 12 percent. If, because of a 50 percent price rise, this income rose to $30,000, the brackets to which each tax rate applied would be raised sufficiently so that individuals with unchanged real incomes would continue to pay 12.0 percent instead of the 14.6 percent applicable to a $30,000 income under an unindexed 1984 tax schedule.

Other major distortions are illustrated by interest-rate regulations. The federal government sets ceilings on interest rates that can be paid on demand, savings, and time deposits (Regulation Q). States have similar ceilings and frequently enact usury laws which set maximum amounts that lenders can charge on loans. These ceilings fail to differentiate between real and nominal interest rates. When inflation premiums are high, savers and lenders subject to the ceilings find they must use nontraditional investment channels to protect their real incomes. They invest directly or buy goods rather than putting their savings into deposits. Some sources of funds dry up. Those who save through traditional ceiling-dominated channels lose purchasing power. Recognition of these conditions led to the Depository Institutions Deregulation and Monetary Control Act of 1980. Its purpose was to phase out Regulation Q over savings and time deposits, but not demand deposits. Many states altered their usury ceilings. Still, enough regulations survive to insure distortions in financial markets. Saving and investment are reduced, causing losses in output and income.

OTHER POLICIES THAT REDUCE OUTPUT

Because inflation is a serious problem, voters want governments to do something about it. In response to public pressure, when governments use policies for the purpose of cutting back demand or of suppressing price increases, further losses in output and income are incurred. Real money growth is curtailed to slow spending. As a result, interest rates rise and output is reduced. The lower output means a loss to the economy for as long as resources remain unemployed. Another result is that investment in capital is reduced. Future capacity and productivity are lower. When the costs of these policies become politically or economically unacceptable, they are reversed. Such "stop-go" anti-inflationary policies add to the losses in output and income. Not only are any gains against inflation nullified, but lost output cannot be recouped, and the diminished capacity and productivity make the next anti-inflation fight more difficult. In addition to reductions in demand, price and wage controls may be used to fight inflation. They distort and lower incomes and production. Output is reduced and inequities arise among groups of workers or among those receiving income from other sources.

Redistribution of Income by Inflation

A third major cost of inflation is a redistribution of income and wealth that seems completely arbitrary in its impact. Some families are able to adjust without too much difficulty to the price changes. Others endure true hardships. It is not easy to generalize about which broad groups in the population win and which lose from inflation. It depends on other factors—on each family's specific job, on its transfer payments, on the amount of property owned, on the amount of debt owed, and on how it spends its income. All of these things change over time.

The income redistribution appears to bear little relationship to an individual's merit or contribution to society. It often appears that in an inflation the bad guys—speculators, tax evaders, opportunists—win, while the good guys—the hard-working, cautious, saving families—lose out. Owners of wealth denominated in dollars will lose, while net debtors gain from an unanticipated rise in inflation. Losers will include holders of savings accounts, insurance policies, bonds, and mortgages which do not have variable rates. (Variable rates are those with interest that moves with prices.) As inflation has become more probable, variable rates have become less unusual. The government, as a large net debtor and with tax revenues that rise with inflation, can also be considered a winner in some ways; yet in the 1980s the pay of bureaucrats failed to keep pace with inflation, and many politicians were defeated because of inflation-related issues.

REDISTRIBUTION DEPENDS ON THE SOURCE OF INCOME

A clue as to who might win and who might lose can be found by looking at the sources of income of various groups in economy. Table 14.3 shows major

TABLE 14.3   **Principal Sources of Income of United States Households by Type, 1972**

	Poor				Upper income			
	Female head		Male head		Female head		Male head	
Type of income	Under 65	65 and over	Under 65	65 and over	Under 65	65 and over	Under 65	65 and over
	(percent)							
Wages	33	4	72	7	86	45	94	54
Welfare	44	12	10	14	*	*	*	*
Social insurance	13	72	11	70	3	13	1	15
Pensions	2	6	3	4	2	11	2	12
Rent, interest, dividends	2	5	2	5	6	29	3	18
Other	6	1	2	*	3	1	*	1
	(dollars)							
Average income	1,771	1,417	2,358	1,779	11,587	12,607	18,365	15,348

* Below .5 percent.
SOURCE: J. L. Palmer and M. C. Barth, "The Distributional Effects of Inflation and Higher Unemployment," in M. Moon and E. Smolensky, *Improving Measures of Economic Well-Being* (New York: Academic Press, 1977).

The table shows large differences among households in their dependence on wages, welfare, social insurance, pensions, and income from assets. Households within each category vary still more from the average of all households. To the degree that inflations alter wealth and income from each source, they cause redistributions of income and wealth.

sources of income for eight separate categories. One division is into households with low incomes—those below the poverty line—in contrast to upper-income households—those whose incomes are at least three times the poverty line. A second division is into househoulds with female or male heads. The final division is by age—under or over 65.

Several factors stand out in the table. Welfare and social security are the main sources of income for the poor, with the exception that for those under 65, wages, although low, are significant. Among upper-income groups younger than 65, wages and salaries form the dominant income source. Those over 65 show substantial returns from wages, but pensions, social security, and property income are most important. All the figures are class averages. In reality, some individuals in each class will depend almost entirely on one particular income source.

How a family is affected by inflation will depend on how prices of different sources of income shift. For example, although individual wage increases vary, most wages tend to rise at about the same rate as inflation. Social security and most welfare payments are indexed; they, too, move with inflation, although with some lag. Pensions, interest payments, and rents are less likely to be indexed. Recipients of income from such sources are more likely to be hurt.

ON AVERAGE, REAL GROSS INCOME AND EXPENSES ARE STABLE

Figure 14.1 presents estimates of how such factors influence average families in each income group. It depicts a study which measures the total impact of a 2 percent price rise on the income and expenditures of different families. A family for whom the effect of inflation raises costs of expenditures at the same rate as income measures 1.00 on the left-hand scale. The curve shows an estimate of how families at different income levels measured by current cash income (census definition) are affected. This census income definition includes wages, business and property income, pension benefits, and transfers. Taxes are not deducted.[1] Inflation does not have a large differential effect when income is measured in this manner. The poorest group in the economy—those with very low incomes—gains slightly, as do those with incomes near the top of the income distribution. Most families fall in the break-even category. Only those whose incomes are low but somewhat above the minimum seem to lose. But estimated changes are small. When families are grouped together at each income level, on average higher costs appear just about to match higher incomes. Gains or losses are only a small fraction of the inflation rate.

The tendency, brought out in Figure 14.1, for the real gross income and expenses of the average family at each income level to be almost unaffected by the rate of inflation follows directly from the circular flow. Income and outlays

1. J. J. Minarik, "Who Wins, Who Loses from Inflation," *The Brookings Bulletin* 15(Summer 1978).

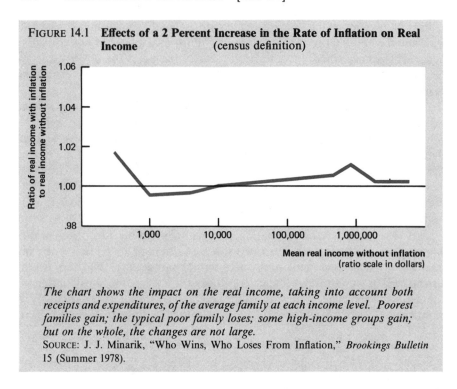

FIGURE 14.1   **Effects of a 2 Percent Increase in the Rate of Inflation on Real Income**   (census definition)

The chart shows the impact on the real income, taking into account both receipts and expenditures, of the average family at each income level. Poorest families gain; the typical poor family loses; some high-income groups gain; but on the whole, the changes are not large.

SOURCE: J. J. Minarik, "Who Wins, Who Loses From Inflation," *Brookings Bulletin* 15 (Summer 1978).

are two sides of the same coin. Some individuals lose if their wages lag far behind the average, but major losses are experienced only by those with incomes from pensions or annuities that are established as a fixed number of dollars.

HOW INFLATION AFFECTS WEALTH

Some families, however, do suffer major losses from inflation for other reasons. As Table 14.2 showed, inflation causes families to pay a higher proportion of income in taxes if rates are not adjusted. In addition, since assets with fixed returns decline in value when nominal interest rates go up, those who hold financial rather than real assets experience a loss in wealth. When interest rates rise, great disparities can develop in the value of different types of assets.

The loss in wealth from inflation can be illustrated by imagining that you deposit $100 in a savings account that pays $5\frac{1}{2}$ percent interest. If inflation is $10\frac{1}{2}$ percent, at the end of the year the amount you have will be $105.50; but it will buy only as much as $95 would have bought at the beginning of the year. The problem with long-term bonds is still worse. An increase in the expected rate of inflation will be added by the market to the preexisting rates reflected in the coupons of outstanding bonds. The bonds will immediately experience a capital loss corresponding to the reduced present value of the future flows being discounted at the new higher nominal interest rates. Such changes in anticipated inflation account for the fact that some U.S. government bonds sell at less than 75 percent of their par value and that some bondholders have received low or negative returns in many years.

Of course, as we have seen, those who owe on debt have the opposite experience. Look at a mortgage as an example. The homeowner who owes money on a mortgage gains in an inflation. This gain is on top of any increase in the price of the house due to inflated building costs. It is easy to see why houses are popular when people fear inflation; owning a house is one of the few ways the average family can hedge against an unanticipated inflation. Of course, if the inflation ends, nominal interest rates will drop. Any inflationary premium paid for the house will be wiped out, and the owner will lose.

A key point to remember is that anticipated inflation gets built into market prices and interest rates. Only unanticipated changes and the resulting moves in nominal interest rates and the purchasing power of assets cause gains and losses. If real interest rates are 5 percent and lenders receive 15 percent in interest, they are fully compensated for a 10 percent rise in prices. It is sometimes suggested that the only sure way to beat inflation is to buy a house. This is an incomplete and incorrect statement. Except in poorly organized markets where sellers accept less than the real value of their assets, prices should reflect anticipated inflation. When you buy a house or other real asset, you protect yourself against an unanticipated increase in the inflation rate. But you take the risk of an unanticipated drop. Since many families hold other assets, such as deposits or life insurance, which react in the opposite way, purchases of real assets may lower their risks through diversification. But they cannot be a sure thing; if they were, they would be bought before you got there.

ESTIMATED LOSSES FROM TAXES AND CHANGED ASSET VALUES

The study on which Figure 14.1 was based also estimated the losses to average families at different income levels produced by inflation through the tax and wealth channels. Figure 14.2 reports the calculated changes in real income after expenses using a second concept of income called *accrued comprehensive income,* or ACI. From the usual measurements of gross income and expenses illustrated in Figure 14.1, ACI subtracts out tax payments and—more importantly—losses or gains in asset values. ACI includes total economic returns. The losses or gains in the market value of an asset due to interest rate changes are added to interest and dividend payments to measure the total accrued changes in income. Thus ACI takes into account the drop in the value of interest receipts and of dollar-denominated securities as well as higher real income taxes on larger incomes and incomes of corporations.

The total ACI line also shows that, as a group, lower- and middle-income families are not greatly affected by inflation. They do not own much wealth, and their real taxes do not rise to any degree. Wages, transfer payments, and home values rise at about the same rate as inflation. But those who hold fixed-price securities and are in the higher income brackets show substantial losses from inflation. The government, both as a debtor and as a tax collector, gains a great deal of this amount. If the redistribution effects through the government were more completely analyzed, conclusions as to who wins and who loses might be altered somewhat.

The second line in Figure 14.2 shows still more clearly the impact of inflation on those who own securities. This line measures the effect of the rise in

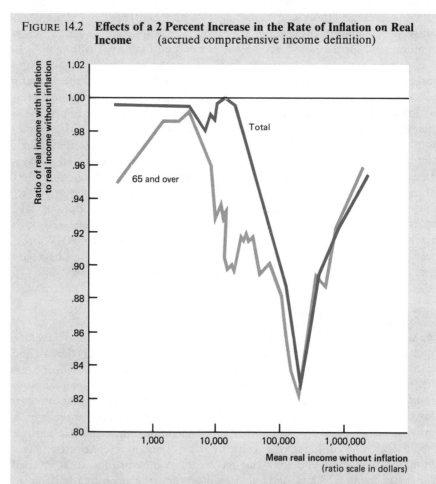

FIGURE 14.2   **Effects of a 2 Percent Increase in the Rate of Inflation on Real Income**   (accrued comprehensive income definition)

When taxes and the impact on wealth are included in a more comprehensive definition of income, losses at higher income levels become substantial. Elderly families particularly lose because more of their receipts come from assets with fixed payments.

SOURCE: J. J. Minarik, "Who Wins, Who Loses From Inflation," *Brookings Bulletin* 15 (Summer 1978).

prices on the accrued comprehensive income of households whose heads are over 65 years of age. Note that in this category, important losses from inflation occur among lower-income groups, and even more so among those in middle-income brackets. More of the incomes of the elderly tend to come not from wages, which move with inflation, but from insurance, deposits, and pensions, which have fixed returns. In the higher-income groups, age does not matter as much because among these classes most income derives from real assets with returns that do increase.

This and other studies show that, on average, the major redistributions which occur as a result of inflation are away from those over 65 to those in younger age groups, as well as to whoever benefits from larger government transfers and expenditures. While these charts present a picture of how inflation losses and gains tend to be distributed among income groups, because they are class averages, they cannot be applied to individual families. How any particular family fares depends on its particular sources of income. Furthermore, this type of study only tells how people may be affected by redistribution due to unanticipated changes; it does not account for the factors in the inflation that lower real income. When average real income falls because of lowered output, lowered productivity, higher real payments to foreigners, and psychological costs, all classes are worse off. Only the lucky few who do considerably better than their class will not lose.

GOVERNMENTS GAIN FROM INFLATION

We have already seen that the United States government gained in several ways from inflation. In the late 1970s the income elasticity of the tax system was estimated at 1.4. Inflation raised federal revenues faster than costs. Tax collections swelled merely because of the rise in prices. Table 14.2 showed that inflation pushed individuals into progressively higher tax brackets, increasing their real tax payments. In addition, corporations paid more taxes because depreciation was allowed only on historical, not on real costs. Taxes on capital gains were inflated because nominal as well as real gains were taxed.

Furthermore, the United States government is a large net debtor. It has both long- and short-term interest-bearing liabilities. To the degree that lenders to the government do not fully anticipate inflation, their interest receipts do not fully compensate them for the losses inflations cause in the purchasing power of their bonds. Since inflation was higher than anticipated in the 1950s, 1960s, and 1970s, the real interest on the public debt was lower than if inflation had been forecast correctly. State and local government profited as well through similar channels.

The federal government also gains in a more subtle way. The monetary base consists of government liabilities which do not pay interest. In contrast to the other parts of the debt, the Treasury receives back semi-automatically most of the interest paid to the Federal Reserve on the bonds bought in open market operations to back currency or required deposits at the Fed. When inflation raises nominal income, the monetary base expands. The amount of debt on which no interest is paid increases. In 1981 the Federal Reserve returned over $11.7 billion to the Treasury.

The questions of the degree to which governments should be allowed to profit from inflation and how the gains should be divided have led to major political controversies. On the strength of jumps in revenues related to inflation, governments received more income without the necessity of voting new taxes. This led some governments (state and local as well as federal) to expand their real expenditures. It was one factor entering into the greater governmental share of the circular flow. It has also led to major battles over what limits are proper for government expenditures. The federal tax changes of 1981 were passed to limit the revenue elasticity of the U.S. government. Initial estimates indicated that after 1984, inflation is likely to cause federal expenses to rise faster than revenues. If inflation continues, either expenditures—primarily those for social security and defense—will have to be cut or new taxes will have to be legislated.

Psychological Costs

Although output losses and redistribution costs may be great, the psychological costs of inflation to individuals may be even more significant. Impacts on future welfare and the political process may be considerable. The psychological costs arise from people's feeling that they are losing out to "the system." Individuals tend to believe that increases in their wages, profits, or income are the fruits of their own efforts, resourcefulness, and skills. Yet when they go to spend their extra income, they find that inflation has robbed them of what they consider a well-deserved increase in satisfaction. They receive no more real goods and services than they did when they worked at a lower-paid job. Rising prices mean that they can buy no more than they could before their hard-earned and hard-fought-for salary increase. Because people are sure that their higher incomes are due to their own merit and hard work and not merely to inflation, they become dissatisfied when real income fails to rise.

Uncertainty is another major psychological cost. In a period of fluctuating prices, individual planning becomes complicated. Many people hesitate to retire or to change their housing or to sell goods because they fear that inflation will worsen. They see people who retired with what seemed like adequate income struggling to make ends meet, as the prices they have to pay rise much faster than their incomes. They don't know what to do; decisions become costly in psychic terms.

The Fight against Inflation

Because inflations are costly, there is an almost universal desire to see them end. Numerous approaches have been put forward as the best way to accomplish the task. We divide the principal suggestions into four categories, analyzing the first three in the remainder of this chapter and the fourth in Chapter 15.

1. *Demand management.* Inflations can be halted if the growth of aggregate demand $(\dot{AD})$ is reduced sufficiently. If demand grows at less than the inflation rate, output will fall below potential and the pace of inflation will slow. How fast success will be achieved and at what costs depend on the dynamics of price determination—short-run expectations-augmented inflation curves. If, in addition, inflation rates are directly influenced, as some believe, by the money stock rather than indirectly through the channels of slack output, then restrictive monetary policy opens up an additional path through which demand management can reduce inflation.

2. *Removal of government-imposed costs and obstacles.* Government programs and regulations may raise some prices, and they may make it harder for competition to fight inflation. If such obstacles are removed, prices may adjust more rapidly.

3. *Incomes policies.* Government actions can be taken to influence prices and wages directly. If successful, they will reduce the rate of inflation with a smaller loss in output.

4. *Supply economics.* Policies can be utilized aimed at shifting the supply curve downward to the right, while increasing the rate of growth in potential output.

Deciding which policies are best has been difficult. Agreement has been lacking as to the costs and benefits each method or combination of methods entails. Each approach differs in its cost to specific segments of the population. Every time particular anti-inflationary policies have been suggested or adopted, the groups in the economy most affected thereby have fought to have their sacrifices minimized. Who pays and who gains from governmental actions is at the heart of the political process.

LIVING WITH INFLATION: INDEXING

To the degree that the major costs of inflation arise from a failure of prices to adjust evenly to anticipated price increases, a system in which all or most contracts are fully indexed could reduce many of inflation's costs. If indexing is inclusive enough, the costs of inflation may be less than waging an all-out war against it. Living with inflation through widespread indexing is a policy that has been followed by many Latin American countries and by Israel. Inflation rates of 50 percent or higher have not halted the functioning of these economies. However, because not all costs are removed, inflations even with indexing cause dissatisfaction and losses in output. They greatly complicate international trade. But the fact that these countries have delayed declaring total war against inflation would appear to mean that they view living with inflation through indexing to be the preferable policy, at least over considerable periods.

In indexed systems, all or nearly all prices, wages, and other types of payments are raised at specific intervals on the basis of a government price index. The government may announce at the beginning of each month the percentage rate of increase in the official index during the past month. All salaries, wages, financial contracts, and prices not set in competitive markets are automatically increased by the same rate or some percentage of the rate by which the index rose. Problems arise due to lags (few durables will be bought near the end of the month), due to differing changes in relative prices, and to the need to enforce the regulations. But despite major problems of these types and widespread dissatisfaction over continued inflation, some countries choose to live with the situation rather than invoke more Draconian policies.

In the United States, in addition to the tax system, indexing is becoming more common in many spheres. In recent years, many leases have been written in which rents rise with a price index. Variable-rate mortgages are another type of indexed contract. Some bonds require that interest rates move with prices. The objectives are similar in all of these cases. People want to enter into a contract which assures them of paying and receiving an agreed-upon amount of real purchasing power. They accomplish this by agreeing on what the real interest rate should be and allowing it to move with prices. As an example, Mary Smith and Paul Jones, who are negotiating a loan, may agree that 5 percent is a fair real interest rate. Because prices have been rising and are expected to rise by 10 percent a year, market interest rates are 15 percent.

$$i = r + \dot{P}e \qquad i = 5 + 10 = 15. \qquad\qquad \textbf{14.1}$$

They agree that at the end of each year Smith will pay Jones 5 percent plus any increase in the price index for that year. If prices rise by 12 percent, the required payment will be 17 percent. If they rise by 5 percent, she will owe him only 10 percent. In either case, the lender receives 5 percent in real interest plus an additional amount sufficient to hold the purchasing power of the principal constant. While some observers believe that a fully indexed economy will operate as well or better than traditional ones, a majority conclude that living with inflation through indexing is a second-best solution. They want to see inflation halted primarily through management of demand.

Demand Management

Earlier chapters showed that the government could reduce the rate of increase in dynamic aggregate demand ($\dot{A}D$) by either fiscal or monetary policy. Chapters 18 and 19 will discuss issues related to proper policy decisions. In weighing the costs and benefits of fighting inflation, we now ask what costs arise from the use of demand management for anti-inflationary programs. These are the costs people think about when they support or oppose particular policies.

Slowing demand through monetary and fiscal policy reduces output and increases unemployment. Restrictive monetary policy raises real interest rates and may cause financial difficulties. How far demand must be lowered and the amount of output that will be lost (as was shown by the discussion of Figure 13.9) are at the heart of the debate over the use of demand management. Those who emphasize expectations and credibility picture an economy in which the growth of demand can be lowered and inflation ended without large losses. The price-wage structure is flexible so that less spending primarily lowers prices, not output. Those who think that a rigid price-wage structure causes the persistence of inflation believe the costs of using demand management may be high.

In its issue of June 20, 1979, *The Wall Street Journal* asked two prominent bank economists, Tilford Gaines and Beryl Sprinkl (who became undersecretary of the Treasury in 1981), together with Robert Solow (president of the American Economic Association) how long they thought it would take to cure inflation and at what cost. Gaines thought that a severe recession with unemployment of 8 or 9 percent could have a significant impact. Sprinkl thought that even with this amount of unemployment it would take several years to reduce inflation back to the 6 to 7 percent range. Solow believed that while a steady state of unemployment could reduce the inflation rate by .5 percent a year, it would take eight years of mild recession for the inflation rate to fall to 5 percent a year. When *Newsweek* (November 19, 1979) asked Paul Samuelson his view of the 1980s, he picked as a key issue probable stagnation costs of hundreds of billions of dollars.

THE CONTRASTING VIEWS OF PRICE RESPONSIVENESS

When growth in demand is reduced, output falls. Slack in output causes the inflation rate to decline. How fast inflation slows depends, as we have seen, on three separate factors in the dynamic process:

1. How much demand is reduced; how far $\dot{AD}$ shifts to the left.
2. The slope of the *IC* curve determines how much the decline in aggregate demand affects output and prices. The principal effect of a movement of $\dot{AD}$ to the left may be to depress output rather than to slow price increases.[2]
3. What the rate is at which expectations will change. Many arguments are carried on over the relationship of expectations to past experience. How important are rational expectations compared with catch-ups in prices and the cost of living?

The contrasting opinions of economists as to these relationships are pictured again in Figure 14.3. The distance between adjacent short-run inflation curves is an indication of how fast the inflationary expectations term might

---

2. An early study of this problem is O. Eckstein and R. Brinner, "The Inflation Process in the United States," in U.S. Congress, Joint Economic Committee 92:2, (February 22, 1972). They found a nearly horizontal short-run Phillips curve subject to numerous shocks.

FIGURE 14.3   **The Slope of Inflation Curves and the Rate of Fall in Inflationary Expectations**

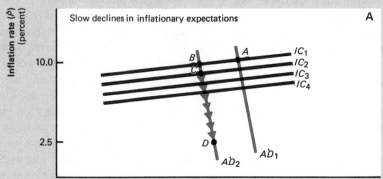

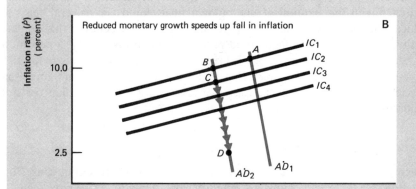

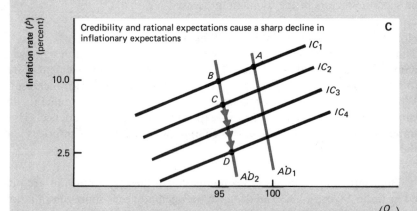

How fast a decrease in demand can end inflation depends on the slope of the IC curves and on how rapidly expectations fall. This example assumes that it takes a year to move down from one IC curve to the next. Inflation drops far faster under the conditions of panel C than under those of A.

drop. Figure 14.4 shows econometric estimates of how long and expensive the cures might be.

Figure 14.3A is basically a pure Phillips curve model. Excess unemployment causes the inflation rate to drop, but at a slow rate. It pictures a very flat short-run *IC* curve and a projected decline that depends almost entirely on the amount of slack in the economy. The downward pressures from decreasing expectations are slight, as indicated by the closeness of the individual *IC* curves to each other. The middle panel, 14.3B, shows a steeper *IC* curve and a more rapid adjustment of expectations. In this model, changes in the rate of monetary growth affect output, expectations, and the rate of inflation. Money has a direct impact on prices in addition to an influence through holding down output. The third panel, 14.3C, is derived from the model used in conjunction with President Reagan's initial presentation of his "Program for Economic Recovery" in February 1981. It is based on the concepts of credibility and rational expectations. The impact of such a program depends largely on how it is received. If enough decision makers agree that inflation is going to end, the decline in price expectations is rapid. The economy soon reaches a point of zero inflation.

ECONOMETRIC ESTIMATES OF OUTPUT LOSSES

Figure 14.4 pictures the losses it would take to reduce the inflation rate by 7.5 percent in accordance with the assumptions underlying the models in the preceding figure. Each line agrees with the panel having the same letter in Figure 14.3. Lines *a* and *b* in panel A are derived from econometric estimates made at the Federal Reserve Bank of St. Louis. The policy assumptions fed into the computer assume policy set so as to hold the economy in a long, shallow recession. Line *c* pictures the information contained in President Reagan's program of February 18, 1981. It assumes that the credibility hypothesis is correct.

Line *a* follows a simple Phillips curve model like those discussed in the last chapter. For the chart, unemployment was assumed to remain 1 percent above its natural rate. According to the model, such slack in demand causes the inflation rate to fall at a rate of approximately .33 percent per year. Such a policy, by itself, would require 23 years to slow an inflation rate of 7.5 percent per year to zero. Tripling the excess slack to a rate of unemployment 3 percent above its natural rate would end inflation in 11 years, but the costs in lost output and suffering would be considerably higher. Recall that the model assumes that the only anti-inflationary force at work is reduced demand. All other policies, such as those to shift expectations or supply-side improvements, merely offset adverse shocks which might otherwise cause inflation to worsen.

Line *a* on the second panel, 14.4B, shows how much output would be lost if this model is correct. The losses in output needed to extinguish inflation are translated from the model's unemployment estimates by an early version of Okun's law. Each 1 percent addition to unemployment causes a 3.2 percent loss

FIGURE 14.4   **Contrasting Estimates of Time and Losses in Fighting Inflation**

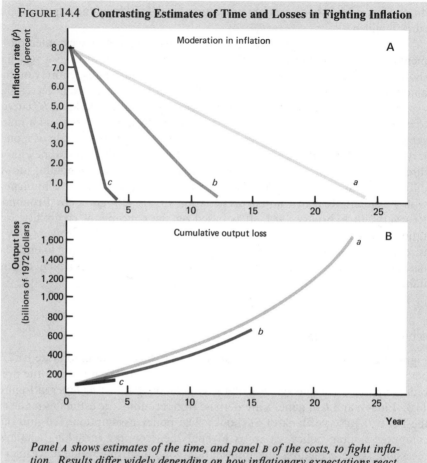

Panel *A* shows estimates of the time, and panel *B* of the costs, to fight inflation. Results differ widely depending on how inflationary expectations react.
To reduce the core rate by 8 percent takes 23 years and cumulative losses of
over $1,600 billion (constant 1972 dollars) under the assumptions of panel *A*
in Figure 14.3. More optimistic assumptions (14.3B) show a 12-year battle
and cumulative losses of $700 billion. If credibility takes hold (14.3C), the
drop takes only 4 years with little or no loss in output.
SOURCE: Lines *a* and *b* adapted from Meyer and Rasche, "On the Costs and Benefits of
Anti-Inflation Policies."

in output. According to the model and chart, the cumulative loss in output
needed to end inflation amounts to over $1,600 billion in constant 1972 dollars.
Initially, output is lost at a rate of about $50 billion a year. But because of the
growth in potential output, 1 percent slack causes an annual loss of $85 billion
in constant 1972 dollars by the end of the period. The present value in 1972
dollars of the total loss is about $1,000 billion.[3]

3. L. H. Meyer and R. H. Rasche, "On the Costs and Benefits of Anti-Inflation Policies,"
Federal Reserve Bank of St. Louis, *Review* 62(February 1980): 3–14.

The second estimate, line *b* on the figure, follows a monetarist model developed by Jerome Stein. This model takes the form:

$$\dot{P} - \dot{P}_{t-1} = a(\dot{M} - \dot{P}_{t-1}),\qquad\qquad\textbf{14.2}$$

or the change in the inflation rate from the previous period is equal to the growth rate of the money stock less the previous period's inflation rate. In this model, the growth in the money supply rather than in aggregate demand drives the rate of inflation and unemployment. The decline in inflation pictured results from holding monetary growth 1 percent below its full-employment path. This model shows that such a policy would extinguish inflation in 12 years. Line *b* on the second panel, 14.4B, pictures the cumulative loss in output engendered by this policy. According to Stein's model, the length of time and the losses from a policy to end inflation are about half those shown by line *a*, the Phillips curve analysis.

Neither of these models allows for shifts in expectations. They assume either that the impact of a reduced rate of inflation on price expectations is minimal, or that the rate at which expectations adapt is slow. In contrast, line *c* assumes that the fight against inflation becomes credible. Inflationary expectations and the rate of inflation drop rapidly to zero. This line is based on the published data of President Reagan's program. Inflation drops by over 7.5 percent in four years. Removal of the pressure of adverse supply shocks in the previous years causes some of the decline, while part is due to slack in the economy. Actual output was estimated to be from 4 to 7 percent below potential. More than half of the improvement, however, would come from a decline in inflationary expectations. Furthermore, as line *c* in panel 14.4B shows, the program projected almost zero costs to achieve these results. While output would be below potential, as a result of supply-side economics, the growth rate of the economy would speed up. Consequently, the actual level of output would be close to the potential projected from previous growth patterns.

The key differences in these various projections arise from the weight they assign to the forces of inertia and expectations. If the underlying core rate of inflation declines because of a drop in inflationary expectations, inflation subsides at a much faster pace. On the other hand, if inflationary pressures stem primarily from the inertia of sectors trying to regain prior income losses, staggered contract renewals make rapid declines in inflation more expensive and less probable.

Table 14.4 compares the expected results of the Reagan program to those projected a month earlier by the outgoing Carter administration. Many forecasters believed the Carter estimates were made slightly optimistic for political reasons. In contrast, when the Reagan projections were published, some prominent supply-side economists indicated they felt that the projected decline in the inflation rate to 5.5 percent for 1984 was too pessimistic. In their view, a successful program would reduce inflation and increase output at an even faster rate. The factors leading to the conflicting predictions are discussed in more detail in Chapter 19. These differences in views led observers to agree that the Economic Recovery Act of 1981 was a great gamble whose pay-off would only be clear as history unfolded.

TABLE 14.4 **Projected Effects of Carter and Reagan 1982 Budget Messages**

		1981	1982	1983	1984
(percent)					
Growth in output	Carter	0.9	3.5	3.5	3.7
	Reagan	1.1	4.2	5.0	4.5
Change in consumer price index	Carter	12.5	10.3	8.7	7.7
	Reagan	11.1	8.3	6.2	5.5
Unemployment rate	Carter	7.8	7.5	7.1	6.7
	Reagan	7.8	7.2	6.6	6.4
(billions of dollars)					
Budgeted surplus (deficit)	Carter	(−55)	(−26)	(−5)	41
(fiscal year)	Reagan	(−60)	(−45)	(−23)	1

The Reagan economic program called for major cuts in federal expenditures and taxes, resulting in increased deficits and aggregate demand. The inflation rate was projected to drop more rapidly because of a reduction in inflationary expectations and increased supply.

UNEMPLOYMENT

The decline in output is not the only cost from slack in demand. Losses also occur because unemployment is higher, capacity utilization is down, profits turn into losses, wealth shrinks, mortgages are foreclosed, and corporations fail. Although some people become better off, on the average people are poorer. The deeper the recession, the more people are hurt. The greater the individual losses, the fewer are those willing to pay the costs necessary to conquer inflation.

Although output turns down before employment and has more widespread impacts, many think of the unemployment rate as a shorthand way of describing recessions. Political decisions on economic policy are especially sensitive to the unemployment rate. Data on lost output, profits, and wealth are less certain, less accurate, and arrive more slowly. The costs of unemployment are high and extremely visible. People without jobs are unproductive. Both their personal incomes and national output are reduced, and the loss is permanent. With few exceptions, idle hours are not recouped.

Unemployment also has a high psychological cost. The inability to find a job delivers a severe blow to one's self-image and sense of worth. In our society, what one does is a basic measure of a person's role. Inability to find a job labels a person a loser. The social and psychological costs are primarily a function of how long a person takes to find work. When unemployment is prolonged, family resources evaporate. For a while, family expenditures may be sustained by receipts from unemployment insurance, by using up assets, or by going into debt. But the longer unemployment lasts, the greater is the likelihood of real poverty. Children and other family members are affected by anxiety and the inability to maintain their position in the community. Homeowners lose their property. Indexes of social well-being and behavior begin to deteriorate. Crime rises; health standards decline.

In nonrecession periods, about half of the unemployed are out of work for 5 weeks or less, while a quarter or less report that they have been seeking work for 15 weeks or more. (This number is split fairly evenly between those in the 15- to 26-week category and those over 26 weeks.) But in a recession, a dramatic change occurs in these ratios. Not only does the number out of work rise, but the percentage out of work for long periods may double. Because of this difference in duration of unemployment, some observers feel that, in normal times, the impact of unemployment is fairly diffuse and may not be too serious, whereas it becomes more devastating in a recession.

The unemployment rate does not reflect the number of people who are no longer counted as unemployed when their failure to find a job causes them to drop out of the labor force. In addition to increases in the number of dis-

TABLE 14.5 **Unemployment Rates among Population Groups**
(percent)

		1969	1975	1979:Q2	1980:Q4
Ages 16 to 19					
Female:	Black	27.6	38.5	38.9	36.6
	White	11.5	17.4	13.9	14.5
Male:	Black	21.4	35.4	31.9	37.6
	White	10.0	18.3	12.8	17.1
Ages 20 and above					
Female:	Black	5.8	11.5	10.2	12.3
	White	3.4	7.5	4.9	5.8
Male:	Black	3.7	11.7	8.2	11.9
	White	1.9	6.2	3.4	5.6
All groups		3.5	8.5	5.7	7.5
Duration of 27 weeks or more		0.2	1.5	0.6	1.1

SOURCE: U.S. Bureau of Labor Statistics.

Marginal groups in the labor force have high unemployment rates, which become much higher in recessions. They did not recover as well in the limited prosperity of the late 1970s. In recessions, the number out of work for over a half-year increases greatly, even though the reported rate is reduced by discouraged job-seekers who drop out of the labor force.

couraged workers, recessions mean that many of the employed will be working fewer hours than they would like to work. Overtime disappears. Undertime—partial work weeks—becomes more common. Human capital is also decreased. Slack demand for labor means less on-the-job training and fewer promotions. Low-income workers have less chance to advance. Future lifetime incomes may be reduced.

Increases in unemployment are not spread evenly. In recessions, those who normally have the lowest incomes are hit hardest. Table 14.5 shows how unemployment differs among groups. Even in prosperity, blacks, women, and teenagers experience higher unemployment rates than adult white males. When recessions hit, their situation deteriorates still further. The table shows that in the fourth quarter of 1980, when average unemployment was 7.5 percent, over 37 percent of black and nearly 16 percent of white teenagers who wanted work could not find it. Over 12 percent of blacks 20 and over were unemployed compared with about 5.7 percent for whites in these age groups. Furthermore, other studies show that within each of these groups, the poorer the worker was to begin with, the larger the loss in income is likely to be as a result of a recession. The costs of unemployment arising from lowered demand and output, like the costs of inflation, tend to be concentrated. Recessions hit especially hard among those who are less well-off before the decline in output.

OTHER COSTS OF RECESSIONS

The unemployment rate is only one indicator, and it will vary as the natural rate of unemployment shifts. An undue emphasis on the unemployment rate leads to a one-sided view of the costs of deflation. When output drops, many firms do not reduce their labor force proportionately. Skilled workers are hard to find and train; it pays to keep them attached to the firm as long as possible.

Failure to sell goods, with overhead and fixed costs continuing, leads to a drop in profits throughout the economy. Firms and financial institutions which seemed to be well-run in prosperous times, although somewhat weakly capitalized, go under in a recession. It is much harder to launch new ventures and innovations. Existing businesses retrench, making future production more expensive. The level of investment in the economy and future capacity drop. Mobility decreases because people can't buy or sell houses and fear to be out of work.

Some economists feel winning the inflation fight and improving efficiency by weeding out the less well-run firms is well worth the costs. Others, concerned with the overall effect on the economy and with losses in output and income as well as with jobs, are more likely to think in terms of John Donne's famous line: "Any man's death diminishes me, because I am involved in mankind; and therefore never send to know for whom the bell tolls; it tolls for thee." These contrasting views lie behind the difficulty of reaching agreement on deflationary policies and on how long to maintain them.

Removing Government Costs and Obstacles

A second category of anti-inflation policies aims at removing government programs which raise costs. Such programs can be divided into three types. First and most prominent are government regulations. Second are taxes that raise the cost of goods and directly impact the consumer price index. Any reduction in these taxes would be felt shortly in the CPI. Third are special programs to aid individual groups or industries and enable them to raise prices; such programs include quotas on steel and autos, restrictions on agricultural production and imports, the minimum wage.

Agreement is nearly unanimous that removing obstacles to a more efficient, competitive economy is worthwhile and should be accomplished as rapidly as possible. What is not as clear is how large the pay-off will be. The hoped-for benefits also depend on how such changes would affect expectations and how expectations influence prices. Inflation is a dynamic process. Table 14.4 showed that President Reagan estimated prices would rise over 30 percent in four years. Even if removing obstacles cut prices by 5 percent over the period, it would mean an improvement of less than one-sixth of the total. To have a truly significant impact, deregulation and similar policies must cause expectations to fall so as to multiply their initial effects.

DEREGULATION

During the 1970s, economists pinpointed 60 or more regulations that they wanted to see abolished or improved. Controls on building and land uses raise housing costs. Higher prices result from agricultural marketing orders, acreage controls, trucking regulations, financial controls, import quotas, and similar programs. In the 1970s, agricultural and housing policies had major inflationary impacts. Swings in food prices and the rising cost of houses boosted inflation and caused counterproductive price increases even in periods of recession. Estimates of the costs to the economy of government regulations vary by several hundred billion dollars, or by more than 10 percent of the GNP. These costs and suggested policies spoken of as deregulation include the programs listed under miscellaneous in Table 14.6. Obviously, the greater the real waste, the greater are potential savings from deregulation.

The Carter administration began the deregulation process with major changes for the airline, railroad, trucking, communications, and banking industries. Attempts were made to apply cost-benefit analysis to regulations over energy, clean air and water, health and safety, and consumer protection. When the Reagan administration took office, they abolished or drastically curtailed many of the regulations in these latter fields.

Everyone can point to inane regulations. No one doubts that bureaucratic overkill commonly occurs in large organizations, and centralized government programs generate more than their share. Every cent saved by abolishing needless regulations or by improving the efficiency of those which remain enhances the national welfare. Improving a regulation shifts the supply curve down and to the right. Greater output is possible at lower costs. The impacts of such changes can be multiplied if they lead to further improvements in productivity or reductions in inflationary expectations.

While such improvements are applauded by all, skeptics believe that what deregulation can do for inflation has been greatly overestimated. For example, the reductions shown in Table 14.6 are not large. While the programs inaugurated by President Reagan differ to some extent, doubters believe their mag-

TABLE 14.6 **Summary of Policy Proposals to Reduce the Price Level**

	Potential reduction	
Proposal	Annual amount (billions of 1977 dollars)	In gross private domestic deflator (percent)
GOVERNMENT REGULATION		
Pursue deregulation of airlines, trucking, and the coastal maritime trade	5.3 to 10.4	.3 to .6
Impose a shadow budget on social regulatory agencies	Unmeasurable with present data	...
Increase federal timber cut	.3	.02
Require fully incremental costing of all imported liquid and synthetic natural gas	Unknown, but up to 36.0	Up to 2.2
Reassess best-available-control-technology amendment to Clean Air Act	1.0 to 2.0	.06 to .12
TAXES		
Social security		
Replace employer and employee payroll taxes with general revenue financing for disability and health insurance (fiscal 1979)	14.6	.7
Sales		
Reduce state sales taxes up to 2 percentage points of personal income	27.4	1.6
Replace federal excise taxes with direct taxes	17.4	1.0
MISCELLANEOUS PROGRAMS		
Agriculture	8.0	.5
Foreign trade	2.3 to 2.7	.1 to .2
Minimum wage	3.1	.2
Hospital cost control	1.5	.09

SOURCE: Compiled from information in the *Brookings Papers on Economic Activity* 2(1978). Based on projection of fiscal 1979 gross domestic private product.

nitudes do not differ greatly from those of the table. Improvements to be gained from deregulation result in a single shift of the static AS curve. Since the deregulations listed in the table would reduce costs about 1 to 3 percent, to exert a larger impact on inflation, the programs must start a dynamic process. Successive downward shifts covering many periods must come about, either through steady improvements in productivity or through a move by the economy down from one short-run Phillips curve to the next as a result of a change in price expectations.

Some fear that the benefits of certain programs slated to be abolished may be underestimated. Gains from clean air or better health and safety do not appear in the National Income and Products Accounts, but the costs of the equipment and manpower required to implement such regulations are counted as part of the costs of production. As such programs grow, measured—but not necessarily real—productivity falls. Abolishing such programs reverses these drops, but the apparent gains from deregulation are overestimated. Others, of course, believe that specific programs confer benefits far outweighing their costs; they had to have majority approval when adopted and should be continued. How much the nation wants to pay for specific public programs appears to vary with shifts in the political climate.

TAXES

Some analysts believe that a proper tailoring of taxes can be as significant in fighting inflation as deregulation. Taxes can shift the static AS curve. Such tax effects, it should be noted, are separate from the effects of reducing taxes on demand or to increase incentives. Chapters 5 and 11 showed that tax cuts that raised demand had partially offsetting revenue effects. The next chapter discusses cuts in taxes aimed at increasing incentives and shifting the supply curve.

Taxes vary in their price impact. Many believe that excise and payroll taxes are more likely than income taxes to lead to higher prices. However, the ultimate effect of sales or value-added taxes is more uncertain. Arthur Okun estimated that a $20 billion tax reduction which was passed in 1975 could have reduced prices by 2 percent if the cuts had been used to lower sales rather than income taxes. In contrast, those who stress incentives would argue that the ultimate effect would be the opposite of his estimate.

Table 14.6 presents an attempt to put dollar values on the three categories of anti-inflation policy proposals. It is not complete because it omits some major regulatory issues. In this sphere the widest range of estimates is found. While many would not agree with the table, the orders of magnitude are of interest. The table estimates that the principal impact of deregulation would be to lower prices by from 1 to 3 percent. The particular taxes listed show an impact of 3.3 percent. The miscellaneous programs equal about 1 percent. One can draw one's own conclusions about the significance of the proposed changes. What the table does show is that efficiency and real output could be increased, making the majority better off if such proposals were adopted. On the other hand, the impact on inflation rates might not be great since, under the best of circumstances, such gains would be spread over several years.

Incomes Policies

Throughout history, governments have acted to influence the rate at which prices and wages are established. In their interventions, the governments have used both the power of persuasion and other inducements, such as granting or withholding government contracts or raising or lowering taxes. They have also used direct fiats—orders to limit price increases. *Incomes policies* are actions by governments to influence the setting of wages and prices. Some policies utilize indirect means for this purpose. When the government issues direct decrees to limit changes, the policies are called *price-wage controls.* Incomes policies are adopted in the hope of reducing the costs of stopping inflation. Successful policies can mean smaller price increases at any level of excess or slack output and unemployment.

POOR TRADE-OFFS LEAD TO CONTROLS

Many situations lead governments to resort to incomes policies or controls. Most common is the recognition of a poor trade-off between prices and output. In the period following World War II, prices periodically rose well before the economy reached the assumed point of full employment. At other times, falling output and rising unemployment have been accompanied by escalating prices. Governments dislike such trade-offs; they want to insure that policies which lower demand reduce inflation without incurring large costs of rising unemployment. Controls are also introduced as a result of wars and emergencies. In such periods, many goods will inevitably be in short supply. In order to spread the burdens of the shortages fairly, controls are adopted, often accompanied by rationing. Rationing is required because the controls do not allow price movements to clear the market. It is assumed that shortages ought to be shared, that those with wealth should not be allowed to obtain the lion's share of scarce goods.

The reasons nations adopt incomes policies, even if reluctantly, have been well stated by Murray Weidenbaum, chairman of President Reagan's Council of Economic Advisers:

> We need to recognize the basic reason that incomes policies—both voluntary and compulsory, both here and abroad—have been resorted to. It is hardly because we as a nation like to interfere with private decision-making or that the citizenry is enamored with the success of government intervention. Rather, it is that citizens and policy makers have not been satisfied with the apparent results of indirect measures such as monetary and fiscal policy and will support at times a more activist policy stance.[4]

4. M. L. Weidenbaum, "Reconciling Monetary Policy and the Institutional Structure," in Center for the Study of American Business. *Alternative Policies to Combat Inflation,* Working Paper No. 40 (January 1979):100.

Such desires for a more activist policy have been worldwide. Hardly a single industrialized nation has failed to adopt some kind of incomes policy or direct controls in the past 50 years. In the United States, controls were imposed during both World Wars, the Korean conflict, and in 1971 under President Nixon. Incomes policies were engaged in by Presidents Kennedy, Johnson, and Carter. Most polls show that a majority of citizens believe controls are the way to end inflation.

In nonwar periods, the situations leading to such policies have followed similar scenarios. Demand appears to be below potential output, but prices and wages continue to rise. Some technique is needed to halt the inflationary process. Prices and incomes chase each other up the spiral. While a few individuals and firms gain from this process, most lose; the nation would appear to be better off if the process could be slowed or, even better, stopped.

REDUCING EXPECTED PRICES

If everyone could be convinced that inflation would end, their principal excuse for pushing up their wages and prices would disappear. This is the basis for the view that direct policies can succeed by lowering expectations of future price increases. Instead of moving down short-run inflation curves anchored to the previous high rate of inflation, the economy can come into equilibrium at a low or zero expected inflation rate.

Others point to the pressure exerted by firms and workers to protect their own incomes. As each firm foresees rising costs, it immediately passes them on to its customers. Each group of workers tries to protect itself by demanding larger wage increases, fearing the loss of real income that accompanies a failure to keep up with the cost of living. If cooperative action could guarantee that prices and costs would rise at a rate slower than that of the past or expected in the future—say 5 percent less next year—all could agree to knock that 5 percent off their own price and wage demands.

Under a voluntary incomes policy, governments try to convince everyone that inflation will be slowed. They announce a specific wage-price-income target to the economy as a whole. For example, in 1979 the government picked as a target a maximum 7 percent increase in wages and prices. Such targets are then translated into specific guidelines or standards for every firm to use in making its own price and wage decisions. Having set the guidelines, the government then uses moral suasion and patriotic appeals, threats of withholding contracts, or any other action it has available to obtain compliance with the guidelines.

TAX-BASED INCOMES POLICIES

It has been suggested that price-wage guidelines might be strengthened through tax incentive programs (TIP) using the tax system to provide tangible incentives to firms and workers who aid in slowing the rate of inflation. Such programs could either raise taxes (a penalty plan) on firms whose wages exceed the guidelines or refund taxes (a reward TIP) for those whose increases were held below the guidelines. For example, taxes could be reduced for firms whose workers received wage increases below the guidelines.

Proposals are usually based on the average change in a firm's salary and wage payments. A firm might be offered tax credits—say, 1, 2, or 3 percent—to the degree that its average increase in payments fell below the standard set in the plan.[5] These credits would then be passed through to the workers, offsetting in part the failure of their wage increases to match the average. The Carter administration suggested real wage insurance as part of such a program. Under this proposal, if prices rose above the target and worker's income did not go up as much, he would be compensated to the degree that his income fell behind inflation. The compensation would be in the form of a tax credit or refund. For example, assume that a worker's income was $10,000 and the target was a price increase of no more than 7 percent. Under a wage insurance program, if prices rose 9 percent, the worker might receive a tax credit of $200. The proposal got nowhere; Congress barely discussed it.

SOME PROBLEMS WITH INCOMES PROGRAMS

The idea of an incomes program seems sensible. That is why so many countries and governments, from the most conservative to the most radical, have tried them. What goes wrong? What problems are encountered in making them work? First problems of equity arise. When a program begins, some firms have just raised prices; others have not. Some new wage contracts have just been signed; others are in the process of negotiation. Some contracts will be reopened for the first time only after two or three years. If the wages of plumbers and carpenters usually move in tandem, carpenters won't be satisfied with a 7 percent increase if the plumbers just got 15 percent. Someone expecting a 20 percent raise to make up for a 25 percent increase in the cost of living since her last raise would feel cheated (legitimately) if she is told she can only be raised 7 percent. These inequities mean that the program must include some way of approving adjustments and allowances for special circumstances.

Relative prices change. When OPEC raised oil prices, costs increased at very different rates for individual firms, depending on how important oil was in their costs. Gasoline stations, petrochemical companies, oil-burning utilities would have cost pressures very different from those of a lumber mill, a doctor, or a movie theater. While this is an extreme case, relative prices are constantly changing. In a market economy, prices signal when production should be raised or lowered. If they cannot move, waste, bottlenecks, and shortages will develop. These facts mean again that procedures have to be built into the system to allow some relative price movements. The longer controls remain in

---

5. Details of such plans, their potential costs and benefits are discussed in the *Economic Report of the President* (Washington: Government Printing Office 1981), pp. 59–68.

effect, the more distortions occur. If they become severe enough, some form of rationing must be imposed, either by sellers or by the government.

When full-scale controls are imposed or guidelines strictly enforced, administrative costs rise rapidly. Thousands—or even hundreds of thousands if rationing is included—of people may be needed to interpret the rules, make exceptions, and enforce them. By the end of World War II, enforcement was an expensive and severe problem. People fear such a growth in the bureaucracy if controls are reintroduced. Either with or without a large administrative staff, people experience a loss in economic freedom. Firms cannot make their own wage and price decisions; they must get legal opinions as to whether or not they are in compliance with the guidelines and regulations. Lawyers and accountants reap a bonanza. There may be threats of pressure by customers, regulatory agencies, and public opinion to hold firms and unions in line. Many negotiating sessions revolve around what the government may or may not allow. Not all of this pressure is bad; it may be easier to agree in the negotiations to a moderate price-wage increase if the guidelines come from outside; but still, the pressures and lack of freedom remain.

With wages and prices set by direct intervention, demand management may receive the wrong cues. In the last half of 1971 and 1972, the Nixon price freeze and wage controls seemed to be successful. However, unemployment was still above the assumed full-employment level. With an election coming up, demand was raised by means of fiscal and monetary policies. These government actions overheated the economy; instead of the control period being one of a successful deceleration of prices and expectations, it ended in a new burst of inflation. The underlying symptoms were hidden by the price-wage controls.

Because of problems such as the foregoing, most analysts and governments are loath to use controls. Some say flatly that controls never have worked and never can. Others agree that they are hard to handle, but hope that with better administration and more knowledge, they can prove successful. In the history of their use in various countries, a number of mild successes have been recorded. The imposition of price-wage controls in January 1951 at the time of the Korean War put an end to speculative price increases. Prices began to fall almost immediately, and the ceilings were barely tested. The Carter voluntary wage policies in 1979 succeeded in holding down the imbedded rate of wage increases below the increase in commodity prices, a large part of which was due to OPEC's raising of oil prices. However, such successes have not been great, and if controls have been maintained for too long, the success dissipates.

In contrast to flat claims that controls will or won't work, other analysts looking at history believe that they can be a useful supplement to demand and supply management. Incomes policies cannot replace demand management, but they can help it to succeed by improving the trade-off between price deceleration and falling output. A danger exists that because controls are in place, demand will expand too much, but proponents hope that with awareness of history, such experiences can be avoided. As long as the trade-off between prices and output appears to be poor and as long as inflation continues to be a problem, some kind of incomes policy is likely to be tried again and again. In fact, to some degree, incomes policies may be forced into existence by a kind of self-fulfilling prophecy. Because everyone recognizes that they may be used, firms and workers anticipate their imposition. They try to obtain their higher prices and wages before controls go into effect. It is like the housewife who buys 200 pounds of sugar to beat the sugar hoarders. As long as people act under such assumptions, the use of incomes policies becomes almost inevitable.

Summary

1. If inflation and all cost changes were correctly anticipated and if costs and income were properly indexed, losses from inflation would be minor. They would be limited to deadweight losses, which arise primarily from efforts to avoid losses from holding noninterest-bearing money.

2. Because prices change irregularly and unexpectedly, in inflations holders of some assets and liabilities gain real income, while others lose. Similarly, some sources of income are slower than others to adjust to inflation or deflation.

3. Inflation causes losses in production because uncertainty makes it harder to plan and to invest. Taxes and the use of historical costs distort investment and production decisions. Wastes are engendered in trying to avoid its impacts. Stop-go policies to fight inflation mean that output is lower on average than in noninflationary periods.

4. Those who lose by inflation have fixed incomes or incomes from dollar-denominated assets bought prior to inflation-induced increases in nominal interest rates. The government gains by being able to increase its noninterest-bearing debt and because many tax rates are based on nominal income.

5. People feel cheated by inflation. They see their nominal income rising but their real income remaining constant. They don't recognize that inflation is raising both their income and their costs.

6. Indexing removes some of the costs of inflation by providing for price contracts, wage bargains, taxes and other prices that change with movements in a general price index.

7. Inflation can be ended by slowing increases in aggregate demand. The effectiveness of slower demand depends on how fast prices slow or output declines. Imbedded price movements place a greater burden on output adjustments.

8. Costs of slowing demand include losses in output, increased unemployment, and financial losses and failures. In addition, sectoral losses, a slowdown in innovations and new industries, and a smaller capital stock occur.

9. Cost curves can be shifted downward to the right by deregulation and cutting certain taxes. To have much effect on inflation, such moves most engender further dynamic increases in productivity or decreases in inflationary expectations.

10. Price-wage controls and incomes policies limit price-wage increases. They are used to stop price increases in periods of severe shortages and to halt the inflationary spiral. Incomes policies can include various types of incentives to restrict price-wage increases. Since controls remove prices as a source of adjustment, the economy loses flexibility. The longer they are maintained, the greater are problems of enforcement.

Questions for Discussion and Review

1. In what sense can it be said that most costs of inflation are due to market imperfections?

2. What are the major costs of inflation? What are the major costs of recession? Which do you think are more severe?

3. Suppose the federal government enacts a plan (in reality, impractical) of issuing at the end of the year to all currency holders an additional amount of currency exactly equal to the decline in the real value of the dollar. What would be the effect on the deadweight loss of inflation?

4. Suppose that prices changed in some simple relation to past changes in one of the monetary aggregates and that this fact was generally known. How would the costs of inflation be affected?

5. How do net debtors gain from an unanticipated increase in inflation?

6. How likely is it that an individual can beat inflation by purchasing a new house?

7. Suppose the universal expectation was that the rate of inflation was going to soar to the rate of 100 percent per day, beginning tomorrow. Discuss briefly the major effects this would have on the American economy.

8. Discuss briefly the problems engendered by a fluctuating standard of value.

9. Discuss what can be concluded about who gains and who loses from inflation.

10. It has occasionally been suggested in recent years that the Federal Trade Commission order the U.S. Treasury's television commercials for savings bonds to be removed as false and misleading. What is the basis for this (half-serious) proposal?

11. What is meant by tax indexing?

12. What are the principal considerations involved in implementing a policy of fighting inflation by lowering aggregate demand?

13. How does the fact that any anti-inflation policy must entail losses for some members of society affect the ability of economists as economists to prescribe a solution?

14. Economists do not agree on how much it is likely to cost to end inflation by curtailing the growth of aggregate demand. Explain the reasons behind different cost estimates. Illustrate your answer diagrammatically.

15. Discuss the effects of the following on the rate of inflation:
    (a) Increasing competition in labor and product markets.
    (b) Indexing of as many prices (wages, rents, interest rates, etc.) as possible.

References

Blinder, A. S. *Economic Policy and the Great Stagflation.* New York: Academic Press, 1979. Chapter 6 analyzes price-wage controls.

Fischer, S., and S. Modigliani. "Towards an Understanding of the Real Effects and Costs of Inflation," *Review of World Economics* (Weltwirtschafliches Archives) 114(1978): 810–33.

Hicks, Sir John. *The Crisis in Keynesian Economics.* New York: Basic Books, 1974.

Lewis, J. "The Lull That Came to Stay." *The Journal of Political Economy* 63(February 1955): 1–15.

Minarik, J. J. "Who Wins, Who Loses from Inflation." *Brookings Bulletin* 15(Summer 1978).

Palmer, J. L., and M. C. Barth. "The Distributional Effects of Inflation and Higher Unemployment." In *Improving Measures of Economic Well-Being,* edited by M. Moon and E. Smolensky. New York: Academic Press, 1977.

Solow, R. M. "Down the Phillips Curve with Gun and Camera." In *Inflation, Trade and Taxes* edited by D. A. Belsey *et al.* Athens, Ohio: Ohio State University Press, 1976.

Tobin, J. "Inflation and Unemployment." Reprinted in *Readings in Macroeconomics: Current Policy Issues,* edited by W. E. Mitchell *et al.* New York: McGraw-Hill, 1974.

15

Aggregate Supply: Problems of Prices and Growth

Supply-side economics is the study of how potential output can be increased and inflation reduced. How fast potential output grows depends on the rate of increase in available inputs and in productivity—the amount of output per unit of input. The Economic Recovery Act of 1981 reflected an enhanced concern over supply in addition to the administration's drive to reduce government programs.

Some economists have narrowed the concept of supply-side economics by using the term to refer primarily to tax changes that increase incentives to work, to save, and to invest. This chapter explores these ideas, together with a broader group of factors that shape supply. Nobel laureate Lawrence Klein, in his 1977 presidential address to the American Economic Association, emphasized the need for a broad approach and the importance of examining the production functions of individual sectors. Materials, capital, labor, and energy can affect output. Productivity can be enhanced by increased education, manpower training, improved research and development, and energy policies as well as by improved relationships among the sectors. The largest increases in productivity have resulted from greater knowledge and improvements in the quality of labor inputs. Attempts to expand supply which concentrate on a limited number of channels may miss some of the best bets for the future.

In this chapter, supply relationships that determine growth and price reactions are examined through the perspectives of three major problems which have beset our economy in the past decade:

1. Supply-demand relationships in individual sectors of the economy can cause sharp increases in production costs and prices. Relative prices rise in specific sectors because of the particular shapes of their supply curves. The parts of the economy producing food, energy, housing, lumber, and steel furnish examples of sharp relative price rises in the 1970s in response to movements

of demand. If falling prices elsewhere had offset these cost increases, damage would have been minimized. But offsets did not occur. Instead, these increases raised the general price level and led to higher inflationary expectations and a stepped-up core rate of inflation.

2. Supply grows when resources of capital and labor expand. In the 1970s and early 1980s both types of inputs grew quite rapidly, but various complicating factors caused growth to slow down. Key questions faced by supply-side economists concern ways to improve the availability and usefulness of labor and capital.

3. One of the reasons for the poor economic performance of the 1970s was that productivity ceased to grow. The economy failed to obtain more output per unit of input. Instead, growth and the anti-inflationary pressure generated by increasing productivity ground to a halt. Why did this happen, and how can the situation be improved in the future?

These three major problems are examined first by seeing how factors other than wages have influenced prices in the post-World-War-II period. The second half of the chapter analyzes in greater depth the forces determining changes in productivity, capital investment, and labor inputs. These are considered in the following framework:

Nonwage influences on costs of output.
Prices and cost increases.
Energy, lumber and steel prices: Case studies of responses to demand.
Growth in potential output.
Increasing investment in plant and equipment.
Ways to increase capital investment.
Other sources of increased growth.
The amount of labor inputs.
What determines the level of unemployment.
Lowering the natural rate of unemployment.

Nonwage Influences on Costs of Output

While emphasizing that wages are a prime determinant of the shape and position of the supply curve, previous chapters also pointed out that the price-wage relationship would differ depending on what happened to productivity and to other costs, particularly those of crude materials, imports, and products sold in contract markets. Prices are not directly dependent on raw wages or compensation, but rather are set to cover **unit labor costs,** the total compensation divided by the total output produced in a period. Since changes in productivity alter the amount of output per unit of labor, productivity directly influences unit labor costs.

The 1970s show that movements in raw material costs and in prices of products from industries with a shortage of capacity can also contribute to a price-wage spiral and inflationary pressures. The prices of energy, food, and other raw materials shot up in 1973, 1974, 1979, and 1980. Higher prices due to supply shocks led to an increase in compensation and, through it, to further price increases. The shocks of the 1970s raised the core rate of inflation while decreasing output.

PRODUCTIVITY AND COSTS

Supply-side economics places great emphasis on the relationships between unit labor costs and productivity. To the degree that productivity rises faster than compensation, costs and prices will be reduced. The deteriorating performance of productivity contributed to the poor price performance of the 1970s. The relationships between workers' compensation, productivity, unit labor costs, and prices are brought out in Table 15.1. In the five years 1960–65, wage increases of 4 percent a year were virtually offset by greater productivity; unit labor costs did not rise. Prices did increase at a rate of 1.1 percent a year, but such minor differences can result from measurement and sampling problems. In contrast, from 1975 to 1980, less than .5 percent of increased compensation was offset by improved productivity.

The decline in productivity also slowed the growth of output. For example, the growth rate of productivity per employee fell by over 1.8 percent between the 1948–73 period and the 1973–80 period. This sharp fall was larger than the entire drop in the growth rate of output, which declined from 3.6 to 2.3

TABLE 15.1   **Annual Rates of Change in Unit Labor Costs and Prices in Private Nonfarm Business, 1960–80**

(percent)

Item	1960–65	1965–70	1970–75	1975–80
Compensation per hour	4.0	6.4	8.2	8.8
Output per hour	3.9	1.1	1.6	0.5
Unit labor costs	—	5.2	6.5	8.3
Implicit price deflator	1.1	4.2	6.6	7.2

SOURCE: Council of Economic Advisers.

Changes in compensation less improvements in productivity (output per hour) shift unit labor costs. (The totals do not add exactly because data are from different sources and are rounded.) The long-term behavior of prices closely resembles that of unit labor costs, their largest component. Movements in raw material prices create short-run differences and can cause an acceleration in compensation.

percent per year. If productivity had continued at its previous pace, the 1970s would have experienced record growth with less inflation. People would have been richer and would have been far less dissatisfied with the performance of the economy.

RELATIVE PRICE MOVEMENTS

Because of supply shocks and unique reactions to changes in aggregate demand, all prices do not change at the same rate. Figure 15.1 brings out differences which can occur in relative price movements. The figure presents several price indexes. Of those shown, the GNP price deflator fluctuates least. It contains a higher proportion of services and of government expenditures. Its weights change with actual output, in contrast to the fixed market-basket weights of the consumer price index. Import prices rose at a very fast pace in the first half of the decade, partly reflecting the revaluation of the dollar in terms of foreign currencies. Prices for foodstuffs moved erratically and with wide swings. Their large increases in the first half of 1971, in 1972–73, and at the end of the decade were particularly important in their impact on expected prices. The movements of crude materials, even if fuel prices are excluded, show similar large swings, although they are more dependent on levels of output.

When relative prices rise, they can lead to an increase in the core rate of inflation. John Scadding has shown that even random price movements may raise the underlying rate of inflation.[1] Even if purchasers form their expectations in a perfectly rational manner, a high variance for prices makes it hard for people to distinguish underlying inflation from random movements. They adjust their anticipations of all price movements more slowly. According to Scadding's estimates, it takes up to five years before a change in the inflation rate fully enters into expected price changes ($\dot{P}^e$). Such delays are rational because of the difficulty of deciding how much of any price change results from a random shock and how much from inflationary pressures.

OTHER FACTORS INFLUENCING PRICES

The shape of the short-run aggregate supply curve reflects the manner in which raw material prices react to shifts in demand. As demand expands and contracts cyclically, the prices of materials rise and then fall. Costs also shift as a result of shocks exogenous to the economy. OPEC increases in energy prices are outstanding examples of such shocks, but poor food crops in the USSR, changing foreign exchange rates, and wars and revolutions are additional examples of changes exerting a decided effect on prices in the United States. Some analysts feel, however, that such movements deserve no more than minor

1. J. Scadding, "Estimating the Underlying Inflation Rate," Federal Reserve Bank of San Francisco, *Economic Review* (Spring 1979): pp. 16.

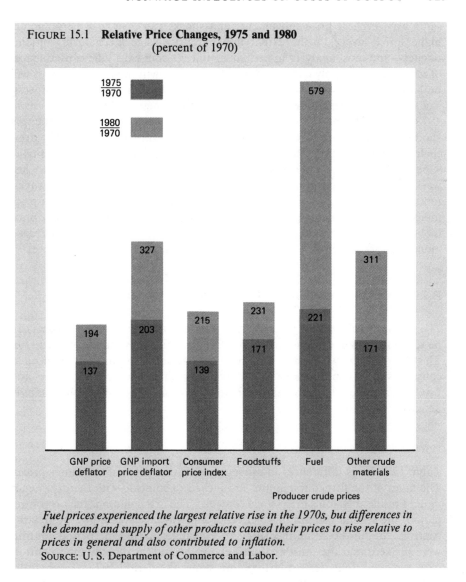

FIGURE 15.1   **Relative Price Changes, 1975 and 1980**
(percent of 1970)

Fuel prices experienced the largest relative rise in the 1970s, but differences in the demand and supply of other products caused their prices to rise relative to prices in general and also contributed to inflation.
SOURCE: U. S. Department of Commerce and Labor.

attention. Cyclical fluctuations are self-reversing; what goes up comes down. They also assume that external shocks are likely to be random; a price level may be shifted down as often as up. Movements in commodity prices are like waves in the ocean; except in the immediate vicinity, they don't affect the general level. Prices and inflation must be explained in terms of unit wage rates, not extraneous movements.

While waves do not change the level of the ocean, they do swamp a number of boats every year and cause steady erosion of many beaches. In the same way, cyclical price movements and shocks can lead to a permanently higher price level. To the extent that our price-wage mechanism contains ratchets—and most analysts agree that significant ones exist—the consequences of moves up the supply curve or upward shifts in it will remain, and prices will be higher. Moreover, such shifts can start or add to an inflationary process. Today's price moves influence tomorrow's. Consumers hit by higher prices in 1973, 1974, 1979, and 1980 did not differentiate between the rises due to supply shocks, to cyclical pressures, and to underlying inflationary trends; they drew their conclusions about the future from the prices they encountered in the supermarket. Their wage demands were based on what happened to last week's paycheck, not on a theory of reversible price increases. When wages, rents, or other costs contain index clauses, establishing new rates when a price index moves, wage demands are linked automatically to even temporary price movements. Furthermore, higher prices are likely to be met by an increased money supply, which will remain even if temporary price pressures abate.

Prices and Cost Increases

The way in which relative price changes can lead to inflationary pressures can be seen through an examination of some of the price movements of the 1970s. This history shows why some economists have strongly emphasized the need to consider supply conditions in specific sectors such as energy, agriculture, and production materials in the all-out battle to reduce inflation through supply actions.

PRICE MOVEMENTS IN THE 1970s

Table 15.2 shows differences in movements among types of consumer prices. The dates of the first four columns are picked to coincide with the experience under President Nixon's price-wage controls. The first column is the precontrol period; the second column, the period of a price-wage freeze and quite strict controls; the third column measures price changes during the period controls were relaxed; and the fourth column, the eight months directly after controls were removed. The next to last column shows the period 1975–78, when the rate of inflation was relatively stable but at the high level of 7.0 percent. The final column covers 1979–80, when prices burst forth again—a major factor leading to the election of President Reagan who ran on a platform which included anti-inflationary programs.

The table reveals significant increases in the general price level accompanying rises in specific relative prices. At different times, food, energy, and homeownership costs rose as a result of their own particular supply-demand relationship—namely, crop failures, OPEC increases in oil prices, and the impact of an interaction of inflation and a tax subsidy on housing. In an economy with generally flexible prices, if the level of spending were held constant, such increases would be accompanied by declines in other prices. The price level would not rise providing enough declines occurred in other sectors to offset the specific price increases. But such declines did not occur. In 1974 and 1975, when the rate of growth of nominal income fell slightly, decreased spending resulted in a fall in real output, not in prices. While other prices rose more slowly than those creating the problem, their rate of inflation did go up, not down. The reduction in output slowed the rate of inflation somewhat. But as a result of the recession, fiscal and monetary policies were relaxed, and spending expanded in 1976. Inflation stabilized, followed by a gradual rise, until it again shot up in 1979.

With hindsight, most observers now wish that the recession had been allowed to continue longer. Lower output for a longer period might have eradicated the core rate of inflation. At the time, however, because the decline in output during the Great Stagflation of 1973–75 had been the deepest and largest of the entire post-World-War-II period, not many disagreed with Presidents Ford's and Carter's desires to have output return toward full employment.

TABLE 15.2   **Changes in the Consumer Price Index, 1970–80**
(average annual rate in percent)

Category	Dec. 1970– Aug. 1971	Aug. 1971– Jan. 1973	Jan. 1973– Apr. 1974	Apr. 1974– Dec. 1974	Dec. 1974– Dec. 1978	Dec. 1978– Dec. 1980
Food	4.0	5.7	18.0	11.7	6.8	10.2
Energy	3.6	3.1	27.8	7.0	8.4	27.4
Homeownership	1.0	4.3	8.7	15.5	8.3	14.1
Medical care	6.3	2.9	6.2	14.6	9.4	10.0
All other	4.7	2.0	2.4	12.6	4.9	3.8
Total consumer price index	3.8	3.2	9.9	12.4	7.0	12.8

SOURCE: U.S. Bureau of Labor Statistics.

Movements in the general price level consist of divergent changes among major components. Relative prices in a sector can rise because of unique supply-demand situations. If not offset elsewhere, such unique movements raise average prices, which feed forward through wage and salary compensation to the rate of inflation.

THE PERIOD OF PRICE-WAGE CONTROLS

One method of analyzing what happens during periods of rapid price increases is to use input-output analysis to trace the effects on final products of changes in the prices of crude materials, imports, and wages. William Nordhaus and John Shoven have conducted such a study of movements on the Bureau of Labor

Statistics's producer price index.[2] Some of their results are contained in Table 15.3. It shows the direct and indirect contributions of crude materials, fuel, imports, and wages to the rise in the total price level in both percentage points at an annual rate and as a share of the total.

The first and fourth columns of the table cover the period during which the Nixon administration decided to impose price controls. For an administration that had promised it knew how to cure stagflation, both the statistics and the dissatisfaction of the country with the economy were a spur to action. Unemployment stood at 6 percent. The GNP price deflator was rising at an annual rate of 5 percent, and the consumer price index was rising at 4 percent. Although the problems raised by these conditions seem mild compared with developments later in the decade, they were serious enough at the time to build up pressures for controls, particularly among business groups. The table shows that at the producers' level, wages and crude material prices were the main factors raising prices. At the consumers' level, food, medical care, and miscellaneous services composed the core of the increases. Prices of other consumer goods were relatively stable. However, the key factor worrying business groups was what seemed to them to be a runaway increase in wages, threatening a price-wage spiral. Increases in money wages were approaching record levels. The dollar was in trouble. President Nixon reacted by introducing a price freeze—followed by a period of controls—and by allowing the dollar to be devalued. The period from August 1971 to November 1972 included a three-month complete freeze on wages and prices followed by Phase II, in which controls applied to about 80 percent of prices in the CPI. During this entire period, prices rose at about the same pace as in the previous nine months.

The second and fifth columns report on the period when controls were in the process of being removed. Most of the price increases in this period occurred among crude materials. Food and lumber prices rose rapidly. (Some products—primarily agricultural—had been excluded from controls either on the assumption that their prices were set in competitive markets or because the costs of controls would outweigh potential benefits.)

Import prices also began to rise, following a 10 percent drop in the exchange value of the dollar. Wages barely went up and other prices were comparatively stable. Some believe the increases which occurred were an inevitable result of controls. Others feel the higher prices simply reflected the increases in crude material and import prices.[3] Still others claim they came about because the Nixon administration was halfhearted in its policies and also relaxed the controls prematurely.

The last half of 1973 and the first quarter of 1974 were marked by the continued relaxation of controls and an acceleration of price rises. All con-

2. W. Nordhaus and J. Shoven, "A Technique for Analyzing and Decomposing Inflation," in *Analysis of Inflation, 1965–1974,* edited by J. Popkin (Cambridge, Mass.: Balinger, 1977).

3. H. Stein, "Price-Fixing as Seen By a Price-Fixer," *Across the Board* 15(December 1978): 32–43.

sumer prices went up rapidly, but food, housing (mortgage and utility rates) and transportation (gas and oil) shot up especially fast. The third and last columns in Table 15.3, based on producer prices, present a somewhat different picture. Because aggregate demand did not grow, prices of foodstuffs and many other crude materials declined during the period. Oil prices, raised sharply by OPEC, were the disturbing element in the first half of 1974. Table 15.3 shows that the largest increases occurred in imports, fuel prices, and in some final energy products included in the "all other" category. Nordhaus and Shoven estimate that in the final period in their table, 55 to 60 percent of the total increase in producers' prices resulted from the direct and indirect impact of the rise in energy prices. A sizable share of other price increases reflected an additional 10 percent fall in the exchange value of the dollar. Note that the impact of wages was up to some extent. However, the history of the period toward the end of and immediately following price-wage controls did not show large swings in wages. Wage increases slowed and then increased slightly. The recession in 1974 caused real earnings of labor to fall from 1972 to 1975.

TABLE 15.3 **Decomposition of Changes in the Producer Price Index by Type of Product**

	In percentage points at an annual rate			*Share of total (percent)*		
Attributable to	*Nov. 1970– Aug. 1971*	*Nov. 1972– Aug. 1973*	*Oct. 1973– July 1974*	*Nov. 1970– Aug. 1971*	*Nov. 1972– Aug. 1973*	*Oct. 1973– July 1974*
Agriculture, livestock, forestry, fisheries	1.34	11.75	−0.68	37.1	66.4	−4.1
Mining and domestic fuel	0.23	0.65	3.37	6.3	3.7	20.3
Imports	0.53	1.95	6.16	14.7	11.0	37.1
All other (includes wages)	1.50	3.35	7.75	41.9	18.9	46.7
	(1.07)	(0.92)	(1.33)	(29.6)	(5.2)	(8.0)
Total	3.60	17.70	16.60	100.0	100.0	100.0

SOURCE: Nordhaus and Shoven, "A Technique for Analyzing and Decomposing Inflation," Table 3.

The table traces the total effects of movements in crude material, mining and fuel, imports, and wages on the general producer price level. How much a change in energy prices influences the price level depends on what happens to prices of gasoline, chemcials, steel, and all final goods affected by fuel prices. Input-output analysis used to derive this table shows these final effects.

Energy, Lumber and Steel Prices: Case Studies
in Responses to Demand

Any individual commodity can cause a shift in the supply curve. In the 1970s, the most critical seemed to be crude oil prices. Figure 15.2 shows changes in OPEC crude oil sales prices. Note the $8 a barrel jump in a few months in 1973–74 and the even larger leap in 1979 and 1980. Both increases were severe shocks to costs and output. Robert Gordon developed estimates similar to those of Nordhaus and Shoven for the private product GNP deflator. He estimates that from the fourth quarter of 1973 to the second quarter of 1974, energy prices rose at more than a 41 percent annual rate. During this period, the private GNP deflator rose at a 10.4 percent rate. Of this increase, he attributes over 25 percent to the change in energy prices.[4] Similarly, in 1979 it was estimated that over 30 percent of the 13.5 percent increase in the CPI was due to higher energy costs.

ENERGY PRICES

The surge in energy prices in 1974 and the later one in 1979 helped cause the recessions that followed. Such supply shocks have at least four major impacts: (1) costs and prices are higher, (2) the new costs are passed through to other prices and then to wages, (3) a redistribution of income takes place, and (4) potential output declines. Oil producers gain income at the expense of consumers. When oil prices rose, most of the higher income went to the foreign sector. The leakage from the income stream resembles taxes and saving. If the receivers buy goods for export, income will not fall, but fewer goods can be divided among domestic producers. Real wages drop in the United States. If the income receivers fail to spend it but, instead, purchase deposits or bonds in the United States, the effect is similar to other saving. Desires to spend on goods fall. Interest rates are lower. The new level of aggregate demand depends on the relative responsiveness of spending to income and interest rates. The negative impact of decreased purchases by consumers with lower incomes can cause inventories to rise and production to be cut back. Downward pressures through income can build up faster than expansion pressures from greater liquidity and lower interest rates.

Monetary policy faces a dilemma. Rising prices reduce the real money supply. Markets experience additional downward pressure. For prices to return to their initial position, the fall in demand must reduce domestic prices and wages sufficiently to offset higher energy costs. To the extent that frictions or ratchets hold back the decline in prices, lower demand results in reduced output. The Federal Reserve is forced to choose (1) whether to furnish enough nominal money to halt the drop in demand by raising real money to its original

4. R. J. Gordon, "The Impact of Aggregate Demand on Prices," *Brookings Papers on Economic Activity* 3(1975):613–55.

FIGURE 15.2   **OPEC Average Crude-Oil Price**

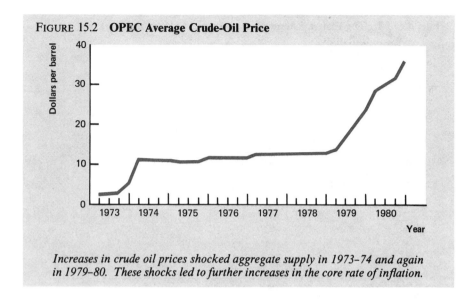

Increases in crude oil prices shocked aggregate supply in 1973–74 and again in 1979–80. These shocks led to further increases in the core rate of inflation.

value or (2) whether to allow output and jobs to fall far and long enough so that the decline in other prices and wages offsets the higher energy prices.

SUPPLY SHOCK AND THE GREAT STAGFLATION

A number of analysts have studied the interaction of the increases in food and energy prices in 1973–74 and the accompanying large drop in output.[5] The Great Stagflation was characterized by a record postwar decline in output accompanied by a rapid inflation. One interpretation of what happened can be demonstrated by the use of the dynamic inflation models developed in preceding chapters. The initial situation of the economy in 1973 is shown at point A in Figure 15.3. The economy is in equilibrium on the line of potential output $\left(\dfrac{Q}{Q^*} = 100\right)$, with an unemployment rate of 5 percent. The curves $A\dot{D}_1$ and IC_1 intersect at this point. An exogenous increase in the costs of crude materials raises the inflation rate above its previous level. This supply shock increases production costs and shifts the economy to the curve IC_2. Following this shock, policy makers face a dilemma. The dynamic aggregate demand curve $(A\dot{D}_1)$ could be shifted upward to the right by more expansive monetary or fiscal policies. If that path were followed, the economy would move up the line of potential output to a new temporary equilibrium at point B. (Recall that the growth trend of potential output will be reduced as a result of higher-cost energy inputs and the tax paid to oil produc-

5. Several of these studies are included in A. Blinder, *Economic Policy and The Great Stagflation*, Chapter 6.

FIGURE 15.3   **The Rise in Energy Costs Reduced Output and Increased Inflation**

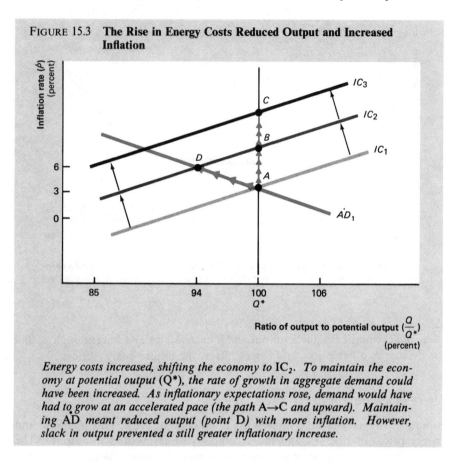

Energy costs increased, shifting the economy to IC_2. *To maintain the economy at potential output* (Q^*), *the rate of growth in aggregate demand could have been increased. As inflationary expectations rose, demand would have had to grow at an accelerated pace (the path A→C and upward). Maintaining* $\dot{A}D$ *meant reduced output (point D) with more inflation. However, slack in output prevented a still greater inflationary increase.*

ers.) An equilibrium at *B* will be only temporary. The increase in prices will raise inflationary expectations, causing a shift to a new curve IC_3. If dynamic aggregate demand is increased again, a steady acceleration of inflation occurs as the economy moves straight up through points *B* and *C* and beyond.

However, this policy was not followed. Instead, the economy stayed on $\dot{A}D_1$. The growth rate of aggregate demand was not stepped up. The economy moved along $\dot{A}D_1$ to a new equilibrium at point *D* on IC_2. A fall in output and additional slack halted any further acceleration in inflation. Rough estimates show that the food and energy shocks increased the inflation rate by 3 percent. Had this move been validated by an increase in demand, higher wage and cost pressures would have raised the inflation rate an additional 3 percent. Instead, the drop in output was just sufficient to hold the inflation rate at *D*. The inflation rate in 1974 rose to the extent of the increases in material prices, but no further upward shove to the core occurred. If slack had been maintained at *D*, declines in the inflation rates of some sectors might have occurred. The movement from *A* to *D* might have been reversed, and the increase in inflation would gradually have been removed. However, no one knows how long that would have taken or how great the costs in lost output would have been. Instead, aggregate demand was increased, moving the economy back toward full employment with a higher inflation rate.

LUMBER PRICES

The 1973–74 supply shocks came from outside sources. However, the supply structure in many industries causes periodic problems resulting merely from the expansion of the economy toward full employment. Lumber and steel are examples. In the lumber industry, the reaction of prices to demand is typical of many raw-material sectors.

Many materials undergo price increases soon after demand for them starts to expand, even though production is far from capacity. In some cases their prices also decline when demand falls, but in others, they may not. Figure 15.4 presents some of the demand-price history of lumber. The figure contains four curves, one for real expenditures on residential construction, one for prices of softwood lumber, one for saw timber prices, and one for the amount of saw timber cut. Lumber prices respond quickly to demand (the amount of residential investment expenditures in the GNP). Lumber is produced under quite competitive conditions. But during the 1970s, prices rose faster than the general price level and higher than cyclical factors could explain. Between 1967 and 1980, lumber prices shot up about twice as fast as the average of all other nonenergy products.[6]

Lumber exemplifies a major sector where supply cannot respond strongly to demand. Nearly 60 percent of softwood lumber grows on public lands and in national forests. How the government regulates its crop determines the response of supply to demand changes. During this period, in deciding the amount to be cut, Forest Service policy gave little or no heed to economics. As a result, the cut of timber on federal lands was only minimally responsive to demand changes. Consequently, lumber prices started up when demand expanded. The price of timber for cutting rose even faster. Price increases accelerated. Imports expanded, but not enough to restrain prices. When demand fell, prices declined. However, during this period, the growth trend of lumber supply was below demand. Declines failed to carry prices back to previous levels. With a declining ratio of supply to demand, lumber price-increases exceeded most others. This was one cause of the extraordinary rise in housing prices during the 1970s.

STEEL PRICES

In 1980 and 1981, steel, autos, and other basic industries were in trouble. Blaming foreign competition, the industries lobbied for import restrictions.

6. See ·Y. Levy, "An Economic Alternative to Current Public Forest Policy," Federal Reserve Bank of San Francisco, *Economic Review* (Winter 1978).

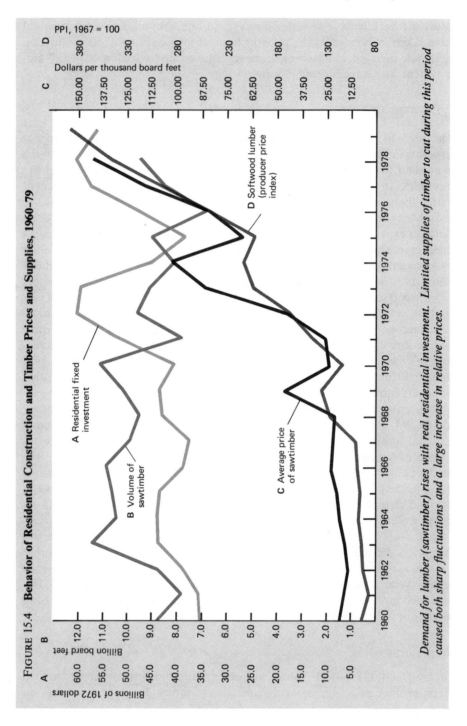

FIGURE 15.4   Behavior of Residential Construction and Timber Prices and Supplies, 1960–79

Demand for lumber (sawtimber) rises with real residential investment. Limited supplies of timber to cut during this period caused both sharp fluctuations and a large increase in relative prices.

They were successful in obtaining so-called "voluntary" restrictions, even though critics pointed out that steel firms were profitable while producing at what had traditionally been considered a low capacity-utilization rate. Furthermore, workers in the industry were among the highest paid in the economy.

Steel is typical of a number of industries that have contract markets and in which prices and wages continue to rise even in recessions. An example of the forces permitting price increases even when demand is down was uncovered in an early study of the steel industry conducted by Otto Eckstein and Gary Fromm.[7] They found that from 1953 to 1958, even though the rate of capacity-utilization was falling, steel prices rose much faster than those of other commodities. In fact, Eckstein and Fromm estimate that the rise in steel prices above those of other wholesale prices accounted for more than 50 percent of the entire rise in the wholesale price index during this period.

Between 1955 and 1960, the wholesale price index of iron and steel rose 21 percent, compared to 8 percent for all wholesale prices. During this time, steel output fell 22 percent, and capacity-utilization was below 80 percent.[8] The authors conclude that prices went up because of "an extraordinary rise in wages which is the result of bargaining between a strong union and a management with strong market power in the product market. Government intervention has probably accelerated this process." Management was able to increase the rate of profits even while paying higher wages with lower output. They conclude that steel prices were a critical inflationary factor that could not be explained by demand, but resulted rather from an exercise of market power.

The degree to which steel is a special situation, as it appeared to be in 1959, is less clear. Observers are no longer surprised to see wages and prices of commodities rising even as demand and output fall. Many markets evidence at least a partial failure of the model of perfect competition. Information costs, transaction costs, and similar factors allow disequilibriums of demand and supply. The slow reaction of contract markets to movements in demand causes many setbacks in combatting inflation.

Growth in Potential Output

A more rapid growth in output is usually included among the nation's primary economic goals. The greater the amount of available goods and services, the better off the average family will be. In addition, growth may aid in fighting inflation. Better supplies of crude materials can reduce the risk of unfavorable supply shocks. An increase in potential output shifts both short- and long-run inflation curves to the right, leading to a smaller price rise for any increase in demand. After examining the factors which have brought about growth in the

7. O. Eckstein and G. Fromm, "Steel and the Postwar Inflation," in U.S. Congress, Joint Economic Committee 86:1, *Study of Employment, Growth, and Price Levels* (Paper No. 2).

8. P. Cagan, *Persistent Inflation* (New York: Columbia University Press, 1979), p. 12.

past, this chapter continues with an analysis of productivity and inputs of capital and labor.

From 1948 to 1973 real GNP grew at a rate of 3.8 percent a year, while inflation averaged 2.8 percent. From 1973 to 1980 GNP growth averaged only 2.3 percent, while the rate of inflation was 7.7 percent per year. How does supply-side economics help to explain these differences? What insights does it provide to aid in reversing the costly deterioration of the economy?

GROWTH IN OUTPUT

The level of potential output depends on available resources—labor, capital, and crude materials, both domestic and imported—and on technology and the organization of the production process. Chapter 12 explained why studies of production concentrated on labor and capital, although raw materials were included in the production function:

$$Q = f(N, K, MR).$$ **15.1**

Output (Q) can increase either (1) as a result of additional supplies of inputs of labor (N), capital (K), and cheaper raw materials (MR) or (2) as a result of using inputs more productively.

Labor and capital inputs grow either because their quantity expands or because their quality improves. Part of the large post-World-War-II growth of the United States economy was due to a rapid expansion of the labor force and of physical capital. However, labor inputs also grew because of improvements in education, training, and other skills. As the quality of work improved, labor inputs rose faster than hours worked. In contrast to such input increases, inputs of raw materials have become less available and more expensive in recent years. Higher priced energy and shortages of land have retarded growth. Capital and labor had to be diverted from raising output in order to perform tasks previously accomplished by the use of cheap energy and cheap land.

Total factor productivity measures the amount of output per unit of all inputs of a given quality. Many studies and discussions of productivity are limited to only part of the total—that of *man-hour (labor) productivity,* which is total output divided by hours worked. Included in gains or losses in man-hour productivity are the results of improved labor quality and additional inputs of capital or materials, as well as from technological changes. Productivity shifts when methods of production (the production function, f) change. Although, obviously, research and development are not free, productivity is sometimes spoken of as the "costless" advances in applied technology, organization, and efficiency. What analysts try to do is to differentiate between growth which results from employing additional inputs and the remaining growth attributable to changes in productivity.

An analysis of past growth can illustrate the relationships between total and labor productivity, while showing the dependence of growth on added resources and advances in knowledge. Edward Denison of the Department of Commerce and the Brookings Institution has prepared extensive estimates of the factors influencing the growth of output.[9] He estimates that between 1948 and 1973, real national income in the business sector grew at a rate of 3.6 percent a year. About 45 percent of this growth, or 1.6 percentage points, came from employing more labor and capital resources. Improved productivity accounted for growth of 2.0 percent a year, or 55 percent of the total. The same data show that labor productivity—output per person employed—increased by 2.4 percent a year. Labor productivity grew faster than total productivity because, in addition to new technology and organization, the quality of labor improved and the amount of capital per unit of labor expanded.

$$\dot{Q} = b_1\dot{N}_1 + b_2\dot{K} + \dot{P}R \qquad 3.56 = .81(1.26) + .19(2.95) + 1.98. \quad \textbf{15.2}$$

Equation 15.2 shows one method of accounting for the 3.56 percent per year growth in total output ($\dot{Q}$ measured by real national income). Resource inputs rose. Growth in units of input equaled the growth in labor ($\dot{N}_1$) times its weight (b_1) plus the growth of capital and land ($\dot{K}$) times their weight (b_2). Weights are based on an input's importance (measured by the share of income it received) in production. Labor inputs ($\dot{N}_1$) grew for two reasons; more employees (N_3) were at work and input per employee (N_2) increased as skills improved, even though employees worked fewer hours. The growth of labor inputs at a 1.26 percent rate times its weight of .81 contributed 1.02 percentage points to the average annual growth in output. Capital and land increased at a rate of 2.95 percent. When multiplied by their production weight of .19, their contribution to growth was estimated as .56 percentage points a year. The final impetus came from the 1.98 percent per year improvement in total factor productivity.

$$\left(\frac{\dot{Q}}{N_3}\right) = b_1\dot{N}_2 + b_2(\dot{K} - \dot{N}_3) + \dot{P}R$$
$$2.44 = .81(.14) + .19(2.95 - 1.11) + 1.98. \qquad \textbf{15.3}$$

Equation 15.3 accounts in the same way for the 2.44 percent per year growth in output per person employed $\left(\frac{\dot{Q}}{N_3}\right)$, one of the measures of labor productivity. The amount of labor input per employee ($\dot{N}_2$) rose by .14 percentage points per year as higher education and greater skills were offset by a shorter work week. Labor productivity also increased because land and capital grew at a faster pace than employees ($\dot{K} - \dot{N}_3$). Added capital per worker raises

9. E. F. Denison, *Accounting for Slower Economic Growth* (Washington, D.C.: Brookings Institution, 1979). The discussion in this section is primarily confined to the data of his Chapter 7—estimates for the nonresidential business sector, which has the most complete information.

marginal productivity. Finally, improvements in technology and organization $(\dot{P}R)$ also increased productivity. Denison does not show changes in the quality of capital independent of its quantity. Other analysts do attempt to measure the quality of capital inputs and therefore the percent of growth which arises from such changes.

ACCOUNTING FOR GROWTH

During the 1970s the growth rate of the economy slowed, even though the expansion of the labor force speeded up. Improvements in total factor productivity dropped almost to zero. These divergent trends are summarized in Table 15.4. This table, based mainly on the work of Denison, also furnishes a framework useful in analyzing the forces behind expansions in aggregate supply. The factors influencing growth in potential output are divided into four categories (as in equation 15.3): (1) the quantity of labor inputs, (2) the quality of these inputs, (3) capital and land, and (4) total factor productivity, which is output per unit of input. Successful supply-side economics acts to increase the growth in each of these categories.

The table, based only on the nonresidential business sector, shows that real national income declined from a growth rate of 3.6 percent a year from 1948 to 1973 to one of 2.4 percent from 1973 to 1980. This decline occurred even though labor inputs—adding both quantities and quality—expanded at a rate of 2.1 percent in the later period, compared to 1.0 percent earlier. While the potential labor force and its educational skills increased rapidly, higher unemployment, a shortened work week, and an unfavorable demographic age-sex trend partially offset these forces for growth.

The next section of the table shows that inputs of capital and land also raised productivity, but their impact was less after 1973. Finally, the largest setback to growth came from the drastic decline in the expansion rate for total factor productivity. Increases in output per unit of factor inputs dropped from a growth rate of 2.0 percent a year to only .1 percent. This decline in productivity contributed to an increase in unit labor costs and to inflation. A return of productivity gains to earlier levels would aid the fight against inflation while helping to achieve the goal of a larger real income.

TOTAL FACTOR PRODUCTIVITY

It is not hard to find 15 or 20 explanations as to why productivity grew so much more slowly in the 1970s than in earlier periods. Among major possible factors that slowed improvements in productivity are a decline in the mobility of labor into more efficient industries, more government regulations, lower real expenditures on research and development, higher energy prices, faster inflation, increased tax disincentives, errors of measurement, and less available real capital. Denison examines these and a number of other ideas. He is able to measure the impact of only a few, but believes he can put logical bounds on

TABLE 15.4   **Accounting for Growth and Productivity**
(percent)

	1948–73	1973–80
Real national income	3.6	2.4
Factor inputs		
Quantity of labor		
Potential	1.0	2.5
Unemployment	−0.1	−0.5
Hours of work	−0.2	−0.5
	0.7	1.5
Quality of labor		
Age/sex	−0.2	−0.3
Education	0.5	0.9
	0.3	0.6
Capital and land	0.6	0.2
Total inputs	1.6	2.3
Output per unit of input		
Resource allocation	0.4	0.1
Economies of scale	0.4	0.2
Legal and human environment	0	−0.5
Intensity of demand	−0.2	0.1
Advances in knowledge and not elsewhere classified	1.4	0.2
Total factor productivity	2.0	0.1

SOURCE: 1948–73, E. F. Denison, *Accounting for Slower Economic Growth,* Tables 7-1, 7-2; 1973–80, author's estimates. Data are for the nonresidential business sector.

Growth in national income results from growth in labor and capital inputs and total factor productivity (output per unit input). The figures in the table are the product of an input's growth times its weight in the production process. Most of technological change is not accounted for separately. It shows up under "Advances in knowledge and not elsewhere classified."

most of them. He concludes that while, in theory, each possibility could account for a decline in growth, no single one nor even a combination of several seems to explain adequately the bulk of the drop. In his mind, the cause of the productivity decline remains a mystery.

Other economists feel certain that Denison's measurements are wrong and that they know why productivity has fallen. Depending on the analyst, it is claimed that half or more of Denison's last category—"Advances in knowledge and not elsewhere classified"—can be accounted for. While various analysts pick different explanations, they tend to emphasize (1) the rise in the cost of energy, (2) the effect of inflation and taxation on effort and incentives, and (3) the failure of capital to grow more rapidly.

DECLINES THAT CAN BE MEASURED

Denison does measure some of the categories which influence factor productivity. Two of these—"resource allocation," or movement among jobs, and "economies of scale"—have undergone sizable declines. These factors together are estimated to have increased productivity by .8 percent a year in the early period, but by only .3 percent between 1973 and 1980. Economies of scale arise from greater specialization and a more intensive use of the capital stock and infrastructure, such as the transportation system and utilities. Productivity also improves when workers move from farms or low-wage industries (such as mama-papa stores) to more skilled employment. The drop from this factor is attributed to the fact that by the 1970s, most potential excess farm labor had already transferred to industry. In contrast, labor was moving at a faster rate into the service industries, where productivity was lower.

Other negative factors are the costs of additional labor-hours required to handle problems of pollution, greater worker safety, and crime prevention in industry. These are included in the category "Legal and human environment." Since labor-hours in these pursuits do not add to measured output (although an improvement in real goods and welfare may occur), expenditures on labor for these purposes reduces productivity. This factor was exceedingly important between 1973 and 1980. It is hoped—but perhaps it is only wishful thinking— that these factors will put less pressure on growth during the 1980s. The changes in intensity of demand reflect a movement from overutilization to some slack.

ADVANCES IN KNOWLEDGE AND NOT ELSEWHERE CLASSIFIED

The final category in Table 15.4 is a grab-bag of individual factors. It includes a good deal of what people think of as technological change. Productivity increases when new knowledge—managerial, organizational, technological—is incorporated into the production process. Some analysts hold that change in this category results primarily from expenditures for research and development. Such new developments as computers, silicon chips, and wide-body airplanes all increase output per hour. Others place more emphasis on managerial ability and know-how as sources of technological change.

Real expenditures for research and development rose rapidly until about 1968. They then leveled off. To those who believe that R and D is critical in advancing knowledge, the correlation between a failure of real expenditures in this sphere to expand and a slowing of growth is no accident. On the basis of his own work and that of Zvi Griliches, Denison believes that R and D contributes only about .3 percent a year to growth. Furthermore, while its growth slowed, it did not actually decline. Therefore, it is unlikely to be a major factor in explaining the productivity slow-down.

Higher energy costs necessitate reorganization of the production process. Dale Jorgenson, Robert Rasche, and John Tatom attribute almost all of the reduction in factor productivity to higher energy prices. Those who hold energy to be the main input, point to Figure 15.5, which shows that the decline in productivity has been general in most industrialized countries. In contrast, Denison cites several other studies which estimate that only about .1 percent per year of the slower growth in productivity resulted from higher energy prices in the period 1973–76. The data of Figure 15.5 can also support the view that inflation has been a critical factor. Chapter 13 pointed out how inflations slow growth. Business planning becomes uncertain. Executives devote more time to avoiding the potentially disastrous effects of higher prices and interest rates. Accounting systems deteriorate as measures of real costs and profits. Real taxes rise. Resources are misallocated. Investment becomes increasingly short-term. The world-wide declines in productivity came at the same time as world-wide inflation.

Denison concludes that the cause of the sharp drop in productivity re-

FIGURE 15.5   **Productivity Growth in Major Nations, 1960–73 and 1973–79**

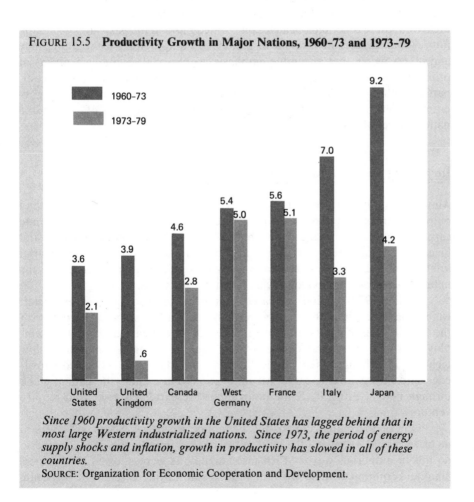

Since 1960 productivity growth in the United States has lagged behind that in most large Western industrialized nations. Since 1973, the period of energy supply shocks and inflation, growth in productivity has slowed in all of these countries.
SOURCE: Organization for Economic Cooperation and Development.

mains unknown. Ways to improve productivity follow closely individual views as to the critical forces in the decline. But to the degree that the fall remains unexplained, prescriptions for a cure must be based primarily on guesses or hopes. There is wide agreement that slowing inflation and reversing regulatory burdens should help. There is also general agreement that productivity will improve with a larger, up-to-date capital stock.

The Humphrey-Hawkins Act put considerable emphasis on capital formation and requires that an investment policy section be included in the president's annual economic report. President Reagan justified proposed tax cuts as a means of increasing investment in order to shift the supply curve to minimize price increases. In contrast, many conservative and liberal economists believe that while more investment will raise productivity, gains will be modest. They fear that an undue concentration on building more plant and equipment will lead to policies that neglect more fruitful paths to improved productivity. They place more emphasis on the need to increase human capital, on research and development and other forms of knowledge, and on government capital. In their view, these other factors have contributed more in the past—and will in the future—than greater investment in plant and equipment. Furthermore, they and others worry that an undue emphasis on personal saving as a means of promoting investment in capital equipment is an inefficient technique compared to other possible policies. They place greater reliance on reducing government deficits and increasing business profits as methods of raising the nation's level of saving.

Increasing Investment in Plant and Equipment

Almost all analysts agree that a larger capital stock will raise productivity and output. Increased investment in plant and equipment can also help alleviate capacity bottlenecks, make it possible to achieve energy independence, and meet the capital needs for combatting pollution and promoting industrial safety. In addition, some estimates show that added capital can reduce the natural rate of unemployment by as much as .5 percent.

In the 1970s capital increased, but because labor grew even faster, changes in the capital-labor ratio were slight. Table 15.4 shows a sharp drop in the contribution of capital to growth. The rate of increase of capital per employee slowed. If capital does not grow rapidly enough, it may also slow technological change. New physical capital embodies more advanced knowledge and improves efficiency. All innovations must enter the capital stock through new investment. Some innovations are extremely risky and require venture capital.

One of the major aims of the Economic Recovery Act of 1981 was to increase capital by raising the level of saving and investment. It attempted to do this in numerous ways. Much faster write-offs were allowed for business plant and equipment. The investment tax credit was increased. The corporate profit tax rate was reduced. Top bracket tax rates on income received from dividends, interest, and capital gains were cut by 28.6 percent. Larger tax-free contributions were authorized for savings through retirement and pension funds. Savings and loan associations were granted a subsidy through removing income taxes on interest received from a special class of saving certificate. This section analyzes the reasoning behind these actions while pointing out the type of gains hoped for from the legislation.

AN INCREASE IN NET INVESTMENT

What would happen if gross investment in plant and equipment rose from 11.0 percent to 12.1 percent of the gross national product, or by 10 percent? Historically, such an increase would be very large. From 1960 through 1980, real business fixed investment ranged from a low of 8.8 percent to a high of 11.0 percent, averaging 9.9 percent of real GNP. In their studies of productivity and capital needs, Denison, Feldstein, and Kendrick estimated independently the effect on productivity of increasing investment by 10 percent. While the range in their estimates makes clear the dangers of trying to be too precise with given data, the pictures they draw of the future are not dissimilar. Denison's data show that such additions to capital would probably raise productivity by about .15 percent for each year of higher investment. Denison believes that no added incentives for investment and saving are necessary. Feldstein finds a gain of .25 percent, while Kendrick's estimate is a gain of 0.30 percent per year.[10] In the long run, these gains would diminish and then disappear because a larger capital stock entails greater depreciation and more gross investment to stay even. If it took 40 years to reach the new equilibrium, at that point total output would be 6 to 12 percent higher than if the lower saving rate of 1950–80 were maintained.

Such estimates are based on analysis like that contained in Table 15.4, which shows the contribution of capital to be between 10 and 15 percent of the total growth in real income. However, other studies show it with far higher weights. Dale Jorgenson, for example, estimates that for the period 1948–76, capital contributed nearly half of all growth.[11] His figures are higher in part because he includes housing and international assets, but primarily because he attempts to measure changes in the quality of capital and in the movement of capital to industries where it is more productive. Neither of these factors is specifically estimated by Denison.

10. E. F. Denison, *Accounting for Slower Economic Growth* (Washington, D.C.: Brookings Institution, 1979), pp. 59, 75; M. Feldstein, "National Saving in the United States" in E. Shapiro and W. L. White, *Capital for Productivity and Jobs* (Englewood Cliffs, N. J.: Prentice-Hall, 1977), p. 136; J. W. Kendrick, "Productivity Trends and Recent Slowdown," in *Contemporary Economic Problems 1979* edited by W. Fellner (Washington, D.C.: American Enterprise Institute), Table 6.

11. D. Jorgenson, "Energy Prices and Productivity Growth" in *The State of the Economy*, Hearings, Joint Economic Committee 96:2 (May 29, 1980): 47–56.

HOW MUCH ADDITIONAL CAPITAL IS NEEDED?

While agreement exists that more capital would be desirable, no consensus has been reached as to how much is needed. Increased investment requires either that current consumption be sacrificed or that wasted resources be put to work. To those who believe that markets are competitive, strong, and adjust well, the concept of a shortage of investment makes little sense. Efficient markets assure interest rates that properly equate saving and investment. A lack of capital can arise only if government programs paralyze investors or interfere in other ways with market operations. If a real need for capital exists, interest rates and profits will rise and attract the necessary saving and investment.

In contrast, supply-side followers and others believe that a positive investment policy is needed. They feel that such steps do not mean government intervention but merely a reduction in governmental impediments. They point to a failure of the capital-labor ratio to grow, to more investment and faster growth in productivity abroad, to temporary shortages of capacity, and to a wedge between saving and investment as indications that action is called for.

Comparisons with the Past.   Figure 15.6 shows that, compared with past performance, the level of gross nonresidential fixed investment in the late 1970s was not low. Investment was slow to recover from the Great Stagflation, but by 1979 it reached record levels. It stood well above the average of the 1948–65 period, when productivity grew at a much faster pace.

While agreeing that investment has been high, many think that there was a failure to meet needs which were growing at an even faster pace. President Carter's Council of Economic Advisers pointed out that the capital-labor ratio had not increased, even with large gross investments.[12] A higher share of investment was concentrated in shorter-term assets. Consequently, the more rapidly depreciating stock meant that less current investment was available to increase net capital. A larger share of investment went to meet requirements of environmental, health, and safety regulations and as substitutions for higher-priced energy. As a result, they estimated that it was desirable to increase gross nonresidential fixed investment by 10 to 20 percent. A 20 percent increase would lift this category of investment to about 13 percent of the GNP.

Foreign Experience.   Initially, some push for greater investment came from a comparison with other industrialized countries. Facts such as those presented in Figure 15.5 were compared with rates of investment among countries. The United States invested a smaller share of its GNP in plant and equipment than any other industrialized nation and had the slowest improvement in productivity. Wouldn't growth in the United States approach that of other countries if it increased its investment to their levels? The answer appears to be no. Although part of the differences in growth rates could be attributed to a faster

12. The *Economic Reports of the President* for 1978–81 include detailed analysis of the issues of investment and capital formation.

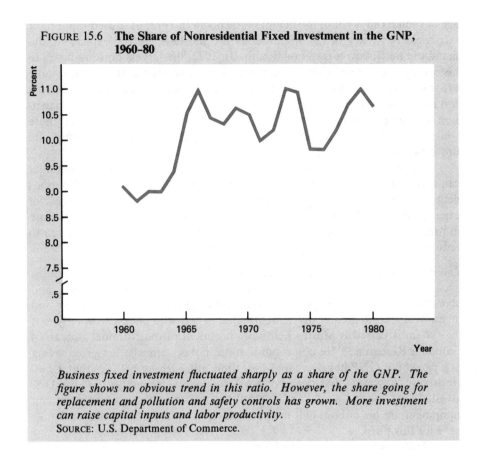

FIGURE 15.6   **The Share of Nonresidential Fixed Investment in the GNP, 1960–80**

Business fixed investment fluctuated sharply as a share of the GNP. The figure shows no obvious trend in this ratio. However, the share going for replacement and pollution and safety controls has grown. More investment can raise capital inputs and labor productivity.
SOURCE: U.S. Department of Commerce.

expansion of capital in foreign countries, not as much came from this source as simple comparisons seemed to indicate.

Other countries started with much lower productivity levels and capital stock than the United States; they had a long way to go to catch up. Among the major developed countries, capital contributed about the same amount to productivity growth in France as in the United States and less in the United Kingdom. Other Western European countries, with the exception of Germany, had results scattered around the United States experience. Germany and Japan, coming out of the war with much of their capital destroyed, had much further to go. Capital did contribute somewhat more to their growth, but in both cases, changing technology was far more important. They gained economies of scale and were able to utilize knowledge from other countries as they rushed to catch up. In the 1970s, their growth slowed sharply.

Temporary Shortages. Since neither the comparison with the past nor to foreign experience provides much insight into how much capital is required, other approaches are called for. Most observers agree that a temporary shortage of capital did occur at the height of the boom in 1973. It caused rapid price increases. A variety of factors underlay the shortage. In the expansion, demand did not follow a traditional path. In 1972, the largest housing boom in history resulted from a sharp increase in subsidy programs and unusually expansionary monetary policies. The demand pressure far exceeded the short-run ability of industry to supply materials. Because the government's expansion of demand preceded the Nixon-McGovern presidential campaign, those who believe in a major political cycle of fiscal and monetary policy often cite this action.

This period appears to furnish evidence that temporary capital shortages can arise and be instrumental in starting an inflationary spiral. In some periods demand will exceed supply, and prices will rise. The smaller the excess of capacity, the more likely are such periods to occur, and the larger will be the rise in prices needed to match demand to supply. More investment is required to reduce dangers of future inflationary pressures.

The Wedge between Saving and Investment.   Another approach to estimating a need for more capital asks whether our system is biased against saving and investment. Would a tax system neutral with respect to both consumption and investment lead to greater investment? One expert who believes strongly that the system is biased is Martin Feldstein, president of the National Bureau of Economic Research.[13] He points out that it is not certain whether gross saving as a percent of GNP has decreased over time, although he believes that it has. He is sure, however, that net saving has fallen. He estimates that the U.S. invested only about 3 percent of its GNP for increasing the stock of plant and equipment; or, only about half the percentage other major industrial countries used for this purpose.

He also believes that our problems are not due to market failures or to any capital shortage. He argues, rather, that personal and corporate income taxes insert a wedge between the national rate of return on real capital and the aftertax rate received by savers. He estimates that current earnings from investment range around 12 percent a year, while the aftertax return on saving is closer to 6 percent. The difference between these rates means that individuals are not rewarded sufficiently for forgoing consumption. The economy could earn up to 12 percent for each additional dollar of investment, but those dollars won't be saved because the aftertax return is so much lower. Feldstein estimates that if this wedge were removed, the rate of return on saving and investment might stabilize near 10 percent. This added return to savers and the

13. See Hearings for the Subcommittee on Economic Growth and Stabilization, U.S. Congress, Joint Economic Committee 95:1, *The Role of Federal Tax Policy in Stimulating Capital Formation and Economic Growth,* particularly the testimony of July 14 and July 19, 1977. Also see M. Feldstein, "National Saving in the United States" in *Capital for Productivity and Jobs* edited by E. Shapiro and W. L. White (Englewood Cliffs, N.J.: Prentice-Hall, 1977), pp. 130–49; *The Wall Street Journal* June 19,1981, p. 26; and D. W. Jorgenson and M. A. Sullivan, *Reforming Capital Recovery Under the Corporate Income Tax* (Cambridge, Mass.: Harvard Institute for Economic Research, 1981).

ability to make investments with a lower marginal efficiency of capital would raise the share of saving and investment in the GNP by about 1.5 percent a year. In addition to the wedge, Feldstein has also stressed that low returns to savers and inadequate capital investment occurred because inflation caused corporations to overstate their profits and so to pay abnormally high taxes. He estimated that in the late 1970s inflation raised the total effective tax rate on the earnings from corporate capital to about 75 percent, while lowering the real aftertax rate of return to 2.6 percent.

These arguments and similar ones led to steady reductions in corporate taxes, both as a share of total revenues and as a share of corporate income. The corporate share of federal revenues fell from above 26 percent in 1955 to 12 percent in 1980 and was projected to drop to under 10 percent in 1985. Meanwhile, even though the statutory corporate profits rate remained at 46 percent, more rapid depreciation allowances and investment tax credits in the 1981 act cut the actual effective tax rate to only 14 percent. As a corollary, Dale Jorgenson, Feldstein's colleague, estimated that the 1981 act produced a government subsidy (a *negative* tax rate) for investment in new capital equipment. Even though other taxes still had to be paid, corporations would receive credits against other taxes if they bought new equipment.

Ways to Increase Capital Investment

The policies adopted in the 1981 act and most similar proposals to increase saving and investment can be classified in four categories: (1) lower taxes on the return from saving and investment; (2) reduce uncertainty, instability, and interest rates; (3) increase incentives for specific types of investment and future saving; and (4) increase the rate of saving by governments.

LOWER TAXES

Supply-side economists testified that the sharp reduction in taxes on saving and investment in the 1981 act would lead to a rapid increase in the rate of investment in plant and equipment pushing it far above the 11 percent of GNP achieved in previous years. Others were less optimistic because they believed that a general decrease in taxes had four potential disadvantages compared to tax reductions aimed at achieving specific results:

1. Prior analysis of the desire to consume and to save brought out that part of the higher aftertax incomes would be consumed. Therefore, the net effect on saving and investment depends on what the government did with the taxes before they were reduced. If they had gone to saving or to nontangible investment, the reduction in taxes could lower productivity.
2. The amount of investment may be more sensitive to demand than to taxes. The danger always exists that with more money available for saving, new equilibrium spending desires may occur at a lower level of investment. The paradox of thrift says that additional desires to save can lower investment.

3. Lowering taxes on saving in general, particularly if consumption taxes are increased, engenders windfall profits and causes a major redistribution of income. The potential cost of such policies can mean that only small productivity gains are realized at a considerable expense, both to equity and to large government programs such as national defense and education. Over time, some of the disparities would be reduced because, with more capital, real wages should rise and the profit rate fall.
4. Unless fully offset by expenditure cuts, the resulting budget deficit will crowd out some investment through higher interest rates.

Such arguments make little sense to those who believe that demand for investment is virtually unlimited or that the present distribution of income is too egalitarian. They are convinced that inflation results from too much demand. There will be adequate demand for capital; increased saving will not be wasted.

DECREASED UNCERTAINTY

While disagreements were common during the 1970s as to whether profits had fallen or were too low, it was clear that uncertainty and high interest rates had reduced the value of business fixed assets as reflected by the drop in real prices of common stock. The ratio of market value to replacement costs had fallen from nearly 1.3 in the mid-1960s to under .75 in the late 1970s. With existing assets worth so little, why should businesses spend money on new capital? This drop in the value of assets was a mystery. Heightened uncertainty about inflation, the world situation, and potential energy shortages, together with a lack of incentives, were all advanced as possible causes. In the absence of agreement as to the cause, reaching agreement as to possible cures was difficult.

Certain policies can minimize uncertainty. The government has guaranteed loans for long-term investments claimed to be vital for the national welfare. A lessening of inflation can decrease uncertainty and raise investment, but not if it results from decreased demand. An obvious requirement is to end stop-start policies, which foster both uncertainty and higher interest rates and discourage investments.

SPECIFIC INCENTIVES

Because of the high cost of general programs aimed at increasing the return on all past saving and investment, many economists advocate instead specific programs geared either to particular needs or to new investment or saving. They point out that in many cases, economics shows that it is far more cost-effective to treat marginal rather than average decisions. The variety of possible specific programs is almost endless. Examples include raising the rate of depreciation allowed for tax purposes on new equipment and structures, increasing the investment tax credit, allowing tax credits for research and development, raising the government's expenditures for research and development back to their previous share of the GNP, subsidizing energy investments, decreasing taxes on small savers and investors, and allowing accumulations of housing downpayments or larger retirement funds to avoid taxation.

Many problems are encountered in trying to evaluate the relative merits of proposals like these. The political process may find it difficult to make such choices. It may be easier to adopt programs with broad appeals, even though their efficiency and ability to accomplish specific tasks may be far lower.

GOVERNMENT SAVING

If the problem is merely one of too low a level of saving, many observers believe that a simple solution would be for the government to run surpluses of the desired size. Instead of reducing taxes, the government could repay more of the public debt. This would avoid many of the issues related to windfall profits and changes in income distribution that arise when specific taxes are reduced.

The advantages of added government saving appear particularly strong to those who believe that social security has tended to reduce the national saving rate.[14] Instead of being largely on a pay-as-you-go basis, the social security trust fund could be expanded. Funds placed in the fund would raise current saving and lower future taxes. Today's savers would help pay for their own retirement—an advantageous program, given an increasing percentage of the population in older age groups.

Arguments against more government saving are voiced by those who fear that current aggregate demand is too low, not too high, and by those who believe taxes are too high. If equilibrium aggregate demand is weak, increased government saving is achieved at the expense of current output and growth. Those who hold this point of view believe that added saving makes sense only if it occurs in response to higher investment demands. Raising saving before investment, they believe, puts the cart before the horse.

Those who feel that taxes are too high see a large potential for raising output and investment by shifting desires through greater incentives. They are not willing to accept past performance as a basis for future actions. They want to probe for new and much more productive possible equilibriums in hitherto unexplored areas of the aggregate supply and demand space. Since their arguments are based largely on faith, counterarguments tend not to shake their convictions. The extremely large 1981 tax reductions were a victory for those holding this point of view.

Because growth can be increased by added investment, some or all of these approaches will be tried. The purpose of the model of aggregate supply and demand is to enable each observer to discover the assumptions behind these policies and to judge how effective they may be.

14. Feldstein, "National Saving in the United States," pp. 130–49.

Other Sources of Increased Growth

While most policy suggestions are directed toward expanding investment in plant and equipment, productivity experts agree that a far broader effort makes more sense. Some urge a greater effort to improve management and overall planning. Studies of successes in Japan and Europe point to the importance of organization in firms and industries. Economists are concerned that too much attention is devoted to old, tired industries rather than to new, dynamic ones. The electronics industry in the United States has felt that most proposals to promote investment in plant and equipment fail to recognize the importance of investment in research. Other experts point out that many other ways of raising productivity have also been left out of the discussions of capital investments. Suggested policies often fail to take into account the wide range of physical capital used in the economy, particularly investments in housing, inventories, international assets, and by governments. While investment in the three private categories together average only about half as much as that going into plant and equipment (fixed nonresidential capital), according to Denison their joint contribution to growth in national income is as great as that from the much larger nonresidential fixed investment.[15] In addition to this other private sector investment, estimates by Kendrick and others show that tangible investments by governments are from one-third to one-half the size of business fixed investment; they too increase private productivity.

HUMAN CAPITAL

An even more serious omission in most discussions is investment in human capital. If investment policies are restricted to business fixed investment, they are limited to between 20 and 30 percent of total capital investment in the economy. For example, Richard Freeman, using the conventional definition of the GNP and a rather narrow definition of investment in human capital and research and development, finds that business fixed investment is less than 30 percent of total investment.[16]

Estimates of the share of total investment in the GNP are set forth in Table 15.5. Freeman's concept of investment in human capital uses only direct educational expenses and forgone income of working-age students. John Kendrick uses a broader definition.[17] He adjusts both the stock of capital and the GNP to take account of the flow of services from this added investment. According to Kendrick, the share of total investment in the adjusted GNP is close to 50 percent. The share of business fixed investment is around 8 percent,

15. E. F. Denison, *Accounting for Slower Economic Growth*, p. 113.

16. R. B. Freeman, "Investment in Human Capital and Knowledge," in American Assembly, *Capital for Productivity and Jobs* (Englewood Cliffs, N.J.: Prentice-Hall, 1977), Table 2.

17. J. W. Kendrick, *The Formation and Stocks of Total Capital* (New York: National Bureau of Economic Research, 1976).

TABLE 15.5 **Investment by Categories as Shares of the Gross National Product 1950–74**

(percent)

	1950	1960	1965	1970	1972	1974
Fixed nonresidential private	9.5	9.4	10.4	10.2	10.0	10.7
Residential, inventories, foreign	10.0	6.6	7.0	4.5	5.8	4.9
Government tangible	2.7	3.3	3.8	3.4	3.1	3.3
Private R and D	0.5	1.0	1.0	1.2	1.0	1.1
Government R and D	0.8	1.7	1.9	1.5	1.4	1.2
Human capital	5.6	8.1	10.0	11.5	11.7	10.9
Total	29.1	30.1	34.1	32.3	33.0	32.1

SOURCE: Rows 1 and 2, President's Economic Report, 1979. Rows 3 to 6 from R. Freeman, "Investment in Human Capital and Knowledge," Table 2.

When investments in research and development, in human capital, and in government capital are included, total investment is three times as large as fixed nonresidential expenditures, which receive most of current attention. Each type can improve productivity and aid growth.

which means that plant and equipment investments are a good deal less than 20 percent of total investment.

The point made by these and other writers on nontangible capital is that many kinds of investment increase our capital stock. This capital produces future output of goods and services in the same way as plant and equipment. While they are omitted from the official Department of Commerce GNP accounts because of difficulties in measurement, these other forms of capital are recognized in economic analysis as playing a most significant role in raising productivity. For example, Table 15.4 showed that investments in knowledge have a major impact on productivity. Improvements in productivity arise from education, from better job training, health, and movements to more productive jobs. Many also believe that the investments in research and development are especially strategic. According to Kendrick, the return on human capital, on both a gross and a net basis, has been higher than that on nonhuman capital. Specifically, in the early 1970s, the net yield on human capital was about a third higher.

When the entire range of capital is considered, the number of opportunities for increasing productivity through investment policy expands considerably. But at the same time, policy problems become more complex. More factors must be considered in deciding what expenditures to support and which to cut. An increase in one type of investment, if it is at the expense of another, may lower, not raise, productivity.

A BROAD APPROACH

Because of the difficulty of raising productivity through traditional capital investment alone, many economists feel that a far broader attack on the problem is called for. A program advocated by Kendrick typifies the thinking of optimists who have examined the problem in depth.[18] Kendrick believes that the rate of improvement in productivity in the period 1980–90 could be returned almost to its level of the 1946–73 period. Broad, active policies to improve productivity would raise it well above its expected normal growth, which would fall between the 1948–73 and the 1973–80 experience.

Where would the increases come from? The largest by far would be from improved knowledge and education. This is one reason Kendrick stresses the need to think of investment in the broadest sense. Additional subsidies and expenditures for increasing investment in human capital and research and development could raise productivity by .5 percent annually, or about 40 percent of the total. Policies to increase investment in plant and equipment and inventories would account for .3 percent. Ending the deterioration in government services and reversing some impacts of regulation would raise productivity by .2 percent per year. Finally, increased output from these three previous factors would lead to greater economies of scale and a further improvement of .2 percent.

The Amount of Labor Inputs

Table 15.4 divided the changes in labor inputs into five categories. In the first period, potential employment grew at a rate of 1.0 percent a year and then leaped to a 2.5 percent rate. Total hours worked did not grow as fast, however, since they were reduced by an upward trend in unemployment and a decrease in the average work week. Meanwhile, labor quality improved as a result of a steady increase in the educational attainment of the work force and a better ability to perform skilled tasks. Some of this improvement was offset, however, as the percentage of new entrants into the labor force grew and more jobs were held by less skilled youth and by women without previous employment experience. In examining labor inputs, this section considers first growth in the potential hours of work and the factors influencing the quality of labor. The chapter concludes with an analysis in greater depth of unemployment.

INCENTIVES TO OFFER MORE WORK

The largest gains in real income between 1973 and 1980 came from the desire of more people to work. In fact, because the sum of all other factors together was negative, output did not keep up with the expansion of the labor force; the average real income per person in the labor force fell slightly. The number of potential workers—counting all those 16 years of age and older—increased by 1.75 million per year from 1948 to 1973, and then by 2.57 million annually from

18. Kendrick, "Productivity Trends and Recent Slowdown," pp. 49–69.

1973 to 1980. The percentage wanting to work rose from 58.8 percent in 1948 to 60.8 in 1973 and to 63.8 percent in 1980. All of this change was due to the greater participation rate of females, which increased by nearly 60 percent, even as the rate of male participation in the labor force fell 13 percent.

While the total number of potential employees grew rapidly, a steady decline in the average work week slowed the rate of increase in labor inputs. United States labor history records a persistent decline in the average number of hours worked per person. In 1980 the average work week was less than three-quarters of its 1929 length. Of course, output would grow faster if this trend of increasing leisure were turned around and if the percentage wanting to work grew still faster. Supply-side economists have suggested that the amount of work would increase rapidly if personal income taxes were cut. Supply-side proponents argued that large reductions in tax rates, such as the 1981 actions to cut tax rates sharply over three years, were needed to raise supply and not, as earlier tax-cut advocates had suggested, to close the gap between actual and potential output. They argued that the tax cut would cause potential output to expand as fast as or faster than demand. One of the theoretical bases for such supply-side tax-cut proposals was the Laffer curve, according to which the disincentives introduced into the economy by high taxes may be so great that raising taxes will lower government revenues, while cutting taxes will raise revenues. The possible relations between taxes and revenues, however, go considerably beyond the direct effect of taxes on the labor supply. Much emphasis is placed on how taxes influence saving, capital investment, and productivity.

Most studies show that tax cuts will increase the labor supply, but only by small amounts. For example, some estimates show that a 10 percent cut in income taxes raises labor inputs by about .33 percent per year, or by about 330,000 more workers. Some claim that lower taxes will raise hours worked by several percent; other studies, however, show that the direct effect of a cut in income taxes is to reduce labor inputs. While a decrease in the marginal tax rate may succeed in increasing hours worked, it may also fail because tax cuts have income effects that work contrary to the expected substitution of labor for leisure. As noted in the discussion of labor supply, the direct effect of a higher wage or price for work will mean more labor offered. Indirect effects, however, go the other way. The reduction in taxes augments take-home pay and income. Some of that increased income will be taken out in more leisure. Will the doctor who plays golf on Wednesday afternoons give up his afternoon off to increase his earnings if his marginal tax rate drops from a maximum 50 percent (on earned income), or will he add a Friday game because the lower rate increases his take-home pay?

Studies of how individuals actually react to changes in wages and tax rates yield ambiguous results. The empirical work has many conceptual and statistical problems. Some studies find that higher wages do increase the amount of labor offered, while others show the opposite. It is probably correct to say that changes in incentives through lower taxes or higher pay make only a slight difference with respect to male workers, but that the amount of work offered by women will rise if incentives are increased. This is because the female labor force has a lower participation rate, more part-time workers, and lower wages. All of these factors should mean that higher earnings would increase the desire to work, while the income effect would be less important.[19] According to this type of analysis, the section of the 1981 act which lowered the marriage penalty (a quirk of the tax which means that when both partners of a couple work, they pay higher taxes if married than if living together unmarried) was expected to be particularly effective in raising labor inputs. The *Economic Report of the President* for 1981 concluded that a 10 percent cut in personal income taxes would increase potential output by a maximum of .2 to .6 percent. By 1985, when most of the tax reductions would be in place, these assumptions as well as the much higher ones from other sources could be tested.

INPUT PER HOUR WORKED

Demographic changes in the labor force reduced labor skills. A higher percentage of youth and of women in the labor force lowered the average experience level and cut growth by about .3 percent per year. On the other hand, the level of education and training of the labor force has risen steadily. Between 1973 and 1980, improvements in labor quality due to education increased inputs by .9 percent per year. In the 1970s this was the largest single growth component. It is expected to remain significant in the 1980s.

Accounting procedures do not attempt to measure effort. Changes in how hard people work affect the rate of change shown in the last line, "Advances in knowledge and not elsewhere classified." Some analysts blame part of the sharp drop in this component on less hard work. For example, Arthur Burns, then chairman of the Federal Reserve Board, stated in 1977, "My own judgment is that we have been undergoing a change in our societal values and attitudes that has contributed significantly to poorer job performance in recent years." Many agree that work effort has deteriorated. Others, however, point out that while people may work less hard than in the past, any such deterioration has taken place gradually over most of the period since 1940; no quantum jump occurred to account for the sharp drop in productivity in the 1970s.

What Determines the Level of Unemployment?

The rate of unemployment also influences growth. Output falls when unemployment rises. If the natural rate of unemployment is reduced or if the economy runs with less slack, output and growth will expand. The level of unemployment is one of the most closely watched indicators of the success or

19. See E. Kalachek, *Workers and the Hours Decision,* Publication No. 26 of the Center for the Study of American Business, October 1979.

failure of economic policy. In addition to causing devastating effects on individuals, idle labor and capital constitute a waste that cannot be made up. The failure of the economy to offer jobs to those actively seeking work reveals that something is wrong. On the other hand, an excess of jobs and a rate of output above potential create the opposite kind of problem: they lead to inflation.

Like Gaul, unemployment can be divided into three parts: (1) unemployment due to frictional, including seasonal, factors; (2) structural unemployment, including locational unemployment; and (3) unemployment arising from a lack of aggregate demand, sometimes called cyclical unemployment. The natural rate is determined by the amount of the first two, frictional and structural unemployment. If they can be reduced, the natural rate will fall and potential output will increase.

Most of macroeconomics has concentrated on unemployment due to cyclical forces. Because the loss of jobs from this source is caused by a drop in demand below potential output and because it is possible to change *AD*, it would seem possible to avoid the economic waste of cyclical unemployment. But when actual unemployment between 1950 and 1980 is analyzed, one finds that by far the largest share was caused by frictional or structural factors. If the natural rate of unemployment could be reduced permanently, the result could be an improvement in future output and income as great as that which would result from a major lessening in the instability of aggregate demand.

FRICTIONAL AND STRUCTURAL UNEMPLOYMENT

Frictional unemployment results from normal turnover and entry into and exit from the labor force. New workers enter the labor force; workers move from one job to a better one, or from one part of the country to another. Some people are unemployed because they quit to look for something better. Others may leave to return to school or to have a baby. When they reenter the job market, until they find a new position they are unemployed. Joblessness may also increase for seasonal reasons, such as bad construction weather or the interval between the harvesting of one crop and the next. Table 15.6 shows the number of people in these various categories. The number of job-leavers, reentrants, and new entrants into the labor force does not appear to vary greatly between periods of recession and relative prosperity. In fact, when jobs were at a minimum in the recession 1973–75, a slightly higher percentage of the unemployed had left their jobs than in the other periods.

The existence of a sizable number of job-leavers, reentrants, and new entrants is a normal attribute of a free market. They are there because they enjoy freedom of choice. Because it promotes a more efficient matching of jobs and skills, some frictional unemployment is not undesirable. Workers can find better jobs or jobs at preferable locations. The first job offered a worker may not suit him well. Unemployment which allows time to search for a better job may pay off. Frictional unemployment is often of short duration and creates few hardships. However, it constitutes a sizable element in reported unemployment.

Frictions increase as aggregate demand falls. The big difference between a recession and more prosperous years in the unemployment data lies in the number who lose their jobs. In the recession year of 1975, this category accounted for over 55 percent of those unemployed, whereas in 1978 it was 41 percent. The fewer the jobs available, the longer the time that must be spent in searching. For this reason, not all frictional unemployment can be considered a normal attribute of the labor market. Furthermore, in a better market with more complete and current information about job availability, the number in this group and the time lost could be greatly reduced. Many European labor markets are far better organized, with a much lower level of frictional unemployment than those in the United States.

TABLE 15.6   **Frictional Unemployment by Cause**
(percent)

	Percent of labor force		Percent of unemployed	
	1975	*1978*	*1975*	*1978*
Job losers	4.7	2.5	55.4	41.6
Job leavers	0.9	0.8	10.4	14.1
Job reentrants	2.0	1.8	23.8	30.0
New entrants	0.9	0.9	10.4	14.3
Total	8.5	6.0	100.0	100.0

A good deal of unemployment is frictional, related to normal turnover and to searching for more suitable jobs. When aggregate demand falls, as in 1975, unemployment rises because people lose jobs and it takes longer to find new ones; this is a sign of cyclical not frictional unemployment.

Structural unemployment is due to rigidities and imbalances in the labor market. Job-seekers do not match available jobs. Workers may be trained as clerks when what is needed are plumbers. The level of this type of unemployment also is much higher in the United States than in other countries. In normal times, there are a large number of unfilled jobs, even while many must hunt for work for which they are qualified. Those seeking jobs may have less skill, less experience, and less education than the available vacancies call for. The job-seekers may also be in the wrong place, or be of the wrong sex or color. As demand expands into the critical zone near full employment, the economy runs out of labor with specific skills. Shortages may also crop up in particular locations. In such a situation, further expansion of demand leads to inflationary increases in those sectors experiencing shortages. But at the same time, other large segments of the labor force, particularly unskilled workers, remain unemployed. A reduction in structural unemployment calls for either better training of the unemployed or a lowering of the level of skills required in particular jobs. It may also call for more capital investment. If expanding demand runs up against capacity constraints, additional jobs are possible only through less efficient and a more inflationary use of the labor force.

If individual frictional and structural unemployment can be reduced, potential output can be raised. The normal amount of unemployment at full employment can be lowered. The government uses the term *interim full employment* to emphasize that there will be fewer unemployed if labor markets can be improved and a better job done in matching skills to needs. For example, if a good enough job were done in lowering frictional and structural unemployment, instead of an unemployment rate of 5 percent at full employment in the 1970s (as estimated in the *Economic Report of the President* for 1979, p. 76), the number of unemployed at full employment might go down to 3 percent. By improving job markets, the unemployment level at which prices start to rise could be lowered. Reducing the level of the natural rate of unemployment by 2 percent would raise potential output by over 75 billions of constant 1972 dollars a year. Clearly, such gains in available goods and services are worth striving for.

WHY HAS THE NATURAL RATE OF UNEMPLOYMENT INCREASED?

When President Kennedy's Council of Economic Advisers first calculated full employment, they estimated that it was marked by an unemployment rate of 4.0 percent. In the 1980s, minimum estimates, including those of the CEA, were that the noninflationary full-employment rate had risen to 5 percent, while many economists estimated it as high as 6.5 percent. What caused these sharp increases in estimated rates and the resulting large losses in output?

The principal cause of differing estimates arises from a lack of agreement as to how sensitive the economy is to inflation. How high does unemployment have to be for demand to be noninflationary? Some analysts attribute much of the inflationary record of the 1970s to excess demand, while others stress supply shocks. Those who see a high natural rate picture an economy extremely vulnerable to inflation. Without a great deal of slack, prices will take off. Those who pick the 5 percent rate point to prior experiences of noninflationary periods. If inflation were behind us, they believe demand would not be excessive at the 5 percent level.

Between the two extremes, many observers agree that the economic system has developed an inflationary bias. More products are sold in contract markets; labor unions and oligopolistic producers have more power; extensions of welfare state benefits have made unemployment less costly to the individual; more output comes from the nonmarket sector, including governments. The result of these factors has not been to shift the point of full employment to the right on the inflation curve, but it makes more likely an upward drift from one curve to the next even before full employment is reached. Those who emphasize the drift rather than an increase in the natural rate believe that incomes policies are necessary to halt the steady upward movements so that full employment without inflation can be achieved at a 5 percent or lower natural rate.

While disagreements continue over the threshold of inflation, most economists agree that at least three forces did raise the natural rate of unemployment above its level in 1956, the base year for the CEA's calculations.[20] The forces which have raised the rate, with fairly low estimates of their impacts, are shown in Table 15.7

Demographic Factors. Differences in unemployment rates by demographic groups are closely related to the structure of labor markets. More skilled and educated workers are less likely to be unemployed. Blacks and females are likely to be discriminated against. On average, young blacks have less training, less education, live in central cities, and are affected by discrimination. All such factors lead to higher unemployment rates. Table 14.5 highlighted significant differences in unemployment rates among demographic age-sex-race groups. Because the groups that include youth, women, and blacks contain more new workers, part-time workers, and less skilled workers, they suffer more structural and frictional unemployment. When rising unemployment heightens competition for all jobs, the employability of those in the higher rate categories drops more than the average.

If all groups in the labor force grew at the same rate, such disparities would not affect the natural rate. But the proportionate growth of the young and of females has far outpaced the total. If one assumes that the same ratio of unemployment by groups found in the 1950s continues to apply in 1980, these demographic factors raise the natural rate by at least the minimum .46 percent found in Table 15.7. In addition, because these groups grew rapidly and have to compete more vigorously for jobs, a further increase in structural unemployment may have resulted. For example, teenagers' share of the labor force grew from 6.3 percent in 1955 to 9.5 percent in 1975. During this same period, the gap between their unemployment rate and that of males 20 years of age and over widened from 7.2 percent to 13.1 percent. Michael Wachter estimated that this crowding-in of teenagers to the labor force added a further .5 percent to the total unemployment rate. The impact of the baby boom over the 20-year period 1955 to 1977 may well have raised the natural rate by 1 percent, or twice the amount shown in the table. Some of this increase is due to a changing age distribution, some to the shifting of participation rates, and some to changes in laws. Because these factors interact, it is hard to assign specific amounts to any one factor.

Unemployment Insurance. A system of unemployment benefits increases frictional unemployment. A father who can feed his family by using unemployment checks is under less pressure to accept a job he feels is unsatisfactory. He can continue to search for a longer period. Others under even less pressure may not look very hard, taking time out to ski or surf. On average, those receiving

20. P. Cagan, *Persistent Inflation,* Chapter 8; M. Wachter, "The Changing Cyclical Responsiveness of Wage Inflation," *Brookings Papers on Economic Activity* 1(1978):115–59; J. Antos, W. Mellow, and J. E. Triplett, "What is the Current Equivalent to Unemployment Rates of the Past?" *Monthly Labor Review* (March 1979): 36–45.

TABLE 15.7 **An Estimate of Structural Change in the Natural Rate of Unemployment, 1956–77**

(percent)

Source of charge	Amount
Demographic	0.46
Unemployment insurance	0.34
Minimum wage	0.63
Other changes	−0.20
Total	1.23

SOURCE: P. Cagan, *Persistent Inflation* (New York: Columbia University Press, 1979), Table 8.1.

The natural rate of unemployment has risen for demographic reasons. In addition, higher unemployment insurance allows a longer job search. Higher minimum wages increase the difficulty of finding jobs for those with a low marginal productivity.

unemployment insurance benefits take two to three weeks longer to find a job than those without benefits. Martin Feldstein has estimated that the total amount of frictional unemployment resulting from unemployment insurance may be as high as 1.25 percent. However, since benefits existed in 1956, their impact was included in the initial full-employment estimate. Table 15.7 contains Cagan's estimate that changes in the unemployment insurance system since 1955 raised the natural rate by .34 percent.

Minimum Wages. Most economists agree that high minimum wages result in fewer jobs for the less well-trained and less-skilled workers. Output depends on skills; firms won't hire people if the revenue from their output falls below their wage. The minimum wage affects unemployment rates in three ways:

1. Some unskilled workers will be unemployed because they cannot qualify for a job. The level of the minimum wage compared to that of real output determines how many will fail to find work. In many periods, when the wage rate was low compared to the value of output, the law had a minimal effect. Major changes in the minimum wage occurred in 1967, 1968, and 1978.
2. When people can't find jobs, they get discouraged and drop out of the labor force. The minimum wage forces the most unskilled out of the labor force. Thus it tends to reduce reported unemployment.
3. Both of these factors have a greater impact in recessions than in periods of high employment. Firms will hire the unskilled and do more training when they can't get the skilled workers they need. Therefore, the figures must be adjusted for cyclical changes.

Table 15.7 estimates that increases in the minimum wage between 1955 and 1975 raised the overall unemployment rate by .63 percent.

Other Changes.   Many other factors have affected unemployment rates. For example, the number of multi-worker families has jumped. If one member has a job, the pressure on a second family worker to find one is lessened. The number of families with more than one worker rose from 38.3 percent in 1956 to 52.9 percent in 1976. This increased the natural rate.

The level of welfare payments also affects unemployment. People who can exist on welfare will not search as hard for work. But many benefits stipulate that one must be actively seeking a job. This causes some to report themselves in the job market and looking for work even though they are not. Work registration requirements for welfare mothers were passed in the 1970s. This would have increased the number reporting themselves out of work, both in total and compared to the 1950s.

Two other factors reduced reported unemployment. (1) Persons in government training programs are now reported as employed rather than as unemployed or not in the labor force. The expansion of these programs reduces the amount of unemployment and increases the labor force. (2) Changes in the survey used to measure unemployment in 1966 and 1970 may have slightly lowered total reported unemployment.

Since these other changes operate in both directions, no one is sure what their net impact may be. Some observers add sizable increases to their estimates because of these factors; others net them out and show small drops. Table 15.7 shows the net effect of these various factors as reducing the natural rate by .2 percent.

The Capital Stock.   One important category does not appear in Table 15.7. The natural unemployment rate can be affected by potential shortages of capital and natural resources. In the short run, production facilities and procedures are established to employ an optimum mixture of workers and machines. Output can expand if workers are hired beyond the most efficient point, but doing so raises costs and prices. Some observers believe that by 1981, the ratio of capital to labor had fallen so far as to raise the natural rate of unemployment by another .5 percent over the 1955 rate.

Lowering the Natural Rate of Unemployment

A key feature of the so-called natural rate of unemployment is that it is not fixed. It is natural only with respect to a particular institutional labor market, to a work force with given skills, to a specific production function. If any of these change, so will the natural rate. Policies designed to alter any of them can increase output and reduce the rate of unemployed resources. Table 15.5 shows that large numbers of the unemployed are seeking new or better jobs. Not all of them were fired; some have left voluntarily. Others are entering or reentering the market. Improved labor-market information and labor mobility, by speeding up their search and ability to find available jobs, will lower the natural rate. Better job knowledge for teenagers and others seeking their first jobs would be especially helpful. These groups, which account for the largest portion of frictional unemployment, have the worst communication system. Poor information also causes significant differences in regional unemployment rates. Some sectors experience severe shortages even as others have large surpluses of workers. Better communications could reduce these differences.

MANPOWER TRAINING PROGRAMS

At full employment, many individuals are out of work because the amount their employment can contribute to a firm is less than the wage attached to the job. In the range of full employment, most of the unemployed are unskilled. Jobs remain available to those with greater accomplishments. By providing workers with necessary skills and education, manpower training can reduce the minimum level of unemployment. Human capital can be enhanced even as mismatches of workers and jobs are eliminated. Improved skills can lead to better jobs with less turnover. Public manpower training programs have been tried frequently. Some observers feel that they have failed and should be dropped. Others believe that the prospective gains from better programs are so great that far more effort in this direction is called for. Many programs have done some good, and some have done much good. It is hoped that examples of successful programs can be used to upgrade others.

One form of improvement may lie in subsidies by the government to private industries to enable them to upgrade training programs. Many programs have failed because the training provided has not related closely enough to specific jobs. Such defects are less likely to occur with on-the-job training. Subsidies can reduce the cost of labor to firms sufficiently to make it worthwhile to hire those whose initial productivity is low. They can then be trained to the point where subsidies are no longer needed. Other subsidies may have a more permanent role. Many submarginal workers exist in the economy. Because of physical or mental shortcomings, their output is worth less than the minimum wage. They could find work if firms or nonprofit institutions are subsidized to make up the difference between their pay and their product.

REDUCING THE MINIMUM WAGE

One of the most controversial issues is whether structural unemployment could be reduced by lowering the minimum wage, particularly for teen-agers. Some people who want to work can't produce enough to earn the minimum wage. In some cases their skills are too low. In other cases, certain jobs which call for low skills—washing cars, keeping cities clean, maintaining yards, custodial work— will not be performed at all if the minimum wage is too high. Some estimates show that 20 percent or more of the minimum level of unemployment may be attributable to jobs removed from the market by high minimum wages.

Whether or not to lower the minimum wage for some or all groups is a political decision. The level has been raised steadily, on the argument that labor markets are imperfect, especially for the unskilled. Because of ignorance among their employees, employers are able to pay less than the marginal product. Others use labor inefficiently, thereby lowering the productivity of their labor force. An increase in the minimum wage forces employers to improve productivity and to pay poor bargainers their true marginal product. A dual structure with a lower minimum for teen-agers or the handicapped is opposed on the grounds that the competition from these groups would lower the pay of those now employed.

Those who believe that markets are efficient reject these arguments. In their view, the chances that people are being paid less than their marginal product or that owners can improve productivity are slight. They therefore stress that every increase in the minimum wage shifts the aggregate supply curve upward and raises the amount of structural unemployment without compensating benefits.

LOWERING WELFARE AND UNEMPLOYMENT BENEFITS

People will spend more time hunting a desirable job if the level of welfare and unemployment benefits is high enough to make it practical for them to do so. As the gap in income between not working and working at a poor job narrows, more people will choose to remain unemployed. The penalty of holding out for a better job becomes lighter. Whether to lower structural unemployment by reducing welfare and unemployment benefits is also a political decision. Improving the design of the benefits system to minimize undesirable effects may be possible. However, this is not the main issue. Most arguments concern what constitutes an adequate level of benefits, given the general wealth and income distribution of the country.

CREATING MORE JOBS

Output can grow and the natural rate of unemployment will decrease if the rate of capital investment expands faster than the labor force. More investment can lower the natural rate of unemployment in two ways. By raising labor's marginal productivity, those with marginal skills will become employed. Perhaps more important, if the investment takes place in spheres of potential bottlenecks and capital shortages, it can shift to the right the range in the aggregate supply curve surrounding the point of potential output and full employment at which price rises begin to accelerate. Shifting this range outward lowers the natural rate of unemployment.

Another potential but controversial source of jobs is through creating temporary jobs in the public sector. The greater the number employed in such programs, the lower is the natural rate of unemployment. However, most economists feel that such programs are flawed. While they are advocated as a means of giving work to the unemployed and supplying needed public services, the efficiency of the system is highly questionable.

Policies to reduce the natural rate of unemployment and other supply-side actions are attractive and are welcomed by all observers. But, as this chapter has brought out, it is far from clear which policies offer the best prospects. Those who believe that inflation results primarily from poor governmental policies would like such programs reduced to a minimum. They place their trust in the existing markets. Government programs to assist investment and saving would improve productivity, but that can best be accomplished by lowering taxes and increasing incentives. The natural rate of unemployment will determine price acceleration or deceleration. It can be reduced by cutting back the minimum wage, welfare, and unemployment benefits.

Economists who believe that poor price-wage performance and slow growth result from the institutional structure of the economy see other possibilities. They would welcome more efficient government programs and policies, but would place more emphasis on improving the market structure and on areas in which government actions can improve on the free market. Their agenda is likely to include greater price competition, better information, increased investment in human capital, government aid to research and development, actions to increase price and supply flexibility in major contract markets, continued government concern with incomes policies and wage-price bargains. They want a more careful evaluation of the social benefits to be gained from regulations such as the minimum wage or unemployment compensation before these laws are targeted for major revisions.

Summary

1. Action to shift the supply curve can increase the rate of growth and can decrease the danger from supply shocks and from shortages and price increases in specific sectors, even as slack characterizes the overall economy.

2. While the general price level over the long run depends primarily on the level of unit labor costs—output per dollar of compensation—shifts in the relative prices of raw materials can cause price increases and inflation because other relative prices continue in an inflationary pattern.

3. Output grows as labor and capital inputs expand and as technology and the organization of production improve. Total factor productivity measures changes in output not due to an increase in inputs. It equals the amount of output per unit of input. Labor productivity—output per unit of labor—is influenced by changes in technology and by the amount and quality of labor.

4. Prices go up and growth declines when improvements in productivity slow down. Education and knowledge raise labor inputs and productivity. In the 1970s productivity fell because of an influx of younger, less skilled workers into the labor force; fewer economies of scale, and fewer workers shifting to better jobs; negative impact of the government; fewer improvements in knowl-

edge; and a failure of capital to expand as rapidly as before relative to labor growth.

5. Saving and investment can be increased by raising the aftertax return to savers and investors, by minimizing uncertainty, by specific tax breaks or subsidies, and by expanded government saving. Total investment and saving will not grow unless the demand for investments equals the increased desires to save at a higher level of aggregate demand.

6. Supply-side economics stresses the effects of tax incentives and disincentives on the amount of work, saving, and investment. How much supply shifts in response to a tax cut depends on how labor inputs are influenced and on the improvements in productivity gained through additional capital investment. The 1981 tax reductions were based on the view that lower taxes would increase the incentives to work, to save, and to invest by a great deal. This would increase output and reduce inflation.

7. When all types of investment and capital are taken into account, the largest share of current output goes to investments in human and other intangible capital. These forms have the highest yields and have led to much of the improvement in productivity.

8. The natural rate of unemployment depends on the amount of frictional and structural unemployment. The rate increased after 1955 because these types of unemployment were raised by demographic factors and disincentives were introduced into the system.

9. The natural rate can be reduced by improving the labor market, by increasing labor skills, increasing capital, and reducing disincentives for work.

Questions for Discussion and Review

1. What events during the 1970s have led economists to examine closely commodity prices when considering the aggregate supply curve?

2. What does making the aggregate supply curve more flexible mean? How might this be accomplished?

3. Why is it that "crude materials react sooner and with greater amplitude than other products to movements in demand?"

4. Explain how a supply shock, such as a sharp increase in energy prices, can trigger a recession. What policy problems are posed by such shocks for the monetary authorities?

5. What are the main factors influencing labor productivity? In particular, how have demographic trends in the 1970s affected labor productivity?

6. Explain the differences between labor productivity and total factor productivity.

7. Discuss the possibility of lowering unemployment by reducing wages.

8. Identify the three different types of unemployment. Are aggregate-demand management policies equally effective in dealing with all three?

9. What determines the natural rate of unemployment? Why has it shown a tendency to increase in recent years?

10. Identify and discuss three proposals for lowering the natural rate of unemployment.

11. Why is productivity growth considered so important? What do you suppose the long-run implications of very low productivity growth might be?

12. Why is there such universal agreement on the benefits of more capital investment?

13. Explain the argument of Martin Feldstein and others that the tax system is biased against saving and investment. What are the estimates of the effect on output of raising the gross investment rate from 10.5 to 12 percent?

14. What are the main proposals which have been advanced to increase saving and investment? Evaluate the probable effectiveness of each.

References

Antos, J., Mellow, W., and J. E. Triplett. "What is the Current Equivalent to Unemployment Rates of the Past?" *Monthly Labor Review* 12(March 1979): 36–45.

Blinder, A. S. *Economic Policy and The Great Stagflation.* New York, N.Y.: Academic Press, 1979.

Brookings Institution. *The Measurement of Productivity* (Reprint 244). Washington, D.C.: Brookings Institution, 1972.

Denison, E. F. *Accounting for Slower Economic Growth.* Washington, D.C.: Brookings Institution, 1979.

Gordon, R. J. "The Impact of Aggregate Demand on Prices." *Brooking Papers on Economic Activity* 3(1975): 613–35.

Nordhaus, W., and J. Shoven. "A Technique for Analyzing and Decomposing Inflation." In *Analysis of Inflation, 1965–1974* edited by J. Popkin. Cambridge, Mass.: Balinger, 1977.

Perry, G. L. "Stabilization Policy and Inflation." In *Setting National Priorities* edited by H. Owen and C. L. Schultze. Washington: Brookings Institution, 1976.

Shapiro, E., and W. L. White. *Capital for Productivity and Jobs.* Englewood Cliffs, N.J.: Prentice-Hall, 1977.

Part 6

The International Economy

16

An Open Economy
and Exchange Rates

Until now, our model of the economy has been presented as though it operated independently of foreign influences. Domestic demand, supply, and prices have occupied the limelight. But the United States in fact buys and sells many goods and services abroad. It borrows and lends in international capital markets. Shocks from these international markets shift domestic aggregate demand and supply. Furthermore, when domestic output expands, induced spending occurs overseas as well as at home.

An economy with flows of goods and capital across its borders is called an **open economy.** A **closed economy** has no such movements. Over the years the United States economy has become more open. In the late 1940s, foreign imports made up less than 4 percent of the GNP. By 1970 this share had risen to 6 percent. By 1980, partly as a result of dependence on foreign oil at ever-increasing prices, the share of imports rose to 12 percent. The greater a country's dependence on foreign trade and financing, the stronger will be the shocks arising from foreign events to the domestic economy. The more interaction that exists with foreign markets, the greater the attention that must be given to the international sector in formulating domestic monetary and fiscal policies. Actions logical in terms of domestic needs in fact may have perverse results because of their effects on the balance of payments.

When foreign trade was a minor part of the economy, the United States had the luxury of being able to neglect the foreign impacts of its policies. But as the foreign sector has expanded, the United States finds itself increasingly in the situation long faced by many other countries with foreign trade comprising as much as 40 percent of their GNP. Our domestic policy can no longer be planned without considering the impact on the balance of payments. Money created to raise aggregate demand will result in more payments overseas. Domestic and international goals and policies may be in conflict. Foreign events may constrain output and income. Furthermore, the exchange rate of a currency affects the ability to buy goods abroad, their prices, and, therefore, domestic prices as well as the relative incomes of people who depend on exports or imports. A dilemma may arise if the equilibrium between aggregate demand and potential output is not at the point where nonofficial foreign payments and receipts are equal. This chapter examines these issues as follows:

Balance of payments.
Foreign exchange markets.
The exchange value of a currency.
Fixed or flexible exchange rates.
The International Monetary Fund and international reserves.
Eurodollars.
Gold.

As the box shows, the chapter is primarily concerned with the balance of payments and how changes in it affect international reserves and the exchange value of a currency. Chapter 17 deals with the relationships between domestic and foreign demand.

Balance of Payments

A country's **balance of payments** *(BOP)* is the measure of the flow of payments between it and all other countries. Payments cover trade, services, or movements of financial assets. The balance of payments accounts, like those of the GNP, are calculated by the Department of Commerce from a wide variety of reports and estimates. Their purpose is to summarize all economic transactions between residents of the United States and those of foreign countries. The balance of payments accounts are based on double-entry bookkeeping; every transaction involves both a receipt and a payment or, in accounting terms, a credit and a debit. The system is set up so that each transaction which provides us with more foreign currency (as, for example, exports) is recorded as a receipt or credit. The export of goods is the debit, and the fund received for the exports are credits and are listed as such in the accounts. Similarly, if the transaction is an import or one like an import—that is, the purchase of goods or services from abroad or investing in a foreign country which requires the purchase of foreign currencies—it is recorded as a payment or debit.

WHY WE CARE ABOUT THE BALANCE OF PAYMENTS

Changes in the balance of payments make news because they say something about the underlying demand and supply for a country's currency. People speak of balance of payments surpluses or deficits even though, by definition, the accounts themselves must balance. The situation is similar to the analysis of income determination. The balance of payments (BOP), like the GNP, is a statistical identity which must balance. However, the accounts may reflect unplanned and undesired accumulations or losses of official reserves. A country may be accumulating or losing claims against the rest of the world. If such changes continue, exchange rates will have to alter, or other action will have to be taken to bring the demand for and supply of foreign currencies back into balance. The difference (surplus or deficit) between a limited number of accounts is selected for special analysis on the assumption that such deficits may reflect a disequilibrium.

The problem is complex because the need for a country to alter its policies when some of its accounts are in deficit will differ widely from one period to another. The need for action depends on how willing other countries are to lend it money and hold its liabilities. In the 1950s, many countries accumulated official claims against the United States because private American firms were buying assets abroad. For a time, U.S. debts were welcomed; other countries wanted to acquire as many dollars in the United States as they could. But as time passed, these accumulations became troublesome. Countries watch each other the way banks watch their customers. Initially, they are happy to lend; but like any creditor, they begin to worry if they see a country's liabilities growing too fast. They wonder if they will be repaid. In this case, foreign countries became less willing to hold U.S. liabilities. The distrust of the dollar was evidenced in the demand of foreign countries that their excess holdings of dollars be purchased by the United States with gold. Under both the Bretton Woods system and the gold exchange standard (both of which will be explained shortly), countries agreed to hold their exchange rates within narrow limits by purchasing the excess foreign credits created as a result of BOP deficits with international reserves. For the United States, this meant selling gold to those countries unwilling to accumulate more dollars.

During the 1960s, the United States tried to adjust this situation by imposing direct controls over certain types of international payments. However, liabilities continued to expand, and foreign countries grew more apprehensive. As more gold was withdrawn, the United States became unwilling to pay its debts at the exchange rates which had been fixed in the immediate postwar period. In August 1971, it refused to transfer gold abroad in payment for foreign balances held in the United States. In December of that year, the United States officially devalued the dollar by raising the price of gold in terms of the dollar. The period of fixed exchange rates came to an end.

The problems facing the United States were signaled by movements in the balance of payments. Deficits led to the devaluation. In the same way, changes in the early 1970s appeared to signal basic disequilibriums between the dollar and the German mark and Swiss franc. The result was a shift in the exchange rate. Those who bought francs and marks and sold dollars in the early 1970s made sizable profits. On the other hand, during the same period, the dollar price of the French franc and the Swedish kroner and other Western European currencies did not change much. In 1981, the dollar strengthened. The price of most currencies in terms of the dollar fell. Some, such as the French franc and the Italian lira, sank to new lows against the U.S. dollar.

BALANCES WITHIN THE BALANCE OF PAYMENTS

Table 16.1 shows the balance of payments of the United States for the year 1980. The form of presentation emphasizes that the total balance of payments consists of many kinds of balances, each of which may throw some light on the question of a fundamental disequilibrium.

Current Account. The first item of the **current account** is one of the most familiar. Figures on exports and imports are released monthly. In 1980 our merchandise exports fell short of our imports by $27 billion. (Petroleum imports alone amounted to almost $80 billion.) The United States had a deficit in its merchandise balance of payments of this amount. But exports and imports of merchandise do not make up the entire current account. United States investments abroad earn income, and foreign holdings here pay dividends and interest. The United States, as a major creditor, earns far more than it pays. The income and payments of income from investments comprise the second row of the table. Tourism abroad has been a major U.S. expenditure since World War II. But in recent years more and more foreign tourists are visiting this country, providing a return flow of currencies. Goods must be transported and insurance on shipments paid. Other services are also bought and sold. Money is spent to maintain military forces abroad and for other related military transactions. All such goods and services are included in the category "Other services." When the total of these other earnings and expenditures is added to the trade balance, the net result is the balance on goods and services.

People in the United States as well as the government send remittances, pensions, grants, and other transfers abroad. These are shown as a separate line in the table. When added to the previous balance, the net is the balance on current account. This is one of the important balances because it must be paid for. If it is negative, the United States must transfer financial assets to foreigners. If it is positive, foreigners must transfer assets to the United States.

The Capital Account. The next major item in the table is the **capital account.** It includes borrowing or lending abroad. If the United States borrows or sells stock abroad, it is exporting securities or receiving credits in the account. Lending or investing abroad creates debits or negative flows. Private direct investments are payments for plants owned by U.S. corporations abroad, such as Ford Plants in England or Germany. The receipts come from purchases of corporate assets by foreign companies. Examples include the takeover and investment in the Saks Fifth Avenue stores by a British tobacco company or the establishment of Volkswagen plants in the United States. Portfolio investments are even larger than direct ones. United States banks lend abroad; foreign

TABLE 16.1   **United States Balance of Payments, 1980**
(billions of dollars)

Item	Credits (receipts)	Debits (payments)	Balance
Current account			
Merchandise trade	221.8	249.1	−27.3
Investment income			32.5
Other services			1.9
Balance on goods and services			7.1
Remittances, pensions, transfers,			
and U.S. grants			−7.0
Balance on current account			0.1
Capital account			
Direct investments	8.2	20.6	−12.4
Portfolio investments	23.2	50.6	−27.4
Government nonreserves	2.4	5.1	−2.7
Statistical discrepancy			35.8
Balance on capital account			−6.7
Balance of official reserve transactions			−6.6
Changes in official Reserve assets			
Increase in foreign official assets in U.S.			14.8
Increase in U.S. official reserves			8.2
Total financing of official reserve transactions			6.6

SOURCE: U.S. Department of Commerce.

Payments abroad for all goods, services, and remittances, as well as for loans, stock purchases, or investments, are debits in the U.S. accounts. Receipts for goods and services sold, lending by foreigners or their investments in the U.S. are credits. Balances on subaccounts are rarely zero. A surplus or deficit in the sum of the current and capital accounts must be balanced by changes in official reserves.

banks lend in the United States. Americans buy Canadian bonds; Canadians purchase stock on Wall Street. Some foreign government entities also borrow and lend here; they may be drilling oil wells or building steel plants. Such operations reflect capital movements by governments, but they are not part of the official reserve transactions.

A statistical discrepancy similar to that in the GNP arises, but it is often much larger. The balance of payments must balance, but reported transactions are frequently incomplete. People who are illegally transferring their money out of a South American or Middle Eastern dictatorship go to great lengths to conceal all traces of their actions. Reports of money spent by tourists abroad are based on small samples with large errors. Importers and exporters may not give accurate data to customs officers. For all of these reasons, statistical discrepancies arise. In years of political turmoil, such as 1980, large amounts of unreported capital are transferred to the United States as a safe haven.

Official Reserve Transactions.   The sum of the balance on current and capital accounts equals the balance of *official reserve transactions.* This is what many people call *the* balance of payments. A negative flow in this account is the most common definition of a balance-of-payments deficit. If the sum of the current and capital account is negative, the deficit must be financed either by transferring official reserve assets to foreign governments or by the accumulation of official reserves in the United States by foreign governments. If the sum is positive, the United States will, on balance, accumulate additional foreign reserves. The funds held by central banks generally acceptable for payments to other governments are called their *international reserves.* These sums are available to cover deficits in the balance of payments. They can be sold either in foreign exchange markets or directly to foreign governments or central banks. The *official reserve assets* of the United States consist of gold, foreign currencies, and its reserve position in the International Monetary Fund (IMF) plus special claims against the Fund called special drawing rights, or SDRs. In addition, foreign governments (including central banks) hold official assets in the United States in the form of currency, treasury notes, or deposits at the Federal Reserve or at commercial banks.

Periodically, experts have revised the way in which the accounts are published, with a view to improving the picture they present. None of these attempts has been successful because the balances which are significant change from period to period. As a result, international lenders and traders stress the need to avoid trying to find a single critical surplus or deficit or to attach too much weight to any single figure. Instead, they emphasize the need to examine the many relationships which can be dug out of the balance-of-payments accounts.

Foreign-Exchange Markets

When New Englanders buy Chevrolets, they pay for them in dollars. Auto workers in Detroit and steel and glass workers in Pittsburgh are paid in dollars. But what if Toyotas rather than Chevrolets are purchased? Japanese auto workers need yen since dollars are not a common medium of exchange on the streets of Tokyo. The problem can be solved by an exchange between those who have yen and want dollars and those who have excess dollars and want yen. Trading of dollars and yen in fact takes place in a worldwide foreign exchange market. The rate at which such trading occurs is called an *exchange rate.* More precisely, an exchange rate is the number of units of one country's currency that exchanges for a unit of another currency. In March 1981, a trader could buy 209 yen for one U.S. dollar, or a yen could buy .48 U.S. cents.

Payment for production of goods in one currency and sales in another can cause problems. A Toyota costs 1.76 million yen delivered in Boston. If the exchange rate for yen fluctuates every day, what dollar price should a dealer quote? To minimize such problems, from the end of World War II to 1973, most trading nations attempted to fix the price of their currencies in terms of the dollar. Central banks stood ready to buy excess dollars or sell their own currencies at a *fixed exchange rate.* The Bank of Japan, for example, stood ready to buy all dollars offered at roughly 360 yen each and to sell all yen demanded for about .28 cents. Since 1973, the industrial democracies have operated instead on a *flexible exchange rate* system. The foreign exchange markets determine the price of currencies, and they move from moment to moment. If they move too fast, however, central banks will intervene. They will buy excess dollars or sell their own currency for dollars or other assets.

The relationship between a country's balance of payments, the exchange value of its currency, and its international reserves is extremely close. If a country runs a balance-of-payments deficit, the exchange rate for its currency will fall unless it can be propped up or the rate can be pegged by the use of international monetary reserves. Unless it can be corrected, disequilibrium in the balance of payments makes necessary a change in the exchange rate. Why do such shifts in the exchange rate matter? Isn't the rate simply a price like many others? Isn't our system run by allowing relative prices to change?

The answer is that the exchange rate is far more significant than most other prices because it affects almost all other prices within the country. If the dollar buys fewer yen, the price of a Toyota will rise compared to American cars. Oranges can be delivered in Japan at lower prices. It becomes easier for the United States to sell machine tools in Brazil in competition with Japanese machine tool-makers. As a result, U.S. exporters are better off and U.S. consumers and importers are worse off when the price of the dollar drops in terms of yen. In addition, fluctuating exchange rates may make trade riskier and will therefore reduce the amount of trade and the advantages to be gained from it. For these reasons, as well as those of international prestige, most countries have felt it necessary to deal with actual or potential movements in exchange rates by employing a wide variety of special policies aimed specifically at the international markets for trade and exchanges.

THE PRICE OF A DOLLAR

In Chapter 2, the price of a dollar was defined in terms of its purchasing power—the real goods it could buy—the reciprocal of its price index. We now define it in a second way which has a close theoretical relationship to the earlier definition, but which can lead to considerable differences in the short or even intermediate run. The price of the dollar in the foreign exchange market is the rate at which it trades with all other currencies. This rate is set minute by minute as the result of supply and demand in the currency markets. While the market for dollars is multilateral, consisting of all foreign demand and supplies, it is simpler to explain what happens in terms of bilateral currency exchanges. For example, we can think of a market as that between the dollar and the yen, or the dollar and the mark. Actually, however, all bilateral exchange markets are intertwined. Arbitrage takes place constantly among all of them. Traders stand ready to buy in one market and sell almost simultaneously in another if they can make a profit. The exchange rate of the dollar today may be sharply affected by sales of South African gold to Saudi Arabia or similar exchanges that have nothing to do with the United States.

The foreign exchange market is diffuse. It consists of the computers, telephones, and telexes in the international banks and offices of the money brokers of the world. They are constantly making trades, buying and selling all kinds of currencies, with most of the trading taking place in terms of dollars. Someone in Germany wanting to buy yen will buy dollars with their marks and then buy yen with the dollars. Foreign exchange markets never close; they move from London to New York to Tokyo to Singapore and back to London. Tremendous amounts of currencies trade daily. The volume of sales has been estimated at over 50 trillion dollars a year, a figure more than 25 times the total amount of international trade.

SUPPLY OF AND DEMAND FOR FOREIGN EXCHANGE

Let us examine an exchange market in more detail. The market for German marks and U.S. dollars is illustrated in Figure 16.1. This diagram shows the quantity of German marks that will be demanded in a time period (a day, week, or year) by holders of dollars at different prices for a mark in dollars. The demand for marks comes from people who want the German currency to buy a Mercedes, to import Rhine wine, to travel in the Black Forest, or to hold marks in a Frankfurt bank as a speculation against a future drop in the value of the dollar. The market's supply of marks comes from those who want to obtain dollars for the marks they now hold. Lufthansa may buy a Boeing 747, a German bank a new computer, a grocer in Hamburg some Florida oranges, or a German tourist may visit Washington and San Francisco. The equilibrium price set in the exchange market is that needed to clear the market at the point of equality between demand and supply. Thus, at point A in Figure 16.1, at a price of 50 cents per mark, all those who want to trade marks for dollars and vice versa are satisfied.

What if the demand for marks rises because sales in the United States of Rhine wine increase or because more Americans decide to travel in Germany? The demand for marks will shift up to the right; this is shown at point B in the diagram. With the higher demand, Americans will have to pay 55 cents for each mark. Germans will pay less for their dollars and, therefore, for American machine tools, computers, chemicals, or whatever else they buy with their cheaper dollars.

FIXED EXCHANGE RATES

What if the German government decides it would prefer to see the dollar price of the mark remain fixed at 50 cents? Many reasons for such a desire can be cited. The government may feel that the rise in the demand for marks is temporary; it may be caused by speculators, or by a poor California wine year,

FIGURE 16.1   **A Foreign Exchange Market**

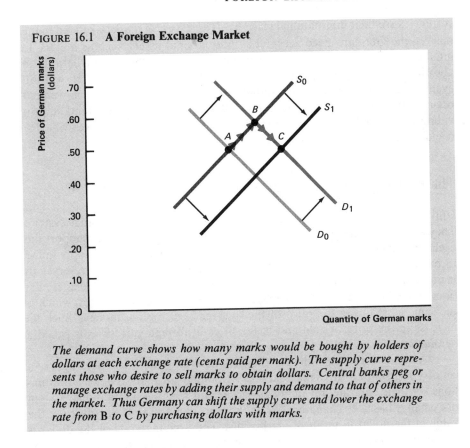

The demand curve shows how many marks would be bought by holders of dollars at each exchange rate (cents paid per mark). The supply curve represents those who desire to sell marks to obtain dollars. Central banks peg or manage exchange rates by adding their supply and demand to that of others in the market. Thus Germany can shift the supply curve and lower the exchange rate from B to C by purchasing dollars with marks.

or by a cyclical peak in output in the United States leading to a surge of orders for German steel. The government may believe that it would be bad for German workers if the Mercedes and Volkswagens were priced out of the U.S. market because of a short-run aberration in rates. The German government can fix the mark-dollar rate by increasing the supply of marks. Every time the price starts to rise toward *B* in the figure, it can increase the supply of marks (increase the demand for dollars) by buying Treasury bills in the United States. In effect, the government action shifts the supply curve to the right by buying dollars for marks; it thus moves equilibrium to point *C*. At that point, more marks are traded, but the price remains 50 cents. If the demand for marks from the private market now falls, and the price begins to decline below 50 cents, the government can raise demand for marks back to the 50 cents level by purchasing marks with its dollars.

Markets where central banks buy and sell their currencies at a specific price are said to have fixed, or pegged, exchange rates. The central banks support the prices of their currencies or hold them down by buying or selling in the exchange market. They add or remove supplies in order to prevent changes in the exchange rate. The funds which central banks use to purchase their currencies are their international reserves. If an excess of marks is offered in the market, the Germans need acceptable international assets, such as dollars, to intervene in the market. If they run out of reserves, they won't be able to absorb all the excess supply of marks. The dollar price of the mark will fall even if the country desires to maintain a fixed rate. The opposite movement occurs if they become unwilling to take additional dollars off the market, providing the United States has no marks or other acceptable reserves which it could use to absorb the excess dollars.

The Exchange Value of a Currency

Until 1971, most major industrial nations operated on a fixed exchange system. They announced the gold or dollar price at which they planned to support the exchange rate for their currency. If at that price the demand and supply failed to balance, they sold or bought their currency with international reserves to maintain the pegged price. If they ran short of reserves, they would increase the price of gold or equivalently increase the price of foreign currencies, which is the same as reducing the price of their currency in foreign money. Such an increase in the price of gold and in the price of foreign currencies is called a *devaluation* of a currency.

An understanding of the forces which determine the exchange value of a country's currency forms a necessary background to an analysis of why devaluations—or their opposite, revaluations—occur and why the international system of exchange has been changing. When the costs of marks in U.S. cents rises, the value of the dollar in terms of marks falls. The exchange rate of the dollar is said to have *depreciated.* The opposite movement, *appreciation,* is reflected by the higher value of the mark in terms of dollars. Between 1968 and 1980, the price of a mark rose from 25 cents to 58 cents. The mark appreciated in value by 130 percent, or the dollar depreciated to where it was worth about 40 percent of its previous value in marks.

THE DETERMINATION OF VALUES IN EXCHANGE

What determines the exchange value of the dollar? One notion is that the exchange rate of a national currency is the price which, in the absence of transportation costs, trade barriers, and differential risks, will cause the price of similar goods in each of the world's markets to be more or less equal. This theory is called the *purchasing power parity theory.* The reasoning behind the theory is intuitively simple. If the prices of similar goods differed significantly among nations, arbitrage opportunities would exist. Traders would buy goods where they were cheaper and ship them to where they would bring higher prices. They would profit thereby. In the markets in which they were buying, prices would rise, while the prices would fall where they sold. Their demand for currency to buy goods would cause the money of the first country to appreciate and that of the second to fall. Goods and currency markets would come into equilibrium when arbitrage was no longer profitable. As we shall see, this explanation has a good deal of validity, but it must be expanded to put more emphasis on capital movements and expectations of future values if it is to explain satisfactorily movements in exchange rates.

THE EXCHANGE RATE AND THE BALANCE OF PAYMENTS

The picture of the demand for foreign goods and capital assets arising from differences in the prices in many nations gives a clue as to the relationships existing among the balance of payments, exchange rates, and international reserves. If a country pegs its exchange rate at too low a level, the demand for its goods and assets will be high. To maintain a fixed rate, it will have to purchase large quantities of international reserves in order to make enough of its currency available to those who want goods at the bargain rate it is offering.

If a country runs a chronic balance-of-payments surplus, its currency is said to be **undervalued.** In the example of Figure 16.1, for Germany to peg the mark at point C when equilibrium was at B would require it to buy and hold dollars. The mark would be undervalued, which is the equivalent of saying that the dollar is **overvalued.** The dollar's exchange rate would be too high (the price of marks in cents too low) to generate the necessary demand for U.S. goods and capital assets.

For a country to maintain an overvalued currency, as a rule it must finance the resulting balance-of-payments deficit. It does this by using its international reserves to buy the excess supply of its money which results from a balance-of-payments deficit at the fixed rate. An exception to this rule requiring a country to have reserves in order to finance its balance-of-payments deficits has been the U.S. dollar. Because most countries accepted the dollar as a reserve which they could trade elsewhere, when the dollar became overvalued in the 1950s foreign countries absorbed—at first willingly, later unwillingly—the excess dollars in the exchange markets.

THE VOLATILITY OF EXCHANGE RATES

A general picture of the exchange value of the dollar is shown in Figure 16.2, which illustrates movements in the trade-weighted value of the dollar. This index averages the changes in the exchange rate of the dollar against ten other currencies. The weights used to make the index are based on the amount of U.S. trade with each of these countries. The value of the dollar fell approximately 20 percent in the two years after the fixed exchange system was abolished in 1971. Its value then rose, but after 1977 it declined again. By the spring of 1981 it had returned to its 1971 value. The drop in the trade-weighted value of the dollar was, however, much less than its drop in the comparison with the German mark. This difference is explained by the fact that the Canadian dollar and the Mexican peso, as well as the currencies of other major trading partners of the United States, experienced still larger depreciations than did the U.S. dollar.

Figure 16.2 shows rapid movements in the trade-weighted exchange value of the dollar. Exchange rates after 1973 show much wider movements than can be explained by the purchasing power parity theory. Ups and downs of 10 or 15 percent in exchange rates within a few months are not unusual. In 1974, the exchange value, corrected for movements in purchasing power (which should be relatively stable since it already corrects for differences in the purchasing power parity) went up and down 10 percent in a few months. From 1976 through 1978, the real value of the dollar, corrected for relative price changes, fell over 20 percent. A comparison of the rates between the dollar and the individual major currencies shows still wider movements. In the last half of 1976, sterling fell 25 percent in relation to the dollar. It then returned to its previous height.

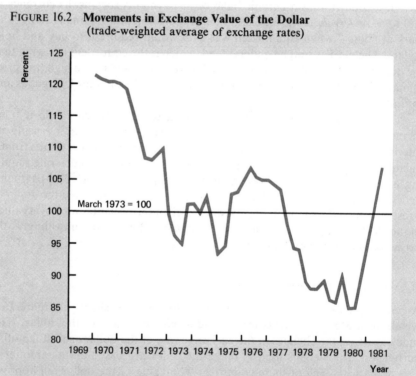

FIGURE 16.2   **Movements in Exchange Value of the Dollar**
(trade-weighted average of exchange rates)

In a world with a multiplicity of exchange rates, movements in the exchange value of the dollar are measured by a weighted average of changes in individual rates. The weights used in the figure are based on the amount of U.S. international trade conducted with each major country as a share of total U.S. trade. Changes in the dollar's exchange value of 5 to 10 percent in a year have been common.

SOURCE: Federal Reserve Bulletin.

Such volatility would seem to suggest that exchange rates must reflect factors other than merely the month-to-month movements in price indexes, which are much smaller than those of the exchange rates. Exchange rates in fact do reflect changes in the underlying demand and supply situation in both the goods and money markets. A good or bad crop year, cyclical changes in income, the rise to power of a new political party, differences in productivity and tastes all influence exchange rates. One factor increasing the magnitude of shifts is that financial assets as well as goods move across borders. Exchange rates must equate not only the relative prices of goods, but also those of money and other assets. Sharp changes in exchange rates occur when investors and speculators reevaluate the desirability of holding their funds in different markets. Values in each market change with expected prices of goods, but also with such factors as interest rates, fear of controls, political instability, and wars. Expectations of such variations can shift drastically, even in the course of a day. This means that sharp movements in exchange rates are not really unexpected.

THE MONETARY APPROACH TO EXCHANGE RATES

One broad view of equilibrium in the exchange markets is the monetary approach. It emphasizes the important influence on exchange rates of money, interest rates, and capital flows. Differences in monetary growth rates among countries cause exchange-rate movements. Since the supply of money affects aggregate demand, it will influence future movements in prices and interest rates and the demand for goods and assets. Exchange rates reflect expectations of future prices and interest rates. Since financial assets can move easily across borders, they play an especially important role in exchange movements. Observers of foreign exchange markets, noting differential growth in the stock of money of two countries, will use this information to predict the effect of the money supply on future demand and prices. They then move exchange rates in such a way as to equate at once both the market for goods and for financial assets. As noted, inventory adjustments in the financial markets are cheaper and more rapid than in that for goods.

The equilibrium between financial assets in two countries requires an adjustment based on two factors: (1) relative interest rates in the two countries and (2) expected changes in their exchange rates. Suppose, for example, that General Motors must decide whether to hold some excess funds in Toronto or New York. It sees no difference in the riskiness of funds in the two markets, and therefore makes its decision purely on the basis of which investment offers the highest return. Which investment is better depends on both interest rates in the two countries and on the expected percentage changes in the exchange rates. Let i_{US} be the rate of return on one-year Treasury bills in New York; i_C is the rate for Canadian bills; and $E\dot{X}C$ is the expected percentage change in the exchange rate. Equilibrium exists when

$$i_{US} = i_C + E\dot{X}C. \qquad\qquad \textbf{16.1}$$

If interest rates in Canada are higher, it will pay to hold money there unless the exchange value of the Canadian dollar is expected to fall. Money should move back and forth between Canada and the United States until the current exchange rate differs from the expected one by just the interest differential.

TWO CAUSES OF DISEQUILIBRIUM

Equation 16.1 shows that movements in current exchange rates (the spot rate) can arise either because interest rates in the two countries alter or because expected future exchange relationships change. Let us consider exchange-rate movements first. New information about relative movements in the money supply of the two countries or in their prices or trade balances or political elections may lead to anticipation that future exchange rates will differ from current ones. This would be reflected immediately in current exchange rates and in decisions by corporations as to where to hold their funds. The spot exchange rates would move, and the move could be very sharp, in order to reflect changed expectations.

But a second possibility also exists. What happens if the Bank of Canada decides to run a tighter monetary policy, with higher interest rates, than the Federal Reserve? Both rates start at 10 percent; the Canadian rates now jump to 14 percent ($i_C - i_{US} = 4\%$). If nothing affects exchange-rate expectations, it would pay firms to move funds to Canada. They could earn 4 percent higher interest rates. But as a result of such movements, the Canadian dollar would appreciate. How high would the Canadian exchange rate have to rise? Equilibrium would exist when current exchange rates exceeded expected future rates sufficiently so that the loss from holding Canadian dollars through the exchange differential would exactly equal the extra amount earned by holding Canadian rather than American financial assets.

The necessary response of movements in assets and exchange rates to interest-rate differentials shows how countries can use domestic monetary policy to increase international reserves. Higher interest rates attract foreign funds from investors who seek the best market in which to hold money. Under fixed exchanges, one of the many adjustment techniques used to reduce a balance-of-payments deficit was to raise interest rates. When sterling was the principal international currency, it was said that a high enough bank rate in London would pull money off the moon. With flexible rates, actions are less predictable, since investors must estimate expected movements in future exchange rates in order to compare them to the interest differential. The effect of an announced change in monetary policy will depend on the market's estimate of how long it will be maintained and how it will affect incomes and prices and, therefore, future exchange rates.

Fixed or Flexible Exchange Rates

Some of the most vehement arguments in the international arena have been fought over the relative advantages of fixed and flexible exchange rates. On the whole, economists have supported a flexible system, while men of affairs— bankers, international traders, government officials—have preferred fixed rates. The background of this debate is the history of the international exchange system, including the gold standard, the gold-exchange standard, the par-value (Bretton Woods) system, and—currently—flexible (floating) exchanges.

Under the **gold standard,** a unit of a country's currency was convertible into a fixed quantity of gold. Governments freely bought or sold gold at a fixed price. The country's money stock was rigidly tied to its gold supply. The **gold-exchange standard** was a modification whereby countries maintained the convertibility of their currencies into a fixed quantity of gold, but also held reserves other than gold (for instance, dollars). The amount of their gold and international reserves influenced but did not control monetary policy.

Under the **par-value** or **adjustable-peg system,** governments established the exchange rate of their currencies in terms of the dollar or of gold. They then intervened in the foreign exchange markets to maintain the exchange rate within narrow limits around its par. If a fundamental disequilibrium developed in their balance of payments, they would adjust the par value (the peg) at which they supported their exchange rate.

Under the **flexible exchange system,** exchange rates are set freely in accordance with the supply of and demand for a country's currency. Governments do not intervene in the exchange market. Most countries, however, use a modified version in which they continue to buy or sell some of their currency in the market to dampen movements. This technique is called a **managed float,** or sometimes a **dirty float.**

THE GOLD STANDARD

For most of the nineteenth and twentieth centuries, major Western industrialized countries operated on the assumption that all would be better off if they maintained fixed exchange rates. Until 1930 most countries maintained fixed rates by operating on the gold or gold-exchange standard. The gold standard acted as a semi-automatic method of insuring that the international demand for and supply of a currency balanced at a fixed rate. Thus, until 1933, the U.S. Treasury would buy or sell to anyone $\frac{1}{21}$ of an ounce of gold for a dollar. In the same way, the Bank of England bought and sold gold at a price of $\frac{1}{4}$ ounce per pound sterling.

The willingness of the two governments to buy and sell gold insured that the dollar price of a pound sterling in the exchange markets would remain just about at parity. Parity could be calculated from the cross rates of each country's currency against gold. In the case of the United States and the United Kingdom, this meant a parity of approximately $5 per pound. If the price of a pound rose above $5 in the exchange markets, traders had an alternative; instead of paying $5.10 for a pound, they could have purchased ¼ ounce of gold for $5, shipped it to London, and then sold the gold to the Bank of England to get their pound. As long as the two countries were willing to buy and sell gold at fixed prices, their exchange rates could not diverge more than the transaction cost of shipping gold in either direction. The actual exchange rates fluctuated within the "gold shipping points," which were a few cents removed from the exchange rate found by calculating the separate parities.

The second feature of the gold standard was the willingness of a country to tie its money stock rigidly to gold. The country's money supply expanded and contracted automatically in conformity with movements of its gold holdings.

LESS RIGID FIXED EXCHANGE SYSTEMS

Because a shortage of gold meant that nations had to economize on the world's gold supply and because countries found that they did not need to adhere to a rigid relationship between their money stock and gold, many countries moved to the gold-exchange standard in the early 1900s. They held some reserves in foreign markets—say, in Treasury bills which earn interest—and made these reserves available when their international accounts were in deficit. The ability of a country to furnish reserves depended on its willingness to alter domestic financial markets, prices, and income when it was losing gold (or the opposite when its gold stock was rising). Chapter 17 explains how countries can shift domestic policy to increase the demand for their currencies in foreign exchange markets. A country which desired to stay on the gold-exchange standard had to operate in accordance with procedures that would insure that it did not run out of gold or other international reserves. These procedures are called "the rules-of-the-gold-standard game." But at critical times, countries would break the rules; they would suspend gold sales. Demand and supply would no longer balance at the fixed price. Exchange rates would move. The Great Depression of the 1930s was closely related to a breakdown of the gold-exchange standard. Countries found that when they had reached the limit of their ability to deflate, they still could not meet international payments at the fixed rate. As a result, most countries either adjusted their purchasing price for gold or completely abandoned the gold-exchange standard.

In 1944, as World War II was drawing to a close, the countries of the free world met in an international conference at Bretton Woods, New Hampshire, to see if they could construct a system that would avoid the pitfalls of the gold-exchange standard while enabling international trade to expand at an optimum pace. The International Monetary Fund and the par-value or Bretton Woods system (as well as the International Bank) were the products of this conference. The Fund and the par-value system made possible readjustments of exchange rates by international agreement. Countries in temporary balance-of-payments difficulty could borrow international reserves from the Fund. If a fundamental change took place in a country's international economic relations, the exchange rate could be altered. It was hoped that by allowing flexible adjustment, a breakdown of the system such as occurred in the 1930s could be avoided.

Under this system, countries agreed to intervene in order to maintain a stable exchange rate for their currencies by buying and selling dollars, usually when their price rose or fell by more than 1 percent from their fixed price or parity. In turn, the United States agreed to buy and sell gold to other countries at a fixed par value ($35 an ounce). The United States was placed at the center of the system because it held most of the world's monetary gold. In effect, every country's currency was convertible indirectly into gold at a fixed price, under the terms of these agreements. If the demand for a country's currency was weak, it had to prevent its currency's price from falling below its lower support price by buying up the excess supply with dollars, as in the example of Figure 16.1. Whether or not a country could intervene depended on its supply of dollars or its ability to get dollars, either by selling gold or by borrowing some from a country with extra dollars or from the International Monetary Fund.

In the opposite case, if a country's currency was strong, it was obliged to intervene by selling its currency (purchasing dollars in the open market) to hold down its price in terms of dollars. If it so desired, it could then use its excess dollars to buy gold from the United States. In theory, the effect of the intervention of central banks in the exchange market through the dollar (the intervention currency) would be the same as stabilizing a country's exchange rate within its upper and lower support prices by shipping gold, as was done under the gold standard.

THE DEMISE OF FIXED RATES

The fixed-rate system came under constant attack during the 1960s. It was generally recognized that the British pound and the American dollar were overvalued. For fixed exchange rates to work, prices and incomes among countries must be synchronized. If prices rise too fast in the United States and exchange rates are fixed, Americans will not be able to sell as much abroad; their imports of foreign goods whose prices are not rising will increase. Large deficits in the balance of payments will have to be financed by flows of official reserves. While a country losing reserves can try to lower prices or income, or can use direct controls or other adjustment mechanisms, it is more likely to decide, as these become more expensive, in favor of lowering exchange rates.

When it becomes clear that exchange rates are probably out of line, speculation makes a change in the rates almost a self-fulfilling prophecy. Firms can see that a country may have to lower the value of its currency in the exchange markets, and they will therefore sell the currency. A U.S. firm, believing that the price of dollars in marks will drop, will buy marks. If the rate is 4 marks to the dollar, the firm can buy 4 million marks with $1 million; if the rate then becomes 2 marks per dollar, it can buy back $2 million with its marks, and it will have doubled its money.

In the 1960s, the dollar was in trouble. Germany and Japan had rebuilt their economies devastated by World War II and were enjoying much faster increases in productivity. This lowered the prices for their goods. A fixed exchange meant that they could sell abroad for less. At the same time, inflation induced by the war in Vietnam raised prices in the United States. Controls were imposed over exports of capital, but still the likelihood that the dollar would have to be devalued rose steadily. Between 1958 and 1971, the United States lost over 60 percent of its gold reserves, as countries used their right under the Bretton Woods agreements to buy gold with the excess dollars they accumulated in the course of buying up the large oversupply of dollars in their exchanges. (They had to purchase the dollars in order to maintain their currency prices at the fixed rate.) But in spite of exchanging the dollars for gold, the dollar holdings of foreign countries continued to grow. They became much larger compared to the remaining U.S. gold holdings. Consequently, central banks felt forced to convert their dollars into gold; they did not want to be caught in line when the gold window slammed down in front of them.

As the situation became increasingly acute, private speculators saw the writing on the wall and began to sell dollars at a rapid rate. Finally, in August 1971, the United States refused to buy any more dollars with gold. In the following two years, many attempts were made to maintain fixed exchange rates at new parities. Official devaluations of the dollar in terms of gold were carried out in 1971 and 1973, but these were not sufficient to bring about exchange stability. The price of the dollar in the exchange markets was then allowed to float.

THE ARGUMENT FOR FIXED RATES

During the period when the dollar was under pressure and in the period of floating rates, there was a running debate between those who felt that the world would be better off if fixed exchanges could be maintained and those who advocated floating rates as the better system. The proponents of fixed exchanges believe that they encourage more and better international trade and constitute a major deterrent to internal inflation. International trade at its best faces many hurdles. Removing the uncertainty of future exchange rates is a big plus. For example, an exporter can plan production, knowing what price he will receive in his domestic currency. Domestic inflation is curbed because, with fixed exchange rates, domestic prices must stay in line with foreign ones. A country cannot resort to inflationary internal policies and at the same time maintain fixed rates. If its prices rise too rapidly, exports will fall and imports rise. While at first, the balance-of-payments deficits may be financed by using available reserves, eventually reserves will run low. To maintain a fixed exchange rate, countries will have to deflate to bring their balance of payments and reserves back into line.

THE ARGUMENTS FOR FLEXIBLE RATES

The pressure to deflate argument for fixed rates was also used against them by the advocates of flexible rates. Fixed rates may require drastic internal deflationary measures to adjust to external price and income pressures. These pressures develop if internal and external incomes and prices move along different paths. Flexible exchanges give countries more autonomy for monetary and fiscal policy. They need not move in lock step with other economies. Flexible rates remove governments from the market. They will not have to develop policies (likely to be controls) to maintain fixed rates. People who fear price fixing and government interference in domestic markets do not see how they can be justified in the exchange markets. A fixed exchange rate is merely another major example of price controls.

A pure flexible-exchange-rate system reduces the need for reserves and BOP policies. Demand can be expanded or contracted to assure a balance of domestic prices and output. Whenever full employment is reached, a floating exchange rate equates the foreign currencies demanded by domestic purchasers of foreign goods, services, and financial assets with the available supply. The exchange rate adjusts to assure that, at the market price, dollars offered exactly equal those demanded.

Floating exchange rates make it less likely that inflation and deflation will be transmitted across borders. With floating rates, if England inflates too much, the value of its currency in foreign exchange will fall. Because it must pay more pounds to obtain an equal number of dollars or marks, the pound price of its imports will rise. Therefore, imports will no longer be a comparative bargain, as they are when domestic prices rise and exchange rates are fixed. The drop in the value of the pound in foreign currencies means that the rising prices of English export goods will be offset. Because Germans or Americans get more pounds in the exchanges, they can pay the higher prices in England without increasing the number of dollars or marks they offer. The delivered price of exports stays stable; they remain competitive in Frankfurt or New York.

However, while floating rates avoid some of the problems of fixed exchanges, they engender other costs. When the value of a country's currency declines, the prices of imports rise, causing increases in the consumer price level. Higher prices reinforce inflationary pressures which arise from more expansive monetary policy made possible by the abandonment of the fixed-exchange-rate discipline. Another difficulty occurs because a rise in the price of foreign currencies reduces the amount of foreign goods that can be obtained in trade for domestic output. Thus it costs a Kansas farmer more bushels of wheat to secure a Toyota pickup truck when the dollar buys fewer yen.

To many, however, the most vital defect in flexible rates is their increased volatility, which results in reductions of international trade. A fluctuating exchange rate hampers international trade because the firms involved in a future international deal will not know what prices they will receive in their own currencies. While such uncertainty can be controlled up to a point, through operations in the forward exchange market, such hedges against future shifts in exchange rates are reasonable only for short periods, primarily three or six months. Figure 16.2 showed that foreign exchange rates have become quite volatile. This means that prices of internationally traded goods also shift. Producers and consumers find that their incomes and the demand for their work fluctuate because of the exchange-rate movements. The greater volatility imposed on domestic output and the resulting income distortions are major drawbacks of the flexible exchange system.

The International Monetary Fund and International Reserves

The previous sections have indicated the importance of international reserves. Countries which have them can use them to maintain a fixed exchange rate or to assure that market changes in expectations will not cause wild day-to-day fluctuations in this critical price. If they have sufficient reserves, they can avoid being forced to take drastic action to adjust their balance-of-payments accounts (see Chapter 17). They can finance their deficits by furnishing the excess of demand for foreign currencies from their existing balances without reducing their exchange rates; or if their BOP is in surplus, they can accumulate additional international reserves.

When countries lack reserves, the system gets into trouble. Recognizing that gold would be inadequate to support the hoped-for postwar level of international trade, the planners at Bretton Woods gave the International Monetary Fund several functions designed to enable it to provide reserves to individual countries when they were in trouble and also to provide the international monetary system with additional liquidity (reserves). The IMF performs three major functions:

1. The Fund provides a machinery for international monetary cooperation, aiding in the establishment and management of exchange rates and exercising surveillance over the exchange rate policies of its members and, consequently, over trade, monetary, and fiscal policies which affect such rates.
2. It furnishes facilities whereby members can borrow international reserves.
3. It acts as a central bank for central banks, creating additional international reserves.

CONSULTATIONS AND CHANGES IN EXCHANGE RATES

The International Monetary Fund has directors elected by its member nations and an expert staff located in Washington. If a country gains or loses large amounts of reserves, it can consult with the Fund to see what actions it might take to improve its situation. Such consultations take into account necessary domestic actions, changes in exchange rates, and possible loans.

Prior to 1973, most major noncommunist countries had entered into agreements with the IMF to establish fixed exchange rates. When a country lost reserves it could agree, as part of its borrowing arrangement, to establish a new exchange rate. Countries which had excessive increases in reserves could also agree to revalue their undervalued currencies, although upward movements were rare. Since 1973, the IMF has been greatly concerned over the amount and type of intervention in which members engage. It is hoped that exchange-market intervention will be kept to a minimum and will not be used to gain unfair advantages through manipulation of the rates in the exchange markets. Group and individual meetings and consultations continue for the purpose of arriving at a better international monetary system.

BORROWING FACILITIES

To give countries more time in which to allow their policies to reduce BOP deficits to work, the IMF established facilities through which countries can borrow foreign currencies. Borrowers are subject to agreements to take action to restore their BOPs to equilibrium without impairing international trade. The IMF receives currencies it lends by deposits or "quotas" from its member countries. Quotas are allocated in accordance with a country's importance in international trade. Initially, they were paid for in gold and a country's own currency. When a country runs a deficit, the Fund can lend it currency from others to use in the exchange markets. Each additional loan of this kind carries more stringent agreements by a borrower to take domestic monetary and fiscal action to bring its BOP into balance.

With time, the Fund has established a number of special borrowing facilities to aid countries faced with special problems, such as a sudden drop in the price of a critical raw material export or the need to pay for petroleum imports when the soaring prices completely disrupted normal balance of payments. The total facilities of the IMF in 1980, including special drawing rights, were about $50 billion.

SPECIAL DRAWING RIGHTS—PAPER GOLD

One of the issues surrounding the founding and operations of the IMF was the degree to which it would act as a central bankers' central bank. Countries can create the reserves they need to operate a domestic banking system because every commercial bank must deposit its reserves at the central bank and must accept the reserves (or the government's currency) when tendered as a payment. In the same way, if all countries agree to accept some form of deposits at the IMF in payment for their BOP surpluses, these deposits have value and become a form of international reserve or money.

Under Bretton Woods, the international reserves of the world were gold, the dollar which could be used to buy gold, and the IMF's lending facilities. As world trade exploded in the 1960s and the dollar grew weaker, a shortage of reserves was feared. Production of gold fell far short of growth in trade.

International negotiations to create new international reserves took place during the last half of the 1960s, culminating in 1969 in the agreement to create *special drawing rights,* or *SDRs,* also known as "paper gold." SDRs are created by agreement of the member countries of the IMF. They are a new form of money, an international reserve asset. They are usable only by governments to settle international debts. The critical point is that members agree to accept SDRs (within negotiated limits) in payment of monies owed them through exchange transactions. The willingness of countries to hold and accept SDRs gives them value.

The price of SDRs was originally set in terms of gold. However, as a result of the semidemonetization of gold in the 1970s, the value of SDRs was reestablished as a weighted average or "basket" of 16 currencies. The dollar price of an SDR varies with the movement of the dollar in relation to the other currencies. Because it is based on an average, SDRs tend to be more stable in value than individual currencies. SDRs have replaced gold as the basic means of accounting and settlement among IMF members. The amount created and allocated to members is subject to negotiation. The SDRs lack the complete freedom of other reserves because countries which use them must agree to repurchase them (reconstitute their balances) over time up to some minimum percentage of their initial allocations.

SDRs also carry interest. The IMF credits countries with interest on their holdings of SDRs. However, countries must also pay interest on the amount they use, including their initial allocation. In effect, countries which actually use SDRs must pay interest to countries which accept and hold them. The interest rate is set at 80 percent of a weighted average in five national markets (the United States, the United Kingdom, Japan, France, and Germany). Because of restrictions placed on transfers of SDRs, because of their lower interest yields, and because of the reconstitution obligation, the SDR, however, is considered to be an inferior reserve asset compared to such currencies as the dollar or the mark.

Eurodollars

One post-World-War-II development that affects both the value of the dollar in international exchanges and its value in the United States is the growth of Eurodollars. *Eurodollars* are deposits denominated in dollars but not held on deposit at banks in the United States. Thus a deposit in Lloyd's Bank in London or in the Bank of Hong Kong and Shanghai in Hong Kong is a Eurodollar (although the latter is often called an Asian-dollar). The Eurodollar market has swelled as a result of the exchange restrictions and interest ceilings in the United States and other countries. It enables those with surplus funds to seek out markets throughout the world. Loans in these markets can be made in dollars rather than in local currencies, thus avoiding one type of exchange risk. Most major banks and multinational corporations engage in the Eurodollar market. Billions of dollars are traded. It is a very efficient market, with narrow interest-rate spreads between borrowing and lending.

A country's banks can issue liabilities in any currencies allowed by its legal system, not merely in its own national currency. Eurodollars are only one example. Bank deposits in currencies other than those of the country in which the bank is domiciled are given the generic term of **Eurocurrencies.** Thus a London branch of Citibank of New York could have deposits in U.S. dollars, German marks and Swiss francs, all of which would be considered as Eurocurrencies. Its pound sterling deposits, however, would not be Eurocurrencies.

The Eurodollar or Eurocurrency market started in the 1950s because the USSR feared it was accumulating dollars which might be subject to expropriation. It needed stocks of dollars if it were to engage efficiently in international trade, much of which takes place in dollars. For anyone in international trade, it is cheaper not to have to buy and sell dollars after every transaction. Exchange costs can be avoided by accumulating dollar balances. But the USSR did not want to hold such balances in the United States for fear of expropriation. (For example, the United States froze all Iranian balances in U.S. banks in 1979.) The problem was avoided by placing the money in English banks, which would accept dollar deposits in London.

THE CREATION OF EURODOLLARS

In Chapter 6 (Figure 6.3), we saw how a banking system can create deposits which holders look upon as money. The amount that can be created depends on the reserves needed to meet withdrawals. In the United States, the required ratio of deposits to reserves is set by Federal Reserve regulations, but in many systems minimum reserves are determined by the banks themselves. The reserves they need depend on how many checks are written against their deposit accounts, how many checks are redeposited in the bank compared with the number requiring funds to be transferred elsewhere, and the degree to which these demands for funds can be matched by claims resulting from deposits based on checks against other banks. In banking systems without legal reserve requirements, banks determine their minimum reserves from their experience with such flows. The deposit-to-reserve ratio for the entire Eurodollar system depends on the share of newly created deposits which remain inside the system compared with how much leaks out as a result of required payments through banks in the United States.

Table 16.2 compares the factors determining the ability to create Eurodollars with deposit expansion in the United States banking system. Figure 16.3 shows how this works. It is similar to Figure 6.3, which explained the domestic creation of money. In section *A* of the chart, Standard Oil of California has a deposit of $100 million with Bank of America in San Francisco It draws a check on this account to buy $100 million of oil from Saudi Arabia. That government, either directly or through its central or a commercial bank, deposits this check at Lloyd's Bank in London. Section *B* shows the new

TABLE 16.2   **What Sets the Limits on Creation of Eurodollars?**

Question	United States banking system	Eurodollar banking system
1. Who can create deposits?	Any bank in the United States	Any bank outside the United States.
2. Where are reserves held?	At the Federal Reserve	At commercial banks in the United States.
3. What reserves are required?	Set by Federal Reserve regulations.	Set by ability of banks to meet demands for funds.
4. What sets limits on expansion?	Amount of legal reserves and legal reserve requirements.	Amount of deposits held in U.S. banks and rate at which funds flow in and out of system.

The amount of deposits created by U.S. banks is controlled by the size of the monetary base and legal reserve requirements. The amount of deposits created by Eurodollar banks depends on the amount of reserves needed to meet demands for funds.

situation: $100 million of Eurodollars have been created as a result of the deposit in Lloyd's in London.

But Lloyd's has not accepted the deposit to hold money in San Francisco. It will make a loan—say, one of $80 million. The situation will be that shown in panel *C*. A total of $180 million Eurodollars has been created. In turn, the people who have received the loan from Lloyd's will spend it. Checks will be drawn and deposits will be made in other banks. They in their turn will make loans and lose funds until an equilibrium situation is reached, as in section *D*.

How many Eurodollars will be created? The answer depends on how fast money leaks out of the Eurodollar banking system and what reserve ratios the banks need to feel safe and able to supply dollars if called upon. The Eurodollar system is not as closed a system as are national banking systems; firms borrow and act in it because they are trading in international markets. Every time someone paid in Eurodollars deposits the funds in the United States, reserves will be lost to the system. When it hits a bank in the United States, the money is likely to be loaned in domestic markets rather than being returned abroad. The leakage is similar to that which happens when currency is withdrawn from the domestic system.

The final section of the figure shows $50 million still held by Eurodollar banks in San Francisco. Assuming that each Eurodollar requires a 20 percent reserve, the banking system will have created $250 million in Eurodollars, having made loans and investments of $200 million.

EURODOLLARS AND THE UNITED STATES MONEY SUPPLY

The existence of Eurodollars lessens the control of the Federal Reserve over the

FIGURE 16.3 **Expansion of Deposits**
(millions of dollars)

| | Bank of America | | Lloyds Bank of London | |
	Assets	Liabilities	Assets	Liabilities
A	Reserves 20 Notes 80	Demand deposit 100 (to Standard Oil of California)		
B	Reserves 20 Notes 80	Demand deposit 100 (to Lloyds Bank of London)	Deposit at Bank of America 100	Demand deposit 100 (to Saudi Arabia)
C	Reserves 20 Notes 80	Demand deposit 100 (to Lloyds Bank of London)	Deposit at Bank of America 100 Loan to Mexico 80	Demand deposits 180 (to Saudi Arabia 100; Mexico 80)
	⋮ ⋮	⋮	⋮	⋮
D	Reserves 10 Notes 40	Demand deposit 50 (to Eurodollar banks)	Deposits at Bank of America 50; Investments 100; Loans 100	Demand deposits 250

The creation of Eurodollars is analogous to that of domestic deposits (see Figure 6.3). However, the level of reserves maintained is set by experience rather than by legal requirements. Moreover, reserves are held in U.S. banks (or in the U.S. money market) rather than at the Federal Reserve.

money supply. Of an estimated total sum of $400 to $1,000 billion Eurodollars, no one knows exactly how much should be counted in the U.S. money stock. A dollar in London or Hong Kong or Frankfurt will not affect spending in the United States to the same extent as a dollar in Boston. But how much less the effect will be is uncertain.

In the 1980 revision of the money supply figures, the Fed removed from $M1$ deposits of foreign commercial banks and foreign governments in the United States; these would include some of the reserves behind Eurodollars: At the same time, it added to $M2$ and L certain Eurodollars held by U.S. nonbank residents abroad. The amounts which could be measured were limited by the availability of data; more will be included in the money stock when improved measurements become possible. Though better than nothing, the solution still leaves important gaps in the measurement of money. Some of the Eurodollars not counted serve as international reserves of foreign governments. Some influence spending in the United States directly. Some react on capital movements of both U.S. and foreign firms. The fact that all of these sums change, as well as their impact on U.S. spending, adds another force tending to create fluctuations in the measured velocity of money in the United States.

Gold

The 1970s began with gold prices making headlines nearly every day. The price of gold, which central banks had fixed for most of the previous 150 years, suddenly took off. The free-market price of gold had averaged $35.20 per ounce in 1969. It then rose to $186 in 1974 and fell to $135 in 1976. Then it began to boom. It rose to over $800 an ounce in early 1980. Gold prices fluctuated at between 10 and 25 times that at which they had been stabilized from 1934 through 1968. The price per ounce rose and fell by as much as $100 a day; often daily fluctuations were greater than the original fixed level. News of gold moved from a small report in the commodity tables carried in only the larger financial papers to the front page of almost every paper in the United States. It became a political issue as well, as supporters pushed for a return to the gold standard. What caused this phenomenon, and what was its significance?

GOLD AS MONEY

Gold has a long history. Egyptian tombs of 5,000 years ago as well as earlier ones elsewhere contained many gold artifacts. Gold is considered beautiful; it is durable, malleable, and easily worked. It does not rust or lose its value. Equally important, gold has always been scarce; it is found only in small quantities and requires a great deal of effort to mine. In the 1970s, gold production averaged under 40 million ounces per year. But gold has not been desired primarily for its worth in jewelry or the arts; its worth stems from its use as a portable store of value acceptable in trade throughout most of the world. The intrinsic value of gold and its monetary value have been closely intertwined.

When countries adopted gold as an international standard in the nineteenth century, they made their currencies convertible into gold. Under both the gold standard and the Bretton Woods system, gold acted as a discipline to maintain a sound currency. Countries could not expand their money stock and inflate their currencies because, if they did, they would lose their supplies of gold. If money income and prices rose too rapidly, they were forced to deflate in order to maintain convertibility; otherwise, their gold would drain abroad to finance their balance-of-payments deficits. For most of the nineteenth and twentieth centuries, the price of gold was fixed by the terms governments established. The industrial use of gold was minor. Some gold disappeared into hoards, but central banks were the marginal buyers throughout the period. The price of gold was that set by governments. Until 1933, the world price of gold was $20.65 per ounce, the price set by U.S. law.

In 1933, gold became nonconvertible in the United States. Citizens could not own or trade in gold except for industrial purposes. In an effort to reflate the U.S. economy and bring it out of the Great Depression, President Franklin D. Roosevelt arbitrarily picked $35 an ounce as the new price of gold. Most economists agree that the theory behind this move was incorrect and that its effect on the economy was not great. The main result was that, with an inflated price for gold, followed by the destructiveness of World War II, gold flowed from the rest of the world into the official reserves of the United States. It was generally recognized to be an overpriced commodity, sold to the buyer who was artificially holding the price up. Gold remaining in private hands was primarily that used for jewelry or in traditional small hoards. A few individuals, however, preferred the security of gold to either money or property in their own countries.

THE GROWING POPULARITY OF GOLD

As the economies of the world recovered following World War II, gold once again came into prominence. World trade expanded rapidly, raising the need for monetary reserves. Some countries which traditionally held their reserves in gold began to accumulate dollars, which they then tendered to the United States for gold. Private owners, fearing renewed inflation, also began to accumulate gold. Demand from industrial users, private hoarders, speculators, and small central banks began to rise. During the 1960s a good deal of current gold production went into these uses and was not available to expand the world's monetary base.

Pressure in the markets for gold developed in two ways. When the private demand for gold exceeded current production, the market price of gold would rise above that fixed in the par-value system. To avoid this danger, the eight major gold-holding countries agreed to peg the price of gold at $35 an ounce (the par value of the U.S. dollar). The system was similar to that for pegging currencies; the central banks, acting through the Bank of England, added sufficient demand or supply to the market to be certain that it cleared at $35. This system broke down in March of 1968, as some central banks were no longer willing to supply the gold needed to match tremendous speculative demands in the market.

The second pressure came from the U.S. balance-of-payments deficits and the accumulation by foreign central banks of more dollars than they wanted to hold. They began to convert their excess dollars into gold. Finally in August 1971, the United States refused to sell any more gold at the $35-an-ounce rate. While gold prices rose, the initial increases were not dramatic. The price of gold reached nearly $200 in 1974. It then fell by half, only to start back up. It averaged over $225 in 1978 and over $650 an ounce in the first quarter of 1980.

THE MONETARY FUTURE OF GOLD

During the entire postwar period, there were widespread controversies over whether or not gold had any role to play in the international monetary system. The sharp run-up and then wild fluctuations in the price of gold intensified the debates. Central banks continued to hold gold in their reserves. When the price of gold rose from $35 to $600 an ounce, the value of this gold climbed by more than $575 billion. This meant that total world monetary reserves were nearly 17 times as great as they would have been if central banks continued to value gold at $35 an ounce, the price which had been set at Bretton Woods.

Some business and government analysts have continued to argue that the world ought to return to the gold standard, with all currencies freely convertible to gold at fixed prices. In their opinion, only such action will insure the necessary discipline on the part of governments to avoid inflation. They believe that if countries are forced to reduce their money supply when gold flows out, they will have to operate under sound fiscal and monetary policies. They point to the period of the gold standard as one during which worldwide inflation was avoided. Prominent among this group are many supply-side economists. As a result of their pressure, the 1980 Republican platform contained an ambiguous plank which some interpreted as a promise to return the United States to the gold standard. In 1981, the Reagan administration and Congress established a "Gold Commission" to consider what role gold should play in the domestic and international monetary systems. The new classicists, who advocate a return to the gold standard, argue that the supply of money ought to be tied to a commodity and not be under the control of the Federal Reserve or the government. Some would tie the price of a dollar to a basket of commodities, but most select gold.

In contrast, most economists probably think that gold should be removed completely from the monetary system. They would like to see all central banks sell their supplies to the market; gold prices would then move like those of any other commodity. They base their views on (1) the lack of stability in the price of gold; (2) the disadvantages of returning to the gold-standard system of fixed exchange rates; (3) the fact that gold is an expensive commodity (maintaining gold reserves mean countries lose interest on the amount paid for it); and (4) the belief that few countries would stick to convertibility if it came to a crunch. If forced to deflate their domestic economies drastically because of an outflow of gold into hoards or to other countries, most countries would devalue. Under a reinstated gold standard, economists fear that there would be frequent runs on countries' gold supplies like those of the 1960s. When speculators smelled blood, they would bedevil individual countries until they could make a kill.

While no general inflation developed in the nineteenth century and the period through 1960, major deflations, large-scale inflations, and even hyper-inflations did occur in specific major countries. This poor past record was one of the factors that led to the demise of the gold standard. Equally important was the fact that gold for monetary purposes was not keeping up with the expansion of output and trade. If countries tried to stay on the gold standard, there was a constant threat of worldwide deflations and depressions. Milton Friedman has argued that a major cause of the Great Depression was the failure of the Federal Reserve to expand the money supply because of a mistaken attempt to assure a sufficient stock of gold to maintain the gold standard. From 1960 to 1980, the supply of monetary gold held by central banks fell. Most countries have price-wage systems similar to that of the United States. As a result, a decrease in wages and prices is extremely difficult to achieve; yet that would be required under the gold standard. If trade and output expand but the amount of gold does not, deflation must follow.

To solve the problem of expanding incomes with a constant gold supply, either the ratio of the money supply to gold must grow or the institutional structure must be improved so that the increased velocity allows more spending to take place. During most of the gold-standard period, increases in income velocity compared to gold did occur. Paper money and then demand deposits became more acceptable mediums of exchange. But such increases in velocity are limited. If the money multiplier on gold continues to expand, the dangers of increasing instability and monetary crises will grow.

Rather than depending on changes in velocity to avoid deflations, another possibility would be to raise the price of gold at regular intervals. If the value of gold held in monetary stores rose periodically, deflationary pressures need not arise. But such periodic price changes might lead to significant speculative movements. The sharp run-up of gold prices in 1979 and 1980 added strength to the negative arguments. If increases in gold prices caused the monetary base of many countries to shoot up, wouldn't inflation go up even more? How much stability can be expected in a system where the value of money and prices is tied to a commodity whose price jumps 5 or 10 percent a day and whose price doubled in a few months? Critics of the gold standard remain convinced that the gyrations in gold prices prove that it has no logical role in the monetary system. Let gold be held by people who can use its portability and durability as hedges against political risks in their own countries. If they are willing to trade other resources in order to hold gold, everyone else will be better off.

As long as gold retains a position half in and half out of the monetary system, it creates problems. Since gold retains its mystique and people watch its movements, reactions in other markets are likely to occur. The U.S. government, as a matter of policy, wanted to apply benign neglect to gold, but the gyrations in its price made that difficult. They threatened to raise monetary and price expectations in the rest of the system. In 1978, 1979, and 1980, because the Federal Reserve worried that movements in gold prices would trigger unwanted fluctuations in exchange rates and in other commodity markets, it imposed more restrictive monetary conditions than would otherwise have been necessary. Because financial markets may continue to be disturbed by gold, some bankers argue that a new international monetary system is needed, giving a more prominent role to gold. Believers in the gold standard would go farther, advocating a return to the system of the nineteenth century. Proponents of free markets prefer to treat gold like any other commodity, assuming that the market system can absorb shocks from gold and that these will diminish as people realize it is no different from other commodities.

Summary

1. The balance-of-payments accounts summarize all economic transactions between domestic and foreign residents. Three principal divisions are (1) the balance on current account, (2) the balance on capital account, and (3) the

balance in official reserve assets, which equals the difference between other payments and receipts.

2. The exchange rate of a currency is its price in terms of foreign currencies. The rate is determined by demand and supply in the foreign exchange markets. Countries influence the rate for a currency by adding to or subtracting from private demands in the market.

3. In theory, exchange rates between currencies depend on their relative prices—their purchasing-power parity. In fact, exchange rates move far more than can be accounted for by current price changes. Exchange rates are also influenced by relative interest rates and by expectations of future prices and interest rates. As in all cases where prices depend on expectations, no one can be sure why rates move at a given time. Speculators base their actions on expectations; so do investors. Whether they are right or wrong, current rates reflect their actions.

4. Under the gold standard and the Bretton Woods agreement, countries fixed, or pegged, their exchange rates; that is, they set the prices of their currencies in terms of gold or other currencies. This was done for the purpose of stabilizing the purchasing power of money both domestically and internationally. The fixed-exchange-rate systems broke down as a result of differential growth, costs, and inflation.

5. Under a floating or flexible rate system, exchange rates move with supply and demand. In theory, governments allow the exchange markets greater freedom to adjust to altered supply conditions. Speculation is made more risky. Exchange rates move instead of income and domestic prices. But a redistribution occurs between exporters and users of imports. Speculation may cause wide swings in rates, making trade and investment more difficult.

6. The International Monetary Fund was established to coordinate exchange-rate policies among countries and to provide borrowing facilities for international reserves. An important development was the creation of special drawing rights (SDRs), which are accounts created by agreement among governments which will accept them in payment for international debts. Their exchange value depends on a "basket" of currencies, as do their interest rates. Future developments depend on a balancing of exchange risks, liquidity, transferability, and interest payments between them and other potential reserves.

7. Eurocurrencies (including Eurodollars) are deposits denominated in currencies other than those of the nation in which the issuing bank is domiciled. In the 1960s and 1970s, an explosion in the growth of Eurodollars occurred. These monies are outside the control of central banks. They are efficient, but they can create problems of inflation and added risks. They complicate the control of the Federal Reserve over the money stock which influences spending in the United States.

8. Gold has played a diminishing role in official monetary reserves and a growing role in private speculation. At some future time, governments will have to make critical decisions as to the role of gold in the world monetary system. This will greatly affect its private values. With widely fluctuating prices, its monetary role is uncertain.

Questions for Dicussion and Review

1. Discuss the role of gold in the international monetary system. Why should gold, as opposed to some other commodity, have this role?

2. What methods exist to finance balance-of-payments deficits?

3. What reasons exist for fixed exchange rates? When is this type of policy likely to lead to problems?

4. How can governments influence the value of their currency? How does this affect other countries?

5. What is the role of the International Monetary Fund?

6. What are Eurodollars? What is the rationale for their existence?

7. Define the following terms:
   a. Balance of payments
   b. Devaluation
   c. Special drawing rights
   d. Purchasing-power parity

8. What are the relationships between exchange rates and interest rates?

9. Why are exchange rates volatile? What is a dirty float?

10. Discuss factors influencing exchange rates.

References

Frenkel, J. "Flexible Exchange Rates in the 1970s." In *Stabilization Policies* (proceedings of a conference) edited by the Center for the Study of Business, Working. Paper No. 53, April 1980.

Frenkel, J., and H. G. Johnson, eds. *The Monetary Approach to the Balance. of Payments.* London: Allen & Unwin, 1976.

Friedman, M. "Exchange Rates: How Flexible Should They Be?" Reprinted in *Readings in Macroeconomics: Current Policy Issues* edited by W. E. Mitchell *et al.* New York: McGraw-Hill, 1974.

Heller, H. R. "International Stabilization Policy under Flexible Exchange Rates." In *Stabilization Policies* (proceedings of a conference) edited by the Center for the Study of Business, Working Paper No. 53, April 1980.

Kreinen, M. E. *International Economics: A Policy Approach,* 2nd edition. New York: Harcourt Brace Jovanovitch, 1975.

17

International Trade and Domestic Adjustments

International trade can lower prices and expand the variety of goods available to a country, but it may also introduce instability through external shocks and make the choice of domestic stabilization policies more complex. Shifts in exchange rates and international trade may have severe impacts on domestic prices and income. To see how international trade and exchange influence an economy, we need to expand the models of the goods and money markets to include movements of goods and capital across borders.

International trade and exchanges add new dimensions to fiscal and monetary policies. A change in the money stock to influence domestic interest rates and credit availability will alter international capital movements and exchange rates. Reactions to international trade and finance shift a country's aggregate demand and supply. They modify the equilibrium levels of the goods and money markets while changing the price and availability of supplies. Both domestic and foreign events can cause disequilibrium in the balance of payments. When imbalances occur, action to adjust international accounts must be taken. There are limits to how long a country can lose or gain official reserve assets. Adjustments may take place through the semi-automatic movements of foreign-currency prices under a system of pure or managed floating foreign exchanges, through action to influence domestic income or financial markets, or through **balance-of-payment policies,** which are actions taken to influence directly the amount of international trade or capital flows.

Policy decisions become more complex because actions to improve domestic stability may cause a disequilibrium in the foreign accounts, while attempts to halt losses of international reserves may lead to domestic recessions or inflations. This chapter examines the interplay of foreign and domestic events and their impacts on output, interest rates, prices, and official reserves through the following topics:

Goods market equilibrium in an open economy.
Money market equilibrium in an open economy.
Why the balance of payments shifts.
Adjusting the balance of payments.
Conflicts between internal and external balance.

Goods Market Equilibrium in an Open Economy

In Chapter 2, as part of the discussion of GNP accounting, we saw that the amount of goods available for purchase in an economy equals domestic output (Q) plus imports (IM). Total spending for goods and services in the United States includes purchases by consumers (C) plus investors (I) plus the government (G) on both domestic and imported goods, and, in addition, monies spent by foreigners on goods exported (X) from the U.S. Thus,

$$Q + IM = C + I + G + X. \qquad \textbf{17.1}$$

When the foreign sector is included, total available goods and expenditures are greater than the GNP (the sum of a country's production of goods and services), since imports are included as an addition to domestic production on the left side of equation 17.1, while expenditures for goods produced abroad are included in $C + I + G$. To correct for this excess, imports can be subtracted from both sides. The resulting equation shows GNP (output and income produced) on the left side and total expenditures for domestic output on the right. Domestic output equals expenditures on domestic and imported goods ($C + I + G$) plus the difference between expenditures from abroad (X) and imports:

$$Y = Q = C + I + G + (X - IM). \qquad \textbf{17.2}$$

At equilibrium, this equation also equals aggregate demand. The decision making process becomes evident when we recognize that AD for output depends on the desire to purchase domestic goods by the spending sectors plus the demand from abroad for export goods and services.

Table 16.1 shows that the balance on goods and services in the balance-of-payments accounts is equal to the difference between exports and imports (defined to include all expenditures on both goods and services). With the addition of the minor items of net transfer payments to foreigners, this also equals the BOP current account balance.

GOODS MARKET EQUILIBRIUM

Equation 17.2 shows that the level of equilibrium income in an open economy depends on the desire of domestic spending groups to purchase foreign goods (imports) in addition to spending money on domestic products. Every dollar spent on imports reduces demand for domestic output. How much is spent abroad depends on tastes, on income, and prices at home and overseas. The demand for imports can be stated as a function similar to the consumption and investment functions. It reflects the decisions by all sectors as to how much spending will be done in domestic and how much in foreign markets. A simple import function can be written as:

$$IM = \overline{IM} + zY. \tag{17.3}$$

Demand for imports (IM) equals an autonomous factor ($\overline{IM}$) plus the marginal propensity to import (z) out of income (Y). The demand for exports (X) depends on the level of income in the rest of the world and also on relative prices (to be discussed shortly). While large-scale econometric models estimate exports in complex international sectors, small models usually treat exports as exogenous.

In an open economy, equilibrium income can be found, as before, by using either the slope-intercept diagram, to see where the total desire to spend equals output, or the injection-leakage diagram, to find the level of income at which they are equal.

The Slope-Intercept.   Figure 17.1 illustrates the addition of the desire to export and import to the domestic spending desires of the three decision sectors. At equilibrium income, Y_{E_1}, the desire to spend (assuming no interest effects) equals output and income earned. When the foreign sector is added, two changes occur. The intercept is shifted upward by the difference in autonomous spending ($\overline{X} - \overline{IM}$), while the slope of the line declines because the marginal propensity to import reduces the marginal propensity to spend (m). The multiplier is smaller because leakages are larger. In a closed economy, the joint desire to spend from income of the three sectors (represented by the slope of the lower line) includes their marginal propensities to spend (m) for all goods. When their marginal propensity to import (z) is subtracted from their total desire to spend, the remaining desire to spend on domestic goods alone must be smaller. The darker line in the figure includes the autonomous spending on exports and imports and reflects the manner in which their desire to spend for domestic goods rises with income. Since interest effects are excluded in this example, the point of equilibrium before the foreign sector is added is[1]

$$Y_{E_1} = k_1 \overline{A}_1 \qquad\qquad Y_{E_1} = 2.5(740) = 1,850 \tag{17.8}$$

---

1. In equations 17.8 and 17.10, the following assumptions are made (see equations 5.1-5.4):

(17.4)	$C = \overline{C} + c(Y - t(Y) - \overline{T})$	$C = 300 + .75(Y - .25Y - 200).$
(17.5)	$I = \overline{I} + d(Y - t(Y) - \overline{T})$	$I = 200 + .05(Y - .25Y - 200).$
(17.6	$T = \overline{T} + tY$	$T = 200 + .25Y.$
(17.7)	$G = \overline{G}$	$\overline{G} = 400.$

FIGURE 17.1   **The Level of Aggregate Demand with the Foreign Sector Added**

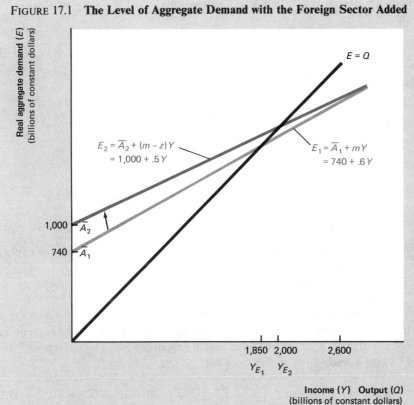

Adding the demand for exports and imports to domestic demand shifts autonomous expenditures, the slope of the real aggregate demand curve, the multiplier, and it may also change equilibrium income.

where

$$k_1 = \frac{1}{1-m} \qquad k_1 = \frac{1}{1-.6} = 2.5$$

and

$$\overline{A}_1 = \overline{C} + \overline{I} + \overline{G} - (c+d)\overline{T} \qquad \overline{A}_1 = 300 + 200 + 400 - .8(200) = 740.$$

The import and export functions are assumed to be

$$IM = \overline{IM} + zY \qquad IM = 30 + .1Y \qquad \qquad \textbf{17.3}$$

$$X = \overline{X} \qquad \overline{X} = 290. \qquad \qquad \textbf{17.9}$$

When the foreign sector is added to equation 17.8, the new equilibrium becomes

$$Y_{E_2} = k_2 \bar{A}_2 \qquad\qquad Y_{E_2} = 2(1,000) = 2,000 \qquad\qquad \textbf{17.10}$$

where

$$k_2 = \frac{1}{1 - m + z} \qquad\qquad k_2 = \frac{1}{1 - .6 + .1} = \frac{1}{.5} = 2$$

and

$$\bar{A}_2 = \bar{A}_1 + (\bar{X} - \overline{IM}) \qquad\qquad \bar{A}_2 = 740 + (290 - 30) = 1,000.$$

This numerical example was chosen to demonstrate three significant points:

1. Autonomous spending shifts by the difference between exogenous exports and exogenous imports.
2. The addition of imports dependent on income lowers the slope of the desire-to-spend line and results in a smaller multiplier.
3. The current balance in the BOP accounts depends, among other factors, on the equilibrium level of income. A drop in income will raise the current-account balance, while deficits increase if incomes rise. The current balance (XS) is ($X - IM$), or in the example,

$$XS = \bar{X} - \overline{IM} - zY \qquad\qquad XS = 290 - 30 - .1(2,000) = 60. \qquad \textbf{17.11}$$

The surplus declines with income because of the assumption that imports depend on domestic income, but exports do not vary with the GNP. (In fact, the decline may be faster because exports may fall somewhat as income rises as manufacturers find it easier to sell at home rather than abroad.)

Injections and Leakages. Figure 17.2 derives the same information by using injections and leakages. The lighter lines are based on the equilibrium when investment plus government purchases equal saving plus taxes, or

$$I + G = S + T = Y_{E_1} - C + T$$

and

$$Y_{E_1} = I + G + C - T. \qquad\qquad \textbf{17.12}$$

Using the information from equations 17.4-17.7, we find, at $Y_{E_1} = 1,850$:

$$I + G = S + T \qquad\qquad 259.4 + 400 = -3.1 + 662.5.$$

Injections equal leakages at an income of $1,850 billion.

When the foreign sector is taken into account, exports must be added to injections because they increase the demand for domestic goods at each income level, and imports must be added to the leakages because they reduce spending. The result of performing these operations is the darker lines in Figure 17.2. Using the equations and the numerical example, the identical results found in the slope-intercept example are obtained:

$$I + G + X = S + T + IM = Y_{E_2} - C + T + IM$$

and

$$Y_{E_2} = I + G + C - T + (X - IM).\qquad\qquad\textbf{17.13}$$

FIGURE 17.2   **Injections and Leakages With the Foreign Sector**

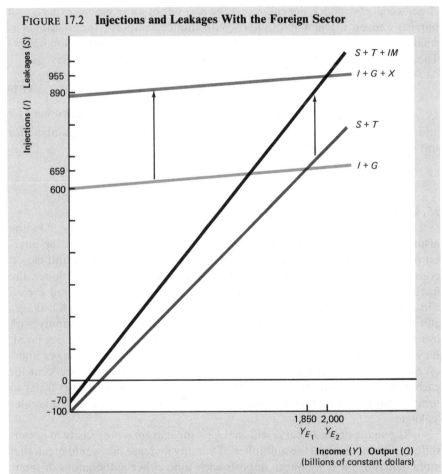

When the foreign sector is included, exports inject additional demand which must be added to investments and government purchases of goods and services. Imports are a leakage in addition to saving and taxes. At equilibrium, total injections and leakages are equal.

Again, by substitution, equlibrium is found at $2,000 billion and

$$I + G + X = S + T + IM \qquad 265 + 400 + 290 = 25 + 700 + 230.$$

THE *IS* CURVE IN AN OPEN ECONOMY

Figure 17.1 and equations 17.10 and 17.13 show how to find an equilibrium in the goods market assuming a fixed interest rate or the absence of interest effects on spending. Just as in the closed economy, interest rates can be varied and their effects on equilibrium spending can be charted to obtain the income-in-terest-rate points of equilibrium in an open economy. Figure 17.3 presents such *IS* curves. What effect does including exports and imports have on the *IS* curve? At each interest rate, the equilibrium of income will differ from that in a closed-economy model, depending on the amount of autonomous exports and imports and on the new multiplier. With induced imports, the multiplier is smaller and the *IS* curve steeper. (This is shown by the IS_1 line in the figure.) The numbers for IS_0 are those found previously for a closed economy.

$$Y_{E_1} = k_1 \overline{A} - k_1 br \qquad\qquad Y_{E_1} = 2.5(740) - 2.5(2,000r). \qquad\qquad \textbf{17.14}$$

IS_1 adds exports and imports according to the assumptions of equations 17.9 and 17.10. Autonomous spending and the multiplier shift. The numbers for this example in the open economy become

$$Y_{E_2} = k_2 \overline{A} - k_2 br \qquad\qquad Y_{E_2} = 2.0(1,000) - 2.0(2,000r).$$

IS_1 has a steeper slope than IS_0 (see Figure 7.3).

Consider a specific decrease in interest rates—say, 1 percent. On the assumption that foreign trade is minimally affected by interest rates, the inter-est-responsiveness of spending (*br*) will be the same in both open and closed economies. However, because the open economy has a smaller multiplier, the increase in income from any change in interest rates will be less, and the *IS* curve will therefore be steeper. Another way to picture this is through leakages and injections. A movement down the *IS* curve in the closed economy with income rising means that leakages from savings and taxes grow. At every point, they are exactly offset by added injections as investment rises with lower inter-est rates. When imports are added to the model, additional leakages occur for each movement down the curve. As a result, interest rates must drop faster to bring about the still larger amount of investment needed to offset the greater leakages.

The shape of the *IS* curve will change if the marginal propensity to import shifts, since this changes the multiplier. Thus any increase in *z* would mean that more demand is leaking out to imports each time either autonomous or inter-est-induced spending changes. Since the multiplier would be smaller, the *IS* curve would become still steeper. If tastes changed and imports became less fashionable, a shift in the opposite direction would take place.

FIGURE 17.3   **Factors Shifting the *IS* Curve in an Open Economy**

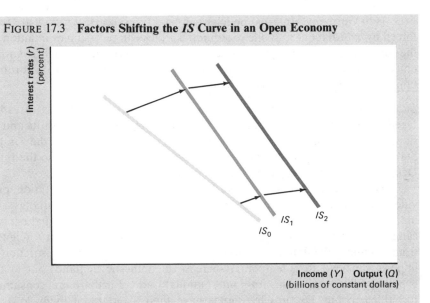

In an open economy, the position and slope of the IS *curve differ from those of a closed economy. Additional forces, such as foreign demand and supply, relative international prices, and movements in exchange rates, cause the curves as well as their slopes to shift.*

SHIFTS IN THE *IS* CURVE DUE TO FOREIGN EVENTS

Added to the numerous domestic factors which can shift the *IS* curve—such as alterations in taxes or government spending and changes in people's desire to save or invest—events in the foreign sector can also cause the curve to shift. In Figure 17.3, the curve IS_2 depicts such a movement. What are some of the international forces that may be at work?

Exports.   The demand of foreigners for U.S. exports may change. In Figure 17.1 and equation 17.10, as well as in most analysis of the *IS* curve, foreign demand is considered exogenous. It depends on events abroad. Foreign countries have import functions much like ours—heavily dependent on income. If Canada, Germany, Japan, and the United Kingdom experience a cyclical boom, their import demand rises. American firms supply more goods to meet this demand. U.S. exports increase, shifting the *IS* curve. Other changes may occur as a result of such factors as weather. When the USSR has a bad crop year, American exports of grain may soar, either directly or into the markets of third countries whose grain the USSR buys.

The recognition that *IS* curves are interdependent—that internal fluctuations in demand overflow into foreign markets—has led the heads of the major industrialized nations to hold periodic economic summits. A decision by France to try to expand demand can be frustrated if it is offset by a drop in

exports to Germany. Internal policies will be more successful if they are reinforced by external ones. While coordinated attacks on recession or inflation by
the major countries appear to be a good idea, differences in each country's
objectives and domestic political considerations make international coordina-
tion of such efforts extremely difficult.

Substitutions.   What happens if U.S. purchasers decide to buy Fords instead of
Datsuns? If U.S. goods are substituted for imports, the *IS* curve shifts and its
slope changes. The level of autonomous spending $(X - \overline{IM})$ in the United
States is higher and the leakages (z) are less. The *IS* curve shifts to the right.
Demand is greater at all interest rates.

Recognition that internal demand can be increased by substitution, provided that exports remain at the same level, leads to tariffs, import quotas, and
indirect pressures against foreign goods. The catch, of course, is that exports
cannot stay at the same level if the restrictions on imports prevent foreigners
from obtaining the dollars they must have to buy U.S. exports. Restriction of
imports can lead to a temporary increase in domestic demand, but at the
expense of long-term gains from international trade. Furthermore, consumers
forbidden to buy Datsuns by quotas have their standard of living lowered
through having to pay higher prices.

Price Effects.   Exports and imports and, therefore, the amount of aggregate
demand also shift if prices in the United States change relative to those of the
rest of the world. Internal rates of inflation affect foreign purchases. If German
prices rise less than those in the United States (and the mark exchange rate does
not change), more of the cheaper German goods will be sold in the United
States. Since American goods will be more expensive in Frankfurt, fewer will
be exported. The drop in exports and rise in imports will shift the *IS* curve to
the left. The level of income will be reduced by the substitution of foreign for
domestic production times the multiplier.

Movements in Exchange Rates.   A drop in U.S. exchange rates, enabling foreigners to buy more U.S. dollars with their currencies, or—the same thing—a rise
in the price of foreign currencies in U.S. cents also shifts the *IS* curve. Exchange-rate movements are equivalent to relative price changes. If the price of
the dollar in francs falls, Frenchmen would find it cheaper to buy U.S. goods,
and exports would rise. French wine would become more expensive; people
would substitute California wines. The *IS* curve would shift to the right.

The addition of the foreign sector to the factors affecting equilibrium in
the goods market complicates both analysis and policies. The next section
shows that this is also true when foreign effects are included in the money
market. The influence of monetary and fiscal policies on the current and capital
accounts contributes to shifting *IS-LM* curves and may reinforce or offset their
domestic impacts.

Money-Market Equilibrium in an Open Economy

The analysis of money-market equilibrium must also be expanded to point up the contrast between an open and a closed economy. International forces influence both the supply of and the demand for money. The shape and position of the economy's *LM* curves reflect both foreign and domestic events. When interest rates or prices or foreign demand change in London, they affect *LM* curves in New York. Chapter 16 showed that movements in price expectations, interest rates, and the money supply cause capital to move among countries. Exchange rates, interest rates, the money supply, and the demand for money are not static.

Let us trace the results of a decision by foreigners to hold more financial assets in New York. Such diverse forces as a U.S. surplus on current account, higher interest rates in New York, or a fear of a Communist take-over could alter the balance of payments. As a result, the United States runs a payments surplus and gains official international reserves. Assume that American sellers of securities or goods accept foreign exchange. They take it to their banks, which credit them with dollar deposits. The banks deposit the foreign currencies at the Federal Reserve, which credits the accounts of the Banks. Banks have added reserves, while the Fed holds the foreign currencies as additional assets. The Fed's additional assets and liabilities mean that the monetary base has expanded. It can either hold the foreign currencies or it can sell them to foreign central banks, which would pay for them with the U.S. Treasury bills they hold as international reserves.

Exactly the same sequence takes place if the U.S. sellers are paid in dollars. To hold the exchange rate steady, foreign central banks must furnish these dollars. They acquire them by selling gold or international reserves to the Federal Reserve. The monetary base expands, as do bank reserves. Instead of allowing its total assets and the monetary base to grow, the Fed can sell some of its bill holdings (open-market operations). Such action to offset the effect of inflows of gold or other international reserves is called *sterilization.* It has been common in the United States but less so in other countries. To the degree that the Federal Reserve sterilizes inflows, the money stock will not expand and the *LM* curve will not shift.

However, assuming that sterilization does not take place, the growth of BOP surpluses and the resulting expansion of the money supply shift the *LM* curve as illustrated in Figure 17.4. The line LM_1 depicts the initial situation. When the stock of money increases, if the demand for money does not change, the *LM* curve will shift downward. LM_2 reflects the altered situation. The additional money created as a result of a BOP surplus can support a larger income at every interest rate.

EXCHANGE RATES, PRICES, AND THE *LM* CURVE

Chapters 8, 12, and 13 showed the dependence of the *LM* curve on prices. Movements in the price level alter the real value of a fixed stock of money. The result of a change in real money balances is a shift in the *LM* curve. Now we see that the prices that determine the real money balances are also influenced by international forces, including foreign prices and the exchange rate. If

FIGURE 17.4   **A Balance-of-Payments Surplus (not sterilized) Shifts the *LM* Curve**

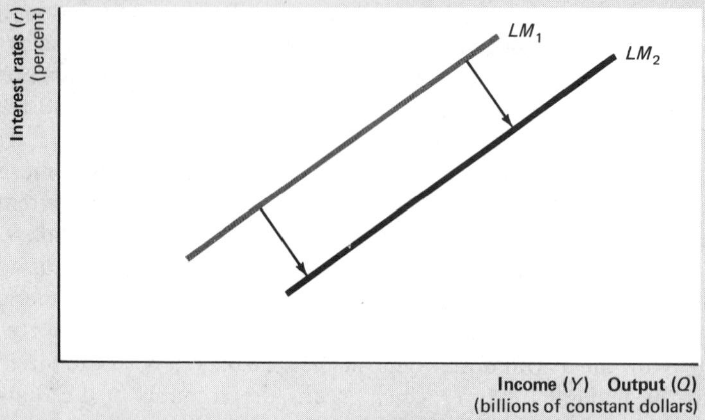

International trade and financial relationships can also shift the LM *curve. Central bank purchases of gold, foreign currencies, or other official reserves expand the real money stock, resulting in shifts in the* LM *curve. Changes in exchange rates and prices of imports and exports alter the price level and, therefore, real money balances and also the position of the* LM *curve.*

Common Market prices fall or if a U.S. dollar can purchase more francs or marks, import prices will decline in the United States. Prices of domestic goods competitive with the imports are also likely to fall. Such price declines increase the real money stock. In Figure 17.4, a larger money supply causes a shift from LM_1 to LM_2.

FOREIGN DEMAND FOR DOLLARS AND THE *LM* CURVE

The position of the *LM* curve depends on money demand as well as supply. Foreign-exchange transactions may require holding money balances. Europeans may shift to holding money temporarily after selling stocks in New York. In 1981, as part of the agreement for release of the American hostages held by Iran, large sums were transferred from New York and from Eurodollar accounts held in London to sterling balances at the Bank of England. Foreign governments holding international reserves in New York may shift their funds among demand and savings deposits, Treasury bills and bonds, and other assets in accordance with their transactions and assets demands. All such actions affect the demand for money, just as do decisions of the domestic sectors. An increase in the demand for money, given a constant money stock, will shift the *LM* curve to the left (see Figure 7.8).

At certain times, the Federal Reserve has estimated that a large share of changes in money-market interest rates in New York resulted from such shifts in foreign demands for U.S. money. Poor methods for measuring such changes compound the problems of formulating monetary policy. If foreign demand for dollars in New York falls, should the Fed reduce the money stock? If it fails to do so, it increases inflationary pressures when the *LM* curve shifts to the right, as shown in Figure 17.4. By following a fixed target for monetary growth, the Fed may allow movements in foreign demand for money to adversely affect interest rates and output, thus frustrating the objectives of monetary policy.

Why the Balance of Payments Shifts

Having seen how international factors affect aggregate demand, we next ask how these and similar forces determine the balance of payments. What are the variables that lead to international payment surpluses and deficits? Among the factors that influence the BOP are:

Aggregate demand.
Aggregate supply.
Prices.
Interest rates.
Exchange rates.
Trade controls—tariffs, quotas.
Export subsidies.
Exchange controls.
Taxes.

We can observe these factors at work by first looking at the balance on current account, including exports and imports of goods and services. We then examine the balance on capital account, including movements in both directions of financial claims and assets. Finally, we analyze the combination of the two as they result in international deficits or surpluses.

BALANCE ON CURRENT ACCOUNT

The balance on current account or export surplus (*XS*) includes all credits and debits of a country for sales and purchases of goods and services, such as merchandise, investment income, insurance, and travel (see Table 16.1). Figure 17.5 shows that the export surplus or deficit depends on the slopes and positions of the export and import functions and on the level of output in the economy. (The figure is an illustration of equation 17.11.) Look at point *B*. Under the assumptions of the figure, when output is at $2,600 billion the current account is in balance.

FIGURE 17.5   **The Balance on Current Account**

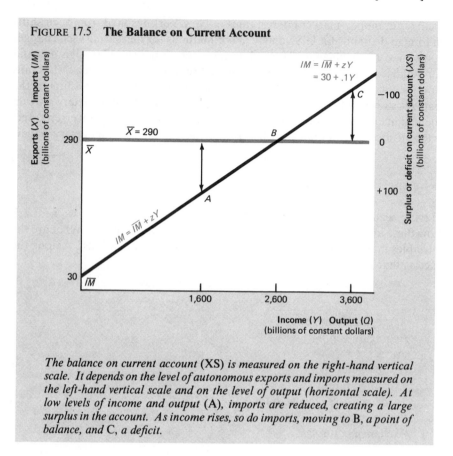

The balance on current account (XS) is measured on the right-hand vertical scale. It depends on the level of autonomous exports and imports measured on the left-hand vertical scale and on the level of output (horizontal scale). At low levels of income and output (A), imports are reduced, creating a large surplus in the account. As income rises, so do imports, moving to B, a point of balance, and C, a deficit.

What causes the current account to change? The component balances vary with output. When output falls, the demand for foreign goods also decreases. Inventories of foreign goods are run off. Domestic sales are filled from inventories instead of by purchases abroad. At point A, the arrow shows an XS surplus larger than that at point B, based on an assumption of no change in exports (foreign countries are not yet affected by the decline in U.S. income) and a drop in imports. An increase in exports may also lead to an enlarged surplus. For example, assume that an exogenous increase ($\Delta \bar{X}$) occurs in exports. Total income will rise by the multiplier times this autonomous change, or by $k\Delta \bar{X}$.[2] There will be an induced increase in imports equal to the size of the marginal propensity to import times the increase in income.

2. There can be a divergence between movements in real exports and imports and the value of exports and imports (quantity times price). For example, the short-run demand for oil has been extremely inelastic. Thus several OPEC countries were able, by raising oil prices, to increase their revenues from oil sales even as their real exports (barrels) of oil fell. In this chapter, we assume that exports and imports are sufficiently price-elastic so that real and nominal exports move together, as do real and nominal imports.

The change in the BOP surplus or deficit will be the difference between the initial shift in exports and the induced imports, or

$$\Delta XS = \Delta \overline{X} - z(\Delta Y) \qquad \Delta XS = 20 - .1(40) = 16. \qquad \textbf{17.16}$$

An exogenous increase in the value of exports raises the BOP surplus or reduces a deficit, depending on the elasticity of the propensity to import and on the size of the multiplier.

Other factors also shift the export and import schedules. Substitutions, relative prices, and exchange rates are among other influences on the current account. If domestic prices can be lowered relative to foreign ones, exports will rise and imports fall (assuming that the combined price elasticities are greater than one). If supply economics works and domestic inflation slows compared with that abroad, both the export and import schedules will shift. Even if output expanded only somewhat, the XS surplus would still grow. A drop in a country's exchange rate has effects on the XS similar to a decrease in domestic prices. If the price of the yen rises in terms of the dollar, Datsun cars cost more in the United States and fewer will be bought. Fords are more likely to be exported to third markets. There will be fewer imports and more exports; the curves will shift. Thus devaluation is always a possible response to a BOP deficit. For this reason, such action was taken by the United States in 1971.

Governments can take direct action to remove BOP deficits and improve the balance of trade by penalizing imports or aiding exports. An increase in tariffs, import quotas, and stricter customs examinations will all shift the import curve to the right. The effect is the same as a change in relative prices or exchange rates. The United States has imposed formal and informal quotas, such as agreements with Japan to limit sales of automobiles, TV sets, and steel in the United States. In other cases quotas have been imposed on imports of meat and cheese. Taxes and tariffs have also been used to raise the cost of imported goods. While the use of import quotas and similar restrictions reduces the need for domestic income cuts, it tends to aggravate inflation. Fewer foreign goods are available to meet any excess of domestic demand. Price competition is cut, causing prices to rise more rapidly. This is an example of conflict between domestic and foreign economic policies.

The United States and most other countries subsidize exports in some form. In the United States, the Export-Import Bank subsidizes credits for exporters. Some countries rebate taxes. All may use foreign service and con-sular officers to drum up trade. All forms of export and import adjustments can become extremely competitive and reduce the advantages expected from in-ternational trade. During the 1930s countries imposed various controls and took action in efforts to improve their BOP at the expense of others. These "beggar-my-neighbor" policies were self-defeating, because they led primarily to reduced international trade among all nations. As noted, after World War II, attempts were made to insure coordinated adjustments among nations. The International Monetary Fund (IMF), the Organization for Economic Cooperation and Development (OECD), and similar regional groups were established to foster coordinated international policies and improve reserve availabilities. Most countries also entered into the General Agreement on Tariffs and Trade (GATT). These are agreements to reduce tariffs on a multilateral basis and to stop imposition of specific trade barriers aimed at helping individual industries or countries.

BALANCE ON CAPITAL ACCOUNT

The second major component of the BOP in addition to the current account (XS) is the balance on capital account (CA). Its size depends on all the factors causing financial assets to move across borders. Interest rates in both domestic and foreign markets are the most important of these, but other variables enter in as well, such as fear, investment climate, relative taxes, and information. Some wealthy families hold assets in many countries for fear of revolution. At times, multinational companies are attracted by the investment climate of particular countries, while at other times they are repelled. High taxes on profits or interest may place barriers between financial markets. Official controls over capital movements are even more common. Figure 17.6 illustrates possible capital-account curves. In the figure, interest rates, measured on the vertical

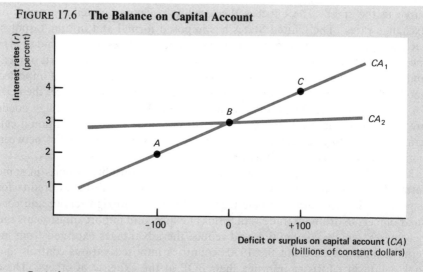

FIGURE 17.6   **The Balance on Capital Account**

Capital-account surpluses or deficits are measured on the horizontal axis. Flows depend on domestic interest rates (vertical axis) for a particular set of conditions relative to foreign markets. Flows on CA_2 are more sensitive to interest differentials. Curves shift as a result of changes in market conditions, such as foreign interest rates or taxes.

axis, influence capital flows which lead to capital-account surpluses or deficits, measured on the horizontal axis. On curve CA_1 the capital account is in balance at B when interest rates are 3 percent. At higher rates, as at C, more funds are attracted from abroad, resulting in a surplus. At lower rates, overseas investments will be more profitable. Citizens of other countries may repatriate some funds; local firms send more abroad.

The line CA_2 shows fund movements which are far more sensitive to interest rates than on CA_1. A small change in rates causes large sums to flow across borders. Sensitivity increases as economies become more open. Each curve results from a given set of conditions abroad. If interest rates change or capital controls are altered or wars threaten, the position of the CA curves will also shift. The curves become steeper as it becomes harder to move funds.

Because capital movements depend on interest rates, the specific position on a curve, and therefore the actual capital-account surplus or deficit, depends on a country's LM-IS equilibrium and its aggregate demand. For example, in the figure, an increased domestic demand for funds accompanied by higher interest rates can cause a move from B to C. Investments will be attracted from abroad. The market for funds is worldwide. If interest rates are higher in New York than in Toronto or London, funds will flow to New York. Assuming that exchange rates are not expected to vary, a change in relative interest rates will cause a capital flow because investors find it profitable to shift the location of their assets. A surplus will develop in the capital account.

Higher incomes will cause similar effects. As incomes rise in the United States, profits also rise. Direct investments will pay more in the United States. German or British firms will invest more in their U.S. subsidiaries, and Ford and IBM will invest less abroad. Perverse possibilities exist, however. If interest rates are raised to reduce income, the lowered profits and reduced stock prices in Wall Street may cause less direct investment in the United States. The ability of higher interest rates to attract funds from abroad will be partially offset.

The position of the CA curve can also be shifted by direct action to control capital flows. Such actions are nearly as common as efforts to affect the trade balance. Most countries at one time or another have imposed direct controls over capital outflows. Special licences are required for individuals or firms to purchase foreign exchange. Every category of request for foreign exchange, such as for travel, dividends, and investments, is likely to have separate rules and availability. In the 1960s, the United States imposed an interest-equalization tax on purchases by U.S. individuals or firms of stocks, bonds, or properties abroad. Similar voluntary restraints were imposed on bank lending and on direct investments of U.S. firms abroad.

THE BALANCE-OF-PAYMENTS CURVE

Together, the current and capital accounts make up the balance of payments.

In the same way, the current- and capital-account curves can be combined into a single *BP* curve showing how balance-of-payments surpluses or deficits are influenced by interest rates, output, and the other factors that cause the *XS* and *CA* curves to shift. Figure 17.7 pictures such a combination. A point is picked at which both the current and capital accounts balance and, consequently, no combined surplus or deficit exists. Point *B* on Figure 17.5 shows the output at which the *XS* accounts balance, while *B* on Figure 17.6 shows the interest rate at which the *CA* accounts balance. These output and interest rates are plotted as point *B* on Figure 17.7. It marks a balance for all three accounts. Every other point on the *BP* curve is plotted in the same way. At each interest rate, the balance in the *CA* account is calculated. It is then matched by a level of output which gives the opposite *XS* surplus or deficit. The two accounts offset one another and the total account balances. Thus, at point *C*, output is higher than at *A*. From Figure 17.5 we recognize that this leads to higher imports and to a deficit in the current account. However, at the same time, interest rates at *C* are higher than at *A*. They lead to a capital-account surplus just sufficient to offset the *XS* deficit. Similar offsetting relationships exist all along the *BP* curve. To test the opposing movements, try relating the *XS* and *CA* surpluses and deficits at point *A* compared with those at points *B* and *C*.

FIGURE 17.7   **The Balance-of-Payments Equilibrium Curve**

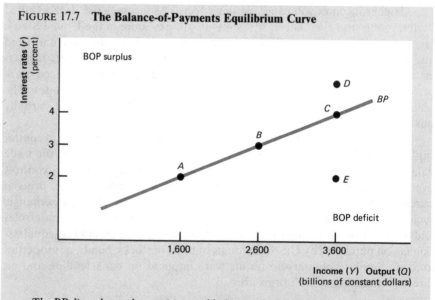

The BP *line shows the sensitivity of balance-of-payments deficits to output and interest rates. Along the line, no changes occur in official reserves; trade deficits at higher outputs are offset by capital inflows attracted by higher interest rates. At all points of* r *and* Q *above the line, the combined accounts are in surplus. At all below, deficits occur.*

THE SLOPE OF THE *BP* LINE

The slope of the *BP* line depends both on how the balance of trade responds to income and on reactions of capital movements to interest rates. If capital markets are very efficient and risks of foreign lending are slight, small changes in relative interest rates would cause large capital flows. The *BP* curve would be nearly flat. But if everyone feared foreign lending and risks were great, the *BP* curve would be more nearly vertical. Large increases in relative interest rates would be needed before capital moved. If small changes in income mean large changes in imports (everyone shifts to Mercedes as incomes rise), the curve would also be steeper. It would take more increases in interest rates to attract enough capital to offset the deterioration in the trade accounts which occurred as income rose.

The *BP* line divides all of the *r, Y* space. At every combination of interest rates and income above the *BP* curve—as, for example, *D*—the balance of payments is in surplus. Compared to *C*, interest rates are higher; more capital will flow into the country. Since at *C* capital inflows were already high enough to offset the deficit on trade, at higher rates they pull in still more funds, causing a surplus. In contrast, each point below the *BP* curve represents a BOP deficit. The effect of interest rates at *E* compared to *C* is to lower capital inflows so that they are no longer great enough to offset the trade deficit. In fact, a comparison with *A* shows that there is a deficit on the capital and current accounts.

Adjusting the Balance of Payments

Figure 17.7 shows the possibility that at many equilibrium levels of aggregate demand, there will be surpluses or deficits in the balance-of-payments accounts. The combined flows on current and capital accounts will not sum to zero. Movements of official reserve assets will be necessary as a counterbalance. A continuation of losses or gains of international reserves calls for action to adjust trade or capital flows. Countries have limited supplies of reserves. If losses occur, when all are spent they will no longer be able to buy foreign exchange to purchase goods, services, or financial assets abroad. Their international trade grinds to a halt unless they can find some lenders willing to make foreign exchange available.

Countries gaining reserves have an easier time. As long as they are willing to hold the reserves in the IMF or in other currencies, pressure to change policies will be delayed. Eventually, however, they too will feel strains and a need to adjust. The gains in reserves mean that they are investing abroad. Such investments may be less satisfactory and may promise less future income than domestic investments. They will also encounter adverse reactions among their debtors, who are likely to prefer a cut in trade to a steady expansion of a foreign debt.

Many adjustment policies are available. Any technique that alters domestic interest rates or output or shifts the *BP* line will change the balance of payments. In addition to the policy of paying for the BOP deficits by using international reserves, a number of other policies may be adopted. Monetary policy can be employed to alter interest rates and aggregate demand by shifting the *LM* curve. Under both the gold standard and the Bretton Woods agreement, the "rules of the game" called for policy decisions to alter the monetary stock. The level of rates under floating exchanges is also partially determined by the money supply. Fiscal policies can shift the *IS* curve and, therefore, the level of aggregate demand. If such shifts aid in achieving domestic goals, no conflict need arise. But if the economy is running a BOP deficit and it is in a recession, the contradiction of objectives will lead to other policies.

Finally, a whole group of policies operate directly on the *BP* curve. Declining domestic prices relative to foreign ones, a drop in the exchange rate, higher tariffs are all examples of actions which shift the *BP* curve down to the right. BOP deficits will be reduced or surpluses increased at each point of equilibrium of the *IS-LM* and aggregate demand and supply curves.

Figures 17.8, 17.9, and 17.10 illustrate how these adjustment processes work. Since they are based on identical assumptions, they show that any of the three techniques can be used to achieve an *IS-LM* equilibrium and a balance in the international accounts. However, they also show that each procedure may result in a different level of output and interest rates. Consequently, depending on which policies are selected to achieve external balance, conflicts with domestic goals of price and output stability may arise.

ADJUSTMENTS THROUGH THE MONEY SUPPLY: SHIFTING THE *LM* CURVE

Figure 17.8 presents a set of *IS, LM,* and *BP* curves in which domestic spending is initially in equilibrium at point *A,* but a balance-of-payments deficit exists, as indicated by the fact that *A* is below the *BP* line. This figure and those which follow show these curves in real terms.[3] In this figure, external imbalances are brought into adjustment through movements in the domestic money market.

Consider the situation at *A.* To finance the deficit, the central bank must sell foreign currency reserves (gold). Such actions reduce the monetary base and the money supply. The *LM* curve shifts up to the left. Income drops and interest rates rise. At lower incomes, imports fall and exports expand, improving the trade balance. Higher rates make holding capital in the country more attractive; more capital flows into the country or less flows out. Eventually, the money markets come into balance at the line labeled LM_2. At point *B* all three

---

3. This avoids the complications of having to analyze and chart different reactions to changes in *AD*. Previous chapters show that movements in *AD* will divide between prices and quantities depending on the status of aggregate supply. When movements in *AD* are analyzed in an open system, the complications and results are similar to those in the closed economy. To avoid these complications, the analysis is in real terms. For completeness, however, the effects on the *IS* and *LM* curves must be transferred to movements in nominal *AD* and *AS*, including the impact of the price changes on the *LM* and *IS* curves.

lines—*LM, IS,* and *BP*—join. An equilibrium level of expenditures and the balance of payments exists. Under the gold standard and fixed exchange rates, such adjustments of internal and external spending were assumed to occur automatically. When a country's income or price level was high relative to other countries, it would lose international reserves and be forced to contract its money supply. Internal demand would fall; interest rates would rise; external balance would be regained automatically.

In fact, because automatic adjustments in response to BOP deficits often took a long time, countries did not wait for reserve losses to tighten domestic money markets. When reserves began to flow out, central banks used open-market operations or raised discount rates to insure that higher interest rates would attract reserves from abroad. Similarly, with floating exchange rates, policy decisions to alter the money supply for external reasons have been common. If internal demand is high and prices are rising relative to the rest of the world, the price of the dollar in the foreign exchange market will fall. Speculation in the exchanges may drive down the price of the dollar even more. Pressure builds from other countries, from U.S. importers, and from those concerned about the international prestige of the dollar to halt its decline. In both the fall of 1978 and 1979, the Federal Reserve took drastic action

FIGURE 17.8   **Adjustments in the Balance of Payments through Monetary Policy**

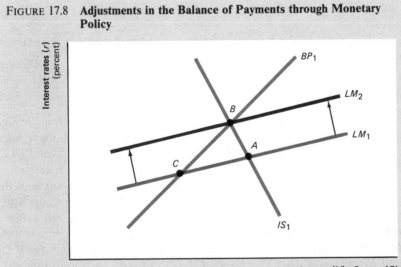

If not sterilized, central bank sales of international reserve assets made necessary by a BOP deficit contract the real money stock. The LM *curve shifts upward to a new* IS-LM *equilibrium at B—that is, on the* BP *curve.* LM *shifts can also result from open-market operations or price changes.*

FIGURE 17.9   **Adjustments in the Balance of Payments through Fiscal Policy**

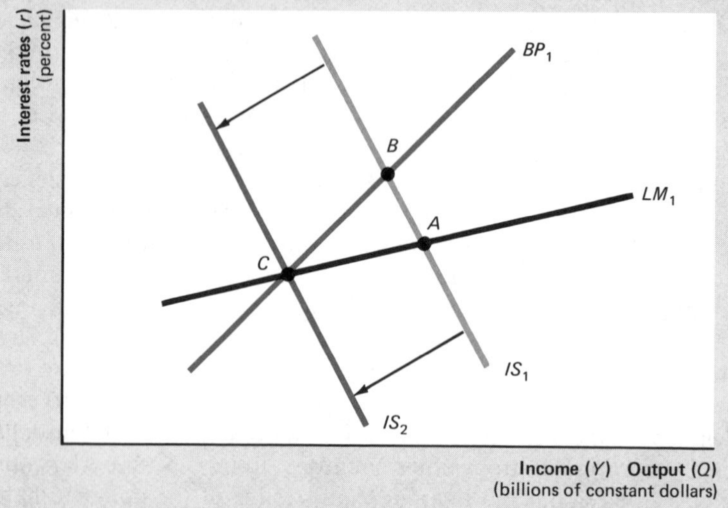

Income (Y)   Output (Q)
(billions of constant dollars)

Shifts in the IS curve alter real aggregate demand and interest rates, thereby changing the international balances on current and capital accounts. The contraction of output from A to C reduces imports and results in a BOP equilibrium.

to reduce the growth of the money stock. In both cases, declines in the external value of the dollar were major factors precipitating these moves.

SHIFTS IN THE *IS* CURVE

A second method of achieving balance in the international accounts is through action to shift the *IS* curve. The results of the use of a contractionary fiscal policy are shown in Figure 17.9. At an initial position, point *A*, an *IS-LM* equilibrium exists, but the balance of payments is in deficit. A reduction in government expenditures or an increase in taxes will shift the *IS* curve to the left. As a result, output and interest rates will decline. The lower level of output will improve the current account, but the lower interest rates will cause a deterioration in the capital account. How far the *IS* curve will have to shift to reduce the BOP deficit to zero will depend on the interest-responsiveness of the *LM* and *BP* curves. Figure 17.9 shows a shift to *IS₂* and an equilibrium at *C*. The drop in output is considerable.

A comparison of Figures 17.8 and 17.9 reveals that a balance-of-payments deficit can be removed by either monetary or fiscal policy. However, the effect on income and interest rates will differ depending on the shape of each of the underlying curves. In this example, the use of monetary policy appears to bring about a smaller loss of output. This need not be true, however. The outcome will depend on the responsiveness of the three curves to interest rates and output. Furthermore, the results abstract from the length of time it takes each policy to reach equilibrium. If lags are long, the costs of each policy will be affected. Because shifts in the *IS* and *LM* curves take the economy down different difficult paths to internal and external balance, a government is unlikely to be neutral in its choice of what to do.

SHIFTS IN THE BALANCE OF PAYMENTS

Many have felt that the policies that will directly affect the balance of payments are better than fiscal or monetary policies for the purposes of achieving internal and external balance. In Figure 17.10, if the curve BP_1 prevails, the BOP will be in deficit at the *IS-LM* equilibrium, point *A*. As noted, to obtain a BOP balance, the *IS-LM* equilibrium could be shifted to *B* or *C* with lower output. Instead, the *BP* curve could be shifted to BP_2, which would allow the three curves to meet at point *A*. No reduction in aggregate demand would be necessary. Balance will be reached at a higher level of real output. If this point is at or below potential output, such a situation will be preferable domestically. Thus, to reduce BOP deficits, governments frequently tend to try to shift the *BP* curve before utilizing policies to raise interest rates or reduce income.

Numerous techniques for shifting the *BP* curve are available. If domestic

FIGURE 17.10   **Adjustments in the Balance of Payments through Balance-of-Payments Policies**

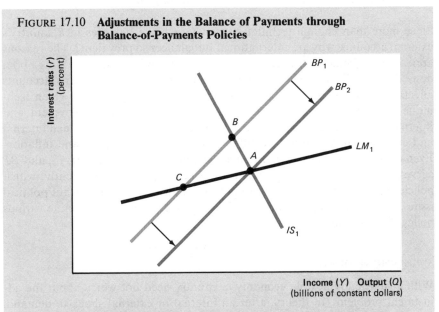

The IS-LM equilibrium remains at A. *The balance-of-payments deficit is removed by policies that shift the economy from* BP_1 *to* BP_2.

prices can be lowered relative to foreign prices, exports will rise and imports fall (assuming that price elasticity is greater than one). The *BP* curve will shift down to the right, as shown on Figure 17.10. Relative prices can be improved either by holding down the domestic rate of inflation compared with those abroad or by reducing the exchange rate. While an improvement in prices will be welcome, a decline in exchange rates may be a costly path because it will tend to increase inflation by raising the costs of imported goods and by reducing their availability. A country fighting inflation will be better off using international reserves or importing capital to pay for additional imports rather than allowing its exchange rate to depreciate.

To avoid the costs of adjustment through shifting prices and incomes, countries tend to seek other methods of shifting the *BP* curve. Controls over foreign exchange and capital movements and actions to curtail imports through tariffs, quotas, threats, and customs delays have all been frequently used. Changes in taxes, export subsidies, and loan subsidies are other techniques that have been employed. In deciding which policies are best, if any, the costs of adjustments through lost output, income redistributions, and inflations must be balanced against the losses in international trade and the inefficiencies of control systems. At many times over the past 50 years, countries have been faced with the difficult problem of deciding whether controls or internal adjustments would be more costly. The tendency has been to opt for controls.

Conflicts between Internal and External Balance

Since more than enough techniques exist to achieve balances in a country's external accounts, why are international imbalances so prevalent? The reasons appear to be similar to the reasons why domestic policies may not bring about desired goals. Every technique for adjusting balance-of-payments accounts affects the internal economy in a different way. How effective a given technique is depends on the lags in adjustments of prices, output, employment, and international trade and finance. Each path to a position of a combined internal and external balance results in different losses in output, jobs, and inflation. Even if countries choose the most effective policies to shift the *LM, IS,* and *BP* curves, large costs to some groups cannot be avoided. Consequently, which policies to select—or whether to use policies at all—become significant political issues. After analyzing the factors behind these costs, we will examine various policy dilemmas in more detail.

ADJUSTMENT PROBLEMS

With a sufficiently flexible economy, a country need not worry about the adjustment problem. In theory, after an internal or external shock to demand, countries can automatically return to an equilibrium for both domestic and foreign spending. If a country's BOP is in deficit, it will lose reserves. Its monetary base and money supply will contract. Spending will fall. Unemployment will rise. Wages and prices will decline. The level of spending will eventually shift to a point where the *IS, LM,* and *BP* curves join. As prices and wages shift, all who want to work will obtain jobs in some time period. But few countries are willing to go through this adjustment process. The actual world is not a frictionless system. Most nations resort to all kinds of means to avoid a reduction in domestic demand because sticky prices and wages, together with high information and transactions costs, may mean that adjustments through movements in aggregate demand entail large penalties.

Arguments over whether or not policies which forestall automatic adjustments do more harm than good are closely related to those over domestic policy. Economists who believe that frictions are comparatively mild and that market operations resemble the simplified theories favor automatic measures in both foreign and domestic policies. Those who see market failures or who believe that political behavior makes interference with automatic systems inevitable favor the development of policies to affect directly the balance of payments instead of reducing aggregate demand when BOP deficits occur. Whichever strategy is adopted, conflicts between internal and external balance can arise.

UNSTABLE BOPS

Countries always cling to the hope that imbalances in the foreign exchange markets are temporary and will be self-correcting. Prices in other countries may rise more rapidly; crops may improve and lower import prices; cyclical movements in income among countries will come into phase. Only when reserves are depleted or become too large will actions be taken to adjust the BOP. Such reluctance may be logical since there is considerable evidence that market adjustments may be difficult. The internal costs of reducing the money supply may be high. Low short-run elasticities of demand for exports and imports may mean that adjustments occur primarily as a result of a drop in domestic output and jobs. People will be out of work even as inflation gathers momentum. Only gradually will foreign demand and supply react. Furthermore, attempts to bring about adjustments through flexible exchange rates may not help. The sharp fluctuations in rates necessary for an equilibrium will have unfortunate effects. A drop in exchange rates will raise prices of imports and related domestic prices.

Instability is caused by the length of time it takes to develop exports and substitutes for imports. American auto manufacturers took a decade to produce a fuel-efficient car. In the interim, Japanese imports continued to expand, even as their prices rose. Unfortunate initial effects can result from inelastic short-run price elasticities in exports and imports. With price-inelasticity, the BOP deficit may grow when exchange rates fall. Only in the long run do

exports climb enough to reach BOP equilibrium.[4] Furthermore, the movements in exchange rates cause internal price movements and income redistributions. Just as with output and interest changes, recognition of this fact
leads to opposition to using exchange movements for the purpose of bringing
about external balance. Devaluations are also opposed because they tend to
undermine national pride. Sovereign nations may take all sorts of actions in
efforts to reverse the situation rather than acknowledging that the international
value of their currency has gone down. Devaluation has often been considered
to be an admission of defeat in the game of international prestige. During the
1960s, for example, devaluation was delayed in England both because of the
fear of raising the cost of imported foodstuffs to the English—with reactions on
internal wages and prices—and because of national pride. In the United States,
pride was also a factor, but in addition, many felt that if the discipline of a
fixed dollar price were removed, international trade and lending, as well as
price stability, would be dealt a major blow.

CONFLICTING POLICIES

One view of how conflicts over policy choices develop can be observed by
studying the full-employment (Q^*) and BP curves in Figure 17.11. The two
lines cross and divide the economy into four sections. At all interest rates and
output levels above the BP line, excess international reserves are being accumulated; below the line, the balance of payments is in deficit. To the left of
Q^*, aggregate demand is inadequate; output is below potential. To the right,
excess demand prevails; the danger is inflation. The policies required to move
the economy to point E, where internal and external balance exists, differ in
each section. In section I, few problems are found. Expansionary policies will
reduce both unemployment and the surplus on international accounts. No
·difficulty exists in section III either, where contractionary policies are desirable.
But let us see what happens in the other two. Suppose the economy is at point
A, with output below potential and the balance of payments in deficit. What
policies could be used to move the economy to a point of internal and external
balance, such as E? (Let us assume that exchange rates are fixed, not flexible.)

Fiscal Policy. In order to reduce unemployment and lost income, fiscal policy
could be used to expand demand and output. Movements would resemble
those of Figure 17.9, but with a major difference. In Figure 17.11, even though
domestic demand is weak, international payments are in deficit. To cure the
BP problem, the IS curve would have to shift to the left to point C—a move
opposite to that needed for domestic balance. A dilemma exists; fiscal actions
taken to cure a lack of internal demand will aggravate the external problem,
and vice versa.

4. Such adverse adjustment lags are sometimes called a *J*-curve reaction. A decline in the
exchange rate means an initial loss of reserves. Only over time do the shifts in relative prices lead
to higher exchange earnings. Plotting such a movement on a chart over time, the initial losses
followed by eventual gains in reserves seem to trace out the letter *J*.

Such conflicting results occur when imports rise rapidly (and exports fall) in response to expanding output at the same time that increases in interest rates cause only mild capital inflows. In the figure, the current-account balance is sensitive to output, while the *LM* curve and the *CA* curve are relatively insensitive to interest rates. If expanded demand raises prices, difficulties are compounded. An increase in prices relative to those abroad shifts the *BP* curve up to the left, while the resulting drop in exports and rising imports make it harder to push the *IS* curve to the right.

Monetary Policy. The conflict will also be troublesome to solve by monetary policy. A decrease in the money stock shifts the *LM* curve to the left so that higher interest rates attract capital inflows and solve the balance-of-payments problem at point *D*; but another result is a decrease in internal demand. Output falls, widening the gap between actual and potential. Similarly, an attempt to solve the internal problem by increasing the money stock and shifting the *LM* curve down to the right expands the *BP* deficit. International reserves are lost. The expansionary program will be defeated by the need for

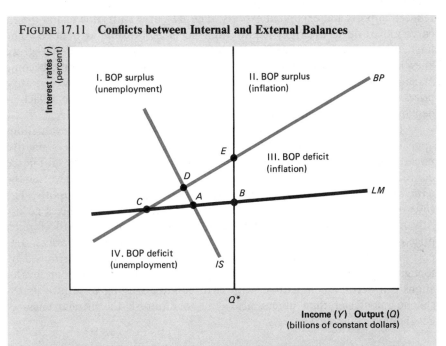

FIGURE 17.11   **Conflicts between Internal and External Balances**

The curves of full employment (Q*) and balance in the international accounts (BP) divide the space of all combinations of output and real interest rates into four sections. In each, the situation differs with respect to an excess or deficit in real aggregate demand and the balance of payments, as well as in possible actions for the economy to move to E, a point of full employment where no gains or losses occur in international reserves.

the central bank to contract the money stock. Because international reserves flow out when interest rates fall, monetary policy cannot be used to meet expansionary internal needs.

Direct Controls.   Conflicts between internal and external balance often lead to imposition of direct controls, tariffs, quotas, or other restrictions, so that losses of international balances can be limited even as the internal economy expands. In Figure 17.11, direct controls can be thought of as actions to shift the *BP* and *IS* curves so that all three curves intersect at point *B*. Controls reduce the sensitivity to domestic output and interest rates of purchases from abroad and capital flows. Controls can be expensive, however; they reduce the advantages of international trade. They are hard to police and may require expensive administrative structures. Because more expensive domestic goods must be substituted for cheaper imports, they raise internal prices. Furthermore, they invite retaliation. Tariff wars or burgeoning controls which make everyone worse off are among the evils that countries hoped to avoid by establishing the IMF and GATT.

Devaluation and Relative Prices.   Conflicts between internal and external balance can be resolved if relative prices fall. Lower domestic prices will lead to reduced imports and expanded exports. The *BP* curve shifts down, and the *IS* curve moves up to the right; equilibrium becomes possible at point *B*. The hitch, of course, occurs if insufficient ability exists to move prices down. If we knew how to do that, inflation would vanish and other problems would become manageable. Decreasing demand and increasing supply work to lower relative prices, but both results may be slow in arriving. In the meantime, a lack of demand and reduced output lower national well-being.

The difficulties encountered in these other actions make devaluations appear attractive. A fall in the exchange rate immediately lowers relative prices. Imports decline and exports rise. Both the *BP* and *IS* curves shift in the desired direction. Unfortunately, however, devaluations are likely to worsen the **terms of trade,** the quantity of domestic goods given up per unit of imports. The costs of servicing or paying off debts which are in foreign currencies go up. Adverse trade-offs lower domestic real income. Furthermore, while foreign price relationships improve, devaluations result in higher internal prices. Import prices rise immediately, even as domestic prices, formerly restrained by foreign competition, also go up. Fear of inflation and recognition that devaluations can become competitive, with each country striving to reduce its exchange rate faster than others, also tend to diminish the attractiveness of devaluation policies.

ADJUSTMENTS WITH FLEXIBLE EXCHANGE RATES

One of the strong arguments for the adoption of flexible exchange rates was the belief that they would do away with the necessity for making difficult policy choices. The exchange markets would be free of controls, while aggregate demand policies could concentrate on obtaining internal balance with full employment, free of inflation. Unfortunately, although flexible exchanges guarantee external balance, the costs of internal adjustment may nevertheless be high. Exchange-rate movements can cause a reduction in international specialization, deteriorating terms of trade, and more inflation. Shifts in capital flows and fluctuating exports and imports may create difficulties—different from but of the same type as those under fixed exchange regimes.

The key point about flexible exchange rates is that the balance of payments must be in equilibrium at all times. Foreign exchange rates must shift to insure a new balance. Suppose that Germans holding capital assets in the United States decide to sell in order to repatriate their funds. The increased demand for marks will cause the price of the dollar to decline. German goods will become more expensive in Chicago, and American goods will sell for less in Munich. These price movements will cause the export surplus of the United States to rise enough to offset exactly the deficit in the capital account.

Such changes can be analyzed in terms of the *IS* and *LM* curves. What happens to exchange rates, balance of payments, output, interest rates, and prices when a monetary expansion occurs with flexible exchange rates? Suppose that in order to increase output, monetary policy acts to shift the *LM* curve to the right. Initially, interest rates fall. However, these lower rates will cause overseas capital flows, as investors seek higher interest rates abroad. Sales of dollars by investors desiring foreign exchange will lead to a decline in the exchange rate of the dollar. Foreign goods will consequently become more expensive in the United States, and American goods cheaper abroad. Imports will fall and exports rise sufficiently so that the improvement in the export surplus will offset the deterioration in the capital account. The amount by which the *IS-LM* equilibrium must shift depends on the degree of international capital mobility. If mobility is perfect, capital flows will continue until domestic and foreign interest rates are equal. While interest rates will not have changed, output and prices will be higher and the exchange rate will have depreciated. The improvement in the balance of trade will offset the outflow of capital.

If capital markets are imperfect or if foreign interest rates move along with those in the United States, other possibilities exist. How far and how fast equilibrium shifts will depend on the degree of international capital mobility, on the price elasticities of exports and imports, on the impact of the change in exchange rates on domestic prices, and on the effect of price movements on the *IS-LM* equilibrium. Since each of the markets may adjust at a different rate, the path to equilibrium may be uneven and perhaps unsatisfactory in the fight against inflation.

THE POLICY OF DELAY

The introduction of floating exchange rates has not solved the problems of policy. Individual countries have somewhat greater freedom to manage their own economies, but their output, investments, and prices are still influenced by events abroad. Cyclical expansions and contractions among major trading partners cause sizable movements in trade and in exchange rates. Capital flows for both economic and noneconomic reasons. Fears, wars, changes in the political climate—all lead to shifts in the desirability of holding capital in particular markets. Under flexible rates, even though most countries intervened quite regularly (dirty floating), exchange rates fluctuated far more than anticipated.

The shifts in exchange rates and in demand from abroad cause instability in domestic prices and output. They affect capital availability and interest rates. Flexible rates do not insulate local from foreign markets. Furthermore, they may increase the costs of servicing existing debts. Because sharp fluctuations in exchange rates and in foreign demand have significant internal repercussions, most countries prefer to delay adjustments to international events for as long as possible. They accomplish this by using international reserves to meet their BOP deficits and by trying to control imports of goods and exports of capital by a variety of official and unofficial devices. The hope is that radical changes in policies can be avoided. Efforts are made to minimize disruptions. A poor crop year or a sharp upturn in copper prices or even a temporary spurt in inflation should not lead to massive unemployment in export or import industries if the situation is expected to reverse.

In such situations, the principal point of disagreement is whether the exchange market, by itself, can be expected to handle the problem. Do speculators take positions that help bring the market back toward equilibrium? Most observers agree that their profit-oriented actions instead can aggravate the market's problems, but it is not clear whether this is a necessary condition or whether governments interfere too soon. The issues are similar to those in the domestic sphere. Is it reasonable to expect that a government would fail to intervene in a critical market if it felt that speculators or incorrect information were causing significant national losses?

Questions relating to long-term adjustment are even more vital. If foreign producers become more efficient, what protection should be given to existing domestic industries, and for how long? The extent of loss from either long- or short-run adjustments depends on how easily an economy shifts factors of production. If unemployed steel workers can produce computers, airplanes, or some other needed product, with few frictional difficulties, damage will be slight. Youngstown and Pittsburg will continue to prosper as growth in Seattle and San Jose tapers off. However, if it is difficult to transform a steel mill into an electronics factory, while steelworkers develop the skilled fingers of those producing silicon chips, the period of transition can be long and fraught with privations.

Many observers believe that frictions are serious. As a result, markets are not left to themselves. Tariffs, quotas, or controls are chosen to ease adjustments. Increasing pressures are felt against the use of high interest rates and reduced aggregate demand as a means of solving BOP deficits. There are conflicts between internal and external balance. Lags, frictions, and problems of retraining and reshaping whole industries produce differential elasticities. Costs may be reduced if transitions are planned and allowed to occur gradually instead of all at once.

Summary

1. In an open economy the demand and supply from exports and imports become part of the equilibrium process in the goods market. Part of domestic purchases (imports) are produced abroad. The propensity to import measures such leakages. Part of domestic output is demanded by foreigners (exports).

2. International trade affects the shape of the *IS* curve. The curve will shift in response to foreign demand and to the domestic desire for imports, but also as a result of movements in exchange rates and relative prices at home and abroad.

3. Capital also flows in and out of an open economy. Shifts in income and interest rates may attract or repel capital from abroad. The movements in official reserves may shift the money supply and the *LM* curves, or they can be offset (sterilized) by actions of governments and central banks.

4. Some level of interest rates and income will balance both domestic and foreign aggregate demand and supply. Higher incomes reduce the balance on current account, while higher interest rates improve the balance on capital account. Changes in relative prices and exchange rates also influence the total flows.

5. Balance-of-payment policies are actions to influence international reserves by directly affecting international trade or capital movements. Tariffs, import quotas, exchange controls, export subsidies, taxes, and customs regulations are all methods commonly used to alter trade. Direct controls over capital movements, differential taxes, and controls over borrowing and lending with foreigners are also common.

6. Shocks to aggregate demand may cause conflicts between achieving domestic goals and a balance in international payments. An expansion in domestic demand to raise output and employment may increase imports and lower exports. The interest rates needed for full employment may cause capital to flow out.

7. Most countries prefer to absorb imbalances in the foreign sector through movements in international reserves (even though this is contrary to the implicit international "rules of the game"). However, countries in deficit will run out of reserves and must take other actions to adjust. They can alter the *IS* or *LM* curves, try to influence prices by supply management or through exchange rates, or they can use direct controls over foreign trade and capital movements.

8. No technique of adjustment is without some cost. Losses occur in efficiency and through costs of surveillance. When short-term shifts in international exchanges occur, governments adopt policies aimed at minimizing their costs, in the belief that markets cannot handle the quantity of needed transactions or that speculation will aggravate instability rather than dampening it.

9. The automatic change in relative prices and the absence of movements in official reserves under a flexible (floating) exchange-rate system reduces the need for balance-of-payments policies. However, international events still influence domestic stability through shifts in the demand for exports and imports and through movements in the price level and the availability of supplies. The effects of monetary and fiscal policies are influenced by their impact on international trade and capital flows.

Questions for Discussion and Review

1. What are the reasons for tariffs and trade restrictions? What effects do they have on other countries?

2. Discuss the impact of the foreign sector on the multiplier.

3. What are the effects of imports and exports on the *IS* and *LM* curves?

4. Define the following:
   (a) Balance-of-payments curve
   (b) Terms of trade
   (c) Sterilization
   (d) GATT

5. Discuss policies that might be invoked to remedy a decline in exports relative to imports. If prices are inflexible, what might be the best policy?

6. Why are balances of payments unstable?

7. How are policies toward internal and external demand conflicting?

8. What are the relationships between the balance of payments and the money supply?

9. Why is the balance-of-payments curve sloping upward to the right? Can it take on any other slope?

References

Dornbusch, R. "Exchange Rate Economics: Where Do We Stand?" *Brookings Papers on Economic Activity* 1(1980): 143–206.

Federal Reserve Bank of San Francisco. "Money, Prices, and Exchange Rates." *Economic Review* (Spring 1979), 5–46.

Frenkel, J. A., and H. G. Johnson, eds. *The Economics of Exchange Rates: Selected Studies.* Reading, Mass.: Addison-Wesley, 1978.

Friedman, M. "The Case for Flexible Exchange Rates." In *Essays in Positive Economics,* pp. 157–203. Chicago: University of Chicago Press, 1953.

Mundell, R. A. "The Appropriate Use of Monetary and Fiscal Policy for Internal and External Stability." *International Monetary Fund Staff Paper* 9(1962): 70–79.

Whitman, M. V. N. "The Payments Adjustment to Balance of Payments: What Have We Learned?" *American Economic Review* 65(May 1975): 133–46.

Part 7

Analysis and Policy

18

Macroeconomic Models and Decision Making

To insure continued prosperity, business executives, investors, and government officials must plan for the future. They face a constant need to decide what, if any, economic actions are desirable. Depending on the future path of the GNP and prices, some projects and some assets will be far more profitable than others. When a new government budget or a change in inventory policy is announced, analysts throughout the business and financial world immediately reexamine the assumptions and projections underlying their current activities with a view to deciding whether plans should be readjusted. Should an investment be made now or should it be delayed? Is this the time to buy or to save? The aim of macroeconomics is to improve economic decisions. Macroeconomic theories and models offer methods for analyzing current events and predicting developments in the economy. Most large corporations purchase forecasts and their staffs use macroeconomics to develop strategic models for future actions.

The discussion in this chapter begins with a description of macroeconomic decision making. Although the example is drawn from the formulation of monetary policy, the process has far wider applicability. It emphasizes the interaction between predictions, analysis of alternative actions, and decisions. Theories based on knowledge of the past are used to formulate plans aimed at improving the probability of reaching a desired objective. The discussion shows how economic theories, together with statistical techniques, computers, and judgment, combine with data to yield econometric models. These models then become the basis for making forecasts. Perhaps even more important, they are used to simulate what future developments can be expected to result from alternative actions.

The monetary sector of a group of models is selected to illustrate the development of models. Previous chapters developed simplified models of the money market. A discussion of actual econometric models illustrates the complex relationships possible between money and spending. Finally, problems of timing and of differences in multiplier estimates are discussed, together with the actual record of econometric forecasts during the 1970s. Because forecasts are not expected to be exact, a good deal of uncertainty remains in predictions and simulations. Everyone making decisions should be aware of their possible errors. Accepting a newspaper story, a forecast, or a theory at face value without considering its underlying model and possible errors can lead to poor and potentially costly decisions.

The topics in this chapter include:

The decision-making process.
Econometric models.
Policy simulations.
Models in use.
The monetary sector. An example of expansion.
Some problems with using models.
The accuracy of forecasts.

The Decision-Making Process

The number of macroanalysts and of large-scale computers and models has grown rapidly as government and business have stepped up their efforts to formulate economic policies to deal with rapid change. Although the underlying assumptions remain controversial, the actual process of decision making follows a consistent pattern. Monetarists and neo-Keynesians, activists and noninterventionists alike use similar procedures to chart the economy, to plot their own investments and policies, or to persuade others that their policies are the best.

DEVELOPING AND APPLYING FORECASTS

Throughout the government, as well as in most major corporations, analysts draw up lists of actions aimed at improving economic welfare or profits. At the heart of the decision-making process are large-scale models which forecast what will happen if the economy continues on its present path compared with the results to be expected if policies change. In addition to preparing forecasts, staffs use their models to predict how the economy could develop under alternative scenarios. Recommendations based on their results are made as to what changes will help achieve goals. In formulating their proposals, the analysts must predict both where the economy will be if no changes are made and how their proposals may be expected to alter the future. Holding in mind how uncertain are future developments, they look at as many combinations as possible in order to pick an optimum strategy. They also peer ahead as far as they can. Planning periods used to extend for only the year ahead; now horizons are more likely to be five years into the future, with decisions covering a minimum of at least eight quarters.

The staffs of the Federal Reserve, the Treasury, the Council of Economic Advisers, and the Congressional Budget Office use large-scale models containing hundreds of equations. In developing their forecasts, the staffs pore over the output of the models, simulate them in various ways, and finally come up with rather detailed forecasts and recommendations. As proposed decisions then rise through the hierarchy, economic detail and a close relationship to any given model diminish. By the time proposals reach the secretary of the Treasury or the Board of Governors of the Federal Reserve System the amount of detail has shrunk. These officials may look at tables presenting alternative projections covering 40 or 50 key series. By the time these recommendations are winnowed down to submit to the president, the entire analysis may be presented on three or four pages containing comments on only five or six key variables, together with attachments of supporting material.

Similar simplifications from large models into concise presentations are found throughout industry as well. The briefing given to a company's board of directors is far different from the report seen by the vice-president for operations. As any recommendation moves up in an organization, the relationship to the underlying model becomes more diffuse, while greater emphasis is placed on individual judgment and opinions.

TRANSFORMING FORECASTS INTO POLICY

Figure 18.1 illustrates the policy-making process. While based on the process used by government officials in making policy, it is similar to those followed in many businesses. It starts with a forecast arrived at by a combination of econometric models with judgmental views. Forecasts take a fairly standard form. They show projected levels of aggregate demand, prices, output, unemployment, balance of payments, and similar critical variables. They contain quarterly estimates for each one of these variables covering the next two or three years, together with annual projections out to five years. Forecasts made for policy purposes normally assume no change from existing policies for the variables under the control of the decision makers. Box 1 in Figure 18.1 shows such a forecast for the major measures of economic activity. Such forecasts must be examined to see if the outcome for the economy meets the nation's goals. Are the projected levels of output, prices, jobs satisfactory? If not, are they so far off base that policy actions are called for? This comparison is represented by box 2 in the diagram.

If the comparison of forecasts and goals seems unsatisfactory, alternative policies will be modeled, with as many logical changes in policy as can be handled. Box 3 of the diagram shows a simulation of alternative actions. Table 18.1, from a January 1980 report of the Congressional Budget Office, contains an example of the results of such modeling. It covers only fiscal policies, the primary congressional responsibility. In this example, the CBO estimated four

FIGURE 18.1   **Use of Models in Decision Making**

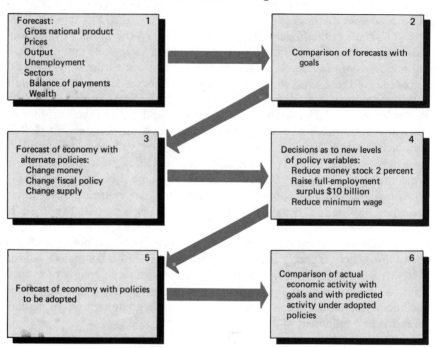

Decision making starts with a comparison of forecasts to goals (1 and 2).
Decisions to act (4) are based on simulated forecasts under alternative policies
(3). New forecasts based on modified policies (5) are tracked against actual
developments (6).

separate possibilities based on combinations of increases, or cuts, in expenditures and lowered taxes. The table shows, using simulations from large-scale
econometric models, how each action would be expected to change equilibrium
income eight quarters after the adoption of the policy. The other columns show
how such changes in spending might divide between movements in real output
and prices, as well as the resulting shifts in employment and unemployment.
On the basis of such simulations and staff reports, policy makers (Congress)
must decide whether it is worth trying, given the expected level of each variable
with or without a policy change, to adjust policies and, if so, which variable to
alter and by how much.

Such comparisons of alternate projections with goals, together with the
costs of change, lie behind decisions as to whether to undertake new policies.
For example, if, on the basis of such analysis the president accepts any proposed policies, they will be recommended either in his annual economic report
or in special reports made if the economy shifts drastically. In the same way,

TABLE 18.1   **Estimated Effects of Four Fiscal Policy Packages after Eight Quarters**

Fiscal packages	GNP (billions of current dollars)	Real GNP (billions of 1972 dollars)	Unemployment rate (percentage points)	Employment (thousands)	Consumer price index (percentage points)
$15 billion personal income tax cut and $5 billion increase in spending	26	11	−0.3	425	0.1
$15 billion payroll tax cut and $5 billion accelerated depreciation	19	13	−0.3	400	−0.2
$10 billion personal income tax cut and $10 billion cut in spending	−1	0	0	−25	0
$20 billion spending cut	−28	−12	0.3	−475	−0.1

SOURCE: Congressional Budget Office, "Entering the 1980s: Fiscal Policy Choices," January 1980. p. xx.

The first column, headed "Fiscal packages," shows four proposals for tax and spending changes. The following columns report how much the GNP, output, unemployment, employment, and prices are expected to change if a program is adopted. Estimated changes are based on simulations with a large econometric model.

further recommendations will be made by congressional budget committees as to the budget resolutions to be adopted by Congress. During these periods, the Federal Reserve continues to consult with the administration and with Congress to make sure that monetary policy is coordinated with the fiscal decisions of the government. Most political debate takes place during the period between the recommendation and the actual adoption of new policies.

The modified policies are shown in box 4 of Figure 18.1. They lead to a new forecast, as shown in box 5. If the decision is not to change policies, the forecast in box 1 will continue in effect. In either case, as the situation develops, new data appear and are compared with the last forecast. If developments are in line with the projections, all is well; but if the economy grows faster or slower than predicted or if the split of aggregate demand between prices and output differs from expectations, the entire process must be restarted. New forecasts must be made and compared again with the nation's goals. Decisions must be taken as to whether to recast the policies in effect.

Econometric Models

The diagram of the policy process shows that it starts with a comparison between where the economy is expected to be and the desired goals. The key element in policy decisions is some type of forecast. Forecasts derive from models, in most cases large-scale econometric models. While the adequacy and the weight to be given to models are constantly under review, just as the nightly weather prediction depends far more on computers and scientific models than on the feeling in someone's bones or corns, economic forecasts have come to depend on econometric models rather than on seat-of-the-pants judgments.

Econometric models are systems of mathematical equations which specify relationships among economic variables that economists believe prevail and will continue to prevail. The coefficients of the equations are estimated from past data. The equations are used to quantify assumed structural relationships. They form the basis of forecasts of what will happen to the economy if certain conditions obtain.

ESTIMATING THE MODEL

At the first stage in the construction of an econometric model, its builders write down general mathematical relationships expressing the structure of the economy as they believe it to exist. Such models are equivalent to the equations for the *IS-LM* and the *AD-AS* curves. Suppose for illustrative purposes that we write down a simple three-equation model, assuming away the financial and price-wage sectors. (Obviously, the simpler the model, the more limited its assumptions, the more restricted is its usefulness.)

$$C = \overline{C} + c_1 Y + c_2 C_{-1} + u_1. \tag{18.1}$$

$$I = \overline{I} + dY - b\overline{i} + u_2. \tag{18.2}$$

$$Y = C + I + \overline{G}. \tag{18.3}$$

Equations like the first two are called *behavioral* because they are derived from theories of the patterns of behavior that decision makers are expected to follow. They explain what determines the level of consumption and investment in any period. The first equation states that consumption depends on autonomous consumption $(\overline{C})$ and on the propensity to consume (c_1) from current income and from previous income (c_2). (This propensity is developed through a lagged relationship to prior consumption levels.) Investment depends on income and interest rates. In addition to the explanatory variables, these two equations contain an error or *disturbance* term (u), which reflects forces not contained in the model. These other forces are expected to operate in a random manner. The third equation is an *identity,* or definitional equation which is always true. It therefore lacks the disturbance term. Income is defined as equal to expenditures on $C + I + G$. The variables $\overline{i}$ and $\overline{G}$ are assumed to be exogenous policy variables. The Federal Reserve determines the interest rate, and the government determines $\overline{G}$.

The model builder selects the particular form and components of the equation so as to reflect the significant factors believed to influence consumption and investment. However, selected variables also depend on current data and what will be available when the model is used. A model builder might believe that expectations outweigh interest rates in determining investment, but since current data on expectations are lacking, this variable either must be omitted or a proxy must be constructed for it from available data. If omitted and if expectations had been correlated during much of the past period with one of the included variables, the assumption that the distubances are random may not be true. If so, even if the model seems to do a good job of explaining past movements, it may not work well for the future.

The final form of the equations also depends on the results the investigator obtains in testing the various hypotheses. The variables which remain in the model will have coefficients that pass the test of statistical significance and which result in the model's having a high explanatory value and a low standard error. Normally, the coefficients will also be tested to make sure that they lead to good forecasts beyond the period of estimation.

SOLVING THE MODEL FOR A FORECAST

Once a system of estimated equations is established, the model can be used for forecasts and simulation. Forecasts are achieved by solving the system for the value of the unknown—*endogenous*—variables, those whose values will be determined by the interactions of the model. Such a solution requires placing four kinds of information in the computer:

1. Most important is the set of equations with their constants and coefficients obtained from prior data by the fitting process. The error term in the equation is set equal to zero. While errors will occur, they have an expected value of zero.
2. Next, assumptions must be made covering each of the *exogenous* variables— those whose values are determined outside the model—for all of the future periods to be forecast. In the example, if a forecast covering each of the quarters for the next two years is desired, the person operating the model must insert expected values for interest rates and government expenditures for each one of these 8 quarters.
3. To start a new forecast, the computer must also be supplied with estimates of the initial values of the *lagged* (also called predetermined) variables. In the simple illustrative model, this is last period's consumption. In more complex models, such lagged variables might include capital stock, wealth, and price changes during each of the last 2 to 20 quarters.
4. Finally, and more controversially, the values of the constants (the autonomous $\overline{C}$ and $\overline{I}$ in the example) may be adjusted. Forecasters commonly test their models by comparing recent solutions with the actual data. If the

solutions diverge from the actual, the forecasters examine the residuals, or the differences between the forecast and actual results, for each equation. Large residuals may indicate that either the model is incorrect or the economy has changed. To correct the model, forecasters may add or subtract sums from the constants of the equations. These **add-ons** or **fudge factors** may be inserted for the first few quarters or the entire period of a forecast. For example, assume that $\bar{I}$ is $200 billion and that a study of the investment forecasts for the last 4 quarters shows they have averaged $50 billion less than actual. The forecaster might add $50 billion to $\bar{I}$ in each quarter for the set of forecasts about to be performed. Such actions assume that the autonomous desire to invest has altered, resulting in a larger $\bar{I}$ than during the period whose data were used to estimate the model—the period of fit.

While add-ons remain controversial, they are used almost unanimously. They provide a technique through which forecasters can use judgment about structural changes or omitted forces that are currently significant. Forecasters are not locked into the relationships which existed in the period of fit. Use of fudge factors has succeeded in greatly improving forecast results compared to similar models run without adjustments. However, they also make it harder to evaluate the correctness of models. The use of discretion means that the forecasts depend partly on the model and partly on the skill and judgment of the forecaster. Better predictions may not mean that a model is better but may reflect the sounder judgment of its user.

Figure 18.2 illustrates how this process works. The inputs include the policy variables $\bar{G}$ and $\bar{i}$, the add-ons to $\bar{C}$ and $\bar{I}$, and the lagged endogenous variable (C_{-1}). Next comes the estimated equations of the model. When the model is run, the endogenous variables are computed. After a first-period solution, the new estimates can be used to update the lagged endogenous variables. The model can then be run for the following periods. Thus, in the simplified model, the estimate of consumption in the first quarter becomes an input into the second quarter's solution, which in turn becomes an input for the third quarter.

When the model has been fitted, it is possible to describe and measure its estimates of how a change in a particular variable affects the economy. This is accomplished by altering the level of a variable and then seeing how this changes the values of all the endogenous variables. Whether what the model shows is a good description of reality depends on how good a job the modelers have performed. The objective is to be able to trace the path—or channel—from the change in a variable to its ultimate impact on the economy. The picture a model draws of a factor's influence on the final equilibrium depends on the theoretical approach and equations adopted. The process of fitting tells whether the analysis seems to make sense and reveals the magnitude of the effects through separate channels of influence. If the equations are illogical, the variables in the fitted equations will lack significance and the simulation will fail to track actual events, both during the period used to fit the equations and in the forecasts. The farther into the future projections go, the greater are the

FIGURE 18.2   **The Making of a Forecast**

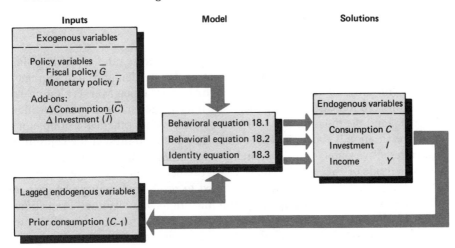

A forecast begins with a model containing constants, coefficients, and lagged endogenous variables estimated from historical statistics. The forecaster can tune the model to recent developments by adjusting the constants through add-ons. The forecaster inserts estimated values for the exogenous variables and runs the model, obtaining predictions for the future values of the endogenous variables as outputs.

chances for error. Exogenous variables are more likely to be wrong. In addition, if the lagged variables begin to wander, their errors will become cumulative. Still, the actual percentage errors for many forecasts tend not to grow much over the first year or two.

Policy Simulations

Forecasts may constitute only a minor part of a model's use. In addition, models provide estimates of expected reactions to changes in policy variables—that is, those which can be changed. They furnish estimates of the economy under alternative assumptions. Such simulations and the analytical discussions surrounding them underlie a great deal of decision making.

The historical discussions in previous chapters often utilized estimates from models as to how the policy variables interacted. While the simple concept of multipliers and the *IS-LM* curve are useful for analytical discussions, policy makers need exact spending estimates for the periods ahead. Figure 18.1 showed that the policy process began with a comparison of projections to goals. Table 18.1 showed an example of simulations of alternative fiscal policies. Such simulations occur when a gap appears to exist between the forecast and hoped-for achievements or when disagreements arise over the probable course of the economy.

A HYPOTHETICAL POLICY PRESENTATION

How the economy reacts to a given change in interest rates or fiscal policy differs depending on the current status of aggregate demand and aggregate supply. Suppose, for example, that when the Federal Open Market Committee meets, the staff forecasts that if policies are not changed, unemployment will be 7 percent and the inflation rate will be 7 percent. A hypothetical example of a staff presentation is shown in Table 18.2. The staff will present the committee with alternative simulations from their models based on the assumptions shown on the left side of Table 18.2. The forecast, predicated on no change in policies, is used as a base, and movements expected to result from policy changes are compared with it. For example, the top line, under the heading "Predictions, State 1," shows no change in policies from the basic forecast. If interest rates remain at 8 percent and no change takes place in government spending, the GNP (Y), output (Q), and price changes $(\dot{P})$ will continue as forecast.

TABLE 18.2   **Examining Predictions of Proposed Policy Changes**
(in percent or billions of dollars)

			Predictions					
	Action		State 1 ($U = 7\%$: $\dot{P} = 7\%$)			State 2 ($U = 8\%$: $\dot{P} = 6\%$)		
Row	$\bar{i}$	$\Delta\text{-}\bar{G}$	$\Delta\text{-}Y$	$\Delta\text{-}Q$	$\Delta\text{-}P$	$\Delta\text{-}Y$	$\Delta\text{-}Q$	$\Delta\text{-}P$
1	8%	0	0	0	0	0	0	0
2		50	+100	+20	+0.5%	+120	+40	+0.3%
3	10%	0	−50	−10	−0.1%	−70	−30	−0.2%
4		50	+25	+15	+0.2%	+30	+20	+0.1%

The rows under action show four fiscal and monetary policy packages measured by the level of interest rates and increases in goverment spending. The predictions show how each package is expected to alter the economy in comparison with row 1. Other factors will cause the economy to vary. The outcome of each policy will differ depending on actual economic developments, as can be seen by comparing a policy's predicted results under stages 1 and 2.

The table also includes a combination of three other policies: (1) interest rates stay at 8 percent and government expenditures are increased $50 billion; (2) interest rates are raised to 10 percent and government expenditures are held constant; and (3) both interest rates and expenditures are raised. The table shows the model's simulation of how such changes would influence demand, prices, and output. The bottom line, for example, projects that with both policies altered, GNP will rise by $25 billion. Increased demand will split between a $15 increase in constant-dollar GNP and a rise in the deflator of .2 percent. With such predictions, the FOMC must decide which policies appear best. If the optimum choice requires a combination of monetary and fiscal policy, they must also determine the chances of negotiating the proposed fiscal policy change with the president and Congress.

Suppose, however, that the majority of the committee think the staff forecast is incorrect. Instead, they believe that unemployment will rise to 8 percent and inflation will decline to 6 percent. They would then ask the staff to simulate these alternative conditions. To perform this task, the initial inputs into the previous forecast must be adjusted. The staff would have to vary their assumptions with respect to the exogenous variables and add-ons so that the forecast of the model will agree with the judgment of the committee. When this tuning has been accomplished, the alternative policies can be simulated again. The right side of Table 18.2, labeled "State 2," shows the results when the model has been adjusted by add-ons or changes in other exogenous variables so that it forecasts 8 percent unemployment and 6 percent inflation, with no change in the monetary target or budget. With the model adjusted to forecast 8 percent unemployment and 6 percent inflation, the policy simulations yield quite different results. The trade-offs between real output and prices would improve under each indicated policy. This follows from the assumption of more slack. With less pressure on supply conditions, the multipliers of aggregate demand and the trade-off between prices and output differ.

With alternative forecasts and estimates of the impact of changes before them, the decision makers must make their choices. Decisions will depend on their individual judgments as to which forecast and which multipliers to accept, as well as on the values they place on particular trade-offs between more output and jobs and more inflation. In addition, in arriving at their decisions, they must constantly hold in mind the probability that there are errors in the underlying assumptions, in the forecasts, and in the multipliers estimated by the models.

Models in Use

The purpose of econometric models is to explain past economic events, to forecast future ones, and to evaluate possible changes. An examination of selected models in more detail imparts a better feel for their content and operation. Early models, originating in the late 1930s, contained from 6 to 12 equations to explain the entire economy. More recent ones, which have grown with computer technology, encompass from 150 to 1,000 equations.

SIMPLE AND MORE COMPLEX MODELS

Not all models have grown, however; some remain small because they are not designed to perform complicated tasks. An example of a small model is the

FIGURE 18.3   **Equations and Flow Diagram of the St. Louis Federal Reserve Bank Monetarist Model**

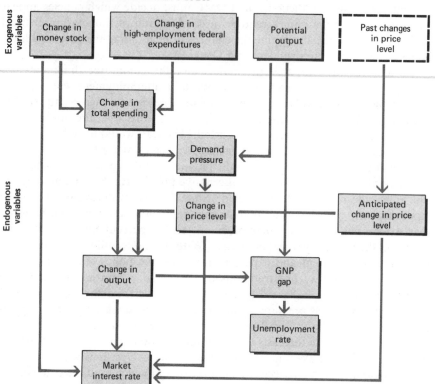

The St. Louis model is based on 8 equations. The exogenous inputs are shown at the top—changes in the money stock and high-employment federal expenditures, the level of potential output, and past changes in prices. When estimated future values for the exogenous variables are combined with the model's constants and coefficients, the model estimates and explains the forces determining nominal GNP, prices, output, unemployment, and interest rates.
SOURCE: L. C. Andersen and K. M. Carlson, "A Monetarist Model for Economic Stabilization," *Monthly Review* (April 1970), pp. 9–10.

well-known one of the Federal Reserve Bank of St. Louis. It contains only 5 behavioral equations and 3 identities. It is not meant for forecasting or to explain the probable sectoral impacts of changes in demand. For this reason, the number of equations has been severely limited. The builders of the model state that it was developed to permit testing of stabilization policies. They assume that the model can measure the relative importance of money and fiscal policies, and they believe that they have succeeded in doing so.[1]

1. L. C. Andersen and K. M. Carlson, "A Monetarist Model for Economic Stabilization," *Monthly Review*, St. Louis Federal Reserve Bank, April 1970, pp. 7–25; and L. C. Andersen and K. M. Carlson, "St. Louis Model Revisited," *International Economic Review* 15(June 1974): 305–27.

Figure 18.3 shows the variables and relationships within the St. Louis model. To make it work, the operator estimates future changes in the money stock, high-employment federal expenditures, and potential output. He must also furnish past changes in prices. With these limited variables and the equations derived from fitting to past data, the model builder can project aggregate demand, output, prices, employment, and interest rates. As shown in the diagram, both money and government expenditures could, in theory, determine aggregate demand. In fact, in the fitted equations, money alone dominates spending. This model indicates a much lower fiscal-policy multiplier than most other econometric models. Fiscal policy has only a limited and temporary effect. While initially changes in spending can alter both output and prices, over time, according to the model, more money only raises prices. The model comes close to describing an economy in which the crude quantity theory applies. Excess spending does not affect real output or employment, since they are determined by supply factors exogenous to the model. Additional spending, except in the very short run, only raises prices.

Most models are more disaggregated; that is, they divide the economy into more sectors and show more detailed interrelationships. For example, Figure 18.4 shows a much more complex model than that of Figure 18.3. The arrows at the left of Figure 18.4 indicate that aggregate demand depends on income, levels of production, prices, and a set of financial variables. In turn, as shown by the arrows on the right, aggregate demand creates movements in production, demand for labor, and income. When demand and output rise, prices, productivity, interest rates, and financial balance sheets are affected.

The top line in the model shows six sectors of aggregate demand. In practice, many current models subdivide each of these. They may include from 4 to 15 kinds of consumption, an equal number of investment categories, plus several types of government expenditures, as well as a further subdivision of the foreign sector. Such models end up with between 10 and 40 equations for final demand. When the other categories are added, it is not unusual to find current models that contain from 100 to 300 equations, even when they include no industrial breakdown. In some cases, where the model attempts to measure demand and supply by industry, several hundred more equations may be included.

In addition to the basic equations, the models require a large number of identities; for example, to translate the current capital stock requires movements in the estimates of investment and depreciation to obtain the next period's stock. These identities may require 50 to 100 equations. Furthermore, from 50 to 100 exogenous variables will be required. These may include some government policies, foreign trade and agriculture, which are hard to model, as well as dummy variables which allow for such factors as strikes and special regulatory changes. Dummy variables take on specified values (usually one) when they are effective (when the strike is on); otherwise they are zero.

THE PURPOSE OF ADDED EQUATIONS

Why has this proliferation occurred? What has been gained, and what lost?

FIGURE 18.4   **Overview of the DRI Quarterly Model of the U.S. Economy**

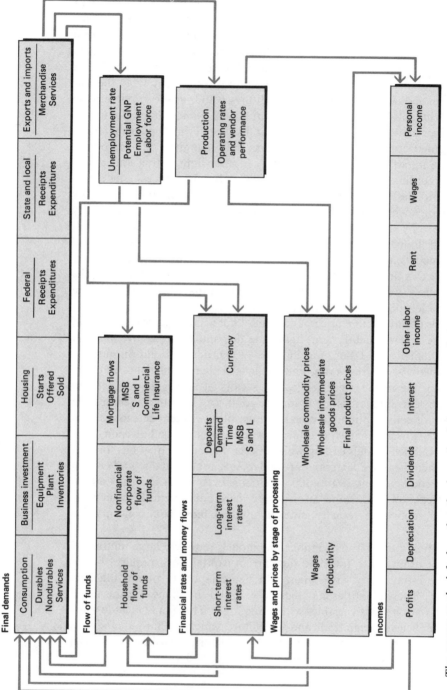

The arrows on the left show that the demands of the sectors result from the interaction of incomes, wages and prices, and financial variables. Their values result from the movements in demand and supply represented by the arrows on the right. Exogenous variables, not shown separately but inserted into specific equations, include the money stock, government expenditures, and taxes. The model contains over 780 separate equations.

The splitting up of each of the principal sectors into component parts is expected to produce a better representation of reality. For example, not all consumption is influenced by the same variables. Autos, clothing, food, and housing services may each be affected by unique factors. With their own estimating equations, these unique features can be taken into account, thereby improving the ability of the model to describe the real world.

Adding components enhances the ability to measure what happens when policies change. If tax cuts are proposed, we would like to know how they affect both supply and demand. Separate equations are needed to show the necessary detail. Some sets of equations have been added to make the model consistent with theoretical developments. The greater emphasis in recent years on the effect of expectations, wealth, and supply has accelerated the search for ways of building these variables into the models. If they are missing or are treated in a purely exogenous manner, information is lost.

More complete equations allow greater depth in analyzing errors. They may also improve the ability to tune the model to recent events. It is easier to explain errors and to decide where add-ons are called for if the specific variables causing the problem can be isolated. For example, without sufficient detail, the effects of higher energy costs are likely to be hidden or misspecified. In more disaggregated models, the impacts of energy prices may be treated separately instead of being lumped together with all other costs.

Some proliferation originates because firms want knowledge of variables most likely to affect their particular operations. For example, financial institutions are interested in many types of interest rates. They are both borrowers and lenders in several markets. For this reason, models may include equations for as many as 20 separate interest rates. Those interested in the stock market and investments want detailed equations showing production, wages, costs, and profits for as many industries as possible.

As disaggregation increases, the number of variables in each equation also tends to expand. It is not unusual in current models to find 8 or 10 independent variables influencing the demand for autos or houses. Many of these variables may also have lagged values covering each quarter in the previous year or more. Some of this disaggregation does not enhance the ability of a model to predict the overall economy. Proliferation of estimates by industry or by different interest rates may contribute very little to accuracy. Moreover, since the model must still be estimated from a limited number of independent observations, the added detail may give a false sense of security. The seeming importance of certain variables may not be very robust; in other words, their coefficients may change rapidly as one or a few more observations are included.

When the complexity of models grows, they become harder to analyze, and it is more difficult to determine what is driving them. Teams of operators become necessary, and it is harder for any one person or for the group as a whole to grasp what the model is actually reporting. No one knows what the optimum amount of disaggregation is. It will vary with changes in the economy. The analysis of aggregate supply is still in its infancy. It is difficult to judge how many more equations will be needed to improve the supply side of the model and make it equivalent to the demand side. Many believe that a model with about 150 behavioral equations plus a similar number of identities could yield most macroeconomic information. With existing data and theories, the main value of further proliferation is to make models more useful to specific firms or decision makers. Such added information, however, may actually work to the detriment of somewhat better overall projections.

The Monetary Sector: An Example of Expansion

The increasing complexity of macroeconomic models becomes obvious if we trace the development from 1960 to 1980 of a single sector. The monetary sector is useful for this purpose. It grew from about 10 equations in the early large-scale models to almost 200 equations in current models. The analysis also shows the many channels of monetary impacts on the economy traced by the modern portfolio theory of demand for and supply of money. This view contrasts sharply with the simple quantity theory of money, in which a change in the money stock will cause over the following year an equivalent change in spending. Current models show changes in money causing a reshuffling of portfolios in all sectors of the economy. These movements alter financial prices, lending, and borrowing. Changes in interest rates, in money balances, and in credit availability cause differential movements in types of spending, depending on how influential credit is in each spending decision.

THE EARLY MODELS

The St. Louis (Federal Reserve Bank) econometric model shown in Figure 18.3 approximates a simple monetarist model of the economy. It has a single monetary variable—the exogenous money supply. This is the prime variable driving the model. Such a paucity of variables and effect is in complete contrast to the development of most modern models, but it is not that different, except in its channels, from the earlier econometric models. In models built prior to 1960, aggregate demand reflected an *IS-LM* concept, but they too contained only a single variable for the monetary sector. Usually this was an exogenous interest rate in an equation similar to that in the illustrative three-equation model. All monetary effects were generated by the effect of this interest rate on investment.

During the 1960s, in the first large-scale model (known as the Brookings Model) and in a later one built by professors at MIT and the staff of the Federal Reserve Board, the financial sector began to expand. These models contained between 10 and 20 monetary supply and demand equations. Monetary policies either changed the monetary base or the federal funds rate. Such changes shifted the supply or demand for money as described in the theory of the *LM* curve. Figure 18.5 illustrates the channels of transmission from one of these

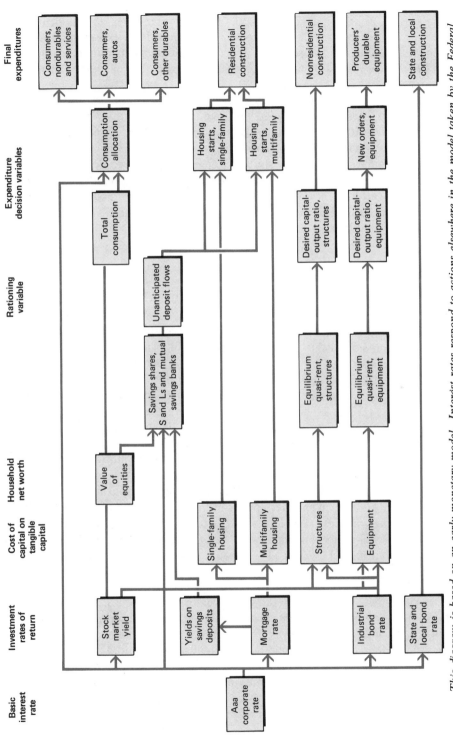

FIGURE 18.5   Flow Chart of the First-Round Effects of Monetary Policy in the Federal Reserve-MIT Economic Model

This diagram is based on an early monetary model. Interest rates respond to actions elsewhere in the model taken by the Federal Reserve, to output, and to the behavior of owners of asset portfolios. Interest movements alter capital costs, wealth, and credit availability. These financial forces influence the desire to spend and expenditures in the GNP, as shown on the right.

SOURCE: F. deLeeuw and E. M. Gramlich, "The Channels of Monetary Policy," Board of Governors of the Federal Reserve System, *Federal Reserve Bulletin* (June 1969), pp. 484.

early models. When monetary policy changed, in order to regain equilibrium, interest rates on corporate bonds, mortgages, savings deposits, and municipal bonds responded, as did stock prices. Deposits in financial institutions changed and stock prices rose. The model shows the responses to the changes in interest rates.

The new interest rates altered the cost of capital and, therefore, the desired level of the capital stock and the investments in plant and equipment needed to bring it to equilibrium. They also increased the demand for state and local construction. New stock prices altered wealth and consequently influenced consumption. Finally, shifting interest rates altered deposits (disintermediation). Such deposit flows, together with changes in the mortgage interest rate, affected housing construction. Thus, in this model, monetary policy influenced final demand through three channels: interest rates, wealth, and credit availability.

A MORE EXTENDED MONETARY SECTOR

This model can be contrasted with the financial sector of the large DRI model as it existed in the late 1970s. At that time, the DRI model's financial sector alone contained 110 behavioral equations and 75 identities. Some of the channels of transmission in this model are traced out in Figure 18.6.

Initially a change in monetary policy alters either the monetary base or the federal funds rate. To bring portfolios back into balance, changes take place in balance sheets of households, nonfinancial corporations, and four separate types of financial institutions. Furthermore, the financing needs of the federal, state, and local governments are affected. In the model, each balance sheet contains 10 to 20 separate items including currency, deposits, bonds, stock, houses, other durables, installment debt, other debt, mortgages, and net worth.

The portfolio reshufflings cause interest rates and various financial ratios and prices to shift. Such changes appear in the third column of the figure. In addition to new interest rates and stock prices, financial institutions become more or less willing to make consumer and mortgage loans and to purchase bonds or other financial assets. The amount of debt held by households and corporations, as well as the ratio of their debt to income and the amount of their required debt repayments, all move.

All of these changes in interest rates, wealth, debt burdens, and cash flows due to the portfolio realignments affect final demand. For example, consumption is influenced by consumer interest rates, the outstanding installment debt, the ratio of debt to net worth held by households, and required debt payments as a percentage of current income. Wealth and expectations are affected through the stock market, as well as through increases in income and new money. Each of these factors in turn has an impact on desires for specific types of consumption expenditures. In the same way, investment responds to move-

FIGURE 18.6   A More Disaggregated Model of Monetary Channels

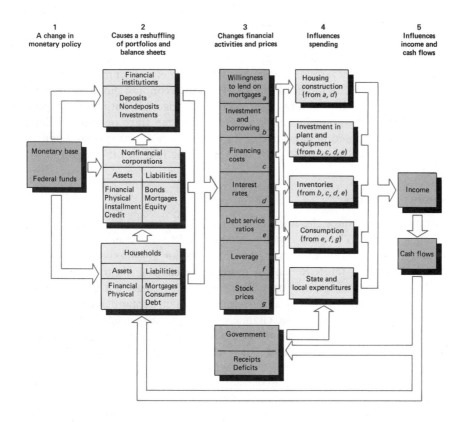

Changes in the monetary base or the federal funds rate cause a reshuffling of financial portfolios. The consequent movements in interest rates, capital costs, wealth, and credit availability, plus government financial requirements, influence decisions to spend, expenditures, and income. Financial sectors, such as this one, may use 200 separate equations to track the forces at work.

ments in interest rates and the cost of capital through financing charges and the discount effect on the rental cost of capital   Furthermore, debt-equity ratios move, as does the willingness of financial institutions to make mortgage commitments. Each of these factors influences investment and the output of investment goods.

Finally, shifts in aggregate demand alter income and cash flows, which also affect the household and corporate balance sheets. State, local, and federal spending are affected by interest-rate movements, as well as in response to income and output effects on their revenues. Fiscal-policy multipliers shift in response to financial factors and interest rates.

In contrast to the early models, in which monetary policy was represented by a single exogenous variable operating directly on final demand, current models are obviously extremely complex. The channels reflect most of the ways in which monetary and financial theory tells us the economy should be affected when monetary policy moves. The computer, together with the complete model of which the financial sector is only a part, can trace out the predicted effect of any proposed policy change, showing how it affects specific financial prices and balance sheets, when the change will be felt, and its magnitude.

AN EXOGENOUS SHOCK

Such models also show the interaction among spending sectors and with the monetary sphere. They can explain instability and cyclical movements in demand. To see how this works suppose that a major automotive innovation—perhaps a decided improvement in gasoline mileage—leads to a 20 percent spurt in the demand for new cars. What do such models tell us? Car sales jump, but they also start a cyclical movement in which demand and output first rise and then fall. What are the channels leading to the cyclical effect?

Higher auto sales raise income and output, increasing through the multiplier desires to invest and consume. In addition, cash flows rise throughout the system, changing balance sheets, the flow of funds, and financial ratios. The financial factors reinforce the expansion. Expectations are raised because higher incomes and rising profits increase stock prices. Since production takes time to adjust, some of the initial demand is met by an unplanned drop in inventories, but later, output expands to return inventory stocks to their normal level.

Now, however, the negative factors begin to take effect. On the assumption that the total number of cars needed has not changed, demand for new auto production after a time will decline. The initial spurt causes an excess of cars in the hands of consumers above their normal desire and this must be worked off. This adverse effect is reinforced since consumers had to increase their installment debt in order to buy the new gas-saving cars. The need to repay this debt holds down future consumption. The size of the necessary cutback is partially reduced because higher incomes accelerate the scrapping of older cars and raise the level of the desired stock. The negative effects are strengthened because the growth in output leads to a greater demand for labor and production and to bottlenecks and shortages which cause costs and prices to go up. In turn, the demand for greater transactions balances and rising price expectations brings about higher interest rates. When prices and interest rates start up, expectations tend to decline. New auto sales drop below normal as a result of lowered expectations, larger stocks in the hands of consumers, greater outstanding installment debts, and higher prices.

Over time, a cyclical pattern develops. Initially, the shock raises demand above its trend, but after a period, fewer autos are sold, and production drops below the long-term trend. Through the multiplier and the inventory cycle, these effects spread to other consumption goods and investments. These cyclical effects tend to dampen out after a specific shock. However, the economy may experience similar shocks in other areas. If they come sufficiently close together, depending on how they interact, a major fluctuation can occur in total demand and in output.

Some Problems with Using Models

Knowledge of how the econometric models work provides a background for understanding part of the decision process and the controversies that surround it. The decision process presented in Figure 18.1 shows that before new policies are adopted, it is necessary to reach a verdict that current actions will lead to unsatisfactory results and that measures are available that would improve the future state of the economy. Agreement must be reached to adopt the new policies, after which they must be properly administered. Difficulties may be encountered at each of these steps.

Three types of forces enter into the ability of models to function as a useful tool in shaping policies:

1. The timing of policy moves determines whether they will be helpful or harmful. Delays in adopting policies and further delays before they become effective may be so great that their impact will be adverse rather than favorable.
2. Changes in policy variables must be of appropriate magnitude. The effect of an increase or decrease in a variable will depend on its multiplier. How much will spending rise or fall per unit change in the policy variable?
3. The final critical factor in decision making is that the forecasts and the model used must be accurate enough so that after any policy is changed, the odds favor the economy's coming closer to achieving the goals sought than if no changes were made. Whether or not this happens depends on the reliability of the forecasts and the models.

THE TIMING PROBLEM: POLICY LAGS

To be effective, demand policy changes must lower aggregate demand when it is excessive and raise it when it is too low. Success depends on the ability to forecast where the economy will be if left to itself, the amount by which the policy change will alter demand, and the time it takes for spending to be modified. Suppose that a continuation of excess demand is forecast. The Federal Reserve then decides to fight inflation by reducing the money supply. A danger exists that spending will decline just as the economy turns down of its own accord. In the same way, fiscal policies modified to raise demand may cause excess spending if other forces work in the same direction.

The shorter the lag between the need for a policy and the time it becomes operative, the more it is likely to be effective and useful rather than harmful. Figure 18.7 illustrates an accepted way of thinking about policy lags. First, time is required before actions are taken; this is called the *inside lag*. Second, after the policy variable is changed, its effect on the economy may be delayed; this is the *outside lag*. If the two lags together take too long, the policy may have adverse and undesired results.

The time required to change a policy instrument comprises several factors. Forecasters must gather data on what is happening. Some information, such as interest rates, is available almost instantaneously. Money supply figures come in weekly; but erratic movements and revisions ("noise") in the data require a longer period before they can be considered significant. Unemployment statistics are available monthly, but again, it takes a longer time to establish a trend. GNP figures come near the end of a quarter, but they are also subject to future revision.

Data once obtained must be inserted into models, and forecasts must be made. It takes time before a high probability can be assigned that the economy has entered a new phase. During this interval, discussion takes place over policy. Congress, the executive branch, and the Federal Reserve all discuss whether policy variables should be changed, and if so, which ones. Great variations are found in the elapsed time between the first indications of necessary action and final implementation of new policies. At times, lags in mone-

FIGURE 18.7   **Components of Lags in Policies**

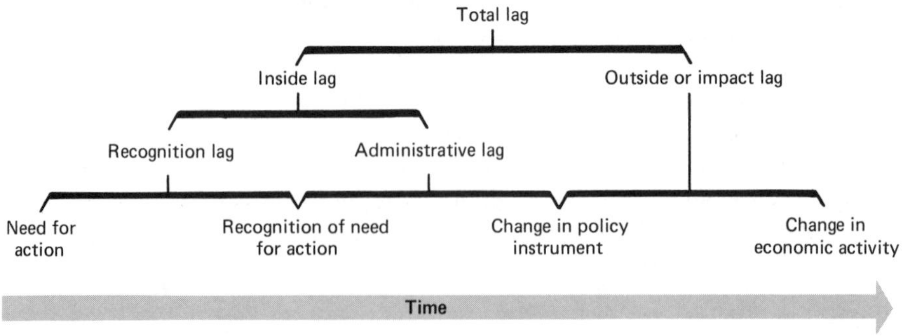

Moving from left to right, policy lags are shown as: the time to recognize the need for action; the time to change the policy instrument (both are part of the inside lag); and the time it takes the economy to react to the changed investment—the outside lag.

tary policy have been short. On the other hand, during the Vietnam War period, fiscal action was delayed for more than two years after most analysts recognized a dangerous inflationary situation.

Once policies have been altered, their impact may be delayed. Changes in the money supply or in taxes or in government spending are not concentrated on a given day. Money-supply growth can be reduced from 5 percent to 2 percent almost overnight, but its effect on spending must build up. Similar problems arise, perhaps to an even greater degree, with fiscal policy.

The problem which can be caused by timing is illustrated in Figure 18.8. Assume that in this diagram, the economy reaches an inflationary peak and then starts down; the colored line shows its path if left alone. An optimum level of aggregate demand over the next several years might be the one illustrated by the black line. To achieve such a desired outcome, policies ought to increase demand after point 2 and decrease it after point 3. But what if delays cause the policies which add to demand not to become effective until point 3? In that case, their net effect (lighter-color line) would be to make the situation worse in comparison to a passive policy.

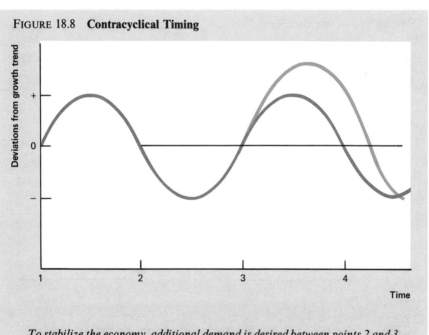

FIGURE 18.8   **Contracyclical Timing**

To stabilize the economy, additional demand is desired between points 2 and 3 in order to fill the gap below the black line, while stability will be enhanced by reduced demand between 3 and 4. Incorrect timing of policy can result in the extra demand being created at the wrong time, as shown by the lighter-color line.

DIFFERING ESTIMATES OF LAGS AND MULTIPLIERS

In addition to timing, the effectiveness of policies depends on which are chosen and on the state of the economy when action is taken. Every instrument has a separate pattern which will vary with the supply situation. Movements in demand, for instance, have different impacts on prices and output depending on the amount of unemployed resources. Thus estimates of multiplier effects— through changes in government spending—must be simulated in models which contain the supply and demand conditions expected to exist when the changes are effective. Furthermore, major models differ in their estimates of magnitudes and timing for the multipliers depending on the theory built into them. The multiplier estimates of any particular group shift every time the model is revised and the state of the economy changes.

Figure 18.9 contains examples of how multiplier estimates depend on the construction of the individual models. For the estimates in the figure, specified changes in government policies were assumed to occur at a certain state of the economy. Each model then estimated the effects of this change. Most models predicted fiscal multipliers of 2 to 2½, with the maximum expansion occurring in

FIGURE 18.9   **Estimated Multipliers**

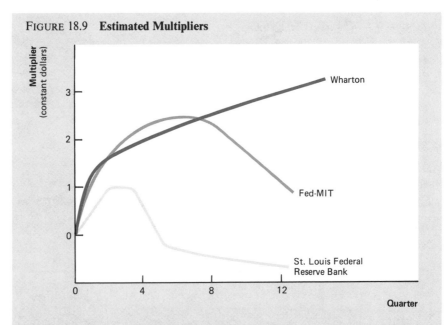

The lines show each model's estimate of how nondefense government spending is multiplied in terms of real output. Thus, with 4 quarters of change, the St. Louis model shows a multiplier of .5 (government spending crowds out private); the Fed-MIT model has a multiplier of 2.2, and Wharton III one of 2.0.
SOURCE: G. Fromm and L. R. Klein, "A Comparison of Eleven Econometric Models of the United States," *American Economic Review* 63(May 1973):391, Table 5.

4 to 6 quarters. The figure also illustrates the minimal effects from fiscal policy shown by the St. Louis Federal Reserve Bank monetarist model, in which the multiplier never exceeds 1 and falls off rapidly. Fiscal changes exert a negative impact on real output by the middle of the second year. At that time, the larger, more detailed models still show multipliers of 1½ to 2. Estimated lags and magnitudes for monetary policy also vary greatly from model to model.

The length and differences in lag estimates raise serious questions as to the possibility of altering policy in time to do any good. If the average interval between the beginning of a contraction and the middle of the next expansion is a year and a half, and if because of both the inside and outside lags, a change in policy exerts most of its effect two to three years after the economy starts to turn down, the lag problem makes fine-tuning appear extremely difficult, if not impossible. The effects of policy changes would come at the wrong time more often than not. If the length of the lags varies over time, difficulties in predicting the effects of policy changes are still greater. It should be recognized, however, that this problem is based on the assumption that the economy will reverse itself and return to the full employment level of its own accord. If inflation or deflation are longer-run threats, the danger of poor timing diminishes rapidly. Action to increase demand would have been helpful at most times between 1931 and 1938.

The Accuracy of Forecasts

Forecasts are not expected to have 100 percent accuracy. The structure of the economy is dynamic. It contains random or chance elements which cause forecasts from even the best of models to diverge from actuality. More important, no model exactly replicates the economy. Simplifications are necessary; model builders make mistakes. The forecasts also depend on the judgments of their operators, who supply the assumptions as to how the exogenous variables, such as expectations, will move during the policy period. They tune the models, using adjustments or add-ons. How well the model is managed influences both the forecasts and the simulated results of policy changes.

THE PERFORMANCE RECORD

Given the importance of models for decision making both in government and in business, it is worth looking at how well or poorly they performed during the decade of the 1970s. In examining their results, we are reminded of the old gag, "Compared to what?" Compared purely to judgmental, intuitive forecasts, or to naïve assumptions that what has been happening will continue to happen, the forecasts have done quite well. Compared to some absolute standard of what we would like, the results may not look as good. Table 18.3 gives the results of two forecasts: one, the official one made and published by the Council

TABLE 18.3   **Mean Absolute Errors of Annual Predictions 1969–1980**
(percentage points)

	Forecast of:		
	Nominal GNP	Constant-dollar GNP	Implicit price deflator
Council of Economic Advisers	1.0	1.0	1.2
ASA-NBER	1.0	0.9	1.1

SOURCE: For 1969–76: V. Zarnowitz, "On the Accuracy and Properties of Recent Macroeconomic Forecasts," *American Economic Review* 68 (May 1978): 314, 316 (updated by author).

Each figure shows the average for 12 separate years of the absolute difference between the forecast and the estimated actual outcome a year after the forecast. Even though the Council of Economic Advisers' forecasts are constrained by the CEA's political position, their forecasting record is only marginally poorer than the consensus forecast.

of Economic Advisers, the other the median of a group of major business and private economists whose forecasts are reported quarterly in advance to the American Statistical Association and the National Bureau of Economic Research. This table compares average errors in forecasts made at the end of one year, covering changes in the GNP in output and prices expected to occur during the course of the next year.

For the 12 years, the mean absolute error for predicting nominal GNP a year ahead for each set of forecasts was about 1 percent of the level of the GNP. For many purposes such a record would be thought excellent, but the average may conceal periods of more serious problems. Furthermore, still greater accuracy is desirable, given the major policy decisions that must be made.

As the period covered by a forecast is extended, the forecast deteriorates somewhat. This fact, as well as the considerable year-to-year variations around the averages, is brought out in Figure 18.10. An average of the forecasts made by five major econometric models for a period 4 quarters ahead is compared with actual results. Again, comparisons are possible for total spending, output, and price changes. The figure shows the percentage error for the median of the forecasts made four quarters earlier. Several points are worth noting. On the whole, the predictions for output—real GNP—have been the best. More than half of the average forecasts for output were within .5 percent of the actual. On the other hand, the forecasts for the 1974–75 recession were extremely poor. The prediction made in the first quarter of 1974, when the recession was just starting, for the first quarter of 1975 was 7 percent too high—by far the worst record of the forecasters. Predictions, however, appear to be improving. The predictions for the recession of 1980 (not shown on the chart) were far better than those for 1974–75.

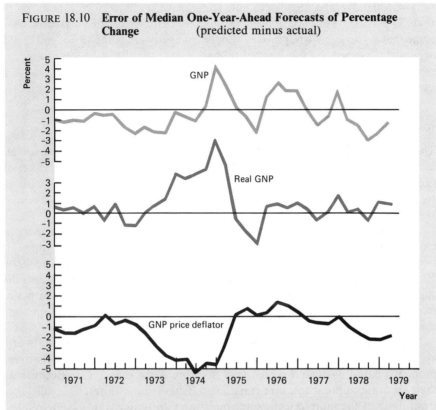

FIGURE 18.10   **Error of Median One-Year-Ahead Forecasts of Percentage Change**   (predicted minus actual)

The three curves show the median percentage error made by the five major econometric forecasting services in their predictions of how the macroeconomy would perform four quarters later. Most of the predictions clustered around the median—some doing better in one period, others in the next. The 1974–75 inflation and recession were missed badly. The revised models then improved significantly.
SOURCE: G. K. McNees, "The Forecasting Record for the 1970s," *New England Economic Review* (September/October 1979), Table 5.

The forecasts for prices have been the poorest. This was especially true at the start of the decade. The models badly missed the effects of the supply shocks and removal of price controls in 1973 and 1974. They also erred in 1978–79, but not as much. In the earlier period, the errors in forecasts of prices and real GNP often offset each other. The predictions of demand were quite good, but the models failed to divide the spending properly into its price and output components. This type of mistake diminished as the models were altered to include more supply-side equations.

When the results of the forecasts are compared to a naïve one which assumes that changes that have been taking place will continue, they do quite well. On the average, they were able to improve on naïve forecasts by more than 50 percent. They were also considerably better than forecasts which assume that if you knew what money supply changes were going to be, you could accurately forecast the GNP (even though in fact the future money supply is not known when forecasts are made).[2] A study by Victor Zarnowitz shows a quite steady improvement in forecasts of nominal GNP over time.

SOME PROBLEMS WITH FORECASTING ACCURATELY

Table 18.3 and Figure 18.10 showed that while forecasts have done rather well in recent years, they are far from perfect. Forecasts miss their mark because of failure in the underlying econometric models or because of faulty judgment as to changes in the exogenous variables. The economy is always subject to shocks. If they are incorrectly anticipated, the forecast will err.

Because analysts talk to each other and share ideas, forecasts tend to cluster around a mean. Still, at any time some forecasters will be indicating the need for a different set of policies than most of the others. If we examined 40 or 50 major forecasts, we would probably find that while a consensus would suggest a certain course of action, some would always be at odds with the majority. Some economists will always throw doubt on proposed changes because they obtain different results from their particular model.

General agreement is lacking as to how systems react to individual variables. If incorrect theories lead to wrong measures of the reaction to changes, proposals based on such a model may do more harm than good. Because of their separate approaches, monetary models have quite different coefficients from those of the more eclectic ones built from an underlying *IS-LM* model. As a result, even when all are forecasting similar movements in the economy, their policy recommendations are likely to disagree.

Such lack of agreement is exacerbated by contrasting views as to how movements in aggregate demand divide between prices and output. Forecasts of aggregate demand were considerably better than were those for prices and output. Initially, the models primarily projected aggregate demand, and they steadily improved their performance of this task. But their modeling of aggregate supply was naïve. As the importance of supply has become evident, greater effort has been devoted to analyzing and modeling the operative factors on the supply side. While it is still embryonic, there is hope that improvements on the supply side will be possible, similar to those made in modeling nominal GNP. During the late 1970s the consensus for a more deflationary policy would have been reached more easily if everyone had been convinced that a drop in

---

2. Examples of evaluations of forecasting performance can be found in S. K. McNees, "The Forecasting Record for the 1970s," *New England Economic Review* (September/October 1979), pp. 33–53; V. Zarnowitz, "On the Accuracy and Properties of Recent Macroeconomic Forecasts," *American Economic Review* 68 (May 1978): 313–19; R. G. Davis, "The Monetary Base as an Intermediate Target for Monetary Policy," Federal Reserve Bank of New York, *Quarterly Review* 4 (Winter 1979–80): 1–10.

aggregate demand would lower inflation more than it would depress output. But because many were sure that prices would continue to rise, with the bulk of the drop in demand acting merely to lower employment and increase unemployment, agreement on what to do was more difficult to achieve.

Furthermore, the models do not do a good job of differentiating among the various theories. The errors in predicting the results of changes are greater than errors in the overall forecasts. Thus, while the forecast for aggregate demand may be accurate within 1 percent, predictions of the effect of changes in the money supply on interest rates or spending may be off by 50 percent or more. Similar errors can arise with respect to other variables.

As Chapters 15 and 19 show, the models have been under still more basic attacks by some of those who emphasize rational expectations and supply-side effects. They point out that the models are based on past performance and past reactions to changes. They believe that experience will have only slight relevance to the future if an entirely new situation develops. While all agree that such drastic changes are theoretically possible, many feel that history ought to be given great weight. They would place low probabilities on the likelihood that any sudden movements of the economy will occur which depart radically from past relationships. How much faith is placed in models is one of the factors underlying the policy differences discussed in the next chapter.

Summary

1. Business and government decisions to act or not to act are based on forecasts and simulations of the expected results of alternative actions. The forecasts and simulations are tempered by judgment. In addition, policy decisions are based on calculations of the economic and political costs of change. Actions must be planned in the light of the uncertainty of the predictions.

2. Underlying most predictions and suggested policies are econometric as well as analytical models of the economy. The models vary in size from only a few equations to as many as a thousand.

3. The models make possible predictions of how the economy will react to policy changes under a variety of possible future states of the economy.

4. In attempts to supply more information about the economy's structure, the effect of different variables, and how to improve forecasts, model builders have disaggregated their models. Some have increased the number of equations a hundredfold.

5. The monetary sector furnishes a good example of disaggregation. In early models, an exogenous interest-rate movement directly influenced investment and then GNP through the multiplier. In later models, changes in monetary policy are traced through impacts on balance sheets, interest rates, liquidity, credit availability, and wealth to a number of final demand sectors, and then through multipliers to the GNP.

6. The record of forecasts is mixed. Predictions have improved on naïve or simple models and on pure judgment and feel. At crucial times, however, errors tend to be large. Forecasts of spending tend to be more reliable than predictions of what happens to sector demand, prices, and the effects of changes in variables.

7. The uncertainty in the timing and magnitude of policies and in the forecasts and simulations increases the difficulty of obtaining a consensus as to desirable moves. Disagreements over predictions exacerbate arguments over theory.

Questions for Discussion and Review

1. Discuss the relationships among the following terms:
    (a) Econometric model
    (b) Behavioral equation
    (c) Endogenous variable
    (d) Exogenous variable

2. What is the role of economic theory in econometric modeling?

3. What are econometric models used for?

4. Discuss the steps involved in making a forecast from an econometric model.

5. What are the advantages and disadvantages to having extremely large econometric models?

6. Discuss the reasons why forecasts from econometric models are subject to error.

7. Why is the St. Louis model regarded as a monetarist model?

References

Andersen, L. C., and Carlson, K. M. "St. Louis Model Revisited." *International Economic Review* 15(June 1974): 305–26.

Intrilligator, M. D. *Econometric Models, Techniques, and Applications.* Englewood Cliffs, N. J.: Prentice-Hall, 1978.

Klein, L. R. "Econometrics." Conference Board *Across the Board* (February 1979): 49–58.

McNees, S. K. "The Forecasting Record For the 1970s." *New England Economic Review* (September/October 1979), pp. 33–53.

Miller, P., and Kaatz, R. *Introduction to the Use of Econometric Models in Economic Policy Making.* Minneapolis, Minn.: Federal Reserve Bank of Minneapolis, May 1974.

Zarnowitz, V. "On the Accuracy and Properties of Recent Macroeconomic Forecasts." *American Economic Review* 68(May 1978): 313–19.

19

Macroeconomic Policies: The Choices

Popular discontent with the economic situation was one of the major factors behind Ronald Reagan's election in 1980. Inflation was too high, and had lasted too long. People were dissatisfied with rising taxes, with the proliferation of government regulations, with stepped-up programs for redistributing income, and with inefficiency in government operations in general. The advent of the Reagan administration represented a turning point in economic policies. President Reagan's "Program for Economic Recovery" had two distinct aspects. The first was based on a desire to reverse the social activism of the previous twenty years. Government programs to redistribute income were to be cut. Federal support for conservation, energy, urban development, education, the arts and science, and transportation were to be slashed. On the whole, cuts in federal transfer payments and nondefense expenditures followed traditional conservative economic doctrine. So did plans for phasing out a host of regulations that were seen to interfere with the workings of free markets. Thus, by curtailing the scope of government, the administration aimed at reducing public spending while giving the private sector greater latitude. How people reacted to this segment of the program depended mainly on their views as to the proper role of the government.

The second aspect of the program consisted of its macroeconomic policies. Inflation was to be slowed and productivity increased by eliminating some government regulations, by lowering taxes, and by curtailing the growth of the money supply. While the emphasis on sound money was traditional, other parts of the macroeconomic program were less so. A balanced budget—a long-standing conservative demand—was postponed in favor of large cuts in personal income taxes. The program embraced supply-side tax incentive ideas accompanied by faith in the ability of rational expectations and enhanced government credibility to reduce the costs of ending inflation.

EMERGING MACROECONOMIC ISSUES

The Reagan programs marked the culmination of a gradual shift in policy trends. At the start of the 1970s macroeconomists divided primarily over issues surrounding the economy's responses to changes in monetary and fiscal policies. Which reactions were most powerful and most predictable? Was the economy inherently stable or unstable? Would it self-correct or not? That the economy would respond to policies was accepted; at issue was whether policies ought to be applied actively with the use of government discretion or passively in accordance with some predetermined rule. During the 1970s, however, inflation led to a reconsideration of some key macroeconomic concepts.

The lesson of Keynes that recessions could be controlled through demand policies had proven correct. Post-World-War-II business-cycle contractions were both much shallower and shorter than in the pre-Keynesian period (Chapter 9). Between 1854 and 1938 the economy experienced mild or severe recessions over 43 percent of the time. From 1938 to 1981 recessions were smaller and they occurred in only 16 percent of the months. But one consequence of the success in maintaining output was more rapid inflation. Convinced that the government would keep recession losses at a minimum and end them quickly, business and labor became unwilling to accept cuts in real prices or wages. Prices and wages continued to rise even when output was not expanding and unemployment surpassed most economists' estimates of the point of full employment.

A severe enough cut in demand might have snapped the price-wage spiral. But no political consensus developed for deflationary actions that would cause higher unemployment and business losses. To supplement demand management, economists sought new policies to solve the stagflation problem. Among those suggested were new measures to shift the aggregate supply curve downward, actions to reduce the inflationary pressures of the price-wage structure through incomes or other policies, and attempts to increase the credibility of the government's anti-inflationary efforts so that rational decision makers would lower their expectations and reduce the pressure for price increases. The two main approaches to combatting inflation have been designated *rationalist,* placing the major emphasis on expectations, and *structuralist,* stressing price-wage relationships. The Reagan program emphasized a rationalist approach, combined with actions to increase supply and adoption of the monetarists' rule of small but constant increases in the money supply.

This chapter examines the debate between the Reagan administration and its critics over the president's new economic program, in terms of some of the key macroeconomic policy issues out of which the program developed. Some of the differences expressed grew out of the earlier arguments of neo-Keynesians and monetarists; some stem from differing theories of the inflationary process; some center around the view developed from rational expectations that government policies are likely to be ineffective. In making policy recommendations, analysts are greatly influenced by their assumptions as to how the economy functions. Is it naturally stable or unstable? How long does it take prices and wages to adjust to movements in demand? How efficient are markets and how good is their information? What is the proper role of the government? Do the indirect effects of the budget on working and investing overwhelm its effects on consumption?

Divergent answers to these and similar questions lie behind the disagreements over the Reagan program and the general usefulness of policies. These issues and how they have influenced current macroeconomic analysis are considered in the context of the following topics:

> Policy options.
> Instability, market failures, and uncertainties.
> The controversy over policy effectiveness.
> Rules versus discretion.
> Political issues.
> Inflation: The economic background of the Reagan program.
> The Reagan "Program for Economic Recovery."
> The outlook for macroeconomics.

Policy Options

The range of policies that can be applied to improve economic performance has been discussed throughout the text. Such policies can be organized into five broad categories:

Monetary policies. Responsibility for planning and implementing government actions to influence the stock of money and of bank assets and liabilities has been delegated to the Federal Reserve. The Fed must however, coordinate its policies with the goals and actions of the president and Congress. Some of the disagreements over monetary policy are operational: What is money and what is the best monetary target? How useful or harmful are sharp, short-run variations in the money supply or in interest rates? Most arguments go deeper, however: What advantages or costs arise in accommodating price and wage increases? If the Federal Reserve followed a rule of a constant growth in some measure of money of 3 or 4 percent, would this insure a stable, noninflationary economy or would it lead to widespread bankruptcies, unemployment, slack output, deterioration of our capital stock, and even slower growth in productivity?

Fiscal policies. As in the case of monetary policies, economists have held differing views on spending and taxing decisions that determine government programs and budget deficits or surpluses for over 50 years. What are the multipliers of government actions? Do increases in government spending crowd out private spending, or does higher demand lead to more consumption, enhanced private investment opportunities, and a larger stock of human and physical capital? Experience shows that fiscal policies can raise demand sufficiently to end a depression and that high government spending can create inflationary pressures. But agreement is still lacking over the limits of contra-cyclical policies, given the problems of timing, since government expenditures cannot be altered rapidly. Furthermore, even though temporary revisions in taxes or transfer payments can be enacted quickly, disagreements remain widespread as to how successful such acts are. Here, too, other issues have moved to the fore. Do fiscal policies have significant impacts on aggregate supply? To the nonspecialist, budget deficits are usually seen as necessarily bad; most economists have not agreed. Are their views converging? Government budgets decide how much of the income stream goes through the government and who gets what. Are fiscal decisions so intertwined with the political process that economic logic will usually have to take a back seat?

Aggregate supply policies. Actions aimed at improving conditions of the supply of goods and services—such as additions to both physical and human capital, reductions in the natural rate of unemployment, increased supplies of energy and other primary products, and elimination of inefficient regulations—have received increasing attention. But what policies will best balance supply? And how much improvement can be expected? Economists who have dubbed themselves supply-siders have emphasized tax incentives, particularly to savers, to higher income groups, and to capital investment. They have promised that such policies would bring about rapid growth and a sharp decline in inflation. Other economists have advocated more direct concentration on investment, on energy, and on human capital and marginal workers. They attach high values to growth, but are dubious about whether it can be increased rapidly over normal development and they are not optimistic over its ability to reduce inflation drastically.

Incomes policies. Government actions to influence directly the setting of wages and prices may be voluntary, as the Kennedy guidelines and the Carter price-wage standards, or mandatory, as the Nixon price-wage controls. Most countries have engaged in such actions because the demand-management programs to fight inflation have seemed slow and costly. Interest in incomes policies rises and falls with the success or failure of other policies. Most economists have opposed such programs; most voters surveyed say they approve of them; political decision makers waver. Recently, innovative programs using taxes as carrots or sticks have been proposed, but these concepts have received minimal acceptance.

Balance-of-payments policies. Controversies have arisen over the extent to which governments should attempt to influence international trade and capital flows by delaying or enhancing the adjustments in the domestic economy needed to balance flows of official international reserves. Should policies try to shield domestic activities by sterilizing the monetary base against flows of international reserves, or should they anticipate necessary corrective action by altering domestic income and interest rates? Such issues are closely related to views as to proper governmental activities in foreign exchange markets. Should governments intervene to peg or manage exchange rates? Or is benign neglect a better policy, allowing rates to float where they will? To what extent must domestic prices and output be subject to instability arising in foreign demands for goods or financial assets? How much harm or good is accomplished by import quotas on steel or automobiles? Some believe the advantages of fixed exchange rates were sacrificed because of the lack of moral fiber to adjust domestic demand. Others feel as strongly that fixed exchange rates are detrimental and illogical and that they fail in most critical situations. The best policy is to keep governments out of exchange markets.

Instability, Market Failures, and Uncertainties

Questions as to which policies to use, if any, and the degree of change appropriate are at the heart of the disagreements common among economists. In the debates between the monetarists and the neo-Keynesians, the issues of the natural stability or instability of the economy and the rigidity of the price-wage structure played central roles. In the 1970s these issues were supplemented— and often supplanted—by the debate between the rationalists and the structuralists. Are expectations or inertia more significant in the inflationary process? Related questions concern the ability of the market to clear. Is the price set in the market one which leaves no unfulfilled demand or supply? Situations in which inertia is important and markets fail to clear arise from the particular structure of the economy. In markets with poor information or where prices are administered or set by contracts, the expected results of any policy change will differ considerably from those predicted for a market with perfect knowledge and competition. If economists believe that economies are basically stable and self-correcting, they see little scope for active policies, concluding that government actions will do more harm than good. Such views are highly correlated with faith in the ability of the market left to itself to arrive at the best solution.

INSTABILITY AND MARKET FAILURES

Will the economy be better off if the government actively changes its policies to influence aggregate demand and supply? Those who believe that the economy is basically unstable and that long periods of unsatisfactory output or inflations are likely to exist in an economy left to its own resources will want to see a more active use of policies than those who believe the economy is stable and that market failures to clear are unlikely to be a problem.

Whether free or controlled, economies have experienced major fluctuations in aggregate demand. Recessions, depressions, financial crises, inflations have occurred over and over again. A principal reason why many economists believe in the need for discretionary policy rather than a fixed rule lies in the history of instability in all industrial economies. Theories based on the past have been developed (and, in the opinion of many, verified) which explain why instability has characterized the economy and will continue to do so. Shocks from outside the system; wars; defense efforts; supply shortages in energy, food, or other raw materials; political crises; changing technologies; shifts in the desires to invest and consume and in money demand—all cause instability. Aggregate demand and supply react to these pressures, leading to inflation and deflation. Furthermore, according to these theories, the economic structure makes it inevitable that shocks cause fluctuations rather than a return to a desirable equilibrium. The multiplier; cycles in inventories, housing, and other investments; changes in expectations; the wide swings in credit, stock, and other financial markets—all these factors contribute to the likelihood that a shock will become cumulative in either an inflationary or deflationary direction.

As important as instability in determining the need for policy changes is the question as to whether the economy, left to itself, will or will not adjust to a noninflationary, full-employment equilibrium. If markets fail to clear, whether because of firm or labor oligopolies, lack of information, transactions costs, or other similar frictions, output rather than prices will fall unless specific policy actions are taken to restore production. Resulting deflationary pressures impose heavy burdens through reduced output and higher unemployment.

In contrast to the belief that markets left to themselves cannot solve the problems of inflation and instability, believers in an inherently stable economy and in the importance of stable money and rational expectations hold that instability is due primarily to incorrect government policies. Without wars, if regulations were minimal and if monetary policy were conducted properly, the economy would be stable and markets would clear. The government has been guilty of both sins of omission and commission. It failed to cut poverty payments when Vietnam costs rose; it failed to expand the money supply during the Great Depression; it imposed controls on gasoline prices, followed by windfall profit taxes when OPEC raised oil prices.

UNCERTAINTIES

Furthermore, a great deal of uncertainty always exists. Forecasts fail as a basis for policy actions because data are not up to date, because expectations shift, because of faulty projections of future shocks, and because of errors in the structure and coefficients of the model. Even though the computers print out specific numbers, they are recognized as estimates containing sizable ranges of uncertainty. The same indeterminacy applies to projected policy effects. A study of past forecasts and policy suggestions shows that economists do better in forecasting the future course of the economy than in estimating how and when policy changes will affect spending. Forecasts of specific policy parameters, such as the velocity of money or of the multipliers of fiscal policy, contain large errors.

On the other hand, uncertainty may make flexible policies more necessary. Almost everyone agrees that at critical times the Federal Reserve must act as a lender of last resort; that is, it must assure liquidity sufficient to avoid large-scale failures of financial institutions and other businesses. If too many go under, the entire system of production and distribution becomes endangered. What is less certain, however, is the maximum number of firms and businesses that should be allowed to fail before the Fed acts. Should the Fed pour in money and liquidity to insure the system against all but a few bankruptcies, or should it stay as close as possible to a monetary rule, letting the market weed out a large number of institutions and firms?

The Controversy over Policy Effectiveness

As described in Chapters 1 and 4, rational expectations is the concept that a free market will act in accordance with the rational deductions of informed individuals on the basis of all available information. Because, in their model, the economy left to itself performs as well as possible, rationalists do not feel that policy changes can aid in achieving national goals. Such opinions conflict with those of the neo-Keynesians and traditional monetarists, both of whom see major shifts in demand accompanying monetary and fiscal policy movements.

RATIONAL EXPECTATIONS AND POLICY INEFFECTIVENESS

The belief of the new classicist proponents of rational expectations in the ineffectiveness of policies is based on two separate premises. The first views any deviations from the equilibrium path of the natural rate of unemployment as due to unexpected and unforseeable events. As a corollary, observed rates of unemployment and slack output are not signs of a gap between actual and potential output that can be narrowed; fluctuations in output result from random and irreducible errors. The market is assumed to be efficient and to make the best decisions because everyone strives to make profits. If useful information exists, someone will exploit it. Anyone who fails to do so will lose out. The idea is similar to that of arbitrage in financial markets. While the market will not necessarily guess right, its prices and outputs will express all of the available information processed in an efficient manner.

The second concept holds that models which are based on past experience and which fail to include rational estimates of expectations cannot predict the effects of a policy change. In their view, the structure of the economy constantly shifts in response to the actions of decision makers. Such shifts are hard for a model to track. Actions will differ from those underlying the model because people shift their ideas of how to beat the game. As a result, the model's predictions will be wrong. Put more strongly, the altered policies will be ineffective because they must depend on models incorporating past actions and the structure estimated from them. When the government tries to exploit this past knowledge, the policy changes cause the structure to shift. Private decision makers will observe what the government is doing and will change their desires. The coefficients of the model on which the government bases its actions will no longer be correct. Robert Lucas and Thomas Sargent, the leading proponents of rational expectations theory, summarize these views as follows:

> *Any* explanation of this general type must carry with it *severe* limitations on the ability of government policy to *offset* these initiating changes. First, governments must somehow have the ability to foresee shocks which are invisible to private agents but at the same time lack the ability to reveal this advance information (hence defusing the shocks). . . . Second, the governmental contracyclical policy must *itself* be unanticipated by private agents (certainly a realized condition historically) while at the same time be systematically related to the state of the economy. Effectiveness then rests on the inability of private agents to recognize systematic patterns in monetary and fiscal policies.[1]

Unemployment Results from Errors.   Rational expectations theorists view unemployment and slack output as due to irreducible errors—imperfect foresight on the part of employers and employees. Output fluctuates as a result of unanticipated price disturbances. No systematic errors can occur in these price forecasts for, if they existed, someone could utilize this fact to increase profits. Nevertheless, divergences between actual and expected prices and wages do in fact arise and these actual errors lead to deviations in output from full potential and of employment from the natural rate.

Effect of Policy Surprises on Output.   Government stabilization policies will be ineffective, except those that come as surprises, if market participants correctly anticipate the full effect of policy changes and immediately take responsive action. Suppose, for example, that the Federal Reserve expands the money supply in order to increase demand, output, and employment. If, except for errors, firms automatically drive the economy to the natural path for output and employment, how can the Fed's action help? It could increase output only if the policy furnished new correct information about real future demand and the natural rate. But would the Federal Reserve be any better than the market at diagnosing real demand and potential? Moreover, the action might be harmful. The market will realize that added money cannot increase output so that, assuming velocity does not change, more money must raise prices ($MV = PQ$). Correctly anticipating this, every business will immediately raise its prices. Thus the market's belief in a price rise promptly becomes a self-fulfilling prophecy.

To sum up, the assumptions are that, except for random errors, the economy always operates on the equilibrium path of the natural rate of unemployment; the market correctly interprets the systematic components of policies,

---

1. R. E. Lucas and T. J. Sargent," 'New' Explanations of the Persistence of Inflation and Unemployment" in *After the Phillips Curve: Persistence of High Inflation and High Unemployment,* Federal Reserve Bank of Boston, Conference Series No. 19, June 1978. (Italics are in the original source.)

and it properly adjusts its intelligent decision-making model to the new policies. If the assumptions are correct, policies will never be effective in closing
any gap between actual and potential output because such slack is merely the
result of irreducible errors.

Some Problems with Rational Expectations Theory.   The acceptance accorded
to the concepts of rational expectations and estimates of their significance differ
widely. Most economists do agree that expectations can shift demand and that
models must be adjusted for these and other structural shifts. Earlier chapters
explained why such tuning of models is necessary and how adjustments are
incorporated into the theories and models. The total errors in the model include those due to incorrect adjustments. Whether they are large enough to
interfere with the model's uses is primarily an empirical question.

    However, most economists disagree with the new classical view of how the
economy operates. The gap between experience and the predictions of these
models is wide. A principal attack on the theory of rational expectations holds
that it neglects the institutional inertia in the price-wage structure. Much of the
economy operates in contract, not auction, markets. Workers remain attached
to firms for considerable periods. Both employers and employees have investments in human capital arising from a history of working relationships and
from skills related to specific jobs. Consequently, wages and prices do not react
rapidly to changes in demand. Declines in output and employment do not
result primarily from errors in price anticipations. Rather, both parties are
better off if they respond to changes in demand by allowing output, not prices,
to shift. Fluctuations in output reflect rational reactions to demand shifts, not
mistakes.

    To date, most empirical analysis seems to find little basis to support the
rational expectations model.[2] Contrary to the theory, studies of price and
output movements show only slow and adaptive changes. While sudden spurts
occur in reaction to expectations, the overall record of gradual movements
appears convincing. Cyclical movements also exist. Movements of these types
are hard to explain in markets which act as pictured by the theory of rational
expectations. Many feel that this theory fails to explain the decline in unemployment during the 1960s and the failure of unemployment to reduce inflation
more rapidly in the 1970s.

HOW DRASTIC SHOULD ACTION BE?

Whether economists are rationalists or structuralists will influence, but will not
necessarily determine, their views as to whether gradual or drastic policies are
best. If failures to respond to demand management reflect rigidities in the

---

2. P. Cagan, *Persistent Inflation* (New York: Columbia University Press, 1979), Chapter 9;
G. Perry, "Inflation in Theory and Practice" *Brookings Papers on Economic Activity* 1(1980):
207–42.

structure, deep recessions are likely to see costs increase exponentially rather than linearly. Institutional rigidities may mean that a depression will cause the economic structure to crack. Under severe pressure, cumulative weaknesses may cause interrelated simultaneous failures throughout the system. In contrast, if difficulties arise primarily from a lack of credibility, a depression may reinforce belief that inflation will end and therefore hasten its demise. The degree of suffering the economy accepts may be a measure of its determination to end inflation.

During the early 1980s, the issue of how much pressure policies should exert on the economy was debated mainly in terms of the proper amount of deflationary pressure. Should policy makers go full speed ahead and bring on a full-scale recession, or should they be gradualists and operate on the theory that the least costly way of ending inflation is by maintaining a lesser degree of slack over a long period? Figure 19.1 illustrates these two possible policy alternatives. Assume that the economy is at point *A* on the inflation curve with a core rate of inflation of 9 percent. The ultimate goal is to reduce inflation to point *D*, close to zero. A decision has been reached that the most effective method of achieving the goal is by lowering demand. The question then is whether the most cost-effective procedure would be to reduce demand to point *B* where the actual-to-potential output ratio is 98 percent or, instead, to move the economy to point *C*, where the ratio is 92 percent.

Two factors enter into determining the best choice: What are the probabilities of success under each program? What are the probable costs? Earlier analysis (Figure 14.4) showed how and why economists differ in their estimates of the time required for slack demand to reduce inflation. One set of estimates—which minimizes the importance of expectations—shows every 1 percent reduction in nominal demand dividing into a drop in prices of .1 to .2 percent and a decline in output of .8 to .9 percent. At the other extreme, the model of rational expectations shows that as soon as a program becomes credible, a 1 percent fall in nominal demand reduces prices by the full 1 percent decline in demand, while output grows at its natural rate.

What do these views imply as to the desirability of imposing larger or smaller cuts in demand? If, because of inertia, the anti-inflationary response of the system is small and slow, policies to halt inflation through slack alone are in trouble. Furthermore, costs will continue to rise at a faster rate than the increase in slack. When output is only slightly below potential—say 2 or 3 percent—losses from reduced output arise primarily from fewer goods and services. But as slack grows—say, to point *C* (the 92 percent ratio in Figure 19.1)—other costs enter. The percentage of long-term unemployment shoots up, as do other economic and social losses. The number of bankruptcies, of cities in trouble, of declines in investment, capital, and growth accelerate rapidly. In turn, large and concentrated losses can trigger political actions to reverse the programs. On the other hand, with only small amounts of slack, chances diminish that the anti-inflationary program will succeed. Favorable demand effects may be offset by adverse supply shocks. Such occurrences

FIGURE 19.1   **How Much Slack in Output Is Best to Fight Inflation?**

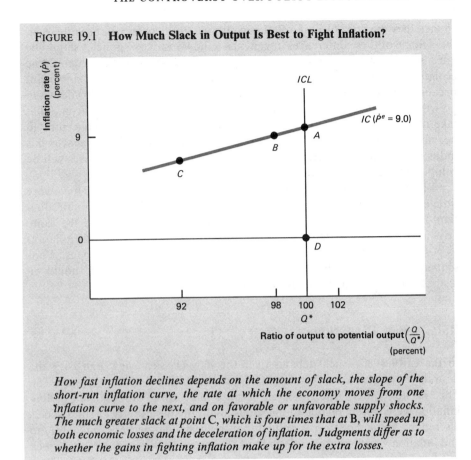

How fast inflation declines depends on the amount of slack, the slope of the short-run inflation curve, the rate at which the economy moves from one inflation curve to the next, and on favorable or unfavorable supply shocks. The much greater slack at point C, which is four times that at B, will speed up both economic losses and the deceleration of inflation. Judgments differ as to whether the gains in fighting inflation make up for the extra losses.

reduced the effectiveness of slack in the 1970s. Because they foresee only limited success for such programs, those who believe in inertia, in adjustment difficulties for the economy, and in heavy costs from curtailed output frequently advocate that gradualism be supplemented by the use of incomes policies and greater efforts to increase supply.

In contrast, believers in credibility, in rational expectations, and in the possibility of large increases in supply are far more optimistic. Many believe that a stable policy, even one with only a minor amount of slack, can gain credibility. They recognize difficulties in shifting expectations and reforming the wage and price system, but are convinced that gradualism can work. However, if credibility turns out to be harder to achieve than they hope, many who accept these models would be willing to see the government, and particularly the Federal Reserve, go full steam ahead in curtailing demand and raising unemployment. In this view, the long-run losses from inflation are so heavy that it is worthwhile undergoing great sacrifices of output and jobs for a period.

In fact, they see no choice; if inflation continues, total losses will be still larger.

Some of these differences in views as to how restrictive policies should be are also related to the importance assigned to the short or long run. Some economists hold that what happens in the short run is extremely significant because of potential losses from slack output and unemployment, slowdowns in growth and therefore in future output, and the redistributions of income that take place in recessions. They see losses in output and income concentrated heavily among producers and workers in durable- and investment-goods industries and among marginal workers. They doubt that these losses will be compensated for in the future.

In contrast, those who believe that, over the long run, policies have very little effect on output and that changes in money alter only prices, not production, are more willing to see restrictive policies. If output will be the same anyway, it would be better to reach long-run equilibrium with as little inflation as possible, thereby avoiding the redistribution effects of price changes. Consequently, in order to halt inflation as soon as possible, demand should be restricted to whatever degree is necessary.

Rules versus Discretion

In the early 1980s, such debates over the new classical view and over the desirability of gradualism tended to supplant previous debates over activism. This was not entirely true, however, because some of the proposals for ending inflation were closely related to questions about the desirability of rules versus discretion. Some monetarists argued that the best—and perhaps, only—way to end inflation was to adopt a rule to limit the rate of growth in the money stock to a fixed, and quite small, percent per year. Some prominent economists have always advocated such passive policies, with the government acting to change fiscal or monetary policies only under unusual circumstances. In contrast, others have pointed out that even the adoption of such rules requires specific agreements on the underlying model of the economy. Because they see such rules as more harmful than helpful and almost impossible to enforce, they have felt that policy changes must continue to be made in a discretionary manner. Both groups would like to see the structure of the economy altered to make it as automatically stabilizing as possible, but believers in discretionary policy find it hard to imagine that the economic structure in any near period will be able to halt inflation and end serious depressions without the help of specific corrective actions. The government must be aware that it is a major influence in determining aggregate demand and supply, and must take cognizance of this fact every time a new budget is adopted.

A FIXED RULE FOR MONEY GROWTH

Those who believe in a rule rather than discretion usually support the idea that policy makers should follow a fixed rule based on the principle of increasing the money supply by some fixed amount per period—week, month, quarter, or year. An optimum fiscal policy should be determined by deciding how large the government should be and whether the country requires a surplus, deficit, or balanced budget. A separate decision is then needed as to whether fiscal policy should conform to this rule in a given year or over several years. Advocates of firm, largely undeviating, passive policies (except for active control of the money stock) advance a number of reasons for their position:

1. The idea that the economy, left to itself, is basically stable.
2. The belief that the market can select the best policies more efficiently than can the government (the concept of rational expectations).
3. The government is a major cause of instability. Curbing government actions would improve the economy.
4. The uncertainties in the models and forecasts are too great to make them dependable.
5. The long run is critical for decisions; too much concern with the short run is self-defeating.
6. Politicians and bureaucrats are self-serving, acting to maximize their own welfare rather than that of the country; therefore they must be controlled.
7. Even if the models were good, they contain long and variable lags, which means that policies are too likely to become effective at the wrong time.

A FLEXIBLE RESPONSE

The possible advantages of firm rules and limited policy changes are more widely recognized now than they were 15 years ago. President Reagan's emphasis on a tight monetary policy with limited growth in the money stock is a clear expression of this fact. Yet, a political majority and probably an equal proportion of economists appear to believe that a need for discretion remains. They find fault with a passive rule because they feel that it neglects significant factors. This, of course, is at the heart of the big debate: Can the majority be convinced that the economy would be better off if a rule were followed?

It has often been claimed that those opposed to a fixed rule favored "fine tuning," the idea that policy variables should be adjusted as often as necessary to minimize the fluctuations of aggregate demand around the level of full potential. If any economists did in fact ever believe in fine tuning, they have long since disappeared. Those who favor discretion and oppose a fixed rule take a far more moderate position. Policies should be changed at times because the economy is operating poorly or because it experiences shocks or changes in its structure. However, because of uncertainty surrounding the models and forecasts, such changes should be undertaken cautiously. The best way to climb a mountain is not to try to go straight up, but rather to follow the natural contours of the terrain toward the desired goal. A better path will be found by use of discretion than by adherence to a fixed rule. Lack of flexibility may lead to disaster.

Analysts in this group believe that neither large, rapid inflations nor heavy losses of output and growth are inevitable. A dynamic economy calls for dynamic policies to keep it on the proper path. An unsatisfactory outlook should and will give birth to actions designed to bring the nation closer to its goals. But because of uncertainty, policies should be adopted cautiously.

Most people agree that under certain circumstances (such as a war, prolonged unemployment, or continuing inflation) any fixed rule will be broken. What is lacking is agreement on when and what economic conditions are sufficiently unusual to warrant action. Believers in discretion feel that it may be easier to agree on flexible rules than to try to set prior conditions for breaking supposedly fixed rules. The supporters of flexible policy responses base their opinions, among other factors, on:

1. The inherent instability of the economy.
2. Past failures of the market to adjust to a full-employment, stable-price equilibrium, and fear of future collapses unless policy action is taken.
3. The belief that policies can lead to more rapid growth and greater stability.
4. The importance of the short run in determining both current and future output, and who pays and who gains from fluctuations.
5. Belief that the political system cannot and will not limit itself to a passive role.

Although a system which operated automatically and did not require policy choices would have many advantages, a dynamic economy and political system may not permit the adoption of a single rule or of passive plans. Free choice in politics has an even stronger appeal than free markets in economics. Policies must be made; therefore, they should be the best possible.

Political Issues

Many political issues surround the selection of economic policies. Among the questions raised are the possibility that difficulties in obtaining a political consensus will result in delays and weak policies; the issue of self-interest on the part of the party in power—the political business cycle; and demands that the government actively fight recessions.

OBTAINING A POLITICAL CONSENSUS

The uncertainty inherent in forecasts of the economy, both with and without policy changes, leads to grave problems in attempting to reach a political consensus about what should be done. Such difficulties are compounded by disagreements as to what the nation's economic goals should be. Some people give a great deal of weight to the costs of unemployment, others may be more concerned about inflation, while still others stress the balance of payments and the foreign exchange value of the dollar. To alter policies, agreement must be reached, either with regard to legislation or to changing monetary reserves. To someone not eager to make a change, any difference of opinion becomes a reason why new policies should not be undertaken. The more bases for lack of agreement that can be found, the harder it is to get a consensus and to change policy.

Tendencies not to act are strengthened by the fact that any policy will be more expensive to some individuals and political groups than to others. For example, even if it is agreed that aggregate demand is too high and the dangers of accelerating inflation are great, one will rarely find builders and the building trade unions conceding that inflation should be fought by making money any tighter. They are aware that such policies cause them to suffer greater losses in income and jobs than are felt by most other sectors of the economy. Consequently, they can always suggest alternative policies to meet the goals, such as adopting price controls on food. Even though a majority wants to fight inflation, if they split between those favoring restricted credit and those advocating direct controls, either action may be postponed. Such considerations lead to delays in the adoption of any policy. The administrative and political process may take so long that by the time the new policies are put in place, they are too late.

THE POLITICAL BUSINESS CYCLE

Closely related to the issue of whether a political consensus can be reached is the danger that the party in power will manipulate the economy with a view to promoting its prospects for reelection. If people are more worried about jobs and output than about inflation, an expansionary policy at the start of an election year could create falling unemployment and rising prosperity through the election period. Inflationary price rises would not be felt until afterward. Of course, such a scenario assumes that the market is not rational and that it fails to recognize the basic thrust of policy.

Some analysts believe strongly in a political business cycle, although this is subject to debate. For example, many observers believe that in the election of 1972, the Nixon administration consciously attempted to shape policies so as to assure their reelection. Federal expenditures expanded rapidly in the first half of the election year; government housing subsidies were raised to a new high; the Fed was attacked publicly so as to obtain a faster growth in the money supply. Production, employment, and spending all grew at a rapid pace. Inflation did not start to accelerate until after the election, at which time the administration reversed policies and put on the brakes. On the other hand, although both the Ford and Carter administrations would have eagerly welcomed lower unemployment, inflation appeared to be more critical. They did not increase demand before their attempts to be reelected. Instead their continuing battles against inflation increased discomfort and contributed to their defeats.

A POLITICAL BASE FOR ACTIVISM

An inability to agree on what policy is best makes the choice of a simple rule difficult. But the political problems of passive policies are yet more fundamental than this. Since agreement is lacking as to which are the best rules and since different rules entail greater costs to some groups than to others, it appears optimistic to hope that any rule can be even semipermanent. Who gets what and when are basic political issues. Işn't it safe to assume that no body politic will abdicate the right to deal with the most critical questions?

The Keynesian revolution occurred because policy makers were able to shift aggregate demand through fiscal policy. Massive unemployment disappeared; bank failures were reduced to a trickle. Large gains in output and wealth took the place of poverty and unemployment. After full employment reappeared, monetary policies were able to reduce aggregate demand and halt undesired expansions. Problems arose, not because aggregate demand could not be influenced but because of the difficulty of arriving at a political consensus as to what steps should be taken to halt inflation. Experience and the knowledge that policies can affect demand and supply seem to insure that activist policies will continue. Even if it were possible to put the genie back in the bottle and to forget that demand can be increased in recessions, a majority of policy makers would most likely not want to do so.

Inflation: The Economic Background of the Reagan Program

The need to identify the causes of and to find a cure for inflation lay at the heart of the critical changes in policy adopted early in the Reagan administration. As illustrated in Figure 19.2, inflation was omnipresent throughout the 1970s. In 1972 price increases were contained by the Nixon price-wage controls. After reaching a low of 3 percent, inflation then began to escalate as controls were removed and the economy experienced a series of supply shocks. Inflation reached a temporary peak at the end of 1974, a year after the recession of 1973–75 had started. The combination of a sharp drop in output and fewer supply shocks caused it to decline until the end of 1976. Inflation then started up again, reaching a peak of 14.5 percent as measured by the consumer price index, which showed a double-digit inflation rate in 1974 and again in 1979–80. The GNP deflator was also above 10 percent in 1974–75 but remained just below that level in 1980. The bias in the CPI appears to have overestimated the actual inflation rate. For the entire year of 1980, the deflator was at 9.0 percent compared with the CPI's 13.6 percent—a difference in estimated inflation of over 50 percent. Both measures show, however, that inflation was rapid and constituted a major macroeconomic problem. Both reveal that, except during the year of strict price controls, inflation was never as low as 5 percent, while it averaged somewhere between 8 and 12 percent for the three years 1978–80.

FIGURE 19.2   **The Rate of Inflation, 1972–81**
(percentage change from four quarters earlier)

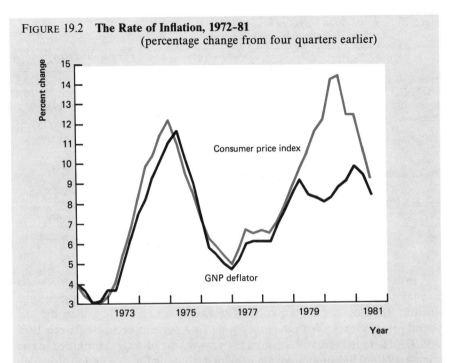

Inflation reached a high in early 1975 and then, as supply shocks diminished, it declined under pressure of excess economic slack. Early 1980 witnessed a new peak, as slack narrowed and a new set of shocks occurred. In 1980 inflation measured by the consumer price index far exceeded the rate recorded for the GNP deflator.
SOURCE: U.S. Department of Commerce and Labor.

THE SUPPLY SITUATION

Movements in the inflation rate appear to be linked to changes in the relative prices of a few key supply components, particularly food, energy, and house financing. In Table 19.1, these individual prices reveal large fluctuations. Their movements help to explain the declining inflation rate in 1976–77 and its rapid run-up in 1979–80. Both food and energy prices have a large exogenous component. By 1980, over 30 percent of farmers' cash receipts came from exports—more than double the percentage from foreign sales in the 1960s. Similarly, energy prices were heavily influenced by foreign forces, notably the changes in OPEC policies. Increases in financing costs were more closely related to domestic events. Demand and supply conditions in the markets for money and houses dominated the cost of financing houses. Both of these markets were greatly affected by changes in monetary policies, as the Federal Reserve sought to fight the outbursts of inflation.

TABLE 19.1   **Inflation in Selected Prices, 1974–80**
(year over year change in percent)

Prices	1974	1975	1976	1977	1978	1979	1980
Consumer price index	11.0	9.1	5.8	6.5	7.7	11.3	13.6
Energy (CPI)	29.3	10.6	7.2	9.5	6.3	25.2	16.7
House financing (CPI)	12.7	11.5	5.4	6.8	13.5	19.8	28.1
Received by farmers	7.3	−3.6	0.5	−1.6	14.8	14.8	1.7

SOURCE: Economic Report of the President, 1981.

Fluctuations in the rate of inflation reflect sharp year-to-year movements of the relative prices in a few critical spheres, as well as slower changes in the underlying trend. The fundamental changes in the inflation rate, however, depend on movements in labor costs, which are influenced by the balance between aggregate demand and supply.

In contrast to the wide year-to-year fluctuations in the relative prices of a few major items, Table 19.2 shows that the basic fulcrum of the price-wage structure—the hourly compensation of workers—varied far less than did the general price indexes. With the exception of a 2 percent decline between 1975 and 1977 due to the Great Recession, the growth rate of wages continued to rise through 1980. High unemployment helped account for the period in which compensation decelerated. So did the slower advance of wages indexed to the consumer price index, as inflation in the CPI (illustrated in Figure 19.2) slowed. Because both of these anti-inflationary pressures were sizable, observers were surprised and disappointed that the decline in wage increases was not greater. The failure of the growth in wages to fall more rapidly in this and similar past periods underlies the econometric estimates which show that wages react only weakly to slack output. These statistical estimates, in turn, are one of the reasons why structuralists fear that it may require a long time and be very

TABLE 19.2   **Changes in Unit Labor Costs, 1974–80**
(year over year change in percent)

Item	1974	1975	1976	1977	1978	1979	1980
Unit labor cost	12.1	7.4	4.7	5.5	8.7	10.4	10.4
Compensation per hour	9.4	9.6	8.1	7.6	8.4	9.6	10:0
Productivity	−2.4	2.1	3.2	2.0	−0.2	−0.8	−0.3

SOURCE: Economic Report of the President, 1981.

Unit labor costs vary with the compensation of labor and with productivity. Short-run changes in productivity primarily reflect cyclical swings in output. Such movements affect prices less than does the underlying trend of productivity.

expensive in terms of lost jobs and output to halt inflation primarily by reducing aggregate demand.

Because, as the table illustrates, sizable year-to-year shifts occur in productivity, unit labor costs fluctuate far more than does wage compensation. The large movements of productivity result from the effects of sharp cyclical shifts in the utilization of capacity and the labor force. Productivity declines with output because firms require time to adjust employment. Price movements, however, do not fully reflect short-run changes in labor costs. Many pricing models show that businesses do not alter prices in response to cyclical movements in productivity. Instead, they appear to average labor costs over a cycle. Note, however, the low growth rate for productivity over the entire period. This apparent decline in the underlying productivity growth rate led to an almost universal agreement that macroeconomic policy should place more emphasis on ways to improve supply.

While the specific reasons for the decline in the growth rate for productivity remained a mystery, at least three separate factors appeared significant. To some, almost all of the drop could be attributed to ballooning energy prices. The Council of Economic Advisers estimated that during the period 1974–80, energy inputs per unit of output fell 19 percent. To cut energy use by this amount required substitutions of both labor and capital. Other analysts emphasized the failure of net investment in plant and equipment. While gross investments remained at or near record levels, the rate of increase in the capital-output ratio slumped to almost zero. A third factor blamed for declining productivity was government regulations. While 1979 and 1980 saw a rapid expansion of deregulation activity, the 1970s as a whole experienced a proliferation of regulations and capital costs, particularly in the sphere of protection of public health and the environment. The problems of deregulation, capital investment, and energy were high on the agendas of most supply-side economists.

THE DEMAND SITUATION

Figure 19.3 shows the 1981 official estimates of the Council of Economic Advisers of the gap between potential and actual output and actual unemployment compared with full employment. The figure does not, however, show the estimated gaps that were in fact used in making policy. During the decade, estimates of potential output were lowered and estimates of actual output were raised. In 1973, the Nixon administration based its policies on a current estimate of a gap in which output was 2.75 percent below potential. The revised estimates in the figure picture output above potential in that year. However, even the revised estimates indicate that demand remained below potential for the remainder of the period. Only briefly in the spring of 1979 did the economy approach full employment.

How inflation could accelerate when aggregate demand was below potential output was a key question for the 1970s. Some economists—particularly

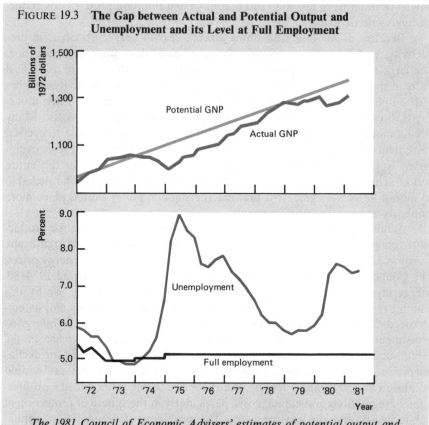

FIGURE 19.3   **The Gap between Actual and Potential Output and Unemployment and its Level at Full Employment**

The 1981 Council of Economic Advisers' estimates of potential output and full employment show considerable slack for every year except 1973. Because inflation accelerated in 1977, 1978, and 1979, some analysts judge that the natural rate of unemployment was at least 6 percent or higher. They believe that the CEA overestimated the economy's output potential.

among the new classicists—would argue that since inflation increased in 1978, 1979, and 1980, the economy must have been above the natural rate of unemployment, with output above potential. Such a failure to agree on whether or not full employment had been attained was one of the causes of conflict over policies. For example, the recessions of 1973–75 and 1980 were imposed by active government planning for the purpose of fighting inflation. Most disputes which arose were not concerned with whether policies were too restrictive, but rather whether demand should have been cut even more, since inflation remained high. Other disputes focused on the fact that output was below potential, raising the question of whether additional policies were needed to supplement those creating slack demand.

THE POLICY RESPONSES

Monetary Actions. Some economists wanted the Fed to restrict monetary growth far more than it did. They argued that the high rates of inflation were possible only because monetary policy was accommodating. Periodically, Milton Friedman in his *Newsweek* articles showed a chart relating growth in money to inflation. Others held as strongly that the Fed was failing to furnish enough money. They pointed out that the slow growth in money appeared to cause high interest rates and reduced output rather than inflation.

Table 19.3 compares growth in nominal and real GNP with measures of growth in the money stock and nominal short-term interest rates. Chapter 6 pointed out that it is hard for the Federal Reserve to reach short-run targets. Over periods of a year or more (such as those in the table), the Fed can come close to its objectives, but data revisions and divergent movements of different money definitions still cause problems.[3]

During the entire recession of 1973–75, the Federal Reserve, contrary to previous policies, continued to fight inflation rather than the growing unemployment. For 1975–76, the rate of growth in the money supply was well below the increase in prices alone. The rate of increase in spending declined, while real output fell markedly. For the remainder of the period, estimates of the growth in money required to maintain a normal growth in output, given the inflation rate, were about 10 percent. The Fed, in order to fight inflation by depressing demand, set upper limits for the growth of M-1 of $6\frac{1}{2}$ to $7\frac{1}{2}$ percent, or 3 percent below the amount estimated as required if output were to grow at its trend rate. Over the seven-year period covered in Table 19.3, while the growth rate of money varied widely, particularly on a quarterly basis, it averaged 5.6 percent. Throughout the period, nominal interest rates were high by traditional standards. Real interest rates appeared high in 1974, 1979, and 1980, but given the rapid inflation rates, not for 1975–78.

Monetary policy became especially restrictive following November 1978, when, in response to large capital outflows, President Carter called on the Fed to go all-out in defense of the dollar's exchange rate. In October 1979, the Federal Reserve shifted to a new operating technique which placed greater emphasis on controlling bank reserves. The result was another decline in monetary growth and a rapid rise in both nominal and real interest rates. A recession began in January 1980, but speculation in commodities, in real estate, and in other goods speeded up. In March 1980 the president issued orders allowing the Fed to place special restrictions (required reserves) against further expansions of some types of credit. Interest rates soared; output fell at an annual rate of 9.9 percent; the demand for money and credit declined temporarily. By

---

3. The data show 1981 estimates. They differ considerably from the data actually used when policies were carried out. Data revisions constantly plague policy makers. They argue for skepticism and cautious action.

TABLE 19.3   **Changes in Selected Economic Indicators, 1974–80**

Item	1974	1975	1976	1977	1978	1979	1980
	(year over year in percent)						
Real GNP	−0.6	−1.1	5.4	5.5	4.8	3.2	−0.2
Nominal GNP	·8.1	8.0	10.9	11.6	12.4	12.0	8.8
Monetary policy							
Money (*M*-1)	4.2	4.6	5.9	7.7	7.1	5.2	4.6
Federal funds (actual interest rate)	10.5	5.8	5.1	5.5	7.9	11.2	13.4
	Federal fiscal policy						
	(billions of dollars)						
Expenditures	299.3	356.6	384.8	421.5	460.7	509.2	602.0
Deficit	−11.5	−69.3	−53.1	−46.5	−29.2	−14.8	−61.2
	Full-employment deficit (−)						
	(percent of GNP)						
1981 estimate	−0.1	−2.2	−1.5	−1.6	−1.1	−0.1	−1.2
Unrevised estimates*	0.2	−0.5	−0.8	−1.3	−0.6	0.4	−1.2

SOURCE: Economic Report of the President, 1981
* From Economic Report of each following year.

In the 1970s, money grew at historically high rates, but not enough to validate completely both the trend growth in output and the rise in production costs. Real interest rates were low or negative for 1975–77, but otherwise quite high. Federal expenditures grew rapidly. The estimated deficits in the full-employment budget indicate a rather expansionary fiscal policy.

December 1980, however, output was again rising rapidly and interest rates reached record highs.

Fiscal Actions.   During this period, inflation also dominated debates over fiscal policy. Was inflation the result of high budget deficits? Did the level of government expenditures and related taxes reduce incentives and aggregate supply? Table 19.3 shows data for expenditures, for the actual budget deficit, plus two estimates for the full-employment deficit—that from the Economic Report of the President for 1981 and unrevised estimates based on data at the end of each year, figures similar to those actually used in policy planning.

During most of the decade, policy makers stated that fighting inflation was a principal goal. Thus in 1974—even in a recession—the full-employment budget was maintained in surplus and the actual deficit (national accounts basis) was rather small. In 1975, however, policy was altered. Falling output caused the deficit to increase sharply. In addition, rising unemployment led to the passage of the Tax Reduction Act of March 1975. Some taxes were refunded; some were cut temporarily; others were cut permanently. The unrevised full-employment budget shifted from surplus to deficit. Revised data show both the full-employment budget and the federal deficit at record-breaking levels. The actual deficit for the calendar year 1975 was over $69 billion, or about 20 percent of expenditures.

Tax reductions made fiscal policy more expansive through 1977. As the economy approached full employment, policy brought about a slow but steady contraction of the deficit, and the full-employment budget consequently went into surplus in the first half of 1979. Its deficit then rose again, but for a peculiar reason. Government interest payments are part of the budget. In 1979–80 much higher than anticipated payments on the debt pushed the full-employment budget back into deficit. In 1980, high interest costs together with revenues reduced by recession drastically raised the actual budget deficit, which had been declining.

While fiscal policy professed to be anti-inflationary, the evidence is questionable. Federal expenditures expanded steadily—triggered principally by rising transfer payments responding to cost-of-living indexing. One key to why fiscal policy behaved as it did was a general ambivalence with respect to proper goals. If the main problem was excess demand and inflation, most economists would argue that a sizable full-employment budget surplus would have been proper. Only if equal weight were given to the failure of the economy to reach full employment could the actual fiscal policy be considered satisfactory.

Looking back at the 1970s, no one is happy with the results of macroeconomic policies; the economy went into the 1980s with the discomfort index at its highest level in over 30 years. Furthermore, for differing reasons, few are satisfied with the way in which policies were implemented. To monetarists, the period proved the long-run relationship between money and prices. A failure to curb monetary growth resulted in inflation. To neo-Keynesians, the period proved the natural instability of the economy, the danger of supply shocks, and how hard it is to reduce the core rate of inflation. Together both monetary and fiscal policies restricted demand below most estimates of full employment. From 1975 through 1980 unemployment averaged over 7 percent, yet the inflation rate (CPI) averaged 9 percent. Because the curtailment of aggregate demand appeared to reduce output more than prices, solutions were sought in placing more emphasis on aggregate supply, on a balanced budget, on incomes policies, and on improving the price-wage structure.

The Reagan "Program for Economic Recovery"

At the start of 1981, as the rates of increase in energy prices, mortgage financing, and housing prices fell, the inflation rate as measured by the consumer price index retreated from the peak recorded in early 1980. However, labor compensation showed that the core rate of inflation continued at a high of just under 10 percent. The shortest recession in history had ended in July; income was expanding rapidly, but the rate of unemployment had declined only slightly, remaining at 7.4 percent. Typical forecasts for the next five years predicted that inflation would decline at an average rate of $\frac{2}{3}$ percent per year; output would grow about 3 percent a year, and unemployment would remain above 6.0 percent. Such were the economic events forming the background against which President Reagan's "Program for Economic Recovery" was unveiled.

A SHIFT IN ECONOMIC POLICY

President Reagan viewed his election as a mandate to revise drastically the thrust of economic policy. Immediately upon taking office, he thus proposed major shifts. The logic and probable results of his proposals became the subject of intense economic analysis. Although the program had to be altered with time and political realities, an examination of how analysts evaluated the proposals provides an excellent illustration of the application of macroeconomic theories. Shortly after its introduction, the president cut his proposed first year's tax reduction in half, but otherwise he was amazingly successful in translating his initial program into legislation.

President Reagan's economic package consisted of three interrelated parts. Most important was reform of government spending programs and of regulations. While objecting to specific cuts or reforms, most observers welcomed actions to improve government efficiency in general. The momentum generated by a shift in administration helped make it possible to rid the system of outmoded practices politically difficult to dislodge under normal circumstances.

The second part of the program was a realigned fiscal policy. Government expenditures were to be cut drastically. However, moves to balance the budget were to be postponed for a time in favor of an even larger cut in taxes. Federal government outlays were targeted to drop from 22.6 percent of the GNP in fiscal year 1980 to 19.0 percent in fiscal 1986. At the same time, a three-year tax-cut plan was designed to increase incentives, productivity, and output.

The third part in the program was the administration's prodding of the Federal Reserve to reduce further the growth rate for the money stock. Administration spokesmen promised to support the Fed in this policy even if it led to high interest rates accompanied by slow growth and higher unemployment. Conversely, they promised to attack the Fed if it maintained previous growth rates of the money supply, even if the Fed believed them necessary to accommodate spending and to lower unemployment.

Table 19.4 presents one estimate of the changes in fiscal policy contained in the new administration's budget. The proposals called for only minor changes in total government purchases of goods and services; the cuts in purchases of civilian goods and services were to be more than offset by higher purchases of national defense items. Most of the cuts would be in transfer payments. Through 1984, roughly a third of the cuts in transfers were to be in grants to state and local governments; a third in payments to individuals, such

TABLE 19.4 **Reagan Administration Proposed Changes in Carter Budget**
(billions of dollars—fiscal years)

	1981	1982	1983	1984
Expenditures				
Decreases	−6	−40	−88	−116
Increases (defense)	6	11	24	29
Reestimates	−7	−15	−21	−33
Total	−7	−44	−85	−120
Revenues				
Personal tax cuts	−5	−55	−86	−125
Business tax cuts	−2	−7	−14	−27
Total	−7	−62	−100	−152
Proposed increase (−) in deficit compared to Carter budget	−0	−18	−15	−32
Estimated surplus (+) or deficit (−)	−55	−45	−23	1

SOURCE: Office of Management and Budget, Proposed 1982 Budget, March 1981.

The Reagan administration proposed sharp cuts in transfer payments, higher defense spending, and a reduced federal share of the GNP. Projections of faster economic growth and lower interest rates accounted for a further reduction in estimated expenditures. Proposed tax cuts were sizable, but not much larger than estimated fiscal drag.

as in social security, medicaid, and food stamps; and the remainder were in other subsidies, such as housing, legal services, and student aid. In addition, interest-rate payments would decline, on the assumption of lower market rates.

Under the administration's proposals and the tax act as enacted, corporations would pay much lower taxes as a consequence of an authorized increase in the pace at which depreciation could be charged against current income and by a decrease in marginal tax rates on profits. Taxes on saving were reduced by slicing the maximum rate on unearned income from 70 to 50 percent. Individual income taxes were cut 25 percent across the board over three years. This was largely to offset so-called bracket creep, in which inflation-swollen increases in income pushed individuals into ever-higher tax levels. Incentives were granted to savers through exempting from income taxes: interest earned on certain saving certificates; dividends on certain public utility common stock; and increased amounts placed in individual retirement accounts. Estate and gift taxes were cut sharply. Married couples with separate incomes were granted some tax relief. Indexing of tax brackets (effective in 1985) was voted. The decreases in taxes would initially exceed cuts in spending, causing an enlarged deficit. Tax reductions were desirable, however, to increase incentives. The program estimated that the extra revenues collected from more work and greater investment would shift the budget into surplus by 1984.

SUPPLY-SIDE ECONOMICS AND CREDIBILITY

The new economic program emerged from the interaction of conservative political views with two major concepts of the new classicists—namely, supply-side economics and rational expectations. Supply-side economics postulated that a reduction in taxes accompanied by a smaller role for the government would rapidly raise incentives to save, to invest, and to work. For example, supply-side economists estimated that investment in plant and equipment would rise from 11.2 percent of the GNP in 1980 to 15 percent in 1986—far exceeding recent levels. Personal saving would increase from 5.6 to 7.9 percent of disposable income, as individuals—particularly at higher income levels—chose to save and invest rather than to seek nonproductive tax shelters. Business saving would grow even faster as taxes on corporations were reduced from 21 to 14 percent of total taxes on profits.

The program was proclaimed as a major break with outmoded Keynesian ideas. The tax cuts were not to increase demand, as had been true in previous administrations, but were aimed instead at a faster growth in aggregate supply. Higher investment and greater willingness to work, following from sharp reductions in marginal taxes and an improved regulatory climate, would assure a more rapid expansion of real output. Table 19.5 compares three sets of economic estimates—those contained in the 1981 Reagan and Carter budgets and a third labeled "alternative." This third line estimates the effect of inserting the Reagan program into a consensus set of econometric models. The contrast between the alternative and Reagan lines shows how much effect the supply-side models predicted the program would have in comparison to traditional theories.

Look at the lines for the real GNP. While the year-to-year differences look comparatively small, their cumulative impact is considerable. A comparison of the Reagan and Carter lines shows that the supply-side economists estimated that the new program would increase the average rate of growth in output by about 25 percent, causing real output in 1986 to be 4 percent higher than the Carter estimates. A comparison of the first and third lines shows that when the Reagan program was inserted into the traditional econometric models, the projected level of output in 1986 was 6 percent less than that estimated by the new classical models.

While the differences in forecasted growth are sizable, they are not extreme compared with normal year-to-year fluctuations. The two models, however, show somewhat larger contrasts in their estimates of future inflation and interest rates. Based on the concept of rational expectations, the administration economists predicted that enactment of the president's program would lead to a sharper drop in inflation. Since everyone would recognize that the government was now engaged in a true anti-inflationary program, it would be rational for labor and management to accept reduced price and wage increases. Underlying the Reagan budget was a projected fall in the GNP deflator of over 50 percent during the next five years. This figure compared with a decline of 30

TABLE 19.5   **Alternative Economic Assumptions of the Reagan and Carter Budgets**
(percent change—calendar years)

Economic variable	1981	1982	1983	1984	1985	1986
GNP, Reagan	11.1	12.8	12.4	10.8	9.8	9.3
GNP, Carter	11.4	13.1	12.3	11.8	11.0	10.2
GNP, alternative	11.8	11.9	11.5	11.4	11.7	10.9
Real GNP, Reagan	1.1	4.2	5.0	4.5	4.2	4.2
Real GNP, Carter	0.9	3.5	3.5	3.7	3.7	3.7
Real GNP, alternative	1.3	2.5	2.7	3.0	3.8	3.7
GNP deflator; Reagan	9.9	8.3	7.0	6.0	5.4	4.9
GNP deflator, Carter	10.5	9.3	8.5	7.8	7.0	6.3
GNP deflator, alternative	10.3	9.2	8.6	8.1	7.5	7.0
91-day Treasury bill (percent)						
Reagan	11.1	8.9	7.8	7.0	6.0	5.6
Carter	13.5	11.0	9.4	8.5	7.7	6.8
Alternative	12.6	13.7	11.5	10.2	9.7	9.3

SOURCE: Congressional Budget Office, *An Analysis of President Reagan's Budget Review for Fiscal Year 1982*, March 1981, Summary Table 3.

Lines 1 and 2 compare the economic assumptions of the Reagan and Carter budgets. The third line—alternative—shows the effect of inserting the Reagan fiscal program into a typical traditional large-scale econometric model. The differences between lines 1 and 3 mainly reflect the divergences between the new classicists' and traditional economists' analysis of the impact of the Reagan program.

percent when this program was inserted in the traditional models. As Table 19.5 shows, the expected drop in short-term interest rates differed even more. The July 1981 budget report showed no basic changes in the administration's views. Inflation was expected to fall somewhat faster and interest slightly less than initially projected.

How the assumptions built into the two types of models were expected to affect the economy can be illustrated by the use of a dynamic aggregate demand and supply curve (Figure 19.4). When 1981 began, the economy was on an inflation curve such as IC_1 with an expected inflation rate ($\dot{P}^e$) of 10 percent. The level of dynamic aggregate demand ($\dot{A}D$) gave an equilibrium point, A, with output below potential. Under the traditional assumptions, slack output would cause the inflation rate to decline, followed by a steady downward shift in expectations and inertia leading to a new equilibrium in 1986 at B on the curve IC_2. The advocates of supply-side economics hypothesized that the cut in taxes would increase aggregate supply at a faster pace, thus causing a more rapid movement to lower *IC* curves. Improved inflationary expectations would also work to speed up declines. Consequently, in 1986 the economy would be at point C on IC_3 rather than at B.

FIGURE 19.4   **New Classicists and Traditional Analysis of the 1981 Economic Program of the President**

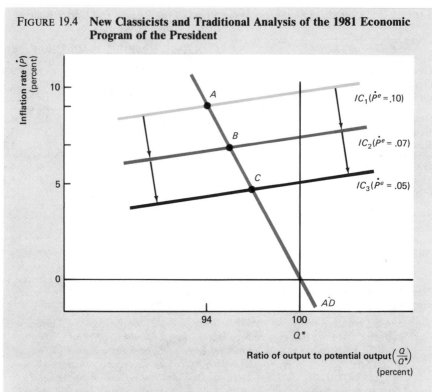

The Reagan program was announced with the economy on a curve such as IC_1 with slack but high expectations of continued inflation. The new classicists said that the program would increase supply and lower expectations, allowing the economy to move to point C. Critics held that the large tax cuts would maintain demand so that the economy would move only to B unless restrictive monetary policy caused a sharper fall in demand.

THE CRITICS OF THE NEW ECONOMIC PROGRAM

Nonadministration economists, particularly those in financial and investment institutions, greeted the administration projections with a great deal of skepticism. In their view, the budget was primarily a political, not an economic document. They heartily approved of the cuts in business taxes, federal expenditures, and regulations, but they feared that the basic macroeconomic policies, especially the large cut in personal income taxes, would either cause a continuation of inflation or very high interest rates. They worried because the program would maintain large government deficits and demands on the money market. According to their analysis, the policies did not provide the additions to planned saving needed to fund the increased demand for investment. Competition for credit among government, business, and consumers would mean that some would have to be crowded out through high interest rates. Given the administration's opposition to any form of credit allocation, the necessary crowding out would require the continuation of record-breaking levels of both nominal and real interest rates.

The new classicists predicted that interest rates would fall rapidly because added saving would come from corporations, from families saving income made available by tax reductions, and from families using current income to purchase the increased public debt. Traditional economists agreed that business saving would rise and that some added personal saving was likely, but they predicted it would not suffice to produce really low interest rates. They pointed out that families with incomes under $35,000 would experience virtually no reduction in taxes because, as a result of continuing inflation, they would move into higher brackets and would also have to pay more social security taxes. According to their projections, the administration was sacrificing a sure source of saving—the reduction in public debt—for a possible one through increased personal saving which they doubted would be as large.

The financial analysts' view was summed up by one of their most noted members, Henry Kaufman of Salomon Brothers. He called the economic program "exceedingly expansionary" because the planned budget cuts would not offset the stimulative effects of the defense spending increases and of tax reductions. He predicted problems in balancing the budget by fiscal 1984 and expected that heavy government borrowing would keep interest rates and inflationary expectations high.[4] Despite the fact that President Reagan made a direct attack on the Wall Street view, interest rates during the period of debate over the program stayed extremely high and well above the predictions of the administration.

The position taken by those who believed that the program would not alter dynamic demand is illustrated by the *IS-LM* diagram in Figure 19.5. When President Reagan took office, aggregate demand was in equilibrium at point A. Interest rates were at record levels. Traditional economists considered output to be below potential with an unemployment rate of 7.4 percent. Since inflation was not abating, some new classicists accepted this as the natural rate of unemployment; others felt the economy might be in a temporary cyclical disequilibrium. The Carter budget urged a retention of tax rates to balance the budget and shift the economy to IS_2 and a new equilibrium at point B. From the traditional point of view, the Reagan tax cuts were dangerous because they would leave an unaltered fiscal demand which would keep the economy at point A, with high interest rates and continued inflation. The only way to halt inflation with these fiscal proposals would be through much more restrictive monetary policies, shifting the economy to LM_2 and an equilibrium at C with higher interest rates and lower output.

Table 19.6 shows the degree to which the administration's projections of a balanced budget depended on falling inflation and interest rates, both of which the traditional approach deemed exaggerated. If the new classicist assumptions

4. *The Wall Street Journal,* May 7, 1981, p. 13.

FIGURE 19.5   **Alternative Views of Interest Rates and Output under the 1981 Economic Program of the President**

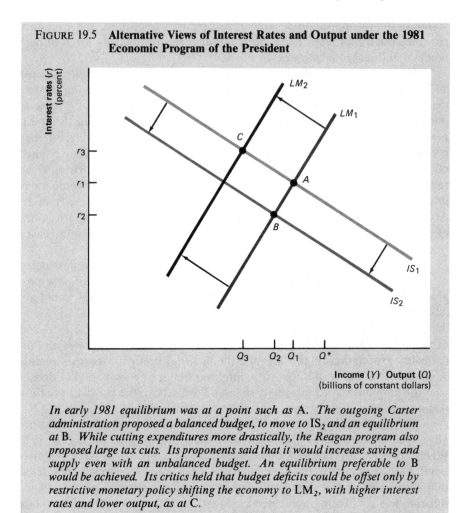

In early 1981 equilibrium was at a point such as A. The outgoing Carter administration proposed a balanced budget, to move to IS₂ and an equilibrium at B. While cutting expenditures more drastically, the Reagan program also proposed large tax cuts. Its proponents said that it would increase saving and supply even with an unbalanced budget. An equilibrium preferable to B would be achieved. Its critics held that budget deficits could be offset only by restrictive monetary policy shifting the economy to LM₂, with higher interest rates and lower output, as at C.

were wrong and the economy followed the alternative projections of Table 19.5, higher expenditures would be required to pay for social security, retirement, defense purchases, and other expenditures indexed to current prices. The bottom line in Table 19.6 shows how much the deficit would increase above the administration's estimates as a result of smaller declines in inflation and interest rates.

Rejecting this analysis, the proponents of the Reagan program held that a higher savings rate would shift the economy in Figure 19.5 to *IS*₂ even if direct fiscal policy did not, and they pointed out the adverse indirect effects of the Carter budget as well. As Figure 19.4 showed, they could also fall back on two other propositions: Even if aggregate demand were not reduced directly, inflation would end because of improvements in aggregate supply and in lowered inflationary expectations.

TABLE 19.6   **The Effect of Economic Assumptions on Budget Estimates**
(Congressional Budget Office estimates minus administration's estimates in billions of dollars—fiscal years)

	1981	1982	1983	1984
Net interest payments	1.2	8.1	13.3	12.5
Social security and indexed	0.2	1.0	3.7	10.9
Other	−0.2	4.4	9.4	12.2
Noneconomic factors	5.3	12.8	7.6	12.0
Total	6.5	26.3	34.0	47.6
Estimated deficit (−)				
Administration	−55	−45	−23	1
Alternative	−63	−67	−59	−49

SOURCE: Congressional Budget Office, *An Analysis of President Reagan's Budget Review for Fiscal Year 1982*, March 1981, Summary Table 5.

The difference in the estimated deficit between the administration and the alternative projections shows the importance of assumptions in budget estimates. The top section shows how much expenditures from a given set of appropriation acts differ depending on what happens in the economy. If the alternative assumptions were correct, the variations in output, prices, and interest rates would cause the deficit to increase by the differences between the bottom two lines.

In addition to their concern about a failure to reduce demand, traditional economists felt that programs to increase aggregate supply were not sufficient. The incentives for some firms to invest in additional plant and equipment were large. Cuts in taxes on large savers would also help. However, the incentives to the dynamic sectors of the economy—high technology firms and research and development—were smaller. Many economists also believed the effect on labor inputs would be slight. Any increased incentives to work through reductions in the higher tax brackets would be more than offset by a sharp increase in potential taxes on the working poor. Curtailment of food stamps and other income supplements to those getting jobs reduced the incentive to work instead of remaining on welfare. A reduction in the marriage penalty would increase time worked by married women, but this would only offset some of the other disincentives.

In the end, how one judged the net effect of fiscal policy in this budget depended on one's theoretical views. To the spokesmen of the administration, the budget was a major innovation. It cut the growth in spending, increased aftertax incomes, and raised incentives. To observers on the sidelines applying neo-Keynesian yardsticks, it was a good start at necessary budget and regulatory reform, but as a fiscal policy, the package offered nothing new. The expected downward trend in prices would continue, but they saw little in the program to speed the decline. In fact, Walter Heller, a chief innovator in fiscal policy as chairman of President John Kennedy's Council of Economic Advisers, seemed to express a widespread view when he stated:

On balance, the demand effects of the fiscal policy in the Reagan budget are more stimulative than those in the Carter budget. Like Kennedy's budget in the early 1960s and Nixon's ten years later, it is a budget geared to promoting a brisk cyclical expansion to high employment.[5]

MONETARY POLICY

Heller's view applied only to the fiscal program; monetary policy, if implemented, would have, without question, a major impact. While the administration's budget appeared conservative, its proposals for monetary policy were a radical departure. They called for a stable monetary growth rate averaging 4 percent a year in M-1 and 6.25 percent for M-2 over the period 1981–84. At the same time, projected growth in spending (Table 19.5) averaged 11.5 percent per year. Since growth in spending must approximately equal that of money plus velocity ($GNP = M + V$), the combined projections required the velocity of M-1 to rise at an annual rate of 7.5 percent and that of M-2 at 5.2 percent. The maximum previous increases in velocity in any four-year period averaged 4.2 percent for M-1 and 1.2 percent for M-2. What could bring about such an increase in velocity? Higher interest rates would be one possibility, releasing money from assets demand. This was one of the forces driving up interest rates in the simulations of Table 19.5. Another possibility would be a downward shift in the underlying demand to hold money, making possible the required increase in velocity without the higher interest rates.

Neither of these possibilities seemed reasonable to monetarists. They supported the Reagan program, but on grounds far different from those of administration spokesmen. According to the point of view of prominent monetarists, the fuss over the budget was much ado about not much. Although significant in influencing the amount of income flowing through the government and, therefore, affecting efficiency, incentives, and income distribution, the proposed fiscal package would exert only a minor impact on the GNP. The heart of the Reagan program was the proposed monetary constraint. It would cause spending to contract and trigger a recession deeper than the administration forecast. Consequently, the government's credibility would rise and rational expectations of inflation would decline. The result would be a faster drop in the rate of inflation than appeared feasible to skeptics whose historical models did not give adequate weight to shifting expectations. Falling prices would allow output to rise without a record-breaking growth in velocity. Monetary policy would save the administration's promises.

The forecasts of the Claremont Economic Institute, a major source of concepts adopted by the administration, agreed that the enactment of the original Reagan fiscal policy would have only minor effects on demand. The proposed expenditure cuts would barely offset the tax cuts, leading to a net

5. W. W. Heller and G. L. Perry, *U.S. Economic Policy and Outlook* (National City Bank of Minneapolis, March 19, 1981).

fiscal restraint of about .5 percent of GNP for 1982, 1983, and 1984. Because of tight money, the actual restraint on demand, however, would be much greater. Unemployment would rise into the $8\frac{1}{4}$ to $9\frac{1}{2}$ percent range. Slack output would cause a rapid decrease in inflationary expectations. The inflation rate would decline to 4 percent by the end of 1985, with the 3-month Treasury bill rate at 5 percent.[6]

The debates over the Reagan program moved macroeconomic analysis into the newspaper headlines and daily TV coverage. Supply-side economics became a familiar term. The conflicts in views dominated the news following the enactment of the Reagan program in August 1981. Instead of the sharp drop in interest rates and improvement in expectations which had been predicted by the administration, long-term interest rates moved to new highs and the stock market fell sharply. The administration agreed that the alternative budget projections shown in Table 19.6 appeared more likely to be correct than their own initial estimates. They proposed additional budget cuts beyond those originally enacted.

The immediate reaction of the analysts and investors in the financial markets was that, while the Reagan administration's gamble might work, the tax-cut was excessive. It would not be matched by a more rapid growth in supply and in revenues. They did not believe in the Laffer curve or that a sizable increase would occur in the desire to save. In their view, the administration's eagerness for a reduction in expenditures and taxes had led it to a policy that depended for its success in fighting inflation on a severe and prolonged period of tight money and high interest rates. They hoped for the success of the program, but because they thought the probabilities were high for either a continued inflation or for considerable financial distress, they preferred to invest in liquid securities rather than in long-term bonds or common stock. Until the success or failure of the program became more certain, they were unwilling to put their money with their hopes for the president's success.

The reactions of the stock and money markets to the program led to high interest rates, a continued weakness of output spreading from the auto and construction to other industries, and a sharp rise in unemployment. Failure of the economy and of income to grow at the rates underlying Table 19.6 threatened to hold down revenues and move the deficits well above those predicted by the critics of the administration's program. A recession and reduced output would take some pressure off interest rates, but policy makers would face a dilemma. Could the Federal Reserve continue to hold the growth of money and credit well below normal without creating still more difficulties? If not, should the Fed accept the view of some monetarists that a sharp or continued recession was a necessity, or should the Fed move partway back toward prior policies by furnishing enough money and credit to avoid severe financial distress while helping the economy to stave off still greater losses in output?

6. *The New York Times,* April 24, 1981, p. 26.

The Outlook for Macroeconomics

As we have seen, macroeconomic theories and policies change constantly in response to dynamic forces in the economy, to new information, to new analytical techniques, and to the tests of time. Today's views differ significantly from those of ten years ago, just as they will differ from those of a decade hence. New ideas come into fashion and then disappear, or perhaps become incorporated into the generally accepted concepts of the field. Specific techniques and problems rise to prominence and then fade. What has not varied is the importance to individuals, businesses, and the economy of overall fluctuations in demand, output, jobs, and prices. The need for better decisions has led to a continuous improvement in macroeconomic analysis. As a result, current techniques do quite a good job of explaining what is happening in the economy. While less accurate than hoped for, forecasts appear satisfactory. The major weakness of macroeconomic analysis lies in the lack of agreement over the effectiveness of policy variables.

While many disagreements persist among macroeconomists, particularly with respect to the elasticities and stability of policy variables, a large number of concepts dealing with the dynamic relationships of the economy are nevertheless generally accepted. Because a large area of agreement does exist as to the basic factors which determine demand and output, macroeconomists do not differ widely in their explanations of economic events themselves. The major divisions arise over what policy actions should be taken. In this sphere, the lack of information, uncertainties, variable lags, and conflicting estimates of policy impacts become critical. History shows that the economy has experienced numerous fluctuations in output. Business cycles have been frequent, and some have encompassed deep depressions.

It is not clear whether the economy, if left alone, would self-correct. Nor are the advantages and disadvantages of the use of monetary and fiscal policies obvious. Because specific knowledge is lacking and forecasts are uncertain, many observers believe in following mixed strategies. If policy changes are called for, a combination may be better than any single policy indicated as best by a particular theory. The choice of a combination strategy is supported by the observation that the costs of using a policy, and especially its chances of error, rise exponentially. For example, the costs of a second equal rise in the real interest rate are far greater than the first. A 10 percent increase in taxes is more than twice as costly to those who bear it and to incentives than a 5 percent increase.

Macroeconomics is still a young science, one whose theories and techniques have improved measurably. As more complex decisions are required, new techniques and methods will develop based on as well as in reaction to those with which we are now familiar. Our present knowledge of macroeconomic analysis will provide the foundations for a better understanding of future economic conditions.

Summary

1. At least five major types of macroeconomic policies are available for governments to use: monetary, fiscal, supply, incomes, and balance of payments. Furthermore, almost unlimited possibilities exist for combining components from each.

2. Neo-Keynesians and structuralists emphasize the natural instability of the economy and the rigidity of the price-wage structure. Because of poor information, the advantages of long-run contracts, and costs of readjusting labor and customer relations, firms alter output as well as prices when demand shifts. A market may be in disequilibrium—failing to clear—with suppliers unable to sell all they desire at the prevailing price.

3. Theories of rational expectations lead to predictions that government stabilization policies will be ineffective. According to these theories, the forces of profit-making in the market push the economy to an equilibrium at the natural rate of unemployment. Deviations are due to unforseeable events. Skeptics who doubt the assumptions of rational expectations point to markets with poor information, long lags, inflationary price-wage inertia, and irrational movements in expectations. In their view, business-cycle history shows long periods of inflation or stagnation, with the economy far from the path of full employment. Government policies can close the gap between actual and potential output.

4. Gradualists believe that step-by-step actions with only minor amounts of slack and lost output are preferable, even if a considerable time is required to achieve objectives. They see real costs accelerating the farther the economy moves from its normal path. Losses from unemployment, bankruptcies, failures to invest, and a smaller capital stock all rise more than proportionally as the gap between actual and potential output grows. Others believe that sharp shocks may be necessary for policies to gain credibility. While deploring the costs of a large drop in output, they believe that total losses from a gradualist policy or from a failure to halt inflation will exceed those from a hard-hitting program.

5. Advocates of a fixed rule want to see a stable fiscal policy and a constant growth rate for the money stock. They emphasize the natural tendency of the economy to move toward full employment. They doubt the efficacy of changing policies because of long lags, implausible models, and distrust of government actions.

6. Those who believe that governments should be able to use discretion in changing policies point to inherent instability, exogenous shocks to demand and supply, the past failures of the economy to adjust to full employment and stable prices, the lack of knowledge as to what rule to follow, and the unwillingness of the political system to endure large losses in output and jobs.

7. President Reagan's election and his proposed "Program for Economic Recovery" were heavily influenced by the apparent failures of economic policies in the 1970s and the stagflation which prevailed. Inflation and unemployment were both high.

8. The "Program for Economic Recovery" called for deep budget cuts in civilian services and transfer payments, accompanied by increases in military expenditures. The share of total federal spending was to fall by about 3 percent of the GNP, while the rate of deregulation would speed up. Taxes were to be cut in order to raise incentives. The budget would be balanced in 1984 if incentives raised output sufficiently and if rational expectations and improved government credibility caused inflation and interest rates to decline faster than prior predictions. Critics claimed that the program depended too much on tight money.

9. The development of a more comprehensive macroeconomic theory has been rapid. Better analyses of aggregate supply and of the inflationary process have been added to the theory of income determination. Both explanations and forecasts of the GNP have been quite good. Disagreements continue because of conflicting assumptions as to: the economy's inherent stability; the time taken by demand, supply, and prices, if left to themselves, to reach a desirable equilibrium; the likelihood that government policies will succeed; the importance of lags and of short-run in comparison to long-run costs; and the shape of the functions which determine the economy's reactions.

Questions for Discussion and Review

1. What are some of the major economic issues facing the country?

2. Comment on the advantages and disadvantages of taking policy actions based on a rule.

3. What is the rational expectations view on the effectiveness of policy actions?

4. Why should the government intervene in economic affairs? Can it remain completely neutral?

5. Comment on the interrelationship between politics and economics.

6. What are some of the causes of the stagflation of the 1970s?

7. What are incomes policies?

8. Discuss the Reagan "Program for Economic Recovery." Include in the discussion what various sources have to say about the program, and why.

References

Each of the following publications consists of a number of articles presenting both sides of the issues discussed in this chapter.

American Enterprise Institute Seminar. "Rational Expectations." *Journal of Money, Credit, and Banking* 12(November 1980).

Brookings Institution. "Tenth Anniversary Issue." *Brookings Papers on Economic Activity* 1(1980).

Center for the Study of American Business and Federal Reserve Bank of St. Louis. *The Supply-side Effects of Economic Policies.* Center for the Study of American Business, No. 39, May 1981.

Federal Reserve Bank of San Francisco. "The Monetarist Controversy: A Seminar Discussion." *Economic Review* Supplement (Spring 1977).

U.S. Congress, Joint Economic Committee. *The Business Cycle and Public Policy, 1929–80.* Joint Committee Print 96:2, November 28, 1980.

Index

GLOSSARY OF SYMBOLS*
(Continued from inside the front cover)

Symbol	Meaning*	Symbol	Meaning*
kD	Deposit multiplier (6)	MY	Real transactions demand for money (7)
kM	Money multiplier (6)	N	Labor; hours of work (12)
kT	Tax multiplier (4)	n	Response of labor supply to real wages (12)
kt	Income tax multiplier (4)	ND	Demand for labor (12)
l	Response of wages to unemployment (12)	NPV	Net present value (9)
LM	Liquidity-money curve; points of equilibrium in real money market (7)	NS	Supply of labor (12)
$\lambda, \mathcal{L}$	Constants (9)	$NSNW$	Real per capita net worth, excluding common stock (10)
M	Nominal stock of money (7)	ODD	Transactions deposits not in money supply (6)
m	Marginal propensity to spend (4) and marginal propensity to spend and tax (8)	P	Price level; the GNP deflator (2)
MA	Real assets demand for money (7)	$\dot{P}$	Percentage rate of change in prices; the inflation rate (8)
$\overline{MA}$	Autonomous real demand to hold money (7)	$\dot{P}^e$	Expected inflation rate from inertia or expectations (13)
MB	Monetary base (6)	P_0	Principal amount at time 0 (5)
MD	Nominal demand for money (7)	p	Response of inflation rate to expected percentage rate of change in prices (13)
$\dfrac{MD}{P}$	Real demand for money (7)		
MEC	Marginal efficiency of capital (9)	$(\ )_p$	Planned spending (3)
mpc	Marginal propensity to consume (3)	PC	Phillips curve (13)
MPL	Marginal (physical) product of labor (2)	PM	Prices of supply factors (13)
MR	Supply of raw materials (2)	PR	Productivity (13)
MS	Nominal money supply (7)	$\dot{PR}$	Percentage rate of change in productivity (13)
$\dfrac{MS}{P}$	Real money supply (7)	PRC	Prices of capital services (9)
MV	Monetary spending (7)	PV	Present value (5)

*Number in parenthesis indicates the chapter in which the symbol is introduced.